The Secret Speeches of Chairman Mao

Harvard Contemporary China Series: 6

edited by
RODERICK MACFARQUHAR
TIMOTHY CHEEK
EUGENE WU
with contributions by
MERLE GOLDMAN
and BENJAMIN I. SCHWARTZ

Published by
THE COUNCIL ON EAST ASIAN STUDIES / HARVARD UNIVERSITY
Distributed by the Harvard University Press
Cambridge (Massachusetts) and London   1989

The Secret Speeches
of Chairman Mao

From the Hundred Flowers
to the Great Leap Forward

The Council on East Asian Studies at Harvard University publishes a monograph series and, through the John King Fairbank Center for East Asian Research and the Edwin O. Reischauer Institute of Japanese Studies, administers research projects designed to further scholarly understanding of China, Japan, Korea, Vietnam, Inner Asia, and adjacent areas

Library of Congress Cataloging in Publication Data

Mao, Tse-tung, 1893–1976.
    [Speeches. English. Selections]
    The secret speeches of Chairman Mao : from the hundred flowers to
the great leap forward / edited by Roderick MacFarquhar, Timothy
Cheek, Eugune Wu ; with contributions by Merle Goldman and Benjamin
I. Schwartz.
        p. cm. – (Harvard contemporary China series ; 6)
    Bibliography: p.
    Includes index.
    ISBN 0-674-79673-X
    I. MacFarquhar, Roderick. II. Cheek, Timothy. III. Wu, Eugene,
1922- . IV. Goldman, Merle. V. Schwartz, Benjamin Isadore, 1916–
VI. Title VII. Series.
DS778.M3A5   1989
951.05'092'4 – dc19   89-497
                                                               CIP

CONTRIBUTORS

TIMOTHY CHEEK is an assistant professor of history at The Colorado College. He is co-editor with Merle Goldman and Carol Lee Hamrin, of *China's Intellectuals and the State: In Search of a New Relationship*, Harvard Contemporary China Series, 3.

MERLE GOLDMAN is a professor of history at Boston University. She is the author of several books on the role of intellectuals in the People's Republic of China, including *China's Intellectuals: Advise and Dissent* (Harvard University Press, 1981). She is currently working on a book about the humanistic elite in post-Mao China.

RODERICK MACFARQUHAR is a professor of government at Harvard University and director of Harvard's Fairbank Center for East Asian Research. Joint Editor of Volume 14 of the *Cambridge History of China*, he is now working on Volume 15 of that series and the third volume of his own *Origins of the Cultural Revolution*.

BENJAMIN I. SCHWARTZ is the Leroy B. Williams Professor of History and Political Science, *Emeritus*, Harvard University. His early, pathbreaking work on Mao Zedong includes *Chinese Commun-ism and the Rise of Mao* (1951). His most recent major book is *The World of Thought in Ancient China* (Harvard University Press, 1985), and his current work has broadened in scope beyond China to theore-tical issues in the concept of culture.

EUGENE WU is Librarian of the Harvard-Yenching Library. He is coauthor with Peter Berton of *Contemporary China: A Research Guide* (Hoover Institution, 1967) and is currently preparing a chapter on American library resources on contemporary China for the forthcoming *American Study of Contemporary China*, edited by David L. Shambaugh.

CONTENTS

THE GREAT LEAP FORWARD

TABLES

TERMS

APC	Agricultural Producers' Cooperative
CC	Central Committee
CCP	Chinese Communist Party
CCRM-ARL	Center for Chinese Research Materials, Association of Research Libraries
CPPCC	Chinese People's Political Consultative Conference
CPSU	Communist Party of the Soviet Union
CR	Cultural Revolution
FYP	Five-Year Plan
GLF	Great Leap Forward
KMT	Kuomintang, or Nationalist party
NPC	National People's Congress
PLA	People's Liberation Army
PSC	Politburo Standing Committee
PRC	People's Republic of China
SSC	Supreme State Conference

UFWD — United Front Work Department
URI — Union Research Institute

PUBLICATIONS

BDRC — Howard L. Boorman, ed. *Biographical Dictionary of Republican China.* 4 vols. New York, Columbia University Press, 1967–1971.

CHOC 12 — *Cambridge History of China,* Vol. 12. *Republican China 1912–1949, Part 1.* John K. Fairbank, ed. Cambridge, Cambridge University Press, 1983.

CHOC 13 — *Cambridge History of China,* Vol. 13. *Republican China 1912–1949, Part 2.* John K. Fairbank and Albert Feuerwerker, eds. Cambridge, Cambridge University Press, 1986.

CHOC 14 — *Cambridge History of China,* Vol. 14. *The People's Republic, Part I: The Emergence of Revolutionary China, 1949–1965.* Roderick MacFarquhar and John K. Fairbank, eds. Cambridge, Cambridge University Press, 1987.

FBIS — *Foreign Broadcast Information Service*

GMRB — *Guangming ribao* (Guangming daily)

JPRS — *Joint Publications Research Service*

Klein and Clark — Donald W. Klein and Anne B. Clark. *Biographic Dictionary of Chinese Communism, 1921–1965.* 2 vols. Cambridge, Harvard University Press, 1971.

New Mao Texts — Collections from which this volume is drawn; publication forthcoming from Center for Chinese Research Service, Association of Research Libraries, Oakton, Virginia.

Origins — Roderick MacFarquhar, *Origins of the Cultural Revolution.* 2 vols. New York, Columbia University Press, 1974, 1983.

RMRB — *Renmin ribao* (People's daily)

SW — *Selected Works of Mao Zedong.* 4 vols. Beijing, Foreign Languages Press, 1975.

SW5   *Selected Works of Mao Zedong,* Vol. 5. Beijing, For-
             eign Languages Press, 1977.
Wansui   *Mao Zedong sixiang wansui* (Long live Mao Zedong
             Thought). 3 vols. (n.p., n.pub., 1967–1969). Three
             separate volumes of apparently original material
             released by the Institute of International Relations,
             Taipei.
XJ   *Mao Zedong xuanji.* 4 vols. Beijing, Renmin chuban-
             she, 1951–1960. These first four volumes of Mao's
             selected works have been reprinted several times.
XJ5   *Mao Zedong xuanji,* Vol. 5. Beijing, Renmin chuban-
             she, 1977.

NOTES ON TYPOGRAPHY AND TRANSLATION

Square brackets ([ ]) are used to enclose interpretative English words inserted by the translators, or the original Chinese words where these may be of special interest to Sinologists. Words inserted to transpose Chinese to English syntax are generally not enclosed. This distinction is, of course, to a considerable degree subjective; but we have tried to err on the side of an over-scrupulous use of brackets, at the risk of distracting readers, rather than on the side of using too few, which would be misleading.

The page number of the original Chinese text is also enclosed in square brackets and printed in boldface. Readers wishing to compare the translation to the original will, therefore, be able quickly to locate particular passages when the originals are published by the Center for Chinese Research Materials of the Association of Research Libraries.

Braces ({ }) are used to enclose passages inserted from a parallel text.

Parentheses are used only when they occur in the original Chinese texts, and all such instances are retained. In some cases, they seem to enclose editorial amplifications rather than words by the Chairman; in other cases, they may be interpolations taken from a secondary transcript or set of notes. We have not attempted to identify the nature of the parenthetical materials.

Angle brackets (< >) are used where square brackets occur in the original Chinese texts.

Italics are used to indicate passages that have already been published in abbreviated or censored versions of a text.

Ellipsis dots occur only where they occur in the original Chinese texts. Three dots are used in the translations, in conformity with American practice; six are generally used in the originals.

An X has been retained wherever one has been used in the Chinese originals to obliterate a character, usually from a numerical figure or someone's name. Where we have been able to make identifications, we have provided them in footnotes. Where we have not been able even to speculate, we have retained the Xs without comment.

Punctuation has been silently altered to meet the demands of English. Quotation marks around individual terms, however, have been retained where they are used (often inconsistently) by the Chinese editors.

Paragraphing follows the Chinese with one exception: Many of these talks include the comments and questions of a moderator or speakers from the floor as well as the words of Chairman Mao. In the original documents, a change in speaker is sometimes indicated by a new paragraph, sometimes only by parentheses within a block of the Chairman's speech. We have consistently set off new speakers in a new paragraph, so that readers can readily find all exchanges. The Chinese editors' parentheses have been retained. The original documents sometimes supply a name or Xs, followed by a colon at the head of a speech or question. We provide within square brackets an identifying word like *Chairman* or *Questioner* or *XX* where needed to accommodate our reparagraphing. Parenthetical indications of laughter from the floor have been left embedded in the Chairman's speech.

Measurements are given in the Chinese, English, or metric system according to the usage of the speaker. For equivalents, see "Chinese Measurements" on the following page.

CHINESE   MEASUREMENTS

Money
100 fen = 1 yuan = US $1 (ca. 1950)
1 jiao = 10 fen = 10¢
1 mao = 10 fen = 10¢
10 mao = 1 yuan = US $1

Volume and Weight
1 dan = 50 kilograms = 110 pounds
1 dou = 1 decaliter = 2.642 gallons or 1.135 pecks
1 jin = 1 catty = 500 grams = 1.1 pounds
1 liang = 50 grams = 1.76 ounces

Distance and Area
1 li = 500 meters = ca. one-third mile
1 mou = ca. one-sixth acre
1 zhang = 3.3 meters = 3.6 yards

PREFACE

This is a volume of translations of hitherto unavailable speeches by
Mao Zedong dealing with key events in the forty-year history of the
People's Republic of China. While documentary collections are normally considered specialist publications, we have attempted through
accompanying articles to paint the background and to elucidate the
importance of these texts for a wider audience.

The speeches all date from 1957 and 1958 and greatly illuminate
two crucial episodes: the Hundred Flowers (1956–1957) and the
Great Leap Forward (1958–1960). Today, when most students and
observers of China are engrossed with the current reform program, it
is important to recall that those thirty-year-old events, like Mao himself, are still vibrant memories for national leaders. Indeed, they still
exercise a powerful influence over their conduct.

The Chinese publications from which the speeches are culled are
being made available to the editors of that admirable, comprehensive
project, *The Writings of Mao Zedong, 1949–1976*, Michael Y. M. Kau
and John K. Leung. But in view of the importance of these particular
texts, we thought it worthwhile to bring them out in a special volume with commentaries.

As the various sources of these speeches gradually became available at Harvard, we decided they demanded a team effort. I made the original selection of documents. Timothy Cheek checked to ensure that they had not appeared elsewhere, and his careful analysis of these documents and Mao texts in general is a major part of the critical apparatus of this volume. He then launched out on the translating, and assembled and supervised a group of hard-working assistants, including Yin Xiaohuang and Mei Jing, to help with this massive labor. When the Zhengzhou and Wuchang texts appeared, Rudolf Wagner kindly agreed to translate them.

Eugene Wu then worked over the translations with great care. Without his unmatched knowledge of this type of source, illustrated in his article here, and without his assistance this would have been a much poorer book. I went over his version and we argued out what seemed to us the remaining conundrums. K. C. Chang next spot-checked the translation of a couple of the texts and convinced us that there were still sufficient problems to justify a further check. Ye Yang then went meticulously over the whole translation and made numerous further corrections and helpful suggestions. For any remaining errors or omissions, I must take the final responsibility.

The footnotes to the translations dealing with traditional culture and history are usually Eugene Wu's; those on the obscurer contemporary literary figures are usually Ye Yang's; those dealing with current politics are usually mine; but Rudolf Wagner and Timothy Cheek also contributed in all categories. The bibliography and the comparison of sources found in the appendix were compiled by Timothy Cheek and Yin Xiaohuang.

As our work progressed, other new volumes of Mao texts surfaced elsewhere; as Eugene Wu points out in his article, with China's opening up, such works can leave the country in a multitude of ways. We are most grateful to Dr. Jonathan Unger, head of the Contemporary China Centre at the Australian National University, for sending us two important volumes, and to Mr. Y. S. Chan, head of the East Asia Library there, who allowed the originals to be xeroxed for us. Michael Schoenhals, author of *Saltationist Socialism: Mao Zedong and the Great Leap Forward 1958,* kindly gave us the titles of Mao collections that have been in his possession for several years, an offprint of his article in *The Australian Journal of Chinese Affairs* on the original text of Mao's "Contradictions" speech, and the text of a 1957 speech by Deng Xiaoping.

All of this took much longer than we had hoped! We all found these Mao texts difficult because none appear to have been formal, prepared speeches; rather, they were rambling monologues. The Chairman was allusive, tangential, colloquial, earthy. Even now, we are uncertain about what he meant in some places (and so indicate). Moreover, some of these speeches were apparently versions taken down by members of the audience whose stenographic skills are uncertain and whose understanding of Mao's meaning may have sometimes been as incomplete as our own. Considering all the problems of interpretation which we encountered, we were very fortunate to have so cheerful and painstaking an editor as Katherine Keenum to ensure that our final product was not merely well laid out, but also comprehensible, and in the English language.

The original texts and first draft translations were made available to colleagues at the Fairbank Center who had agreed to write commentaries. I did not ask for detailed analyses of the texts. Rather I wanted to elicit the reflections of specialists reviewing the period in the mirror of the new documents. Benjamin I. Schwartz and Merle Goldman are both veteran analysts of the events to which these speeches relate, and their articles illustrate how the passage of time and the availability of new material can modify perceptions. My own contribution attempts to describe the contemporary scene for the benefit of those, both Sinologists and more general readers, who have not fought this territory before; it is in my footnotes to the documents that I try to pinpoint key issues and revelations. The reader may detect some differences of emphasis and analysis among us all; if so, it only proves that at least at Harvard, the spirit of the Hundred Flowers lives on! Finally, our thanks go to Daniel Bell, who settled a long-running argument by suggesting the title of this book.

R.M.

PART ONE

Introductory Chapters

CHAPTER ONE

The Secret Speeches of Chairman Mao

RODERICK MACFARQUHAR

During his years in power, Mao Zedong initiated three policies which could be described as radical departures from Soviet and Chinese Communist practice: the Hundred Flowers of 1956–1957, the Great Leap Forward of 1958–1960, and the Cultural Revolution of 1966–1976. Each was a disaster: the first for the intellectuals, the second for the people, the third for the party, all three for the country.[1]

This volume retells the story of the Hundred Flowers and the

---

[1] Each resulted also in severe damage to Mao's standing. Had he died as soon after the revolution as Lenin, none would have taken place. Had Lenin lived to the same age as Mao, he would have died only seven weeks before Stalin!

Great Leap Forward, mainly through the words of Mao Zedong. It contains contemporary speeches of the Chairman which have never been published before, at least not in their original form, either in China or the West. While many other *in camera* speeches of Mao's have become available to Western Sinologists, the fact that these speeches have surfaced only after thirty years suggests that their circulation even among the Chinese elite was very limited, testimony to their embarrassing content. The major speech from the Hundred Flowers period is full of revelations which were cut out of the official version; the major speeches from the Great Leap period were not even bowdlerized for public consumption, so hyperbolic had Mao become at that time.

I

The term *Hundred Flowers* is used loosely by Sinologists to describe the period from January 1956 to early June 1957 during which Mao initiated a series of "liberal" policies towards the intellectuals. He was encouraged to do so by a series of successes in the struggle for socialist transformation. A speech by the Chairman in July 1955 had inspired a highly effective rural collectivization drive in the fall. By the end of the year, China had nearly completed this key task, without either the savagery or the chaos that Stalin had inflicted on Soviet agriculture a quarter of a century earlier. The nationwide victory of socialism, as defined by ownership of the means of production, was then secured by the virtually overnight conversion of private businesses into joint state-private enterprises and of handicraft trades into cooperatives.

Long before the last collective was formed, Mao proclaimed that China had undergone a "fundamental change"[2] and turned his attention to a new task, production. The first Five-Year Plan (FYP) (1953–1957), published in mid 1955, was insufficiently ambitious for Mao in his new mood. Increased output was needed both to prove the efficacy of socialism and to propel China faster along the road to wealth and power.[3] In January, Mao put together a utopian, forty-

[2]Mao, "Preface," in *Socialist Upsurge in China's Countryside*, quoted in *Origins* 1, p. 15.
[3]For a confirmation that the pursuit of wealth and power (*fu qiang*) was an essential motive for the Hundred Flowers, see Lu Dingyi, "'Bai hua qi fang, bai jia zheng ming' de lishi

article Twelve-Year Program for Agriculture and in April revamped industrial policy in a speech entitled "On the ten great relationships."[4]

To further his grandiose schemes for what was later known as the "little leap" of 1956, Mao needed to harness the enthusiasm and talents of the intellectuals, broadly defined to include the non-communist politicians who participated in Beijing's "united front"; scientists, engineers and managers, and the academics who trained them; as well as writers, artists, and actors who had the skills to help mobilize the "broad masses" for the production drive. Together these people constituted a relatively small group: 3,840,000, according to official statistics, including 100,000 "higher" intellectuals. More reason for Mao to court them. In January 1956, Premier Zhou Enlai promised them improved living and working conditions, higher status, more responsibility, and better pay.[5]

But the intellectuals had cause to be wary. The criticism and self-criticism sessions of the ideological remolding campaign unleashed on them in 1951 had imposed a humiliating acceptance of intellectual conformity. As recently as 1955, Mao had denounced the "anti-party" writer Hu Feng, whose sin was to seek greater room for maneuver for the intellectual within the Chinese Communist Party (CCP) and under the broad rubric of Marxism. The campaign against Hu Feng had epitomized the party's demands for total subjection to its dictates. To restore the intellectuals' confidence and arouse their creativity, more was needed than higher salaries.

The Chinese were encouraged to consider relaxing controls over intellectuals by the post-Stalin "thaw" in the Soviet Union. This de-Stalinization process was hastened by Nikita Khrushchev's "secret" speech to the Twentieth Congress of the Soviet Communist Party (CPSU) on 25 February, in which the Soviet first secretary denounced the late dictator and his deeds, root and branch. Khrushchev's diatribe was leaked to the West and published by the

---

huigu" (Historical review of 'Let a hundred flowers bloom, let a hundred schools contend'), *Xinhua wenzhai* 7:1(1986).

[4] For a fuller account and analysis, see *Origins* 1, pp. 15–32, 57–74.

[5] Zhou Enlai's report is translated in *Communist China, 1955–1959: Policy Documents with Analysis* (Cambridge, Harvard Univ. Press, 1962), pp. 128–44; the original text can be found in *Zhou Enlai tongyi zhanxian wenxuan* (Selected writings of Zhou Enlai on the united front) (Beijing, Renmin chubanshe, 1984), pp. 273–307.

United States government, causing immense confusion and questioning within the world communist movement.

Mao and his colleagues had their own reasons for not remembering Stalin with affection: He had interfered disastrously in the Chinese revolution, given the wrong advice in the civil war, imposed humiliating conditions before agreeing to a treaty with the new China, and godfathered a war in the Korean peninsula which had cost the infant People's Republic of China (PRC) much blood and treasure. But they realized that demolishing the "personality cult" of the god-like colossus would undermine the movement's morale and momentum. To restore balance to the appraisal of the dead despot, on 5 April they published "On the historical experience of the proletarian dictatorship." This critical editorial in the *People's Daily* acknowledged that Stalin had made mistakes, but asserted that his achievements were primary. Implicitly, it also absolved Mao himself of fostering an equally menacing personality cult.[6]

Mao's next moves were almost certainly prompted more by domestic imperatives than foreign stimulus. In his speech "On the ten great relationships," he not only set out new economic policies, but also proposed "long-term coexistence and mutual supervision" with China's non-communist political parties, which had been allowed to survive as a symbol of the united front. Their members also happened to constitute a large proportion of the country's managerial and technical experts.

A week later, on 2 May 1956, developing themes laid out earlier, Mao enunciated the policy "Let a hundred flowers bloom, let a hundred schools contend." His object was to encourage debate among intellectuals of all types. The Chairman realized that economic progress would be held back if the regime persisted in imposing a stultifying conformity on its best brains.

This landmark speech has never become available, but its main themes were elaborated three weeks later by the director of the Central Committee's Propaganda Department, Lu Dingyi.[7] As Lu confirmed, this was a policy "to mobilize all the positive elements." A "strict distinction" had to be made between the battle of ideas

---

[6]See *Origins* 1, pp. 43–8.
[7]Lu Dingyi, "Let a hundred flowers bloom, let a hundred schools contend," *RMRB*, 13 June 1956; trans. in *Communist China, 1955–1959*, pp. 151–63. See below, p. 88, n. 30.

"among the people" and the struggle against counterrevolutionaries: "Among the people themselves there is freedom not only to spread materialism but also to propagate idealism."

Even this ringing declaration failed to convince large numbers of senior intellectuals. The point was that the party retained the right to define where the boundary line between the people and counter-revolutionaries should be drawn and who fell into which category.

So, few flowers bloomed; and the schools that contended disputed only minor issues. The intellectuals' caution was justified by the storm of criticism that greeted the publication in September 1956 of a short story entitled "Young newcomer to the Organization Department." Its young author, Wang Meng, dared to describe cynicism and demoralization in a Beijing party organ.[8] At the CCP's Eighth Congress that same month, delegates indicated their unhappiness with the Hundred Flowers campaign and the order to work with non-party people.[9] In January 1957, four senior officials of the propaganda department of the General Political Department of the People's Liberation Army (PLA)—Chen Qitong, Chen Yading, Ma Hanbing, and Lu Le—attempted to bury the flowers and schools policy once and for all by pointing to the emergence of unhealthy literature of the Wang Meng type.[10]

Repeated references to them in the documents in this collection suggest that Mao was infuriated by the temerity of Chen and his colleagues in questioning the Hundred Flowers and felt compelled partially to defend Wang Meng as a symbol of that policy. It is sometimes argued that Wang's sufferings during the Anti-Rightist Campaign would have been far more severe but for Mao's favorable mention of him. Possibly Wang Meng reflects on this today when he makes his own pronouncements as Minister of Culture.

By the time Chen Qitong and his colleagues ventured to attack the Hundred Flowers, Mao had more compelling reasons to focus on how to deal with potential intellectual dissidents. In October 1956, the Polish communists had defied the CPSU by rehabilitating a lead-

[8]Trans. in Hualing Nieh, *Literature of the Hundred Flowers*, vol. 2. (New York, Columbia Univ. Press, 1981), pp. 473–511.
[9]*Origins* 1, pp. 110–16.
[10]See the discussion in Merle Goldman, *Literary Dissent in Communist China* (Cambridge, Harvard Univ. Press, 1967), pp. 181–2; D. W. Fokkema, *Literary Doctrine in China and Soviet Influence, 1956–1960* (The Hague, Mouton, 1965), pp. 124–7.

ing victim of the postwar Stalinist purges, Wladyslaw Gomulka, and making him party first secretary. Defense Minister Marshal Rokossovsky, Polish-born but a longtime Soviet citizen who had been imposed on Warsaw by Stalin, was dropped from the Politburo and sent home. For a brief period, it looked as if Khrushchev, who had flown secretly to Warsaw in a vain attempt to prevent the return of Gomulka, might try to overthrow the new Polish leadership by force. The Chinese protested behind the scenes against any such display of what they called "great nation chauvinism." From their own experience, the Chinese believed that independent communists were more effective than Soviet puppets.

Meanwhile, in Hungary, Khrushchev's "secret speech" had set off even greater ferment. Students and intellectuals expressed deep dissatisfaction with the rule of the Hungarian Stalinists, Mátyás Rákosi and Erno Gerö. In July, Rákosi was forced out. Much of the Hungarian debate took place in the Petöfi Circle, a discussion group named after a nineteenth-century patriot, which had been formed within the official youth federation after the CPSU's Twentieth Congress. For Mao, as his speeches in this volume underline, the Petöfi Circle came to symbolize the power of students and intellectuals to mobilize the people against communism once party leaders had destroyed their own legitimacy by oppression and terror.

On 23 October, two days after the "Polish October," Hungarian students and intellectuals staged a massive demonstration in Budapest demanding free elections and the removal of Soviet forces. New leaders were installed and Gerö followed Rákosi to exile in Russia. Soviet troops began to withdraw, but by the end of the month were quietly returning. Perhaps it was this that spurred Premier Imre Nagy, another recently rehabilitated victim of postwar Stalinist purges like Gomulka, to announce on 1 November that the Hungarian government wished to withdraw from the Warsaw Pact, the Soviet bloc military organization.

The Chinese vacillated in their response to the unfolding Hungarian drama, reflecting uncertainty about what was happening and where it would all lead. But once Nagy had opted to leave the Warsaw Pact, the Chinese wholeheartedly supported Soviet suppression of the revolt. They had not fought a costly war to save communism in North Korea only to tolerate erosion of the communist bloc in Eastern Europe. Early in the new year, after the Soviet Red Army had crushed the Hungarians and executed Nagy, Zhou Enlai interrupted an Asian tour to visit Warsaw and Budapest and confirm Chinese backing for the Soviet actions. He told the Polish Politburo that Moscow's leadership was essential for bloc unity and indicated to the Hungarian people that Beijing endorsed the Moscow-installed regime of Janos Kadar (who would survive as first secretary in Budapest until 1988).

The Hungarian revolt caused even more heart-searching and defections than the secret speech had within the ranks of non-ruling communist parties, especially in Western Europe. President Tito of Yugoslavia compounded the confusion by accepting the need to suppress the revolt in order to preserve socialism, but denouncing both the Stalinist errors that had led to the revolt and the Soviet-style bureaucratic system which produced them.

Again the Chinese felt obliged to buttress the gravely damaged authority of the CPSU. In an editorial entitled "More on the historical experience of the proletarian dictatorship," published on 29 December, they reemphasized the achievements of Stalin, but, more importantly, rejected Tito's allegation that Stalinism was an inevitable outgrowth of the Soviet system. The Chinese explained that even with the right system, there could still be human error. Incorrect behavior on the part of leaders such as Stalin could lead to "contradictions between the government and the people in socialist countries."[11]

This was the first time that communist ideologues had admitted that such contradictions could occur, a notion that Khrushchev later rejected. The correct handling of "contradictions among the people" (or "internal contradictions") was to be the subject of a major Mao speech in February 1957, which is included in this volume, and the basis of the subsequent Rectification Campaign.[12] Rectification of work style (*zhengdun zuofeng* or *zhengfeng* for short) was a well-tried method pioneered by Mao in the early 1940s as he sought to impose his leadership and to eradicate the wilder leftism of his Moscow-

---

[11]"More on . . ." is translated in *Communist China, 1955–1959*, pp. 257–72.

[12]Mao's first mention of correctly handling internal contradictions was in a letter, dated 4 Dec. 1956, to a leading businessman, Huang Yanpei; see Li Weihan, *Huiyi yu yanjiu* (Recollections and research), xia, (Beijing, Zhonggong dangshi ziliao chubanshe, 1986), p. 825; and, for the full text of the letter, *Mao Zedong shuxin xuanji* (Selected letters of Mao Zedong) (Beijing, Renmin chubanshe, 1983), pp. 514–5.

appointed predecessors.[13] As early as mid 1956, there were hints that a new rectification movement would be needed to accustom party cadres to working more cooperatively with non-party people. At the CCP's Eighth Congress that September, Deng Xiaoping had suggested that the party's ruling position could lead cadres to abuse their power, and reasserted the need for "supervision" of the party by non-communist parties.

The upheavals in Eastern Europe had no parallels in China. But Mao's speeches in this volume confirm that the People's Republic of China, too, experienced strikes by workers and students in 1956. Mao indicated that he believed these strikes were largely the product of bureaucratic mishandling and even oppression. He was increasingly concerned to avert the error described by Chinese theoreticians in the second editorial on the historical experience of the proletarian dictatorship, namely to prevent abuse of power from spreading and becoming systemic. Party rectification was too urgent, he evidently concluded, to be delayed till its originally scheduled start in 1958.

In the speeches translated here, Mao repeatedly alludes to massive opposition to his rectification plans. Indeed, these documents reveal that in March Mao thought of launching rectification only "informally" in 1957 and formally in 1958.[14] Since rectification had been carried out on a number of occasions since the first 1942–1944 campaign, albeit on more limited scale, and was thus an accepted tradition within the party, this is curious. The likely explanation is that Mao's colleagues may have accepted the need for rectification, but objected to its proposed form.

Previous rectifications had taken place inside the party. This time Mao wanted non-communists to participate. This was consistent with his advocacy of "long-term coexistence and mutual supervision," but was hardly to be welcomed by cadres who could expect non-communists to repay long years of oppression during obligatory and protracted criticism and self-criticism sessions.

Awareness of the party's hostility to his proposed campaign may

[13]For the documents and a discussion of the earlier Rectification Campaign, see Boyd Compton, ed., *Mao's China: Party Reform Documents, 1942–44* (Seattle, Univ. of Washington Press, 1952).
[14]See Text 13, n. 5.

have led Mao to elaborate his new theories before a non-party body rather than the Central Committee (CC). "On the correct handling of contradictions among the people," published here in its original spoken version for the first time anywhere, was delivered on 27 February to the institution which it was Mao's prerogative to summon as head of state rather than party chairman, the Supreme State Conference. Mao's warmth and frankness captivated his audience. He admitted that the regime had killed some 800,000 citizens in its various drives against counterrevolutionaries and other putative opponents, but seemed to promise that violent forms of class struggle were at an end. The reactions among Mao's colleagues are less easy to calibrate, but an unexplained absentee from the front-page *People's Daily* picture of the Supreme State Conference podium was Mao's heir apparent Liu Shaoqi. In recent years it has been possible to establish that Liu did attend at least part of the four-day meeting but left before the end on a tour of the southern provinces. Why Beijing's propagandists did not publish a picture of him beside the Chairman on the occasion of Mao's most important speech since the establishment of the PRC remains unexplained.

One theory is that party cadres who resented Mao's intended use of non-party critics against them saw Liu Shaoqi and Beijing Mayor Peng Zhen as their allies.[15] The 1957 documents in this volume do not confirm this hypothesis conclusively, but they do reveal a strength of party resistance to Mao's policies that would be hard to explain if he had a united Politburo behind him. It turns out that in addition to his major speech to a central propaganda conference on 12 March 1957—translated long since and so not included here[16]— Mao made several other speeches to smaller groups at that conference,[17] and followed this up with a whistle-stop tour during which he gave four more speeches in major cities. Mao was hustling on behalf of his policies, but at the end of the tour he confided to Mao loyalists in the Shanghai party *apparat* that the majority was still against him.

[15]See *Origins* 1, passim.
[16]See *SW5*, pp. 422–35.
[17]One of Mao's main supporters at the conference sessions was Kang Sheng, an alternate member of the Politburo, who emerged a decade later as an ultra-leftist during the Cultural Revolution. This reinforces the notion that, in Chinese politics, it is not what you support but whom you support that is crucial. Kang Sheng's seasonal changes duplicated Mao's; his loyalty was repaid.

Wary intellectuals underlined his dilemma with references to "early spring weather," the period when a sudden frost may nip early blooming flowers in the bud. They apparently were not sure that Mao could restrain his colleagues if the intellectuals spoke out.

We now learn that as late as 20 March Mao did not expect to be able to launch the Rectification Campaign before the originally agreed date in 1958. Indeed, the ideas laid out in the party chairman's "Contradictions" speech had received no publicity in the chief party organ, the *People's Daily*, presumably a reflection of both intra-party antagonism to them, and the absence of any formal party decision on rectification. As Timothy Cheek has established, on returning to Beijing from central China in early April, Mao called in the paper's editor, Deng Tuo, and harangued him in his customary earthy language for this lapse.

The decision to issue a rectification directive on 27 April 1957 and launch the campaign immediately thereafter on the 30th, was taken very late, probably no earlier than 23 April.[18] During the preceding weeks, Liu Shaoqi was away much of the time. It seems unlikely that he could have participated in detailed preparations for the campaign. On 30 April, Mao summoned non-party dignitaries for one final briefing before they took up his offer to criticize his party colleagues. In that speech, which for good reason was not included when Beijing published the fifth volume of Mao's selected works two decades later, Mao made the explosive undertaking that the widely resented party committee system on campuses could be reexamined, and asked Deng Xiaoping to take charge of the discussion.[19]

The 30 April speech was Mao's last in the Hundred Flowers vein: our selection for that period ends with it. There followed the exuberant spurt of "blooming and contending" in May and early June. Forums were held up and down the land, some convened by the CC's United Front Work Department, at which non-communists and even party intellectuals attacked aspects of CCP rule, some even rejecting

[18]For the importance of 22–23 April as a turning point, see *Origins* 1, pp. 208–10. For a discussion of the significance of the revelations in these documents about the launching of the Rectification Campaign, see below, Text 13, n. 5.

[19]See Text 16 in this volume, and Li Weihan, xia, p. 831. Li Weihan was director of the CC's United Front Work Department at the time, and presided over the major series of forums in May 1957 at which non-communists made their complaints.

it totally. By mid May, students were beginning to join in. Mao, either alarmed at the rising tide of criticism or pressured by more anxious colleagues or both (scholars still debate this point) began to issue warnings against excesses. CCP leaders probably remembered the effectiveness of their own student agitation, and when campus unrest escalated, an Anti-Rightist Campaign was launched and a leading "bourgeois rightist" was denounced for espousing Mao's last concession, the offer to reexamine the running of campuses. By then it was no longer attributable to the Chairman.

The Anti-Rightist Campaign was a major defeat for Mao. His vision of a benevolently-run communist society had to be abandoned in yet another assault on the luckless bourgeoisie and unwary party members. It was the end of the line for non-communist government ministers like Luo Longji, Zhang Bojun, and Zhang Naiqi who had nominally shared power with the CCP. It was the beginning of two decades of hard labor and internal exile for communist writers like novelist Wang Meng, journalist Liu Binyan, and the doyenne of Marxist feminists, Ding Ling, as well as over 550,000 lesser-known rightists.[20]

During the Anti-Rightist Campaign, Mao tried to maintain that it had always been part of his plan to lure "poisonous weeds" into the open in order to cut them down. This unconvincing subterfuge may have persuaded lower-level party members; but insofar as it was believed by the intellectuals, it could only have served to disillusion them further about the abortive Hundred Flowers policy. Later Mao argued that the hundred schools were in reality only two, the proletariat and the bourgeoisie.[21]

---

[20]All three were fully rehabilitated only after Mao's death. Indeed virtually all rightists were later exonerated, many during the early 1960s. Only a few like Luo Longji and Zhang Bojun, supposedly co-conspirators, seem still to be considered guilty men, presumably to preserve a fig-leaf of justification for the Anti-Rightist Campaign, currently criticized for being excessive but not as totally unnecessary. For the present official appraisal, see Zhonggong zhongyang wenxian yanjiu shi (CCP CC Documentary Research Office), *Guanyu jianguo yilai dangde ruogan lishi wentide jueyi, zhushiben (xiuding)* (Resolution on certain historical problems of the party during national construction, Annotated volume [revised]) (Beijing, Renmin chubanshe, 1985), pp. 317–8. For the total number of rightists, see Li Weihan, xia, p. 839.

[21]See Lu Dingyi, "'Bai hua qi fang, bai jia zheng ming,'" p. 3.

II

Mao desperately needed a new initiative to restore his tarnished credibility. Surprisingly, since he and his colleagues were already disenchanted with Soviet leadership of the communist bloc and the Stalinist economic model, Mao found inspiration in Moscow.

We have not translated the full texts of his speeches during his visit to the Soviet capital in November 1957 for the fortieth anniversary celebrations of the Bolshevik revolution, because they are now available in English.[22] The crucial point about Mao's visit for understanding the Great Leap Forward was his decision, taken apparently in the heat of the moment and in response to Khrushchev's boast that the Soviet Union would overtake the United States in the output of major products in fifteen years, to commit China to a similar competition. Mao simply substituted the United Kingdom as the yardstick.[23]

The little leap of 1956 had quickly petered out. By June that year an irate Chairman had felt compelled to allow his economic ministers, headed by Premier Zhou Enlai, to rein in the production drive because of the economic dislocation it was causing. But as he later indicated, he never really accepted the necessity of this step backward and continued to yearn for rapid economic progress. In October 1957, at the height of Mao's discomfiture over the termination of the Rectification Campaign and the counterattack on the rightists, the Chairman revived the over-ambitious Twelve-Year Program for Agriculture, presumably in an attempt to divert attention to production. Now, in the homeland of the Stalinist model, the Soviet leader was advocating a campaign approach to economic development. Mao must have felt vindicated.

Initially, as in 1956, Mao appears to have assumed that the production drive would be managed by the normal economic organs. But while party colleagues like Liu Shaoqi embraced his plan wholeheartedly, the economic ministers mouthed the slogans without making the upward revision of targets that they implied. Mao gave his reluctant colleagues a tongue-lashing, but it is not clear what would have happened if he had not come out with an alternative development model.

---

[22]See Michael Schoenhals, "Mao Zedong: Speeches at the 1957 'Moscow Conference,'" *The Journal of Communist Studies* 2.2:109–26 (1986).
[23]See *Origins* 2, pp. 15–9.

During the slack agricultural season in the winter of 1957–1958, the party led a massive water-conservancy drive in the rural areas, mobilizing large battalions of peasants to dig irrigation ditches and build reservoirs. Corvée labor was a Chinese imperial tradition to which the communists brought impressive organizational techniques; that winter they outdid themselves. Out of this achievement emerged an idea for a new rapid route to economic development: the substitution of labor for capital.

If agriculture was failing to keep up with the demands of industrialization and an expanding population, then China's hundreds of millions would be organized and mobilized to liberate themselves from the thrall of poverty by manual labor. If steel targets could not be met in conventional plants, then peasants (and everyone else) would be set to making it in primitive backyard furnaces. Since the bourgeois experts vital to a planned economy had been deemed politically unreliable in the Anti-Rightist Campaign, this abandonment of the Soviet model in favor of a Chinese road was timely as well as nationalistic.

This strategy was never formulated very precisely; it gradually evolved in a series of top-level work conferences from January 1958 on: Hangzhou, Nanning, Chengdu, Hankou. The Great Leap Forward was formally launched at the second session of the CCP's Eighth Congress in May, but was sent into orbit with a second-stage boost at the Beidaihe work conference in August, after a big summer harvest gave promise of a bumper crop year. At Beidaihe, too, a decision was taken to combine the recently-established rural collectives into People's Communes whose greater size, the theory went, would make it possible to mobilize bigger battalions for the tasks of the leap, as during the water-conservancy drive.

More importantly, the communes were viewed as engines of ideological transformation, combining agriculture, industry, commerce, education, and military affairs. They were also intended to obliterate the differences between manual and mental labor, between rural and urban ways of life, and to enforce egalitarianism between poorer and better off villages.

At Beidaihe, it has long been clear, Chairman Mao and many of his colleagues finally took leave of reality. With the publication here of Mao's speeches at that conference we can grasp the Chairman's pivotal role in inducing a party-wide euphoria which translated into an overnight attempt to transform the People's Republic into a communist utopia where egalitarianism would be combined with plenty. Interestingly, characteristically, Mao's style was not overtly demagogic. He was no rabble-rousing orator. His technique was to provide the spark to start the prairie fire. The apocalyptic mood within the CCP was exacerbated by an East-West crisis over the Middle East. Angered by what he saw as Soviet appeasement, Mao ordered a massive bombardment of the KMT-held offshore islands to demonstrate the right stuff. Amid fears of a clash with the United States, China launched an "Everyone a soldier" campaign and trumpeted the militarization of the communes.

What sometimes saved Mao from his own wilder flights of fancy were his acute political antennae, which alerted him to looming dangers. Beijing soon cooled the Taiwan strait when superior US firepower gave support to the Kuomintang; and when Mao, on his inspection tours, realized the negative impact on incentives of an egalitarian "supply system" which redistributed income from families that produced more to families that produced less, he rethought his earlier utopianism.[24] Two months after the triumphant conclusion of the Beidaihe conference, Mao began to draw back on both his production and ideological goals as the full texts of his November speeches to conferences in Zhengzhou and Wuchang here demonstrate. Another high tide had begun to ebb.

Our volume ends at this point, with Mao withdrawing in good order. Mao's speeches for the rest of the Great Leap are already available.[25] As the full impact of the first leap year became apparent in early 1959, he was forced into a hastier retreat. But his retirement as head of state, which party cadres had been warned of before the leap started, was in no sense an admission of defeat; and disaster might have been avoided but for the fateful clash over who was to blame at the Lushan conference in July-August that year. In defensive reaction, Mao relaunched the leap under far less favorable conditions, setting off events which led eventually to millions of deaths.[26]

[24]See Chen Shihui, "The party's earliest attempts to correct the 'Great Leap Forward' and the commune movement," *Dangshi yenjiu* (Research into party history) 5:27 (1983).

[25]See for instance, *Wansui* (1967), passim; *Wansui* (1969), pp. 259–319; and translations in *Miscellany of Mao Tse-tung Thought (1949–1968)*, vol. 1 (Arlington, Va., JPRS, 1974), pp. 133–236. See also *The Case of Peng Teh-huai (1959–1968)* (Hong Kong, URI, 1968); *Chinese Law and Government*, 1.4 (Winter 1968–69); 9.4 (Winter 1976–77).

[26]See *Origins* 2, parts 3 and 4.

III

The Hundred Flowers and the Great Leap Forward continued to have resonance, informing the policies of officials and attitudes of intellectuals. The thirtieth anniversary of Mao's hundred flowers speech in 1986 called forth a spate of articles which helped fuel the growing demand for greater democratization. When students went on the streets to promote this cause, the regime reacted as sharply as thirty years before: The demonstrations were quelled.

But the official response was far more restrained this time round, precisely because Deng Xiaoping, a key actor now as then, remembered the disastrous impact of the Anti-Rightist Campaign which brought the original Hundred Flowers to a close. Thirty years ago, several hundred thousand "rightists" were punished in various ways; this time a handful of intellectuals were expelled from the party. One example: the crusading journalist Liu Binyan was packed off for labor reform in 1957; in 1987, again crusading, he was expelled from the party, but remained at large and was allowed to come to Harvard.

Other veterans of 1956–1957 reenacted their earlier roles in 1986–1987. Hu Yaobang was first secretary of the Communist Youth League then and was regarded as being quietly in favor of reform; he was perhaps lucky to retain his job after young people went on the rampage. Three decades later, now CCP General Secretary, he was probably less discreet and certainly less fortunate, for this time he did lose his job. Peng Zhen, a senior Politburo member on both occasions, was consistently hard-line in wanting a crackdown against "dissidents."

The terrible famine produced by the Great Leap Forward was an even more searing experience for China's leaders. While Mao sat glumly by, Deng Xiaoping, Chen Yun, Li Xiannian, Bo Yibo, and other leaders still alive today guided China out of the economic depression by restoring material incentives and diminishing the powers of the communes. But Mao restrained them from introducing true private enterprise in the countryside or from abolishing the communes, and during the Cultural Revolution economic pragmatists were largely disgraced or demoted while Mao's allies tried to turn back the clock.

After Mao's death, all the old comrades who survived him agreed on the desperate need to revive the reform experiments of the early sixties. In the Chairman's absence they took them much further. They abolished the communes and unleashed private enterprise. They set aside egalitarianism, proclaiming that "To get rich is glorious" and that some must get rich first. They abandoned the ideological hyperbole of the leap and the Cultural Revolution, and substituted the slogan: "Practice is the sole criterion of truth."

Along the way the reformers split. "Conservatives" wanted to go back to the future: Chen Yun, Li Xiannian, and Bo Yibo probably in order to restore a version of the pre–Great Leap economic order, Peng Zhen probably to restore a version of the pre–Hundred Flowers political order. Unlike them, Deng Xiaoping supported both the Hundred Flowers and the Great Leap when Mao launched them, presumably because he, too, wanted to change an unsatisfactory political and economic order. Mao's experiments failed, but Deng still wanted to transform China in the search for wealth and power and pressed forward with his startlingly different experiment. Those momentous events thirty years ago helped to define its parameters.

But Mao's legacy is a complex one and the lessons can point in different directions. The Cultural Revolution was a more traumatic experience for the Chinese leadership than even the Hundred Flowers and the Great Leap Forward. When the death of Hu Yaobang in mid-April 1989 sparked massive student demonstrations in the heart of the capital in defiance of martial law, China's old guard evidently believed that they faced a threat similar to that unleashed by Mao in 1966. Deng Xiaoping, Chen Yun, Peng Zhen, Li Xiannian, Bo Yibo, and others set aside their differences, agreeing that the leadership of the CCP over China must not be threatened again by mob rule: hence the fateful decision to send in troops and tanks into Tiananmen Square on the night of 3–4 June 1989 to suppress the demonstrators by force and thereafter to hunt down their leaders.

Less than three weeks later, the regime was proclaiming that the unrest was over and expressed the hope that economic advance could resume. But this new Tiananmen "incident" would almost certainly have the same numbing effect on China's intellectual elite as the Anti-Rightist Campaign, and could deter rural and urban entrepreneurs and foreign investors. If that were to happen, the lessons of the Hundred Flowers and the Great Leap Forward would have been learned in vain, and the Communist regime's most hopeful decade would have come to an abrupt end.

Thoughts on the Late Mao – Between Total Redemption and Utter Frustration

BENJAMIN I. SCHWARTZ

I will confess at the outset that, for this reader, a perusal of these hitherto unpublished, informal utterances of Chairman Mao delivered
before a variety of audiences during the crucial period running from
the early months of 1957 to November 1958 do not, on the whole,
enhance his stature.

What strikes one most forcibly is the fact that the style, the tone,
the rhetorical devices, and the modes of reasoning that we find here
link this Mao to the Mao of the entire body of documents previously
drawn from Red Guard materials and made public under the title
Long Live Mao Zedong Thought (*Mao Zedong Sixiang Wansui*, hereafter *Wansui*), which is why it may be legitimate to refer to the "late
Mao" even though he had two decades still to live. Like the previous
Red Guard materials, these new documents are records of the

informal Mao "thinking out loud"; and as Timothy Cheek remarks elsewhere, this Mao is markedly different from the Mao whom we find in the various heavily edited and much more clearly articulated collections of his *Selected Works*.[1] To the extent that one can speak of a logical evolution of ideas and intellectual coherence of vision in Mao, these can be found most clearly enunciated in the official works.

The ideas that we find in the official writings are all here, but some-how these rambling and fascinating disquisitions tend to shift our at-tention from the implications of ideas as such to the constantly shifting states of mind of the Chairman during a period running from the beginning of the Hundred Flowers campaign in 1956 to his death. I use the vague term "states of mind" to refer to the evidence of shifting moods, of deep anxieties, soaring exaltations, injured pride, deep resentments, and unexamined complacencies. Our attention tends to be drawn to his affective reactions to emerging and often un-anticipated situations. While never believing that Mao the political leader was ever an Olympian social philosopher whose thoughts could be divorced (in the manner of Spinoza in his garret) from his political life, while realizing that the problem of the relationship of thought to states of mind is a problem for all of us, I must confess that these materials raise serious questions, at least for me, about the degree to which "Mao's thought" of the later years had any auton-omous, inertial weight of its own which set bounds to his shifting states of mind.

When the first *Wansui* documents were published in 1974 many readers found them fresh and even charming. They are, to be sure, rambling and full of bizarre associations of ideas, but most of us might not fare much better if our unedited conversations were to be recorded for posterity. Stuart Schram remarks that in contrast to the often wooden, ideological Newspeak of the official utterances, here we find the real "flesh-and-blood" Mao.[2] We are struck by the odd, wild, and sometimes whimsical trains of association; by the revela-tion of the degree to which the personal culture of Mao draws most of its imagery, metaphors, and historic examples from the Chinese

[1] For a comparison of official Mao texts, as well as previous *Wansui*, with the newly avail-able collections upon which our translations are based (some of which are also *Wansui* volumes), see Timothy Cheek's chapter.
[2] Stuart Schram, *Mao Tse-tung Unrehearsed* (Harmondsworth, Penguin, 1974), p. 8.

culture of the past (a fact that by no means guarantees their accuracy). His humor—earthy and otherwise—is very much present here in the newly available documents as in the previous *Wansui* documents; but on second reading, one is more struck by the menacing and bullying tone of his sarcasm directed against individuals and groups. Above all, one is struck by the cavalier freedom and looseness with which he handles not only the categories of Marxism-Leninism in general but even his own ideas. These materials underline, on the one hand, the degree to which Mao's intellectual universe is shaped by Marxist-Leninist categories and the degree to which he genuinely regards himself as an integral Marxist-Leninist, and, on the other hand, the plasticity and malleability of his entire arsenal of categories, which seems to offer little resistance to manipulation in the interest of his very immediate preoccupations. Does this indeed point toward a "liberal" openness to new ideas or to a kind of despotic capriciousness and arbitrariness?

Finally, we also find in these documents, as in the others, Mao's disarming readiness to admit his own past mistakes (in his speech at the Lushan conference of 1959 he even speaks of "crimes"). Yet one cannot escape the conclusion that the mistakes and "crimes" of the supreme leader are essentially venal. They do not touch the core of his being, since they are mistakes that flow from his essentially correct "general line." The fact that they may lead to unfortunate results may be due in large measure to the exaggerations and distortions of those below who implement policy and are often motivated by less than ideal motives—such as a yearning for recognition or a craven fear of attack. In Text 19, he admits that he himself may have been a "bit adventuristic" in the apocalyptic fervor of his speeches at Beidaihe a few months earlier in August 1958 but he claims that he had been essentially right in his effort to stimulate enthusiasm and a sense of infinite possibilities. Was it his fault that the local cadres had implemented his ideas in a "forced" manner and even resorted to "commandism"? Furthermore, the Chairman has always known how and when to correct his own mistakes. His mistakes are never such as to transfer him from the ranks of the people to the ranks of the enemy.

As stated, given the modes of rationalization and rhetorical devices used in this material, one finds oneself driven to focus as much on the Chairman's shifting states of mind as on the implication of his ideas. The reconstruction of states of mind is, of course, a highly hazardous and fallible undertaking. Yet one can hardly avoid it in dealing with the older Mao. This does not mean that the "thoughts" themselves have lost their significance as thoughts or that the ideas are simply to be treated in terms of psychological states. What becomes questionable is the degree to which the thought as thought established controls over and constraints on his shifting moods.

Mao had first asserted his claim to be an ideological leader during the Yan'an period—a claim that seems to have been accepted more or less by the other party leaders. Whether the Mao Zedong thought during this period was wholly his own creation or whether it was, to a degree, collectively shaped by the party leadership as a whole, as is now being maintained in China, is a matter which I shall not attempt to deal with here. What marks this thought in the late thirties and forties, however, is the awareness of the degree to which vast "objective" political, military, and economic forces impose severe constraints on the actions of the leadership. The ideological categories are used to adjust to a real and recalcitrant environment. No doubt, the faith in the ultimate triumph of socialism and communism which had played a role in Mao's original conversion continues to act as a sustaining faith, but there is no evidence that it shapes his immediate strategic thinking. There was as yet no anticipation of a speedy communist triumph, and it is highly doubtful that the Mao of the Yan'an period as yet saw in the Yan'an experience itself prefigurations of the ultimate communist utopia. Whatever one may think of the appropriateness of the Marxist-Leninist categories Mao used to analyze situations, the categories were related directly to current economic, political, and military realities. It is perhaps in these circumstances that Mao's talents as a political strategist were most effectively exercised.

It is noteworthy that the Yan'an strategies not only proved effective in winning victory in the civil war but were applied, with due adjustment, to new realities in the initial period of state consolidation (roughly 1950–1952) when general "law and order" were speedily established. The continuation of the "New Democratic" policies in the economy had something to do with the success of the measures taken in these years to bring about an initial economic and financial stabilization. To be sure, this "pragmatic" program of adjustment by no means precluded the vast blood-letting of Land Reform and the movement against counterrevolutionaries. Yet, on balance, this probably did not prevent the People's Republic from establishing its general authority and the bases of the legitimacy it has enjoyed ever since.

No doubt, the speed with which effective government was established led to an enormous growth of confidence on the part of both Mao and other party leaders that it was possible now to proceed very quickly to both economic development and the "transition to socialism." The fact that the two goals could be so readily coupled probably explains one of the main attractions of the Stalinist model, which so effectively combined both goals. Even the Mao of Yan'an, who resisted Stalin's claim of authority as a strategist of the Chinese revolution, found Stalin's *Short Course on the History of the CPSU* utterly convincing on the question of building socialism; and indeed it was used as a major text in cadre education. Mao was among those who genuinely accepted Stalin's role as a teacher in this area.

He no doubt wholeheartedly accepted two of Stalin's "contributions to the storehouse of Marxism-Leninism," namely, the notion that socialism can be achieved long before the full development of industry as well as the notion that industrialization can itself be carried out by "socialist methods" in an underdeveloped country. This acceptance, it would appear, even extended to the priorities of Stalin's socialist "development model." To be sure, the speedy achievement of political control in China may have suggested the thought that in China this model might be applied with greater success and without the depressing side effects of the Soviet model in the Soviet Union itself. It was no doubt this optimism which led the Mao of 1955 to believe that, in China, agricultural collectivization would be achieved without any of the distressing concomitants of Soviet collectivization and would even lead to a phenomenal rise in agricultural production.

On the other side, the wholehearted acceptance of Soviet ideas on the "building of socialism" in many ways marked a continuation of the Chairman's acceptance of external constraints—in this case the constraint of Soviet wisdom in the matter of "building socialism." Indeed, in the entire period stretching from Yan'an until the abrupt demise of the Hundred Flowers campaign, Mao seems to have remained genuinely modest in the acknowledgement of his own limitations in the fields of technology and economics. Indeed, in the

1952–1955 period he seems to have deferred to Soviet superior authority not only in the field of technology and economics but in all other fields of modernization as well. When one looks back over this period, it would appear that a good deal of his own energy during this period from the Wu Xun affair of 1950 to the Hu Feng affair of 1955 was devoted to preventing "bourgeois" literary-cultural intellectuals from exercising a harmful spiritual effect on the march toward socialism.

When viewed against this background, one is strongly inclined to agree with Roderick MacFarquhar that Mao's basic sense of liberation from major external limits and constraints on his role as a creative spiritual leader in his own right came in the latter months of 1955 with his initiative in accelerating the collectivization of agriculture. The apparent success of the drive, which was carried out without any of the horrors that had accompanied Soviet collectivization, as well as the presumed voluntary acceptance by the "national bourgeoisie" of "socialist transformation," seems to have convinced him that in China, socialism had basically, speedily, and decisively triumphed.

To be sure, the definition of socialism was still quite conventionally institutional in the Soviet manner. It meant, above all, the nationalization of private property. Yet the manner in which socialism had been "basically" achieved must have induced in him an exultant sense that China was after all different from the Soviet Union and that these differences could be related in retrospect directly to some of his own Yan'an ideas. The fact that the peasant masses had willingly embraced socialism and that even the "national bourgeoisie" had "been persuaded" to accept socialism certainly seemed to lend support to the hint in his "On Coalition Government" of 1945 that in China the entire people (all four classes) might positively participate in the building of socialism. This, when taken together with some of the new winds blowing in the Soviet Union after Stalin's death, may even have led Mao to contemplate the possibility that Stalin may not have said the last word on how a socialist economy must be built, thus opening up a new space for Chinese contributions even in the area of "socialist construction."

All of this was to lead to what was to become a central dyadic formula in Mao's thought during the Hundred Flowers period (a formula that figures prominently in our documents) namely the antithesis between the tasks of class struggle and the tasks of production.[3] By 1956, we are told, "antagonistic" class struggle between the "enemy and ourselves" had been brought to an end and the barriers to soaring victories in the battle of production had all fallen away. It was China's great fortune that all the four classes of the people could now be united to carry forward the tasks of production. It was within the context of this mood of elation that Mao was evidently persuaded by Zhou Enlai and others that the "bourgeois intellectuals," who had been the object of his most vehement animus as late as the end of 1955, must be allowed to play a vital role in the tasks of production. If China were to develop its own new model of a socialist economy, the skills and cultural capacities of the intellectuals would be indispensable.

At this point, however, the willingness to recognize the existence of independent sources of knowledge and skills not available to Mao or the party reflected not simply a modest recognition of limitations but also a soaring confidence that a party which had "basically" achieved victory in the area of "antagonistic class struggle" and "basically" achieved socialism could afford to recognize the contribution that "intellectuals" might make to a Chinese socialism which might even represent an advance over the Soviet model. The same Mao who had a few months before regarded the literary views of Hu Feng as a fatal threat to socialism and who had treated Hu Feng as a deadly enemy was now ready to assign both the cultural and scientific intelligentsia to the ranks of the people. This meant that even the "wrong" views of the intellectuals could be tolerated on the assumption that basically they were patriots and had willy-nilly come to accept socialism. Even wrong views ("poisonous weeds") among the people were no longer an infallible sign of enemy status. The older intellectuals and party cadres were, of course, acutely aware of the contrast between the treatment of Hu Feng, who still languished in prison, and the Chairman's new line on bourgeois intellectuals. The Chairman, however, easily proceeded to solve the problem by inventing the fiction that Hu Feng had not only held false views but had actually created a political conspiracy.

As a politician, Mao is not unique in his ability to construct "best-case scenarios." In these writings, however, one has the feeling that

---

[3]During the period 1952–55 he seemed, on the main, to have accepted the Stalinist assumption that the two—class struggle and production—went hand in hand.

having constructed his scenario, he then proceeded to believe it forthwith as a faithful depiction of reality. In the early months of 1956, he probably genuinely believed that "bourgeois intellectuals," being patriotic and having either genuinely accepted socialism or having realized that they had nowhere else to go, would accept the tasks assigned to them in the fields of culture, science, and technology. Presumably all their contributions would be made strictly within the boundaries of a socialist economy. Yet even here there was some implication that a space existed for flexibility now that Mao himself no longer seemed to be fully committed to the Stalinist model (as is made somewhat clear in his speeches of April and May 1956, which became "On the ten great relationships"). Much of his discussion with "intellectuals," however, is characteristically addressed more to the literary and cultural intellectuals than to the scientists and technologists. As a poet and man of letters he continues as in the past to assign an extraordinary weight to literature as a force in human society. What is more, one senses that, on one level, he acutely feels the truth of Hu Feng's charge that Marxism-Leninism in China had failed to produce a living literature, and that without a sense of life no literature can serve the ideological cause. It may have been his sensitivity to the essential truth of Hu Feng's charge that particularly infuriated him. Yet in the early months of 1956 he seems to have been sublimely confident not only that a literature which combined good writing with sound doctrine was eminently attainable but also that even where "poisonous weeds" appeared they could do no harm to the impregnable structure of an achieved socialism. In general during the early months of 1956, Mao's best-case scenario seems to have remained untroubled by major obstacles, even though the intellectuals were responding very cautiously to his overtures; but this, he probably believed, would soon change.

Developments in Moscow and the communist bloc were doubtless also read by the Chairman at this time as favorable to his scenario despite the unease occasioned by Khrushchev's shocking speech on Stalin at the Twentieth Congress of the CPSU. If there is one point that is underlined by these documents, it is the fact that Mao continued to be enormously concerned with communist bloc politics and ideology, continued to regard China as an integral part of that bloc, and continued to see an intimate link between his domestic and his bloc concerns. Thus, in the early months of 1956, he seems to have interpreted the new trends in the Soviet Union after Stalin's death as generally favorable to his best-case scenario. While this is not yet the apocalyptic Mao of the fall of 1958, we find here a Mao now fully confident of his claims as spiritual leader and highly hopeful that the Hundred Flowers scenario will lead to success.

As we move toward the latter months of 1956, however, we find the emergence of many unanticipated, troublesome circumstances both in China and in the communist bloc as a whole. The Twelve-Year Program for Agriculture, it became obvious, would not soon lead to a productive explosion. The area of agriculture, it is to be noted, was an area in which his feelings were particularly sensitive given his previous triumph in collectivization. The CCP's Eighth Congress in September had raised serious questions about the implications of Khrushchev's speech on Stalin for his own claims as spiritual leader of the party. Finally the Hungarian Revolution seems to have had a radically ambivalent effect on the whole subsequent development of his outlook. The very thought that an established communist regime might actually disintegrate was no doubt profoundly disturbing. Whatever his doubts about the new Soviet leaders, he continued to believe that China's fate was solidly bound up with the fate of the communist bloc. Although the thought that an established socialist system might be systematically defective was unacceptable, the notion that even the right system might be wrongly applied because of ongoing non-antagonistic contradictions between the leadership and the people provided Mao with a space for criticizing the Rákosi leadership in Hungary and for reasserting the CCP idea of party rectification, which had its roots in Yan'an. The intellectuals in Hungary may have, on the one hand, reinforced Mao's strongly held feelings carried over from the past that intellectuals were not to be trusted and could under some circumstances prove to be enormously dangerous. On the other hand, he was able to persuade himself of the decided difference between the Hungarian intellectuals and China's intellectuals who had "basically" accepted the system and were basically patriotic—basically, "part of the people."[4]

In sum, I would suggest that, in the documents of the early months of 1957 included in this volume (Texts 1–14), we find a Mao determined to move forward with the Hundred Flowers "scenario"

[4]See *Origins* 1, p. 173.

but a Mao already deeply disturbed and worried by the developments of the latter months of 1956. There can be no doubt that he
meant to go ahead with the Hundred Flowers and with party rectification or that he was indeed profoundly irked by those top party leaders who were strongly resisting his policies, particularly after the
disturbing events in Hungary; yet oddly enough, in some ways, he
also continued to identify with the suspicions and resentments of the
average party cadre against the intellectuals. While some of the
themes in these talks seem to foreshadow the final Cultural Revolutionary assault on the party, this reader does not see as yet a prefig-
uration of the Mao of the Cultural Revolution, who was to set
himself against the entire party apparatus. Nor do I see a Mao really
aligning himself unambiguously with non-party intellectuals against
the party.

In fact, one is struck by the relatively negative tone of much of
what he has to say about them. He very much stresses the seemingly
unalterable "bourgeois" nature of most of the intellectuals. He is still
willing to concede their patriotic loyalty; but, in discussing their
acceptance of socialism, he more often stresses their lack of alternative rather than their sincere commitment.[5] Whatever hopes he cher-
ished in 1956 about winning most of them over to Marxism seem to
have greatly diminished. The core of his argument in his talks with
party cadres is the inescapable fact that both he and they still have
much to learn from intellectuals in the realms of science, technology,
and culture. Until such time as new "proletarian intellectuals"
emerge, he and the other party cadres will have to "toughen their
scalps." They will have to grin and bear it.

When he rebukes the party cadres for feeling bitter that "we" who
have fought through all the bitter years of class struggle must now
defer to intellectuals who had done little in the revolution, this may,
of course, simply be regarded as a rhetoric used to convince the
cadres to mend their ways. Yet the use of the personal pronoun "we"
suggests that the Chairman himself may share their resentments.
When he speaks about the intellectuals lifting their tails high and of

---

[5]We nevertheless find the odd notion that Hungarian intellectuals were particularly unruly
because of their worker-peasant origins while Chinese intellectuals were "safer" precisely
because of their "bourgeois" background. Here we have the thought that even intellectuals
who spring from the masses may be incalculable and dangerous.

the need to kowtow to them at least for a time, one senses something of himself in this heavy sarcasm, although he is also probably quite sincere in insisting that the cadres themselves, many of whom had become indolent bureaucrats, should cease resting on their laurels.

Most revealing of the chairman's profound ambivalence in the early months of 1957 are his remarks on the famous story by Wang Meng, "Young newcomer to the Organization Department." This story, which had been published in September 1956 and had presented a most vivid negative portrayal of middle-level bureaucrats, had become a symbol of the problems of "blooming" in the field of literature.[6] By January and February of 1957 it had become a main target of anti–Hundred Flower sentiment within the party press. Although the upshot of Mao's remarks in Text 1 of February 1957 is to defend the right of Wang Meng's story to exist, it cannot be said that they do much to encourage cadres to think well of such stories. He cannot help admiring its lively style, but he is profoundly uneasy about the unalloyed negative depiction of party cadres and the lack of anything positive which would demonstrate that justice is ultimately served in a socialist system. On balance, he leaves the impression that despite its vivacity the story may be one of those poisonous weeds which must be endured. In his talk on literature to literary and art circles, we find him criticizing a film that portrays a thoroughly reprehensible bureaucrat in the role of director of a railroad bureau: "Since [sic] the writer has described him [in this way], and then he is still retained as a bureau director—this type of cadre should be dismissed!"[7] That is how matters would work in a true socialist system. He implies that any literary work which is to be considered a true flower must be firmly within the bounds of socialist realism but that essential writing skills may be learned even from the weedy contributions of bourgeois writers.

If his remarks about bourgeois intellectuals in the texts seem far less reassuring to the intellectuals than official speeches might lead us to believe, his advice to party cadres about how to avoid the pitfalls of "dogmatism and subjectivism" are almost totally lacking in sub-

[6]For a discussion of the story see Merle Goldman, *Literary Dissent in Communist China* (Cambridge, Harvard Univ. Press, 1967), pp. 179–80. The story is translated in Hualing Nieh, ed., *Literature of the Hundred Flowers*, vol. 2, (New York, Columbia Univ. Press, 1981), pp. 473–511.

[7]Text 7, p. 218 below.

stantive advice or concrete, substantive illustrations. This is particularly evident in his discussions of March 10 with "Press and publishing circles" (Text 8). Here again, we meet the large dyadic formulas such as "dogmatism versus right opportunism" with the sage advice not to fall into either extreme. Again the editors and publishers are exhorted to use persuasion rather than a policy of striking blows, but there is a notable absence of concrete advice to cadres whose whole training had led them in the opposite direction on *how* to persuade bourgeois intellectuals. In the end, the burden of his message is that in dealing with concrete circumstances they should rely on their own best judgment. This might seem to indicate an admirable willingness to grant independence to the lower cadres, but the advice is proffered without any assurance that they will not suffer direct consequences for exercising bad judgment. To those not inclined to take new initiatives, there was nothing in the Chairman's advice that was likely to move them toward boldness.

We are thus not surprised that during these months leading well into April neither the top party leaders nor the lower cadres nor the intellectuals themselves were inclined to move ahead. The rhetorical signals conveyed in these informal talks were by no means sufficiently unambiguous to send a clear message to any of these groups. Even the speaking notes on the "Correct handling of contradiction among the people" (Text 3) seem much more ambivalent than the officially published text of the speech (that is, the first part of the published text, unmodified by the added "Six criteria"). Yet there can be no doubt that, despite his worries, the Chairman was determined to go ahead with the Hundred Flowers formula. He did not depart from his basic assumptions: 1) that the party needed the skill and knowledge of the bourgeois intellectuals; 2) that the intellectuals would cooperate with the state either for reasons of genuine patriotism or because of their realization that they had no alternative or both; and 3) that the party, the state, and the masses were solid enough in their unity to withstand any "bourgeois" criticism, no matter how poisonous. What were crucial were the differences rather than the similarities between China and Hungary.

It is clear, however, that by April and May, the Chairman's growing exasperation with the massive resistance of the party on all levels to the kind of persuasive rhetoric contained in Texts 1–12 finally led him to greater exasperation with the party than with the intellectuals—hence the new stress on party rectification and the even more fateful heightened encouragement of non-party intellectuals to participate in the rectification process. The Chairman's message was now clear and incisive (even though he probably continued to believe that the criticism that would emerge would be like a "gentle breeze and mild rain"). Now his policy line became sufficiently forceful to demonstrate once more (as in the collectivization speed-up of 1955) that his pre-eminent authority, when asserted unambiguously, was adequate to override the resistance of his party colleagues.

In light of the above, one finds it difficult to imagine the depth of the fury and exasperation which he probably experienced in May and early June 1957 after the unbridled flood of "blooming and contending" that emerged particularly among the students whose entire life experience had been shaped in the post-Liberation period. After having vehemently insisted again and again that the party could withstand any criticism no matter how bourgeois and how poisonous, it suddenly became obvious that the questioning by the students of the very principle of "party leadership," which he had, it is true, always mentioned, was something he had utterly failed to anticipate. In all the talk of "mutual supervision" between democratic parties and the Communist party it was evidently simply assumed that the Communist party would decide which criticisms were acceptable and which not. The claim of the "hegemony of the CCP within the United Front" was a claim to which he expected no challenge. Yet what the students were now demanding were tangible limits on party authority. Here was a weed sufficiently poisonous to transfer its propagators back to the ranks of the enemy. Despite all of Mao's conflicts with other party leaders and with lower party cadres, I find no indication that he could as yet disentangle his personal claim to authority from the authority of the party as a whole.

While he continued to employ the vocabulary of the Hundred Flowers for a time (he could not drop it immediately in the face of party leaders who were drawing satisfaction from his mistakes), it was quite obvious that his best-case scenario assumptions had collapsed. The sharp dichotomy between the class struggle of the past and the struggle for production of the future was no longer viable. The intellectuals had again proven themselves to be a dangerous "antagonistic" bourgeois element. This new view had even deeper implications. The conventional institutional definition of socialism in terms of public ownership of the means of production was obviously grossly deficient. Not only could capitalist "antagonistic" consciousness survive the inauguration of a socialist system, it could even threaten socialism. The fact that even a sector of the party and of the communist literary intellectuals had accepted the bourgeois critique was the ultimate proof of the sinister, dynamic power of bourgeois ideology. A further implication was thus a marked broadening of both the negative and positive roles of the conscious factor in human affairs. Bourgeois consciousness was not simply a passive remnant; it could become a threatening force. At the same time, on the positive side, the survival of socialism (and attainment of communism) was not assured by the socialization of property. Only the internalization of a socialist (and communist) ethos could assure ultimate victory.

The Chairman was soon able to convince himself, however, that while the bourgeois intellectuals had proven their perfidy, the entire history of the People's Republic had proven that the broad masses of workers and peasants were, in contrast, ready to accept the leadership of Mao and the party with total faith. They had proven their readiness to internalize a socialist ethos. The signs of discontent among the collectivized peasants in 1956 and 1957 could thus easily be attributed to the influence of rich peasants and "departmentalistic" cadres. The masses as a whole remained loyal.

In turning from his previous emphasis on the need to rely on intellectuals as a source of indispensable knowledge as well as from the cautious assumption that acquisition of knowledge in the realm of science and culture would be a cumulative and slow process, Mao eliminated one of the last external constraints on the sway of his spiritual authority. He was able to accomplish this shift not by explaining his change of mind but simply by turning to certain alternate themes and notions already available to him and again by invoking the Yan'an experience as a model. This time, however, Yan'an emerged as a model of a proto-communist society in which the masses had sacrificed themselves selflessly to achieve military victory—a victory won basically by mass solidarity and moral incentive. The masses were the source of an incalculable "nuclear" power, which, once released, would manifest itself not only in physical labor but in the ability to master technology by swift empirical methods of "learning by doing." After all, "the inventor of the sleeping pill was not even a doctor. He was only a pharmacist. . . . I am told that penicillin was invented by a man who worked as a laundryman."[8] Once imbued with a proper communist spirit, the masses will be able to overwhelm most obstacles in the "war on nature" without the need to place total reliance on the fussy and pompous "science" of the academic scientists.

As we move from the later months of 1957 to the early months of 1958, Mao soon accumulated what he regarded as much empirical confirmation of his new best-case scenario. The campaign against the Four Pests became almost, in miniature, a highly plausible model of all the principles which were to underlie the Great Leap Forward. The party's ability to consolidate the enthusiasm and energy of the masses in the war against natural pests and the capacity of the masses to develop simple and yet ingenious methods for dealing with these crucial problems of public health and production could be applied across the board to all sectors of government. The same release of the "nuclear" energies of the masses would soon manifest themselves in the mass production of steel and in the emergence of the communes themselves. Wherever the Chairman discerned an experimental effort that at first glance seemed to confirm his vigorous new faith in "revolutionary romanticism," there seemed to be no further need of sustained close scrutiny and investigation. Finally, with the promise of an amazingly abundant harvest in 1958, all inhibitions on his new Great Leap vision seemed to evaporate.

In the remarkable talks at Beidaihe in August 1958 (Text 17), we find Mao at the very pinnacle of his most apocalyptic expectations. It is now entirely obvious that the Chairman was himself the fountainhead of the notion that communism was close at hand. The real problem was to conceal the fact from the Soviet Union, which would be highly displeased with the news. The vast increase in grain production and the soaring expansion of steel production finally had proven that the Chinese masses (peasants perhaps even more than workers) could now be easily imbued with a communist ethic.[9] "[We've] drawn water up hills from the Tiao River in Gansu [province]; the completion of such a large project is the result of the party's leadership and the people's communist spirit . . . We are one party with

[8]Schram, p. 119.
[9]Text 17, p. 397ff.

one 'ism,' [and] the masses support us. We have become one with the masses . . . "[10] It is also important to note at this point that Mao was still relying wholly on the party as the instrument for internalizing the communist spirit in the masses and was even able to convince himself after all the tensions of the Hundred Flowers period that "[s]ince rectification, the system of bourgeois right has been almost completely destroyed; leading cadres no longer lead by virtue of their power and prestige [or] bureaucratic airs, but [instead] rely on serving the people, seeking benefits for the people, and on persuasion."[11] In the apocalyptic mood of August one hardly doubts the sincerity of these statements. What one does doubt, however, is the enduring depth of his commitment to them.

The sincerity of Mao's utopianism as depicted in the texts was in these years immensely attractive to radicals abroad. Here was a communist leader who truly seemed to believe in the reality of the communist vision of the good society and who was even willing to dare to believe in its imminent realization. Whether Mao's dream of the good society was indeed the same as that of Marx, it was similar in one respect. Unlike the painstakingly detailed utopias of "utopian socialists" like St. Simon and Fourier, Marx's image for the future is, in the end, drawn from what one might call an eliminative utopianism. Once the capitalist mode of production and private ownership of the means of production had been eliminated from the stage of history, the roots of social disharmony would have basically disappeared. The good society would emerge as a total integrated state of affairs. Mao's utopia is also eliminative. There are, to be sure, profound differences. The older Marx relied fundamentally on the impersonal forces of material history to bring about the elimination of the obstructive forces while the older Mao's main reliance is on the transformation of consciousnesses initiated by a virtuous elite. To be sure, in the decidedly more sober reflections of his November 1958 "Talks at the Wuchang Conference" (Text 19), he points out that communism would be marked by an extreme abundance of products[12] as well as by ownership by the whole people. Yet in Text 17 and even

---

[10]Text 17, p. 413.

[11]Text 17, p. 414.

[12]In the "Talks at Beidaihe" he seems to assume that the forthcoming staggering harvests of 1958 and the astronomical rise in steel production were already a sign that such abundance was almost immediately available.

Texts 18 and 19, it is implied that in China the speedy internalization by the masses of a communist ethic would itself be the precondition for the achievement of these tangible goals. If the peasant masses had already in Yan'an in their "rural work style and guerrilla practices" manifested the sprouts of communist ethic, "Why is it that building communism doesn't work? Why do [we] have to use a wage system?"[13] "Restoring the supply system seems like 'retrogression'; [but] 'retrogression' means progress, because we've retrogressed since we came into the cities."[14]

The apocalyptic frame of mind which we find here, in some ways, seems to resemble the soaring optimism of the beginning of the Hundred Flowers movement. Yet, in the end, one feels that the vision of the Great Leap Forward is much closer to the heart of his being than the Hundred Flowers movement, which from beginning to end seems to have involved an uncomfortable and grudging concession to the intellectuals and to the notion that they were the custodians of an autonomous wisdom of their own. With the new vision that promised the fusion of what he now saw as the communist ethos of Yan'an days with the speedy achievement of a wealthy and powerful China, one might say that he had attained his final spiritual resting place. Whether this clinging to his ultimate utopian vision really manifests his profound commitment to the well-being of the masses as flesh-and-blood human beings or whether it has become an abstract projection of his own imperial ego is a question I shall not attempt to answer. Yet while the faith in the vision seems to have survived in some form to the end, it by no means put a stop to his continued cavalier manipulation of his categories, which were to prove as malleable as ever in the face of changing political circumstances.

It would now appear that between the August meeting at Beidaihe and the November meetings at Zhengzhou and Wuchang (Texts 18 and 19) Mao himself became unavoidably aware of enormous dislocations, false reporting, coercive methods used by local cadres to implement the "communist wave," and so forth.

Mao was even prepared to admit that he himself may have been a "bit adventuristic." The local cadres were now belatedly informed that despite the "sprouts of communism," the "laws" of the socialist

[13]Text 17, p. 417.
[14]Text 17, p. 418.

stage of development described by Stalin in his *Economic Problems of Socialism in the USSR* would not so speedily disappear. It might take considerably longer for the sprouts to grow than had been suggested in the Beidaihe talks. Peasants still require rest. Commodity production cannot yet be totally eliminated, and so forth, and so on. The incessant accordion-like game with numbers continues. At Beidaihe, we are told that "[p]robably in about ten years our produce will be very bountiful [and the people's] morality will be very noble."[15] At Zhengzhou there is talk of two decades. After the extravagant claims about the communist propensities of the vast mass of peasants at Beidaihe, the Mao of the talks at Wuchang suddenly reminds the cadres of all the strictures to be found in Marx concerning peasants (not just rich peasants). Peasants will hold back their grain and think of their own family and village interests. "Once the heaven-storming enthusiasm of the peasants emerges, it's easy to think of them as workers, [and] to consider the peasants to be superior to the workers."[16] But, after all, peasants are not workers. Why the cadres should *not* have believed that they were, after Mao's Beidaihe's projection, remains a puzzle. When the circumstances seemed favorable, the peasants were proclaimed to be more open to communization than city people. When circumstances were unfavorable, the local cadres were to be sharply rebuked for ignoring all of Marx's strictures concerning the petty bourgeois nature of the peasantry.

The documents in this volume carry us to the end of 1958. As we know, the increasing frustrations already visible in Texts 18 and 19 were to grow in magnitude as we move into 1959, finally reaching the crisis of the Lushan Conference of 1959. The Chinese communist leadership, which had seemingly been itself swept up in varying degrees by Mao's apocalyptic vision after Beidaihe, soon became deeply concerned by the news from the field. In the end, however, it was clear that Mao, despite all his admissions of errors and "crimes," would not renounce his ultimate vision, in which he now had the kind of personal investment that he had not had in the cause of the intellectuals in the Hundred Flowers period. In his amazing speech at Lushan in 1959, which provides a vintage example of some of the most spectacular rhetorical devices of the aging Mao, he freely

[15]Text 17, p. 419.
[16]Text 18, p. 476

admits "mistakes" and even "crimes." Yet his basic commitment to the Great Leap vision remains essentially intact—even reinforced by his towering fury directed against the party "rightists." It is during this conference indeed that we begin to discern the first glimmerings of the full-blown Cultural Revolutionary doctrine that the final and most formidable obstacle to the achievement of the good society is, after all, the corporate membership of the party itself.

During the remaining months of 1959 and even the early part of 1960, the fundamental rhetoric of the vision remains in place; and in 1960 there is even the campaign to extend the vision to the urban sector in the form of the "urban communes." Once again the Chairman demonstrates his capacity to prevail over the other party leaders.

With the devastating economic disasters of 1959–1961, the Chairman nevertheless also displayed his now long-proven ability to retreat *in extremis*. We now hear little of the imminence of the communist stage. Indeed we are even astonished to hear that "with regard to socialist construction we still lack experience."[17] "As for the construction of a strong socialist economy, in China fifty years won't be enough; it may take a hundred years or even longer."[18] These statements represent an astonishing manifestation of discouragement and modesty, and no effort is made to relate them to the credo of the Great Leap Forward. Yet despite this moment of deep discouragement concerning the domestic scene, in retrospect, it would seem that he never really abandoned his Great Leap vision. It was, in fact, to prove to be his final spiritual refuge.

When the economic recovery of 1962 led him to discover his own voice once more, he was easily able to convince himself that while he had indeed miscalculated the imminence of the arrival of communism, while he was now willing to speak of fifty or even a hundred years of socialism, he really had not abandoned the Great Leap as his long-term trajectory. He now returned with growing vehemence to the rhetoric of "class struggle, socialist education and politics in command." Thus when the party leadership seemed in the next years to move precisely in the reverse direction toward what he regarded as a Soviet- and Western-influenced "bourgeois revisionism," his frustrations now tended to focus on the party membership itself. The party,

[17]Schram, p. 173.
[18]Ibid., p. 174.

it is true, had always presumably been open to rectification. Indeed his remarks on the success of rectification as late as 1958 were particularly exuberant and extravagant.[19]

If we speak of Mao's final synoptic vision, it is one of ongoing battle between bourgeois revisionism and the continuing revolution to communism. "Bourgeois revisionism" seems to emerge as a formidable disease of the collective consciousness, able to manifest itself in ever new embodiments and guises. In the case of the Cultural Revolution it embodies itself in the collectivity of the party itself. Later, Lin Biao, Chen Boda, and a section of the military would become the embodiment if not of "bourgeois revision" then of "feudal reaction." The forces of revolution would, on the other hand, find their carriers first among a vision of the uncorrupted young, in the military and finally in the so-called Gang of Four.

The final dominant abstract formula is that of the everlasting Manichaean contradiction. The content of the two terms of the contradiction remain as vague and shifting as ever. The relationship of *bourgeois revisionism* and *revolution* to the concrete realities of the situation remains as indeterminate as ever. The categories offer little guidance in predicting the Chairman's concrete responses to circumstances. Even the Mao of the last years did not completely lose his instinct for politics as the art of the possible. This instinct would lead him after 1970 to make tacit concessions to party and army groups who despised the Gang of Four. Such compromises, as well as his willingness on the international scene to accept the overtures of Richard Nixon, may in some fashion be reconciled with his "high doctrine"; but neither could have been predicted by the Cultural Revolutionary vision. In the end, on the level of his final abstract vision, Chairman Mao may be not so much "alone with the masses" as alone with himself.

[19]See above, p. 34.

Mao's Obsession with the Political Role of Literature and the Intellectuals

MERLE GOLDMAN

The Hundred Flowers policy of relaxing the party's control over intellectual life in 1956 and the first half of 1957 was China's first major liberalization since the establishment of the People's Republic in 1949. Because of previous campaigns to indoctrinate intellectuals with every new twist in the party line and to switch their orientation from the West toward the Soviet Union in this period of Sino-Soviet alliance, the party in the mid 1950s was confronted with a passive intellectual community. In urgent need of their services as it was about to begin its industrialization drive, it launched the Hundred Flowers in order to encourage a degree of intellectual freedom and criticism of bureaucratic repression in the expectation that the intellectuals would participate more actively in the party's program for modernizing China. This policy was espoused by most of the top leaders, but Mao pushed it much further than most of his colleagues wished it to go. He sought to extend the campaign into the political as well as the intellectual sphere and to encourage criticism of the party by non-party people, thereby sanctioning criticism outside normal inner-party channels.

The original drafts of Mao's talks during the Hundred Flowers, especially in the early months of 1957, reveal his obsession with the political role of literature and intellectuals in general. This obsession was already evident when he presented his "Yan'an Talks" on art and literature in 1942, in which his policy toward writers became the framework for the party's political control over the intellectuals. The use of literature and intellectuals for political purposes is not unique to Chinese communist leaders; they were used by China's dynastic rulers as well as by the leaders of the Soviet Union and of Eastern Europe. What was different about Mao was his total preoccupation with the political-literary nexus in particular periods, especially in the Hundred Flowers and later in the early phase of the Cultural Revolution. He attributed enormous power to a literary work, whether it were a short story, play, or literary criticism, as if such a work could make or break his policy or his political prestige. Most of the talks here translated from early 1957 were to literary and artistic intellectuals—writers, artists, musicians, publishers, journalists, social scientists, and propagandists—those who interpreted his policies to the public. Even such a powerful leader as Mao was ultimately concerned about public support for his policies. He belittled party bureaucrats for worrying about the effect of student demonstrations and workers' strikes on the party's authority, but he incessantly complained that a literary criticism that did not conform with the Hundred Flowers policy expressed opposition to his policies.

Since literary intellectuals have no independence or power base in the PRC, it would appear that Mao ascribed inordinate power to them. Yet, perhaps he had cause. Since there are no elections and no freedom of speech in the People's Republic, the major channel for expressing divergent views was, and is, through literary works. Controversial issues that cannot be resolved behind closed doors in inner-party circles are debated obliquely and indirectly in literary forums. Thus, a political faction within the leadership may use literary intellectuals and literary means to express dissent or opposition to policies with which it disagrees. And this is what happened in the

Hundred Flowers. A group within the party used a discussion of literature to oppose Mao's interpretation of the Hundred Flowers.

Not all literature was the tool of political factions. Sometimes literature was simply literary. Sometimes a group of writers had genuine grievances that did not represent the views of any political faction, as was true of the left-wing writer Hu Feng, who in the early 1950s asked for more intellectual freedom. Yet even though they acted on their own initiative, Hu and his disciples were accused in the ensuing campaign against them in 1955 of representing all kinds of counterrevolutionary forces. Often, however, literature under Mao was a facade behind which political battles were fought.

Mao was instinctively attracted to literary issues, perhaps because, in his youth, literature was the main source of his education. Yet, despite his love of literature, he harbored a disdain for most people employed in literary pursuits. With some important exceptions, such as China's great modern writer Lu Xun, he seemed to regard literary intellectuals as effete and inept in the revolutionary struggle. He associated them with the traditional literati whose rule he believed had brought China to such a sorry state. Even in his Hundred Flowers talks, in which he urged intellectuals to join in his battle against bureaucracy, he revealed an underlying distrust of intellectuals. He claimed that their acceptance of socialism was due to the fact that "they have no alternative; they cannot but accept [it]. But in [their] minds [they] are not convinced."[1]

Thus, when the intellectuals did not prove effectual in helping him rectify the bureaucracy and, in fact, criticized even himself as well as the party bureaucracy, he turned against them in the subsequent Anti-Rightist campaign with a vehemence born of disillusionment. Once more he put his faith in the "masses" as his main support. His distrust of the intellectuals deepened until it exploded in the Cultural Revolution into a violent attack on virtually all intellectuals.

THE UNEVEN COURSE OF THE HUNDRED FLOWERS

Even as the party was carrying out its relentless campaign against the nonconformist writer Hu Feng and his disciples, it became interested in the second half of 1955 in using the intellectuals more rationally as

[1]Text 5, p. 198.

it moved from a period of class struggle to socialist construction and economic modernization. A survey conducted in the fall of 1955 by the People's Congress and the People's Political Consultative Conference disclosed that bureaucrats were preventing intellectuals from using their expertise. Consequently, bureaucrats were directed to relax their controls and allow intellectuals a degree of independence. The de-Stalinization underway in the Soviet Union in the mid 1950s also had a liberalizing impact on China's intellectual community. Even though China's intellectuals resented having to follow the lead of Soviet academics, many of them in the literary realm sought to emulate the participants in the Soviet "thaw."[2]

Zhou Enlai's report to the Central Committee on 14 January 1956 endorsed the relative relaxation in the intellectual sector already underway. Always Mao's dedicated follower, Zhou prefigured what Mao was to say to the same conference on 20 January.[3] Mao also wrote on 19 February 1956 to other party leaders, among them Liu Shaoqi, Peng Zhen, Deng Xiaoping, Lu Dingyi, and Chen Boda, urging them to encourage intellectual debate.[4] Subsequently, these party leaders made similar speeches, and party organizations at various levels were directed to allow intellectuals to express themselves more freely in their areas of expertise.

Despite these high-level efforts, the Hundred Flowers did not really begin until May 1956, when the slogan "Let a hundred flowers bloom, let a hundred schools contend" was set forth. The two parts of the slogan had been coined separately and on earlier occasions in the party's efforts to deal with cultural and academic controversies.[5] In 1951, at the China Research Institute of Traditional Operas, there was a dispute over Peking Opera, a controversial subject even before the Cultural Revolution. One group wanted to transmit the traditional operas totally and uncritically; another group wanted to reject them completely because they were derived from the old society. At

[2]See Rudolf Wagner, "The Chinese Writer in His Own Mirror: Writer, State, and Society— The Literary Evidence," in Merle Goldman, Timothy Cheek, and Carol Lee Harmin, eds., *China's Intellectuals and the State* (Cambridge, Council on East Asian Studies, Harvard, 1987), pp. 197–203.
[3]*Wansui* (1969), pp. 28–34.
[4]See *Mao Zedong shuxin xuanji* (Selected letters of Mao Zedong) (Beijing, Renmin chuban-she, 1983), p. 510.
[5]Gong Yuzhi and Liu Wusheng, "How the 'Double Hundred' slogan was put forward," *GMRB,* 21 May 1986.

that time Mao took a middle position and resolved the dispute with the slogan, "Let a hundred flowers bloom, weed out the old and raise the new." This meant that the traditional operas were to be performed, but with discrimination, which signified that they were to be rewritten and made ideologically acceptable. The slogan, however, did not originate with Mao, but had been expressed at a meeting on traditional operas and reported back to Mao by the cultural czar, Zhou Yang. The other slogan, "Let a hundred schools contend," arose in a debate between two Marxist historians, Guo Moruo and Fan Wenlan, over how to periodize Chinese history. When a committee set up to resolve the dispute asked him for instructions, Mao, who was close to both men, came down on neither side. He declared that "Let a hundred schools contend" should be the guideline.

Consequently, the two slogans became appropriate for a policy that encouraged debate, criticism, a variety of views, and professional standards in academic and cultural circles. Director of Propaganda, Lu Dingyi, quotes Mao to have said, "Even if you had Marx as head of your department and Engels and Lenin as deputy heads, they would still not be able to solve so many academic questions."[6] In his 2 May 1956 speech to the Supreme State Conference, when he first presented the slogans, Mao insisted that party officials should not poke their "noses into academic debates."[7] He was referring to the various disputes then raging in academic circles, such as the debate between Western-trained geneticists and those following the Lysenko theory of genetics pushed by Stalin in the Soviet Union. At the same time that Mao was beginning to question the Stalinist economic model in this period, he also questioned Stalinist scientific methods, specifically in the field of genetics. He encouraged those who challenged the policy of blindly following Stalinist academic views and urged newspapers and journals to publish the views of those who held alternate positions.[8] Henceforth, he said, questions of right and wrong in the arts, social sciences, and sciences were to be debated without the imposition of official directives.

[6]*GMRB,* 7 May 1986, p.1.
[7]Gong Yuzhi and Liu Wusheng, *GMRB,* 21 May 1986, p. 1.
[8]See Gong Yuzhi, "The only way to develop science—Introducing Comrade Mao Zedong's letter and editorial note for the reproduction of the article 'Talking about contention among a hundred schools of thought in the context of genetics'," *FBIS,* 13 Feb., 1984, pp. K16–9 (*GMRB,* 23 Dec. 1983, p. 2).

This did not mean that ideological remolding of intellectuals would be discontinued, but that it would be carried out through discussion and persuasion rather than through administrative orders and mass campaigns. The goal was still ideological conformity, but it was to be achieved voluntarily rather than forcibly. The Hundred Flowers policy was predicated on the belief that a genuine exchange of ideas and the criticism of repressive officials would ultimately lead to ideological unity.

Mao's policy of advocating pluralism within a framework of broader conformity to his version of Marxism-Leninism led to one of the major controversies of the Hundred Flowers, that over the story "Young newcomer to the Organization Department."[9] Its author, Wang Meng, was one of a group of young writers in 1956 who specifically answered Mao's call to expose and criticize bureaucraticism that prevented others from fully using their talents. The story, like those of several of his literary cohorts, was about an idealistic youth who struggled against the entrenched bureaucracy in a party district office in Beijing. Although Wang Meng was not mentioned by name, the story became the focus of an attack by four members of the Propaganda Department of the People's Liberation Army (PLA)—deputy-director Chen Qitong, Ma Hanbing, and two others—in the *People's Daily* on 7 January 1957. The fact that it was published in the party's preeminent newspaper indicated that it had the support of some in the party's inner circle. Though their article ostensibly criticized writers for writing satire and descriptions of everyday life rather than depicting socialist-realist worker, peasant, and soldier heroes, in reality it opposed the Hundred Flowers policy.

Following the publication of the article, the Hundred Flowers, which hitherto had been almost exclusively a campaign against bureaucratic dogmatism and repression, increasingly became a justification for denouncing "rightist" deviation and "democracy in the extreme." Whether one approved or disapproved of Wang Meng's story became the criterion by which one approved or disapproved of the Hundred Flowers. Debate raged in literary journals, such as the authoritative *Wenyi bao* (Literary gazette) and *Wenyi xuexi* (Literary study), the literary journal of the Youth League. Another conspicuous critic of Wang Meng was Li Xifan, who had become famous as one of the young

---

[9]*Renmin Wenxue,* (People's Literature), September 1956, trans. in Hualing Nieh, *Literature of the Hundred Flowers,* vol. 2 (New York, Columbia Univ. Press, 1981), pp. 473–511.

co-authors of the attack on the famous literary critic Yu Pingbo's interpretation of the *Dream of the Red Chamber* in 1954. Li's attack on Wang
Meng insinuated that because Wang Meng's story was set in Beijing, it
implicated the top party leadership. Moreover, because the author at
that time was working at the Beijing district office of the Youth League,
his story had caused friction between the party and youth.

It was within this context of increasing party opposition to the Hundred Flowers, expressed most openly against specific literary works,
that Mao gave a series of talks to intellectual groups, propaganda
officials, the press, and local officials, in February, March, and April
1957, in an effort to resuscitate his campaign. His talks urged criticism
of officials in the political as well as the cultural-academic realm, in
order to hit back at bureaucratic and party opposition. Mao claimed
that nine out of ten ministers and eight or nine out of ten old cadres
opposed the Hundred Flowers and sympathized with the criticism of
the four PLA writers. He also complained that lower-level officials
relayed to their constituents Mao's comment that the four writers were
"well-intentioned," but did not also tell them that Mao had denounced
their views. In response to Li Xifan's implicit criticism that Wang
Meng was attacking the top leadership, Mao declared that it was "precisely the Central Committee which has produced bad people." He
called for criticism of "senior" leaders, as well as junior officials, saying
that "from Marx onward, never once has it been said that junior and
senior cadres should be distinguished, [or] said that only junior cadres
can be criticized [and] senior cadres cannot be criticized."[10]

Although Mao implied that Wang Meng's negative depiction of
bureaucratism might have gone too far, he himself used the four PLA
writers' criticism of the Hundred Flowers to symbolize the repressive
nature of bureaucracy. The fact that the four writers held power,
Mao claimed, in and of itself produced dogmatism and the use of
ruthless methods against those with whom they disagreed. This
theme, that political power is inherently dogmatic and repressive,
runs through most of his talks in early 1957. Mao granted that the
bureaucratism could not be easily eliminated, because "our party is
so big . . . and the country is so large,"[11] but held that it must be con-

[10]Text 3, p. 171.
[11]Text 13, p. 353.

stantly exposed and criticized. Consequently, he was furious with the four PLA writers for attacking Wang Meng, whose exposure of bureaucratism was "very good."[12] No matter what the occasion, in virtually every speech in this period, he held them up as examples of those who oppose criticism of the bureaucracy. He even referred to their superior, the head of the Cultural and Propaganda Department of the Military Affairs Commission, Chen Yi, as a "leftist," a term he considered an epithet of abuse during the Hundred Flowers period. In actuality, "orthodox Marxist-Leninist" would be a more appropriate description of the four PLA writers, in that they opposed open criticism of the party, considering it a threat to the party's infallibility.

In contrast to his denunciation of the four PLA writers, Mao repeatedly endorsed Wang Meng's story and student demonstrations, workers' strikes, and peasant agitation, because they warned the leadership of impending problems that had to be resolved. Even though he acknowledged that hundreds of thousands had demonstrated the previous year, Mao believed that such activities should be permitted within certain limits in order to help the party avoid incidents such as the Hungarian uprising that had occurred in the fall of 1956. Mao's commitment to the Hundred Flowers may also have been due to Khrushchev's denunciation of Stalin at the Soviet Party Congress in February 1956, which revealed that Stalin's forceful imposition of only one school of thought had made it impossible for the Soviets to face their problems realistically. Mao's constant reference to the Hungarian upheaval and the revelation of opposition to Stalin's repression expressed Mao's as well as the party's worry that similar occurrences could happen in China. But, as opposed to most of his party colleagues, Mao believed these events had a positive as well as negative aspect, because of their educational value.

Mao's more positive view reflected his confidence that if the party used the Hundred Flowers methods of exposure, persuasion, and discussion, rather than bureaucratic repression and Stalinist violence against those who differed from it, then China could avoid a Hungarian-like uprising. Pointing out that the party did not share his confidence, he repeatedly ridiculed the four PLA writers and, by implication, the party for acting as if "[t]he nation is going to perish" simply because of criticism of bureaucratism, expression of differing

[12]Text 1, p. 114.

ideas, and demonstrations of students and workers.[13]

In the belief that a Hungarian uprising would not happen in China, Mao insistently called on non-party persons to criticize the party's dogmatism, privileges, and separation from the masses. Mao's encouragement of criticism by non-party persons is especially evident in the original draft of his speech "On the correct handling of contradictions among the people"—much more evident than in its revised, sanitized version, published after the conclusion of the Hundred Flowers. In contrast to the opposition Mao found in the party to the Hundred Flowers, he claimed that there was no such opposition outside the party. He urged the Western-oriented intellectuals in the powerless small "democratic" parties, left over from the Republican era, to participate actively in the Hundred Flowers. He was even willing to grant the "democratic" parties a definite political role: "As long as they are not counterrevolutionaries, people should have the freedom to speak not only on purely scientific and artistic problems, but also on matters of a political nature in terms of right and wrong."[14] Of course, it is still necessary to draw "a line of demarcation between party and non-party personages," but "there should not be a deep trench between them" so that people will not fear to criticize, speak out, and express opinions.[15] He assured his party colleagues that they need not fear a Petöfi Circle, a group of Hungarian writers who were the intellectual backbone of the Hungarian uprising. With a few exceptions, he repeatedly told them, the majority of intellectuals might not believe in Marxism, but they were patriotic and also wanted a strong and rich China.

High-level intellectuals hesitated to participate in the Hundred Flowers, Mao complained, because they feared being criticized politically. He acknowledged that some thought the Hundred Flowers was a trap to lure them out so that they might be attacked and reeducated ideologically. He did not deny that this effort was also to bring views out into the open so they could be reeducated, but he promised that the forceful methods of the past would no longer be used. The party had now to use its "mouth" instead of its "hands."[16]

[13]Text 7, p. 222.
[14]Text 13, p. 358.
[15]*Ibid.*, p. 361.
[16]Text 5, p. 204.

At the same time that he assured the intellectuals, he also assured party officials that they themselves would be treated gently. He urged the intellectuals to criticize the officials gently: "There will be a little drizzle and a little breeze. It will blow away our bureaucratism and subjectivism . . . and arrive at a new unity through proper criticism."[17] Thus, in the Hundred Flowers, as opposed to the preceding period and later period, Mao espoused moderation.

In another contrast to the earlier and later periods, Mao expressed an appreciation for the importance of professional and academic skills for modernization. He directed party officials to give intellectuals free rein in their areas of expertise and acknowledged that the party and he "simply don't understand natural science."[18] He even admitted in a talk with representatives of the press that party people are not so able as non-party people in running newspapers, schools, and publishing enterprises. Even in the area of literature, in which he had considered himself *the* authority ever since his "Yan'an Talks" on art and literature in May 1942, he said that those outside the party knew more. He acknowledged that "we are now laymen leading experts."[19] Whereas in the sciences and even the arts, he allowed that there were many schools, in the social sciences there were only two schools—the bourgeoisie and the proletariat—contending with each other. Nevertheless, though he said the goal was one truth (presumably the proletarian truth), in the interim various truths were to be allowed. "Our very purpose is to let people think for themselves, hold forums by themselves, and talk things over among themselves."[20]

At this time, unlike other periods, Mao was open to the world beyond China, and even beyond the Soviet Union. He admitted he did not read much literary and art criticism, an area of his supposed interest, but did read the *Reference News*, translations of the foreign press, every day. Even though the Soviet Union was still the chief source of information, Mao declared that China must also learn from the United States. He explained that it would be very dangerous "to stay behind closed doors, shut our eyes, and stop up our ears."[21]

[17]Text 11, p. 320.
[18]Text 5, p. 208.
[19]Text 8, p. 263.
[20]Text 10, p. 292.
[21]Ibid., p. 291.

THE CONTRADICTORY NATURE
OF MAO'S HUNDRED FLOWERS

Mao sounded tolerant, moderate, and open in the early months of 1957. Moreover, he clearly acknowledged sensitive issues, specifically that a powerful political position led to oppression of others. Yet, almost invariably in the very same speech and sometimes in the very same sentence in which he called for criticism and tolerance, he qualified what he said in ways that undermined and even contradicted his main argument. Even when he praised Wang Meng's exposé of bureaucratism, he criticized Wang Meng for writing insufficiently about positive characters and disregarding the socialist realist formula for model heroic figures.[22] Moreover, though he welcomed Wang Meng's fictional criticism of bureaucracy, he rejected that of another controversial writer of the Hundred Flowers period, Liu Binyan, who similarly wrote of idealistic youth struggling against entrenched bureaucrats. In his article, "Shanghai is pondering," Liu attacked the literary bureaucrats, including the senior literary bureaucrat Zhou Yang and the Shanghai cultural bureaucracy, for not implementing the Hundred Flowers and for suppressing creative talents. Liu pointed out that "people think the reason why there cannot be anyone today who would oppose Zhou Yang as Lu Xun did some twenty years ago is that the relationship between the writer and the head of party propaganda is quite different from what it was."[23] Liu implied that the Propaganda Department now had so much more power than in the past that even such a prestigious writer as Lu Xun would not be able to thwart it at present.

Liu saw himself as carrying out Mao's Hundred Flowers policies. But whereas Mao, in his Hundred Flowers talks, praised Lu Xun for his contentiousness, particularly with the party officials in Shanghai in the 1930s (chief among them the very same Zhou Yang), shortly after Liu's article appeared, Mao condemned Liu's contentious nature and accused him of provoking disunity.[24] Mao's anger at Liu, in contrast to his approval of Wang Meng, may have been due to Liu's

---

[22]Text 1, p. 114.

[23]Liu Binyan, "Shanghai is pondering," *Zhongguo qingnian bao* (China youth news), 13 May 1957. I wish to thank Rudolf Wagner for bringing this article to my attention.

[24]Author's interview with Liu Binyan, July 1986.

attacks on Zhou Yang, who had become Mao's obedient spokesman, and to Liu's attacks on the Shanghai cultural bureaucracy led by Zhang Chunqiao (later of Gang of Four fame), under the Shanghai Party head, Ke Qingshi, a close friend of Mao's. In other words, it was appropriate to attack top bureaucrats, unless they were closely associated with Mao.

At the heart of Mao's Hundred Flowers policy was a fundamental ambiguity: He called for the expression of *all* points of view, but would not tolerate the articulation of basic disagreement with the policy itself. Thus, everyone supposedly could contend—except the four PLA writers and like-minded people, because they did not agree with his interpretation of the Hundred Flowers. All views were possible, except those that disagreed with Mao's. This paradox also explains why Mao was deeply annoyed with the *People's Daily* for publishing the four PLA writers' article. He saw the *People's Daily*, the principal mouthpiece of the top leadership, as opposing his policies.

He also complained that in a 20 June 1956 editorial opposing conservatism and impetuosity, *People's Daily* quoted him out of context. Mao said of the editorial that seemingly it opposed both aspects; in fact, it opposed leftism. The editorial had criticized high-level cadres who carried out programs impetuously, without regard to objective conditions; and it called for careful, concrete study before enactment of policies. Mao declared that it hadn't a single bit of Marxism, that in fact some of it was anti-Marxist. He was particularly incensed with the paper's editor, Deng Tuo. True, the editorial had been written by Deng, but it had been revised by Lu Dingyi and approved by Liu Shaoqi. But Mao did not criticize these higher-level officials directly; only Deng Tuo bore the brunt of his anger.[25]

According to the reminiscences of two of Deng Tuo's associates at that time, the philosopher Wang Ruoshui and the editor Hu Jiwei,[26] who accompanied Deng to an audience with Mao in his bedroom at his official residence in the Zhongnanhai compound in central Beijing in the late morning of 11 April 1957, Mao was very angry with

[25]This episode is analyzed in detail in Timothy Cheek's doctoral dissertation, "Orthodoxy and Dissent in People's China: the Life and Death of Deng Tuo," (Harvard, 1986), pp. 193–196.
[26]This story comes from, Timothy Cheek, "Habits of the Heart: Intellectual Assumptions Reflected by Mainland Chinese Reformers from Teng T'o to Fang Li-chih," *Issues and Studies* 24.3:31–32 (March 1988).

Deng because the *People's Daily* had not given sufficient coverage to the Hundred Flowers and Mao's efforts to push the campaign.

Mao lost his temper. "In the past I've called you 'the pedant editor,'" Mao said to Deng Tuo, "but I was too easy on you. Really it's a case of 'a dead man running the paper.'" Mao then made his complaint that non-party papers like Shanghai's *Wenhui bao* had managed to promote the new Hundred Flowers policy, but the *People's Daily*, the newspaper of the Communist Party, hadn't said a single word on the topic! Mao fumed. "You know," he said to Deng Tuo, "you have depreciated (*zhejiu*). You're not worth what you used to be." Mao, in classic form, summed up his complaint, in his well-known earthy style. "Shit, or get off the pot!" he said to the editor of the *People's Daily*.

Deng tried to explain to Mao why his speeches of 27 February and 12 March 1957 had not been publicized. At present, Deng said, they were at the Propaganda Department, and he was waiting for the department's approval before proceeding. (In fact, propaganda official Hu Qiaomu was sitting on them.) Mao was incensed, finding Deng's explanation both patronizing and insubordinate. Moreover, it reflected bureaucratic obstruction to Mao's policies, the very phenomenon that he was opposing with his Hundred Flowers campaign. He proceeded to shout at Deng, at which point, Deng offered to resign, saying, "If things are like this, I can't continue my job." Mao then exploded: "Are you a party member or not?" Thus reminded of his communist duty, Deng Tuo continued on as editor for a while, but it was clear his services were no longer wanted. He applied for a transfer, claiming health reasons, and was seen in a hospital in the summer of 1957, recovering from migraines.

Despite Deng's explanation that the *People's Daily* had not publicized Mao's speeches because they were simply wending their way through bureaucratic channels, Deng, like some of the more traditional Marxist-Leninist party leaders, was not enthusiastic about Mao's encouragement of non-party criticism of party leaders in those speeches. Not only had the *People's Daily* not publicized Mao's two major ones—"On the correct handling of contradictions among the people" of 27 February and the speech before the propaganda conference on 12 March—at the time they were given, it also did not give much attention to the Wang Meng case until April 1957. It was only on 13 April 1957, two days after Mao's confrontation with Deng, that a *People's Daily* editorial, written by Wang Ruoshui, under Deng's direction, focused on Mao's two speeches and talked about bringing criticism into the open. But even the 13 April editorial Mao considered "too little, too late."[27] By contrast, Mao repeatedly praised the non-party newspaper *Wenhui bao*, which was associated with the "democratic" parties, and the *Guangming Daily*, the paper for the intellectuals, for doing exactly as he asked by giving full coverage to non-party criticism of bureaucratism and echoing his suggestion that the professionals be in charge of academic affairs.

While it is true that Deng Tuo went along with the orthodox party and Marxist-Leninist position in this period, he, like Hu Yaobang,[28] then head of the Youth League, encouraged and protected two of the most outspoken and daring participants in the Hundred Flowers: the prominent student activist Lin Xiling, of People's University, whose article Deng withheld from publication just as the Anti-Rightist Campaign was to be launched; and the controversial writer, Liu Binyan, whose Hundred Flowers critique of high leaders particularly incensed Mao. Deng's rhetoric and some of his actions might have been orthodox in the Hundred Flowers, but some of his actions were unorthodox even by Mao's Hundred Flowers standards.[29]

Although Mao comes across as relatively "liberal" in the Hundred Flowers, he invariably qualifies his "liberalism." Thus, the Hungarian uprising served a positive purpose in teaching how to avoid a similar uprising, but it was positive only as long as it happened in Hungary, not in China. China could have demonstrations as long as they stayed within bounds, which he never defined. He accepted Khrushchev's negative appraisal of Stalin, but criticized Khrushchev for dealing with Stalin in "one blow." Likewise, while he asserted that the natural sciences should be left alone because they did not deal with political issues, he added that because they were carried out by people, they "can still be tainted with some people's class conscious-

[27] According to Wang Ruoshui, interview with Timothy Cheek (Fuzhou, May 14, 1986).
[28] For Hu Yaobang's support of young critics, see Yang Zhongmei, *Hu Yaobang: A Chinese Biography* (Armonk, N.Y., M. E. Sharpe, 1988), pp. 94–8.
[29] Even some of his writings were unorthodox; see "Discard the politics of simpletons," written under penname Bu Wuji, *People's Daily*, 11 May 1957; tr. in *Chinese Law and Government* 16.4:31–3 (Winter 1983–4).

ness."[30] Moreover, Mao added that even though most party members did not understand the natural sciences, this did not mean that the party should not exert leadership over them. "[W]hen it comes to the overall development of science, we are capable of assuming leadership, that is to say with politics and state plans."[31] In time, party members would learn science and technology and take over technologically as well as politically.

An irony of Mao's Hundred Flowers policies, particularly the criticism of bureaucratism and demand for openness and professionalism, was that they were the very same policies that the writer Hu Feng had recommended to the party in a report to the Central Committee in 1954, for which he and a number of his disciples were imprisoned. Mao had been instrumental in the campaign against Hu Feng and written the editorial notes that accompanied the publication of Hu Feng's correspondence with his disciples. In his Hundred Flowers talks, furthermore, Mao continually denounced him, saying, for instance, that Hu Feng sits in prison but "his ideas have not perished yet. They still exist in many people's minds."[32] Certainly, intellectuals must have been as frightened by such rhetoric as by their actual repression by bureaucrats.

To set their minds at ease, Mao promised that as long as they did not engage in destructive acts or were not members of secret groups, then they could express themselves freely. But how does one interpret *destructive* and *secret*? Hu Feng had not destroyed anything, nor had he and his followers been a secret group. They were simply a literary coterie whose members wrote letters to one another commenting on the party's literary policy, which they found oppressive, a policy as much a product of Mao as of the cultural bureaucracy. When they tried to express their views diplomatically in public forums and in the media, they were punished for their efforts. They had done exactly what Mao was urging intellectuals to do in the Hundred Flowers. Their only crime was that they had expressed their views before Mao had sanctioned them.

Another example that Mao used to reassure intellectuals was that

[30]Text 5, p. 197.
[31]Text 10, p. 288.
[32]Text 10, p. 289.

the Hundred Flowers was similar to the Yan'an Rectification of the early 1940s, with its use of the "moderate" methods of criticism and self-criticism. But the Yan'an Rectification, which had originally called on intellectuals to criticize bureaucratism, had turned into a campaign against the critics themselves. One of those critics, Wang Shiwei, was arrested and executed in 1944. Zhou Yang was to compare Liu Binyan with Wang.[33] Such analogies could provide little assurance to any knowledgeable intellectual.

Mao comes across in these talks of early 1957 as contradictory, repetitious, and obsessed. At times he appears to have babbled on and on. The interjections of various members of the audiences reveal an effort to figure out what exactly was his policy. These interjections also reveal the sycophantish manner with which even China's most prominent intellectuals and officials treated Mao. In fact, there was none of the Hundred Flowers spirit of "contending and blooming" in Mao's discussions with intellectuals and cadres. In Tianjin, when he asked for questions, none was forthcoming. When someone interjected, it was usually to expound on what the Chairman had already said. Even though his audiences were usually composed of prominent intellectuals, they expressed no independent ideas of their own. They were probably well aware that Mao might ask for criticisms and divergent views; but when confronted with them directly, he would humiliate and punish the questioner.

The fawning manner toward Mao was not surprising in an official like Kang Sheng, always obedient to the Maoist line and later to be put in charge of Public Security. Actually, his interjections during Mao's discussions expressed the relatively more liberal aspect of Mao's policies at this time. What is disillusioning is the sycophancy of a number of prominent and supposedly independent intellectuals. One of them, however, the famous writer Mao Dun, whose works in the 1920s and 1930s were influenced by Western values, appeared to diverge from Mao's Hundred Flowers views and expressed views similar to those of the four PLA writers. He criticized young writers for rejecting ideology in their descriptions of reality and he claimed that readers found writing about everyday life dull, preferring work with an ideological content. While Mao agreed with Mao Dun that socialist realism still remained the main literary form, he countered that it

---

[33] Author's interview with Liu Binyan, July 1986.

was all right for writers to write about trivia and not to identify directly with workers, peasants, and soldiers.

Despite the contradictory nature of Mao's talks in this period, he had one constant concern throughout, a concern with the bureaucracy's dogmatism, privileges, repression, and separation from the masses, evils that reached up to the top of the party. This concern grew from this time on into an obsession that in the Cultural Revolution exploded into a fierce attack on the party as a "new class." The difference is that in the Hundred Flowers, Mao's remedy for bureaucratism was non-violent; in the Cultural Revolution, it was violent. Yet Mao's agents for change were similar—forces outside the party. In the Hundred Flowers, it was the intellectuals and students; in the Cultural Revolution, the Red Guards. Another consistent strain was Mao's faith in "new-born forces," a faith that led, for instance, to his support for Wang Meng's challenging the bureaucrats. Mao observed that "young people are not so afraid of opposing bureaucrats because they have not yet held any office."[34]

Many of the proponents and antagonists of the Cultural Revolution are already in place in the Hundred Flowers. Mao's dislike of Deng Tuo, who was to be an early victim of the Cultural Revolution, was already evident in the disdain with which he referred to him. Similarly Deng Tuo's dislike of Mao was already evident in his reluctance to give coverage to Mao's speeches and his characterization of Mao's "impetuosity," his disregard for objective limitations, as dangerous. It was a warning that Mao *consciously* ignored in launching the Great Leap Forward and Cultural Revolution, much to the grief of millions of Chinese. It is safe to say *conscious;* for in repeating his criticism of the *People's Daily* in January 1958, Mao added "[I]n the future do not raise [the issue of] 'opposing adventurism'; don't do it under any circumstances."[35] Another major figure of the Cultural Revolution, the literary critic Yao Wenyuan, caught Mao's eye in the Hundred Flowers period. Mao refers to his articles as "written quite convincingly."[36] Always compliant with the twisting Maoist line, Yao wrote articles wholeheartedly promoting the Hundred Flowers.

Also already evident in the Hundred Flowers was Mao's willing-

[34]Text 1, p. 126.
[35]Text 16, p. 396.
[36]Text 7, p. 234.

ness to go outside regular party procedures in order to push policies he wanted implemented. He accepted procedures if they suited his purposes, as when he castigated the four PLA writers because they had not followed the regular practice of submitting their article to the Propaganda Department before it was published. But he totally disregarded procedures when they might obstruct his own policies. This was most obvious in his encouragement of outside criticism of the party, as opposed to the more orthodox Marxist-Leninist, inner-party criticism. Also evident in these Hundred Flowers talks was Mao's tendency to go straight to the "people," when he was blocked in the party from carrying out his policies. In a chat with a group of writers and artists on March 8, a writer from Guangdong complained of bureaucratic opposition to the Hundred Flowers and asked that the Central Committee issue specific directives and make explicit decisions at the upcoming Third Plenum of the Central Committee about the Hundred Flowers policy. Mao replied, "Don't wait till the Third Plenum; you relay and implement [the results] as soon as you return."[37] His joining with the "people" against the party in what he perceived as party opposition to his policies began in the Hundred Flowers.

On 8 June 1957, Mao, along with the party, switched from a policy of tolerance and moderation to one of persecution and intransigence. His sudden switch had less to do with the party hierarchy's prevailing upon him than with the fact that the Hundred Flowers itself began to turn against Mao as well as the party. Mao's call for non-party criticism of the party and criticism of top leaders opened the way for criticism of Mao himself by late May and the first week in June 1957. Even before that, articles appeared, criticizing Mao's "Yan'an Talks" on art and literature. In fact, one writer, Liu Shaotang, said of Mao's talks that they had "now become conservative, far behind the situation now developing."[38]

Perhaps even more shocking to Mao, his trusted youth—the new-born forces—also turned against him. At Peking University some questioned the Yan'an Rectification and emulated Wang Shiwei's criticism of bureaucratism. Calls to reopen the Hu Feng case became a

---

[37]Text 7, p. 240. Lawrence Sullivan called this passage to the author's attention.
[38]Liu Shaotang, "The development of realism in a period of socialism", *Beijing wenyi* (Beijing literature), No. 4:9, 11 (1957).

cause célèbre. There were large-scale demonstrations and wall posters in defense of Hu Feng. Lin Xiling, the student at People's University whom Deng Tuo befriended, led a demonstration demanding an open trial for Hu Feng, an indictment of the party's and Mao's procedures, and pointed out that the Hundred Flowers was an implementation of Hu Feng's ideas. The public association of Hu Feng with the Hundred Flowers policy may have been more than Mao had bargained for. Having overestimated the effectiveness of the former indoctrination, Mao found that his Hundred Flowers released more pent-up dissatisfaction and bitterness than even he had anticipated.

As Mao and the party were to discover whenever they allowed criticism, it could not be confined within specific limits. Thus, when Mao called for criticism of senior cadres, he found that he was not excluded. Clearly disturbed by this development, Mao, in a talk on 13 November 1957, characterized May and June as "a time when the skies were covered with dark clouds,"[39] especially at Peking University, where demonstrations and wall posters denounced the party and their contents then published in *People's Daily*. He did not mention that he himself had also been denounced. The Democracy Wall and Democracy Square established by students at Peking University in May 1957, which spread to other universities, may have finally convinced even Mao that China might be on the verge of a Hungarian-type uprising.

The Anti-Rightist Campaign that followed had a dual purpose. One was to silence the critics Mao had summoned to criticize by labeling them "rightists." Student leaders, such as Lin Xiling, were imprisoned. Even though Hu Yaobang tried to protect Liu Binyan, who worked on the *China Youth News*, a newspaper under his jurisdiction, Liu underwent many years of harsh labor reform and imprisonment. Mao at first had tried to protect Wang Meng, most likely because he was a symbol of his Hundred Flowers policy; but with prodding from Peng Zhen, head of the Beijing Party Committee about whose bailiwick Wang Meng's story had been written, he also underwent labor reform, though less severe than that of Liu. The other purpose was to damage the prestige of intellectuals and reim-

---

[39]Mao Zedong, "Talk to Chinese students studying in Moscow," 13 November 1957, *Mao Zedong sixiang wansui* (May 1967), p. 56. This will be Vol. 5 in the CCRM publication of our collection of New Mao Texts. See Table 1 in Timothy Cheek's chapter.

pose even tighter controls over intellectual life, a policy that finally culminated in Mao's fiercely anti-intellectual Cultural Revolution.

Mao clearly saw that China had to deal with the problem of bureaucratism in order to modernize, but his contradictory methods of the Hundred Flowers—encouraging while at the same time manipulating the intellectuals—backfired. His disappointment with the intellectuals ultimately led to the large-scale persecution of the intellectuals in the Cultural Revolution, along with Mao's other obsession, the bureaucrats. The irony is that Mao's Hundred Flowers criticism of Stalin in his later years also became the epitaph for Mao's later years. He criticized Stalin for suppressing differing ideas and mistaking "contradictions among the people for those between ourselves and the enemy."[40] Such policies, Mao said, led to the "killing of numerous important people in the Central Committee." Mao added, "We didn't do this sort of thing."[41] Yet, within these Hundred Flowers talks, and even beginning with his policies in the Yan'an Rectification, were the ideas and practices that were to result in similar consequences. Unlike Stalin, who personally directed the Soviet purges, Mao unleashed the chaotic destructive forces of the Cultural Revolution—but his actions were as tragic for Chinese society as Stalin's action had been for the Soviet society.

[40]Text 13, p. 353.
[41]Text 3, p. 142.

Contemporary China Studies: The Question of Sources

EUGENE WU

Until the late 1970s, American scholars on contemporary China relied primarily on library resources outside of the People's Republic of China (PRC) for their research. There was no access to libraries in the PRC, no interaction with Chinese scholars there who had similar research interests, and no firsthand knowledge of the events that were shaping Chinese society under communism. Refugee interviews, conducted mainly in Hong Kong, provided some additional data that were useful for cross-checking the published sources, but the latter remained the basic materials for research. The situation has changed today, now that scholarly communication between the United States and the People's Republic of China has become firmly established. While access to library resources and scholars in the PRC has been more or less routinized, and in some cases field work has also become possible, the fundamental importance of the documentary base of contemporary China studies has not diminished. Libraries thus press on in their search for more materials, and the efforts waged by American libraries in this respect had been quite successful. The materials that are translated in this volume are a good case in point.

Indeed, major American libraries have been diligent, for more than four decades since the end of World War II, in their effort to develop and maintain an essential corpus of research materials on contemporary China, including the history of the Chinese communist movement. Today, the combined strength of such resources in the United States is probably the strongest and the most comprehensive in the Western world. How this came about, what the major problems have been, and what the prospects for the future are are the questions this essay attempts to address.

Chinese studies as an area study in the United States developed slowly but steadily in the years following World War II.[1] American library resources up to that time had been developed primarily in support of traditional Sinological research, and collections of social science materials were much weaker by comparison. The post–World War II expansion of Chinese studies provided the necessary impetus for libraries to begin strengthening their social science collections, and much attention has since been directed toward the collecting of both pre- and post-1949 publications on Chinese communism. Leading the way in this latter effort was the late Professor Mary Clabaugh Wright, then the Curator of the newly established Chinese Collection of the Hoover Institution at Stanford University. Her acquisitions in China, particularly in Yan'an, in the immediate post–World War II years, yielded many rare contemporary Chinese communist publications, the best known of which was probably the almost complete set of the *Jiefang ribao* (Liberation daily), the organ of the Chinese Communist Party (CCP) published in Yan'an. Later on she acquired the Harold Isaacs Collection and the Nym Wales Collection in the United States. The former consists of mostly underground Chinese communist pamphlets and journals published (many are mimeographed) from the late 1920s to the early 1930s, and the latter includes a number of original Chinese communist docu-

---

[1]See John M. H. Lindbeck's excellent study, *Understanding China: An Assessment of American Scholarly Resources* (New York, Praeger Publishers, 1971).

ments of the mid 1930s.[2] The Hoover Institution's collections of Chinese communist documentation was further enriched in 1960 when the present author, then Curator of its East Asian collection, arranged for and supervised the microfilming in Taiwan of the Chen Cheng Collection consisting of some 1,500 Chinese communist documents relating exclusively to the Jiangsi Soviet period just prior to the Long March.[3] These three collections and other materials, especially those published during the War of Resistance (1937–1945), which in the meantime had also been collected by other American libraries, constituted the first significant body of primary sources for the study of the Chinese communist movement in its early phase to become available in the United States.

The 1945–1949 period saw the publication of many books, journals, and newspapers, either under the direct sponsorship of the Chinese Communist Party or its front organizations. While the coverage of these publications by American libraries is by no means comprehensive, many of the more important sources such as *Jiefang* (Liberation), a weekly published in Yan'an and the predecessor to the Yan'an *Jiefang ribao* already mentioned; *Xinhua ribao* (New China daily), the CCP organ published in Chongqing; *Qunzhong* (The masses), successively published in Hankou, Chongqing, Shanghai, and Hong Kong; and the many publications and documents issuing from the Communist-controlled "border areas" are all readily available.[4]

[2] All items in the Harold Isaacs Collection and those in the Nym Wales Collection are listed in Chün-tu Hsüeh, *The Chinese Communist Movement, 1921–1937, An Annotated Bibliography of Selected Materials in the Chinese Collection of the Hoover Institution on War, Revolution, and Peace* (Stanford, Hoover Institution, 1960), and its sequel, *The Chinese Communist Movement, 1937–1949, An Annotated Bibliography of Selected Materials in the Chinese Collection of the Hoover Institution on War, Revolution, and Peace* (Stanford, Hoover Institution, 1962.

[3] For a bibliography and complete checklist of all the documents in the collection, see Tien-wei Wu, *The Kiangsi Soviet Republic, 1931–1934, A Selected and Annotated Bibliography of the Chen Cheng Collection* (Cambridge, Harvard-Yenching Library, 1981). Copies of the microfilm of the Chen Cheng Collection were made available to other American libraries by the Hoover Institution soon after its acquisition.

[4] For library holdings of these materials, consult the published catalogues of the following libraries: East Asiatic Library, Univ. of California, Berkeley; Far Eastern Library, Univ. of Chicago; Wason Collection, Cornell Univ.; Harvard-Yenching Library, Harvard Univ.; Hoover Institution, Stanford Univ.; Library of Congress; and Asia Library, Univ. of Michigan. The UC-Berkeley, Chicago, Hoover, LC and Michigan catalogues are published by G. K. Hall & Co. in Boston; the Cornell catalogue by the CCRM; and the Harvard-Yenching cat-

Of particular relevance to the present volume among these publications may be mentioned the following early editions of *Mao Zedong xuanji* (Selected works of Mao Zedong): (1) the July 1945 edition (*juan* 1 only) published by Suzhong chubanshe; (2) the March 1945 Jin Cha Ji reprint (*juan* 2 only) of the 1944 Jin Cha Ji edition, the earliest edition published; (3) the August 1946 Dalian edition in 5 *juan* (also a reprint of the 1944 Jin Cha Ji edition); (4) the March 1947 third printing of the August 1946 Dalian edition, also published in Dalian; (5) the March 1947 Bohai edition (a reprint of the 1944 Jin Cha Ji edition); and (6) the March 1947 Jin Cha Ji expanded edition.[5] While these early editions represent the edited version of only a very small number of Mao's writings, spanning over a period of forty years from the 1920s to the 1940s, the newly acquired Mao texts, from which selections are translated in this volume, are by and large unedited and also very much larger in volume, covering the period from 1949 to 1967, with a heavy concentration on the later 1950s to the mid 1960s.[6] Indeed, the sheer bulk of this one-time acquisition of Mao's works is quite unprecedented in American libraries' collecting experience. Not meant for public distribution, these new texts are internal documents in the tradition of similar publications, such as the *Gongzuo tongxun* (Bulletin of activities) published by the Gen-

---

alogue by Garland Publishing, Inc., in New York. It should be noted that the LC catalogue contains only materials catalogued since 1958. For LC holdings of Chinese periodicals and newspapers, see Han-chu Huang, comp., *Chinese Periodicals in the Library of Congress* (Washington, LC, 1978); and Han-chu Huang and Hseo-chin Jen, comp., *Chinese Newspapers in the Library of Congress* (Washington, LC, 1985).

[5]The July 1945 Suzhong chubanshe edition is in the Yushodo microfilm collection (see note 9), which is available in several libraries. The March 1945 reprint (*juan* 2 only) is available at the Harvard-Yenching Library, the Hoover Institution, and the Library of Congress. The August 1947 Dalian edition is in the East Asian Collection, Yale University Library; its third printing edition is in LC and Harvard-Yenching, the latter also having the March 1947 Bohai edition. The March 1947 Jin Cha Ji expanded edition is in the Hoover Institution and the East Asiatic Library, UC-Berkeley (reprinted in 1970 by CCRM.)

For a discussion of the history of these early editions, see Gong Yuzhi, "Tong Shi Lamu jiaoshou di tanhua" (A conversation with Professor Schram), in Zhonggong zhongyang wenxian yanjiu shi, comp., *Wenxian he yanjiu (1984 nian huibianben)* (Documents and research [1984 selections]) (Beijing, Renmin chubanshe) pp. 243–60; and Timothy Cheek's chapter in this volume.

[6]For a detailed analysis of the early Mao's selected works and the presently available new texts, see Timothy Cheek's chapter in this volume.

eral Political Department of the People's Liberation Army.[7] As such, they provide a much more candid view of the state of affairs both within the CCP and the PRC than previously available from open sources. To what extent these newly available texts might shape future research on contemporary China, however, it is too early to say; for, on the one hand, these documents are most likely not the last such collections, and, on the other hand, it may turn out that, apart from materials translated in this volume, the texts are largely repetitive and thus unlikely to have any impact on future research. Only time and more careful mining of these new texts will help us make any final judgment.

Since the early 1960s, scholars also have had access, in addition to what is available in American libraries, to three very important archival collections in Taiwan, namely the Kuomintang Archives, the Library of the Bureau of Investigation of the Ministry of Justice, and the Library of the Bureau of Intelligence of the Ministry of National Defense. The Kuomintang Archives (officially the Historical Commission of the Kuomintang Central Committee) contains much documentation on the 1924–1927 period during the KMT and CCP collaboration.[8] The Bureau of Investigation Library, which has a collection of over 100,000 volumes, is the largest depository in Taiwan of primary historical documents on the Chinese communist movement, mostly dating from before 1949.[9] This collection contains documents from "almost every level of the Chinese Communist Party and affiliated organizations" and includes "internal communications as well as published books, periodicals, posters, letters, and handbills from the Central Committee and from provincial, county,

---

[7]For a description of *Gongzuo tongxun*, see discussion below and n. 24.

[8]Materials in the Kuomintang Archives catalogued as of the late 1960s are listed in Zhongyang yanjiu yuan, Jindai shi yanjiu suo, *Zhongguo xiandai shi ziliao diaocha mulu* (Catalogue of source materials on contemporary Chinese history), 11 mimeographed vols. (Taipei, 1968–69). Vol. 3 lists documents on the 1924–36 period.

[9]For a description of the bureau's collection, see Peter Donovan, Carl E. Dorris, and Lawrence R. Sullivan, *Chinese Communist Materials at the Bureau of Investigation Archives, Taiwan* (Ann Arbor, Center for Chinese Studies, Univ. of Michigan, 1976). Some 400 items from this collection, mostly documents from the War of Resistance period (1937–45) and with some CC documents from 1932–33, have been microfilmed. The microfilm, in 20 reels, is available from Yushodo Film Publications, Ltd., in Tokyo under the title *Yūkan Chūgoku kyōsanto shiryō* (Materials on the CCP). An alphabetical list of this microfilm by title has been prepared by the Harvard-Yenching Library.

city, and district committees, from local branches, and from many special units of the CCP."[10] The Library of the Bureau of Intelligence of the Ministry of National Defense also maintains an important, albeit much smaller, collection of some one thousand items of original Chinese communist documents, mostly from the 1940s, a large number of which originated from the Shandong area.[11]

The availability of such resources has been further enhanced during the last few years when microfilms of a number of the Chinese communist journals and newspapers published in the 1930s and the 1940s as well as many documentary compilations on the history of the CCP have been reissued or published for the first time in the PRC.[12] Thus, a great wealth of primary documentation now exists outside of China in the United States and elsewhere for the study of the Chinese communist movement prior to the founding of the People's Republic in 1949.

Since 1949, American libraries have maintained a rigorous acquisitions program for publications from the PRC on contemporary China. The results have been remarkable in spite of the many problems.[13] For three decades, until the late 1970s, it was not possible to buy directly from the PRC; instead orders had to be placed with dealers in Hong Kong and Tokyo. Local newspapers were not available for subscription by foreign libraries, and exchange was limited to the National Library of Peking (since renamed the National Library of China). Although indirect buying was a nuisance at best, the dealers did offer all that was allowed for export. The problem was that many

[10]Donovan, Dorris, and Sullivan, p. 2.

[11]For a catalogue of these items, see *Gongfei ershi niandai zhi wushi niandai yuanshi wenjian yu shukan (Original Documents and Publications of the Chinese Communist Regime During the Period Between the 1920s and 1950s)* in Chinese and English compiled by the Bureau of Intelligence, Ministry of National Defense, 1970. Donovan, Dorris, and Sullivan (pp. 89–90) also provide a brief description of this collection.

[12]For microfilm reproductions see, for instance, the various catalogues issued by the China National Publishing Industry Trading Corporation. New documentary compilations include early CCP Central Committee documents, political reports by party leaders, documents from the first six CCP congresses, archival materials on communist activities in the provinces, and various other "study materials" on party history. For sample titles of these compilations, see publication notices in *Dangshi yanjiu* (Research on party history), especially no. 3 (1981) p. 53. Many of these publications carry the *neibu* classification, but have found their way to the West.

[13]The listings in Peter Berton and Eugene Wu, *Contemporary China, a Research Guide* (Stanford, Hoover Institution, 1967) provide some idea as to the richness of American libraries' collections of PRC publications issued before the Cultural Revolution.

of the local publications were published in small press runs; and even when cleared for export, they were often difficult to obtain; those having a *neibu* (internal) classification were (and still are) not available at all, at least not officially. Furthermore, since commercial dealers depended upon Chinese publishers for supply, the vicissitudes experienced by the Chinese publishing industry in those years naturally set the limit on what and how much the dealers had to offer. For example, during the 1950s when the Chinese publishing industry enjoyed a period of rapid expansion, the supply was plentiful both in volume and variety. But, when book production went down either because of a shortage of materiél, as occurred throughout China in the early 1960s, or because of political upheavals, as took place during the Cultural Revolution, the selection became first scarcer and less diverse and then practically nonexistent.[14] Exchange with the National Library of Peking alone proved unsatisfactory; for the items they provided were also easily available from book dealers, and their offerings to American libraries never compared either in volume or in variety with what they were sending to libraries in the Soviet Union and Eastern Europe when China's relations with those countries were still friendly, as this author found on a visit in 1964 to the Soviet Union, Czechoslovakia, Poland, and East Germany. Fortunately, there were other sources from which important research materials from the PRC could be obtained during this period.

In the earlier years, the single most important open source for materials not available through commercial channels was the Union Research Institute (URI) in Hong Kong. For many years URI was an indispensable source for Contemporary China scholars, its clippings file of newspaper and journal articles being of particular value. It also published the *Union Research Service* containing translations of important PRC documents as well as news analysis, and the *Biographical Service*, which provided biographical sketches of prominent leaders of the PRC. Equally important were its topical documentary compilations such as *The Case of Peng Teh-huai, 1959–1968; Docu-*

---

[14]In 1958, a total of 45,495 books, 822 periodicals, and 491 newspapers were published; in 1961, 13,529 books, 410 periodicals, and 260 newspapers. In 1967, a year after the start of the Cultural Revolution, production dropped precipitously to 2,925 books, 27 periodicals, and 43 newspapers (excluding Red Guard tabloids). See Zhongguo guojia tongji ju, comp., *Zhongguo tongji nianjian, 1984 (Zhongwen ban)* (China statistical yearbook, 1984 [Overseas Chinese edition]) (Hong Kong, 1984), pp. 501–3.

*ments of the Chinese Communist Central Committee, September, 1956
to April, 1969*, covering the Eighth National Congress and the
Eighth Central Committee; and *CCP Documents of the Great Proletarian Cultural Revolution, 1966–1967.*

Throughout this period, a very large number of extremely important CCP documents were released in Taiwan, among which the "Lien-
chiang Documents" and the famous "571 Engineering Manual," Lin
Biao's crude plan for an armed uprising against Mao, are probably the
best known.[15] Other documentary collections compiled and published in Taiwan include *Liu Shaoqi wenti ziliao zhuanji* (A special collection of materials on Liu Shaoqi); *Gongfei wenhua da keming
zhongyao wenjian huibian* (A collection of important documents on
the Cultural Revolution of the Chinese Communists), *Wang Hongwen Zhang Chunqiao Jiang Qing Yao Wenyuan fandang jituan zuizheng*
(Criminal evidence against the anti-party clique of Wang Hongwen,
Zhang Chunqiao, Jiang Qing, and Yao Wenyuan);[16] and *Dalu dixia
kanwu huibian* (A collection of Chinese mainland underground publications) which reproduces unofficial magazines and wall posters of
the late 1970s and early 1980s, of which twenty volumes have so far
been published. Of direct relevance to the present volume are two
editions of *Mao Zedong sixiang wansui* (Long live Mao Zedong
Thought), two collections of mostly unpublished speeches of Mao
Zedong published in 1967 and 1969 respectively in the PRC and
reprinted in Taiwan.[17]

[15]Many of the single documents, especially the CC directives, have been reproduced in
Wenti yu yanjiu, Zhonggong nianbao (Yearbook on Chinese communism), and other journals dealing with the PRC published in Taipei. English translations of these documents can
be found in *Issues and Studies,* the English-language edition of *Wenti yu yanjiu.*

The "Lien-chiang Documents," dating between 1962 and March 1963, were captured by
Nationalist commandos in a raid on Lianjiang County on the Fujian coast in 1964. They
deal with various policy statements and production plans and the socialist education campaign during that period. For an English translation of most of the documents with an
introductory analysis, see C. S. Chen, ed., and Charles P. Ridley, tr., *Rural People's Commune in Lien-chiang, Documents Concerning Communes in Lien-chiang County, Fukien Province, 1962–63* (Stanford, Hoover Institution Press, 1969).

[16]The trial records of the Gang of Four have also recently become available in the United
States. This *neibu* publication, *Zhonghua renmin gongheguo zuigao renmin fayuan tebie fa-
ting shenpan Lin Biao Jiang Qing fangeming jituan an zhufan jishi* (Records of the trial of
the principal criminals in the case against the Lin Biao and Jiang Qing Anti-Revolutionary
Cliques at the special tribunal of the Supreme People's Court of the PRC) (Beijing, Falu chubanshe, 1982) was reprinted by CCRM in 1986.

[17]The 1967 edition contains a selection of Mao's speeches of 1959–61; the 1969 edition

In the 1950s book stores in Japan, particularly Daian and Kyokutō Shoten, had some offerings of PRC publications unavailable elsewhere. Research institutes and libraries such as the Ajia Keizai Kenkyūjo, the Tōyō Bunko, and the National Diet Library were also accessible to China scholars. But the most important Japanese contribution to Contemporary China Studies has to be the monumental *Mao Zedong ji* (Collected works of Mao Zedong) edited by Professor Takeuchi Minoru and others.[18] Stuart Schram describes it as "a meticulously edited critical edition of Mao's works, which not only makes conveniently available a very large number of items hitherto to be found only in scattered and sometimes illegible sources, but indicates all the changes which have been made in those items included in the official 1951 edition."[19] And as such, this compilation "will constitute for many years to come the standard work used by all those concerned with what Mao said and wrote prior to the establishment of the People's Republic of China."[20]

The United States government in the meantime also made available to the academic community a large number of translations of PRC publications as well as some Chinese-language research materials. The *Survey of China Mainland Press, Selections from China Mainland Magazines, Current Background,* and *Extracts from China Mainland Publications,* all published in English translation by the American Consulate General in Hong Kong, were for many years a major source for research. The first two series cover newspapers and news releases and periodicals, respectively. The latter two contain

---

those of 1949–68. A number of speeches are given only in summary or abbreviated form. For a discussion of these and the other editions of *Mao Zedong sixiang wansui* see Timothy Cheek's chapter in this volume.

[18]Takeuchi Minoru, ed., *Mao Zedong ji* (Collected works of Mao Zedong), rev. ed., 10 vols. (Tokyo, Sōsōsha, 1983); *Mao Zedong ji bujuan* (Supplement to collected works of Mao Zedong), 9 vols. (Tokyo, Sōsōsha, 1983–5); and *Mao Zedong ji biejuan* (Appended volume to collected works of Mao Zedong), (Tokyo, Sōsōsha, 1986). This last contains a chronology of Mao's writings.

[19]*The China Quarterly* 46:368–9 (June, 1971).

[20]*The China Quarterly* 97:111 (March, 1984). For a collection of Mao's writings from 1949 until the end of his life, see Helmut Martin, ed., *Mao Zedong: Texte,* 6 vols. (München, Carl Hanser Verlag, 1979–82) in German and Chinese. For English translations of speeches covering Sept. 1949–Dec. 1955, see also Michael Y. M. Kau and John Leung, eds., *The Writings of Mao Zedong, 1949–1976,* Vol. 1– (Armonk, N.Y., M. E. Sharpe, 1986–); reviewed by Andrew J. Nathan, in *The Journal of Asian Studies* 47.2:352–3 (May 1988).

materials devoted to single events or topics. Supplementing them were the translations by the Joint Publications Research Service (JPRS) of source materials and other data selected from PRC publications. In addition, the *Daily Report, Foreign Radio Broadcasts* prepared by the Foreign Broadcast Information Service (FBIS) was an equally important source.[21] Early in 1960, the U.S. government also released to the Library of Congress its holdings of some 1,200 Chinese local newspapers published before 1960. While the great majority of them are incomplete files and many were very fragmentary (some containing just a few issues), the significance of this release cannot be overemphasized, as none of the titles was available for foreign subscription at the time, and a great many still are not.[22]

In 1963 the U.S. State Department released more materials to the Library of Congress. This release was a set of secret Chinese military papers, which *The China Quarterly* described as "the most illuminating first-hand material that scholars have had on the Chinese Communists since the Hoover Institution acquired the Yenan Documents in the mid-forties."[23] The papers consisted of twenty-nine issues of the secret military journal *Gongzuo tongxun* (Bulletin of activities), covering the period from 1 January to 26 August 1961. Edited and

[21]For a detailed discussion and listing of these translation services, see Berton and Wu, pp. 405–36.

[22]All titles, including holdings information, are listed in Han-chu Huang and Hseo-chin Jen, comp., *Chinese Newspapers in the Library of Congress* (Washington, LC, 1985).

The Library of the School of Oriental and African Studies, Univ. of London, also acquired a large number of Chinese local newspapers, some of which are more complete than what was available in the United States. Its holdings of 22 such newspapers covering 1951–1966 were made available to CCRM, which has microfilmed them for wider distribution, with some gaps filled with issues obtained from other sources, including the LC and the Institute of Scientific Information on Social Sciences of the USSR Academy of Sciences. For a listing, see CCRM *Newsletter,* No. 40 (Spring 1986).

In 1987 the Universities Service Centre in Hong Kong acquired from the PRC complete sets of 39 national, provincial (except Qinghai), and municipal newspapers, some dating from 1949, the others from the early 1950s, which represent the most complete file of PRC local newspapers outside of China. The newspapers, together with all of the other holdings of the Universities Service Centre Library, have been donated to the Chinese Univ. of Hong Kong, and will be available for use by scholars beginning in the spring of 1989.

A ten-year run (1977–86) of *Jiefangjun bao* (Liberation army news) has been recently acquired by the Australian National Univ. Library. This newspaper has been declassified and offered for foreign subscription as of 1987, but no American library has actually received any issues of it.

[23]*The China Quarterly* 18:67 (April–June 1964).

published by the General Political Department of the People's Liberation Army, the Bulletin was distributed to officers at the regimental level or above, with the top secret issues distributed only to divisional officers. One issue, No. 9, which presumably is such an issue, is missing from the set and was not acquired by the State Department.[24]

The severe disruption of the publishing industry brought about by the Cultural Revolution has been noted earlier. The almost complete halt in the publication of scholarly and research works during those years forced American libraries to place a high premium on the collecting of all kinds of Red Guard publications. Although some of these materials are highly polemical, most contain a great deal of valuable information not available elsewhere. For example, there are directives from all levels of the party leaders, including a good many by Mao Zedong, all from this period; "negative materials" on those being purged; documents on party history; and "news flashes" on people and current events. Initially, libraries competed with each other in the acquisition of the limited number of such publications that were available in Hong Kong, and the prices soared. At the request of China scholars, the State Department agreed to release its collection of Red Guard materials to the academic community. The releases were first made through the Harvard-Yenching Library, and when the Center for Chinese Research Materials (CCRM) of the Association of Research Libraries was established in 1968, subsequent releases were made to CCRM. In 1975 CCRM reproduced these releases, along with some additional materials acquired from other sources, in nineteen volumes for general distribution; in 1979 a general table of contents to the nineteen volumes was also issued. In 1980 CCRM published another eight volumes as a supplement. Together they rep-

---

[24]For an English translation of the papers, see J. Chester Cheng, ed., *The Politics of the Chinese Red Army: A Translation of the Bulletin of Activities of the People's Liberation Army,* (Stanford, Hoover Institution, 1966). For analyses of the documents, see John Wilson Lewis, "China's Secret Military Papers: 'Continuities' and 'Revelations,'" *The China Quarterly* 18:68–78 (April–June 1964); Alice Langley Hsieh, "China's Secret Military Papers: Military Doctrines and Strategy," ibid., pp. 79–99; and J. Chester Cheng, "Problems of Chinese Military Leadership as Seen in the Secret Military Papers," *Asian Survey* 4:861–72 (June 1964). Another *neibu* publication recently available from Japan is Zhongguo renmin jiefangjun junshi kexue yuan, *Zhongguo renmin jiefangjun dashiji, 1927–1982* (A chronology of the Chinese People's Liberation Army, 1927–1982), (n.p., 1984).

resent the single largest collection of Red Guard publications in the Western world.[25]

It should be noted that additional Red Guard publications, such as those from which the translations in this volume are taken, have made their appearance on the academic research scene in the post-Mao period. Besides those used in preparation of this volume, others are probably available in the West.[26] Publication and distribution of Red Guard materials were originally subject to practically no control, and the treatment of what is left of these materials in China remains casual even today.[27]

As has been mentioned, acquiring research materials from the PRC has become much easier since the late 1970s. The Chinese publishing industry has once again regained its vitality.[28] Documentary sources, memoirs of party leaders, new journals, and other scholarly works which for one reason or another could not be published in the past have all appeared in quantity. New types of publications such as yearbooks, statistics, and legal materials also have proliferated.[29] Direct purchases from China have become routine; Chinese libraries are now permitted and are eager to enter into exchange arrangements

---

[25]See *Hong weibing ziliao* (Red Guard publications), 20 vols. (Washington, D.C., CCRM, Association of Research Libraries, 1975). The 8-volume supplement is entitled *Hongweibing ziliao xubian I* (Red Guard publications: supplement I). Most of the materials in both editions were originally published in 1967–8; some were issued in 1966, 1969, and 1970. For a guide to the 20-volume set, see Hong Yung Lee, *A Research Guide to Red Guard Publications 1966–1969* (Armonk, N.Y., M E. Sharpe, forthcoming).

[26]The Menzies Library of the Australian National Univ. kindly shared with us copies of two volumes of *Mao Zedong sixiang wansui* (New Mao Texts, vols. 11A and B). The Swedish scholar, Michael Schoenhals, in *The Journal of Communist Studies* 2.2:109–126 (1986), cites another *wansui* volume and other Red Guard collections (unavailable for inspection as of this writing), which appear to be different from the material we have come upon.

[27]Visiting a Chinese friend who was an ex–Red Guard, a Western student in China recently commented on a volume of *Mao Zedong sixiang wansui* carelessly piled with odd books in the corner of the room. "Oh, that," the Chinese replied. "Who believes in that stuff any more. It's useless. You want it? Take it."

[28]Book production increased from 17,212 titles in 1979 to 45,603 titles in 1985; periodicals from 1,470 to 4,705 and newspapers from 69 to 698 for the same period. See Zhongguo guojia tongji ju, comp. *Zhongguo tongji nianjian, 1986* (China statistical yearbook, 1986) (Beijing, Zhongguo tongji chubanshe, 1986), pp. 781–2.

[29]See, for instance, Barry Naughton, "The Chinese Economy: New Sources and Data"; William R. Lavely, "Chinese Demographic Data: A Guide to Major Sources"; and Tao-tai Hsia and Wendy Zeldin, "Legislation and Legal Publication in the PRC," *China Exchange News* 15.3–4:8–16 (Sept./Dec. 1987).

with foreign libraries; some local newspapers are available for foreign subscription for the first time; book fairs have been held in China and abroad; visitors to China are free to purchase publications in state-run book stores as well as at privately managed book stalls, which are set up on sidewalks in most major cities; visiting scholars are also accorded the privilege of photocopying at their host institutions. As a result, during the last several years American libraries have been able to greatly strengthen their holdings of research materials on contemporary China.

Yet, against this encouraging background of vast improvement, certain problems remain. Firstly, the wide and continuing use of the *neibu* (internal) classification persists for many scholarly works and even reference books. It is baffling, to say the least, to see publications which contain no sensitive material whatsoever bearing this classification. Once so classified, the publication in question is usually not listed in dealers' catalogues, and even when sent on exchange by a Chinese library, invariably stopped by the customs and returned to its sender. Ironically, many of such publications find their way to the outside world anyway, and those reaching the hands of commercial dealers, especially the reprint publishers in Hong Kong, are then reprinted and sold at very high prices without any royalties accruing to the original publishers. It is usual nowadays to see a large number of these *neibu* publications on the shelves of American libraries, and the number is growing.

Secondly, the quality of service provided by the export organizations dealing in publications leaves much to be desired. It is not uncommon to place an order only to find out six to twelve months later, and sometimes never, that the order cannot be filled. In the meantime one often misses the opportunity of obtaining a copy from another source while it is still available. This is a particularly serious problem with regard to local publications, which are usually issued in small press runs and are therefore in limited supply.

Thirdly, while some local newspapers are now available for foreign subscription, the majority of them, especially those below the provincial level, still are not. Fourthly, there is the problem of exchange. The price differential between Western and Chinese publications is such that no Chinese library would agree on any exchange that is based on equal value. For the same reason, American libraries are unwilling to enter into any agreement that is purely on a volume-for-volume basis. Consequently, exchanges are conducted by "gentlemen's agreement," with each side exercising its own discretion as to what constitutes a fair exchange. While some Chinese libraries do oblige requests for publications issued in their respective localities, their standard exchange offerings, more often than not, primarily consist of publications from national publishing houses, which are easily available from commercial dealers.

Lastly, the reluctance of Chinese export companies to search for out-of-print publications and the absence of well stocked second-hand book stores in China combine to make the job of securing such books and journals an extremely frustrating and almost impossible task. Given these problems, American libraries have supplemented the usual and more formal channels of acquisition by relying heavily on the assistance of individuals who travel to China and on personal relationships formed with Chinese colleagues. These private contacts have been very productive, and will certainly continue to be a significant factor in the further expansion of research sources for the study of contemporary China in the United States in the years to come.

Looking to the future, it seems that, if the kind of research and publication activities that we have seen taking place in the last few years in the PRC continue, we should see a further increase in the availability of research sources. As more Chinese scholars venture into the more controversial areas of research, such as those related to the history of the Chinese Communist Party, the continuing assessment of Mao Zedong's leadership in the Chinese Revolution, and the like, new documentary evidence and other primary sources are bound to be introduced. We have already seen developments of this kind in the publication of such materials as the Zunyi Conference documents, documentary histories of the provincial CCP committees, biographies of party leaders, eyewitness accounts of important historical events, and the various editions of "study materials" and "study selections" from which Mao's speeches translated in this volume are selected.[30] Of course, it would be unrealistic to expect, for instance, that the Central Party Archive would be open to all at any time in the future, but there is also no reason to believe that the prac-

---

[30]For a discussion of these *xuexi ziliao* (study materials) and *xuexi wenxuan* (study selections), see Timothy Cheek's chapter in this volume.

tice of releasing historical documentation to justify policy will be a thing of the past.[31] It is always risky to speculate about the future, but for the moment the future prospects of having access to more and better documentation in and from China on contemporary Chinese affairs look very encouraging in spite of the previously mentioned problems which American libraries are likely to continue to face in their acquisition efforts.

[31]The Standing Committee of the 6th National People's Congress passed an archives law at its 22nd meeting, 28 Aug.–5 Sept. 1987 (effective on 1 Jan. 1988), which provides that "state archives will generally be open to the public after 30 years" and that "archives related to state security or other major national interests, as well as those unsuitable for the public, can remain confidential after 30 years"; see *Beijing Review* 30.38:6 (21 Sept. 1987). According to another report, "China has already opened to the public more than 3,000 of its archives recording events before Liberation in 1949"; see *Ta Kung Pao English Weekly*, 24 December 1987, p. 7.

CHAPTER FIVE

Textually Speaking: An Assessment
of Newly Available Mao Texts

TIMOTHY CHEEK

Our translations come from twenty-three volumes of talks and writings by Mao Zedong that have become available in the West over the course of the past few years. The precise provenance of these volumes, which have arrived through various channels, cannot be documented; and since they were never intended for public distribution, they do not contain the bibliographic information page normally found in books published in the People's Republic of China.

The author gratefully acknowledges the guidance and encouragement of Roderick MacFarquhar and thanks the following people for their criticisms and suggestions: David Bachman, Bill Brugger, Merle Goldman, Michael Y. M. Kau, Katherine Keenum, Michael Schoenhals, Stuart Schram, Lawrence Sullivan, Frederick Teiwes, Jonathan Unger, Hans van de Ven, and Eugene Wu.

The historian's first task, therefore, is to evaluate their reliability before offering interpretations of what they have to tell us about Mao, the Chinese Communist Party (CCP), and modern Chinese history. This chapter provides a preliminary critique of the texts, considering the evidence for their authenticity and the topics they are likely to enlighten. It begins with an assessment of the new volumes, then comments generally on the texts we have translated, and finally discusses some of the issues involved in interpreting what is found in them.

Although the final selections were made from only ten of the twenty-three volumes, all twenty-three were examined and compared by the Harvard team, and numbered for convenience. All twenty-three will be published by the Center for Chinese Research Materials in Oakton, Virginia. Together, they contain some five thousand pages of speeches by Mao, verbatim transcripts of meetings at which he was the principal speaker, letters by him, and other similar documents. With the exception of Volume 15, all the collections were made during the Cultural Revolution, when Mao's admirers among the Red Guards were eager to preserve his every word unchanged. By their sheer quantity, therefore, and even more by their rawness, they provide much valuable new data by which we can discover more about Mao's own ideas on China's revolution, his relationship to his colleagues, and the foibles of our own interpretations.

THE NEWLY AVAILABLE MAO TEXTS

Most of the newly available collections of Mao writings are independent volumes rather than parts of a coherent series, even though four bear the same title, *Xuexi wenxuan* (Study selections), and nine share the title *Mao Zedong sixiang wansui* (Long live Mao Zedong Thought) with previously available books.[1] Some of the new volumes, however, are indeed connected, and our numbering groups them together. Volumes 6A and 6B are simply the first and second volumes of one title, with continuous pagination. Volumes 11A and

[1]See *Mao Zedong sixiang wansui* (1967, 1969) in the reference bibliography. Jonathon Unger has kindly called my attention to two further Taiwanese releases of *Mao Zedong sixiang wansui*: "disan ji" (Vol. 3), which features numerous brief texts from 1934 to 1966, and "disi ji" (Vol. 4), which continues in similar format for 1966 and 1967.

11B are clearly a chronological series. Another chronological series, Volumes 12A–12C, was produced by one editorial group; and Volume 13, which is titled as a supplement to it, may have had the same editors, but we have no way of knowing. Volumes 15A–15E, the Peking University textbooks, we are certain are a series and the editors are known. We have ordered the volumes and numbered them in rough chronological order, although it is impossible to determine with accuracy the publication dates of most. They are listed below in Table 1 according to our own numbering of the volumes, with relevant bibliographic information and whatever comments are printed in them as well as brief comments on their contents.

This is a massive amount of material, some 5,500 pages,[2] which forms a veritable new archive of Mao writings. Yet it comes with precious little explicit bibliographic information. A few volumes carry a 1967 publication date and Volume 14 contains material up through 1969; it is reasonable, therefore, to conclude that these were compiled between 1967 and 1969, during the Red Guard phase of the Cultural Revolution.[3] What may we expect of texts published at the height of the Cultural Revolution, and how reliable are they? A number of volumes bring to mind their namesake, the well-known two volumes of *Wansui* reproduced in Taiwan in the early 1970s.[4] The new materials greatly expand the number of Mao texts from "Red Guard" editors available to scholars; but in contrast to the early 1970s, when the first *Wansui* appeared in the West, now there is also a greatly expanded corpus of Mao texts with which they may be compared—not only the 1977 Volume 5 of *Mao Zedong xuanji* (Selected works of Mao Zedong) but Mao publications from the 1980s as well. What is the relationship between the well-known *Wansui* and the newly unearthed material? And what is the relationship of these unofficially published materials to official publications of works by Mao Zedong? The explosion of materials on party history coming out of China in the post-Mao period allows us to view all Mao publications in a fresh light.

[2]This calculation does not include the 1,048 pages of Vol. 14, which is largely a chronology, though it contains many Mao quotations.
[3]With the exception of Vols. 15A–E, which were produced as limited circulation reference materials at Peking University in the post-Mao period.
[4]See n. 1.

TABLE 1 The Newly Available Mao Volumes

Volume	Bibliographic Data	Chinese comment	Contents
1	Xuexi wenxuan (Study selections) (n.p., n.pub., 1967), 415pp.	On title page: Neibu ziliao qingwu waizhuan (Internal materials, please do not circulate)	Texts from 1949–July 1957, most from 1956–7
2	Xuexi wenxuan (n.p., n.pub., n.d.), 322pp.		Texts from 1957–8, most from 1958
3	Xuexi wenxuan (n.p., n.pub., n.d.), 348pp.	On title page: Neibu zilao bude fanyin (Internal materials, do not re-print)	Texts from 1959–63, two-thirds from 1959–60
4	Xuexi wenxuan (n.p., n.pub., n.d.), 153 pp.; appendix, 83 pp.		Texts from 1964–7, over half on 1964, 1966. Includes talks with Wang Hairong, Mao Yuanxin, Wang Dongxing, Zhou Peiyuan, Edgar Snow, CR elite. 83-page appendix of selections on philosophy, political purges, and public health issues, 1954–66
5	Mao Zedong sixiang wansui (Long live Mao Zedong Thought) (n.p., n.pub., May 1967), 218 pp.		Texts from 1950–65, including "Ten great relationships," "Summer '57," "Moscow talks," "Sixty work points of 1958"
6A	Mao Zedong sixiang wansui (n.p., n.pub., June 1967), shang, pp. 1–216	On title page: Neibu zilao, bude waizhuan, bude yinyong bude fanyin (Internal materials, do not circulate, do not cite, do not reprint)	Texts from 1949–58, broad selection
6B	Mao Zedong sixiang wansui (n.p., n.pub., June 1967), xia, pp. 217–379	On title page: Neibu ziliao, bude waizhuan, bude yinyong bude fanyin	Texts from 1958–65, including several around 1959 Lushan plenum; broad selection

TABLE 1 (Continued)

Volume	Bibliographic Data	Chinese comment	Contents
7	*Mao Zedong sixiang wansui* (n.p., n.pub., July 1967), 187 pp.		Texts from 1951–67, most from 1966–7. Compilation of Mao's sayings on the CR, pp. 183–7. Duplicates of 1957 speeches in vols. 1, 9.
8	*Mao Zedong sixiang wansui* (n.p., n.pub.,n. date), 192 pp.		4 talks (including Moscow, Nov. 1957); "Notes on political economy," pp. 81–192; brief selections on purging counterrevolutionaries
9	*Mao Zedong sixiang wansui* (n.p., n.pub., Sept. 1967), 336 pp.		Texts from 1950–65, mostly from 1955–8. Duplicates of several texts translated here; compilation of Mao's sayings on philosophy, pp. 294–332
10	*Mao Zedong sixiang wansui* (n.p., n.pub., n.date), 411 pp.		Texts from 1953–65, most from 1957–9
11A	*Mao Zedong sixiang wansui, 1949/9–1957/12* (Long live Mao Zedong Thought, Sept. 1949–Dec. 1957) (n.p., n.pub., n.date), 234 pp.		
11B	*Mao Zedong sixiang wansui, 1958/1–1959/12* (Long live Mao Zedong Thought, Jan. 1958–Dec. 1959) (n.p., n.pub., n. date), 252 pp.		
12A	*Xuexi ziliao, 1949/10–1956* (Study materials, Oct. 1949–1956) (n.p., n.pub., n.d.), 307 pp.		Texts by date, including prefaces to *Socialist High Tide*, pp. 175–226

TABLE 1 (Continued)

Volume	Bibliographic Data	Chinese comment	Contents
12B	*Xuexi ziliao, 1957–1961* (n.p., n.pub., n.d.), 518 pp.		Texts by date
12C	*Xuexi ziliao, 1962–1967* (n.p., n.pub., n.d.), 314 pp.		Texts by date
13	*Xuexi ziliao, xu-yi* (Study materials, Supplement One) (n.p., n.pub., n.d.), 383 pp.		Texts from 1949–67, most from 1957–60, 1964; latest item, 7 July 1967, p. 375
14	*Mao zhuxide geming luxian wansui: Dangnei liangtiao luxian douzheng da shiji (1921–1969)* (Long live the revolutionary line of Chairman Mao: major events in the two-line struggle inside the party, 1921–69) (n.p., n.pub., n.d.), 4 pp. 8 pp. 1048 pp.		Mammoth chronology with quotations
15A	*Mao Zedong zhexue sixiang jiaoxue cankao ziliao* (Reference materials for teaching Mao Zedong's philosophical thought), ed. Peking University Department of Philosophy, Mao Zedong Philosophical Thought Research Room, vol. 1 (July 1983), 113 pp.	Note on cover: *Neibu ziliao, tuoshan baocun* (Internal materials, be careful to preserve)	Texts from 1948–65; letter to Ai Siqi. NB: "Why do people make mistakes?" (undated), pp. 69–106

TABLE 1 (Continued)

Volume	Bibliographic Data	Chinese comment	Contents
15B	*Mao Zedong zhexue sixiang jiaoxue yanjiu cankao ziliao* (Reference materials for teaching teaching and research on Mao Zedong's philosophical thought, ed. Peking University Department of Philosophy, Mao Zedong Philosophical Thought Research Room, vol. 2 (October, 1983), 100 pp.	Note on cover: *Neibu zilao, tuoshan baocun*	Epistemological and dialectical text-book materials
15C	———, vol. 3 (October, 1983), 41 pp.	Note on cover: *Neibu ziliao, tuoshan baocun*	Series from 1956–65 of 1- to 3-page selections on philosophical problems
15D	———, vol. 4 (October, 1983), 95 pp.	Note on cover: *Neibu ziliao, tuoshan baocun*	Three texts on contradictions and practice; speaking notes of the 27 Feb. 1957 text
15E	———, vol. 5 (October, 1983), 92 pp.	Note on cover: *Neibu ziliao, tuoshan baocun*	Bibliography of studies on Mao's philosophical thought

Since the advent of "Mao Zedong Thought" in the early 1940s,[5] Mao's writings have been published in China in three kinds of collections. These may be distinguished by the intent of their editors and called "collective wisdom" editions, "genius" editions, and "historicist" editions.[6] First, beginning in 1944, volumes of *Mao Zedong xuanji* began to appear by the order of one or another high level CCP institution. These were edited by committee according to a "collective wisdom" criterion: the idea that Mao "represented" the summation of Sinified Marxism-Leninism and thus should reflect the consensus of the party leadership. That this editing relied most heavily on Mao's voluntary acquiescence and that the process was highly distorted as early as 1960 did not weaken, in the minds of the editors, the attempt to make official Mao works a "collective" enterprise. Second, during the Cultural Revolution and particularly at the height of the Red Guard movement in 1967, Mao writings were published by a confusing array of unnamed editors based on the idea that the Chairman was a lone genius not subject to revision by any collective leadership, least of all by a party riddled with "capitalist roaders." Finally, since Mao's death, party historiographers have published both restricted circulation and publicly available collections of Mao writings that reflect in varying degrees an "historicist" urge to understand the past as it really was and to place Mao and his individual writings more firmly in the historical context. The twenty-three new volumes of Mao texts come from the second, "genius"-edition, group, except for Volumes 15A–15E, which are "historicist" editions from the 1980s. A review of the three kinds of Mao collections will help us to understand the strengths and weaknesses of each.

[5]Before the 1940s Mao was simply one among many leading party figures who published in the periodical press and even produced a few limited collections in the late 1930s. There were at least two such early editions of Mao's writings, both apparently edited by his secretary, Chen Boda: *Mao Zedong lunwen ji* (Shanghai, 1937) and *Mao Zedong lun* (Xi'an, 1939). See the reference bibliography. These are analyzed by Raymond F. Wylie, *The Emergence of Maoism* (Stanford, Stanford Univ. Press, 1980), pp. 60–1; and Helmut Martin, *Cult and Canon: The Origins and Development of State Maoism* (Armonk, N.Y., M. E. Sharpe, 1982), pp. 11–12.

[6]These are my categories and not Chinese ones, though they correspond (in order) to the Chinese categories of official (published by the Mao committee), unauthorized, and reference (*yanjiu*, literally "research") in the publication of Mao's writing.

"Collective Wisdom" Editions

The first official edition of a *Mao Zedong xuanji* (hereafter *Selected Works*) was published in the Shanxi-Chahar-Hebei border region in May 1944. At the order of Nie Rongzhen, the military commander of the area, and the Jin Cha Ji branch (*fenju*) of the Central Committee, it was edited by one of their ranking party journalists, Deng Tuo, who had never met Mao. It was designed to facilitate cadre study in the new Rectification Movement, and included a selection of twenty-nine items by Mao in five sections (*juan*), mostly from the war period, but also including some earlier pieces, such as his 1927 report on the Hunan peasant movement. Its last piece was his May 1942 "Talks at the Yan'an Conference on Literature and Art."[7]

In fact, however, according to a senior party historian, Gong Yuzhi, subsequent Mao collections grew out of another series of study materials, *Liuda yilai* (Since the Sixth Congress). This two-volume compendium of some 500 party documents dating from 1928 onward was first printed in December 1941 by the Higher Party School in Yan'an as a source book for cadres students to study in the Rectification Movement. It appears that one of the major functions of the collection was to provide the original views of party leaders and show why Mao, Liu Shaoqi, and their associates were better

---

[7] *Mao Zedong xuanji* (n.p., Jin Cha Ji xinhua shudian, 1944) is not readily available in the West. There is a copy at the Fairbank Center Library, Harvard, and in the reading room of the Literature Department of Tokyo University. This edition was updated at least once in a Dalian edition published in Aug. 1946 with several later printings. This revised edition added his 25 April 1945 "On coalition government" and two other texts. It also edited Deng Tuo's preface to suit the new historical period (references to the anti-Japanese war were removed). See *Mao Zedong xuanji* (Dalian, Dazhong shudian, 1946; 3rd printing, March 1947) in the Harvard-Yenching Library. Gong Yuzhi says that the original Dalian edition was made after 15 August 1945; see his "Tong Shi Lamu jiaoshou de tanhua" (A conversation with Professor Schram) *Wenxian he yanjiu: 1984 nian huibianben* (Documents and research: 1984 selections) (Beijing, Renmin chubanshe, 1986), p. 244. Presumably this August 1946 edition is what he means. Information on early *Selected Works* is also found in Liu Lantao, et al., "Sishi nianqian de yibu *Mao Zedong xuanji*" (An edition of the *Selected Works of Mao Zedong* from 40 years ago), *Liaowang zhoukan* 17:11 (1984); "Deng Tuo yu diyibu *Mao Zedong xuanji*" (Deng Tuo and the first *Selected Works of Mao Zedong*), *Dang shi xinxi* (Information on party history), Sept. 1, 1986, p. 1; and Zhonggong zhongyang wenxian yanjiu shi, eds., *Guanyu jianguo yilai dangde ruogan lishi wenti de jueyi zhushiben (xiuding)*. [Annotations (revised edition) on the resolution on certain historical questions of the party since the founding of the nation] (Beijing, Renmin chubanshe, 1985), pp. 505–506; hereafter *Zhushiben*.

equipped to lead the party than their competition, particularly Wang
Ming and Bo Gu.[8] The collection included, says Gong, a number of
writings by Mao and these became the basis for the 1944 and all later
Selected Works.[9] A review of *Liuda yilai* confirms Gong's remarks,
although the publisher turns out to be the CCP Secretariat.[10]

The 1944 Jin Cha Ji edition of Mao's *Selected Works* was one of
what Gong Yuzhi identifies as five "systems" (*xitong*), or original editions, of Mao's *Selected Works* before 1949.[11] Not many of these pre-
1949 editions are available in the West, though the expanded and
revised 1947 Jin Cha Ji edition is.[12] Essentially, different base areas
under CCP control either edited or reprinted a *Selected Works* as part
of the necessary study materials for rectification study between 1944
and 1948.

Two conclusions can be drawn from the history of pre-1949
Selected Works. First, we see the institutional continuation between
the study of generic party documents (resolutions, directives, various
leaders' writings) and the study of one man's writings. This is the documentary trail of the emergence of the Mao cult, and the genesis of
what Helmut Martin calls the official "Mao canon."[13] Just as 500
party texts in *Liuda yilai* were supposed to guide leaders at the

[8]Frederick Teiwes, interviews with party historians, Beijing, 1985–6. I am grateful to Dr.
Teiwes of Sydney University for sharing his notes.
[9]Gong Yuzhi, pp. 243–4. I am grateful to Dr. Schram for pointing out this interview to me.
[10]Zhonggong zhongyang shujichu, eds., *Liuda yilai—dangnei mimi wenjian* (Since the 6th
Congress—secret inner party documents) (Beijing, Renmin chubanshe, *shang* and *xia*, preface dated Feb. 1980). The preface to both volumes is signed by the Central Archives and
gives details of the 1945 and 1952 revised editions and post–1941 documents added to the
volumes. The current edition does not reprint those Mao writings found in his *Selected
Works* (hereafter, *SW*), but does note them at the appropriate place in the table of contents.
[11]Gong Yuzhi, pp. 244–6.
[12]*Mao Zedong xuanji* (Jin Cha Ji, March 1947), reprinted by ARL-CCRM, 1970 (M19). The
5 "systems," or original editions, from which numerous reprints are identified by Gong, are
(1) the 1944 Jin Cha Ji edition; (2) a 1945 Central Soviet edition by the New Fourth Army,
which appears to be the July 1945 edition at Harvard-Yenching, microfilm: FC-2185; (3) a
slim 1947 edition published in Shandong under the title of *Mao Zedong wenxuan;* (4) a
thick 1948 volume in 6 *juan* published in Harbin and widely distributed; and, by far the
largest, (5) a restricted-circulation edition in 2 volumes published in 1948 in the Jin Ji Lu Yu
Base Area, which Western scholars hope some day to view.
[13]Martin, p. 4. Excellent studies of the emergence of Maoism include, Wylie (1980) and
Noriyuki Tokuda, "Yenan Rectification Movement: Mao Tse-tung's Big Push Toward Charismatic Leadership During 1941–1942," *Developing Economies* 9:1 (1971).

Higher Party School in Yan'an, so 29 writings by Mao Zedong in the first *Selected Works*, with later additions, were held to suffice for lower level cadres from 1944 on. The rise of Mao Zedong Thought (*Mao Zedong sixiang*) in the mid 1940s has been no secret to historians, but we now see the institutional ramifications more clearly. One man's writings replaced 500 institutional documents as the core of study materials; that is a tremendous change.[14] This leads to the second point. Mao's *Selected Works* were aimed at the public, the compendium of party decisions was not. The *Liuda yilai* was reprinted at least twice, and we can presume it was part of the course of study for at least senior CCP members. What we see then is a division of audiences—the laity gets a wise father figure, the priesthood can review the notes of the Curia. This shift from authoritative institutional documents to the writings of a single genius nicely suited the beginning of a massive effort at popularizing Marxist-Leninist ideology beyond the ranks of the party and leftist intellectuals. To the uninitiated, loyalty to Mao was considerably easier than an emotional attachment to the Politburo.

The party, however, felt its collective leadership should have a say in how this father figure was to be presented to his public. The now well-known series of *Selected Works* began publication in 1951. In all, five numbered volumes of Mao's *Selected Works* have been edited by the Mao Zedong selected works publications committee of the Central Committee in Beijing.[15] According to Michael Y. M. Kau and John Leung, as many as 236 million copies of the first four volumes alone were published in China during Mao's life.[16] A pair of supplementary volumes were issued by a subcommittee in April 1965,

[14]Of course, these were not the only study documents for party cadres. Aside from the *Liuda yilai* and presumably numerous other restricted collections, the famous public set of "rectification documents" (*zhengfeng wenjian*) published for the 1942 Yan'an rectification included authoritative writings by other Chinese leaders (e.g. Liu Shaoqi) and Soviet leaders. See Boyd Compton, *Mao's China* (Seattle, Univ. of Washington Press, 1952).

[15]The committee is Zhonggong zhongyang Mao Zedong xuanji chuban weiyuanhui. The first edition of each of the numbered volumes appeared in order in October 1951, April 1952, April 1953, September 1960, and April 1977. In the 1970 reprint, the dates of first publication given for some of the first four volumes differ slightly from those found in the actual first edition.

[16]Kau and Leung, eds., *The Writings of Mao Zedong, Vol. 1: 1949–1956* (Armonk, N.Y., M. E. Sharpe, 1986), p. xxvi.

including the revised version of Mao's February 1957 "On The correct handling of contradictions among the people" and other texts from the previous four volumes and elsewhere.[17] According to Gong Yuzhi, Mao personally revised the post-1949 official publication of his works.[18]

Since Mao's death there have been both restricted and openly published collections of his writings. Most important among these post-Mao publications is Volume 5 of his *Selected Works*, published in 1977. A few volumes of his writings on a specific theme have been published in the mid 1980s. It is debatable, however, whether these contributions should be classified with "collective wisdom" versions of Mao Zedong Thought. The editors of Volume 5 fully intended it to be a contribution to the "Mao canon," but this volume has been subject to severe criticism for distortions in its selection and editing.[19] The publicly distributed (*gongkai*) Mao collections of the 1980s, although clearly released to support current policy, for the most part seem intent on demythologizing Mao, on giving his thought relative rather than absolute value, and on stressing the collective efforts of the party. Internal (*neibu*) documentary collections seem even further intent on this historicist mission. These collections are therefore discussed below under "historicist" editions.

There are two striking characteristics of the "collective wisdom" editions of Mao's *Selected Works*. First, the texts have been freely edited to conform to what the editors consider to be the needs of changing circumstances. That is, in contravention of Western standards of accuracy in reprinting historical documents, the texts have been altered. Many well-known studies have documented this phenomenon. Jerome Chen's analysis of the revisions of Mao's 1927 "Report on the Hunan Peasant Movement," and Bonnie McDougall's study of the 1943 newspaper version and the 1953 "committee" version of Mao's "Talks at the Yan'an Conference on Literature and Art" are two examples.[20] The prodigious Japanese collection, *Mao Zedong ji*, by

---

[17]*Mao Zedong zhuzuo xuandu (jia/yi zhong ben).* (A reader of works by Mao Zedong: supplementary volumes A & B) (Beijing, Renmin chubanshe, 1965).
[18]Gong, p. 246.
[19]Gong, pp. 251–2; a good review of the circumstances and political motivations surrounding the compilation of Vol. 5 is given in Martin, pp. 50–68. Teiwes' interviews with party historians (see n. 8), also records views supporting this criticism.
[20]Jerome Chen, *Mao Papers: Anthology and Bibliography* (London, Oxford Univ. Press,

Takeúchi Minoru and his colleagues, makes a careful comparison of all his pre-1949 works.[21] Among the more common changes are the deletion of positive comments about the Kuomintang (KMT, Nationalist party), infelicities in doctrinal language or earthy language, references to policies that did not work, and specific details. No serious scholar interested in the meaning of a piece by Mao in historical context can avoid consulting the original publication, since the *Selected Works* version is likely to be edited, often without notice.[22]

Secondly, official editions of Mao's writings published before his death in 1976 are considered by the CCP leadership to represent "the crystallization of collective wisdom in the CCP" (*Zhongguo gongchan dang jiti zhihui de jiejing*).[23] Such has unequivocally been the case since Mao Zedong Thought was officially designated as the guiding thought of the CCP in the June 1945 Party Constitution passed at the Seventh Congress of the CCP in Yan'an.[24] This is the corollary of letting Mao speak for the party—it can check what is said. This control in fact did not always happen, for who was about to correct

---

1970), introduction; Bonnie S. McDougall, *Mao Zedong's "Talks at the Yan'an Conference on Literature And Art": A Translation of the 1943 Text with Commentary* (Ann Arbor, Michigan Paper in Chinese Studies, No. 39, 1980).

[21]See Takeuchi Minoru, ed., *Mao Zedong ji*, 10 volumes (Tokyo, Hokobosha, 1971–3); and supplementary volumes in the reference bibliography.

[22]One further example of significant change is the *SW* version of Mao's 1940 essay, "On new democracy." See Mao Zedong, "Xin minzhu de zhengzhi yu xin minzhu de wenhua" (New democratic politics and new democratic culture), *Zhongguo wenhua* 1.1:1–24 (Yan'an, February 1940). A copy is in the Harvard Yenching Library. Takeuchi makes a careful comparison of texts in *Mao Zedong ji*, Vol. 6. Gong Yuzhi (pp. 247–8) acknowledges, without much helpful detail, the alterations made to these three texts as well as others.

[23]Locus classicus is par. 28 of the 1981 "Historical Resolution"; see the Gong Commentary, *Zhushiben*, p. 507ff. Ye Jianying declared this to be the case in 1979 (*RMRB*, Oct. 3, 1979); see Martin, p. 137. Shi Zhongquan emphasizes it; see *GMRB* (18 December 1985) as translated in *FBIS-CHI*, 2 January 1986, pp. K13-6; and *Jiaoyu yu yanjiu* (Teaching and research) No. 3 (May 1985) as translated in *JPRS-CPS-85-113* (7 November 1985), pp. 24–34. See also Fang Daming, "Mao Zedong sixiang kexue hanyi" (The scientific significance of Mao Zedong Thought), in Liao Gailong, ed., *Zhonggong dang shi wenzhai niankan: 1982* (Annual selection of articles on CCP history: 1982) (Hangzhou, Zhejiang renmin chubanshe, 1985), pp. 46–8.

[24]Calls for such a role for Mao's "thought" date to at least the efforts of party theoretician Zhang Ruxin in 1941, to Wang Jiaxiang's apparent first coining of "Mao Zedong Thought" (*Mao Zedong sixiang*) on 5 July 1943, and to Deng Tuo's preface to the 1944 edition of *SW*. See Pang Xianzhi, "Guanyu Mao Zedong sixiang tichu de lishi guocheng" (On the historical process through which Mao Zedong Thought emerged), in Liao Gailong (1985), pp. 48–50; *Mao Zedong xuanji* (1944); and Wylie, pp. 154–7, 171–5.

the Chairman? As Frederick Teiwes has noted for Mao's behavior in general before 1955, the inner-party democracy of the CCP, which would allow this collegial vetting of Mao's publications, was more a matter of "a democracy of the Chairman's self-restraint."[25]

There are two ways to achieve "collective wisdom." One is to edit the Chairman. Gong Yuzhi relates a few instances where Li Da and later some unnamed comrade induced the Chairman to revise "On Practice" and other writings before putting them in the early 1950s *Selected Works*.[26] It now appears that Liu Shaoqi chaired the committee to edit Mao's works before the Cultural Revolution.[27] Mao probably submitted to this because a consensual approach to his own deification had contributed so successfully to the CCP's struggle for power in the 1940s.

The other way to achieve "collective wisdom" was to feed the Chairman with ideas. This appears to have been the more usual method. Post-Mao historiography is awash with revelations of who contributed what.[28] Aside from the input of top leaders such as Liu Shaoqi and Deng Xiaoping, there is a growing list of consultants and editors. Ai Siqi seems to have been part of a brain trust of advisors to Mao in Yan'an, in the mid to late 1930s, which guided Mao's thinking about Marxist-Leninist theory. Mao's short letter in 1937 to Ai acknowledging "the deepest impression" Ai's book *Philosophy and Life* made on him would seem to support this.[29] Hu Qiaomu, Mao's secretary, was in charge of collating the speeches that became "On the ten great relationships" and it turns out that the famous "Critique of Soviet economics" are Hu Sheng's notes from Mao's 1959 study group—Hu Sheng rearranged Mao's comments and Mao never reviewed them.[30]

[25]Frederick C. Teiwes, "Mao and His Lieutenants," to be published in *The Australian Journal of Chinese Affairs* 19 & 20 (January-July 1988).

[26]Gong, pp. 250-1.

[27]Martin, p. 160.

[28]*Zhushiben*, pp. 507-12; Shi Zhongquan, op. cit.

[29]See Joshua A. Fogel, *Ai Ssu-Ch'i's Contribution to the Development of Chinese Marxism* (Cambridge, Harvard Council on East Asian Studies, 1987), pp. 11-2, 82-3. For Mao's letter to Ai, see New Mao Texts, Vol. 15A in Table 1 above.

[30]Interview with Gong Yuzhi, Harvard University, 13 November 1986. See also Gong (pp. 251-2), which says that what became Mao's *Shida guanxi* was put together by Hu Qiaomu in 1975, based on a number of speeches Mao gave in spring 1956, but particularly two: his 26 April speech to an enlarged meeting of the Politburo and a 2 May speech to the Supreme State Conference.

Clearly, the "collective" nature of official Mao publications was more an ideal than a reality. Yet, official Mao essays could not be published without bureaucratic approval, as well as, of course, Mao's own approval. This minimal agreement began to break down by 1957. Mao's 27 February 1957 speech to the eleventh session of the Supreme State Council, "On the correct handling of contradictions among the people," is a case in point. The Central Committee did not approve it for publication until their hand was forced by the publication of portions of a leaked draft in the *New York Times* on 13 June 1957. The revised edition (and it is so marked in the 1965 *Reader* and 1977 *Selected Works*, Volume 5, editions) was published in the *People's Daily* on 19 June and was quite different from the original.[31] Comments by cadres involved in the process have confirmed that this speech went through at least three rounds of editing among the highest leadership before publication.[32] That many of the major talks by Mao from 1957 to 1958 did not appear officially might suggest that Mao and his colleagues had come to a stand-off. It may simply have been, as in the case of the 1957 "Contradictions" talk, that his editors did not understand the Chairman's words!

Later, Mao's ardent speeches of the Great Leap Forward at Beidaihe and during the autumn of 1958 were not officially published. This time, however, it was not the bureaucracy that caused delays. Preparations were made for a Volume 5 of Mao's *Selected Works* in 1961, but it was Mao who delayed publication. According to Party historians, he wanted to make further corrections.[33] Further official publications did come, as in the two supplementary readers of 1965; and Mao continued to express himself in public, but he sanctioned no further *Selected Works*. The impasse—a bewildered bureaucracy and a Mao unsure of which mood he wished to set in stone—was broken in the Cultural Revolution, when party discipline went to the four

[31]See Text 3. For an analysis of the differences, see Michael Schoenhals, "The Original Contradictions—On the Unrevised Text of Mao Zedong's 'On the Correct Handling of Contradictions among the People,'" *The Australian Journal of Chinese Affairs* 16:99–112.

[32]Personal communication; it seems that it was Hu Qiaomu's unenviable task to coordinate this. Gong Yuzhi (p. 247) touches on the revisions briefly. The *Zhushiben* goes over this in more detail, discussed below under "historicist" editions. For a study of the controversy at the time, see *Origins* 1, pp. 184–217, 261–9, esp. 267. The *New York Times* text is compared with the official June version in Roderick MacFarquhar, *The Hundred Flowers Campaign and the Chinese Intellectuals* (New York, Praeger, 1960), pp. 265–277.

[33]Teiwes, interviews (see n. 8, above).

winds. Young radicals who saw Mao as separate from and superior to the party gained access to Mao's unofficial oeuvre and set about publishing them without, needless to say, asking Mao.

"Genius" Editions

The most famous of the Cultural Revolution collections of Mao's writings are the two *Mao Zedong sixiang wansui* volumes from 1967 and 1969. Since they were not publicly released by the CCP but emerged from the Institute of International Relations in Taipei, there was a natural concern that the texts might be forgeries or highly edited. Scholarly opinion has come down on the side of those who believe that such an enormous bulk of internally consistent material could not easily be forged.[34] Stuart Schram's comments on the *Wansui* texts apply to the texts in the present collection: "[T]he real flesh-and-blood Mao revealed in these uncensored utterances, Rabelaisian in speech and forthright in his criticism of both himself and others, is not only more believable, but far more impressive, than the plaster saint worshipped by some of his self-appointed disciples."[35] Yet, there is a difference. The Mao revealed in the current translations is impressive, but as Benjamin Schwartz reflects in his chapter, the impression is a rather humbler picture of a man who appears fickle in 1957 and certainly more wildly headstrong in 1958 than we had previously imagined. The point is, that these "genius" editions of Mao's works give us access to the *man* far better than the homogenized "collective wisdom" editions.

Who published these "genius" editions? At present, we do not know precisely, but we have an idea. According to Hu Hua, it is common knowledge that radical Red Guard groups published volumes like these based on materials they captured when they occupied ministries or other government offices, and especially when they raided (*chadui*) the homes of leading officials. In such files, the Red Guards found a range of internal (*neibu*) copies of Mao's writings and lecture notes of talks by Mao.[36] Some Red Guard groups obtained documents, by Liu Shaoqi and others as well as by Mao, straight

[34]See "Notes on the Texts" in Stuart Schram, ed., *Mao Tse-tung Unrehearsed: Talks and Letters 1956–71* (Harmondsworth, Penguin, 1974), pp. 49–50.
[35]Ibid., p. 8.
[36]Interview with Hu Hua, Harvard University, 20 May 1987. The late Mr. Hu, although a

from the Party Center, presumably from members of the Central Cultural Revolution Group (some of whom are now known as the Gang of Four).[37] The utter lack of coordination of texts among the twenty or more known *Wansui* and other Red Guard collections and the high degree of repetition of key texts and minor variants noted in the ones we have translated all support the picture of competing groups churning out the Chairman's wisdom based on whatever materials they could expropriate.

Are these editions reliable? In addition to the textual comparisons given in the next section, we can add a few comments on this question. When asked if the Red Guard editors would fabricate Mao's writings, Hu Hua responded with a laugh, "They worshipped him (*geren chongbai*)! So, they just printed it without changing it." On the other hand, many of these texts appear to be lecture notes and Mao certainly had no opportunity to correct them.[38] In short, these volumes are full of what Mao said off the top of his head; they are more of what Stuart Schram has aptly called "Mao unrehearsed," a lot more.

This does not mean that the Cultural Revolution period editions of Mao's writings are not subject to editorial slant in their selection or to censoring. Repeatedly in the texts we encounter "X X" where a proper name should appear. These are deliberate omissions by the editors. In addition, names of the Cultural Revolution leadership, particularly Kang Sheng and Yao Wenyuan, appear so frequently that it is hard to imagine anything other than bias in selection or editing of the texts could produce a frequency of appearance higher than much more important figures, such as Liu Shaoqi or Zhou Enlai, in the period 1957–1958. An awareness that the present texts were selected and edited with the faith that Chairman Mao was a genius in need of no committee revisions and the desire to build the reputation of his followers in the Cultural Revolution group—such as Lin Biao, Kang Sheng, Yao Wenyuan—will help the reader to judge what may be suspect and what seems reliable. Nevertheless, we believe the texts them-

---

leading party historiographer, claimed no special expertise on such volumes. His comments were given in general and not as an assessment of the volumes at hand.

[37] According to former Red Guards interviewed by Michael Schoenhals. I am grateful to Dr. Schoenhals for sharing this information.

[38] See n. 36.

selves, when read critically and in the light of all available evidence, are reliable records.[39]

"Historicist" Editions

Official publications in the 1980s of Mao's writings are very sober by comparison. Most reflect a desire to humanize Mao, to bring him back to earth and back into history as a great, but not divine, contributor to Chinese Marxism. Aside from the controversial Volume 5, there have been no further *Selected Works*.[40] In the mid 1980s a number of "special volumes" (*zhuanji*) appeared, covering Mao's writings on journalism and village economics, and his personal letters (see reference bibliography).[41] Only in 1986 did the two-volume *Mao Zedong zhuzuo xuandu* (Mao Zedong reader) appear with selection of Mao's "most important writings" from 1921 to 1964. Its copious (488) and lengthy endnotes reflect a desire to reconstruct the reality of the past, albeit as a way to determine more accurately the contribution of these past texts to a universal and timeless truth. In 1987 a massive two-volume index to books and articles on Mao's life and works appeared.[42] We must assume, based on previous experience, that public editions of Mao's writings are released to support current

[39]The example of Text 3, Mao's "speaking notes" of 27 February 1957, which was printed not only in one of the "genius" editions (New Mao Texts, Vol. 1) but also in the "historicist" 1983 Peking University study notes *in identical form* is a strong case in point, as are the increasing number of extracts of these 1957–8 Mao texts being published in China today (see Table 2).

[40]There are tell-tale signs of a *SW,* Vol. 6, in a highly restricted draft form now, but no Western scholar has yet reported seeing the actual volume.

[41]Gong (pp. 253–8) discusses the publication plans for most of these and future volumes, which are to include Mao on art and literature, his poetry, his military correspondence, his writings on base area economy, his early works, and his reading notes; *zhuanji* is Gong's term for these collections. To my knowledge, none of these planned volumes has yet appeared, although a collection of 14 articles on Mao's reading habits was published in September 1986; see Gong Yuzhi, Peng Xianzhi and Shi Zhongchuan, eds., *Mao Zedong de dushu shenghuo* (Mao Zedong's reading life) (Beijing, Sanlian shudian, 1986).

[42]*Mao Zedong shengping, zhuzuo yanjiu suoyin* (Index to research on Mao Zedong's life and works) (Beijing, Guofang daxue chubanshe, 1987). Although this impressive guide to some 14,000 studies also reflects a similar urge to respect "the facts" and includes a long list of Cultural Revolution period works, I have not located a single title attributed to either Zhang Chunqiao or Yao Wenyuan—two leading theorists of the period who wrote, *ad nauseam*, on Mao (see n. 56, below).

CCP policy.[43] Nevertheless, the public analysis of Mao's role (discussed below) and the documents and publications available in restricted circulation relentlessly put the man in perspective and seek to separate many of his radical ideas from the "collective wisdom" corpus, at the same time emphasizing the contribution of others to "Mao Zedong Thought." Documentary collections such as *Before the Sixth Congress, Since the Sixth Congress,* and *Selected Documents from the CCP Central Committee* provide ample material for assessing Mao's place; and analyses such as appear in Liao Gailong's *Annual Selection on CCP History,* the Central Party Documentary Research Office's *Documents and Research,* and journals such as *Party History Research* seek to do so.[44]

This seeking of truth from facts has always been conducted within the guidelines set through "historical resolutions" by the CCP Central Committee, first in 1945 and most recently in 1981.[45] It is now possible to describe how this works. The current guide for permissible interpretations of party history and, of course, Mao's writings is the "Resolution on some historical questions in the party since the founding of the nation," which was adopted after years of internal bickering at the Sixth Plenum of the Eleventh Central Committee of the CCP in June 1981.[46] As a compromise document intended to define the extent and limits of official criticism of the Cultural Revolution and of Mao Zedong, it is somewhat vague. Implementation

---

[43]Martin (pp. 56ff., 83ff.) and Kau and Leung (pp. xxvi–xxvii) give detailed analyses of the political use Mao "releases" were put to between 1977and 1979.

[44]In order mentioned, these publications are: Zhonggong zhongyang shujichu, ed., *Liuda yiqian* (Beijing, Renmin chubanshe, 1980); *Liuda yilai* (see n. 11); and Zhongyang dang'anguan, ed., *Zhonggong zhongyang wenjian xuanji* (Beijing, Zhongyang dangxiao chubanshe, 1982–); Zhonggong zhongyang dangshi yanjiu shi, eds., *Zhonggong dang shi wenzhai niankan: 1982 nian* (see n. 23; Liao Gailong is listed on the cover as chief editor); Zhonggong zhongyang wenxian yanjiu shi, eds., *Wenxian he yanjiu.* For information on *Dang shi yanjiu* and similar party history journals, see Weigelin-Schwiedrzik, "Party Historiography" (see n. 45). My thanks to Hans van de Ven for sharing the Party School and Liao Gailong volumes.

[45]Susanne Weigelin-Schwiedrzik, "Party Historiography in the People's Republic of China," *Australian Journal of Chinese Affairs* 17:82–8 (January 1987). She has also translated relevant historiographical documents in "Party Historiography," *Chinese Law and Government* 19.3:12–119 (1986).

[46]This text is widely available. The official translation appeared in *Beijing Review* 27:10–39 (July 6, 1981). It is reprinted in Martin, pp. 180–231; Martin details the political in-fighting that went into the drafting of the resolution (pp. 133–9).

of its mandate to revise party historiography began in August 1981 with a series of national work conferences held in Beijing, which gave specific instructions to various research institutions.[47] Much of this work is carried out and disseminated inside the party apparatus and in internal (*neibu*) publications, of which only a portion comes to Western attention. Nonetheless, it is clear that through the 1980s this work has proceeded apace. In June 1983, the restricted circulation official commentary on the 1981 Historical Resolution was produced by the Central CCP Documentary Research Office under the editorship of a senior party historiographer, Gong Yuzhi. After soliciting comments from relevant schools and research groups (and one may presume, party leaders) *Annotations (Revised Edition) on the Resolution on Certain Historical Questions of the Party Since the Founding of the Nation* (hereafter, *Annotations*) was openly published in September 1985.[48] Its major topics, the further elaborations of the guidelines, were spelled out in the periodical press: the collective wisdom basis of Mao Zedong Thought, the difference between Mao "the man" and his "Thought," the importance of proper historical method, the mass line, and independence and self-reliance.[49]

Clearly there is a tension between the explicit calls in these public historiographical guidelines to "seek truth from facts" and the implicit message to stay within the guidelines which legitimize the CCP today, as demonstrated by the careful implementation of guidelines from the 1981 resolution through the 1985 official commentary on it. It is prudent, therefore, to compare such official interpretations within unofficial ones written inside China. For example, Lin Xiling, one of the student activists of the Hundred Flowers in 1957, contradicts firmly the official view of the Anti-Rightist Campaign as "basically correct."[50] However, Western studies using CCP historiog-

[47]See the administrative account in the conference volume from the August 1981 meetings, translated by Weigelin-Schwiedrzik, *Chinese Law and Government* 19.3:112–9 (1986). It is worth noting, as David Bachman has pointed out, that this mandate has not extended to re-editing Vols. 1–4 of *SW.* In other words, "historicist" editions are still subordinate to "collective" editions.
[48]*Zaiban shuoming* (An explanation upon republication), in *Zhushiben,* p. 1.
[49]Shi Zhongquan, op. cit.
[50]Lin Xiling, "Letter to Deng Xiaoping," *Guang jiaojing* (Wide angle), Hong Kong, Nos. 9 & 10 (1983), in *Chinese Law & Government* 19.4:27–9 (Winter 1984–5). See also *Resolution on CPC History (1941–81)* (Beijing, Foreign Languages Press, 1981); p. 27 gives the official verdict.

raphy have noted that most post-Mao histories produced under this rubric are not gross misrepresentations of history such as we associate with the worst of Cultural Revolution polemics or Stalinist or Nazi propaganda.[51] Perhaps the best preliminary metaphor for the issues surrounding historicist party history writings in the 1980s, including those specifically on Mao's writings, is that of academic theology in the Christian and Jewish traditions where "scientific" linguistic and historical analyses seek to contribute to a living faith. With the picture in mind of liberation theology and the movement for ordination of women to the priesthood and rabbinical orders, we should not be surprised at the turmoil such "historicist" analysis of the roots of PRC state ideology can produce in China. From this perspective of current party historiography, the new Mao "genius" editions become source material for constructing "historicist" texts.[52]

In sum, we can say of the volumes on which this book is based that they are authentic "genius" editions (except for Volumes 15A–15E, as noted) of remarks and writings by Mao Zedong and lecture notes from those who heard him speak. Such texts can tell us a great deal about Mao's own thinking at the time and can provide a wealth of incidental data—names and details about events in the Chinese Communist movement that scholars have long yearned to know for certain.[53] Consequently, we can learn a great deal about CCP politics, ideology, and policy formation from them. But they do not speak for the collective leadership of the CCP. They cannot be considered part of the orthodoxy of China, Marxism-Leninism-Mao Zedong Thought, until such time as some authoritative representative of the CCP, such as the Mao publishing committee or a Central Committee

[51]Hans van de Ven in particular has made good use of Mao texts of the 1919–1927 period available in internal party history collections; see his 1987 Harvard PhD thesis, "The Founding of the Chinese Communist Party and the Search for a New Political Order, 1920–1927," pp. 40–4, 103–11, 194–9, 340–4.

[52]Indeed, this is precisely what we see in the restricted circulation Peking University textbooks, where the identical version of the "genius" text of Mao's February 1957 "Contradictions" speech appears next to a selection from "On practice" and the August 1938 text of "Law of unity of contradictions" (see New Mao Texts, Vol. 15D).

[53]For example, Mao's December 1964 talks with Liu Shaoqi and others, "Guanyu siqing wenti de taolun jiyao" (Notes of a discussion on problems in the Four Clean-ups), New Mao Texts Vol. 4, pp. 56–72, identifies more of the speakers than the version "Zhongyang gongzuo zuotanhui jiyao" (Notes from a central party work conference) in the Taiwan-released *Mao Zedong sixiang wansui* (1969), pp. 578–97.

resolution similar to that of 1981, determines them to be officially canonical. Here we have the raw data to compare against what was and will be taken as official Mao Zedong Thought. Thus, they not only tell us a great deal about Mao and his times, but will allow us to understand better the formation of ideology in Chinese Marxism.

THE INDIVIDUAL TEXTS

If we can give the volumes the benefit of the doubt, we can subject the individual texts to a more rigorous inspection in order to assess their authenticity. Although none here translated has appeared before in the West as far as we know, a large proportion of the other texts in the twenty-three volumes appear in either the previously released *Wansui*, other "Red Guard" collections, in the *Selected Works*, Volume 5, or in the specialized Mao volumes of the 1980s. Not every one of the approximately 5,500 pages of newly available Mao texts has been thoroughly compared with available publications for newness or significant variants. All, however, have been examined and compared to some degree; and Volumes 1 and 2 (from which we began our translations) have been subject to a particularly careful comparison.[54] Comparison revealed that approximately half of the items in these first two volumes were newly available texts, fuller texts of which only brief extracts had been previously available, or significantly variant texts. We feel we have translated the most interesting of the new or variant ones. Those remaining, although rejected for translation, help authenticate the newly available speeches, letters, and records of meetings.

A small but significant number of the texts in Volumes 1 and 2 of the present collection have been officially published in *Selected Works*, Volume 5; *Mao Zedong on Journalism*; and the new *Mao Reader*. A greater number, approaching a third, appear in the *Wansui* editions printed in Taiwan, particularly the large 1969 volume. Our translations for 1957 use most of the texts between pages 190 and 322 of Volume 1, which include the original version of the "Contradictions" speech of 1957 and Mao's provincial tour speeches of March 1957. A careful comparison of the new and extant texts leaves the

[54]As other volumes came to our attention, we used whatever version seemed the most complete. Editorial remarks at the start of each text provide the details.

very strong impression that Volume 1 represents part of an archive drawn upon by the other publications (see Appendix). Table 2 presents in outline form the relation among our translations, their sources, and previously published editions.

This textual comparison not only adds concrete detail to the impression that the texts in this new collection are authentic Cultural Revolution editions of Mao's works, but also highlights the significance of the first series of translations in this volume, the ones from early 1957. To date, editors of official Mao collections have chosen not to include even edited versions of the nearly one hundred pages of speeches by Mao given in Beijing and the provinces in March 1957, save for nine pages from Mao's 10 March talk to journalists and four pages from the Jinan and Nanjing talks.[55] This gap in *Selected Works*, Volume 5, resulted from the bias of the editors, who wished, according to Helmut Martin, "to mute the abruptness of the about face" of June 1957.[56] A newly available teaching text from Peking University (New Mao Texts, Volume 15D), however, both confirms the authenticity of the major piece from this period, the February contradictions speech "speaking notes," and suggests that resolution of this problem is underway in internal publications in the 1980s. The speaking notes are presented along with Mao's essay "On practice" and the original, seven-point, 1938 version of "Law of unity of contradictions."[57] Thus, the speaking notes are available in internal teaching materials at the university level with other "original" versions of Mao's philosophical writings.

A last form of verification of the texts is internal repetition. That is, for all texts (except the one-page Text 4) at least two versions are available in the volumes at hand. The four speeches from Mao's provincial tour in March 1957 that appear in Volume 1 also appear in Volume 10, which was likely to have been based on a different "archives." The same is true for the long, August 1958 "Talks at the Bei-

---

[55]See Table 2. The selections from Mao's provincial tour are titled by the editors, "Uphold arduous struggle, intimately link with the masses"; they hardly convey the anti-establishment and "democratic" themes Mao struck in his spring 1957 talks; see *Mao Zedong zhuzuo xuandu*, vol. xia (1986), pp. 799–802; or *XJ5*, pp. 419–22.

[56]Martin, pp. 132–3, citing the Hong Kong press.

[57]*Mao Zedong sixiang jiaoxue yanjiu cankao ziliao* (Teaching and research reference materials on Mao Zedong's philosophical thought), Beijing daxue zhexue xi, Mao Zedong zhexue sixiang jiao-jiu shi, yin (1983/10), Vol. 4. These three texts compose the entire volume.

TABLE 2 Sources and Translations of New Mao Texts

Text	Short Title and Date	New Volumes[a]	Official Editions and Translations	Unofficial Translations
1	Talk at Yinian Tang, 16 February 1957	9, 6A†, 7		
2	Talk to National Student Federation (extracts), 24 February 1957	1, 6A		
3	On the correct handling of contradictions among the people (speaking notes), 27 February 1957	1, 15D	SW5: 384–421*, XJ5: 363–402*	
4	Talk to committee of the National Student Federation, March 1957	1		
5	Talk to provincial and municipal heads of propaganda, culture, and education departments, 6 March 1957	9, 1†, 6A		
6	Talk at party conference on propaganda work, 7 March 1957	1, 6A	Peking Review 13 September 1968, p. 26†	Starr and Dyer: #160A/B†
7	Talk with literary and art circles, 8 March 1957	7, 9		
8	Talk with representatives of press and publishing circles (summary), 10 March 1957	9, 7	Xinwen: 186–194	
9	Letter to Zhou Enlai and other comrades, 17 March [1957]	1, 6A		

TABLE 2 *(Continued)*

Text	Short Title and Date	New Volumes[a]	Official Editions and Translations	Unofficial Translations
10	Talk to cadres in Tianjin municipality, 17 March 1957	10, 1		
11	Talk to cadres of Shandong provincial organs, 18 March 1957	1, 10	*Xuandu:* 799–800†; *XJ5:* 419–20	
12	On ideological work, 19 March 1957	1, 10	*Xuandu:* 800–802†; *XJ5:* 420–2	
13	Talk to cadres in Shanghai, 10 March 1957	1, 10		
14	Talk to responsible democratic personages, 30 April 1957	1, 10, 12B		
15	Talks to Hangzhou Conference (draft transcript), 3–4 January 1958	2, 6A, 12B		
16	Criticism of *People's Daily* (draft transcript), January 1958	9, 1†, 6A†		
17	Talks at the Beidaihe Conference (draft transcript), 17–30 August 1958	2, 10		Starr and Dyer: 224 (17th)
18	Talks at first Zhengzhou Conference, 6 November 1958	2, 13; 9†		*Wansui* (1969): 247–51†
19	Talks at Wuchang Conference 21–23 November [1958]	2, 10, 13		

Notes and special abbreviations: [a]The new volume from which the text for our translation is drawn is listed first.
†Partial extract only.   *Highly edited.
Xinwen = *Mao Zedong xinwen gongzuo wenxuan* (1983); see Bibliography, I.   *Xuandu* = *Mao Zedong zhuzuo xuandu* (1986); see Bibliography, I.
Starr & Dyer, see Bibliography, III.

daihe Conference," which appears in both Volumes 2 and 10. Here competing, or at least different, editors of the "genius" persuasion serve to reconfirm or question the text of the other editors.[58] The repetition of texts in a number of different volumes of the same title, as occurs with the 8 March 1957 "Talk to literary circles" and the 10 March "Conversation with press and publishing circles," which appear in both Volumes 7 and 9 (these are the July and September 1967 versions of *Wansui*, respectively), tends to confirm the impression that although a number of the twenty-three volumes share the same title, they do not share editors.

Our translations are presented in chronological order. The "genius" editions from which these texts come give us not only an uncensored picture of what the Chairman was saying in 1957 and 1958 but also an unedited one. What is a gold mine of political and psychological data for Mao studies is also a cesspool of run-on sentences, obscure grammar, and simple nonsense for the translator. These were difficult texts to translate. As one senior Chinese translator, who had lived as an adult through these years, said, "Now I can see what Lin Biao meant when he said, 'Even I sometimes do not understand what the Chairman says'!" The frustration was balanced, of course, by the fascinating picture that emerged. As did the 1967–1969 *Wansui* collections assessed by Stuart Schram, these texts maintain Mao's earthy and informal language. Therefore, in the English we have attempted to capture some of that by using colloquial contractions, such as "can't" and "wouldn't we." In several places, the texts were not immediately intelligible. Long consultations have been held to divine the Chairman's meaning, and our best guess has been given. Naturally, these passages have been clearly marked and annotated in accompanying footnotes, so that the reader will be alerted to the possible confusion. Finally, we have clearly marked our interpolations by placing them inside square brackets. This has been our compromise between smoothness and accuracy. All other parenthetical marks are in the original Chinese texts. We have marked the page number of the source text throughout the translations inside square brackets to facilitate reference to the original.

---

[58]Notes to each text draw attention to minor differences; larger differences between available versions are pointed out at the start of a text.

INTERPRETATIVE ISSUES

A broad look at these texts brings a number of interpretative issues to mind. Three examples can give a sense of how rich (and how immense) a vein or ore we have before us. First, the sometimes incoherent and often mysteriously layered language of Mao's texts highlights the power of his charismatic authority in the Cultural Revolution. That such inconsistent and rambling texts were used, for a time, as the font of wisdom, as *the authority* for political action, underscores the weight of his charisma. Certainly, careful reading of these texts does not encourage faith. The logical and systematic weakness of Mao's uncorrected talks and notes highlights the fact that his authority lay elsewhere. This was not simply the product of teen-worship by Red Guards; it was rife throughout the establishment. Since at least 1957, and arguably since the founding of the PRC, senior party theoreticians and propagandists below the top leadership have wrestled with Mao's increasingly erratic and unorthodox ideological pronouncements. Even devotées of Leninism, such as party school director Yang Xianzhen, could not bring themselves—or more importantly, could not bring a like-minded group of orthodox Marxist-Leninists—to refute, displace, or at least ignore their chief executive when he "misspoke."[59]

Secondly, we can use these previously unavailable texts to assess current party historiography. In this way we may be able to generate some rules of thumb to use in interpreting party historiography when we do not have twenty-three volumes of raw data against which to test its conclusions. For example, we can take the "speaking notes" (*jianghua gao*) of Mao's February 1957 "Contradictions" speech and compare the *Annotations'* assessment of its fate. The *Annotations* concludes that there were differences, "a reorganization [*zhengli*] and some revisions and additions." These notes give the his-

---

[59]Carol Lee Hamrin, "Yang Xianzheng: Upholding Orthodox Leninist Theory," in Carol Lee Hamrin and Timothy Cheek, eds., *China's Establishment Intellectuals* (Armonk, N.Y.: M. E. Sharpe, 1986), pp. 61–9; I find a similar pattern in the case of *People's Daily* editor, Deng Tuo (ibid., pp. 92–123). Lawrence Sullivan argues that these well-known tensions from the GLF period can be traced back at least to the early 1950s; see "Leadership and Authority in the Chinese Communist Party: Perspectives from the 1950s," *Pacific Affairs* 59.4:605–33 (Winter 1986–7). Frederick Teiwes, "Mao and His Lieutenants," op cit., suggests a more complex picture.

torical background of the Polish and Hungarian incidents and the numerous student and workers' strikes inside China in late 1956 in neutral terms. They also name the cities of Mao's provincial trip in March 1957 and cite, albeit in passing only, "handwritten speaking notes by Mao" from them that stress his themes: bureaucratism, the "two kinds of contradictions" (antagonistic and non-antagonistic), and the need for education and broader democracy. The notes admit that the revisions of Mao's February talk were influenced by the Anti-Rightist Campaign of June, revisions not in the spirit of the original. Nonetheless, it concludes that the public version and the *jianghua gao* share the same underlying spirit and constitute a significant "contribution to Marxism-Leninism."[60]

Readers may now judge for themselves how accurate an analysis this official commentary makes. My impression is that, while the notes are often vague (Mao's calls for supervision of party committees in the speaking notes is stunning), with some gaps (they mention the provincial tour but not the resistance of *People's Daily* to publish the speech nor Mao's anger over this),[61] they are at root accurate. When the *Annotations* slights the historical record, it is by the sin of omission, not commission; by generalizations, not by fabrications. There are enough hints left in the interpretations offered here by Gong Yuzhi and his colleagues, which become clear as greater detail becomes available, to prevent one from thinking that such current party historiography is "propaganda" in the negative sense of distortions churned out by totalitarian minions for some Orwellian ministry of truth. There are echoes in these notes, however mute, of the universal human search to come to terms with major historical issues, to figure out first what happened and then to contemplate why.

What can we generalize about party historiography from this case? We can infer that other similar party histories from the 1980s will give broadly accurate pictures subject to the parameters set by the 1981 resolution. If the topic is controversial in the Historical Resolution and its official commentary, the *Annotations*, we will have to doubt the party historiographer, since he or she is clearly unable to go beyond it. Yet, though only time and experience will identify them, the more committed historians among party history writers

[60] *Zhushiben*, pp. 527–35.
[61] For a vivid picture of Mao's anger at Deng Tuo, see the chapter by Merle Goldman.

will no doubt push the limits and leave hints. Because such carefully produced texts as the *Annotations* are unlikely to have careless phrases, a matching of key phrases such as "basic spirit" and "influenced by" can help us read between the lines in other cases. Finally, a prudent way to assess the amount of positive spin put on topics approved by the resolution (or its successor), and negative light on "bad things," is to compare such official party historiography with unofficial analyses produced inside China.[62]

Finally, an assessment of these texts would not be complete without at least a reference to the continuing debate in Mao studies in the West over the interpretation of texts. The chapters by various authors in this collection, naturally, provide some examples and guidance. The reader should, however, be aware of a few issues in order to mine the texts independently. Stuart Schram's basic text, *The Political Thought of Mao Tse-tung*, as well as his collection of other Cultural Revolution "genius" editions of Mao's works in *Mao Unrehearsed*, provide ample background, along with his biography of Mao. In addition he has produced a review of the current literature, "Mao Studies: Retrospect and Prospect" (1984), which raises problems of interpretation (particularly pp. 118–125). More provocatively, Nick Knight, another Mao scholar, challenges the reader to confront the problems of relativism and unconscious assumptions in analyzing Mao texts. In particular, he demonstrates the fallacy of analyzing Mao according to Mao's professed epistemology, since Mao clearly did not obey his own rules.[63] These last two reviews along with the translations at hand should enable readers to make their own assessment of the "genius" of Mao.

---

[62]Two thoughtful "dissident" critiques of recent political history in China are those by the Li Yizhe group; see Anita Chan, Stanley Rosen, and Jonathan Unger, eds., *On Socialist Democracy and the Chinese Legal System: The Li Yizhe Debates* (Armonk, N.Y.: M. E. Sharpe, 1985); and Liu Guokai, "A Brief Analysis of the Cultural Revolution," in *Chinese Sociology and Anthropology*, 19.2 (Winter 1986–7).

[63]Nick Knight, "Mao and History: Who Judges and How?", *The Australian Journal of Chinese Affairs* 13:121–36 (January 1985). Dr. Knight has pursued this line of analysis, *ad absurdum* I fear, in "The Marxism of Mao Zedong: Empiricism and Discourse in the Field of Mao Studies," *The Australian Journal of Chinese Affairs* 16:7–22 (July 1986), which is part of an important new set of studies, "Mao Zedong: Ten Years After," appearing in the same issue.

PART TWO

The Texts

The Hundred Flowers

TABLE 3 Date Summary, 1956–1957

	1956
January 14–20	Conference on the intellectuals, where Mao and Zhou speak.
February	Conference in Yinian Tang; "Let a hundred schools contend" is formulated as CCP's science policy.
February 25	Khrushchev denounces Stalin in "secret speech" to CPSU's 20th Congress.
April 5	*RMRB* editorial on the question of Stalin: "On the historical experience of the proletarian dictatorship."
April 25	Mao gives the speech "On the ten great relationships" and proposes the policy of "Let a hundred flowers bloom, let a hundred schools contend."
May 2	Mao reiterates Hundred Flowers policy to SSC.
May 25	Lu Dingyi, director of CC's Propaganda Department, publicly enunciates the Hundred Flowers policy.
September	Wang Meng's "Young newcomer to the Organization Department" is published.
September 15–27	CCP's Eighth Congress.
October 19–21	Polish CC meets; Khrushchev delegation to Warsaw fails to prevent Gomulka's becoming First Secretary.
October	Liu Shaoqi is secretly in Moscow to confer on Poland.
October 23	Hungarian Revolt breaks out.
October 31	Soviet forces return to Hungary to quell revolt.
November 10–15	CC's Second Plenum: Liu Shaoqi reports on East Europe.
November 11	Tito's Pula speech attributes events in Hungary and Poland to fundamental defects in Soviet system.
December 29	*RMRB* editorial "More on the historical experience of the proletarian dictatorship" rebuts Tito; first exposition of theory of contradictions between leaders and led in a socialist state.

	1957
January 7–11	Zhou Enlai visits Soviet Union, Poland, Hungary.
January 7	Chen Qitong, Chen Yading, Ma Hanbing, and Lu Le publish article critical of Hundred Flowers policy in *RMRB*.
January 12	Mao sends his poems in classical style to *Poetry*.
*February 16	Mao's Yinian Tang speech, in which he defends Wang Meng.

TABLE 3 *(Continued)*

*February 27	Mao's speech "On the correct handling of contradictions among the people" delivered to SSC.
March 5–April 14	Liu Shaoqi's southern tour.
March 5	Zhou Enlai reports to CPPCC on East European trip; Lu Dingyi article on 15th anniversary of original rectification campaign.
*March 6–13	Central propaganda conference, which Mao addresses several times.
March 12	Mao's main speech to propaganda conference.
*March 17–20	Mao speaks in Tianjin, Jinan, Nanjing, Shanghai.
March 20	Mao says rectification campaign scheduled for 1958.
April 1–7	Mao admits widespread opposition to his policies.
April 9	Zhou Yang, deputy director of Propaganda Department, criticizes Chen Qitong group in Shanghai *Wenhui bao*.
April 10	*RMRB*'s first editorial criticizing Chen Qitong group.
April 11	Mao berates Deng Tuo and Wang Ruoshui on *RMRB*'s failure to publicize his views on internal contradictions; *RMRB* republishes Zhou Yang's *Wenhui bao* interview.
April 13	*RMRB*'s first editorial on contradictions.
April 20	Peng Zhen addresses Beijing propaganda conference on internal contradictions; Jian Bozan article on "early spring" weather.
April 22–23	CC directive on checking up on the solution of internal contradictions.
April 22–27	Liu Shaoqi in Shanghai.
April 23	*RMRB*'s editorial on solving internal contradictions.
April 25–29	Peng Zhen escorts Soviet President Voroshilov around China.
April 27	CC rectification directive completed.
*April 30	Mao addresses non-party people; proposes a conference under Deng Xiaoping's leadership to study the question of party leadership in universities; CC rectification directive issued.
May 1	Rectification Campaign starts.
May 19	Campus agitation starts.
May 25	Mao warns youth league that words and actions departing from socialism are wrong.
June 8	*RMRB*'s first editorial on counterattacking critics; start of Anti-Rightist Campaign.
June 13	*New York Times* publishes quotations from "Contradictions" speech, leaked in Warsaw.

Table 3 *(Continued)*

June 18	Official text of Mao's "Contradictions" speech issued.
September 23	Deng Xiaoping reports on Rectification and Anti-Rightist Campaigns to CC's Third Plenum.

Notes: Good sources for dating events not made clear in the contemporary record are: Zhonggong Zhongyang Dang Shi Yanjiu Shi (CCP CC's Party History Research Office), *Zhonggong dang shi dashi nianbiao* (Chronological table of major events in CCP history) (Beijing, Renmin Chubanshe, 1987); *Zhongguo gongchandang liushi nian dashi jianjie* (A synopsis of the major events in sixty years of the CCP) (Beijing, Guofang Daxue chubanshe, 1985); Fang Weizhong, ed., *Zhonghua renmin gongheguo jingji dashi ji (1949–1980 nian)* (Record of major economic events of the People's Republic of China, 1949–1980) (Beijing, Zhongguo Shehui kexue chubanshe, 1984); Hu Hua, ed., *Zhongguo shehuizhuyi geming he jianshe shi jiangyi* (Teaching materials on the history of China's socialist revolution and construction) (Beijing, Zhongguo Renmin Daxue chubanshe, 1985).

*Texts from these dates are translated in this section of Part Two.

Talk at Yinian Tang

16 FEBRUARY 1957

[33] (This talk was given prior to the Central Committee Propaganda Work Conference. The Chairman called this conference to talk with writers, philosophers, and educators on cultural and ideological problems. He particularly emphasized problems of literary criticism.

This material was compiled on the basis of three transcripts of relayed reports. Whereas it is based mainly on one transcript [34], it

Sources: 9:33–44; alternate text, 7:8–17. Related text: 6A:38–41, "Discussion with scientists and writers on contradictions among the people (16 February 1957)," appears to be an abstract taken from this text. Two other related texts, based on the January 1957 Conference of Provincial and Municipal Party Secretaries, give related material. They appear in 1:169–187, but are not here translated because they appear in *Wansui* (1969), pp. 73–90, and are translated in *JPRS* 61269-1. An official version exists in *SW5*, pp. 350–83. Yinian Tang is a hall inside the Zhongnanhai compound in Beijing, where many top CCP officials live and work.

uses square brackets[1] to supplement the main transcript with materials from the other two transcripts. This is for reference only, no copying is permitted.)[2]

Today I will talk about problems regarding the policy of letting a hundred schools contend in literature and the arts and in academic thought and so on, and how to treat shortcomings in literature and art.

Wang Meng wrote a story. Those who approve of him do so very vigorously. Those who refute him also do so very vigorously. The attitude of those who refute him, however, is not quite appropriate.

<Wang Meng's "Young newcomer to the Organization Department" is currently under discussion.[3] The question at issue is critical attitudes. The story exposes bureaucratism. Very good. Although the exposure is not profound, still it's very good. Liu Binyan's story does not criticize bureaucratism in its entirety.[4] Wang Meng's story has its one-sidedness: he has not written sufficiently about the positive forces. This should be criticized. There should be criticism, but there should also be protection. The positive character, Lin Zhen, appears weak, whereas the negative characters come through as having quite a bit of initiative. >

Our bureaucratism has not yet been demolished [lit. rectified out of existence]; it still needs criticism. In the past, the film (i.e., "To Whom Does the Honor Belong") was not screened. This was not because it criticized old cadres and old cadres should be protected, but because in that film the bureaucratism was not demolished.

In *Xing Xing* (the Sichuan poetry magazine)[5] there are a few

---

[1]NB: In our translation angle brackets indicate the location of square brackets in the Chinese text. Figures in bold indicate Chinese text page numbers.

[2]This editorial note from the Chinese text appears at the end of the alternate text, 7:17. Otherwise, the two texts appear almost identical.

[3]Translated under a slightly different rendering of the title in Hualing Nieh, ed., *Literature of the Hundred Flowers*, vol. 2, (New York, Columbia Univ. Press, 1981), pp. 473–511.

[4]Presumably refers to Liu Binyan's "The inside news of the newspaper," abridged and translated in Nieh, vol. 2, pp. 411–64.

[5]*Xing Xing* (Star Star) was a poetry magazine founded in January 1957, which lasted only for a short period. One of its editors was Liushahe (pseudonym of Yu Xingtan, b. 1931). Immediately following the publication of the first issue, he and the magazine were severely criticized, especially for his five short prose poems, "Pieces on plants" (*Caomu pian*). Liushahe was made a "rightist" and suffered much humiliation for two decades, until he was rehabilitated in 1978. See "Liushahe zi zhuan" (Autobiography of Liushahe) in *Liushahe shi ji* (Poetry of Liushahe) (Shanghai, Wenyi chubanshe, 1982), pp. 1–10; and the biographical notice in Nieh, vol. 2, p. 580.

poems that are relatively good and a few that are not good. We should deliberate a bit and not condemn in haste.

<*Xing Xing* is shouting out. [But there's] no hurry, calm down. Deliberate a bit and don't meet the enemy attack in panic; don't fight a war unprepared. In the case of "critical" articles in the past, those among the masses who voted for us were few.>

The authors who've written bad works need help, need investigation.

Even General Fu Zuoyi who revolted and crossed over to us and [people like] Rong Yiren, we helped, remolded (*gaizao*), so that they could cooperate with us.[6]

So long as the authors of bad stories, even if they contain bourgeois thought and idealism, cooperate with us politically, they should be distinguished from Hu Feng[7] and should not be clubbed to death with a single blow.

[35] Wang Meng doesn't know how to write. He can write negative characters, but he can't write positive characters well. Not writing well has its root in one's life, in one's viewpoint.

Li Xifan[8] says that the location of Wang Meng's story is not right, that it's not a typical environment. He says that the Center[9] is in Beijing. Could it be that it is impossible [for the Center] to produce this kind of problem? This is not convincing. It is precisely the Center which has produced bad people, such as Zhang Guotao, Gao,

[6]Fu Zuoyi was the Nationalist general in charge of North China during the Civil War. His surrender of Beijing (then Beiping) enabled the capital to escape destruction. He was at this time Minister of Water Conservancy and a vice chairman of the CPPCC. See *BDRC* 2, pp. 47–51, and C. P. Fitzgerald, *Revolution in China* (London, Cresset, 1952), pp. 108–14.

Rong Yiren was a leading Shanghai businessman, who had been a strong supporter of the communist regime from its inception. In 1986, over 200 of his family members from all over the world gathered in Beijing for a reunion with him and met Deng Xiaoping.

[7]Hu Feng was a leading CCP writer who came under strong attack in 1955 led by Mao personally; see Merle Goldman, *Literary Dissent in Communist China* (Cambridge, Harvard Univ. Press., 1967), Ch. 7; and *SW5*, pp. 176–83.

[8]Li Xifan was a young literary critic who sprang to prominence in 1954 when still a student with a joint article (with Lan Ling) attacking Yu Pingbo, the most prominent authority on the Chinese classic novel, *Hong lou meng* (usually known as *The Dream of the Red Chamber*, most recently translated as *The Story of the Stone*); see Goldman, pp. 115–25.

[9]The "Center" (*zhongyang*) is used loosely by Chinese communists. It may signify the CCP's Central Committee, its Politburo, the Politburo Standing Committee, leading members of those bodies like Mao himself, or more generally central party or government departments in Beijing. In this context, it probably signifies the Central Committee, formally the CCP's supreme organ.

Rao, Li Lisan, Wang Ming.[10] What do we do if there are more such bad people? According to their opinion they should be boiled in oil.

< Li Xifan's article is not convincing. The view that no bureaucratism could exist in any district committee in the place where the Center is located is incorrect. Even the Center produced Gao and Rao, so it's not strange that district committees (have bureaucratism); this is the "theory of inevitability." (In Lin Zhen[11] the theory of inevitability also applies).[12]

Many comrades actually have not understood the policy on how to handle mistakes among the people. Out of every ten ministers [or department heads, lit., *buzhang*] probably nine oppose this policy.

<The problem is that the author (Wang Meng) does not understand clearly contradictions among the people. Consequently his story has a negative impact. We haven't understood clearly, either. Just because it's written about Beijing and (the location) is too concrete, and thus is not a typical character in a typical environment, this kind of (criticism) will not convince people. >

There is bourgeois ideology in Wang Meng's story. He doesn't have enough experience, either. But he represents a new-born force; he should be protected. The articles criticizing him have had no intention of protecting him.

Sure, there's bureaucratism. Our party has high prestige, yet bureaucratism plays the tyrant and violates the law by taking advantage of the party's prestige. Should this be exposed or not?

---

[10]Zhang Guotao, like Mao a founding member of the CCP, lost the struggle with him for the leadership in the mid 1930s, left the party's Yan'an base, and was expelled from party membership; see his autobiography, Zhang Guotao, *The Rise of the Chinese Communist Party*, 2 vols., (Lawrence, Univ. of Kansas, 1971, 1972).

Gao Gang and Rao Shushi were purged in 1954 after their abortive attempt to ensure that the former (and not Liu Shaoqi or Zhou Enlai) succeeded Mao; see Frederick C. Teiwes, *Politics and Purges in China* (White Plains, M. E. Sharpe, 1979), Ch. 5.

Li Lisan's "leftist" line dominated the CCP in 1928–30; see Benjamin I. Schwartz, *Chinese Communism and the Rise of Mao* (Cambridge, Harvard Univ. Press, 1951), Chs. 9 and 10.

Wang Ming (Chen Shaoyu) was the Moscow-trained official whom Mao defeated in the struggle for the leadership of the CCP in the late 1930s and early 1940s; for a succinct account, see Richard C. Thornton, *China: A Political History, 1917–1980* (Boulder, Westview Press, 1980), pp. 105–10, 119–21. Both Wang Ming and Li Lisan had been re-elected to the Central Committee at the CCP's Eighth Congress in September 1956.

[11]Lin Zhen is the "young newcomer" in Wang Meng's story.

[12]The open parenthesis mark is misprinted in the main text; this sentence is taken from the alternate text, 7:9.

China is a great kingdom of the petty bourgeoisie. In all there are as many as 550 million [members of the] petty bourgeoisie . . . [13] and this is an objective reality.

<China is a great kingdom of the petty bourgeoisie; [so] it's impossible for there to be no petty bourgeoisie in the party.>

The view that says that the shortcomings of the Communist party can't be exposed is incorrect.

Actually very few people endorse the party's United Front policy. Very few truly understand this policy. [36] Punishment cannot convince people.

<Not many among cadres truly understand the United Front policy. We should help others remold in order to achieve true unity. [We have done] far from enough to help remold everybody's thought in this way. The usual method is to resort to punishment. It's quite easy, but it's not a good method. We shouldn't use "punishment" [*zheng*]. It cannot unify.>

Now Wang Ming can still vote. Isn't he still a citizen of the People's Republic of China? He has not been summarily kicked out.

"To kick out summarily" is the old way. That's easy. Those who like to use this method might as well fire guns, fire machine guns, since this is the method of the Nationalists [Kuomintang].

. . .

<That China is a great kingdom of the petty bourgeoisie is an objective reality. The working class is only 24 million, half of whom are industrial workers and the other half of whom are cadres. This is one pole. The other pole is about 30 million landlords, rich peasants, and bourgeoisie. The 550 million between these two poles are all petty bourgeoisie. Even the 12 million cadres have not all been proletarianized. Perhaps around 2 million have authentically changed. Thus, the problem of literature and art must be viewed from the perspective of this reality.> [14]

This is a time of great turbulence. Some people are dissatisfied. In the collectivization of agriculture, the well-to-do middle peasants are dissatisfied.

<The children of the landlords, rich peasants, and bourgeoisie make up 80 percent of the university students. All are non–working-

---

[13]Ellipsis dots appear in the original Chinese version.
[14]A condensed version of the preceding, which includes the figure 12 million for the number of true proletariat, appears in the related talk with scientists and writers; see 6A:38.

class people. That young people have more problems is not at all strange. Very few amongst them want to produce a Hungarian incident; the majority support communism. >

However, even those who were dissatisfied in the past supported the war of resisting the United States and aiding Korea [i.e., China's intervention in the Korean War]. They don't [want to] produce a "Hungary." Of course, some individuals who wish to produce a Hungarian incident do indeed exist.

Our comrades are simply afraid; they fear a Hungarian incident. In my view the Hungarian incident was not necessarily bad. We must talk about dialectics, we must understand the dualism of all things. Without a disturbance like this, there would be no truly good Hungary.

[37] . . . < Contradictions will sooner or later become apparent, so it's good to create a disturbance. A disturbance is one-sided. If we oppose one-sidedness with one-sidedness we can't resolve problems. >

Our comrades use dogmatism. They use one-sidedness to oppose one-sidedness and use metaphysics to oppose metaphysics.

Wang Meng's story has its one-sided qualities, it also has its anti-bureaucratism side. I think his article is quite well written, though not superlatively.

He exposes our shortcomings. Criticism like Li Xifan's can't be used on him.

< Many critical articles are correct in their standpoint, but they oversimplify matters. >

Li Xifan is now in a high-level organ, a member of the Chinese People's Political Consultative Congress. He is fed by the party and follows party orders, and [so] he's become an authority figure.[15] [Therefore] his articles are no longer lively and are hard to read. The first half of his article [that I just mentioned] is hard to understand.

Who's Ma Hanbing?[16] He's also some sort of official. Perhaps a cadre of army-commander rank. His article in the *Wenhui bao* is not well written; it's dogmatism.

< The standpoint of the article written by Chen Qitong and three

---

[15]Literally "grandmother" or "mother-in-law"; used as a metaphor for an authority figure, as in an extended family.

[16]One of a group of four army writers who collaborated on an article critical of the Hundred Flowers policy in *RMRB* on 7 January 1957. Mao dealt with this article at some length in his "Contradictions" speech; see Text 3, under "Blooming flowers and contending schools."

others,[17] is good. It was OK for the *People's Daily* to publish it. But it's not convincing. It seems to say that since the adoption of the Hundred Flowers policy everything has gone wrong. This is dogmatism. It is impossible that every flower be fragrant.[18] Dogmatism has no force. One of the reasons why it has developed is because the Communist party has come into power. Marx and Engels criticized Dühring, and Lenin criticized Lunacharsky.[19] They had to exert great effort to outargue them. Stalin was different (he was in power). So his criticism was not balanced and was very similar to a father scolding his son. [It's like the saying:] "As soon as he has power in his hands, he rules by fiat." Criticism should not rely on state power; it should use truth. If you use Marxism, if you apply effort, you can prevail. >

<You can't use dogmatism to criticize others, because it has no power. See how Lenin wrote his empirio-criticism. Later on Stalin was different. He didn't discuss problems [with others] on an equal footing. He didn't air his opinions only after collecting large quantities of materials. Some of the things he wrote were good, others he wrote as if he were sitting on a hillock and picking up stones to hit people. One is uncomfortable after reading [such writings]. >

[38] The article jointly signed by four people, including Chen Qitong and Ma Hanbing, didn't clearly state the issues; it's too bad. Chen Yi,[20] how many articles have you written? Do you have dogmatism or not? Put out a volume of selected works! Let's have a complete check-up.

Dogmatist articles are dull, oversimplified, and unconvincing.

---

[17]Another of the four army writers; see previous note.
[18]The current text lacks the negative, which makes this sentence out of step with the paragraph. The alternate text, 7:11, gives the sensible version, "duoduo xianghua shi *bu* kenengde," which we use here.
[19]Mao is referring to *Anti-Dühring*, Engels' 1877 attack on a German positivist, to which Marx contributed a chapter on political economy. Anatoly Vasilievich Lunacharsky (1875–1933), was a devoté of Avenarius' philosophy of empirio-criticism and the first Commissar of Education in the Soviet Union. He crossed swords with Lenin over revolutionary tactics in 1908, before either man was in power, and Lenin produced *Materialism and Empirio-Criticism* in part to refute Lunacharsky. See Isaac Deutscher, "Introduction," in Lunacharsky, *Revolutionary Silhouettes* (New York, Hill and Wang, 1967), pp. 14–5.
[20]See note 16, above. Chen Yi (b. 1912) was at that time in charge of cultural affairs in the General Political Department of the PLA. He is not Marshal Chen Yi who later became Foreign Minister. This Chen Yi suffered, was condemned as a "rightist" because of his opposition to Mao at this time, but emerged as an unpopular "leftist" propaganda chief in Shanghai in 1979, stepping down in 1982.

Dogmatism has developed because [we] have come into power.

Marx and Engels put a lot of thought into refuting Dühring. But Stalin in power was different. He cursed people, was inequitable, so he couldn't be convincing.

We should study articles that analyze other people.

Once in power, to curse people like dressing down a son is no good.

The relationship between the people and the party in power shouldn't be one between the people and their master. We shouldn't curse.

Dogmatism is not Marxism.

The criticism of Hu Shi in the past was very successful.[21] At the beginning we said Hu Shi couldn't be completely negated. He served his purpose in the Enlightenment Movement in China. Nor can Kang Youwei and Liang Qichao be negated.[22]

Hu Shi said I was his student.[23] He was a professor, and I was a petty clerk. Our salaries were different, but I was not his student.

---

[21]Hu Shi was a dominant literary and academic figure in the May Fourth Movement. Although never close to the KMT, he served as China's ambassador to the U.S. from 1938 to 1942. In early 1957, he was in retirement in New York, but eighteen months later he went to Taiwan to take up the presidency of Academia Sinica. His ideas and influence are explored in Jerome B. Grieder, *Hu Shih and the Chinese Renaissance: Liberalism in the Chinese Revolution, 1917–1937* (Cambridge, Harvard Univ. Press, 1970).

[22]Kang Youwei was a leading advocate of thoroughgoing reforms in the last decades of the Qing dynasty. After he had passed the examination for the third and highest degree (*jinshi*) under the imperial system, his reform proposals began to reach the Emperor. In 1898, he reached the apogee of his power and influence, when he became the Emperor's principal adviser during the abortive "100 days reform." For a brief account of his life and a translation of his principal work, see Lawrence G. Thompson, '*Ta T'ung Shu': The One-World Philosophy of K'ang Yu-wei* (London, Allen and Unwin, 1958); also Kung-chuan Hsiao, *A Modern China and a New World: K'ang Yu-wei, Reformer and Utopian, 1858–1927* (Seattle, Univ. of Washington Press, 1975).

Liang Qichao was originally a follower of Kang Youwei and another influential reformer of the late Qing and early Republican period. See Philip C. Huang, *Liang Ch'i-ch'ao and Modern Chinese Liberalism* (Seattle, Univ. of Washington Press, 1972); and Joseph R. Levenson, *Liang Ch'i-ch'ao and the Mind of Modern China* (Berkeley, Univ. of California Press, 1967). In his late teens, Mao Zedong posted an article on the wall of his school advocating that the Qing dynasty be overthrown and that, under the presidency of Sun Yat-sen, Kang Youwei should become Premier and Liang Qichao Foreign Minister. See Edgar Snow, *Red Star Over China* (London, Gollancz, 1937), p. 136.

[23]For a discussion and dismissal of this claim, see Grieder, pp. 298–9. Mao later admitted, however, to being an admirer of Hu Shi during the early Republican period; see Snow, p. 146.

It isn't necessary to rehabilitate Hu Shi's reputation now. In the twenty-first century we can look into the problem again.

(In the past, because we were engaged in struggle, we talked about Hu Shi's shortcomings. Today it still isn't necessary to rehabilitate him. Today he is a running dog of imperialism. Wait till the twenty-first century; history should make this clear.)

([We] make arrangements for and transform the landlords, rich peasants, and bourgeoisie. Why not the petty bourgeoisie? We often show no mercy in our articles. The techniques of dogmatism are putting on caps, cursing people, one-sidedness. Their starting point is not unity, their goal is not unity. [39] They do not help transform shortcomings to reach true unity.)

< We must strictly distinguish the way we handle mistakes among the people from the way we handle the mistakes of the enemy (essays that are wrong [in their approach] do not make this distinction). Ruthless struggle against the enemy, but towards the people we start from unity, go through struggle, and arrive at a new unity. Otherwise we could easily kill people. >

We should "stay the execution as the axe is raised."

. . .

During the Rectification [Movement] in Yan'an, didn't we say "learn from past mistakes to avoid future ones, cure the illness to save the patient"? Some of our comrades don't like to cure the illness to save the patient. Rather, they act like quacks killing patients. We should apply proper methods towards the petty bourgeoisie to transform them. <We depend for food on so many of the petty bourgeoisie, that we need to transform them into the working class. >

About 50 to 60 percent of our comrades do not understand this policy of the Center: Criticize to unite, cure the illness to save the patient.

They simply fear disturbances.

A student at Qinghua University spoke of the need to kill tens of millions of people. This is too many.[24] This student should not be expelled from the school.

Students have reasons to cause disturbances. But [no one] advocates a general student strike. They have developed a habit [of opposition] from their opposition to the Nationalists.

---

[24]Mao is being ironic. See below his similar treatment of the same incident in his "Contradictions" speech, Text 3, p. 134.

It is incorrect not to allow workers to strike. The constitution does not ban strikes. Putting up posters is the freedom of speech; holding meetings is the freedom of assembly.

We shouldn't have all those who caused disturbances write a statement of repentance; neither should they all be made to write articles of self-criticism.

Since there are problems, it's good to have a bit of disturbance.

Students making a disturbance is not equivalent to rebellion.

In a population of 600 million, to have one million cause trouble in a year is normal; one out of six hundred.

Those who create disturbances cannot be called counterrevolutionary at all. Possibly one or two of them may be counterrevolutionaries.

[40] The best way to deal with bureaucratism is to strike, to hold student strikes, and to brandish shoulder poles, because problems remain unsolved for so long!

Of course, I am not putting up posters calling for a national strike.

These contradictions are temporary in nature, not basic contradictions.

When problems occur, both sides should be looked at. (Those who create disturbances also have a dual character. They give us warnings. A pustule will be all right once the pus has been discharged.)

If you say, "I am a 'veteran revolutionary,' I can't be opposed," [well,] the Nationalists are also "veteran revolutionaries," more veteran than we are. We can't adopt the same attitude as the Nationalists use towards the people.

Marxism has always developed through struggle with the enemy, through struggle with bourgeois ideology, by extracting the rational elements of bourgeois ideology. Only in this way has Marxism been shaped.

The current danger is the belief that everything in the garden is lovely.[25] So when you read Wang Meng's criticisms, you are unhappy.

Only striking [people down] cannot steel literature and art.

Should we or shouldn't we permit only fragrant flowers to exist and not permit poisonous weeds?

(Under [the policy of] "Let a hundred flowers bloom," we should permit poisonous weeds to exist, permit styles to be different.)

---

[25]Literally, *tianxia taiping le:* all is peaceful under heaven.

Poisonous weeds can poison people, but fragrant flowers can grow only through struggling with poisonous weeds.

There are many weeds in the grain fields. The crops grow only by struggling with the weeds. The Soviet Union has been undergoing socialist construction for decades, and it still has weeds in its fields. Never mind the weeds: turn them in and they'll become fertilizer.

If it's a poisonous weed, you can say so. Some people advocate writing: "This is a poisonous weed. Don't try it." The Soviet way is to have only fragrant flowers and no poisonous weeds. In reality many poisonous weeds live in disguise under the name of fragrant flowers. We advocate that "poisonous weeds and fragrant flowers blossom together, that rosy clouds in the sunset and the solitary duck fly together."[26]

[41] Stalin had his Idealism and his materialism; he had a one-sided character.

< Metaphysics has Idealism as well as materialism. Stalin had both. He had dialectics as well as metaphysics. Precisely for this reason he had both merits and demerits; his merits surpass his demerits. >

Soviet comrades find it difficult to change; they like to use high-handed methods.

The methods of dogmatism are the methods of metaphysics.

Both praise and denunciation of Wang Meng's writing are one-sided in nature.

Wang Meng has a dual nature: One is his good points; the other is his shortcomings.

One point contains two points,[27] and one material thing contains two different aspects.

Commodities have a dual nature, so does Wang Meng.

Yao Wenyuan's article in the *Wenhui bao* is very good. ("Dogmatism and principle" is very convincing.)[28]

---

[26]Mao is evidently doing a take-off of a piece of parallel prose celebrated down the centuries: "Rosy clouds in the sunset and the solitary duck fly together; the autumn water meets the horizon in one color." The original, from an essay by Wang Bo (648–675), had purely scenic significance.

[27]*Yi dian you liang dian.*

[28]Published in January 1957; reprinted in Yao Wenyuan, *Lun wenxue shangde xiuzheng-zhuyi sichao* (On the revisionist thought tide in literature) (Shanghai, Xin wenyi chubanshe, 1958), pp. 3–11. Yao's article is subtitled: "A discussion with Mr. Yao Xueyin," and refers to

We cannot say that everything in the past was dogmatism. The Nationalist party was once the only school. After we overthrew them, the Communist party was for a period the only school. Having a sole school was necessary. But now it is different.

(Disturbances have emerged in Eastern Europe for precisely this reason. Now circumstances have changed, and it is necessary to let a hundred schools contend. If we want to contend, then we must prepare. It is through contending that we obtain education and transformation, not through liberalism. Nothing should be disposed of with one kick. We should criticize mistakes, but should recognize their dual character.)

We can explain to everyone that we do not want to meet an enemy attack in a hurry, we don't want to write articles in a hurry. When fighting, don't we say we fight no battle unprepared and fight no battle we are not sure of winning? Uncertainty is the same as unpreparedness. Our present battle is simply an unprepared battle.

There are vestiges of the bourgeoisie, the landlords, and the rich peasants. There are petty bourgeois intellectuals who come from these. We have the responsibility to carry out ideological struggle and educational work with them.

What we have now is the minority educating the majority.

Don't use simplistic methods to expel people.

[42] They can become teachers; such teachers are hard to find.

Ma Hanbing's and Li Xifan's articles also have dual characteristics. They're dogmatist, but they can alert [people]. They actually don't endorse the policy of letting a hundred flowers bloom and a hundred schools contend.

In reality, there will still be non-Marxist ideas ten thousand years from now.

What's more, Marxism itself will come to an end some day. What can be imagined for five hundred years from now? Nowadays five hundred years counts for as much as tens of thousands of years in the past.

In the world of the future, class struggle will end. Some aspects of Marxism will become useless.

---

a veteran left-wing writer. Yao Wenyuan was a young Shanghai literary critic who later became a leading polemicist of the "Gang of Four," and whose attack on the historian Wu Han initiated the Cultural Revolution. This article may have first brought him to Mao's attention.

Anyone proclaiming himself as [expounding] eternal truth is no Marxist.

In the future there will be no class struggle, but there'll be new struggles. By then new theories should have emerged in the field of social science.

Of course, certain things can't be overthrown, such as the earth turns and the sun does not, that the earth revolves around the sun and not the sun around the earth. All the same, the earth will rot one day.

Humanity may also be negated. Some day our kind of human will no longer fit in, and all will be exterminated. But this will be good for the evolution of the universe.

Three thousand years ago humanity still used stone. Later they progressed to the use of copper and iron down to using machines. Zhang Taiyan has already discussed the 500 thousand years of human history in his *Qiu shu.*[29] The bronze age negated the stone age. Humanity passed its days on earth digging in the dirt. No one ever elected humanity to be the master of the earth. The multitudes of the animal kingdom didn't elect us; neither did the bacteria. Perhaps only the plants are not against us. When we die, we can provide them with nourishment. They can also use our excreta.

Humanity itself will evolve; so, too, must Marxists.

How to construct a huge country like this is a new question for Marxists. How can we reduce the chances of taking roundabout courses? Marx didn't envision this huge country of ours with a population of 600 million, and neither did Lenin. He was involved in the construction of a socialist state for just a few years.

[43] Our population of 600 million will one day in the future have to line up when we go out in the street. In the future the streets will be jammed with people. How will we distribute newspapers? How will we go to the movies? How will we go to the park? All these will become problems.

We can't say all problems have been solved. There are still many questions awaiting identification and solution.

---

[29]Zhang Taiyan [Zhang Binglin] (1868–1936) was a renowned classicist and noted anti-Manchu racist active in the late Qing reform movement. The book Mao mentions here was a 1902 exposition of Zhang's anti-Manchu views based on a study of human evolution strongly rooted in Chinese interpretations of Darwin. The title is obscure, but can be translated as "Book of raillery." See Charlotte Furth, "The Sage as Rebel," in Furth, *The Limits of Change* (Cambridge, Harvard Univ. Press, 1976), pp. 113, 131–2, 375.

Don't be afraid of evil trends. There are always two kinds of trends, one evil and the other healthy.[30]

There has been a great flood in Jilin this year, simply because there has been too much rain. Two currents, one cold and the other warm, have met. They didn't meet above Heilongjiang, nor did they meet over Liaoning. They just met over Jilin, and they put up a fight and from this it rained heavily. It's not good for it to rain too much. But if it doesn't rain, there is drought. The two currents need each other. It won't do for one to be lacking.

The more the struggle, the more enriched [life will become], then new truth will emerge.

(XX: Currently there has been a trend to write about love.)

[Chairman:] Without love, humanity would become extinct.

(XX: There is the "theory of inevitability" in essays.)

[Chairman:] More "theory of inevitability" should be published. In this way people's attention will be aroused.

Holding power has its dual characteristics. Many people simply fear "blossoming" and "contention" no matter what.

<We should especially (note that) after gaining power we attempt to use simplistic methods to put down others. Why (do some people) fear letting a hundred flowers bloom? They fear their rice ladle will cross the river.[31]

Young people are not so afraid of opposing bureaucrats because they have not yet held any office. Bureaucratism has not yet come to roost on them.>

The type of intimidation used recently lacks persuasion and reasoning. It's not too wise. We should give people a way out, help them.

(XX: Wang Meng has asked for a discussion [of his works].)

[Chairman:] Two points: one, good, he opposes bureaucratism; two, his writing still has shortcomings.

---

[30]*Xie* and *zheng* also mean "heterodox" and "orthodox."
[31]Presumably Mao means they fear they will lose their comfortable jobs.

[44] Wang Meng is very promising, with the force of the newly born. People with an aptitude for writing are hard to find.

Bureaucratism just can't be touched now. It seems that to curse bureaucratism is to curse yourselves. Well, since you have admitted to bureaucratism, you'll have to be cursed.

We cannot say Beijing can't be criticized; we cannot say the party's shortcomings can't be written up.

(XX: There is talk that we no longer promote [the interests of the] workers, peasants, and soldiers.)

[Chairman:] Don't promote [their interests]? The whole country is left with only workers, peasants, and soldiers, plus intellectuals.

(XX: If the work of workers, peasants, and soldiers is done well, the people will welcome it.)

[Chairman:] Right. For so many years we have been opposing Dühring, yet we still don't know what he's like. Can we find a book by him?

(XX: He talked about the relationship between dialectical logic and formal logic.)

[Chairman:] < Hegel and Mach, too. Zhou Gucheng[32] discusses Great Logic [*da luoji*] in *New Construction,* and he makes some sense. >

< Schools only follow the president's opinion, and not those of the students. This isn't right. >

---

[32]Zhou Gucheng (b. 1910), historian.

TEXT   TWO

Talk When Receiving Committee Members of
the National Student Federation (Extracts)

24 FEBRUARY 1957

[189] [After] our generation dies, the difficulties will be yours. At
that time you will have a much better foundation. Our foundation
now is not good. There are very few college students, very few intellectuals: 40 million[1] school-age kids cannot go to school. To have all
the school-age kids in school is, I'm afraid, impossible even in a hundred years. Even the Soviet Union has not done that.

So far the Soviet Union has resolved only the problem of the
seven-year [schooling] system. It has not succeeded [in implement-

Sources: 1:189; alternate text, 6A:37, which gives the date as 14 February.
[1]The alternate text says 400,000, which is clearly incorrect. In 1956 there had been about 60
million children in primary schools, or 52% of the primary-school-age population; see
CHOC 14, pp. 211, 214.

ing] the ten-year [schooling] system . . . We can issue directives, [and] let local party committees make reports to students. [We] have already pointed out this problem at the conference of party secretaries from provincial and municipal party committees held recently. [We] told them to pay attention to strengthening work in the school [system]. If the political classes are boring, make people doze off, then it's better not to discuss [politics]. It would be better just to doze off. [Dozing off] can save energy [and] maintain [your] vigor. (Whether you want to relay these few words is up to you.) You are all leaders. I think you definitely don't approve.[2]

[2]It is not absolutely clear whether Mao thinks the student leaders disapprove of boring lectures, dozing off, or his own radical suggestion to abolish classes—but, most likely, "dozing off."

TEXT THREE

On the Correct Handling of Contradictions
among the People (Speaking Notes)

27 FEBRUARY 1957

CONTRADICTIONS AMONG THE PEOPLE

[190] Comrades:

I am going to talk about the following problem: how to handle correctly contradictions among the people. Among the problems I have encountered, the problem of contradictions among the people is an important one, which occupies much of our time and has caused lots of difficulties. Of course, there are two types of problems—

Sources: 1:190–232; alternate text, 15D:54–95. This talk was delivered to the Supreme State Conference. These are the "speaking notes" (*jianghua gao*) of Mao's famous speech to that conference. This text had been unavailable for scholars in the West until the version trans-

contradictions between the enemy and ourselves [and] contradictions among the people—and, in fact, I want to talk about both, not just the one. However, since today we want primarily to talk about the second problem, we will not emphasize the question of the enemy and ourselves, though I will discuss both. These two types of problems are of a different nature, [and so] the methods of resolving them are different. We have discussed this before with two slogans: "Clearly distinguish between the enemy and ourselves," "Clearly distinguish between right and wrong";[1] [separate out] who is the enemy, who are the people. To distinguish clearly right and wrong, well, that's to discuss what's among the people, and the problems among the people are problems of right and wrong, not problems between the enemy and ourselves. If that's so, then are [problems] between the enemy and ourselves also questions of right and wrong or not? They are, but they are problems of right and wrong of a different nature. In common parlance we talk of them as contradictions between the enemy and ourselves (our custom of comparing the two [types of contradictions] makes things clearer). One type is antagonistic contradictions: contradictions between the enemy and ourselves, or antagonistic contradictions. Contradictions among the people are non-antagonistic contradictions. The *People's Daily* carried an article, "More on the historical experience of the proletarian dictatorship".[2]

---

lated here was circulated in 1985. Since then an identical copy has appeared in the Peking University teaching materials (New Mao Texts, vol. 15D). A third version has been reported, but to date has been unavailable for comparison: See Michael Schoenhals, "Original Contradictions—On the Unrevised Text of Mao Zedong's 'On the Correct Handling of Contradictions Among the People,'" *The Australian Journal of Chinese Affairs* 16:109, n. 2 (July, 1986). The highly edited official version that appeared in *RMRB* (19 June 1957) has been reprinted officially several times, most recently in *SW5*. The versions differ significantly. The speaking notes are about 28,000 characters in length; the official version in *XJ5* is some 24,000. Language, emphasis, examples and numbering of points differ among versions, but the rough organization is the same. The rambling, ungrammatical nature of many passages makes us believe Text 3 is a transcript based on a tape recording.

For the reader's convenience, we have inserted headings before each of the numbered points. They do not appear in the original.

[1]Two slogans: *Fenqing di wo* and *fenqing shi fei*.

[2]For a discussion of the circumstances surrounding this article, published 29 December 1956, see *Origins* 1, p. 272ff. The article was a rejection of the speech Tito made in Pula, Yugoslavia, on 11 November 1956, in which he stated that the problems within the Soviet bloc were due not just to the errors of Stalin but more fundamentally to the system which made them possible. The Chinese rejected Tito's views in "More on the historical experi-

That *People's Daily* article primarily discussed international problems. When it discussed these two types of contradictions, it was in regard to international affairs. It didn't say much about domestic affairs. Moreover, on actually how to resolve contradictions among the people it offered no detailed analysis but only an explanation of the principle. [191] And that is the proletarian dictatorship, and the differences between the systems of dictatorship and democratic centralism. What does dictatorship do? What areas does dictatorship control? Dictatorship is used to handle [contradictions] between the enemy and us. To solve contradictions between the enemy and us is a matter of forcing others to submit, but it is not completely a case of so-called total repression. For instance, we speak of denying them the right to vote or the freedom to publish newspapers. Antagonistic classes—for example, the landlord class or imperialist elements—may not freely publish newspapers among us, nor may Taiwan. To prohibit the landlord class from publishing newspapers, to deprive them of freedom of speech and the right to vote all fall within the scope of dictatorship. The exercise of dictatorship must also make use of democratic centralism. Who is to exercise dictatorship? It must be the people! Class dictatorship is the dictatorship of one class over another. If you want to control him, kill him, seize him, naturally you must go through the People's Government, and moreover, you must have the people [on your side]. What we now call the system of democratic centralism applies only to the ranks of the people. If it is not the enemy, then it is the people; and in that context it is not a question of dictatorship nor of who exercises dictatorship over whom. The people do not exercise dictatorship over themselves; for they have the freedom of speech, the freedom of assembly, the freedom of association, and the freedom to demonstrate which are written into our constitution. This is a problem of democracy. Democracy is democracy with leadership; it is democracy under centralized leadership, not the democracy of anarchism. Anarchism is not what the people want.

---

ence of the proletarian dictatorship," in which they suggested for the first time that contradictions could exist inside as well as between socialist countries. For the Pula speech, see Paul E. Zinner, ed., *National Communism and Popular Revolt in Eastern Europe* (New York, Columbia Univ. Press, 1956), pp. 516–41; for "More on . . . ," see *Communist China, 1955–1959: Policy Documents with Analysis* (Cambridge, Harvard Univ. Press, 1962).

The problem of big democracy [*da minzhu*] and little democracy [*xiao minzhu*].

Some people have been delighted by the occurrence of the Hungarian and Polish incidents: Come on, [they say,] let's bring in big democracy! In their so-called democracy hundreds of thousands go out onto the street seemingly delighted by this. There are a small number of people who call this big democracy; [but] as I have just said, dictatorship is the people exercising dictatorship, a class exercising dictatorship, one class exercising dictatorship over another. Throughout history all so-called big democracy, mass democratic movements, dealt with antagonistic classes. Some of our friends outside the party, naturally few in number, do not understand this clearly; in addition, there are a few people with hostile feelings who hope to use big democracy **[192]** somehow to punish the People's Government. They exist. "The day we model ourselves on Poland, model ourselves on Hungary, and punish the Communist party, I will rejoice. We can't go on with this Communist party, the dictatorship is too severe." One university student issued a call. He wants to kill lots of people, to kill several hundred people. [To say] several hundred is an underestimate; [he] wants to kill several thousand, tens of thousands, millions, tens of millions. Of course, this is a bit of hyperbole. Even if he is allowed to kill, I fear he won't be able to kill quite so many! But this indicates something of what is on his mind. In addition, there are also a few naive people who do not understand the concrete situation in the world, who imagine that European democratic freedoms are wonderful and that we haven't enough of them. They like parliamentary democracy and say that the National People's Congress suffers in comparison with Western parliaments. [They] advocate the two-party system, like the two-party systems of foreign countries: this party on top, that party down, and then vice versa. [They] want two news agencies in competition with each other. Some people propose abolishing the dictatorship sooner; some say democracy is the goal. We say to them: democracy is a means, you can also say democracy is both democracy [an end?] and a means. But in the final analysis Marxist political economy tells us that human [society], this superstructure (To which category does democracy belong? It belongs to the superstructure, belongs to politics), serves the economic base. Thus, as soon as you say democracy is a means and not an end, then [they] don't feel so comfortable; you've got to say democracy is the end before [they'll] feel a little happier.

Freedom. Some people say the freedoms in foreign countries are wonderful and ours are very few. We say to them: freedoms abroad are not all that numerous. Their parliamentary freedom is just a facade for others to see, is only freedom for the bourgeoisie. There is no freedom in the abstract, only class freedom; to see freedom in its most concrete form, look at which class or group [has it]. In England the Conservative party has freedom of the Conservative party, the Labour party has the freedom of the Labour party. Conservative party freedom wants to attack the Suez Canal; the Labour party proclaims that the Canal should not be attacked. A group of men have split from the Conservative party, such as Anthony Eden's assistant, [Anthony] Nutting, Minister of State in the Foreign Office. He wrote articles propagandizing his point of view.[3] Thus, [193] Eden has Eden's freedom, Nutting has Nutting's. In class freedom you have this kind of group freedom and even individual freedom for a very small number of individuals. There has never been such a thing as abstract freedom in the world.

Ideological problems, problems among the people, cannot be solved by crude methods. To use crude methods to resolve ideological problems, problems in the mental realm, or problems among the people, is a mistake. All attempts to use administrative fiat or compulsion to solve ideological problems are not only ineffective, but harmful. For instance, religion. It cannot be abolished by administrative fiat, nor can people be compelled not to believe [in it]. [We] cannot compel people not to believe in Idealism. In all questions of an ideological nature, the way to make the people believe you is to use the methods of discussion, debate, criticism, education, and persuasion.

Where do we put the national bourgeoisie? In the first type of contradiction or the second? "More on the historical experience of the proletarian dictatorship" did not discuss this Chinese question. But, we all know that the national bourgeoisie cannot be put in the first type, in the category of contradictions between the enemy and ourselves. [This is] because the national bourgeoisie has a dual character: they are willing to accept the constitution, to accept socialist

---

[3]Anthony Nutting was a protégé of Premier Eden's who seemed destined for a brilliant political career, until he broke with him over the Anglo-French invasion of Egypt to recover the Suez Canal in October–November 1956. The articles Mao refers to were written after Nutting's resignation.

transformation, to walk the road to socialism. For these reasons the national bourgeoisie is different from imperialism, bureaucratic capitalism, and feudalism. Having these differences, the national bourgeoisie is willing to accept socialist transformation. The working class and the capitalists, that is to say the national bourgeoisie, are two antagonistic classes. They are antagonistic; but antagonistic contradictions, if properly handled, can become unantagonistic, they can be transformed into non-antagonistic contradictions, from the first type of contradiction into the second. If we handle them improperly, if we do not use such policies as uniting and educating, then [the contradictions] must move toward antagonism. If we put them [the national bourgeoisie] in the first category, then we will turn them into the enemy. [It won't do] to run things in defiance of reality, in a country like China, with a national bourgeoisie like China's, [194] a national bourgeoisie with an anti-imperialist mindset. A moment ago I brought up this question of how to handle contradictions among the people. The question of how to handle contradictions among the people is a new question. Historically, Marx and Engels talked very little about this problem; Lenin discussed it, but briefly, saying that while antagonism in socialist society has vanished, contradictions still exist. That is to say, what we call the antagonism has been vanquished, the capitalist class has been knocked down, but there are still contradictions among the people. Lenin [himself] said contradictions among the people exist, but Lenin did not have time enough to analyze this question fully. As for antagonism, is it possible for contradictions among the people to be transformed from non-antagonistic contradictions into antagonistic ones? It must be said that it is possible; but in Lenin's time this had not yet happened, and perhaps he did not watch this problem carefully since he had such a short time [as leader of the Soviet Union]. After the October Revolution, during the period when Stalin was in charge, for a long time he confused these two types of contradictions. Problems like bad mouthing the government, talking about the government, being dissatisfied with the government, being dissatisfied with the Communist party, criticizing the government, criticizing the Communist party, are in origin problems among the people. But there are two types of criticism: There is the enemy criticizing us, the enemy being dissatisfied with the Communist party; and there are the people criticizing us, the people being dissatisfied with us; and the two must be distinguished. Stalin for so many years did not make such distinctions, or rarely did. A few [comrades] who have worked in the Soviet Union for many years have told me there were no distinctions; you could only talk about good things, not bad; you could only sing praises, not make criticisms; whoever made a criticism was suspected of being an enemy and ran the risk of imprisonment or execution. These two types of contradictions have always been easy to mix up, easy to confuse. We, too, have sometimes failed to avoid confusing [them]. In suppressing counterrevolutionaries we have taken, indeed have often taken, good people for bad and rectified them, and suspected [those] who never were counterrevolutionary to be counterrevolutionaries and struggled against them. Isn't this so: It happened in the past and is still happening now. The point is, we have a rule: Clearly distinguish between the enemy and ourselves; where there is suspicion, then struggle; where there are mistakes, redress them. Moreover, government offices and schools in the Yan'an period had a rule: Counterrevolutionaries in offices, schools, the armed forces, organizations, and people's organizations, even if they were bona fide counterrevolutionaries, were not to be killed; minor counterrevolutionaries **[195]** were not to be killed, nor were major ones to be killed. In practice they carried out this rule, even though it was not stipulated by law. Because there are exceptions to the law, a small number of exceptions are inevitable. But in practice we did not kill. Not even one. With this rule we are guaranteed that in the unlikely event of a mistake, we still have room for redemption. How easy it is to mix up is seen, too, in the two factions, leftists and rightists. People with rightist tendencies in thought make no distinction between the enemy and ourselves, take the enemy to be us. There are still people who make no distinction between the enemy and ourselves. We still have such people among us now. In our view, in the view of the broad masses, they are the enemy, [but] in the view of these few people they are friends. For example, I have a document here, a comrade wrote me a letter and now it has been distributed to you. He opposes the release of Kang Ze.[4] In his view, Kang Ze is an enemy. This person

---

[4]Kang Ze (1904–73?), who had been one of the leaders of the notorious Blue Shirts groups and a close confidant of Chiang Kai-shek, was a KMT general captured in 1948 by the CCP armies. A Whampoa Academy graduate, he had studied in Moscow. See Lloyd Eastman, *The Abortive Revolution* (Cambridge, Harvard Univ. Press, 1974), pp. 36–7, 71–4.

[the letter-writer], who was a representative at the [second] Congress last December of the All-China Federation of Industry and Commerce, is from Xiangyang district.[5] Kang Ze previously worked in Xiangyang. (He killed the [letter-writer's] son) and so he [the letter-writer] opposed Kang Ze's release; but those who had been Kang Ze's friends had a different view; they thought and felt differently, and therefore their [position] diverged greatly from that of the people. It does not distinguish the enemy from us. The American moon and the Chinese moon are no different, [but] some people even say the American moon is better than the Chinese moon. I believe the American moon and the Chinese moon are the same moon, but to say the American moon is better than the Chinese moon I just can't believe. Why should your moon be better than mine?

"Left"-ists, "left" opportunists. So-called "leftists" are "left" in quotation marks, not the true left. These people excessively emphasize antagonistic contradictions between the enemy and ourselves. For example, Stalin was this kind of person; we, too, have such people who stress [them] to excess, mistaking the second type of contradiction, contradictions originally among the people, for the first type, mistaking them as [contradictions] between the enemy and ourselves. In the campaign to eliminate counterrevolutionaries this emerged time and again. As I have already said before, this is "left". In the Yan'an period, in 1942, we put forward the slogan of calling for unity-criticism-unity as a principle for resolving contradictions among the people. We worked out this formula. More precisely this means to start from the desire for unity, pass through criticism or struggle, to arrive at a new unity on a new foundation. Later, we [used this] to resolve intra-party contradictions, contradictions within the Communist party, **[196]** that is, the contradiction between dogmatism and the broad mass of party members, and the contradiction between dogmatism and Marxism. The policy previously employed was the one brought back from the Western Paradise.[6] That "Western Paradise" was Stalin,

---

[5]Xiangyang is a county in northern Hubei province, touching the Henan border. We do not know who the letter-writer is.

[6]Mao appears to be combining at least two Buddhist allusions here: (a) the "Western Paradise" presided over by the Buddha Amitabha (E-mi-tuo-fo in Chinese); (b) the journeys to the west (i.e., India) of Tang dynasty monks, notably Xuanzang (Hsuan-tsang), who brought back sacred texts from the homeland of Buddhism and translated them into Chinese. The famous fantastical novel *Xi you ji* loosely based on Xuanzang's exploits has now

and [the policy] was called "ruthless struggle and merciless blows." Seeing that this was not suitable, when we later criticized dogma-tism, we discontinued using the method of "dealing with a man as he deals with you" [i.e., 'an eye for an eye']. [We] chose another method, another policy, which is to unite with them, to proceed from the de-sire for unity, to go through criticism or struggle, to achieve unity based on a new foundation. This policy was apparently [sic] raised in the 1942 Rectification [Movement]. After a few years, in 1945, at the time of the Seventh Party Congress, the goal of unity was reached, while the intervening period had been of criticism. Why do [we] want the first unity, want to have the desire for unity? If you do not have the first unity, do not have the desire for unity, once you start to struggle, you will be bound to struggle to a total mess, with no way to stop. Isn't that still "ruthless struggle and merciless blows"? Be-cause subjectively you didn't have such a desire, you have not pre-pared to unite with them; you therefore need to go through the process of first uniting, then criticizing and struggling, finally reach-ing the result of unity. From going through this process we have ob-tained this formula: unity-criticism-unity. Later this was extended outside the party, [then] step by step extended to Beijing. We advised the democratic parties also to adopt this method of criticism. . . . With capitalists, that is, exploiters, we can use this method. To get Tai-wan to use [it], will, I think, be more difficult! Because they are ex-ploiters, [but] they are a different type of exploiter. It wouldn't work for Chiang Kai-shek to use it. Chiang Kai-shek and Hu Shi are of the other type. The struggle between the two men,[7] can it be like us want-ing to criticize John Foster Dulles; should we start from the desire of unity, go through criticism and on a new foundation reach unity? Impossible. (Laughter) But it's possible [to do so] with the national bourgeoisie; this has been completely verified. People who have made mistakes, people with various types of petty-bourgeois thought, people with capitalist thought, Idealists, people with metaphysical thought, [as well as] religious circles, in all these cases one can use this

---

been translated in full in Anthony C. Yu's *The Journey to the West*, 4 vols., (Chicago, Univ. of Chicago Press, 1977–83). An earlier, much abbreviated translation was published by the late Arthur Waley under the title *Monkey* (London, Allen & Unwin, 1942).

[7]This was an obscure passage, but Mao seems to be referring to his belief that the USA was using Hu Shi to isolate Chiang Kai-shek.

method, popularize this method, [and] expand it throughout the ranks of the people. Schools, factories, cooperatives, shops, all can use this [197] method. Among a population of 600 million [it] can be used even with disarmed enemies, enemies who have been relieved of their weapons. For instance, in the past we treated prisoners of war [POWs] this way. The way we treated POWs after they had been disarmed as compared to before they were disarmed are two [different] kinds of attitude. Before they are disarmed, it's soldier against soldier, general against general, you die and I live; once they have been disarmed, we use a different attitude to handle them. With regard to those criminals sentenced to remolding (*gaizao*) through labor, we also use this method, starting out from the desire for unity. A POW, a disarmed enemy, a disarmed spy, whom [we] clearly recognize as such, we decide not to kill. So what then? Remold him. To remold is to proceed from the desire for unity. You let him live, don't wipe him out. Last year, on 2 May 1956, I spoke of ten items [*shi tiao*] at a session of the Supreme State Conference. At that conference I discussed one [set of] ten items, among which were two items (many of you here today also attended that meeting); one item was the enemy and ourselves; one item was right and wrong. One item was the relationship between the enemy and ourselves; one item was the relationship between right and wrong. This relationship between right and wrong is none other than mutual relations among the people, contradictions among the people.[8]

---

[8]The text of Mao's speech to the SSC is not available in full, but the circumstances surrounding it are discussed in *Origins* 1, pp. 51–6. The 2 May speech officially launched the slogan, "Let a hundred flowers bloom, let a hundred schools contend." A brief extract is translated in *Survey of China Mainland Press* 4000 (U.S. Consulate General, Hong Kong), p. 16. Mao's reference above to "ten items" brings to mind his closely related and more famous speech to an expanded Politburo conference on 25 April 1956, which officially appears as "On the ten great relationships" (*Shi da guanxi*), in *SW5*, pp. 285–307, and is discussed in *Origins* 1, pp. 48–51. The two items (*tiao*) Mao mentions, as well as his use of the term "relationship" (*guanxi*) to describe them, seem to refer to items 8 and 9 from this earlier speech. Whether there is a confusion of the April and May speeches here, or whether the same or a similar ten-point format was used in May, as this passage implies, is unclear. In fact, the officially printed "Ten great relationships" is apparently a conflation of these two speeches done by Mao's secretary, Hu Qiaomu, in 1975 in preparation for *SW5*. See Gong Yuzhi, "Tong Shi Lamu jiaoshou de tanhua" (A conversation with Professor Schram), *Wenxian he yanjiu: 1984 nian huibianben* (Documents and research: 1984 selections) (Beijing, Renmin chubanshe, 1986), pp. 251–2.

What I have said above is part one, the beginning. The problem of two types of contradictions.

Secondly, I'll discuss the problem of eliminating counterrevolutionaries.

ELIMINATING COUNTERREVOLUTIONARIES

The problem of eliminating counterrevolutionaries is a problem of the first type of contradiction [i.e., between the enemy and ourselves]. Speaking comparatively, in the last analysis how has our country handled the work of eliminating counterrevolutionaries? Poorly or well? In my view there have been shortcomings, but in comparison with other countries we have done relatively well. Better than the Soviet Union, better than Hungary. The Soviet Union was too leftist, Hungary was too rightist. We have drawn a lesson from this; it's not that we're especially clever. Because the Soviet Union has been too left, we have learned something from that experience. We ourselves have committed leftist excesses, too. During the period of the southern base areas, when we were still rather ignorant, we suffered losses and every base area without exception used the same Soviet method.[9] Later [we] put things right, and only then did we gain experience. In Yan'an [we] finally enacted some rules. Not a single person was to be killed and the bulk [of offenders] were not to be arrested. Once in Beijing [i.e., after the 1949 Communist victory] there were some improvements, though naturally there are still shortcomings, errors. Still, by now progress has been made. Compared with the Soviet Union, it is two lines[10] **[198]** (this refers to the past, not the present, namely the time when Stalin was in power; he did things badly). There were two sides to him. One side was the elimination of true counterrevolutionaries; that was the correct side. The other side was the incorrect killing of numerous people, important people. For example, a high percentage of delegates to the Communist Party [National] Congress were killed. How many in the Central Committee did he kill? He seized and killed XX percent of the Seventeenth

[9]This refers to the late 1920s and early 1930s.
[10]Mao appears to be saying that the CCP and the CPSU had pursued two very different policies towards "counterrevolution," at least until recently.

Party Congress delegates, and he seized and killed XX percent of the
Central Committee members elected at the Seventeenth Congress.[11]
We didn't do this sort of thing, having seen his example. Have there
been any people unjustly killed? Yes, at the time of the great [cam-
paign] to eliminate counterrevolutionaries [*sufan*], 1950, 1951, 1952,
in those three years of the great *sufan*, there were. [When] killing
local bullies and evil gentry [*tuhao lieshen*] in [the campaign against]
the five types of counterrevolutionaries, there were. But basically
there were no errors; that group of people should have been killed.
In all, how many were killed? Seven hundred thousand were killed,
[and] after that time probably over 70,000 more have been killed. But
less than 80,000. Since last year, basically we have not killed people;
only a small number of individuals have been killed. So people say,
"You people are so capricious; if you had known it would come to
this, why did you start as you did? And now again you want no more
killing." In the past four or five years we've only killed several tens of
thousands of people. From last year we more or less haven't killed,
only killing a small number, a few individuals. In 1950, 1951, 1952,
we killed 700,000. The Hong Kong news papers expanded that estimate (at that time we didn't need to reckon accounts with them);
they said we killed 20,000,000. If we subtract 700,000 from
20,000,000, that really leaves a remainder of 19,300,000. They were
19,300,000 over. "The tyrant Zhou cannot really have been as wicked
as all this."[12] How could we possibly kill 20,000,000 people? It is true
that 700,000 people were killed; [but] if they had not been killed, the
people would not have been able to raise their heads. The people
demanded [*yaoqiu*] the killing in order to liberate the productive
forces. They [those killed] were fetters on the productive forces. "Evil

[11]The CPSU 17th Party Congress was held in 1934. The excisions of the precise figures
were presumably made by the compilers of this unofficial volume. Another version of this
text in *Mao zhuxi wenxian san shi pian* (Thirty texts by Chairman Mao) (Beijing, Beijing
Teshu Gangchang Xuanchuan Qinwuzu, n.d.), pp. 96–7 gives figures at this point: 80% of
the delegates and 50% of the CC killed. Unfortunately that text is not currently available,
but is discussed in part (including the quotation and citation of this passage) in Schoenhals,
"Original Contradictions."

[12]The quotation refers to the notorious last ruler of the Shang whose crimes were held to
have been the reason for the collapse of the dynasty in the 12th century B.C. See Arthur
Waley, *The Analects of Confucius* (London, Allen and Unwin, 1938). Luo Ruiqing, one-time
Minister of Public Security, reportedly said in 1964 that 4 million people had been executed
from 1948 through 1955 (a figure excluding battle deaths).

despots"—the Eastern despot, the Southern despot, the Western despot, the Northern despot, the Central despot,[13] the backbone elements of the five types of counterrevolutionaries.

Now a few people want to reverse this verdict, a few friends want to reverse this verdict. It's wrong to reverse the verdict of that time; I don't think it is worth reversing. If it is reversed, the people will rise up and strike us with their carrying poles, the peasants will rise up and strike us with their carrying poles, the workers will grab some weapon, grab iron bars and beat us.

[199] Hungary, for instance, Hungary basically did not eliminate counterrevolutionaries. They killed Rajk; [they] actually killed some revolutionaries but very few counterrevolutionaries.[14] Thus emerged the Hungarian Incident. Looking at our country, following incidents like that in Hungary, people say conditions in China are very stable. Foreigners who have seen [things] here also agree, [and] we, too, feel this way.

Since the Hungarian incident, has China had any disturbances?

We have had a few small disturbances. "A breeze about to rise blows ripples over a pool of spring water."[15] Those spring waters were whipped up, but there were no great waves like that sucked up by a force-7 typhoon. For what reason? Several reasons. The cam-

---

[13]The term is *e ba* or *ba tian. Ba* is normally translated as "hegemon"; but in this case Mao is not referring to the ancient warlords but employing a popular term for "local despot" used in a series of Peking operas, such as the operas based on the Qing novel, *Shi gong an* (Cases of Lord Shi), of which one was *Si ba tian* (The four celestial despots). This usage of *ba tian* was current among peasants to describe village despots during the early 1950s campaigns against counterrevolutionaries.

[14]László Rajk was hanged in 1949 after a Soviet-style show trial, at which the former Politburo member and Interior Minister made the unlikely confession that he had plotted with Tito to overthrow the Soviet-backed Budapest regime and take Hungary out of the communist bloc. Like similar high-ranking victims in other East European countries at that time, Rajk was a scapegoat in Stalin's drive against the specter of "national communism" in the wake of Yugoslavia's defiance of his orders and expulsion from the bloc in 1948. See Hugh Seton-Watson, "Introduction," in Melvin J. Lasky, ed., *The Hungarian Revolution* (London, Secker & Warburg, 1957), pp. 18–9; and Ernst Halperin, *The Triumphant Heretic* (London, Heinemann, 1958), pp. 188–95. In the Chinese text, Mao actually says "he" killed some revolutionaries, which could conceivably refer to Rajk's activities as Interior Minister; but the sense of the passage is clearly that Rajk was one of the wrongly executed revolutionaries and that *ta* ("he") should be read *tamen* ("they").

[15]*Feng zhaqi chui zhou yichi chunshui.* This is a quotation from the Five Dynasties period poet Feng Yansi (903–960). The translation is from Daniel Bryant, *Lyric Poets of the Southern Tang* (Vancouver, Univ. of British Columbia Press, 1982), p. 35. The same phrase is mentioned again by Mao below on p. 206 of the Chinese text.

paign against counterrevolutionaries basically eliminated the counter-revolutionaries; only a few remained, only a very, very few. This is one [reason]. But this is not the primary reason! Primarily [because] the base areas, the Liberation Army, the Communist party, and the democratic figures have emerged from decades of revolutionary steeling; coming out of decades of steeling through struggle, our party has taken root, our army has fighting power, we have passed through the gradual development of the base areas, [and] did not suddenly take control of China. Democratic figures, too, have gone through steeling, have shared the hardships. Students have [participated in] in the December Ninth [Movement], the September Eighteenth [Incident], the May Thirtieth Movement, the boycott of Japanese goods, [and] the May Fourth Movement. Beginning with the May Fourth Movement, various kinds of student movements have been in the anti-imperialist tradition. The what-you-call-it, the people's vanguard corps, were the first. They were the first to become steeled during the long period of struggle against imperialism, bureaucratic capitalism, and feudalism. The people have learned [from this]; the intellectuals, too, have learned [from this]; the self-education of intellectuals is none other than self-transformation. But Hungary doesn't have this. The second [reason] is our virtual elimination of counterrevolutionaries; naturally there are other reasons, as well. For example, [our] economic measures, our policy towards the national bourgeoisie: [the policy of] uniting with the national bourgeoisie, uniting with the democratic parties. Now in our universities, what is the composition of the student body? Even now 80 percent are the sons and daughters of landlords, rich peasants, and capitalists. But Hungary's university students are 60 percent the sons and daughters of workers and peasants. The sons and daughters of the workers and peasants are big on going on strike, big on demonstrating, listening to the orders of the "Petöfi Circle."[16] Our [200] sons and daughters of landlords, rich peasants, and capitalists—we don't have a "Petöfi Circle," naturally—love their country. Except for a very few who mouth strange words, complain, and advocate big democracy, advocate killing people, the great major-

---

[16]This writers' organization, named after a 19th century revolutionary poet who became a symbol of Hungarian nationalism, played a leading role in demanding democratic reforms in the months leading up to the Hungarian revolt; see Lasky, pp. 21, 47. Mao became quite obsessive about the Petöfi Circle syndrome.

ity are patriots, [who] approve of socialism, [and] want to make China into a great nation; [and because they] have this kind of ideal, we are better off than Hungary. Comparatively speaking, our elimination of counterrevolutionaries was not as leftist as the Soviet Union's, and not as rightist as Hungary's. Our policy is, Purge counterrevolutionaries, correct errors; if there are counterrevolutionaries, they must be eliminated; if there are mistakes, they must be corrected!

Have there been excesses? Yes. Have there been omissions? Again, yes. Excesses and omissions both exist. The line we pursued relied on the masses to purge counterrevolutionaries. This line naturally has its defects, but in the main it is better . . . the masses have gained experience, in the midst of struggle the masses have gained experience. [If] a mistake is made, the masses gain the experience of making a mistake; it is known as making a mistake; [if] things get done right, [then the masses] gain the experience of getting things done right. We hope that these mistakes in the work of eliminating counterrevolution will be corrected. The Communist Party Central Committee has already adopted measures to rectify these defects. We propose that this year and next year (if possible these two years; if it is done well, then it can be completed this year) to carry out a great investigation, an overall investigation, a summing up of experience. [In the case of investigations in] central [organizations], the standing committee of the National People's Congress and the Chinese People's Political Consultative Congress will take charge [*zhuchi*]; [in] the localities the standing committees of provincial and municipal People's Congresses and Political Consultative Congresses will take charge. Individual investigation may not be effective, [where we wait for] someone to write a letter saying he has a problem and then make an investigation. Our current goal is, first, not to pour cold water on [cadres]; [and], second, to help them. To throw cold water on the majority of cadres is not good. [If one says,] "[You're] all wrong," "It was you who did things wrong," the result will be that no cadre will dare to raise his head. First, don't pour cold water. Second, whenever a mistake occurs, it certainly must be corrected, that mistake must be corrected. This includes [mistakes in the work of] the Ministry of Public Security and the Ministry of Supervision.[17] Also the departments in

---

[17]The latter ministry was formed in 1954 from the People's Supervision Committee. It was abolished in 1959 with no indication that its functions were being assumed by a new body.

charge of remolding through labor have numerous defects.[18] The standing committee of the National People's Congress and the standing committee of the CPPCC are to be charged [with the conduct of the investigations]; moreover, we hope members of these standing committees, the National People's Congress representatives, and CPPCC committee members, can also join in; specifically, all who can manage it can join in the investigation and make a comprehensive investigation. This will help our legal work. In local regions there are regional People's Congress representatives and [201] Political Consultative Congress committee members to join in.

There are still counterrevolutionaries, but not many. These are two sentences expressing two things. Firstly there are still counterrevolutionaries. Some people say there aren't, the world is already peaceful and tranquil. We can stack the pillows high, high.[19] This does not accord with reality. On the globe there is a China, China has a Beijing, Beijing has an Institute of Aeronautics, the Institute of Aeronautics has a Communist party branch in it, the Communist party branch has a deputy secretary—what is this man called? We ought to let this man's name be known (off stage [somebody yelled]: Ma Yunfeng). Ma Yunfeng wrote a slogan: It said, "Oppose the Soviet Union sending troops into Hungary." Not only did he, a branch deputy secretary, not consult with the party committee, he [also] secretly wrote numerous posters, [and] pasted them up everywhere. In reality this Communist party member was approving a counterrevolutionary insurrection, approving Western nations going in to "assist" Hungary. Therefore we must affirm, there are still counterrevolutionaries. Excesses and omissions both exist. A person like him is not necessarily counterrevolutionary, [although] he has reactionary thoughts; later this man was expelled from the party. But he was still kept there [at the Aeronautical Institute] to study. Even though he has reactionary

---

See Klein and Clark 2, p. 1113. Its abolition may have reflected the generally tougher handling of political crimes after the Anti-Rightist Campaign.

[18]Mao uses "remolding through labor" twice. Possibly he meant to specify both "remolding through labor" (lao gai) and "rehabilitation through labor" (lao jiao). For the difference between these punishments, see Jerome Alan Cohen, The Criminal Process in the People's Republic of China, 1949–1963: An Introduction (Cambridge, Harvard Univ. Press, 1968), pp. 258, 260.

[19]This refers to the Chinese idiom, gao zhen wu you ("to sleep on high pillows without anxiety," "free from cares") originating in the Zhan Guo Ce (Stories of the warring states).

behavior, to say he is a man sent over by Chiang Kai-shek or some such is not right. [We have] discovered many reactionary posters, in Beijing's schools. Factories and schools both have them. Therefore "the theory of the nonexistence of counterrevolution," or the idea that all under heaven is at peace, this idea is wrong. Secondly: but not many [counterrevolutionaries exist]. That is, counterrevolutionaries are very few. These two aspects must both be affirmed. If [you] say there are still many counterrevolutionaries now, this opinion is incorrect; the result of it will be to cause chaos. When I say [from] ten fingers, take away nine, [and] at least one is left over, it doesn't mean there are still 10 percent counterrevolutionaries.[20] It could be [that there are] only 1 percent counterrevolutionaries; [if] there are 100 counterrevolutionaries, it could be only 0.1 percent; in sum, not many.

Should there be a general amnesty? A general amnesty involves many problems. [Some] friends are interested [in this]. I am in general not a supporter of this [idea]; [I am] a negative element. (Laughter) So it is hard to avoid a tiny bit of friction with a few friends. A general amnesty should never be granted. The constitution stipulates [this]. Since you serve as Chairman, how could you not abide by the constitution? I say, there is no need to use this term. In fact, a general amnesty is possible; but there is no need to use the term, general amnesty, [in which case] all counterrevolutionaries must be released at once. [202] If there is a general amnesty, then it must include Kang Ze, Wang Yaowu, the Xuantong Emperor [Pu Yi], Du Yuming.[21] [If] these men are all to be released, the common

[20]The nine fingers/one finger formula was one of Mao's favorite devices for minimizing problems. Here he clearly feels the need to elaborate in order to prevent hard-liners from taking him literally.
[21]For Kang Ze, see n. 4 above. Wang Yaowu was an ineffective Nationalist general whose half-hearted leadership as governor of Shandong contributed greatly to the loss of that province to communist forces in 1948. See Jacques Guillermaz, *A History of the Chinese Communist Party, 1921–1949* (London, Methuen, 1972), p. 403; Lloyd E. Eastman, *Seeds of Destruction* (Stanford, Stanford Univ. Press, 1984), pp. 163, n. 14, 261–2. Pu Yi was the last emperor of the Qing dynasty, whose abdication in February 1912 brought the imperial era to a close. In 1934, he became "emperor" of the Japanese puppet state of Manchukuo (Manchuria). After World War II, he was imprisoned by the Russians and in 1950 handed over to the new Chinese Communist government. After ten years of imprisonment (labor remolding) as a war criminal (toward the end of which he was frequently offered for interview to foreign visitors as an example of the regime's magnanimity), he was pardoned at the end of 1959. He became a member of the National Committee of the CPPCC and wrote

people will surely oppose it. Even now, criminals undergoing remolding through labor are saying, "You have pardoned all the big counterrevolutionaries, why haven't you pardoned me?" The criminals all
speak this way. [If there is an amnesty] the courts will have no work
to do, the procuratorial organs, too, will not be needed, because even
Kang Ze can be pardoned! Some people say, "Even Taiwan can be pardoned, even Chiang Kai-shek can be pardoned, so why can't people
like Kang Ze be pardoned?" Who pardoned Chiang Kai-shek? There
is no pardon for him, the National People's Congress has not decided
to pardon Chiang Kai-shek! [What] we really did was to propose to
Chiang Kai-shek, If you rise in revolt, you will become in insurrec-
tionary general, [and] then [you] will have [earned] the right to receive a pardon. You people on the Taiwan side must revolt. Now we
don't say bandit Chiang, [or] "Bandit clique of Chiang Kai-shek," but
he is different: Daily [he] calls us "communist bandits," [and] he's not
polite to the democratic personages, either, calling them "traitors,"
for example "Traitor Zhang Zhizhong"[22] and such like are published
in the newspapers.

So we can't release [people]. Does that mean we can never release
[them]? Of course not. I think, [they] should be released slowly.
Secretly release one, openly release another; today release one, tomorrow release another. In any event, we don't put it in the papers nor

his autobiography: Aisin-Gioro Pu Yi, *From Emperor to Citizen*, 2 vols. (Peking, Foreign
Languages Press, 1964, 1965). His life was recently depicted in the award-winning Berto-
lucci film, *The Last Emperor*. Du Yuming, one of Chiang Kai-shek's favorite generals, was
captured while trying to escape from the battleground in Jan. 1949 after surrendering the
Nationalist rearguard to the Communists in the Huai-Hai campaign. See *BDRC* 4, pp.
326–8; and J. A. Fyfield, *Re-educating Chinese Anti-Communists* (New York, St. Martin's
Press, 1982), pp. 13–7. This latter volume also has a chapter (pp. 56–66) on Fushan prison
where Pu Yi was held. Wang, Pu Yi, and Du were all pardoned along with many others at
the same time (Pu Yi, p. 477).

[22]Zhang Zhizhong, a leading Nationalist general, was close enough to Chiang Kai-shek to
be entrusted by him with negotiating with Zhou Enlai in the abortive talks at the end of
World War II. In early 1949, he led a mission to negotiate peace in the civil war; but when
the Communist terms were rejected by acting president Li Zongren, Zhang bowed to the inevitable, stayed on in Beiping (as it was then called), and later helped the Communists take
over his former bailiwick, the Northwest. At the time of Mao's speech in 1957, he was a
member of the standing committees of the NPC and the CPPCC, and the holder of the
PRC's Order of Liberation, First Class. Zhang's autobiography, *Wo yu gongchan dang* (The
Communist party and I) (Beijing, Wenshi ziliao) appeared in 1980. See also *BDRC* 1, pp.
41–6.

[do we] send down a directive. [The release of] a small number of famous names will be considered in the future. For example, how should one handle the Xuantong emperor? He is the emperor, my direct superior. (Laughter) People over the age of forty or fifty are all his subordinates, all his people; but this Xuantong emperor has also offended the people. In the future he can be released, but now he can't be released. At present there still can't be any general amnesty. A pardon is of no benefit to him; [it] is of no benefit to Kang Ze, either, nor to Du Yuming. The people will not [understand the release of these men]. We can invite them out for a visit to see the Gate of Heavenly Peace, the big Wuhan bridge, the factories and the villages. The Xuantong emperor has [been out and] seen things and Kang Ze, too.[23] Study, education, read the papers, research. We can think about whether it's possible to find a bit of work to give them to do. [One can] even give them a little work inside prison. Gradually release those few criminals who have reasonably thoroughly repented. Those who have repented reasonably thoroughly, the ones whose crimes were not serious, gradually release them. Release [them] in this manner from now on; don't print it in the papers, because this is a problem concerning the people; [otherwise] the peasants will grab their poles and the workers will grab their iron bars **[203]** and attack; we won't be able to stand it, our hands lacking the strength to truss a chicken. This is the second question.

SOCIALIST TRANSFORMATION

Third is the question of socialist transformation. [I] will discuss just a few points; one question is collectivization.[24] Since the second half of last year, after the high tide of the first half of the year, people have coolly reflected, and a few questions have emerged. In the first half of the year the superiority [of the APCs] was immense, by the second half of the year the superiority of the APCs became very small; a

---

[23]Pu Yi was permitted a three-day inspection visit in Fushan early in 1956 and another longer one, again in the Northeast, in the second half of 1957; see Pu Yi, vol. 2, pp. 408–16, 444–53. The justification for pardoning him and Nationalist generals in 1959 was magnanimity on the occasion of the PRC's 10th anniversary; ibid., pp. 466–7.

[24]The term is actually cooperativization (*hezuohua*), for Chinese collective farms were called Agricultural Producers' Cooperatives (APC). For the significance of the collectivist high tide of 1955–6, see *Origins* 1, p. 15 ff.

wind arose, not a typhoon, but a breeze which carried the message, Collectivization won't work! Among the documents distributed today, one concerns the Wang Guofan APC; please look at it.[25] Here [we] lack a bad, a bad model. In the future [we] should search for a few [different] types of models; [here] is a good model, it is the best model of arduous struggle. APCs must certainly be established through arduous struggle; every undertaking has difficulties, [and] the growth of newly emerging things [xinsheng shiwu][26] must proceed through twists and turns, must undergo criticism. People are not accustomed to collective life; collective life is an unaccustomed thing to people, especially well-to-do middle peasants. Well-to-do middle peasants are the most unaccustomed. Who are the people who support APCs? The poor peasants and the lower middle peasants. Who are the people dissatisfied with collectivization? In addition to the landlords and rich peasants, it is the well-to-do middle peasants. Those who are very dissatisfied with cooperatives are only about 1 percent of the entire peasantry in some places, in some places [they] are 2 percent, in some places 3 percent, in some places 5 percent, [but] in all it is only a few percent. Because in the first few years when a well-to-do middle peasant is in a cooperative it does not live up to his expectations, it's worse than when he worked on his own, because he can't hire laborers! He can no longer hire labor, neither long-term nor short-term hands! So, how long will it take for the APCs to be consolidated? The great majority of APCs in existence throughout the country have a history of only one year, just last year, [plus] the winter of the year before. In a history of only a bit more than a year, how can we demand that they be perfect? This just won't do. Only gradually can they be consolidated. Probably five years will be needed; last year was one year, [so] four more years beginning with this year. For example, the Wang Guofan cooperative has been in existence for five years. This cooperative which is in Zunhua county, Hebei province, near the Great Wall and Rehe, is com-

[25]The Wang Guofan or "paupers" APC was one of Mao's favorite examples for showing what could be done with determination and hard work. The document distributed at this meeting was probably an updated version of the chapter in *Socialist Upsurge in China's Countryside* (Peking, Foreign Languages Press, 1957), pp. 11–6. The Chinese edition of this book, which Mao edited personally, appeared in January 1956.
[26]This term was often used approvingly by Mao's propagandists, such as Yao Wenyuan, in the Cultural Revolution, and earlier in the 1964 attacks on Zhao Shuli.

pletely consolidated.[27] Have there been changes for the better in the lives of the peasants? There have been changes for the better. In the past seven years, starting from 1950, in the past seven years grain [production] has increased by [204] 140 billion catties of grain; in 1949 there were only 220 billion catties of grain. The output of grain nationwide by the peasants increased by 140 billion in the past seven years. At present we have 360 billion catties of grain; last year we had 369 billion catties of grain.[28] So the life of the peasants has changed considerably for the better. To say that the life of the peasants has not changed for the better does not accord with the facts. For some peasants, life has not changed for the better; households lacking grain are probably around 10 percent, in some areas 15 percent, in some areas a few percent. I think it will take three or four years for the households lacking grain gradually to disappear. Didn't we say the consolidation of the APCs would take five years? After five years, households lacking grain will have disappeared. Later, the state monopoly for purchasing and marketing [of grain] will become a monopoly only for purchasing and not marketing, [and] we will no longer sell grain to the peasants. We are prepared in the next few years not to increase the amount of our purchases of grain, [that is] to increase production [but] not purchases. How much grain is in the hands of the peasants now? 360 billion catties. The small part [of production] that the state collected as land tax was nothing but a tiny portion; the largest portion was paid for, was obtained through purchases. Taxes and purchases, the land tax and grain purchases together, added up last year to 80.2 billion catties. Of the 320 billion catties [sic], the state had in its hands 80.2 billion catties. How much [of that] did the state sell in the villages? In the entire nation [to the] households lacking grain and peasants in disaster areas—for instance, peasants who grow cotton—[we] sold only 39 billion [to] 40 billion catties; the [remainder of] 80 billion catties [went to] cities and exports.

[27]Zunhua county is some 95 miles East North East of Beijing. "Rehe" was the old province in that area (now divided between Liaoning and Hebei provinces), a name which would have been familiar to Mao's generation of Chinese, who would have composed the bulk of his audience.
[28]A *jin* or cattie is approximately one pound or half a kilo in weight. Thus, 140 billion catties would be about 70 million tons, 369 billion catties about 185 million tons. Mao is clearly hazy about the precise 1956 output which was officially estimated at 365 billion catties; see *Ten Great Years* (Peking, Foreign Languages Press, 1960), p. 119.

Exports were only 3.8 billion catties, [or] 4 billion catties; the total of grain consumed or stored by urban people was only 40 billion catties or a little more. In the next two or three years, if only this much grain is levied, then the peasants will all become prosperous; they will be able to raise more pigs, raise more draught animals; the peasants will be able to put a part [of the grain] in reserves. Thus, to say the life of the peasants has not changed for the better, to complain of the hardship of the peasants, [saying that] the bitter cries of the peasants [can be heard] everywhere, is incorrect, it's impossible. We have a few cadres who also cry out [about this hardship]. Some of them in reality represent the well-to-do middle peasants. Because [when] these cadres have a little money, they send some home, a little this year, a little next year, within a few years their families will get rich and become well-to-do middle peasants. Well-to-do middle peasants complain the most, [and this] influences our cadres; democratic personages are influenced by them, too, and they probably have relatives and friends among these people. This deserves analysis. [Among] democratic personages, Communist party [members], and non-party [members], there are some who've joined [with the well-to-do middle peasants] in crying out that APCs are not **[205]** superior. I think [APCs] are still superior. If you don't believe it, take a look at the Wang Guofan cooperative. Why haven't Hungary and Poland made collectivization work? In Poland only 6 percent of the peasant population joined collectives. A gust of wind blew away most of them. One speech by Gomulka toppled them. Of over ten thousand collectives, only a few more than a thousand survived, 90 percent were blown away. There are many reasons why in our country so quick a collectivization was possible: First, the most basic reason is the lack of land and the large population. [So] terribly large [is the population that] everyone has very little land, [and] combining [it] is better. Second, are the steps taken by our party and People's Government. Because [we] did it step by step, in several steps, our process of collectivization was different from the Soviet Union's. For several years their collectivization instead of increasing production kept bringing it down. Our collectivization increased production; for example, last year we increased production by 2 billion catties. Aside from the complaints of well-to-do middle peasants, which have influenced comrades inside and outside of the party, there is still a partial reason [for legitimate complaint] and that is peasants are truly [suffering] bitterness, namely the few percent of households lacking grain which I just mentioned. There is yet another [reason for complaint] and that is the comparison of town and country. Wages in the urban areas are relatively higher. Currently the average annual income of peasants is 60 yuan; there are some above 60 yuan, there are some below 60 yuan, for example 50 yuan, 40 yuan [which] are still acceptable, [but] 30 yuan is not enough; still there are [annual incomes of] 20 yuan [or] 17 yuan. [For] a family of four [if each member gets only] 17 yuan, 4 times 7 give 28, [it] will have to live on 68 yuan for an entire year.[29] [This] is the most bitter case, but there are instances [of annual income] which could be as high as 100 yuan and more. Are there cases of [earning] more than 200 yuan? There are cases of [earning] 200 yuan and more. There are [even] cases of one man [getting] 1,000 yuan, so a household of four will get 4,000 yuan. After a few years, you will see, the peasants will become richer than the workers. Workers, you see, except for some unskilled labor and temporary work for which wages are inappropriate, [get] 80 yuan a month as soon as they come to the city. Some of these wages are inappropriate. Compare this with the peasants, and, the peasants get upset. But the city and the countryside are two kinds of life. For example, in the countryside if every person has 50 or 60 yuan in cash, in a year a household [of four] will have 240 renminbi, and one can get along [nicely] on that. In one area [individual income] has been calculated at 48 yuan in cash, each person with an income of 48 yuan; a household with four people each [earning] 48 yuan, would lead a very good life. In the rural villages there are lots of things that one doesn't have to buy with cash, while in the city, everything requires money. Thus, they are two [different] situations, [and] **[206]** to confuse these two situations is inappropriate.

TRANSFORMATION OF CAPITALISM

Fourthly, concerning the transformation[30] of capitalism. I haven't researched [this], but my nose has smelled out something, so [I'll] say

[29]Here Mao first multiplies the units column of 4 × 17 (i.e., 4 × 7 = 28) and in the next phrase gives the full product, 68.
[30]In the following passage, we have translated the Chinese term *gaizao* by either "transformation" or "remold" according to what seems the more appropriate English term.

a few words here. In the area of the transformation of capitalism there is also a small wind; once again it's "A breeze about to rise blows ripples over a pool of spring water." What it says is that capitalists need not be remolded, [that they] are more or less like the workers, even to the point of saying that the capitalists are a bit wiser than the workers. There are some people who talk like this; naturally it is possibly [only] a small number of people who have this type of thought: "If transformation is needed, why does the working class not remold?" Who says the working class doesn't need to remold? The working class needs to remold. In the course of class struggle the working class not only transforms society but also itself. This is what Engels said. In the course of class struggle the working class not only remolds other people, [it] also remolds itself. Moreover, if the proletariat does not liberate the whole of humanity, then they themselves cannot be liberated. They [the proletariat] make overall plans taking all factors into consideration [*tongchou jiangu*]; this is a strategic objective. Speaking of our China, if the population of 600 million is not liberated, well, then, the working class itself cannot be liberated. Thus, in the course of class struggle all are remolded, for example, we who are present here [today]; every year we make some progress, [and] this is also one type of transformation. I myself originally was an intellectual, had all kinds of thought. Mr. Shirob Jaltso,[31] [following] your Buddhism we prayed to bodhisattvas; once I also made a pilgrimage to the Southern Peak,[32] to fulfill my mother's promise; I believed in anarchism. Hey! That anarchism is great; [I] also believed in the Idealism of Kant. You see what a complicated man I am. Only later did Marxism really penetrate me, change my mind; we call this remolding which is achieved mainly in the course of class struggle. During past decades have the capitalists been so wise that they don't have to remold even a little bit? I don't think so. Even I need to remold [myself.] Don't you need to remold [yourselves]? (Laughter) Do you not have a two-sided character? [Do you really] have only a one-dimensional character? That is a metaphysical view-

[31]Shirob Jaltso was a Tibetan Living Buddha and chairman of the Chinese Buddhist Association. As a major non-communist "personage" and a member of both the NPC and the CPPCC, he was an obvious invitee for a session of the Supreme State Conference. For more details about him, see Klein and Clark 2, pp. 766–8.

[32]Hengshan, which Mao calls by its alternative name, Nanyue shan, is one of the five sacred peaks in China, in Hunan not far from Mao's home village.

point. With only a one-dimensional character, analysis of material things is impossible. There are always weak points. The theory of the two aspects.[33] Strong points, weak points. Moreover, the roots of the capitalist class have not been severed; the capitalist class has not yet removed [its] cap; it still requires a period of thought remolding [before] the cap can be removed. If the theory [advocating] the abolition [of remolding] wins, then the capitalist class will have no more responsibility to study. [But] now all of us study! Even government people [207] are studying! [If] on the other hand, the capitalist class doesn't need to study, then it is unnecessary to have those short term training institutes. This does not conform with the wishes of the majority of industrialists and merchants. They are willing to study. Study for forty days and return to the factory [and] things take on an entirely new look; there is [now] a common language.[34] Private and public representatives previously were like square pegs in round holes—you are a capitalist, I am a public representative, both people are very polite, seemingly in harmony but actually at odds, on the same bed but dreaming different dreams. Now are you considered a capitalist or am I a capitalist? Am I [really] considered a capitalist? Since I came back from the forty-day training course, [we] have had a common language. Some people become afraid as soon as they hear the word remolding. We have such people. This thing, remolding, the Americans call it brainwashing. We call [it] remolding. I think the Americans are the real brainwashers, Americans can really do a good job of washing [brains]. We here are a bit more civilized. According to this kind of discussion [i.e., that remolding is unnecessary], the constitution will need to be changed; for in the constitution it says the alliance between workers and peasants which is led by the working class is the basis of the people's democratic dictatorship, [but in this view] they are all the same. Not only are the workers the same as the peasants, [they] are moreover the same as the capitalists. Thus, the leadership of the proletariat will be abolished. I have just now made clear that this is not the opinion of most people. It is what a few people say.

[33] *Liangdian lun.*

[34] After the incorporation of all private enterprise into the state sector in early 1956, businessmen were sent on ideological courses to ensure that their thinking was in tune with the new era; see Robert Loh and Humphrey Evans, *Escape from Red China* (London, Michael Joseph, 1963), pp. 158–66.

INTELLECTUALS AND STUDENT YOUTH

Fifth, the question of intellectuals and student youth. We said earlier that our 600 million people have made great progress; the national bourgeoisie has made great progress; the workers have progressed; the peasants have made great progress; the intellectuals and student youth, as well, have made great progress, but [they] also have incorrect thought, evil winds, too; [there] have been some disturbances. Since the occurrence of the Hungarian incident there have been some strange discussions. As I have already said, disgust with Marxism, only wanting to perfect one's professional capabilities, talking about the future [in terms of] earning one's salary, which is simply in order to eat; in addition to this there is also taking a wife, taking a husband. In general [they] live for these two things: one, to eat; the other, to have children. As to any politics, any future or ideals, that's not important. It seems as if this Marxism was popular for a while, [but] from the latter half of last year it has become less fashionable! Since weak points do exist, [we] must strengthen ideological work, strengthen political work. Among our youth, among the intellectuals, self-remolding needs to be furthered; [we] still need to bring up [the question of] remolding, [we] should not avoid this [question of] remolding. In the past such **[208]** thought remolding was a bit rough, in some cases people got hurt. Now [we] don't want to carry out that kind of remolding. Study diligently; aside from [making progress in one's] specialty, make progress ideologically, progress also politically, study a bit of Marxism, study a bit of current affairs, study a bit of politics; these things are very necessary. If [you] don't have these things, then [you] won't have a soul. [It is maintained by some that] if [you] study only that single specialty, [you'll] never run out of [food] to eat. No political work, don't do political work. Recently political and ideological work have weakened, the education departments do not supervise political work. If the education departments do not supervise it, who will? The Ministry of Higher Education should supervise political work. I think the Communist party should supervise [it], the Youth League should supervise [it], the administrative departments should supervise political [work]. What used to be moral education, intellectual education, [and] physical education, we have now changed to two educations. Intellectual education is devoted to intellectual education; beyond that add a little gymnastics, that's called physical education. Moral education is discarded. So-called moral education is to study a bit of Marxism, to study a bit of politics, to study a bit of this sort of thing.

INCREASING PRODUCTION AND PRACTICING ECONOMY

Sixth, increase production and practice economy and oppose extravagance and waste. [You say,] Yet again! Haven't we put it right [already]? Now once again [we] oppose extravagance and waste. All the Communist party [does] is this stuff; moreover, [they've] figured out that the Communist party after all can only do this stuff, after a few months there'll be no problem [i.e., it will pass]! Now we have this kind of talk, is this true or not? I think it is partially true. The one time of genuine opposition [to extravagance and waste] was the Three-Antis.[35] During the Three-Antis extravagance and waste, [and] corruption and degeneration were combatted, [but] the fight didn't continue after that. One year the practice of economy was championed, but what was being economized? That was economizing on non-productive basic construction, lowering standards; in the year before last it saved over 2 billion [yuan], a lot of cash. But in some areas the economization was inappropriate, with the result that the engineering projects were no good; [it was] excessive economizing. In addition, the economizing in the area of materials for production went so far as to lower quality; that is, the quality of basic construction was lowered [and] the quality of production [in general] was lowered. These were the shortcomings of that time; but the accomplishment was great: over 2 billion [yuan] was saved. Other [work units] generally did not economize; [government] offices, schools, factories, cooperatives, commercial systems, and transportation systems all did not institute [economizing]. Now we want to champion economizing; now we want to launch a nationwide movement to increase production and practice economy [and] to oppose

[35]The "Three-Antis," or *sanfan* campaign was launched in August 1951 against corruption, waste, and bureaucratism within official ranks. From January 1952, it was merged into a "Five-Antis" (*wufan*) campaign against bribery, tax evasion, stealing of state property, cheating on government contracts, and stealing state economic intelligence, mainly on the part of businessmen; see A. Doak Barnett, *Communist China: The Early Years, 1949–55* (New York, Praeger, 1964), pp. 131–71.

extravagance and waste. In this way, as we put it into effect now, tables, chairs and benches [i.e., office furniture] are not bought any more; carpets—nobody wants 'em. I've got some carpets **[209]** for sale, are there any customers here at the meeting? I think if you [the customers] don't want them, then there's nothing I can do. Everybody champions the increase of production and the practice of economy; I've got loads of carpets—[it's] scandalous. Now opposition to [extravagance and waste] applies to me! This time [the opposition to extravagance and waste] could be implemented a bit more thoroughly. If it's not completed this year, do it again next year. I'll make an analogy; it's like washing your face. How does each of you wash your face, do you wash it once a week? (Laughter) Most of the folks I know wash their face once a day, at least. Some wash it several times a day. For what reason? Why wash the same face day after day; what are they up to? Does it increase production or [improve] the practice of economy? It's for nothing more than making one's face look a little better, making your honorable visage a bit better. Washing your face once a day, no matter if it's communist or non-communist everybody does it! It's not because the communists champion face washing that one does it; ever since ancient times [we've been] washing our faces! The current opposition to extravagance and waste, this thing is equivalent to washing your face. People indeed regularly want to wash their face. People are not [like] other animals; other animals do not wash. People are superior animals, so they want to wash their face. Our party, various political parties among the democratic parties, democratic figures without party [affiliation], intellectuals, industrialists and merchants, the working class, peasants, artisans—a population of 600 million. Let's champion the practice of economy. Now it's not being done to standard, [because] for many people no more has developed than the thought of winning a promotion and getting rich. Last year's grading [of cadres] created a problem. The grading served nothing more than a scramble for fame and profit.[36] Vie for a name at court, scramble for profit in the market.[37]

[36]For a brief description of the regime's regularization of the system of cadre grades in 1956, see A. Doak Barnett, *Cadres, Bureaucracy, and Political Power in Communist China* (New York, Columbia Univ. Press, 1967), pp. 41–3.
[37]Mao uses a common saying here, *zheng ming yu chao, duo li yu shi*.

OVERALL CONSIDERATION AND
PROPER ARRANGEMENTS

Seventh, unified planning with due consideration for all concerned [and] appropriate arrangements.[38] This is a strategic policy. The so-called unified planning with due consideration for all concerned is [aimed at] the population of 600 million. All the comrades [present] are responsible comrades, taking responsibility for the nation. Our plans, work, [and] thinking all should start from the [awareness] that we have a population of 600 million. Our nation which has such a large population, this is something other nations in the world do not have; ours has so many people, a population of 600 million. Here [we] need birth control; it would be great [if we] could lower the birth [rate] a bit. [We] need planned births. I think humanity is most inept at managing itself. It has plans for industrial production, the production of textiles, the production of household goods, the production of steel; [but] it does not have plans for the production of humans. This is anarchism, no government, no organization, no rules. (Loud laughter) If [we] go on this way, I **[210]** think humanity will prematurely fall into strife and hasten toward destruction. If China's population of 600 million increases tenfold, what will that be? Six billion: at that time [we] will be near destruction. There'll be nothing to eat; and with advances in hygiene, sanitation, inoculations, the babies will be so many that it will be disastrous, with everyone being of venerable age and eminent virtue. (Loud laughter) I won't dwell on birth control today, because our own Mr. Shao Lizi is a famous specialist! (Loud laughter) He is a graduate of university training.[39] (Laughter) He's brighter than I am. There's also Minister Li

---

[38]The shorter heading above is from the official version of this speech; see *SW5*, p. 407. This expanded wording is more self-explanatory.

[39]Shao Lizi (1881–1967) passed the imperial examination for the *juren* degree in 1903, graduated from Fudan University in 1907, and subsequently studied journalism in Japan. His level of education under the old and new systems was thus higher than Mao's. But as in all his dealings with intellectuals, the Chairman's mock humility here is two-edged; in effect he is saying—"You may be more learned, but I have the power."

Shao was an early supporter of Sun Yat-sen, and later served the Nationalist government as Governor of Shaanxi (1933–6) and ambassador to the Soviet Union (1940–1). After 1949, as a leading non-communist working with the new regime, Shao became a senior member of the NPC and the CPPCC and thus a regular participant at Supreme State Conferences. Shao had been the first prominent Chinese publicly to advocate birth control,

Dequan.[40] [She] also pays great attention [to the subject]: Perhaps this government should establish a department, establish a planned birth department—would that be a good idea? (Loud laughter) Or how about establishing a committee, a birth control committee, to serve as a government organ, [or we could] organize a people's group? Organize people's groups to advocate [birth control]. Since [we] need to solve a few technical problems, [we will have to] provide funds, think up methods, propagandize. Now I won't talk about this much; what [I want] to talk about is still strategic policy. For example, a few affairs of our own. Disaster relief. Every year throughout the country there are disasters, there are many disaster victims. [We] should give them grain, as in unified [state] marketing [tongxiao]. The Soviet Union has never done this. Every city and village, including households without grain and households lacking grain, we take them all into consideration. For example, [we] arrange jobs in industry and commerce, [we] arrange work for the unemployed, [our] unified [state] purchasing, [our] unified planning in various areas—all these are unified planning with due consideration for all concerned and appropriate arrangements. Last year alone over 3 million people were employed. There were hassles and major problems. According to the plan, the original plan was [for] 800,000 [to be employed]; but in fact the increase ran to about 3 million people, an excess of over 2 million, so the wages paid out were greater. Not only have those 800,000 people [seen their wages] increase, [but] the wages for the original 18 million people have more or less increased; the new increase [in employment] last year was about 3 million [people]. That's a very heavy burden. But has unemployment been totally eradicated? Not yet. For example, Guangzhou still has quite a number of unemployed;

---

shortly after the completion of the report on the 1953 census; see Leo A. Orleans, *Every Fifth Child* (London, Eyre Methuen, 1972), p. 39. He was criticized then; but as top-level backing for the proposal developed, he spoke up again. The "loud laughter" that greeted Mao's mention of his name here was probably occasioned by Shao's insistence that even old wives' remedies, such as the swallowing of tadpoles, should be investigated; see William Stevenson, *The Yellow Wind* (London, Casell, 1959), pp. 315–6. In fact, an unsuccessful experiment with the tadpole method of contraception was carried out later in 1957.

[40]Li Dequan, the widow of the warlord Feng Yuxiang (known as the "Christian general"), served as Minister of Health from 1949 to 1965; see Klein and Clark 1, pp. 531–4. Her ministry spearheaded the birth control campaign in 1956–7 and set up a research committee on the subject; Orleans, pp. 39–40.

they say [they] must think of [various] ways [to deal] with the problem]; every case can't be treated the same. Shanghai, too, has some unemployed; other areas still have some—some more, some less. But the unemployed have already decreased. Some people suggest letting five people eat the food of three people. This method is worth considering. [We'd] rather lower salaries a bit; for instance, we have not talked about raising our salaries for ten or eight years. As I bring this up, perhaps **[211]** most of you will oppose, or perhaps you will approve. If salaries are not raised for ten years, [if] high officials' salaries are not raised for ten years, I don't think it will kill anyone, it can't kill! With not killing people as the principle, one's age can be venerable, one's virtue can be eminent. Why eminent virtue? Isn't not raising salaries virtuous? (Sounds of laughter) When [salaries] are raised again, let the lower levels be raised a bit.

What to do about the student problem? Of school-age kids, 40 percent have no school [in] this the People's Government is not an omnipotent government, the People's Government cannot reach the sky in a single bound. Currently there still are 40 percent of the people who have no school to go to. In addition there is another matter: This [can be] called the 4 million. This year there are 4 million graduates from higher primary school who cannot advance to middle school, there's no way to advance to middle school, no space, no funds. Aside from those who should advance, aside from this year's plan for advancements, there are 4 million who cannot advance. Graduates from higher primary school will return to production units, including those in the rural areas. How many graduates from lower middle school cannot advance to higher middle? 400,000. How many higher middle school graduates cannot advance to university? One estimates 40,000, one 80,000, one 90,000. (Premier Zhou [says] 800,000 lower middle school [students] not 400,000) Ai! 800,000 lower middle [school students], not 400,000, an [estimate] made in the morning is superseded by evening.[41] (Sounds of laughter) Eight hundred thousand lower middle [school] students unable to advance [in their] studies, a great many of them have problems with finding employment, too. [They] must wait for employment. Eight hundred thousand is so many! There are 90,000 higher middle school students

---

[41]Either the bureaucracy had got the figures totally mixed up, or Mao misremembered and excused himself with a quip at the bureaucracy's expense.

unable to advance to university; this, too, has created an employment problem. To wait until later is one kind of arrangement. For example, buying pork. [You] wait at the end of a snaking, long line, and up front [the pork's] already sold out: Best just to go back home—after all, [the pork] couldn't be bought! This is quite a big problem, [and I] want to ask you all to think it over; the government, too, should think it over. In sum, this year's plan is for just so much money. In a word, with only so much money, only so much can be done. Let's take a break.

(15 minute recess)

BLOOMING FLOWERS AND CONTENDING SCHOOLS

Eight, I'll talk about the questions of letting a hundred flowers bloom and a hundred schools contend, and about long-term coexistence, [and] mutual supervision.[42] This is a question of contradictions among the people—didn't Lenin say so? There are contradictions among the people, contradictions remain while antagonisms within socialist society disappear. I [have] said that in Lenin's time, he would not fully investigate this question; [and still] lacking experience, he [212] died. For a long time Stalin did not admit that socialist society had contradictions, but in his later years—he died in 1953—in '52 he wrote a book called, *Economic Problems of Socialism in the USSR*.[43] In that book he recognized contradictions between the relations of production and the forces of production. If the two are handled well, contradictions will not develop into antagonistic contradictions. [If they are] not handled well, they will become antagonistic.

(Premier Zhou: He used the word "conflict" [*chongtu*], but in fact it is "antagonism" [*duikang*]).

[42]The policy "Let a hundred flowers bloom, let a hundred schools contend" was first adumbrated by Mao on 2 May 1956, as part of his attempt to encourage greater liveliness in literature and the arts ("flowers") and in academia ("schools"). The policy is discussed in the introductory articles in this volume and in *Origins* 1, pp. 5–56. The policy of "Long-term coexistence and mutual supervision," designed to chart the future relationship between the CCP and the "democratic" non-communist parties, was spelled out in Mao's speech on the "Ten great relationships" in April 1956; see *Origins* 1, pp. 48–50, 112–6.
[43]Mao's remarks here anticipate his more detailed critiques of Soviet economic thinking in subsequent years. See *Mao Tse-tung: A Critique of Soviet Economics* (New York, Monthly Review Press, 1977).

[Chairman:] That they develop into conflict, he [Stalin] had already seen this point. We have been learning from the Soviet Union for about forty years. The Chinese Communist Party [and] Marxists led the revolutionary struggle, from the creation of the base areas—[in] 1927, or ten years behind [our] Soviet comrades. They were victorious in 1917, the revolution was victorious, the revolution began to be victorious. [Whereas] we only began in 1927 to establish base areas in various places. 1927, '37, '47, '57, we also have thirty years of experience. [We] should affirm that contradictions in social-ist society exist; these are basic kinds of contradictions, namely, contradictions between the relations of production and the forces of production, [and] contradictions between the superstructure and the economic base. These contradictions all appear as contradictions among the people. Because at this time socialist society does not have exploiters, the system of ownership is that of the whole people or col-lective [ownership]; there are no private capitalists, no private land-owners, no private factory owners [or] enterprise owners. Therefore Stalin, we say that Stalin was somewhat deficient in dialectics, but [not that he] was without dialectics. In the *People's Daily* editorial we said he partially but seriously turned [his] back on dialectical mater-ialism. That's what [we] said. Under his influence a book was writ-ten, called *A Concise Dictionary of Philosophy*, written by two men.[44] Of the two, one is the Soviet Ambassador Yudin.[45] It [was written] under Stalin's influence, [and] in the context of discussing identity [*tongyixing*]—he had a topic called identity on which he rambled on and on—[he] refuted formal logical identity, [but] failed completely to analyze clearly whether formal logical identity and dialectical iden-

[44]Mao was quite upset with this dictionary and the implied criticisms of Chinese policy it contained. Through Chen Boda, Mao later asked Yang Xianzhen, head of the Central Party School, to write a rebuttal of the Soviet interpretation of "identity" (*tongyixing*), which was to devolve into the internal Chinese philosophical debates of the 1960s. See Carol Lee Ham-rin, "Yang Xianzhen: Upholding Leninist Orthodoxy," in Carol Lee Hamrin and Timothy Cheek, eds., *China's Establishment Intellectuals* (Armonk, N.Y., M. E. Sharpe, 1986), pp. 62–4.

[45]Pavel Yudin, Soviet ideologist, was at this time ambassador to China. In the early years of the PRC, Mao allegedly consulted Yudin on doctrinal points; see *Khruschev Remembers*, tr. and ed. by Strobe Talbott (Boston, Little Brown, 1970), pp. 464–5. In April 1957, Yudin departed from Soviet orthodoxy to admit that Russia like China had contradictions between leaders and led, something Khruschev later denied; see Roderick MacFarquhar, *The Hundred Flowers Campaign and the Chinese Intellectuals* (New York, Praeger, 1960), pp. 31–2, 306.

tity are the same thing or not. Then [he] quoted Engels to say, Engels said there is no such identity, in reality everything exists in change, in objective reality [213] there is no such identity. Then he brought up some metaphysics; he says things in opposition, mutually repellent opposites, cannot be said to have identity. For example, the bourgeoisie and the proletariat, these two classes in a single society, they have no identity, have only mutual rejection, have only struggle. War and peace have no identity; life and death have no identity. To say these things have identity is a mistaken concept. After Stalin died, Soviet philosophers, the Soviet Union began to change on this question. I haven't read much, but I can see they have changed. In philosophy Stalin had a rather metaphysical outlook. The so-called metaphysical outlook [means that things] have no change, war is war, the bourgeoisie is the bourgeoisie, the proletariat is the proletariat. Our theory is different: The bourgeoisie becomes the proletariat; the oppressed proletariat transforms into the proletariat which rules the nation. War turns into peace, peace turns into war, life turns into death, death turns into life. In the midst of identity, after quoting what Engels said (what Engels said had no metaphysics), he [the Soviet author] brought up a piece of metaphysics, these two things short of change cannot have unity, cannot be transformable, but Stalin in his book on economics said socialism has contradictions, between productive forces and productive relations, [and] moreover [that] if [the two] are not handled well, they can become antagonistic. This is well said; nonetheless it is not thorough. I say his dialectics are bashful dialectics, are coy dialectics, or could be called hesitant dialectics. As we look at this question now, we should recognize socialism contains contradictions; the basic contradiction is the contradiction between relations of production and productive forces. The ideologies of the superstructure (politics, law, religion, philosophy, these various ideologies) should serve the economic base; [they] should match the economic base. If [they] do not match [it], then contradictions emerge. Letting a hundred flowers bloom, letting a hundred schools contend, long-term coexistence—how did these slogans come to be put forward? It was in recognition of various different contradictions in society. In the arts and literature it is expressed in letting a hundred flowers bloom. This hundred flowers blooming includes this sort of thing, that is, various different kinds of [214] flowers; but it also includes one kind of qualitatively different flower.

For example, [we] say that among the hundred schools contending there is Idealism, [and among] the hundred flowers blooming it is possible that, although Hu Feng sits in prison, his spirit still lives in the world, writing Hu Feng kinds of works. But one requires only that he refrain from destructive acts. What was Hu Feng all about? He organized a secret group; that's not good. So long as he does not run secret groups, you [Hu Feng types] can cultivate that little flower; [since] our China's area is so big, 9 million square kilometers, what's so serious about this little flower blooming? Cultivate that little flower for everybody to see, [and] people can also criticize flowers like his, saying I don't like your flower. [We're] talking about weeds and fragrant flowers. Some are poisonous weeds. If you want only grain, want only barley, wheat, corn, rice, millet, and absolutely don't want any weeds, that's unachievable. Every year the peasants have to weed; if you don't believe it, go out at this year's spring ploughing and take a look; weeds will have grown on that land, [and] you wouldn't know where such weeds could have come from. In short, the yearly growth of weeds is just like the daily necessity of washing [your] face. Year after year the peasants must weed. To ban all weeds, not allowing their growth, is that possible? In reality it is not; they will still grow, [and] you will still have to hoe [to get rid of them], and that's that. If someone were to send down an order, [that] weeds should stop growing, that of course would simplify matters and the peasants would be ever so grateful. But in reality so many weeds compete with grain, [and] among them are poisonous weeds. A fragrant flower, a poisonous weed, I say you are, of course, a fragrant flower. But dogmatism certainly is not a fragrant flower. What kind of flower is dogmatism? Is dogmatism Marxism? Dogmatism certainly is not Marxism; dogmatism is a petty bourgeois [and] bourgeois thing. The method of dogmatism is the method of metaphysics, one-sided, isolated; to do things one-sidedly is unanalytical; metaphysics, this "learning" was present in ancient times, but [it] developed particularly during the bourgeois period, in foreign countries, and in China, too. It is difficult to distinguish fragrant flowers from poisonous weeds. Previously in the eyes of the people, many things at the time of their first appearance, many newly emerging things—in the old society seemingly all newly emerging things—were bound to be attacked. Take for example Marxism. Marxism was seen by people as a weed, [and] considered a poisonous weed. The Nationalist party [Kuomintang], the United League [Tongmeng hui], in the days of the Qing government, Sun Yat-sen was seen as **[215]** a poisonous weed! The Communist party was called the bandit party, the Communist bandits! Having dealings with the Communist party was called connections with bandits [*tong fei*]! Our meeting here today comes from poisonous weeds turning into fragrant flowers: But in Taiwan, they still call us poisonous weeds, still call [us] communist bandits. Confucius was also unrecognized. Confucius that venerable master, in his whole life did not achieve his desires, nobody took up his principles. Jesus, Jesus at first was not recognized by society. How about Buddhism, how about Sakyamuni? [He], too, went through this process, suffered oppression, a lack of social acceptance. When Christianity came to the Protestantism[46] of Martin Luther, it, too, did not have social acceptance. Monkey,[47] why was Monkey awarded [the title of] Master of the Imperial Stables [*Bimawen*]? Calling Sun Wukong Master of the Imperial Stables was simply not to recognize him. His own title, his self-assessment (cadre appraisal), he identified himself as the Great Sage of Heaven [*Qitian dasheng*]. The Jade Emperor appraised him and made him Master of the Imperial Stables, that is saying [Monkey] was a poisonous weed. Xue Rengui[48] served as an army cook, didn't Xue Rengui serve as an army cook? This is the appraisal given to him of Zhang Shigui.[49] The astronomy of Copernicus, for a long time [no one] dared publish. Only many years after [his] death, was [his theory] recognized by people. The physics of Italy's Galileo, Darwin's theory of evolution, at the start

[46]Mao is loose with his terminology here. He uses *Yesujiao*, the Chinese term for Protestant Christianity, to refer to the pre-Reformation Catholic Church; then he uses *xinjiao*, an alternative term for Protestantism, to refer to Luther's religion.

[47]Monkey, also known as Sun Wukong, is the famous fictional character from *The Journey to the West*, and a favorite metaphor in Mao's writings. See n. 6, above. *Bimawen* was an insignificant title, so Monkey took offense.

[48]Xue Rengui (614–83) was a famous and popular general in the early Tang Dynasty, whose distinguished service in campaigns in Korea saved him from execution when he was later badly defeated by the Tibetans; see C. P. Fitzgerald, *The Empress Wu* (London, Cresset, 1956), pp. 57, 71–3, 80. Xue's career was often depicted in a fictional manner; see C. T. Hsia, *The Classic Chinese Novel* (New York, Columbia Univ. Press, 1968), p. 331.

[49]Zhang Shigui was once Xue Rengui's superior officer who repeatedly claimed credit for himself for Xue's military feats, and was eventually exposed and executed. He figures in the novel, *Zheng dong quan zhuan* (Story of the Eastern Conquest) and in a number of Peking operas based on it. Zhang also appears in a similar discussion in Mao's 8 March 1957 "A talk with literary and art circles" (Text 7).

people did not accept them. I read a scientific booklet, the history of sleeping pills: who invented sleeping pills? A pharmacy clerk in Germany invented them. Germans wouldn't give [the stuff] recognition, [but] the French did. They invited him to France; later it was recognized. There was a Chinese, Li Liejun, who was a central committee member of the Nationalist party; he is dead now. The first time he went from China to *Ma-sha*[50] [phonetic rendering, i.e., Marseilles], from Marseilles riding the train to Paris, he took a sleeping pill. He said this stuff was indeed good, [it] helped people to sleep.[51] There was an American dancer, a dancer called [Isadora] Duncan. She had children, the birth of the first child was very painful, [so] for the birth of the second child she took a sleeping pill. What I am saying is that all inventions in the world [be they] political, scientific, [or] literary and artistic, in the beginning none are recognized. Sima Qian's *Historical Records* at first was not accepted by people! He could only "Hide it [in] a famous mountain, pass it on to other people"; [he] wasn't able to publish it; at that time there were no publication organs, people made copies by hand, but transporting scrolls upon scrolls was difficult. In sum, for newly born forces to be recognized by society, [they] must pass through arduous struggle.[52] Our society is a little different, **[216]** [it's a] socialist society; but there are still numerous new things that are held back. [They] run into bureaucratists, run into the diehards. After all what is to be called a fragrant flower? What is to be called a poisonous weed? Stalin in the past was 100 percent a fragrant flower; Khrushchev in one stroke turned him into a poisonous weed. Now [Stalin] is again fragrant.

Most recently there have been some criticisms. I'm talking about [what's happening within] the Communist party; in the Communist party there are also leftists and rightists. In the central Propaganda Department there is a cadre, Zhong Dianfei.[53] He wrote some articles

---

[50]The note taker has mistaken the second sound of this phonetic rendering for Marseilles and put down the wrong character.

[51]Li Liejun's biography is in *BDRC* 2, pp. 312–6. It is not clear from where Mao got this anecdote.

[52]Mao was always impressed by the role of outstanding individuals in history. In his Chengdu speeches a year later, he emphasized the youth of some of these same people when they made their contribution; see Stuart Schram, *Mao Tse-tung Unrehearsed* (Harmondsworth, Penguin, 1974), pp. 118–20.

[53]Zhong Dianfei (1919–87), an editor of *Wenyi bao* and famous film critic, was later denounced as a rightist, particularly for his article "Drums and gongs of the film circles."

under a pseudonym, saying [our] past was a complete mess; he negated everything. Now these articles have drawn criticism, sparked debate. But Taiwan really appreciates these articles. In addition, some leftists, namely the head of the Cultural Department under the Political Department of the Military Affairs Commission, Chen Yi, and his subordinates, Chen Qitong, Ma Hanbing, and a few other comrades published a declaration in the 7 January [1957] *People's Daily,* signed by the four men as authors.[54] [Its thrust] is to cast doubt on the policy of letting a hundred flowers bloom and a hundred schools contend. It maintains that ever since this policy was introduced there have been no significant works [produced]. That conclusion is a bit premature, because comrade Lu XX's[55] article was written in June and published in July of last year [1956]. August, September, October, November, December—when did these four comrades publish [their] article? It was 7 January. In only five months, how could an article of several tens of thousands of words be finished? So [they] said that there were no significant works, no significant works being produced ever since [the policy of] letting a hundred flowers bloom and a hundred schools contend was put forward, that we no longer produce Marxist works, no longer use socialism or realism, only do bad stuff. Up to now, it has been a while [since the hundred flowers policy was introduced and] what the attitude of our *People's Daily* is remains unclear to me. At the meeting of provincial and municipal secretaries in late January,[56] I had this four-man declaration copied and distributed to everyone. There were comrades from the *People's Daily* there at the time. What did they say? They expressed no

---

See *The China Quarterly* 2:70 (April –June 1960); and D. W. Fokkema, *Literary Doctrine in China and Soviet Influence, 1955–60* (The Hague, Mouton, 1965), p. 155. See below, Text 5, note 12.

[54]See Text 1, note 6. For details of these men and their article, see also Fokkema, pp. 124–7; Merle Goldman, *Literary Dissent in Communist China* (Cambridge, Harvard Univ. Press, 1967), pp. 181–2, and *Origins* 1, p. 179. In fact, Chen Qitong was the senior author of the group; perhaps Mao misremembered; more likely he wished to slight him.

[55]Clearly Lu Dingyi, the propaganda chief, but his explanation of the Hundred Flowers policy was given as a speech on 26 May 1956 and published in the *People's Daily* on 13 June; see *Communist China, 1955–1959,* pp. 151–63. Lu Dingyi's name is partially omitted because, by the time this collection was issued, he had been purged.

[56]Mao's summation of this January 1957 meeting appears in *Wansui* (1969), pp. 81–90; translated in *JPRS* 61269-1 (20 February 1974), pp. 54–62.

attitude. Now a month has passed, more or less. What should be done? Did you publish that thing to approve or oppose it? It there anyone from the *People's Daily* here today? Sooner or later you're going to have to deal with this matter! Or you should talk it over, if you can't make up your minds; find [some] leading comrades in the [party] Center[57] and discuss it! See how to handle the situation. I will now express my attitude: I do not approve of that article, that article is wrong. But **[217]** there are many different things in this world; different people like what they like. Taiwan likes Zhong Dianfei's articles. Socialist countries like Chen Qitong's and Ma Hanbing's article. *Pravda* published it, but *Pravda* did not publish Lu XX's article, "Let a hundred flowers bloom, let a hundred schools contend." [They] liked Chen Qitong's, Ma Hanbing's—the four comrades' [article]. In addition, Czechoslovakia published [it]; Rumania published [it]; [it won] quite a market.

(Offstage someone said, The *Literary Gazette* published it, not *Pravda*)

[Chairman:] It was the *Literary Gazette*? Not *Pravda*? Then that's better.[58] (Laughter) "Birds of a feather flock together, people split into [like] groups"; different [people] like different things, like two of a kind[59] Dogmatism likes dogmatism, opportunism likes opportunism. I'm afraid I must make a criticism now. There is a young writer, Wang Meng. [He's] not called Wang Ming,[60] but probably is Wang Ming's brother. (Laughter) [He] wrote a piece titled, "Newcomer to the Organization Department"[61] which caused a furor. Some approved of it, some opposed it. Later it was believed that this [newcomer] was also a Communist party member [and the story was about] the Communist party, attacking the Communist party, [and

---

[57]The Chinese use the term 'center' (*zhongyang*) loosely. See Text 1, n. 9.

[58]Mao says "that's better" ironically, because *Literary Gazette,* though the main Soviet cultural newspaper, did not carry the official weight of the party newspaper *Pravda.*

[59]This phrase and the one in quotation marks above carried a negative connotation, certainly at the time Mao was speaking, though in recent years it has gradually lost this. The *Hanyu chengyu cidian* (Shanghai, 1978), p. 679 gives for the former: "An analogy for evil people colluding with each other." Chinese dictionaries make clear that these refer to the combination of ideological work style and personal tastes and interests.

[60]See Text 1, note 10, above.

[61]Mao has got the title of Wang Meng's short story slightly wrong. See Text 1, note 3.

the critics] said he [Wang Meng] did not have a single good point. Among these was Ma Hanbing's criticism. Others criticized, saying Beijing is the site of the [party] Center, [how can] there be bureaucratism in a district Communist party committee in Beijing? Thus the background of his [Wang Meng's] model was badly chosen, perhaps best to choose Shanghai [for the story]. This place of ours [Beijing] won't do. X X place won't do, because it is the site of the [party] Center. I could never figure out where this principle [used by the critics] came from. I haven't studied much Marxism, but I have never seen [this opinion] in it (Laughter), saying the site of the [party] Center does not produce bureaucratism? Even the [party] Center produced bureaucratism, why can't the site produce it [too]? What kind of people has the [party] Center produced? The [party] Center has produced Chen Duxiu, produced Zhang Guotao, produced Gao Gang [and] Rao Shushi; [it has] also produced Li Lisan, Wang Ming, so many![62] So this principle [that the site of the party Center does not produce bureaucratism] is a mistaken notion.

Marxism still develops; Marxism is not [something] that is finished once studied. There is still the need to continue studying, [because] circumstances change. Dogmatism is not Marxism. Dogmatism is anti-Marxist. Opportunism, too, is anti-Marxist. China with a population of 600 million is a kingdom of petty bourgeoisie; it's a mighty kingdom. [There are] 500 million peasants, over 10 million handicraft workers, [and then] shopkeepers, peddlers, landlords, rich peasants; [218] the bourgeoisie probably make up a population of 50 million, the petty bourgeoisie make up a population of 500 and some tens of millions. This is an objective reality. You want all these people not to express opinions, to have them completely gagged, only letting [the gag] off a little when they eat, and as soon as they've eaten gag them up again. How can that work? I say the mouth has two functions, one is to eat, the other to talk. It's very difficult to gag it. The bourgeoisie and petty bourgeoisie must certainly reflect their ideological consciousness; moreover, [they] must express themselves, using various methods, staunchly—in a thousand and one ways [they must] express themselves. We cannot use coercive methods to stop them

---

[62]Chen Duxiu, first general-secretary of the party, was dismissed and disgraced in 1927; see Lee Feigon, *Chen Duxiu* (Princeton: Princeton Univ. Press, 1983). For Zhang Guotao, Gao Gang, Rao Shushi, and Li Lisan, see Text 1, n. 10.

from expressing [themselves]; [we] can only debate with them at the time of their expression. [We can] say, Comrade, what you say is a bit inappropriate; [then we] make an analysis, [and] write articles of criticism. These articles [should] not be dogmatic articles, [they] cannot use metaphysical methods, but should use dialectal methods. [They] should be convincing, [they] should be fully convincing. Can senior cadres be criticized? [On] this problem of criticism, from Marx onward, never once has it been said that junior and senior cadres should be distinguished, [or] said that only junior cadres can be criticized [and] senior cadres cannot be criticized. Our constitution stipulates that people are equal before the law, so when it comes to the problem of committing errors, [or] incorrect thought, Communist party members [and] non-party members must be equal. There is a group of people—for example, senior Communist party cadres or senior cadres of the democratic parties—[simply] because they have seniority, they have the right to freedom from criticism. Is that permissible? I think that won't do. If while you are living you receive no criticism, after you are dead, people will still criticize you.⁶³ We have criticized the dead, [we have] criticized Confucius: Down with the house of Confucius!⁶⁴ Even a man who has been dead for several thousand years, [we] still criticize! Now Confucius is a bit better. Stalin was also criticized after his death! Living people can be criticized, [and] dead people can also be criticized. There [should be] no distinction between major and minor official positions, or [between] old and young, elder and junior. Isn't it true that, the older you get, the more [you] live in ease and comfort, avoiding criticism? After committing an error, one should always be criticized. Is it acceptable that someone should eat by relying on seniority? OK, you have seniority, that [we] recognize. Because he is old and lived to such a great age, and doesn't die, he thus has a small qualification, a little usefulness. [He] can still play bit parts,⁶⁵ wave flags [and] cheer, applaud, and lend a hand. I think Mei Lanfang⁶⁶ has played bit parts, cooperating with other people, blade in hand, **[219]** standing there [on stage]. Is

---

⁶³A prophetic utterance!
⁶⁴This was one of the famous slogans of the May Fourth period.
⁶⁵This term, *pao long tao*, means a minor actor, but can also mean a stagehand.
⁶⁶Mei Lanfang (1894–1961) was the doyen of Peking Opera stars and one of the great figures in Chinese theater in the pre-1949 period, known for playing female roles (*qing yi*); see his biography in *BDRC* 3, pp. 26–9. Mao mentioned him several times in his speeches

Mei Lanfang here today? I think that at the age of eighty you can still have a role, at least in a bit part. My own role can only be that of a bit part; the leading part I won't sing: that [is for] people like our Premier Zhou. (Laughter) You all [should] sing.⁶⁷ In *Xi xiang ji* the singer is that Hong Niang; I can't sing [that part]. (Laughter) That old lady in *Xi xiang ji,* she comes out [on stage] and sings those few lines, makes a few turns, [then] retires backstage.⁶⁸ If you do not stop singing, [and] sing too much, people will boot you out. (Laughter) Moreover, old-timers no matter how old you are, you must handle [your] work correctly, [you] must be right. You [could] live in righteousness to the age of ninety-nine; but [if] on the day you turn a hundred you do some foul deed, then you won't be acceptable. What good deeds has Rákosi⁶⁹ done in the past? I don't know. If Rákosi hadn't done anything wrong, but at the very last did some evil deed, [then] he couldn't escape criticism just because he was an old-timer. New cadres naturally are the same, too; [if they're] wrong, [they] must be criticized. Lenin said God forgave him; God can still forgive young people because of their youth, [but] with old-timers [we] should be strict. With old cadres it's like that, [and] with young cadres one should be strict, too; [but we] should help them as well. If [we] are strict with young cadres, [we] should also patiently give

---

in 1957–8; see below, Texts 11 and 12. He was 62 at the time of this speech and was almost certainly in the audience.
⁶⁷Mao was in the process of withdrawing to what he called the "second front" during this period, a fact that was known to his senior colleagues but became publicly visible only when he handed over the post of head of state to Liu Shaoqi in the spring of 1959. The idea was to establish his successors firmly in authority so that China could avoid the kind of struggle for power that followed Stalin's death; see *Origins* 1, pp. 152–6. In fact, as his colleagues later discovered to their cost, Mao was never prepared to relinquish power totally. An interesting aspect of his remarks here is that he singles out Zhou Enlai (China's No. 3) and not Liu Shaoqi (the No. 2) as an example of a leader who would take over a leading role from him; this may have been because Liu was not on the rostrum (see *Origins* 1, pp. 250–2).
⁶⁸*Xi xiang ji* (Record of the West Wing) is a famous musical drama of the Yuan period by Wang Shifu. The character Hong Niang is the maidservant who helps bring together her mistress and the leading man. The old lady is her mistress's mother. See Lai Ming, *A History of Chinese Literature* (London, Cassell, 1964), pp. 242–5.
⁶⁹Mátyás Rákosi was the Stalinist Hungarian leader dismissed in July 1956 in the aftermath of Khrushchev's "secret speech." Mao seems to be hinting in this passage that Rákosi was basically a good man who was rightly criticized for a few mistakes in his later years, whereas he in fact presided over all the brutality of post–World War II Hungary. Mao's aim may be to minimize any internal justification for the Hungarian revolt.

[them] long-term education. Many cadres among us, in fact, do not approve of the [party] Center's policies—the policies of letting a hundred flowers bloom and a hundred schools contend, [and] of long-term coexistence, [and] mutual supervision. Am I overstating the case? I say that among high-level cadres nine out of ten do not approve or [only] half approved, or do not understand well. [Those] who really understand, really think this policy is correct, are a minority, so there is a real need to work [at this], to work at persuading [people]. [We] must [criticize] the antagonists of dialectical materialism: For instance, those who mouth Idealism must be criticized; not to criticize [it] is incorrect. But dogmatic criticism does not solve problems. On the contrary, it fosters the growth of those bad things. This is a policy, one of [getting] self-education and the development of one's career within the ranks of the people. Correct things develop from struggle with incorrect things; Marxism is like this. In this world every new thing, every living thing, no matter what, everything develops through struggle with old objects, old things. [220] Marxism developed through struggle with capitalism. We Chinese Marxists have had to grow up on Chinese soil [where] some [things] don't conform to Marxism, some don't conform a great deal, some [just] a little, [but] some are even antagonistic. All these fragrant flowers and poisonous weeds that have grown up—what is there to fear from their growth? There is nothing to fear; I feel there is nothing to fear. Every year weeds grow; in China they have already grown for several hundred thousand years, [and] aren't they still growing today! Suppose you send down a directive prohibiting whatever flowers [there are] from blooming, whatever weeds from growing—[well,] among the bad flowers there might be some good flowers [too], such as [if we look back] in history, the theory of evolution, Galileo, Copernicus, flowers like these. Flowers that wear the cap of Marxism sometimes are not necessarily Marxist. [Like] Stalin, [he] was 70 percent a Marxist, 30 percent not a Marxist. [He] was 30 percent bourgeois, 70 percent Marxist. This is a basic principle. The life of Marxism (we now are continuing to evolve) is a struggle with different things. Only within mutual criticism, in the midst of criticism can [it] develop. Now our comrades cannot connect these points of view. I don't know how many times, for how many years [I have] talked about this. [The principles of] the united front, long-term coexistence, learn from past mistakes to avoid future ones, cure the

illness to save the patient, mutual supervision, let a hundred flowers
bloom, let a hundred schools contend, oppose metaphysics, oppose
dogmatism, all these are forgotten when it comes time to write articles, give speeches, hold meetings, [or] make comments. There is no
intention of curing the illness to save the patient, no intention of
helping other people, [only] of clubbing [those who err] to death
with a single blow. Leaving this aside, this question reminds me of
smallpox vaccinations. Why give smallpox vaccinations? Have you
all had it? I have—[but] what I got was not smallpox, it was [a disease]
something similar to smallpox—the germs made the disease grow
inside the human body where the body and these germs struggled.
The result of the struggle is immunity from the disease; if there is no
struggle with the germs, then there can't be immunity from the disease. Therefore, those who do not contract disease in their lives run
a great risk; it is dangerous; getting sick regularly is a good thing, it
can produce immunity.

STRIKES AND DEMONSTRATIONS

Ninth, how to handle the problems of strikes, student strikes, demonstrations, [and] petitions. Probably among your documents, comrades, are a few concerning such problems. Why hasn't Kunming's
[221] Aeronautical Institute had any disturbances? ([Here we] lack
materials on disturbances; it would be best to go find a typical case of
a disturbance and print it [for distribution and study].) It is [the]
absence of bureaucratism; if school administrators all did their work
according to this [model], that would be good! This is the Marxist
method of operating a school; [it] recognizes the ideological state of
current youth. The Central Committee of the Youth League has provided a document: Last year among universities and middle schools
in 28 cities there were reportedly over 7,000 students involved in disturbances in 29 schools. The analysis in this material is pretty good:
The cause of the disturbances was nothing more than bureaucratism
and student naiveté; youth, workers, [and] students did not understand the complexity of the world, did not understand arduous struggle. At the same time, the school authorities [and] the administrators
used various methods to deceive them [and] didn't share weal and
woe with them. Then there's also the business of workers' strikes
[and] petitions. Partial statistics in the report of the [All-China] Fed-

eration of Trade Unions [show] some fifty strikes; among these there were [strikes] of a few people, some with scores of people, the largest one had over a thousand people on strike. How are contradictions amongst the people to be handled? I say contradictions constantly occur within the ranks of the people. Strikes, student strikes, peasants hitting out with their carrying poles, [these] happened last year, [and] they are likely to happen this year, too. They [also] took place several years ago, [so] they all can't be blamed on Hungary, [with the excuse] that since the Hungarian incident, things have been difficult to manage in China. You see thousands of students on strike, a portion of the workforce on strike, demonstrations: What [should we] do? I've worked out a few points on this problem. [I will] pose four points; see if they are right or not.

Point one. Work hard to overcome bureaucratism, then people won't strike! Appropriately resolve contradictions, then people won't go on strike, won't make disturbances.

Point two. If bureaucratism has not been overcome [and] they want to make a disturbance, what [should you] do? Permit the disturbance or not? One [way] is not to permit disturbances, to say all agitators are counterrevolutionaries, to say [they] want to rebel. As I have already said, there are counterrevolutionaries, but they are very few. [We] can't say that these agitators are mainly counterrevolutionaries. On the contrary, it is mainly the defects in our work: We don't know how to educate, we don't know how to lead. To permit or not to permit disturbances? I say it's better to permit disturbances. After all, workers want strikes; peasants want to make a din; students want strikes; the peasants want to hit someone with their poles!

Point three. When a disturbance occurs [and there's a confrontation], is it right to call it off in a hurry? There are also two policies [on this]. [If] **[222]** after only two or three days of disturbance, [when] the agitators haven't satisfied their craving [but] the authorities urgently want to end it, this produces a contradiction, how should it be resolved? I say let them agitate to their hearts' content. Mr. Shi Fuliang[70] created disturbances, apparently in Zhejiang; I, too,

[70]Shi Fuliang was an early member of the CCP, who renounced his party membership in 1927. In 1945 he helped organize the China Democratic National Construction Association, one of the democratic parties in post-1949 China. At this time, he was a member of the standing committees of both the NPC and the CPPCC and was presumably in Mao's audience.

created disturbances at school, because problems couldn't be resolved! Moreover we wanted to agitate to our hearts' content. If one week is insufficient, two weeks; if two weeks are not enough, three weeks; if three weeks are not enough, four weeks. In sum, [when they've] satisfied themselves, [they] won't agitate any more. Make the process of the disturbance serve as an educational process, serve as a political course. Our political work has been insufficient, [our] ideological work hasn't been done well; [this is] bureaucratism. [We] must look upon strikes, student strikes, [and] the peasants waving their poles as the process of remolding our work, [and] educating workers [and] students.

[Point four.] Should the chiefs and leaders of a disturbance be expelled or not? I think [they] shouldn't be expelled. Aside from a few exceptions, if [they] kill someone, then [they] should be put in jail at the Public Security Office. [That's] because [they] murdered, committed crime. If you don't hit people, murder, [do] nothing serious, then [you] shouldn't be expelled. Expelling leaders of strikes and student strikes, this is a bourgeois method; in general [they] shouldn't be expelled. Leading persons, both correct and incorrect, should remain. Why should we help the incorrect ones? They should be kept as "instructors."[71] Because [they] have committed errors, [say] a few individuals have been identified as spies, should they be kicked out of school? I think let [them] study, just so long as they're not active criminals. What's wrong with a school having a few spies in it? Will you be comfortable only when it is scrubbed spotlessly clean? So, that student at Qinghua University who wants to kill thousands of people now remains there; he is an "instructor," because he published that famous proclamation. [People like him] are hard to come by. I have discussed these four points: The first point is work hard to overcome bureaucratism to stop disturbances; second, if [they] want to agitate, let them agitate; my third, [if they] feel they haven't agitated enough, let them agitate to their hearts' content; fourth, don't expel. Expulsion is the method of the Nationalist party; we want to proceed in opposition to the Nationalist party's ways. I think that in the future there will still be many problems; the will of the people isn't uniform; in a population of several hundred million there are going to be lots of people with ways of thinking different from ours.

---

[71]*Jiaoyuan* is a general term for teaching professionals inside and outside formal education.

That's one aspect. The second aspect is that our working personnel, responsible people at schools, in factories, in APCs, in [government] offices, come from [223] very many different areas, and many of them have a low educational level; even those people with a high educational [level], even intellectuals, too, cannot avoid committing errors. Sometimes in comparison with those of a low educational level, the intellectuals make the more severe mistakes. In the "leftist" and rightist [errors] which our party has committed, intellectuals have been numerous: Chen Duxiu, an intellectual; Li Lisan, an intellectual; Wang Ming, an intellectual; Zhang Guotao, an intellectual; Gao Gang, doesn't count; Rao Shushi, an intellectual.

ARE DISTURBANCES GOOD OR BAD?

Tenth, is creating a disturbance a bad thing or a good thing?

As to this problem [of] strikes, student strikes, marches, petitions, demonstrations, I think there are both good and bad, [because] they have a dual character! Things like strikes and student strikes have a dual character, too. [The incident in] Hungary has [its] dual character. Do you think the Hungarian incident was good or bad? I say [it] was both good and bad. Of course it was bad, since they had disturbances. But Hungary did one very good thing; the counterrevolutionaries really helped us. Since the end of the Hungarian incident, things have been more secure than before. Hungary now is better than the Hungary of the past when there were no disturbances—all in the socialist camp have learned [from Hungary's experience]. Thus I say the Hungarian incident has a dual character, both good and bad. An anti-Soviet, anti-communist current has arisen in the world. For the first time, especially with regard to the recent instance, it was worldwide [in nature]. How do we look on it? Naturally, I think it's not good. Secondly, [it] is good; this is a good thing. Because imperialist anti-Sovietism and anti-communism steels the Communist party. The French Communist party has destroyed its party newspaper; the Swiss Communist party is doing particularly badly; [their] general secretary is hiding in the mountains, hiding in our embassy, afraid to see [people], afraid to go out. [If] people see [him, he'll] get beaten up. Many party members have left the party. In Holland and Belgium a good many have left the party. England's intellectuals, the more intellectual [they are], the more they want to leave the party.

Thus there are two types of intellectuals; the more important they are in stature, the more they disapprove of the Communist party. [Even] old party members who have muddled along [in the party] for several years or decades want to leave the party, too. Is leaving the party good or bad? Both good and bad, but mainly it is good. If you leave, what's wrong with that? Our China has this gentleman Hu Shi, who is writing lots of articles at present. We've proposed letting a hundred flowers bloom and a hundred schools contend. He says he has already suggested letting a hundred flowers bloom and a hundred schools contend. (Laughter) How [should we] look on the criticism of Stalin? We [humans] are also commodities **[224]** of dual character. The criticism of Stalin has a two-sided nature. One side has real benefit; one side is not good. To expose the cult of Stalin, to tear off the lid, to liberate people, this is a liberation movement; but his [i.e., Khrushchev's] method of exposing [Stalin] is incorrect; [he] hasn't made a good analysis, clubbing [him] to death with a single blow. On the one hand, this provoked the worldwide currents of the latter half of last year; on the other hand, it later also provoked the Hungarian and Polish incidents. But he [Stalin] had his incorrect side; although our published articles have not pointed at the [CPSU] Twentieth Congress, in fact [we've] talked about it. What have we discussed with the Soviet comrades face to face? About how the Stalin problem has not been handled appropriately; [we] discussed our great-nation chauvinism. I think the United States' non-recognition of us also has two sides. Not recognizing us is, of course, not good; [we] can't enter the United Nations; they say there is no such country [as us] in the world. We should be recognized and they won't recognize [us], this naturally isn't good. But there's also been a great benefit; the United States does not recognize us, [but] we are [still] very comfortable. I have exchanged opinions with numerous friends, and, in sum, I have not convinced them that this is the case. I feel that [since] the United States does not recognize [us] now, it'd be best if [after] six years, when the second FYP is completed, at least after six years [they will] recognize [us]. It's better like this. The best would be after eleven years, when the third FYP is completed; at that time make them obtain legal status in China, [that] would be advantageous for us. Without them we are still able to carry on with [economic] construction. [Let's] wait until we have more or less completed construction,

[and] ask them to come take a look. (Laughter) It will be too late [for them] to regret it! (Laughter) Still the United States raises its tail, obstinately saying it doesn't recognize [us]; [they're] so happy. The United States more or less wants to recognize [us], [and] I worry on their behalf, but this is an American affair. The US Chief-of-Staff is an American, not our Nie Rongzhen.[72] Nor do we have to give him advice, but [we'd] better be prepared. If recognition comes quickly, what to do? Accept their insistence on recognition? I say that wouldn't do. But there is the Taiwan question; Taiwan must be returned to us. This thing is a problem to work on; if Taiwan is not returned, I don't care about your recognition. England recognizes us, but we won't establish diplomatic relations with you, [we establish] semi-diplomatic relations, [we] won't send a formal representative, only a chargé d'affaires. Because she [England] votes for Chiang Kai-shek in the United Nations.[73]

We have articles, [but] it's OK to publish a few wrong articles. Didn't I just **[225]** criticize a few comrades? At the same time [I] should thank them. Wrong articles have done good work, because they've given us some grounds, given our criticism an object, [including] dogmatist articles, opportunist articles. This article appeared in nine sections, and still should produce a few more. Not only is its nature no good, not only is [it] incorrect, but in addition it has a service [to give]. It gives us the possibility to counter-criticize. What do [we] do about the lack of significant works [and] good movies? I say this is a bad thing. There are no significant novels, few good movies. This will itself produce significant works [and] good movies. Because there are none? [After] a long period of dearth, eventually [it] will come; things will develop in the opposite direction when they become extreme; the more that bad things are done, [ultimately] the good will emerge. This dialectical method was not invented only

[72]Nie Rongzhen, one of China's ten marshals, had been acting Chief-of-Staff from 1949 to 1954. The current Chief-of-Staff was actually General Su Yu.
[73]Britain recognized the PRC in January 1950; and, but for the Korean War, Ji Pengfei (later Foreign Minister) would have been the new regime's first ambassador in London. After the 1954 Geneva Conference, at which premier Zhou Enlai and Foreign Secretary (as he then was) Anthony Eden had struck up a cordial working relationship, the minimal level of diplomatic relations was raised to the chargé-d'affaires level. Ambassadors would not be exchanged until 1972.

in Marxism-Leninism. Our China's Lao Zi—the one who regarded himself as the number one authority under heaven[74] (Laughter)—spoke like this long ago. He said in every bad thing one should see good; in the good, one should see bad. In misfortune there is fortune, in fortune there is misfortune; when the old man of the frontier lost his horse, who could have guessed it was a blessing in disguise;[75] when the old man of the frontier loses his horse, congratulate him [and] say it was good to lose the horse, it was well lost. In the past there were people who even went to give congratulations when another man's house burned down. When Japan beat China, the Japanese called [it] a victory; the greater half of China was occupied. China called this defeat. But that defeat for China contained a victory, the Japanese victory contained a defeat. [Though they] occupied the greater part of China, plus the Philippines, Indonesia, [and various] countries in Southeast Asia, [their] victory contained defeat. The result indeed was victory transformed into defeat, whereas the occupied countries, like China, transformed defeat into victory. Isn't this so? [When] Hitler's armies approached the cities, Leningrad, Moscow, Stalingrad, all of Europe was occupied; [they] were just on the point of victory, but this contained defeat, and occupied Europe, [and] the greater half of the Soviet Union still contained the inevitability of victory.

Should [we] fight World War III at this time?

You wait, this will be discussed later. Our China has two things: one, poverty; two, ignorance.[76] [You] say Chinese are smart, but the Chinese are illiterate. On the one hand, the standard of living is not high; on the other hand, the educational level is not high: The standard of living is very low; the educational level is very low. This circumstance, too, has its dual character. Our revolution relies on these two things: one, poverty; two, **[226]** the low educational level. If China becomes prosperous, just like the standard of living in the western world, then [people] will not want revolution. The western

[74]Mao is simply enjoying the pun on *lao zi* here—both the name of the ancient philosopher and the "authority" of the phrase he quotes.
[75]This refers to a traditional story in which an old man loses his horse, only to have it return a few months later with a host of fine horses.
[76]This recalls Mao's commoner characterization of China as "poor and blank"; see for instance, Stuart Schram, *The Political Thought of Mao Tse-tung* (Harmondsworth, Penguin, 1969), pp. 351–2.

world is rich, [but] has its shortcomings; its shortcoming is [being] non-revolutionary. [Their] standard of living is so high, their weak point is [being] non-revolutionary. This is not as good as our illiteracy; I think after all illiteracy is better. (Laughter) Naturally illiteracy must be eradicated. I am not here advocating continuing to preserve illiteracy. Our socialist transformation has proceeded so quickly—this is precisely because China is too poor. What if [we] fought World War III? [What if we] started fighting right now; [if] for example, after the meeting [we] heard on the radio [that] World War III had begun? What do we do? You all haven't thought about it? Do you have [any] mental preparation? I think preparation is necessary. If [you] want to fight, fight. Just like student disturbances: If [you] want to agitate, then agitate; that is a contradiction among the people. This [war] is a contradiction between the enemy and ourselves. If [you] want to fight, then fight. What choice do we have? [If] the whole world fights another round, World War III, humanity will be reduced by a half; some people say the entire [human race] will be wiped out. I don't accept this argument. Nehru[77] and I have debated this. The prime minister of Pakistan and I have also debated [this]. As regards fighting World War III, I say that in the first place we do not welcome [it], [but] it's OK [too]. (Laughter) I say that after World War I, there emerged the Soviet Union with a population of 200 million; after World War II, many [socialist] countries appeared, with a population of 900 million; after World War III, [the socialist camp will number] probably at least 1.5 billion or 2 billion, not many will be left out. Thus, war has dual characteristics. [It] has a destructive side; at the same time [it] also stimulates people's activism, arouses people's consciousness, makes revolution erupt. What position do you take on fighting World War III? How will you handle [it]? Do it again, just as with Japan's occupation of China? What about having Beijing, Zhengzhou, Wuhan, Guangzhou all occupied again? Everyone will wail and cry [if] that situation comes to us; we will have one long face; we won't be as good as Generalissimo Chiang Kai-shek; but Generalissimo Chiang did not have a long face. We have all gone through this, [we have had] no long faces. If World War III is to be

---

[77]Jawaharlal Nehru (1889–1964), Prime Minister of India from independence in 1947 till his death, was the first major Third World figure to pursue a neutralist foreign policy, eschewing alliance with either the West or the communist bloc.

fought, let it be fought. How many atom bombs do you have? We have none, [just] millet and rifles; but the eventual outcome of the fighting will be that you are defeated in battle, because you are reactionary [and] backward; even though [your] economy is advanced, [your] civilization advanced, yet [your] politics are backward, you contravene the will of the people. In the whole [227] world there are only two countries that [cannot] be destroyed: one is the Soviet Union, the other is China. The Soviet Union is adjacent to the Arctic Ocean, we are adjacent to the Kunlun Mountains (Sounds of laughter), indestructible. So if World War III is to be fought, I think [it,] too, has a dual nature. Japanese say to me that they are very sorry for attacking us. I say, Friends, you did a good thing. They really became confused [at this]. I say, If you had not attacked, had not occupied so much land, [then] the Chinese people wouldn't have been educated. I say, You were our teachers, motivating all the Chinese people to oppose you, this is your contribution. International affairs influence each other, permeate each other. Someone wrote a poem in the past: two bodhisattvas, smashed into pieces, remixed with water, again molded into two bodhisattvas.[78] Thus I am part of you, [and] you are part of me. Now the world, too, is like this, the world is two mud bodhisattvas. There is something of us inside the capitalist mud bodhisattva, and something of them inside the socialist bodhisattva. Thus inside you is me, [and] inside me is you. Now the world, too, is like this; the world is two mud bodhisattvas. There are more Hungarys; there are more [people] who listen to what they say. Various nations in Eastern Europe listen to their broadcasts; the Soviet Union, too, likes to listen to the Voice of America [and] European radio [stations]. Our China, too, has this kind of person, [who] is influenced by them. There are spies as well; they daily calculate [the date of] their arrival. Some landlords cling on to business documents [and] land contracts; some Nationalist party members retain their party identification cards as proof, waiting for that day when they come, [to say]—[Look], we have party cards! Prepare for the worst; [in] fighting a big war, [you] either fight or don't fight. First, [you]

---

[78]This allusion in verse recalls a poem attributed to the wife of the renowned calligrapher Zhao Mengfu (1254–1322). She dedicated it to him, celebrating their inseparableness. Over the centuries, this inseparable you-me relationship was often referred to on the basis of her original theme. The incorporation of bodhisattvas came in a later corrupted version.

prepare for him to strike, in case he goes crazy! Naturally in the end we will be victorious. Now we [the socialist camp] have a population of 900 million, double that is 1.8 billion. Secondly, I don't think there will be a war for a long period of time, perhaps giving us a [breathing] space of a dozen or more years. First, let's talk about losing the war, not an entirely bad thing. Even a good thing. What about [economic] construction? Construction stops. [We] devote all our energies to fighting the war. But under current circumstances what is it that this imperialism is doing to us? Mutual infiltration with the socialist camp. They hope to see Polish and Hungarian [-type] incidents occur. What is the main contradiction in the world today? It is imperialism battling for colonies, battling for Asia [and] Africa. American and European imperialism, British, French, and the like, this is their **[228]** main contradiction. [There are] three forces: one is the force of socialism; one is the force of the national independence movement; one is the force of imperialism. These three forces do battle [with each other]; and the second force, the national independence movement of Nasser, and others,[79] can cooperate with us on various problems, on the problem of peace, on the problem of imperialism; the degree [of collaboration] is not [always] the same but [they] can cooperate with us. There is no great benefit for the imperialists in going to war. The results of [such a] war would not be of great advantage for them. What if [they] don't go to war? [They] can fight among themselves for the loot; the Americans battle the English for Asia and battle the French for Africa. I think [they will] adopt this method. In oil baron Rockefeller's letter to [President] Eisenhower, his policy is just what we estimated: It seems what [China] tells him to do, he does. His primary goal is not to attack us, but to punish England [and] France. There are three types of country [according to Rockefeller]: one type is Soviet-leaning Pakistan; another type is the neutral states like India; [yet] another type is the colonies with absolutely no independence, countries like Morocco and Algeria. Rockefeller's letter to Eisenhower was written in January of last year [1956], [and] this year—who knows from where [they

---

[79]Gamal Abdel Nasser (1918–70) was the president of Egypt, the leading Arab statesman, and, with Nehru and Tito, one of the architects of the non-aligned or "neutralist" movement. He had met Premier Zhou Enlai at the 1955 Bandung conference and established diplomatic relations with China a year later.

obtained it] and it was published in a German (East German) paper. We have now published it and it's very much worth a look.[80]

NATIONAL MINORITIES

The eleventh problem, the problem of national minorities and great Han chauvinism [and] the problem of Tibet. China has several tens of millions of national minorities; the land that the national minorities occupy is vast, some 50 or 60 percent [of all China]; [their] population is about 6 percent [of China's]. That's why I had a section of my "Ten great relationships"[81] saying that the relations between the Han and the national minorities should be conducted well. This is principally the resolution of the problem of Han chauvinism. Has it been resolved? It still has not been resolved well. The Communist party is preparing to hold a meeting this year, a plenum of the Central Committee, specifically to discuss the United Front and the national minority problem. [We] must certainly change this great Han chauvinist work style, [these] ideas [and] sentiments, monopolizing matters that ought to be done by others [i.e. the minorities themselves], the disrespect for national minorities. There's a group in Tibet who want to set up an independent kingdom. Currently this organization is a bit shaky; this time India asked us to let them return. We permitted the Dalai [Lama] to go to India; he has already gone to India. Now [he] has already returned to Tibet. America does [its anti-communist] work. There is a place in India called Kalimpong, **[229]** [where they] specialize in sabotaging Tibet. Nehru himself told the Premier [Zhou Enlai], that this place is a center of espionage, primarily American [and] British. If Tibet wants to be independent our [position] is this: [If] you want to agitate for independence, then agitate; you want independence, I don't want [you to have] independence. We have a seventeen-point agreement. We advised the Dalai [Lama] that he'd be better off coming back: If you stay in India, then go to America, it might not be advantageous [to you or Tibet]. Premier [Zhou] has spoken with him several times.

---

[80]We have not traced the Rockefeller letter.
[81]The speech was made on 25 April 1956 to an enlarged Politburo meeting, but did not become widely available until circulated by Red Guards during the Cultural Revolution. The official text is translated in SW5, pp. 284–307.

Also with other independence movement people, a group of those residing in Kalimpong, [the Premier] has also talked with them, [saying] they'd do better to return. As for reform, the seventeen points stipulate that reforms be made; but the reforms need your agreement. [If] you don't want reform, then we won't have any. If in the next few years you don't [want] reforms, then we won't have any. This is the way we have spoken to them just now. There'll be no reform under the second FYP, in the third FYP we will see what you think; if you say [let's] reform, then [we'll] reform; if you say no reform, then we'll continue not to reform. Why [do we have to be in] such a hurry?[82]

THE SOVIET ROAD AND THE CHINESE ROAD

Lastly, the twelfth point. The face of China may gradually change within three or four five-year plans. The Soviet Union has one road to industrialization, [but] the road we are currently taking is not completely the same as the Soviet Union's. I think there are some differences. In the "Ten great relationships" there are some items, some of the great relationships [that] discuss this problem: The ratio of heavy [industry], light [industry], and agriculture; the ratio of investments in heavy industry, light industry, and agriculture should be substantially adjusted in comparison with the past. The Soviet Union's [ratio of investment] is nine to one, 90 percent to 10 percent. That is to say

[82]After considerable hesitation, the Chinese government had finally allowed the Dalai Lama to accept an Indian invitation to attend celebrations of the 2,500th anniversary of the birth of the Buddha. He had arrived in India late in 1956 and immediately indicated to Prime Minister Nehru his wish not to return home. Among his reasons were the Chinese imposition of "democratic reforms" in eastern areas of Tibet, which had provoked a revolt by the Khampa people in 1955–6; it was to be the Khampas' second revolt in 1958–9 that would lead to the Dalai Lama's flight to India in March 1959. But in 1956, Nehru urged the Dalai to return and after conversations with premier Zhou Enlai, who visited India at this time as part of an Asian tour, the Tibetan leader went back to Lhasa in April 1957. Perhaps he was encouraged by reports of Mao's remarks on this occasion. But Mao's statement that the Dalai Lama had already returned either indicates misinformation or may have referred to a commitment by the Dalai to return. See John F. Avedon, *In Exile from the Land of Sorrows* (New York, Knopf, 1984), pp. 44–7. For the text of the 17-point agreement signed by Tibetan representatives and the Chinese, see *Tibet, 1950–1967* (Hong Kong, URI, 1968), pp. 19–23. For the use of Kalimpong (situated near Darjeeling at the southern end of the Indian trading routes into Tibet) as a spy center, see Neville Maxwell, *India's China War* (Harmondsworth, Penguin, 1972), p. 101; and George N. Patterson, *Peking versus Delhi* (London, Faber, 1963), pp. 250–5, 289–90.

90 percent is [investment in] heavy industry, 10 percent is investment in light industry and agriculture. [This] skims off a bit too much from agriculture, [though] naturally the money skimmed off is used for construction and is not simply pocketed. Herein lies a problem: The activism of the peasants is not high, and so the market does not flourish. Where is the market for heavy industry? The market for heavy industry is light industry [and] agriculture. The market is these hundreds of millions of people, among whom are 500 million peasants. [In] our first FYP the [ratio of investment] was 8 to 1; when it came to implementation it was 7 to 1, better than the Soviet Union. Wasn't the Soviet Union's [ratio] 9 to 1? Heavy industry 9, light industry [and] agriculture 1. We [set] heavy industry at 8—

(Premier Zhou: Agriculture is not included, only heavy versus light [industry].)

[Chairman:] Agriculture's not included; [if] we add in agriculture, then that ratio will have to be recalculated. I think [we should give] further consideration to this ratio in the second FYP. [230] In sum, [we] should help light industry [and] agriculture develop. Light industry [and] agriculture are more or less the same thing. Without agriculture there would be no light industry; without light industry there would be no agriculture. One is the raw material; the other is the market. Agriculture provides the raw materials; light industry uses the rural areas as its market. Should heavy industry take precedence in development? Well, 6 to 1 is still taking precedence, this side stands at six, that side stands at one! [That's] still taking precedence. Heavy industry still takes precedence. But by taking the new road, will the rate of industrial [development] be quicker than the Soviet Union's or not? It may look a little slower, [but will be] a little faster. That is where we place our hopes. I think after all [we] may be a bit faster than them. Because the Soviet Union in twenty-one years—take steel as an example, [their] old base production figure was 4 million tons; ours was 900,000 tons. At the time of [World] War [I] in 1913, the Soviet Union's steel [production] was 4 million tons. Nineteen seventeen was the year of the Revolution; and we won't count 1918, 1919, 1920, the three years of civil war. Counting from 1921, from 1921 to World War II (1941), that was twenty-one and a half years. In that twenty-one and a half years, 14 million tons [of steel]

were added to the 4 million tons, making in all 18 million tons. Our
old base production figure was 900,000 tons, not speaking of 1949
but of our highest annual level. Most of it was Japanese; very little
came from Chiang Kai-shek—only a few score thousand tons. If we
calculate from that year, calculate from 1950, what year will be the
twenty-first? Is it possible that the imperialists will give us twenty-
one years? I've already said it was possible. There are two possibilities:
one that [they] don't give [that much time]; the other that [they] do.
[If they] don't give it, then [we] fight, an earthshaking fight, [then]
the world [will be] in total chaos. The result is the world goes red, if
not the whole world the greater part of the world. After fighting,
start construction again. This is also one way. [If] they want to fight,
what choice do we have? The stronger possibility is that they won't
fight, [and] very likely they will give us the time. Twenty-one years,
such as the Soviet Union had, [from] 1950, twenty-one goes to 1970,
[and] the third FYP goes to 1967. Sixty-eight, '69, '70, still three more
years [after it]. We say industrialization [will take] three Five-Year
Plans or a little longer, I think it's about right. In twenty-one years
I'm sure our steel [production] can develop from 900,000 tons to over
18 million **[231]** tons, perhaps over 20 million tons. If we follow our
currently adopted policy. Give it a bit of flexibility; do more work
on markets; let the peasants eat their fill, let the peasants have purchasing power, develop light industry; the peasants [will] produce
even more raw materials for industrial use and produce even more
food. [If] peasants increase [their] purchasing power, [then] light
industry will have both materials and a market, [and] heavy industry
will have a market, too. Chemical fertilizers will have a market;
trucks will have a market. Investment in water conservancy requires
steel, [so] steel will have a market. Electric power enterprises will
have to develop for use in light industry and agriculture. [I] don't
intend to talk any more on economic questions, and anyway there is
no time for it. We still lack experience in this problem, having
worked [on it] for only seven years. [We] have more experience in revolution, [on] how to make revolutionary struggle, [we have] political
experience; we have gone through reverses, made mistakes. But we
don't have much experience in running the economy. I hope we don't
have to learn [as in] the revolutionary struggle, having to go through
great reverses, losing all the southern bases, going on the Long March,
ending with only the Northern Shaanxi base. Ninety percent of the

army was lost; 90 percent of the party, too, was lost; work in the White Areas was almost a 100 percent write-off.[83] [We had to have] that kind of lesson to educate us. But in economics is it possible to shorten that time a bit? [We should try to] shorten it substantially, not take so long; the losses from committing errors should not be so great. The price [we] paid for the experience gained in revolution was too high. We only ask this much [i.e., that the price may not be too high.] But we now still lack experience; in the end what [will be] appropriate, on so many things we still need to collect experience.

Should [we] learn from the Soviet Union? Is the Soviet Union good or not? Now it seems [it's] not good. I think it is still a good country. Who designed and assembled so many factories for us? Did America do it for us? Did England do it for us? Did Japan? Did France? None of them did it for us. Who designed for us our military factories, airplanes, artillery, tanks? Also the Socialist Soviet Union. That the Soviet Union has shortcomings is one thing. They are a socialist country, we are the same type of country as they are. We are socialist, they are also socialist. Only that one country helped us, isn't that true? [We should] learn from all countries, [we should] learn also from the United States, this point is certain. Only to study the Soviet Union is not [232] what [I] am talking about. All countries should be learned from: English should be studied; French should be studied; German should be studied; Japanese should also be studied. It's not enough just to study Russian. But primarily we should learn from the Soviet Union. Because only they gave us these things; only they dispatched engineers to design for us, teaching us to be able to make designs ourselves; only they were able to give us equipment, and the same in scientific cooperation as well. In nuclear power, aside from the Soviet Union, what country will help us? so the Soviet Union is the key point in our study. Learning has two approaches: One is to learn everything—dogmatism, bad experience, inappropriate experience, everything is to be transplanted, good and bad all are transplanted. This is one attitude. This kind of attitude isn't good. [What] we are talking about is learning from the Soviet Union's advanced experiences. Who asks you to learn from backward experiences? We certainly have never put forward the slogan to learn

---

[83]"White Areas" refers to places controlled by either Japanese or the Nationalists during the revolution.

from the Soviet Union's backward experiences; we have never put it in the papers, either. But sometimes, in fact, a few experiences that are backward experiences, are labeled as advanced experiences, [though] in reality they are backward experiences. We shouldn't have learned from them, yet we have, and not just a little. This should be avoided. [We] should unite with the Soviet Union, unite with all socialist countries; that is a basic, because we can only rely on these people. The countries of Asia and Africa come only second. As for the imperialists, those people have no conscience, their conscience is questionable. Does Dulles have that much conscience? I don't believe it. You don't give us help, [you] don't send us machines: Where's your conscience in that? Every day [you] curse us, occupy Taiwan and won't leave, won't let go. Comrades, [I've] talked too much. What time is it? Seven o'clock. Three o'clock, four o'clock, five o'clock, six o'clock, seven o'clock: [I] won't talk anymore.

Talk when Receiving Members of the Second Committee of the National Student Federation

(MARCH 1957)

[233] After Lin Zexu burned opium in 1840, China had 110 years of revolution; and during those 110 years [we] did no more than make revolution, overthrow the Qing dynasty, the northern warlords, [and] Chiang Kai-shek's government. But the relations of production

Source: 1:233. A national propaganda conference was held 6–13 March 1957, in the aftermath of the Supreme State Conference to convey Mao's "Contradictions" speech and its policy implications to key officials. Texts 4–7 are various remarks by Mao and conversations he had during this time. A related text is Mao's main speech to the propaganda conference on 12 March (9:90–112); it is not translated here, as it appears in *SW5*, pp. 422–35. Also relevant is the "Concluding speech at the Supreme State Conference" of 2 March 1957, known as the contradictions summing-up speech (New Mao Texts 10:64–74); it is not translated here, as it appears in *Wansui* (1969), pp. 90–9 and is translated in *Issues and Studies* 10.12:110–5 (Sept. 1974).

had still not changed. The transformation of the relations of production came later. Only after 1949 did [we] undertake land reform in the whole nation; socialist transformation came even later. Considering that [we've had] such a long [history] of revolution [but] only a few years of construction, how can we not have difficulties [i.e., in economic development]? We have a population of over 600 million people; it's impossible not to encounter difficulties if one wants to construct socialism in so densely populated a country. Construction is even more difficult than revolution.

The difficulties are [what you] young people [will have to deal with]. The young people must succeed the older generation. Therefore, you should be well prepared. It's you who will manage the country in the future.

Talk at the Forum of Heads of Propaganda, Culture, and Education Departments from Nine Provinces and Municipalities

6 MARCH 1957

[44] [XX:] (With regard to how to hold meetings, we've listened to the recordings of the Chairman's report;[1] [there's] substantial content [in it]; [we] should digest it well; it's best to hold more small meetings [and] fewer large conferences.)[2]

Sources: 9:44–55; alternate text, 7:18–28.

[1]This almost certainly refers to Mao's "Contradictions" speech of a week earlier, tape recordings of which were played to selected audiences across the country; see Robert Loh and Humphrey Evans, *Escape from Red China* (London, Michael Joseph, 1963), pp. 218–22.

[2]This paragraph was evidently spoken by an official chairing this session for Mao, perhaps Zhou Yang, deputy head of the CC's Propaganda Department. We have interpreted many subsequent paragraphs, which are printed within parentheses in the original Chinese texts, as being interjections, with responses by the Chairman. Accordingly, whenever there is an apparent change in speaker, we have provided the word *Chairman* or names where the speaker can be identified and *XX* where they cannot.

[Chairman:] Right, [we're] going to have a one-week meeting. If that's not enough, [we'll] extend it for two or three more days until [all] problems are resolved. [We should] hold more small meetings.

[XX:] (In various localities non-party personages attend the meetings, whereas those of us who've come [today] are all of one suit.)[3]

[Chairman:] Even within the party [there] can't be all of one suit.

[XX:] (As for the article written by the four people [including] Chen Qitong,[4] listening to the recording of the report [its thrust] is different from that transmitted from the last conference of party secretaries of the provincial and municipal party committees.)[5]

[45] [Chairman:] They [Chen Qitong et al.] sallied forth in the guise of defenders of traditional moral principle; [their] methods are dogmatist; [their] mentality is factionalist. [This] won't [serve to] defend [anything]. [What I] said last time was [just] a few remarks, maybe [we] missed something.[6]

[XX:] (What about the question of the various departments of party committees dividing up and running political and ideological work, [while] various specialist government departments do not pay attention to political and ideological work.)

[Chairman:] First secretaries must pay attention to ideology. Go back and tell them that [we] hope the first secretaries will pay attention to ideological work. [Only if] the first secretaries [take charge, will ideological work] then succeed; even with second [secretaries in charge, ideological work] won't succeed. The propaganda departments by themselves alone cannot handle [the work] well. If [you]

[3] The phrase "all of one suit" (*qing yi se*) is from ma-jong and, like its counterpart in Western card games, means "homogeneous."

[4] See Text 1, n. 16; and, for the major discussion, Text 3, under "Blooming flowers and contending schools."

[5] The article referred to basically opposed the Hundred Flowers policy; this passage suggests that its viewpoint was not condemned at the conference of CCP provincial secretaries two months earlier. Mao's "Contradictions" speech reaffirmed the Hundred Flowers.

[6] Mao may mean that his very brief remarks endorsing the Hundred Flowers at the provincial secretaries conference (see *SW5*, p. 359) had evidently been insufficient to quash Chen Qitong et al.

manage [your] professional duties very well [but] don't manage ideological work, then [you] could end up being kicked out when big democracy comes along.[7] [All] the various departments and party organizations must manage ideological work. Provincial party committees, especially [their] first secretaries, must pay special attention to ideological work; the various offices and bureaus [of provincial government] should all manage ideological work.

[XX:] (There have been many problems since the policy of "Let a hundred flowers bloom, let a hundred schools contend" was put forward.)

[Chairman:] There are many problems; [we] must loosen up; there are advantages [to that].

[XX:] (The work of criticism has not been done well.)

[Chairman:] In fighting a big war, [you] often can't avoid loosing a few battles at first; when [you] have some experience [you'll] win.

(Kang Sheng:[8] [We say] unity-criticism-unity,[9] yet often after we've made criticisms, [we] don't achieve a new [level of] unity; [we drive it] back with criticisms. [It's done] in a big hurry, mainly because [we] do battle in haste.)

[Chairman:] The leadership should study and analyze problems; only [in this way can they] resolve problems.

[XX:] (According to Shanghai reports, party members are fighting one another in the newspapers.)

[Chairman:] Thinking within the party is also very confused; [but] don't be afraid; [let's] loosen up, [what's there] to be afraid of? Can the globe explode?

[7]By big democracy (*da minzhu*) Mao means street demonstrations or mass meetings to denounce people rather than small private criticism sessions; see *Origins* 1, pp. 178, 212.
[8]Kang Sheng, at this time an alternate member of the Politburo, had been trained in Moscow and Mao came to rely on him heavily in ideological matters, notably in the nine polemics against the Soviet Union in 1963–4 and during the Cultural Revolution.
[9]See Text 13, p. 359.

(Kang Sheng: People outside the party are also afraid—afraid of sectarianism;[10] [party members] don't let others contend.)

[XX:] (Some report that senior professors hesitate to "contend." It's not easy to write articles. The article is published on day one—on day two it'll be criticized; [as a result] the students no longer respect them.)

[Chairman:] **[46]** In that case [the senior professors can] write another article to rebut the criticism on day three.

[XX:] (Some raise [a question about] the problem of Chen Qitong's article: At the conference of provincial and municipal party committee secretaries one aspect was stressed, at the Supreme State Conference another aspect was stressed—was this because there were non-party personages at the Supreme State Conference?)

[Chairman:] [We] should have [people] within and outside the party talk about it together; if [you] shut [your] door, [say things] differently to outsiders, or if [you] talk to the non-party [personages] alone, it won't work. [We] should have [people] within and outside the party talk about it together.

[XX:] (The problem of disturbances.)

[Chairman:] Of course, the few exceptional law-breaking elements should be treated according to law. In general, those who cause trouble need not be kicked out; after all, [they] can't be kicked out of the People's Republic of China: [they] will always need a foothold. Where else [will they be] if not in schools, [government] organs, factories, or cooperatives? In Xian more than a hundred hooligans were seized, the public was very pleased. But student "hooligans" are different from the hooligans in society [at large]; the intellectuals do not [go in for] that type of "hooliganism." So long as [they] don't break the law, [they] still need not be kicked out. . . .

---

[10]Sectarianism, one of the three evils combatted in the CCP's Rectification Campaign later in 1957, specifically meant discriminating against non-party people; see *Origins* 1, pp. 54, 113–6.

[XX:] ([I] hope [we] will talk a bit about the relationship between the superstructure and the base. Some traditional-style painters say that flowers and plants have no class nature; there is also the problem of natural science.)

[Chairman:] Natural science is not [part of the] superstructure; but [because] it still requires people to do it, [it] can still be tainted with some people's class consciousness.

[XX:] (Can we generalize the current ideological struggle as the struggle between proletarian and bourgeois ideologies or not?)

[Chairman:] Ma Hanbing's article is dogmatist; in comparison, Zhong Dianfei is rightist. We need to criticize both parties . . . The basic orientation of the article, "Drums and gongs of the film [circles]," is incorrect.[11]

(Zhou X:[12] The above-mentioned weaknesses indeed exist; but the sentiments of some comrades from "Central Film" are incorrect. The department[13] disagrees with that article.)

[Chairman:] That proletarian ideology should struggle with bourgeois ideology is perfectly correct, but [we] must adopt the method of persuasion and education. In the course of letting a hundred flowers bloom, bourgeois ideology will emerge more frequently; but not everything [that comes up] is bourgeois ideology, not everything is undesirable. [If you] put a label on [everything], [you] could scare people [away]; it's not necessary to refute every article as soon as it appears.

[47] (Lu XX:[14] The generals should not say [they'll] sally forth, should not lead the charge. Let the non-party personages speak first.)

[Chairman:] Marxism is the proletarian ideology. In China, there

[11]Zhong Dianfei wrote "Drums and gongs"; see Text 3, n. 53.
[12]This must be Zhou Yang, then a deputy head of the CC's Propaganda Department, concerned particularly with writers and artists, by many of whom he was disliked and feared.
[13]Probably the CC's Propaganda Department or the Ministry of Culture.
[14]Lu Dingyi, head of the CC's Propaganda Department.

are few intellectuals; to get them to believe in Marxism is not easy. If one-third of the intellectuals believe in Marxism within three five-year plans, it'll be a great victory. The intellectuals can accept socialism, because they have no alternative; they cannot but accept [it]. But in [their] minds [they] are not convinced.

(XX: The Chairman of the Department of Philosophy of Peking University[15] declared in public that he believes in Idealism.

[Chairman:] They can follow us politically, but to convert them to Marxism-Leninism is no easy business—some have worked on Kant and Hegel for decades; [they] can change gradually; some may never change throughout their lives.

(XX said: [They] even have apprehensions about [the policies of] letting a hundred schools contend, fearing [they might] transform a problem of right and wrong into a problem between the enemy and ourselves.)

[Chairman:] [They] fear escalation.

[XX:] (Witnessing the emergence of so much bourgeois thinking since the initiation of the policy of letting a hundred flowers bloom and a hundred schools contend, some people feel as if all [our] past work was wasted.)

[Chairman:] [When bourgeois thinking is] not exposed, it looks as if it doesn't exist; once exposed, there is much. As to whether or not [our] past work was wasted, it's only been six or seven years since liberation—how can there be no bourgeois thinking? It's good that they speak [their minds]; [that way] we get an opportunity to educate them. The problem is that some of our articles are still not convincing; [they] try to suppress. Suppression is not convincing. The struggle between proletarian ideology and bourgeois ideology will last decades, and [so we] should only criticize after research; to crack down with big clubs is not the way; it can't solve problems. [We]

---

[15]Peking University retains the old romanized form for the national capital even though the city in which it is located is now romanized as Beijing.

achieved success in ideological transformation in the past; then [it was a time of] big storms;[16] [our methods] were rough and ready, [but we] basically solved [the problem of] distinguishing the enemy from ourselves [and] picking out those who had knives to kill people with. This [we] know.[17] Now it's [a matter of] distinguishing right from wrong; [we] have to explain [things] concretely, carefully explain one thing after another, just as in mathematics, physics, and so on . . . Also with regard to each school [of thought], [we] must distinguish right from wrong on the basis of evidence.

[XX:] (Some ask, how does one manage right and wrong? For example, there are debates about journalistic work. Chairman, please talk a bit [about this].)

[Chairman:] I'm not a journalist; you are the experts; XX,[18] [for instance,] is an expert. What we should talk about are the major [questions] of right and wrong, [that is, we] should distinguish the enemy from ourselves. [Those who] are not spies, **[48]** [and those who] have the right to vote, they have freedom of speech under the Constitution; therefore we have to let them speak [their minds]. I can criticize him; he can also criticize me—this is freedom of speech. Some ask whether Marxism can be criticized. If Marxism can be totally refuted, then it deserves to be; it'd prove that kind of Marxism useless.

[XX:] (Hubei province reports five reasons for section-level cadres in the Lower Party School debating [whether to] demonstrate in the streets, in opposition to bureaucratism.)

[Chairman:] [Once] bureaucratism is corrected, people will stop demonstrating. Therefore [we] should strengthen the education of party members.

[XX:] ([There's] ideological confusion now. What's the reason in

[16]Mao is referring to the denunciations at mass meetings, often followed by executions, characteristic, for instance, of land reform and the campaigns against counter-revolutionaries in the early 1950s. This was when the regime was eliminating those it saw as its principal opponents.

[17]*You shude*, literally "has been counted" or "enumerated."

[18]Mao may be referring to Deng Tuo, then editor-in-chief of the *RMRB*.

fact? Some say it's bureaucratism; others say [they] want democracy, freedom, [and] individualism [and] don't want centralization, dictatorship, and homogeneity [gongxing]. The leaders want discipline, homogeneity, and centralization, [whereas] the cadres who are led want the other side. [Still] others say [the confusion arises from] bourgeois ideology and so on.)

[Chairman:] If you call everything "anti-socialist," and say it's bourgeois ideology, it's inappropriate; for the problems in the schools have not been resolved, hence the disturbances. For instance, what is the [nature of] the problems in the Hubei Party School? [We] should analyze [it].

[XX:] (What is the main content of ideological work? What [should we] advocate? What [should we] oppose? [Should we] oppose bourgeois ideology or petty-bourgeois ideology? [Or is it a matter of] bureaucratism? . . .)

[Chairman:] [They] all exist. [We] cannot use one simplified slogan to cover everything. Today it's different from the past when we opposed imperialism. [Rural] collectivization will have to be managed well for several years; there are [indeed] contradictions between the individual and the collective. The bourgeoisie and bourgeois intellectuals still need to reform. This is called a transition period. (. . .) [We] should undertake concrete analysis of concrete problems.

[XX:] (Formerly Lanzhou wanted to expel some dozens of students from school, now [it's] not going to expel [them]; [it's] calling off a battle in too much haste.)

[Chairman:] To expel dozens of students is the Nationalists' method. If a situation is wrapped up without the problem's being resolved, in the future [there'll] certainly be disturbances again. For instance, if we're talking about cheating in student enrollment in the Lanzhou School of Forestry and the [Lanzhou] School of Hygiene [and] of student disturbances [as a consequence], I take the side of the students. Didn't you cheat [to begin with]?

[49] (Kang Sheng: Cheating is violating the law; [people] can sue [you] in court; it's a crime.)

[Chairman:] For schools like these, what do you think the problem is? [In the case of these two schools] it's bureaucratism; cheating; and then bureaucratism again. Communist party members who work like this must be rectified. Without boycotts of classes, how can one rectify bureaucratism? Many students are of bad class status; but they will say, "OK, I'm classified as landlord, but why did you cheat me?" We should tell both party and non-party [people that] there is no so-called dictatorship among the people [and that] it's wrong to talk of dictatorship among the people. When did Marx say that the people exercise dictatorship over themselves? The few who violate the law are exceptions. [If people] don't commit crimes, [you] can't use legal sanctions!

[XX:] (All party schools use outlines[19] in lectures. Does contending apply to Marxist-Leninist education within the party?)

[Chairman:] Marxism is one school only. If different interpretations exist—there was the Second International [and] Lenin's Third International; Stalin had Marxism-Leninism, also had dogmatism.

[XX:] (The teaching outline was called "law" in the past; [it] was changed to "reference" later.)

[Chairman:] In the past [it was] called "law"; now [it's] called "reference." So this "law" is apparently not so serious.

[XX:] (Sichuan originally thought of banning *Xing Xing*[20] magazine.)

[Chairman:] *Xing Xing* still should not be banned. Following this conference, bourgeois and petty-bourgeois thoughts will crop up again; relax. We're not in a hurry to control it; it'll become active again. Didn't you report that some professors said "Let a hundred flowers bloom, let a hundred schools contend" is [designed to] lure the enemy in deep? We apply two principles to bourgeois and petty-

---

[19]It is not clear to what *dagang*, "outline" or "outlines," the speaker is referring here. *Dagang* refers to a general outline including a clear statement of principles. Most Chinese cadres, even today, feel much more secure when such a *dagang* is provided as a guide to policy.
[20]See Text 1, n. 5.

bourgeois ideology: First, [we] must criticize [it]; second, [we] must do well in criticism; therefore [the criticism] must be well thought out [and] must be convincing. Poisonous weeds have grown in China for thousands of years; it does not matter [if they] grow for another seven or eight years. Besides, we still have business to attend to. They're full of pent-up anger; [we] can let them speak out. Poisonous weeds are not frightening; if [we] use the method of suppression, [they'll] still turn up.

[XX:] (Some say two of the seven so-called *Xing Xing* gentlemen nurture hatred because their fathers were killed.)

[50] [Chairman:] In this case, there's a historical reason for the things appearing in *Xing Xing*. How should we treat incorrect thinking? [We] should have a method. [We] should not be impetuous [or] simplistic. [We] should research ways and means. There are tens of millions of landlords, rich peasants, the bourgeoisie, and intellectuals in China; 80 percent of the students in the schools of higher education are their children. Those who feel hatred because their fathers were killed—how could [they] not hate [and] curse us? But we must take into consideration that the majority of the intellectuals who spring from the exploiting classes can be won over. There are still not many workers' and peasants' children in schools of higher education; they are in primary and middle schools. In Hungary, 60 percent of the students were workers' and peasants' children, and yet rioted against the Soviet Union [and] against communism; [whereas] with us 80 percent are those kinds of children,[21] [yet they] still have not caused disturbances. In vocational schools the main [problem] is bureaucratism; in addition there is deception [i.e., of the students by the school authorities]. There's also bureaucratism in factories. [With the launching of the policy of] "Let a hundred flowers bloom, let a hundred schools contend" there are certainly weeds [appearing]. [They] cannot be in the majority. What [small] percentage [do they] comprise? The peasants and small handicraftsmen are all petty-bourgeoisie . . . At present it's the transition period, the period of great transformation; [they're] bound to express [themselves] ideologically; but 90 percent or even a bit more can be educated. The prob-

---

[21]I.e., children of landlord and other types of bourgeois families.

lem is in the method [of education]; [it] consists of writing convincing articles; it consists of school teachers, and cadres in factories, being able to give explanations clearly, [and] being able to convince students [and] workers. [With] suppression alone, [how] can [one] convince people?

[XX:] (In the course of one hundred schools contending, there are people within and outside the party who habitually accuse [us of practicing] vulgar sociology.)

[Chairman:] Oversimplified slogans can't scare [people]. We should study Marxist aesthetics [and write] convincing articles. If everyone thinks it's right [and] only one person is a dogmatist, then the problem is resolved; [but] if the majority [of people] say you are a dogmatist, then [it] won't do. The landlords, rich peasants, bourgeoisie and their children, [as well as] the intellectuals, can be transformed; the problem is in the method [of education]. [Only] a very small number of people cannot be educated; perhaps only a few per thousand. But [they're] of no consequence as long as they don't grasp their knives. The "Pieces on plants" in *Xing Xing* should be criticized;[22] if [you] don't criticize [it], [you are] really letting poisonous weeds grow. Zhong Dianfei's article is also a poisonous weed, it's a flower [springing from] opportunism.[23] Ma Hanbing's article is a flower of dogmatism.[24] In Ma Hanbing's article there is a sense of— Who the hell are you? It's I who fought and won power; how dare you say whatever you please? We must gain experience **[51]** [and] learn how to handle [the situation]. We have had experience in dealing with Chiang Kai-shek [and] imperialism, [and we] handled [them] well. [We've] also [been able to] handle the Hungarian problem. Therefore, [we] must investigate problems, use [our] brains, study; the important [thing] is to obtain experience through struggle. there are two points: First, [we have] overestimated the poisonous weeds. [They have been there] for thousands of years; how can people be poisoned that easily? The people have the ability to distinguish [them from the flowers], have no fear! Let them bloom a bit!

[22]By Liushahe, see Text 1, Note 5.
[23]Zhong's article, to which Mao here refers, is probably "Drums and gongs"; see above, Text 3, n. 53.
[24]Mao discussed these points in his major "Contradictions" talk; see Text 3, pp. 167–9.

The party members (leading cadres) should not speak first; first let democratic personages write articles; let non-party [personages] have a full discussion. Second, we had [proper] methods for waging class struggle in the past; now [it's] ideological struggle, [and we] can no longer use the old methods [we used] in overthrowing Chiang Kai-shek, or in the War to Resist America and Aid Korea, in the Three-Anti and Five-Anti [campaigns,] in land reform, and so on. Now it's ideological struggle, it's different. In ideological struggle [you have to use your] mouth rather than [your] hands; [and you] have to use [your] mouth properly at that, rather than adopt the methods of dictatorship. [We] should not overestimate the enemy and underestimate ourselves; there's nothing to fear. Last year when some vocational schools chose the method of deception, seven thousand people from seventeen schools staged student strikes. There are five million middle school students nationwide. The school principals and the party secretaries should investigate how to run the schools well. [If] five million students were to cause disturbances, it wouldn't be easy to handle [the situation].

[We] should investigate methods for leading the ideological struggle. In the past it was a struggle against the enemy, and [we] had the Three Main Rules of Discipline and the Eight Points for Attention.[25] Now the problem is [more] complicated: there's science, culture, and art; schools of higher education, and the "Pieces on plants." They can write; we can't. What are the *Book of Songs* and the *Poems of Chu*?[26] Most of them are pieces on plants, aren't they? They set themselves against us, but don't be afraid. Sichuan is a big province with a population of 90 million people. Eight or nine out of ten of the old cadres sympathize with the article by Chen Qitong and the other three. But outside of the party [it's] not agreed with; [as a result,] the party has become isolated.

We should mobilize the intellectuals to discuss "blooming again."

[XX:] (The problem of Zhang Yunfeng,[27] a deputy party secretary

[25]Rules of conduct for the military formulated by Mao on Jinggangshan and formulated in their final form in 1947; see John Gittings, *The Role of the Chinese Army* (London, RIIA/Oxford Univ. Press, 1967), p. 102.
[26]For translations of these ancient Chinese anthologies, see Legge, *The Chinese Classics*, vol. 4, *The She King* (Taipei, Southern Materials Center, 1983); and David Hawkes, *Ch'u Tz'u: The Songs of the South* (Oxford, Clarendon Press, 1959).
[27]See discussion of this case, above, Text 3, where his name is given as Ma Yunfeng.

of a party branch of the Institute of Aeronautics writing reactionary posters.)

[Chairman:] He wrote "Soviet troops get out of Hungary." [Whereas] we want them to "get in," he wants them to "get out." [But] in actuality, how many at the school agree with this opinion? One per thousand is possible.

[XX:] (Some suggest there is still much muddled thinking.)

[Chairman:] This is obviously a question of an antagonistic [con-tradiction]; probably it's one in a thousand who has muddled think-ing, [and that] doesn't count. There's much more at large in the world.

(XX: the party branch [52] took a vote on expelling Zhang from the party; five for, four advocated placing [him] on probation. The voting was taken after the responsible comrades had announced expulsion.)

[Chairman:] [Of] nine party members, five for, four against; [this] shows the time was not yet ripe, [so] what's the hurry! If Zhang had a different opinion, [he] could have talked about [it] openly in the party branch—why put up posters secretly? This is abominable [be-havior]! We can still investigate the experience [and decide] whether or not to expel [him]. If it's expulsion, [then] when do we expel [him]?

The bourgeoisie has a bourgeois ideology; the sons of the bour-geoisie also have a bourgeois ideology. Talking of this, the bour-geoisie are fewer in number in China. There are few like Zhang Yunfeng.

(XX: Someone like Zhang Dongsun[28] for several years now, he's still teaching there; still not posing any harm to us. Many professors say publicly, "[It's] a gross injustice for the Communist party to win."

---

[28]Zhang Dongsun (1886–1962) was one of the most influential Western-oriented Chinese philosophers of the 20th century. The translator of Plato's *Dialogues*, Zhang derived his phi-losophy from Kant and in the 1930s bitterly criticized dialectical materialism. Later, how-ever, he was drawn to Marxism through study of the sociology of knowledge and stayed on in Beijing. See Wing-tsit Chan, *A Source Book in Chinese Philosophy* (Princeton, Princeton Univ. Press, 1963), pp. 744–50.

We still adopt the policy of combining earnest criticism with patient education. Recently he criticized himself in public. This shows [our methods] are still effective, harmless for the party. [He] even participated in the conference of intellectuals last year.)

[Chairman:] [His] salary has even been increased. Ideological struggle is "civilized."[29] [We] should learn from past mistakes to avoid future ones, cure the illness and save the patient, [form] a united front [and have] unity, criticism, unity. We are doctors; the purpose of surgery is to save the patient (. . .)

[XX:] (Some teaching staff don't think it's necessary [for them] to continue to remold [themselves]).

[Chairman:] Don't need to remold? I'm sixty years old and still need to remold [myself]. In ten thousand years there will still be a need to remold. [As long as] humanity wants to strive forward, [it will] need to remold; this conforms to [objective] law. If [you] still [use] the old stuff like [what you used] fighting Chiang Kai-shek on horseback in the past, [it] won't work; then [you'll] have to remold. The Communist party after all still has certain sensibilities; it is [here] to get things done. Speaking of scholarship, some say we "have neither learning nor skill." Indeed we don't have much in this respect; therefore [we] badly need to study and research.

[XX:] (Some senior intellectuals say your politics serves professional [work]).

[Chairman:] Right; politics serves professional [work].

(XX: [One] should say so within certain limits.)

[Chairman:] Politics is superstructure, [it] serves the base. We put forward [the slogan of] "Advance in science" [and] the "Twelve-year

[29]Mao uses the term *wen*, traditionally also connoting civilian as opposed to military (*wu*). He possibly means to underline the contrast with more violent class struggle during which, as in war, people were killed.

Plan" [for the sciences];[30] as for transistors, atomic energy and so on, [the work] needs to be done by you [intellectuals]; I know nothing [of that]. In the past we were [involved in] class struggle, it was an **[53]** offensive; they did not have any alternative, but [they] were not comfortable. Now [we] have construction, so the intellectuals in the interest of reform come forward to criticize our bureaucratism. It's good they've made criticisms; why can't [we] tuck [our] tail between our legs and come forward? [We] must study, [we] must do research. (. . .)

[XX:] (The problem of new and old intellectuals; the old [intellectuals] fear the criticism of the new ones.)

[Chairman:] That's the way it is: the later generation, after learning from the earlier generation, then criticizes the earlier generation. Marx was like this. If the later generation were [exactly] like us, what would be the benefit?

[XX:] (They don't publicly profess Idealism; instead [they] mix Idealism with materialism [and] confuse [things]; [they] try to build up Idealism in the name of opposing dogmatism. That's their aim [with respect to] the hundred schools contending.)
As for the policy of let a hundred flowers bloom, let a hundred schools contend, everyone has [his] own aim. But the result will be that our aim will be achieved.

(XX: Some people suggest that [the slogan] "Let a hundred schools contend" is not as clear as "Let a hundred flowers bloom" or "Weed out the old to bring forth the new." Should one add "Eliminate the false and retain the true" or "Seek truth from facts"?)

[Chairman:] To seek truth from facts is Marxist method; Idealism seeks truth by falsifying facts.

[XX:] (Some scientists think the party cannot lead science.)

---

[30]The science plan was drawn up in 1956.

[Chairman:] Can the party lead science or not? [It] can; [we should] give it a try. If [it] can't [provide] leadership, it won't work either. [What] we [do] is to lead science from the political [perspective]. [We] launched a Twelve-Year Plan, [put forward the slogan of] advancing on science—can't we even lead this?

(XX: Last year we attended to [their needs]; [we] did the work of a director of general services.)[31]

[Chairman:] We [act as] a director of general services and add on Li Fuchun's [first FYP];[32] [the] first is for eating; the second is for planning. In scientific research at present, we just don't have that many party members to go and head [research] institutes; no point in arguing about this. [We] should not contest this point. I simply don't understand natural science; [we] must invite them to be [our] teachers. [We offer] Li Fuchun, plus our [acting as] a director general of general services—do I really not lead at all? In the natural sciences the teachers are still yourselves.

[XX:] (Has the Soviet Union made the transition to communism or not?)

[Chairman:] Not yet.

[54] [XX]: (About the problem that Comrade Chen Boda put forward at the conference on intellectuals that the intellectual can arrive at Marxism through two routes.)

[Chairman:] It's through their own professional practice that natural scientists reach Marxism—this refers to the individual route they go through; it doesn't mean [they] don't need leadership. Some intellectuals agree in words that the party can't lead; in reality we do lead.

---

[31]This interjection refers to the determined efforts initiated by the CCP in January 1956 to improve the status, wages, living conditions, and working conditions of the intellectuals; see *Origins* 1, pp. 33–5.

[32]Li Fuchun, Chairman of the State Planning Commission, had unveiled the 1st FYP (1953–7) in 1955. Mao's point is that the CCP has initiated a national development effort and is looking after the intellectuals whose skills are critical to its success, and that this is appropriate and effective leadership.

Did Lenin understand transistors? Yet [he] still [provided] leadership. There are so many fields in the natural sciences that even the scientists themselves understand [only] this one and not that one. Mei Lanfang can lead in Peking Opera: Can [he] lead in modern drama? He plays the female roles: Can he lead the clowns? [Can] he lead Cheng Yanqiu? That would still be laymen leading experts.[33] Politics is leadership. In reality they are talking about this one problem. "The Communist party does not yet have scientists." The situation in the Soviet Union is different from ours; they already have a large number of party members who are scientists.

[XX:] (The professors say: Politics serves education.)

[Chairman:] Politics serves education. The whole People's Government serves exactly the workers and peasants. Does it serve science and technology as well? [It] does. [If politics is] done better, [they'll] develop a little faster. [This] is serving them, and serving [them] whole-heartedly at that.

[XX:] (How should we handle the students, workers and party members who caused disturbances? There are difficulties.)

[Chairman:] There are difficulties; [but we should] look at [whether they] have justification or not. If [they] have justification, then the party members should stand on the side of the masses; [they] should oppose totally rotten bureaucratism. Of course, [we] first of all should try our best to settle the situation peacefully rather than [have] strikes and boycotts of classes. As for [those who] have no justification, [you should] not get involved. For [those] with justification, [be they] party members, labor unions, or student unions, [then] one should stand on the side of the masses.

[XX:] (Should the press intervene in life?)[34]

---

[33]Cheng Yanqiu (1904–58) was a player of female roles in Peking Opera whose talents and popularity rivaled Mei Lanfang's. For Cheng's biography, see *BDRC*, pp. 292–3.
[34]This questioner apparently wants to find out whether journalists should be permitted to expose bureaucratic malpractices through investigative reporting.

[Chairman:] [As for] propaganda in the press, one must see whether [it] benefits the people or not. There is no freedom of speech in the abstract; there's only freedom of a certain class, the freedom of [certain] cliques within a class. When there are classes, [it's] the classes that run newspapers; as for treating newspapers as classless, that's in the future; not now.

[XX:] (Some point out that [in reports] relayed in the provinces [it was said that] the article by Chen Qitong and others was correct.)

[55] [Chairman:] I have said on several occasions in supplementary remarks that "these few comrades are loyal and devoted to the party, that [they] are committed to the party's undertakings; but [their] article cannot [serve as] advice." This [last qualifying] phrase was cut out [when transmitted down].

(Kang Sheng: [This] probably reflects the mentality of the comrades who attended the conference: the first part was easy to accept, the last sentence was easy to ignore.)

[Chairman:] Their article reflects a hatred for antagonistic ideologies; and if there were no [such hatred], that would be serious, and we must protect it. [But] the problem is that they are dogmatists [and their] methods are wrong. [With regard to] letting a hundred flowers bloom [and] a hundred schools of thought contend, there's not too much blooming at present; there's too little. [We] should bloom again. Of course, any wrong things [that appear] in the course of blooming should be criticized. Has there been enough blooming [up till] now? Enough contention? Not enough. People are still guessing at our intentions, thinking we are "luring the enemy in deep." That's why [we] must bloom again. Now [we are] holding a propaganda conference; all of us agree to this policy; [we] should study methods well. First, party members should be in no hurry to write articles; let the non-party [personages] write first; of course, [we] should provide leadership. Second, party members should also write articles, but [the articles] must be convincing, researched, and with analysis, rather than metaphysical and dogmatist in methodology. To be analytical is to be convincing; we should adopt the attitude of helping people correct their errors rather than that of clubbing [them] to death with one fell stroke.

[XX:] (What about the resolution of the Eighth Party Congress [and] the debate caused by the problem of the contradiction between the [social] system and productive forces.)

[Chairman:] There are contradictions, but not serious [ones]. But in protecting the development of productive forces, [we] cannot compare the future with the present, nor can [we] compare the United States with China; this is inappropriate. China fifty years from now will be different. The Soviet Union has been around for forty years, [its relations of production] are still appropriate. As for the contradictions, [they] exist now, [they] will be more serious in the future; now [they] are less serious. This sentence had previously been deleted from the resolution, but it was printed and distributed [and we] realized [this] only on the eve of the Congress.[35]

[35]For a discussion of this issue, see *Origins* 1, pp. 119–21. The importance of this particular remark is that it confirms that the mistake in the political resolution at the 8th Congress was not attributable to a plot by Liu Shaoqi as alleged during the Cultural Revolution.

Talk with the Heads of Departments and Bureaus of Education from Seven Provinces and Municipalities During the Party's National Conference on Propaganda Work

7 MARCH 1957, EVENING

[236] Is it appropriate to have a unified national teaching plan and teaching material? Jiangsu province differs from Hunan province: Is it advisable for each province to have some supplementary material [for its own use]? Do you people from different provinces feel restricted?

Last year quite a few schools were set up, some of which had disturbances, mainly owing to the poor living and study [conditions].

Source: 1:236–8; alternate text, 6A:43–4. This "talk" seems to be a report of the same occasion as that covered in "Directive on educational work" in 6A:45–8, though Mao may have met separately with different groups of provincial leaders on the same evening to discuss issues of common concern as was normal during big conferences: See also the translation of a third version in Michael Schoenhals, "Mao Zedong on Education," *The Stockholm Journal*

The method of setting up "capped [schools]" is a good one.[1] [It is] an advanced experience. It's convenient for peasant children to go to schools close to where they live. After they graduate from school, they can easily return to the farm. Try to send some people from the better middle schools to those "capped schools," to even out the inequalities between them.

The problem of quality: Our main [concern] at present is the problem of spreading education and not [so much] emphasizing quality. We have allocated 30 million yuan to set up "capped schools." The curriculum should be neither too heavy nor too advanced. It should be cut in half; eight courses are enough.

The problem of promotion to schools of higher ranks: Basically [graduates/schools leavers] will have to return home to participate in production.

The problem of financial aid: Financial aid should be granted according to financial need. Within the next three years the peasants will still be very poor. Between 70 and 80 percent of students should get financial aid. [Those] in most difficult circumstances [account for] 15–40 percent and 35–40 percent are slightly better off but still in need. The financial aid [problem] should be handled according to this standard.

The rate of primary-school graduates going up [to middle schools]

---

of East Asian Studies 1:89–95 (1988).

In both reports, Mao is said to have met with officials from seven municipalities and provinces, though 6A:45–8 names only six. On 1:236 Mao refers to Jiangsu and Hunan provinces, quite likely because representatives from them were present. Jiangsu is one of the provinces listed as being represented at the start of the 6A version; Hunan is not, but it might be the seventh missing province, especially as it is referred to by Mao on 6A:47.

Additional material of interest in the 6A report: (1) Henan and Shandong representatives reported on their student disturbances (p. 45); one of the Henan trouble spots was apparently Xuchang (p. 46). (2) After an unnamed vice-minister of education had estimated a need for additional educational expenditure of 80 million yuan, the Chairman increased it by 25% to 100 million yuan (p. 46), the figure mentioned in the translated text. (3) Political classes had been dropped from the Chinese school curriculum in favor of classes on the constitution in line with changes in the Soviet curriculum (p. 47). (4) One Hu XX is mentioned a number of times and towards the end of the session is directed by the Chairman to prepare a *RMRB* editorial (p. 48). This is Hu Qiaomu, then as now a prominent propaganda expert, and at that time one of Mao's secretaries; see Schoenhals, p. 94.

[1]"Capped schools" (*dai maozi xuexiao*) are those with an additional higher grade attached to them. They are usually primary schools, and such schools would have the first grade of middle school attached to them as a "cap."

is close to that of last year. Increasing the enrollment by 400 thousand students requires about 10 million yuan; increasing faculty positions requires about 13 million yuan. Both should be solved within the supplementary budget of 100 million yuan.

[237] The problems of schools run by APCs and by the people: Where conditions [are appropriate] such schools should be allowed. Try to mobilize everyone to discuss how to run schools. Our national income last year, owing to natural disasters, was only so much; the budget for this year is [thus] limited. We must understand the overall economic situation.

The problem of schools run by [state and other] organs and by industrial [enterprises]: We should summon all heads of education bureaus and tell them, We want students to maintain discipline, [live a life of] arduous struggle. Schools should be run with the students. Creative work should be promoted. [We] advocate that teachers and students should share comforts and hardships and run the school together. Deceiving students is not permitted. Boasting when enrolling students is not permitted [either]; one must not skirt around difficulties and talk only about [the school's] good points. A cold douche as fair warning is necessary.

To all the people, cadres, students, workers, peasants, to all alike, we should propagandize [a life of] arduous struggle. Education about arduous struggle must be carried out in all the schools—more in universities, less in high schools, less still in primary schools. Young people lack experience [and] learn from their teachers; and the teachers are also influenced by [our] newspapers.

Political and ideological education should be reinforced. Each province should appoint a propaganda chief and an education bureau chief to take charge of ideological education and give it leadership.

[Where] county leaders are not attending to their duties, they must do so within a certain period of time.

First secretaries at the provincial, prefectural, and county levels should concern themselves with education. They don't have to do it every day; a few days in the first half of the year and a few days in the second half of the year, seven or eight days a year [would be enough]. The phenomenon of disengagement from education is unacceptable.

Call a meeting and listen to people's complaints; jot them down and write an editorial.

Establish a bureau of education at the county [level]. The staffing [problem] can be solved by hiring from among those who are cut [from other organizations].

Lower and higher middle schools should increase political classes. Textbooks on politics should be compiled.

Administrative work should give way to the compiling of texts.

[The amount of] teaching material should be less heavy, [the number of] courses should be reduced. Classical literature should be reduced. Most of the *Book of Songs*[2] has no poetic quality. Reducing the number of classes and the amount of material is for the sake of all-round development [of the students].

You people here are all in charge of education, [but] is the Ministry of Education the Chinese Ministry of Education or the Soviet Ministry of Education? If it is the Soviet [Ministry], then your Ministry of Education should be abolished.

Why isn't teaching material patterned on that of the Liberated Areas?[3] Teaching material should have its local **[238]** characteristics. Each province should add a course on provincial geography [to the school curriculum]. A textbook on agriculture should be compiled by each individual province. A sample text is needed. [You] can talk all you want [about other things], but [you] cannot as a consequence not comprehend [your] own province. A bit of local literature should be taught. The basic principles of natural sciences and mathematics, physics, and chemistry are much the same throughout the country. Teaching some local literature in classical literature [classes] will be more interesting.

An overloaded curriculum and a low standard of teachers, both causes [of educational problems] exist.

Enrollments in primary schools can be increased by two to three million.

In sum, [we will] use over 100 million yuan to solve [all these problems].

---

[2] *Shi jing*, see Text 5, n. 26.
[3] For a comparison of education in the pre-1949 Liberated Areas with that in the PRC in the 1950s, see Suzanne Pepper, "Education for the new order," in *CHOC* 14, pp. 185–217.

A Talk with Literary and Art Circles

8 MARCH 1957

[28] Chairman: How many days has [this] conference been going on? How is it going? I've read all those thirty-three problems of yours.

(Lu XX[1] reports on the status of the [National] Propaganda Work Conference.)

Chairman: (To Central [Committee?] comrades): Which of you is attending the conference?

Sources: 7:27–46; alternate text, 9:56–74. The alternate text has been used to correct a few obviously erroneous characters in the primary source.
[1]Clearly this is Lu Dingyi, head of the CCP's Propaganda Department.

Kang Sheng: I was with the Shanghai group yesterday morning, the Tianjin group in the afternoon, the Ministry of Higher Education this morning, [and I] passed myself off as a writer [and] participated in the literature group this afternoon.

Chairman: What kind of problems do they all have?

Kang Sheng: The discussion in the literature group was very lively. In the end Lao X[2] raised a question which prolonged [the discussion] for another half hour; even then [people] still didn't want to break up.

Chairman: (Asking XX)[3] What was the question?

XX: [It's] about writing tragedies [and] whether tragedies can be written. For instance, there are some people whom the writers hate passionately: Can [they] write about their failure [and] death?

Chairman: What kind of people do [they] hate?

[29] Kang Sheng: Bureaucratism.

Chairman: Bureaucratism should be criticized, of course. There's a film, *To Whom Does Honor Belong,* in which there's a director of a railway bureau. Even with that kind of bureaucratism, [he] is still the director. Since [sic] the writer has described him [in this way], and then he is still retained as bureau director—this type of cadre should be dismissed! [But] for the sake of curing the illness to save the patient, he could be sent to study. This is called not getting to the bottom of things, [or] lack of thoroughness. [We] must be thorough in opposing bureaucratism. Is he not [guilty of] bureaucratism? [He] is none other than that.

Kang Sheng: Some people in the Nanjing group asked whether

[2]Probably Lao She (Shu Qingchun), author of *Rickshaw Boy* (*Luotuo xiangzi,* published in 1936–7), and one of the great novelists who emerged in the 1920s. He was at this time a vice-chairman of the Chinese Federation of Literature and Art Circles (the "Wen-lian"). He died in the early months of the Cultural Revolution as a result of Red Guard harassment. See *BDRC* 3, pp. 132–5.
[3]Probably Lao She himself.

there should be discipline in the schools. For example, can [those] students [who] violate school discipline, commit errors, and refuse to mend their ways despite repeated admonitions be expelled? Another example: [can] there still be discipline [if we] don't kick out those who write reactionary posters?

Chairman: To discipline is to criticize. Everyone helps him correct [his] mistakes]. Some are not really spies. [Their] ideological understanding is confused. It's OK to record a major demerit. It's easy to expel people, but where will they go if they're expelled? They have to end up somewhere. Is it appropriate to give [them] to you people in the [All-China] Federation of Literary [and Art] Circles or to the Writers' Union? China is so big, [we] are always going to have to keep them somewhere, [whether] in the army, in factories [or] in APCs. [If] you expel them here [and] someone else takes them in, how do you think they'll manage? Since [our] schools are so good, why can't we have a few bad students staying there? Those who run schools simply want to expel people.

Kang Sheng: The universities also have some suggestions. [They] say it's not good to have scientific research concentrated in the Academy of Sciences,[4] [that] the universities should also conduct research; [they] want to do research as well as teach.

Chairman: What problems are there in literature and art?

XX:[5] [Some] comrades among the writers as well as [others] from various places are quite confused in their minds about socialist realism. [Do we] still need socialist realism? Some maintain [we] don't; others maintain that [we should] safeguard [it].

Lu XX: It's also difficult to write essays [*xiaopin wen*].

Chairman: Which one of you knows how to write essays? There must be a guilty person.

---

[4]This allocation of research to the Academy of Sciences followed the Soviet pattern.
[5]Probably Zhou Yang.

Hu XX:[6] Comrade Mao Dun[7] wrote quite a few in the *People's Daily* initially, but there are almost no essays in the *People's Daily* nowadays. Initially many people paid attention to page eight;[8] then some said there were too many articles criticizing shortcomings, so [writers] stopped writing [for it].

Mao Dun: A few essays extol new things less because [they] expose shortcomings more often.

[30] Ba X:[9] This time we are all discussing "How to reflect [or express] contradictions among the people?" For instance, everyone feels it a headache, [feels it] very difficult to depict bureaucratism; everyone is unhappy [about it].[10] Also about essays: some in Shanghai say [essays] should be comprehensive [i.e., not one-sided]; others say [they] can't be. Lu Xun's essays only talk about one thing [at a time].

Chairman: [I'm] afraid we need big democracy[11] for things to work! Within the party [we] have proposed criticizing subjectivism, bureaucratism, [and] sectarianism. [The policy] has not been implemented yet. The Central Committee must hold a session [and] issue a directive, [ordering] preparation this year [and] beginning [the campaign] next year. This also requires a period of deliberation. The resolution must be passed in the first half of this year. At present, thinking within the party has not yet been unified [as to] what is bureaucratism [and] how to criticize [it]. [It's] still not yet unified. [We] need a rectification campaign; then [it'll] be easy to criticize. Just now, as soon as some criticisms have been advanced, Ma Han-

[6]Almost certainly Hu Qiaomu.

[7]Mao Dun, a leading realist writer famous since the late 1920s, had been Minister of Culture since 1949 and was also Chairman of the Writers' Union.

[8]At this time, p. 8 was usually the last page of *RMRB* and was devoted to short literary pieces.

[9]Clearly this is Ba Jin, who achieved fame in the early 1930s as a novelist committed to anarchism. At this time he was Vice-Chairman of the Writers' Union. See Olga Lang, *Pa Chin and his Writings* (Cambridge, Harvard Univ. Press, 1967).

[10]Ba Jin appears to be hinting that writers fear writing about bureaucratism for fear of retaliation.

[11]For "big democracy," see Text 3, p. 134; and Text 5, n. 7.

bing [and] Chen Qitong issue a statement.[12] [This] is nothing but [an attempt at] restraining [the policy of] "Let a hundred flowers bloom, let a hundred schools contend."

(A comrade from the Center interrupted: Actually this was Chen Yi's idea.)

Chairman: [In] the rectification [campaign we'll] rectify subjectivism [and] the emphasis will be on dogmatism; [we'll] rectify sectarianism. They always want one school to dominate; they always feel 600 million people are too many [and] it's better to have fewer. [We must] rectify bureaucratism; there's an awful lot [around]. [We] haven't had a rectification [campaign] for quite a few years. Since the Rectification [Campaign] in 1942, have [we] had any rectification?[13]

XX: There was some during the Three-Antis.[14]

Chairman: In the Three-Antis [we] rectified waste in [government] organs; [we've] not had any rectification for the four years, '53, '54,

---

[12]For a discussion of this article, which appeared in *RMRB*, 7 Jan. 1957, see above, pp. 168–9. For a discussion of the rescheduling of the Rectification Campaign from 1958, as envisaged here, to 1957, see Text 13, n. 5.

[13]The 1942 Rectification Campaign was directed against three evils: subjectivism, sectarianism, and party formalism. Subjectivism comprised dogmatism and empiricism. Dogmatism, the more serious and more common failing, meant blindly applying theory (or the Soviet model) without regard to the actual situation; empiricism meant totally ignoring theory. Sectarianism meant discriminating against, even conspiring against, fellow party members or non-party people. The campaign was designed to eliminate the kind of bitter intra-party struggle that some Soviet-trained leaders took as the norm and also to encourage a more friendly attitude towards outsiders at a time when United Front policies were crucial to CCP success. Party formalism referred to turgid and jargon-ridden documents and speeches, incomprehensible to most of their target audience. For documents of the 1942 campaign with an introductory analysis, see Boyd Compton, *Mao's China* (Seattle, Univ. of Washington press, 1952). Frederick Teiwes, in his study of rectification, gives a detailed presentation of its theory and practice in the 1940s; see his *Politics & Purges in China* (White Plains, NY, M. E. Sharpe, 1979), pp. 15–101.

In the 1957 campaign, the first two evils were as before, but party formalism became bureaucratism, the issuing of orders and general conduct of affairs from one's office without concrete investigation; more importantly, it referred to the abuse of the party's position in power by its officials. For a discussion of the different approaches of various leaders to the relative importance of each of the three evils, see *Origins* 1, pp. 110–9, 210–2.

[14]For details of this series of campaigns in 1951–2, see Text 3, n. 35.

'55, [and] '56. There has been less corruption since the Three-Antis, but waste is still very serious; and as for rectification, [we] simply have not carried it out. Some of [you] who are present are party [members], some are non-party [personages]. You understand something of the principles of the Communist party, namely that it wants to move things along, unify thinking, have a common language. Otherwise [when] you say [it's] bureaucratism, he says [it's] not. You say, "Let a hundred flowers bloom, let a hundred schools contend"; he says, don't bloom. [When we] bloom a bit, and there are some bad results, [they] start running around in circles. Chen Qitong and three others seem to declare, "Disastrous! The nation is going to perish!" [They] didn't even [bother] to check it with the Propaganda Department with a telephone call. "Let a hundred flowers bloom" was not the [personal policy] of Lu XX. They don't allow a single word in [their] article to be changed. It can't be right for these people not to become emperors!

[31] In brief, [they're] just very scared. [As far as] letting a hundred flowers bloom is concerned, [they're] very scared of the hundred flowers; the [appropriate] atmosphere has not been created yet. [Without] rectification [within] the Communist party, the rectification of China won't work; [after all] there are many people in the Chinese Communist Party.

There are also quite a few problems with the Film Bureau. It seems to me many of the criticisms are correct; [the problems] should be handled according to the facts. (Asking Zhao X): How's your relationship with the Film Bureau?

Zhao X:[15] Some criticisms are not entirely reasonable.

Qian XX:[16] The Film Bureau has already changed a great deal. Some criticisms are true, but others are too harsh.

Chairman: Hit back [if] it's too harsh.

(Lu XX: They hit back quite a few times.)

---

[15]Possibly Zhao Dan (1915–80), a famous movie star, who at this time was a film director at the Shanghai Film Studio.
[16]Probably Qian Junrui, a Vice-Minister of Culture.

Chairman: [We] must be convincing; I don't think Chen Huangmei's[17] article is appropriate. In short, there's a degree of chaos [*luan*] [both] inside and outside the party. There's great disorder in the land [*tianxia daluan*].

Kang Sheng: [It's] not yet great disorder in the land.

Chairman: Indeed, [things] aren't as chaotic as in Hungary, [but] still [there's] quite a lot of disorder. Thinking is not unified, [there's a] lack of a common viewpoint. At the meeting you raised thirty-three problems, from which [we] see that problems are numerous. [You] want answers. How can one person answer [them]? I still think [it's better to have] self-assessment and public discussion: One person reads, everyone discusses and answers. Some want Lu XX to answer.

(Lu XX: I alone cannot answer [all of them].)

[Chairman: We] want everyone to answer, [to conduct] self-assessment and public discussion [as to] how to write essays, how to criticize bureaucratism. [Where] criticism is incorrect, counter-criticism [should] be prepared; where criticism is correct, it won't do for you not to accept it. Those questions, let Lu XX answer; I am also not the one school, and I can't answer each and every one. Those four papers [indicating the report on conditions],[18] one [of you] read and everyone answer.

Kang Sheng: I suggest another two days of small group meetings, and let the small groups provide the answers.[19]

Chairman: Any other questions?

Mao Dun: There are now some people [who] have a one-sided understanding of writing about reality. Some young writers say [one] should write whatever one sees, [whatever] exists in reality can be

[17]Chen Huangmei (b. 1913) is a film critic, and was at this time Director of the Film Bureau in the Ministry of Culture. It is unclear to which of Chen's articles Mao is referring here.
[18]It is unclear precisely what these "four papers" are.
[19]These "small groups," meeting in between plenaries of the larger meeting, enabled more people to have their say in less daunting surroundings.

written about. That is to say that ideology can't guide creation; it's somewhat similar to Hu Feng's theories.[20] [They] say a poem is for describing emotions (the seven emotions), such as [the poem] "Kiss." [They] deny that writers need ideological guidance in observing life.

[32] Chairman: This kind of viewpoint is related to the incorrect view toward socialist realism; [I'm] afraid it's probably impossible to have all writers accept the Marxist world outlook. [It'll] probably take decades before the majority can [accept it]. In the period in which [you] still have yet to accept the Marxist world outlook, as long as [you] don't follow Hu Feng and form secret cliques, you [may] describe your [own views], each [can] have [his] own truth. [But] in this, [they] must still have help [i.e., to understand Marxism]. Some truly endorse Marxism, others endorse reluctantly. [As for] these national bourgeoisie, how can they be willing and glad [if] you communize their means of production? [They] must inevitably be somewhat reluctant. But there are also some who are not too reluctant. In transforming the social system with several hundreds of millions of people [involved], [moving] from private to public ownership, from individual to collective [ownership], inevitably some will be reluctant. (To Zhou XX):[21] Your drama troupe has [changed] from individual to collective [ownership], from private to state management.

(Zhou XX talks about [his] troupe.)

Chairman: In short, the change of system is a major change; [they] have to endorse it [albeit] reluctantly, because of the nationwide trend. Currently thinking is so confused; many of the problems in the four papers [indicating the reports] reflect precisely the changes in the social base. Our country was not a socialist country in the past; [it] was a semi-feudal, semi-colonial state. After overthrowing imperialism, bureaucratic capitalism, [and] feudalism, we were left with the national bourgeoisie and several hundreds of millions of the

[20]On Hu Feng, see above, Text 1, n. 7.
[21]Possibly Zhou Xinfang (1895–1975), a Peking Opera star, was at this time Director of the Shanghai Jingju Theater and Vice-Chairman of the Chinese Association of Performing Artists.

petty bourgeoisie; and we still wanted to transform the ownership system. Going by class origin, 80 percent of the intellectuals are the children of the landlords, rich peasants, and capitalists. Of course, [they again] can be differentiated as big, middle, or small [landlords; rich peasants; and capitalists]. University students can be counted as intellectuals. Given the nationwide population of 600 million, [if] one percent are intellectuals, [then] there are 6 million intellectuals. Not all of them are university educated. Comrade Xiao Chu'nü[22] never went to a school. He was a waiter in a teahouse in Wuchang; he is self-educated, but is still counted as an intellectual. Last year it was reckoned that there were 100,000 higher intellectuals. Possibly in our society one percent are intellectuals. I estimate there are 5 million including elementary school teachers, teaching personnel [in general], [and] some administrative personnel [in government organs], [and] some in the PLA, commercial banking personnel, engineering and technical personnel, design personnel, also news (reporters), physicians . . . about 5 million [of them]. How many in the 5 million believe in the Marxist world outlook? Are there 10 percent? Ten percent amounts to 500,000 [of them] who believe in Marxism and understand [it] quite well [and] use [it] to guide their actions. Subjectivism and dogmatism can't be counted as understanding Marxism. If [33] there are 10 percent that's good. How many are there in literature and art circles?

(Zhou X and Qian XX:[23] Altogether 250,000 people, including those in the literary and art circles as well as performing artists.)

[Chairman:] There are more intellectuals in literature and art circles—are there 50,000? [Let's] reckon there are 50,000. Can [we] calculate that 10 percent [of them] understand Marxism quite well and use [it] to guide [their] actions? It would be very nice to have that 10 percent. [It would] be 5,000 out of 50,000; [but] dogmatists don't count; subjectivists don't count; [those that follow Marxism] in name don't count. Are there [5,000] or not?

The majority of people still resist the Marxist world outlook.

[22]Xiao Chu'nü (1897–1927) was a founder of the Chinese Communist Youth League, later executed by the KMT. See Klein and Clark 1, pp. 327–8.
[23]Again, probably Zhou Yang and Qian Junrui.

Moreover, there are still [people] hostile to the socialist system, which is not just not following the Marxist world outlook. However, they're neither spies, nor do [they] kill with knives; they only grumble and sometimes write an article or two. This type of person is also in the minority; are there 10 percent [of them] or not? Most of these people don't say anything, resisting in silence, hoping always for the outbreak of World War III, wanting Chiang Kai-shek to return.

(Hu XX: This type of people does not make up 10 percent.)

[Chairman:] Perhaps there are not [as many as] 10 percent at either end. [Those who] follow Marxism do not make up 10 percent either: [If we] don't count [those who] follow [Marxism] in name, and dogmatism, can we reckon there are 10 percent [of the intellectuals] altogether inside and outside the party? There are some inside the party who don't believe in Marxism; [and] on the other hand there are some outside the party who believe in [it]. Now cut off the two ends, [and we're] left with the 80 percent in the middle, still the great majority, most of whom support the socialist system but do not necessarily believe in Marxism, and there are even fewer [who] use [it] to guide their creative activities. So socialist realism[24] cannot be forced upon them. Then what can be done about this type of writing? [Those that are] not socialist realists [we'll] have to publish as long as [they] are not at that end [of the spectrum] that hopes for World War III. Marxist writers—if it's dogmatism—people won't want to read. Is dogmatism Marxism? No, dogmatism is anti-Marxist. [We] need good, genuine Marxism—genuine socialist realist [writings]—even if the number is smaller, just a few of [them], if you could write relatively well; and in a few decades [you would] influence that 80 percent, because [what you write] is to serve the workers, peasants, and soldiers.

Mao Dun: Some say [they] don't even want the orientation of [serving] the workers, peasants, and soldiers.

Chairman: It can't be wrong to serve the workers, peasants, and

---

[24]The text actually says "socialism, realism"—presumably a mispunctuation.

soldiers, can it? There's one sentence about serving the workers, peasants, and soldiers in the article by Chen Qitong and the three others, which is correct. Who else are you going to serve if not the workers peasants, and soldiers? The bourgeoisie will be transformed into the working class, the intellectuals will also be working class; [if] you say not [34] to serve them, [well] there's none else in China [to serve].

Zhou X:[25] Some say that literature and art should have no purpose; once there's a purpose, then [literature and art] become conceptualized.

Chairman: Can't we publish some of the [writings] with no purpose? [We'll] publish two types [of writings], one kind desiring purpose. OK? In short, it's a long process to educate the people. Dictatorship, arbitrariness, and suppression cannot be applied to ideological problems. [If you] want people to obey, [you] have to persuade rather than coerce [them]. Unless [they] take up knives, we must choose between two ways. [People] like Ma Hanbin don't do much reasoning, [they just insist] you have to listen to me.

Mao Dun: According to the comrades of the editorial [departments] of the four publications (meaning those [sponsored] by the Writers' Union), quite a few of the manuscripts they receive write about love for the sake of writing about love [and] about household affairs for the sake of writing about household affairs, [but] not many have been published. Readers don't like dull writings; nor do they accept works without ideological content.

Chairman: Literature and art will perhaps also have to go through the process of steeling. Some people are not conscious [of what they're doing], [they've] not yet been tempered. Those who advocate [that] literature and art should have no purpose actually do want a purpose, [but] they don't want your purpose; under the protection of no purpose they have their own purpose—namely they want petty bourgeois and bourgeois purposes. The bourgeoisie [have gone] from private to state-run [businesses] and the petty bourgeoisie from

[25]Probably Zhou Yang.

individually to collectively run [farms and shops]. What else do you want [of them]?

Some ask about the distinction between the bourgeoisie and the petty bourgeoisie. I can't distinguish them myself. The bourgeoisie and the petty bourgeoisie are in the same category economically. Judged by class origins, the petty bourgeoisie can also be quite ferocious [when they] become reactionary. In the past, quite a few peasants became bandits or professional brigands; [they] were rascals, thieves, leaping onto roofs and vaulting over walls, with quite remarkable ability. The intellectuals of bourgeois class origin are quite revolutionary [once they] accept Marxism; I also belong to this category. Zhou X,[26] you, too, don't you? [When talking of] bourgeois intellectuals, [we] should not only look at class origins; I am referring to those who receive education in bourgeois schools. The bourgeoisie educate us according to their interests. Accepting Marxism [is something that is required] later. Therefore, I think it's very difficult to differentiate bourgeois and petty bourgeois ideologies.

[When] I say educate the people, I have as my object these people [who] number hundreds of millions. The workers need education as well. There are only 12 million workers at present; things would be a lot easier [if] there were 50 million workers in a country like ours. Apart from the workers, there are 1.7 million administrative personnel, an army of 3.8 million, over 2 million cultural and educational [35] personnel, [and] also over 2 million commercial and enterprise personnel. Quite a proportion of [all] these have not been tempered [and their] thinking is quite complicated. These people are [those who] educate others; the power is in the hands of these people. I think there are too many functionaries; [we] don't want so many; [we'll] cut, beginning this year. Currently, there's a "plague of merchants": in one county with a population of 1.7 million there are 18,000 (or 1,800) commercial personnel [renyuan] and 500 functionaries [gongzuo renyuan]. Too many. If someone lets this information out, I would welcome it. [We] must simplify [administration]. This is a period of great social transformation. What system of establishment is appropriate after all? [Our system] has not [yet] got on the right track and we should investigate [this]. All we do is issue a directive. You crowd me [and] I crowd you. But anyway, these party and

---

[26]Possibly Zhou Xinfang; see n. 21.

administrative functionaries are those who lead the country, [and] educate the people. The newspapers, literature, art, broadcasting, cultural troupes, [and] theatrical troupes all educate the people. Some say: "Don't say education, it's better to say entertainment." [This] is also OK. But [when] you put on a show, [you're] bound to influence people and make them believe you. Therefore the educators should first of all receive education. This is what Marx said. People like us should receive education. The idea that no education is needed is untenable. The capitalists now admit they have a two-sided character. Some say it's one-sided. These people who educate others—speaking broadly, it's an education process. It'll take decades to educate 600 million people. [I] said just now that thinking in literary and art organizations and newspapers and other educational organs is rather confused; the impact of the Hungarian incident is not the main [cause].

After the October Revolution, the Soviet Union from 1917 to 1927 was in a more chaotic [state] then we are now. Dogmatism was also very serious. For example, the literary organization RAPP[27] coerced others on how to write their works. [I] have heard that there was still some freedom of speech at that time; there were still fellow-travelers. The fellow-travelers still had [their own] publications, [and] said [they] were for propagating the truth. [In our case], we don't let others run [any publications]. Can we let others run publications that would sing different tunes? [We] could reach an understanding with them, have an agreement; as long as [they] are not like Taiwan, it would be OK.

(Hu XX: If you want them to sing a different tune in public, they won't [want] to run [their own publications].)[28]

[Chairman:] There's no harm in [their] singing [a different tune] publicly. At that time in the Soviet Union some people publicly

[27]RAPP, the Russian Association of Proletarian Writers (or LAPU, as it is abbreviated from the Chinese phoneticization), was a militantly leftist organization which terrorized fellow-traveling authors who were members of the other major literary organization, the All-Russian Union of Writers; see Max Hayward and Leopold Labedz, eds., *Literature and Revolution in Soviet Russia, 1917–1962* (London, Oxford Univ. Press, 1963), pp. x–xiii.

[28]Again, probably Hu Qiaomu. Hu evidently had a shrewd idea as to the cautiousness of writers after earlier ideological campaigns, such as the 1955 campaign against Hu Feng.

admitted they were fellow-travelers. One can see [we are] different on this point. The preparation for the revolution in the Soviet Union was not as long as ours. They waged revolution to overthrow feudal oppression. We had, in addition, national oppression. Imperialism controlled us for a long period of over one hundred years, so the intellectuals hated imperialism passionately. Furthermore, we did not [enforce] uniform confiscation toward the bourgeoisie; [our] economy was not destroyed on so large a scale as theirs [i.e., the Soviet Union's]. Later they started the New Economic Policy, [but] declared its conclusion in two or three years. Why such a hurry? Lately I had a conversation with Ambassador [Pavel] Yudin.[29] [36] He said [the country that] thoroughly implemented the New Economic Policy was China; we have already implemented [it] for three years. [We'll implement [it] for another seven years, thirteen years, [and] continue [it] for another two or three years if necessary. The Soviet Union was in too much of a hurry, [with the result that] it still affects [the production of] its commodities today—the insufficiency of consumer goods. The market is not prosperous either. They [have existed for] forty years. Nowadays we complain daily about shortages; their shortages are even worse. Then take rural policy; they made mistakes. Commandism was very serious. After collectivization, production decreased for several years. The elimination of counterrevolution was quite "leftist" in [its] later [stages]. After Kirov's assassination, everyone came under suspicion.[30] In the first few years, it was still possible to sing a different tune, to have some freedom of speech; later one was allowed to say only good things about the party and government; no criticism was permitted or possible; so [they] practiced a cult of personality. Stalin often confused the two types of contradictions. For this reason, economic policies apart, we don't adopt their methods [in formulating our] cultural and educational policies; we've adopted "Let a hundred flowers bloom, let a hundred schools contend" with guidance. So far [we] haven't created an environment for

---

[29]See Text 3, n. 45.

[30]S. M. Kirov was the head of the Leningrad party organization when he was assassinated in 1934 by a disgruntled ex-Bolshevik. It is widely assumed that his killing was ordered by Stalin out of fear of a potential rival. See Strobe Talbott, tr. and ed., *Khrushchev Remembers* (Boston, Little Brown, 1971), pp. 75–8, especially the editor's note on p. 77. For a more sensationalist "insider's" account, see Anton Antonov-Ovseyenko, *The Time of Stalin* (New York, Harper Colophon Books, 1983), pp. 84–104.

"blooming"; there's still not enough blooming—a hundred flowers want to bloom but dare not bloom; a hundred schools want to contend but dare not contend. I've read twice the article by Chen Qitong and the three others; they're full of anxiety [*you xin ru fen*] that there'll be massive upheaval in the land. [We] must size up the situation in China; the two ends are small and the middle is big [with] such a large number of the petty bourgeoisie. [What's] known as ideological confusion demands elucidation.

I'm saying [all] this in order to exchange opinions with [you] comrades to see if the objective reality is like this. Ten percent of the intellectuals believe in Marxism—[that's] 500,000. Are there so many? Those who don't believe [in it] are so numerous. [But] this can't be forced [upon] them. If after three or four five-year plans one-third of the people believe in the Marxist world outlook and it isn't dogmatism or opportunism, then [that'll] be good.

Lu Xun[31] was not a Communist party member, [but] he understood the Marxist world outlook. He took some pains to study [it]; and by putting it into practice [he came to] believe that Marxism was truth. His essays [*zawen*], especially those his later years, were very powerful, [and] his essays were powerful because they were imbued with the Marxist world outlook. In my opinion, [if] Lu Xun hadn't died, [he'd] still be writing essays; [but I] fear [he'd] no longer be able to write fiction; [he'd] probably be chairman of the Literary and Arts Federation. He would speak at meetings on the thirty-three questions; [and] as soon as he'd spoken or written essays, the problems would have been solved. [I'm] sure he'd have had something to say; he would definitely have spoken and, what's more, would have been very courageous.

True Marxists don't fear anything or anyone. [They] don't worry about [**37**] whether or not someone's going to punish them; at worst [they] won't have food to eat, [they'll have to] beg, [they'll be] punished, jailed, beheaded, or wronged. I've never gone begging for food; [but] if one wants revolution, one has to be prepared to be beheaded. It's not unworthy to be beheaded by the enemy, [but it is] by one's

[31]Lu Xun (1881–1936), probably the leading essayist and short story writer of the 1920s and 1930s until his death, had long been for the communists a paragon of the revolutionary intellectual, partly because Mao chose to canonize him. See Lu's biography in *BDRC* 2, pp. 416–24.

own people, as in the Soviet Union. Therefore we have one principle: Kill no one. But it's possible that we send some people to jail; it's necessary for an individual to get punished a bit in [his] life. Last time I mentioned Xue Rengui and Sun, the novice monk [Sun Wukong, the Monkey King][32] – it was all in the recording, wasn't it? . . . This is also grading cadres. Xue Rengui was sick, [yet still] won battles. [But] the credit was given to others. Sun Wukong was also treated unfairly. Of course, he was seriously prone to individualistic heroism; he considered himself the great sage under heaven. What's more, not a single member of the masses in his kingdom of *Aolai* – those monkeys – had any disagreement [with him]. The Jade Emperor was unfair; [he] only offered him [the position of] "Master of the Imperial Stables" [*bimawen*]. So he attacked the heavenly court to oppose bureaucratism. I think there are both sectarianism and subjectivism. Zhang Shigui[33] had both sectarianism and subjectivism. [If] your name is Xue Rengui, [then we] have two Gui's [here]. Sacrilegious! [This is] sectarianism. Zhang Shigui really existed. [He] was an official in Sichuan; [I] don't know how the author put him together with Xue Rengui. How's literary criticism going? [We] should also keep in mind [the concept of] small at the two ends and big in the middle. This is why [we] must adopt the policy of "Let a hundred flowers bloom, let a hundred schools contend." Then why fear blooming? Just as soon as there's blooming, [they say]: "Master, a disaster is imminent!" "What's so alarming?" "There are monsters around!"[34] – There are indeed monsters; but the majority of intellectuals want to follow the socialist [road]; [they] want the country to be rich and powerful [*fuqiang*], the people's life to be good [and] the cultural level improved. . . . [These will be possible] only through their educating hundreds of millions of the Chinese people. There are 250,000 people in the literary and art circles of whom 50,000 are intellectuals. [There are] 2 million teaching and administrative staff, 5 million middle school students, and 200,000 university students. In a few years, many people will become intellectuals. [If you] want to investigate

[32]For Xue Rengui, see Text 3, n. 48. For Sun, see Text 3, ns. 6, 47; here "*Sun xingzhe*," lit. "Sun the traveler," which conveys the sense of a novice monk who travels on foot to beg for alms.
[33]See Text 3, n. 49.
[34]A pastiche of the traditional dialogues between masters and subordinates in Chinese opera.

[their] class origins, 80 percent of the university students are the children of landlords, rich peasants, and capitalists, [and it's] 50 to 60 percent of the middle school students. [If] you don't want them, who do you want? These people can be re-educated; the problem is whether or not [we] trust [them].

I would like to talk about the problem of literary and art criticism. I haven't read very much, but [I've] read some. [I] feel there's not much appropriate criticism, [that is, criticism] made after research that is analytical, which is preceded by [the critics'] consulting the authors, [criticism which] truly helps the author rather than giving [them] a scolding. [These] indeed aren't numerous, are they? Some criticisms are throughout very rude. Lu Xun had a way of dealing with this type of criticism, which was, ignore [it].

(Mao Dun: The excessively rude criticisms are not so numerous now; [but] there's a kind of criticism that scratches the itch from outside the boots, **[38]** [as they] can't get at the itch. They are only vague and general criticisms.)

[Chairman:] In that case there are now three types of criticism: One type is able to get at the itch, undogmatic, helpful; another type scratches the itch from outside the boot, vague and general, not helpful; to write [these types of articles] is equivalent to not writing at all. Still another type is dogmatic, rude, wants to club people to death with a single blow; [this] prevents literary and art criticism from developing, doesn't it?

(Mao Dun: This is perhaps also [a case of] small at the two ends and big in the middle. [Those that] can't get at the itch and give vague and general [criticisms] are in the majority.)

[Chairman:] I noticed the encirclement of Wang Meng in literary criticism; that's why I wanted to hold this propaganda conference. From [what I can] see from the criticism of Wang Meng, [his] critics haven't bothered to find out [anything about him], how tall or how big. He lives right [here] in Beijing. [Yet] those who want to write critical articles don't even consult him. When you criticize him, is it still for the sake of helping him?

Have you read the essay "Having tea at Hui spring" in *Xin*

Guancha [New Observer]? [It's] in the second of the January issues;
[you] can take a look. The author's name is Yao Xueyin:[35] What kind
of person is [he]?

(People give some information about Yao.)

[Chairman:] [Is he] counted a middle-of-the-roader or as on the
right? I'm quite interested by his depiction of tea-drinkers. His article
says many people don't know how to drink tea; it says he himself
does not know how to drink tea, yet they seem to enjoy themselves
quite a bit when drinking [it]. He also criticizes the shortcomings of
this badly managed cooperative teahouse. This conclusion is correct.
In many cases, after the changeover to joint state-private management, previous strong points were discarded. This should be corrected in the future. But he's not right to despise the masses who
drink tea; this [smacks of] the [old] idea of the "superior man" [*junzi*]
and the "mean man" [*xiaoren*]. The "superior man" is drinking tea
there, [then] the "mean man" also comes along; the article makes
clear that this writer is aloof [when] among the masses.

(Zhou X:[36] He also wrote a treatise in the *Wenhui bao*, saying the
writers didn't need to go among the masses to experience life. He said
we don't respect the experiences of the veteran writers.)

[Chairman:] I've also read articles refuting him. There's a [certain]
Yao Wenyuan[37] who's written quite convincingly. [This kind of arti-
cle] I can read, [but] I simply can't read Ma Hanbing's article. But
[we] should still help him. Be it bourgeois ideology or petty bourgeois ideology it's still the dominant [trend] among the intellectuals.
They still have not identified [themselves] with the masses. **[39]** A

[35]Yao Xueyin (b. 1910), a novelist, the author of the once popular historical novel, *Li Zecheng*, about the rebel who sacked the Ming capital in 1644 and briefly proclaimed his new dynasty before he had to retreat before the invading Manchus. Since 1978, Yao has been Chairman of the Hubei Federation of Literary and Art Circles and has become some-thing of a "leftist," active in the assault on reformist intellectuals in the spring of 1987. Mao had commented positively on 16 Feb. on a criticism of Yao Xueyin by the young radical lit-erary critic, Yao Wenyuan, see Text 1, n. 28.
[36]Probably Zhou Yang.
[37]See Text 1, n. 28.

certain Lü Ban[38] writes in *Zhongguo Dianying* [China cinematography], saying he still can't become one with the masses [even though] he's tried for so many years. I know him; [he's] become a Communist party member [but] still can't identify with the workers, peasants, and soldiers. I think only by identifying with the workers, peasants, and soldiers can [one] have a way out. [If you] can't identify with [them], what can you write about? Write only about those 5 million intellectuals and the trivial matters to do with [them]? [You] can't write only about these people all the time, [for] they will also change. Literary and art works will always be about the relationship between this section and that section of the people. [Writers in] Shanghai can write a bit about Shenxin No. 9 Factory; the capital owned by that capitalist Rong Yiren[39] is equal to one-and-a-half times the capital of Beijing. [If] you want to write about him, Rong Yiren, then you'd have to write about the relations between him and [his] workers. [We] can also allow some people to write about trivial matters to do with him. If [the writers] don't go to identify with the workers, peasants, and soldiers, they don't go; [but] on the other hand [they] can write—what can you do? In such a large country, there'll always be people like this—this is also an objective reality. But we still should help them, influence them; [if they] don't accept [our help, we] can't do anything. [We] can [still] publish their books.

Observing and learning from real life can take a variety of forms; [if they] don't do it right [you'll see] the common people will not open [their] hearts to the intellectuals. At present [when] intellectuals go down to observe and learn from real life, the common people think of it as a disaster. Especially at the famous factories and APCs: [they're] really afraid [that] you are going to investigate [something there], [and their reaction is] we just won't tell you anything. The common people have a variety of ways of dealing with you. In some places there are "plagues of journalists." A physician from Baiyangdian once returned to the countryside to see a friend. [The friend] was a Xiang [township] secretary, whose job was filling out forms. [When] the physician saw him filling out so many forms [and] doing

---

[38]Lü Ban (1913–76) was a stage and screen actor, and at the time a film director in the Northeast Film Studio.
[39]See Text 1, n. 6.

it so neatly, [he] said, "How well [you've] done them!" The friend replied: "[These forms are] false; higher authority want [them], [so I] have to fill them out." This is called township administration identifying with the district administration to manufacture false reports. (Everyone laughs).

Do the critics have an organization?

(Zhou X:[40] There's no expert organization [of the critics]. They're all in the Writers' Union. There's a theoretical group which meets often to study [the situation]. Among the essays criticizing Wang Meng's story, one entitled "A clear current with no spray" published in *Yan He* [*Yan River*] is not bad.)

[Chairman:] *Yan He*—[since it] flows from the Yan River, it has to be more correct. [If you] want to criticize someone's article it's best to have a chat with the person to be criticized, let him read [your] article. The purpose of criticism is to help the criticized. [We] can encourage this atmosphere.

[40] (Hu XX:[41] [We] did this in criticizing Zhu Guangqian;[42] but although he took in all the good points offered by others, [he] still didn't say so!)

[Chairman:] So there's also a group of people [who] don't show anyone [their] articles beforehand lest others would draw [benefit] from [their] good points.

(Lao X:[43] The cultivation of critics is very important. In the history of world civilization many writers have been produced, but very few critics. Not many critical articles have survived [the test of time] for the benefit of posterity. The good ones all display a pro-

[40]Probably Zhou Yang.
[41]Almost certainly Hu Qiaomu.
[42]Zhu Guangqian (1897–1986), a professor at Peking University who focused on aesthetics and was attacked for his close attention to Western literature and his idealistic viewpoint; see D. W. Fokkema, *Literary Doctrine in China and Soviet Influence, 1955–60* (The Hague, Mouton, 1965), pp. 93–7.
[43]Probably Lao She (Shu Qingchun).

found understanding of their own national cultural traditions [and] are all truly for the people and for democracy.)

[Chairman:] When does the history of Chinese literary criticism begin? From [when] Emperor Wen [187–226] of the Wei dynasty [220–65] replied to Yang Xiu [173–219] on literature? Later there were the *Essays on Literature*[44] and the *The Literary Mind and the Carving of Dragons.*[45] Han Yu [768–824] advocated the ancient style [*guwen*]; his was actually a neo-ancient style, without much to it. An essay only had to be new [in form]—if people said it was good, he'd say it was bad; if people said it was bad, he'd say it was good. The *Wen xuan* [Literary selections] also contains [literary] criticisms. [For instance] Zhaoming Taizi[46] wrote in the preface "Matter is the product of profound thought," which pertains to ideological content; and "Principles belong to the realm of literary elegance," which pertains to artistic quality. Theory alone he didn't want. Both ideological and artistic aspects are necessary. Are there other questions?

(Lao X:[47] Among outsiders there's a feeling that writers live well. Actually, not many live really well. [They've] become professionalized. The Writers' Union has some credit available; but most people don't want to borrow, [they] want to live on what [they] earn.

Ba X:[48] The writers have become professionalized, [but] the paper for printing is relatively short; some books [because of] the paper shortage are very slow to come off the presses or don't get published at all. [This] has [adversely] affected the writer's life. While the paper

---

[44]*Dian lun lunwen,* by Cao Pi (187–226). The "Lunwen" is a chapter of Cao's only partially extant work, *Dianlun* (Classical treatises). See, David R. Knechtges' "Introduction," in his *Wen xuan, or Selections of Refined Literature* (Princeton, Princeton Univ. Press, 1982), p. 2.
[45]*Wen xin diao long,* by Liu Xie (465–522). For a translation, see Vincent Y. C. Shih, *The Literary Mind and the Carving of Dragons* (New York, Columbia Univ. Press, 1959).
[46]*Wen xuan* was compiled by Xiao Tong (501–531) who was known posthumously as the Crown Prince of Resplendent Brilliance (*Zhaoming taizi*). For a translation, see David R. Knechtges, *Wen xuan,* vol. 1.
[47]Probably Lao She (Shu Qingchun).
[48]See n. 9.

shortage is a general situation, the distribution of paper is also not equitable.)

[Chairman:] Can the Writer's Union start its own paper mill? [We'll] allocate you some machinery [and] raw materials. (Asking Qian XX)[49] How's the situation with paper?

[If] the works of professors and scientists temporarily cannot be published, they still have their salaries from the Academy of Sciences or the universities to support [themselves]. It's different, though, for the writers. They live on this remuneration as authors. If the publishing house or publications do not have the paper to print [them], then the [writers] without remuneration have no means of livelihood. [If] the [supply of] paper is so tight, what are you (indicating Qian XX) going to do?

(Qian XX reports on the distribution of paper nationwide; quite a bit has been distributed for use in the society [at large].)

[41] (Kang Sheng: The use of paper in society includes paper for office work and for industrial packaging and so on.)

[Chairman: Since the supply of] paper is so tight, give less for social use [so as to] prevent them from making false reports.

(All laugh; then there were two more reports on the printing and distribution of books.)

[Chairman: When I say] the Writers' Union [should] start a printing house by itself, of course, [I don't mean] to have Messrs. Lao She [and] Ba Jin run it; let Zhou X[50] [and] Shen Yanbing [Mao Dun] plan and do [it]. I am for strikes under certain circumstance, [that is, when] bureaucratism is extremely serious. (Asking Zhao X:)[51] How are you in the film circles in Shanghai doing?

(Zhao X says there are no major problems.)

---

[49]For the Qian XX who is questioned here and makes a report in response, see n. 16.
[50]Probably Zhou Yang.
[51]For the Zhao X who is questioned here and responds, see n. 15.

[Chairman:] The film [circle] is also one school. (To Cai Chusheng.[52] You represent them; what do you want to say on their behalf?

(Zhao X: We in Shanghai Film Studio have already done our best to adopt effective measures to improve [our] work.)

(Cai and Zhao: More than 30 feature films were produced last year.)

[Chairman:] Which country produced the most movies last year?

(Zhou, Cai and others: Last year Japan produced the most; [it] shot more than 300 feature films. The second was India; the third was the United States.)

[Chairman:] Our producing something over 30 feature films a year is too little; you'd better produce over 300 of them. Japan [has a] population of more than 80 million [and] it produced more than 300 movies. China [has a] population of 600 million; [whereas it] produces something over 30. (Asking Zhao) Sun X[53] did not manage well, did [he]? You cooperated with him [once].

(Zhao X: Sun X has high blood pressure [and] has rested for a long time. He's written a film script; now [he's] directing; [he] has assistants to help him.)

[Chairman:] That's good.[54] You two . . . once received criticism; that's nothing. [If] a work is not well written, then write another! You always should write it well. (Asking Zhou Gangming)[55] Which

---

[52]Cai Chusheng (1906–68), a famous scriptwriter and film director.

[53]Evidently Sun Yu (1900–85?), a film director in Shanghai who studied literature and drama at the University of Wisconsin in the 1920s. The film he made in 1948, *The Life of Wu Xun (Wu Xun zhuan)*, starring Zhao Dan as Wu Xun, was attacked in the media in 1951. Mao himself wrote an editorial attacking the film for *RMRB* on 20 May 1951; see Mao *SW5*, pp. 57–8. For general accounts of the Wu Xun affair, see Merle Goldman, *Literary Dissent in Communist China* (Cambridge, Harvard Univ. Press, 1967), pp. 90–3, and Theodore H. E. Chen, *Thought Reform in the Chinese Intellectuals* (Hong Kong, Hong Kong Univ. Press, 1960), pp. 38–42.

[54]The text says *shao*; we assume it is a typographical error and should be *hao*.

[55]Zhou Gangming (b. 1909), a writer, was for a time a vice-chairman of the Guangdong Federation of Literary and Arts Circles and a leading official in the Guangdong Provincial Bureau of Culture.

region do you belong to? If [you] have any problems, talk about them.

(Zhou Gangming: I'm in the Guangdong [group]. In order for us to implement the policy of "Let a hundred flowers bloom, let a hundred schools contend" more effectively [when] we return and in order for us to shatter the obstacles [that we] may experience [when we] relay [the results of this conference] upon our return, we hope that the Central Committee [can issue] directives to the party committees of various levels and [can] make explicit decisions at the Third Plenum of the party's Central Committee, which will be held imminently. Only thus [can] this policy be thoroughly implemented.)

[Chairman:] Don't wait till the Third Plenum; you relay and implement [the results] as soon as you return. Perhaps there's a fear of blooming in your place?

[42] (Hu XX:[56] In many places the Chairman's talk at the conference of provincial and municipal party secretaries was relayed incorrectly.)

[Chairman:] My report will be printed soon; my speech at the conference of provincial and municipal party secretaries was only a few side remarks. [I] did not talk specially about the problem of the article by Chen Qitong and the other three. In general [I] talked about the need for [the policy of] letting a hundred flowers bloom to be implemented. There are many high-ranking cadres about the rank of prefectural administrative commissioner [zhuan yuan] or party secretaries—an administrative commissioner is the prefect [taishou] of the old days. There's one writer, Yang Gang,[57] whose father was a prefect in the past. There are over 10,000 cadres about the rank of administrative commissioner. [It's] very hard to say whether there are 1,000

---

[56]For Hu XX here and in the next several speeches, see n. 6.

[57]Yang Gang (1901–57) was at this time a deputy director in chief of *RMRB*. She had been a reporter for the *Dagong bao* in the United States in the 1940s, and then worked as a secretary for Zhou Enlai in the early 1950s (The notetaker here mistakenly uses the masculine form of the third person pronoun, *ta*.).

[of them who] support [the policy of] "Let a hundred flowers bloom, let a hundred schools contend"; the other nine-tenths still don't support [it]. These are all high-ranking cadres! I say [we] must bloom! If they come up with a rebuttal, that's OK. In sum, they think it's disastrous; [those that] conform to their standards, [they] publish; [those that] don't conform to their standards, [they] suppress. I don't think it'll work. You see, [they've] suppressed for so long, can [they] make it work?

The Soviet Union is still suppressing, too; but lately there seems to be a little leeway. Shepilov[58] said in his speech (referring to the news [report] published on the 4th in the *People's Daily*) that socialist realism was good, but [different] schools could be allowed [to exist]. < Is this more lenient? But [they] seem also first to put on a label before allowing [other] schools [to exist]. >[59] (Asking Zhou X)[60] How did they put it at the two writers' congresses in the past?

(Zhou X: That [different] schools could be allowed to exist within socialist realism.)

(Hu XX: in other words, first putting on a label before allowing [different] schools to exist. In reality, literary works can't be pigeonholed in categories like drawing a map.)

(Zhou X: Ehrenburg[61] said [they] could only say that socialist realism was the writers' social outlook; Shepilov criticized this viewpoint.)

[Chairman:] Did Ehrenburg maintain [they should be] more lenient or stricter?

---

[58]Dimitri Shepilov, former propaganda chief and editor of *Pravda*, was at this time Foreign Minister and a candidate member of the CPSU Presidium (Politburo). A few months later, he deserted his patron Khrushchev during the latter's struggle against the "anti-party group" consisting of Molotov (whom Shepilov had replaced at the Foreign Ministry), Malenkov, and Kaganovich. Khrushchev's ultimate victory resulted in all four being expelled from the CPSU Central Committee.
[59]The passage is taken from a very similar version of this text in New Mao Texts 9:72.
[60]For Zhou X here and in the next few speeches, see n. 5.
[61]Ilya Ehrenburg, a leading Soviet novelist and poet, occasionally challenged the official literary line, though never in a way to endanger his position. His novel, *The Thaw* (1954–6), gave its name to the post-Stalin relaxation.

(Hu XX: Ehrenburg maintained [they should be] more lenient; yet [he] still upheld the socialist world outlook.)

(Zhou X made some supplementary remarks saying that Qin Zhaoyang[62] writing under the pen name He Zhi had discussed socialist realism. He was criticized by some as being opposed to socialist realism; he became very nervous. [Zhou X] also said that Zhang Guangnian[63] wrote an article criticizing him.)

[Chairman:] To which school does Zhang Guangnian belong?

(Hu XX: Orthodoxy, [I] guess.)

[43] [Chairman:] The question of socialist realism can't be clarified all at once at this conference. No conclusion can be made, and [people] needn't be nervous; [we] can study and discuss [it].

(A comrade from the Cultural Bureau of Shenyang [Municipality] suggested that the Chairman talk about the question of carrying forward the [cultural] heritage. [He] also mentioned that some people [in] relaying [instructions] said the Chairman had stated that to put on a few shows of monsters and demons in the repertoire didn't matter, that [they] wouldn't affect the APCs [to the extent of] decreasing production. Thus, people don't know what to make of this issue.)

[Chairman:] I do not approve of monsters and demons; [but] let them be put on [so that they can be] criticized. In the past the method was suppression; now [people are] scared when [they] emerge. There is indeed a lot of poison and dross in the heritage!

(Some comrade says there are now people who value every bit of the heritage as treasure.)

---

[62]Qin Zhaoyang (b. 1916), a protégé of Zhou Yang, had until recently seemed a supremely orthodox writer; but during 1956–7, as editor-in-chief of *Renmin wenxue* (People's literature), he emerged as a spokesman for greater creative freedom. See Goldman, *Literary Dissent*, pp. 166–70.

[63]Zhang Guangnian was at this time Secretary-General of the Union of Chinese Stage Artists, Deputy Director of the Ministry of Culture's Art Bureau, and a secretary of the Secretariat of the Chinese Federation of Literary and Arts Circles.

[Chairman:] We banned some [plays in the] traditional repertoire for a few years in the past. Some people were averse to this. Now [we're] relaxing [our policy];[64] [you] can still criticize [them], but must do so with reason.

(Zhou X: [It was] not banning in the past, but suppression. As soon as a show was put on, [people] abused [it], to the extent that no one would dare put it on [again].)

[Chairman:] Some shows with monsters and demons can also be watched. We watched *The Metamorphosis of the Lords*.[65] Is it not [about] monsters and demons? There are monsters and demons in society; [it's therefore] not strange to have [them] in plays.

(Zhou Gangming:[66] Could the Chairman please talk about the problem of developing the literature and art of the national minorities; in our area there are quite a few minority nationalities. [If] the Chairman was to discuss [this] it would give great encouragement to the development of national minority literature and art. [It'll be] a great encouragement.)

(Zhou X, Hu XX: The literature and art of the national minorities are indeed very important; quite a few [items] have been unearthed and processed.)

[Chairman:] So many monsters and demons in society! The Chinese do not necessarily believe in ghosts, [so] putting [them] on stage [for people] to see is not that terrible. (Laughing toward

[64]Two months later, on 10 May 1957, the Ministry of Culture made a decision to lift the ban on 26 Peking Operas that had been considered to be "unhealthy" and banned in the early 1950s, including *A Visit to the Netherworld* (*Tan yin shan*), *Cleaving the Coffin* (*Da pi guan*), etc. On 14 May the ban was formally lifted. See *Liushi nian wenyi da shi ji: 1919-1979* (Chronology of major events in literature and art: 1919-1979) (Hong Kong, Xiandai Zhonguo wenxue yanjiu zhongxin, 1979).
[65]*Feng shen yanyi*, one of a number of Peking Operas based on a 100-chapter Ming dynasty novel of the same title, written by Xu Zhongling during the Wan Li period (1573-1619). It is about the war between King Zhou of the Shang Dynasty and King Wu of the Zhou Dynasty and contains many fantastic stories about "demons and monsters."
[66]See n. 55.

Zhou XX[67]) Haven't you performed in plays in which there were monsters and demons? Would you please say something [on this].

(Zhou XX: In the past when there were restrictions on the repertoire, the plays that could be staged were few. That has affected the income of the troupe and hampered the artists' livelihood. [Since] the relaxation of restrictions on the repertoire, the number of plays has been increased, business has taken a turn for the better, [box-office] takings have gone up, and so the lives [of the artists] have changed for the better as well. But as to how to improve the repertoire, many artists still don't have enough awareness.)

[Chairman:] It doesn't matter if one relaxes [restrictions]. Many young people don't understand what the monsters and demons are about; it doesn't matter [if we] let them watch.

[44] (Zhou continued to report.)

[Chairman:] [It's] not quite normal. In the past [it was] suppression [that] left the artists without anything to eat; now with relaxation, they can eat, but monsters and demons have come out. There are problems.

(Zhou says: Some plays I would not advocate performing.)

[Chairman:] You don't approve of monsters and demons? Is *Si Lang Visits his Mother* still being performed? Was the Empress Xiao of the frontier tribe of the Qitan nationality? More likely Manchu. Probably that's embarrassing to the Han. Ha, ha. Si Lang was traitor to the Han, was he [not]?[68]

(Zhou continued to give his opinions on the current repertoire and the study of art.)

[67]For Zhou XX here and in the reply, see n. 21.
[68]*Si Lang tan mu;* translated in A. C. Scott, *Traditional Chinese Plays* (Madison, Univ. of Wisconsin Press, 1967), pp. 19–91. The play was performed for the first time in the PRC in May 1956 (ibid., p. 23). The embarrassment Mao talks of could appear to be that of Han people at the idea of having an alien mother.

[Chairman:] [If you] can substitute something better that would, of course, be very good; but since you can produce nothing, let them carry on performing! You can produce nothing; you don't perform on stage yourself either, [you] have no choice but to let them perform.

(Zhou went on to say that the repertoire was not well developed; there were not enough actors to fill all the roles. There are no standards for how many people [there should be in a troupe] and are needed.)

Theatrical troupes should have a sense of independence. [They] can't have a four-year system (voice unclear). This you should decide for yourselves after [due] consideration.

(Kang Sheng: At the moment some theatrical troupes have broken [their] original rules.)

[Chairman:] You still [should] observe your own rules, OK; [if it's] still not enough, you should give them enough [personnel].

(The director of the Cultural Bureau of Shanghai Municipality said that the Shanghai Peking Opera Troupe needed an annual subsidy of over 300,000 yuan; in addition there was inequality in wages and salaries. [He] also said that there were more than 300 units, 17,000 people directly under the Cultural Bureau of Shanghai; the unfair high salary system existed in many theatrical troupes.)

[Chairman:] You have more than 300 units with 17,000 people, [this is] truly great chaos under heaven. But [they're] approaching resolution; you'll have to rectify [the situation].

(Fang X[69] reported on the situation of artists in Tianjin and said that the policy of "Let a hundred flowers bloom, let a hundred schools contend" could not be put on the agenda of the party committee's work on literature and art work on a day-to-day basis.)

---

[69]Probably Fang Ji (b. 1919), a writer and Yan'an veteran who was at the time Chairman of the Tianjin Federation of Literary and Arts Circles and a vice director of the Propaganda Department of the Tianjin Party Committee.

[Chairman:] In that case, you just rebel! . . .

My views on the article by Chen Qitong and the other three were relayed incorrectly; [it's] an error of the times. I have also some responsibility [for I] did not express myself clearly at the time. But I did say there must be blooming. There is truly great chaos under heaven. You see even before Hungary was in chaos, one-third of China had already become chaotic. These people are too scared. Can [our] country perish [if there's] a bit of blooming? Didn't Japan come to occupy more than half of China? I just don't believe [our] country would perish. **[45]** [They're] also scared of student rebellion, [so they] want to expel the students. Where [do you] let them go after [you] expel them? All this amounts to the practice of using one's neighbor's field as a drain.

Xu Maogong was a prime minister in the Tang dynasty; but before that he had been in the Wa Gang [rebel] camp.[70] People called him a bandit of Southern Hill before [he was] fourteen years old. He became a general only when he was twenty-four; so you can see that everyone goes through a period of development. When the student youth rebel, they are showing their spirit, not to mention that they are rebelling against bureaucratism and being deceived [by the bureaucrats]. I often say that these young people may take our positions in the future; among them in the future there will also be committee chairmen, committee vice-chairmen, premiers, [and] vice-premiers.

[They] say that I said the article by Chen Qitong and the other three was good; that's really strange! What I said was there must be blooming!

(Kang Sheng: This is because they have doubts about the policy of "Let a hundred flowers bloom, let a hundred schools contend." The article by Chen Qitong and the others is thus very much to their liking.)

[Chairman:] That's why I smelled it at [that] conference. [As for] monsters and demons, you may watch the plays but need not believe

---

[70]Xu Maogong was the "style" (*zi*) of Xu Shiji (594–669), a general who turned over from the Wa Gang camp to the emperors Tang Gaozu and Tang Taizong. During the reign of Tang Gaozong, he was promoted to the position of prime minister. He is also a figure in the popular historical novel, *Shuo Tang* and accordingly a figure in many Peking Operas based on the novel.

in the ghost. The common people believe in the Dragon King when there's a drought; [as soon as] the weather's fine, they stop believing. [If] there's a lot of rain, they believe even less. [They] make a fuss when [there's] just a bit of blooming; this is not trusting the people, not trusting the people to have the ability to discriminate.

Don't be afraid. [If there's] monsters and demons on every stage [don't you think] the people will object? Why be so alarmed just because of the publication of some essays similar to the "Pieces on plants"?[71] Do you think the *Book of songs* and the *Poems of Chu*[72] are [similar to] "Pieces on plants" or not? Can the first chapter of the *Book of Songs* be entitled "Kiss" or not?[73] It just can't be published [as such] now, can it? The first poem in the *Book of Songs* I don't think is all that poetic. Don't be that alarmed because there are [works like] "Pieces on plants" and some monsters and demons.

Dogmatism is [our] "teacher"; their articles others don't read.

[71]Mao is referring to Liushahe's essay, see Text 1, n. 5.

[72]Mao had raised these examples two days before; see p. 204.

[73]The first poem in the first (*zhou nan*) section of the *Book of Songs* is entitled "Guan ju" (Crying osprey) and is apparently a courting song traditionally thought to be celebrating the virtue of the bride of King Wen, who laid the foundations for the Zhou dynasty (1112–255 BC). *Jujiu* (ospreys, or fishhawks) are taken as the symbol of virtue because they are believed to practice a formal separation of sexes; see Vincent V. C. Shih, *Literary Mind*, p. 195, n. 5.

TEXT EIGHT

Summary of a Talk with the Representatives of Press and Publishing Circles

10 MARCH 1957

[75] From 3:00 to 7:00 P.M. on 10 March, Chairman Mao held an informal discussion in his office with representatives of the press and publishing circles. Participating in this informal discussion were Jin Zhonghua,[1] the representative of Shanghai's *Xinwen ribao* [Daily

Sources: 9:75–90, alternate text, 7:46–59. A truncated version of this exchange has been published in *Mao Zedong xinwen gongzuo wenxuan* (A selection of Mao Zedong's writings on news work) (Beijing, Xinhua chubanshe, 1983), pp. 186–95. The excisions made in the 1983 version seem designed to gloss over contemporary political problems. An even briefer version of this text appears in the restricted circulation publication, *Wenxian he yanjiu: 1983 huibianben* (Documents and research: 1983 Selections) (Beijing, Renmin chubanshe, 1984), pp. 54–62. That this last *neibu* version is less complete than the public version serves as a warning that "restricted circulation" does not guarantee greater completeness.
[1]Jin Zhonghua (b. 1902) was one of China's leading journalists. He had worked in the 1930s

News] and China News Service; Wang Yunsheng, representative [of] *Dagong bao*,[2] [and] Shanghai **[76]** *Wenhui bao's* representative, Xu Zhucheng.[3]

To start the discussion, the Chairman first invited the non-party personages from Shanghai to speak. The Chairman asked when Shanghai's *Shen bao* was abolished. [When he] heard the reply that *Shen bao* stopped publishing after Liberation, the Chairman remarked: There was no reason to abolish *Shen bao*, so old a paper of several decades' standing. What newspaper has it become?

(Someone replied: Changed into *Jiefang ribao* [Liberation daily].)

Chairman: It was probably not good to have changed it. [But] if [we] changed it back, it would appear to be a restoration. But this problem needs to be studied.

Next Xu Zhucheng of *Wenhui bao* raised [some] problems. He said that, following the changed format of the *People's Daily* last July, newspapers in Shanghai also made changes; but there were still many problems following the change. *Everyone felt his level of Marxism was low [and] was uncertain as to how to run newspapers in a socialist society.*

Chairman: [You're] uncertain now, but gradually [you'll] become certain. All matters are uncertain at the beginning. We never thought things through before we started fighting guerrilla warfare; [only

---

for *Shijie zhishi* (World knowledge). From 1944 to 1948, in Chongqing and then in Shanghai, he was in charge of press translations for American missions. He was editor of *Xinwen ribao* from 1949 to 1952. In 1955, he became chairman of the board of *China Reconstructs*. He replaced Xu Zhucheng (see n. 3) at the helm of *Wenhui bao* when Xu was purged.

[2] Wang Yunsheng (b. 1899) had been editor-in-chief of *Dagong bao* before 1949, and resumed that post from 1949 until 1953, when he became a director of the paper. A long-time communist supporter, he was a delegate to the National People's Congress. See *Who's Who in Communist China* vol. 2 (Hong Kong, URI, 1969), pp. 705–6.

[3] Xu Zhucheng, a graduate from Peking Normal University in 1927, became editor of Shanghai's *Wenhui bao* in 1938. He was purged as a rightist in 1958, but is an active journalist in China today. He recalls some of his experiences in the "Hundred Flowers" in *Baohai jiu wen* (Old stories about journalism) (Shanghai, Renmin chubanshe, 1981), pp. 313–5.

*when we were] forced to rebel⁴ and had to fight [did we] brace ourselves
for battle. Of course, fighting battles isn't fun, but with experience [one]
gradually becomes more knowledgeable [about it]. Who is there who can
be certain on newly emerging problems? I'm not certain either. Take the
Korean war for example: Fighting American imperialism is different
from fighting Japan. Initially [we were] uncertain [there] also. After one
or two battles, [we became] certain. Now we need to resolve the problem
of contradictions among the people; unlike when waging class struggles
in the past (of course, a certain degree of class struggle is also involved),
being uncertain is natural. It doesn't matter if we're uncertain; we can
take the problems and thoroughly examine them. Although many books
on socialism have been published, there are none that teach us how to
engage in socialism; even when Russia was engaged in the socialist revolution, there were none. There are also books that cover everything in
socialist society but those are about utopian socialism, rather than scientific socialism. Even if we can make a prediction before something
takes place, that is not equivalent to putting forward concrete policies
and methods for resolving [problems].*

[77] *Insufficient understanding of Marxism is a common problem. To
resolve this problem, the only [way] is to study conscientiously. Of
course, studying should be voluntary. [I've] heard that some writers thoroughly dislike this Marxist stuff, saying that it's hard to write fiction. I
think this is also a "conditioned reflex." In every case, when an old habit
takes a grip, new things can't break in, because old thoughts obstruct
them. To say it's hard to write fiction after learning Marxism, perhaps
[it's] because Marxism has met resistance from their old thoughts; so
[they] can't write anything.*

Our China has about five million intellectuals. There are advantages and disadvantages in having many intellectuals. The disadvantage is that they are grouped together. The *People's Daily* is an
example; the intellectuals there are grouped together; therefore troubles build up; but grouping together has its advantage, that is, the concentration of knowledge. *It's imperative to promote the study of
Marxism among the intellectuals; [we] should suggest that everyone
study it for eight to ten years. When more is learned about Marxism,*

⁴Mao uses the phrase *bi shang Liangshan,* a reference to the rebels of Liangshanbo, the heroes of one of his favorite classical novels, *Shuihu zhuan* (translated by Pearl Buck as *All Men
are Brothers*).

[it will] crowd out the old thoughts. But an atmosphere should also be created for the study of Marxism; without the atmosphere, [no one] can learn it well.

Currently there are two ideological tendencies: One is the type of dogmatism represented by Chen Qitong, Ma Hanbing[5] and several others; *the other is the type of right opportunism* represented by Zhong Dianfei.[6] *The characteristic of right opportunism is to negate everything.* Zhong Dianfei's article simply negates everything. *Dogmatism, on the other hand, spurns with a blow everything that is suspect; [it] affirms everything.* [I've] heard that this Chen Qitong is not a bad guy, but Ma Hanbing is very overbearing. He ran with this article to the *People's Daily,* [and] with one shout of "The Imperial Edict has come," Deng Tuo[7] groveled on his knees.

(XX[8] interjected: When he came in with his article, [he] said they had some complaints and wanted to contend a bit [and they] hoped no changes would be made in the article.)

[Chairman:] Ma Hanbing's article is very dogmatic. I found it difficult to finish it; [it was] tantamount to compulsive indoctrination. Zhong Dianfei is a strange name, but his article is readable. *Both dogmatism and right opportunism are one-sided; [they] use the ideological methods of metaphysics to observe and understand problems one-sidedly and in isolation. Of course, [it's] difficult to avoid one-sidedness completely, but ideological* **[78]** *one-sidedness and isolation have a direct relationship to not studying Marxism well. We should take eight to ten years to study Marxism earnestly to break away from the ideas and methods of metaphysics step by step. That way our ideological outlook will become very different.*

[5]Mao first mentions Ma Hanbing et al. in Text 1. See also Text 3 for a longer discussion. See Text 1, n. 16, and Text 3, n. 54.

[6]See Text 3, n. 53.

[7]Deng Tuo, editor-in-chief of *RMRB,* was the recipient of several tongue-lashings by Mao at this time. Mao was also unhappy with the paper's staff; see Text 16. For a full discussion, see Timothy Cheek, "Orthodoxy and Dissent in People's China: The Life and Death of Deng Tuo (1912–1966)" (PhD thesis, Harvard, 1986), pp. 192–201.

[8]XX: Quite possibly Deng Tuo trying to excuse himself. The ellipsis dots at the end of the first paragraph of this text suggest that there were additional people present at the meeting.

At this point, the Chairman asked Xu Zhucheng to go on. Xu Zhucheng said: Now there are also difficulties in promoting criticisms in the press; rebuttals are often oversimplified [and] too rude. [When] discussion of the problems of the movie [industry] was initiated in *Wenhui bao*, veteran actors and directors were extremely enthusiastic about participating in the discussion; later the comrades of the leading departments overseeing the movie industry wrote articles to hit back at the criticisms with a single blow. They [i.e., veteran actors and directors] then greatly regretted it all, believing they had been duped into taking the lead in airing opinions.

The Chairman spoke: *The criticisms of the movies this time have been very beneficial, but the door of the film bureau is not open enough. Their articles have the tendency to affirm everything. [But] other people's criticism is very beneficial. I for one don't like the films now; of course, there are good [ones and we] shouldn't negate everything. Any criticism that tallies with the facts, the film bureau must accept; otherwise there can't be any improvement. Among the articles your paper [Wenhui bao] has published, there were more criticisms in the initial period, and there was more affirmation in the second period. Now [you] can organize these articles and put them together, affirm the good [ones] and criticize the bad [ones]. That the film bureau ignores [criticism] is incorrect. Problems have been exposed following this debate; [it's] beneficial to the film bureau as well as to the people who wrote the articles.* [I] heard that Zhong Dianfei is dismissed from [his] position: Is it so?

(XX replied: It's he who wanted to resign from the position of commentator on *Wenyi bao* [Literary gazette].)

Chairman: I don't think it necessary to dismiss [him]; the problems in film [circles] are many to begin with; the veteran actors and directors are pent up with anger; [we] should let them vent their feelings.

Xu Zhucheng spoke: The readers have different opinions about things published in the newspapers; some young people say they don't want to read things dealing with the fancies of men of letters[9] published in the *Wenhui bao*; [they've] written letters to protest.

---

[9]*Qin qi shu hua*, lit., "lute, chess, books, paintings."

The Chairman spoke: *Your newspaper is edited in a lively manner. I like to read about the fancies of men of letters. Young [people] don't have to read [about them if they] don't like [them]. Everyone has his own "conditioned reflex." Not everyone likes to read the same type of thing.*

[79] Jin Zhonghua of *Xinwen ribao* raised the [following] question: When a shortage of daily necessities occurs in daily life, the masses put forward many opinions in their letters. When the newspapers publish not a single one, the masses complain; [but if] the newspapers published [them] the government and the relevant departments would not approve, saying it would incite the masses [and] cause an even tenser [situation]. One doesn't know what to do to get it right.

Chairman: *Try and see.* (Meaning [they] can publish some to see the reaction.) *[If] the government and the relevant departments have complaints, the newspapers can talk [it] over with them, [print] explanations in the paper, and see what happens. [It's] not too good not to publish any [of the masses' letters]; that way the departments can become bureaucratic [and] not improve [their] work.*

The Chairman inquired about the sales of newspapers in Shanghai.

Jin Zhonghua replied: Since the *Xinmin wanbao* [New people's evening news] expanded its coverage, [sales] have increased a lot.

At this point someone in the audience referred to the cynical remark that with the superior in mind, [you'll have] no freedom in editing [and] the readers won't want to read; with no superior in mind, [you] have freedom in editing [and] the readers want to read.

Wang Yunsheng interjected: This saying is wrong in principle.

Chairman: This should also be analyzed concretely. *The newspapers need leadership; but that leadership must be in tune with objective situations. A Marxist [style of leadership] runs things according to the circumstances, [and] those circumstances include the objective effect [of doing things]. [If] the masses like to read [the newspapers], [then it] proves the leadership has [led] well; [if] the masses don't like to read [them], [doesn't it show] that the leadership is not all that wise? There's correct lead-ership [and] incorrect leadership. Correct leadership does things according to the circumstances, conforms to reality; the masses welcome [it]. Incor-rect leadership does not do things according to the circumstances [and is] divorced from reality; [it] makes the editors feel they have no freedom, [and] the masses don't like to read the newspapers [thus] edited. This [kind of] leadership is unquestionably dogmatic. We need to oppose dogmatism.* In the Chinese revolution it was like that. Without the demise of the Third International, the Chinese revolution could not have suc-ceeded. When Lenin was alive, the Third International was well led. After Lenin's death, the leaders of the Third International were dog-matic leaders (for instance, leaders [like] Stalin, Bukharin[10] were not that good). Only the period under Dimitrov[11] was well led. Dimitrov's reports were well reasoned. Of course, the Third Interna-tional had [its] merits as well, for instance, helping various countries to establish a [communist] party. Later on, [however] the dogmatists paid no attention to **[80]** the special features of various countries [and] blindly transplanted everything from Russia. China [for one] suffered great losses. *We used the rectification pattern for more than ten years, cri-ticized dogmatism, [and] did things independently and on [our own] ini-tiative according to the spirit and essence of Marxism. [Only then] did [we] achieve the victory of the Chinese revolution.* Lenin likewise did not recognize the Second International. As a result, the October Rev-olution succeeded. I don't think we should have any more [commu-nist] internationals. Ever since its foundation, the Cominform[12] has done only one thing: that is, criticize Yugoslavia.

[10]Nikolai Ivanovich Bukharin (1888–1938) became General Secretary of the Comintern after the defeat of Zinoviev in 1925; see Stephen F. Cohen, *Bukharin and the Bolshevik Rev-olution* (New York, Vintage books, 1975), p. 216.

[11]Georgi Dimitrov, a Bulgarian communist who had been the principal defendant at the Nazis' Reichstag Fire trial, became General Secretary of the Comintern at its 7th Congress in July-August 1935, by which time Bukharin had fallen. Mao's friendly memories of Dimi-trov were doubtless attributable to the fact that, at the 7th Congress, the Comintern adopted a popular front policy which dovetailed neatly with the CCP's desperate need for a united front with the Nationalists against Japan in order to obtain a breathing space from Chiang Kai-shek's attacks. See Adam B. Ulman, *Expansion and Coexistence* (New York, Praeger, 1968), pp. 230–1. But in fact Stalin still directed the affairs of the Comintern, even after Dimitrov's elevation.

[12]The Comintern was dissolved by Stalin in 1943 in order to prevent his allies against Ger-many (the United States and Britain) from thinking his long-term goal was still subversion of the bourgeois West; see Jane Degras, ed., *The Communist International, 1919–1943*, vol.

(Kang Sheng interjected: [It] also criticized France and Japan.)

[Chairman:] But [it] does not mean [we] don't want to have [it] for-ever; but [if we are to] have [it], [we'd want to] have the [type] in the initial stage of the Third International [when] various countries [had their] independence, exercised their own initiatives, [and] did things according to their own circumstances and not interfering with others' [business]. I've talked this way with many Soviet comrades, with Yudin and Mikoyan.[13]

Someone asked whether the newspapers should become special-ized.

Chairman: *It would be good to have some specialized newspapers such as* **Dagong bao.** *[When] free markets were opened, I for one liked to read it, because it published many things on that subject and was quick in its reporting.*[14] *But [if] too specialized, [the papers] can become dull sometimes and reduce people's interests in reading [them]. [Besides], the specialists should also read things outside [their] specializations.*

Some made the point that the things currently published in the newspapers were too stiff, [and] reported on some opinions discussed lately in Shanghai regarding the problems of the newspapers. For

---

3 (London, Oxford Univ. Press, 1965), pp. 476–81. In 1947, however, Stalin set up the Cominform (Communist Information Bureau), an association of the Soviet, East Euro-pean, French, and Italian parties. Though it expelled Yugoslavia in 1948, it never attained the importance or functions of the Comintern, its main activity being the publication of a paper bizarrely entitled *For a Lasting Peace, for a People's Democracy;* see Hugh Seton-Watson, *The Pattern of Communist Revolution* (London, Methuen, 1953), p. 328. The organ-ization was dissolved after Stalin's death by Khrushchev; see Ulam, pp. 460–1.

[13]For Pavel Yudin, then Soviet ambassador to China, see Text 3, n. 45. Anastas Mikoyan, with 40 years' service in the CPSU Politburo or Presidium, was at this time Khrushchev's most important supporter and possibly the man who spurred him into making his "secret speech" denouncing Stalin at the Party's 20th Congress in February 1956; see G. F. Hudson's "Epilogue" in MacFarquhar, *The Hundred Flowers Campaign and the Chinese Intel-lectuals* (New York, Praeger, 1960), pp. 298–9. Mikoyan had led the CPSU delegation to the CCP's 8th Congress in September 1956, but seems to have left early after a snub by Mao; see *Origins* 1, pp. 169–70.

[14]Peasants were allowed to sell privately produced items in free markets till 1956. Such mar-kets were closed down in August 1957 in the course of the Anti-Rightist Campaign.

example: "[If] there is too much ideological content, [then] the newspapers aren't lively." Also, some have raised the slogan "Gentler, gentler, and still gentler."

Chairman: *A socialist state's newspapers are invariably better than those of a capitalist state. Although Hong Kong newspapers are without the ideological content we are talking about, [they're] not all that interesting, either; what they say is not truthful, [it's] exaggerated [and] spreads poisons. Our newspapers contain fewer poisons, [and] are beneficial to the people. It [would be] correct [to say] that the articles in the newspapers should be "Shorter, shorter, and still shorter!" [But] we should think more about whether they should be "Gentler, gentler, and still gentler." [Articles] should not be too stiff; when they are, people don't want to read [them]. [We] can combine stiffness and gentleness together. [If] articles are written so as to be popular, intimate, proceeding from small [matters] to talk about major [ones], proceeding from things close at hand to talk about far away [matters], [and thereby be] interesting and absorbing, that would be very good.*[15] *Do you agree with Lu Xun or not? Lu Xun's essays were neither too gentle nor too stiff, were not difficult to read. Some say light essays [zawen]*[16] *are hard to write; the difficulty is precisely in this [combination]. Some ask* **[81]** *what Lu Xun would be like now were he to be alive. [If] Lu Xun were alive, I think he'd both dare and not dare to write. He would probably not write in an unsettled atmosphere. But the more likely possibility is that he would write. As the saying goes, "He who does not fear being cut to pieces dares to unhorse the emperor." Lu Xun was a genuine Marxist, a thoroughgoing materialist. The genuine Marxist [and] thoroughgoing*

[15]These stylistic attributes are, of course, the classic definition of a *zawen* (see n. 16) from Lu Xun in the 1920s and 1930s, to Zhu Ziqing in the 1940s, to Deng Tuo and Wu Han in the early 1960s. Mao's guess, here, at what Lu Xun would do if he were alive, is ironic considering what he had Deng Tuo and Wu Han, among others, subjected to in the Cultural Revolution for taking his advice here. As we see in Mao's late-1958 efforts (Texts 18 and 19) to distance himself from the heady rhetoric of Beidaihe (Text 17), Mao is here being somewhat disingenuous.

[16]*Zawen* (lit. "miscellaneous essays") were made popular by Lu Xun in the 1920s and 1930s and have remained a politically significant form of writing in the PRC. Western scholars have variously translated *zawen* as "polemical essays," "miscellaneous essays," "light essays," or simply as "essays." We have chosen "light essays," since *zawen* are not always polemical, and to remind the English reader that Mao is referring to *zawen* and not other types of essays or articles in the PRC press. Chinese writers generally consider *zawen* to be a subset of *sanwen*—"lyrical essays" or "essays."

materialist fears nothing, so he can write. Nowadays some writers dare not write [owing to] two circumstances: One is that we have not created for them an environment in which they dare to write; they're afraid of being punished. The other circumstance is that they themselves have not learned materialism thoroughly. [If they were] thoroughgoing materialists [then they'd] dare to write. In Lu Xun's era, to be punished meant to be put in jail and beheaded; but Lu Xun was not afraid. [We] still have no experience as to how light essays should be written now. I think [we should] bring out Lu Xun [to let] people study and learn from him. His light essays covered many subjects, such as politics, literature, art, and so on. Especially [in his] later years, [he] talked most about politics; only economics did he fail to discuss. All of Lu Xun's pieces [he felt] compelled [to write]. Marxism he learned also [because he felt] compelled to [do so]. He came from a gentry family; people said he was [part of] the dregs of feudalism, and that he wouldn't amount to anything. My townsfolk [tongxiang] like Cheng Fangwu[17] *and others weren't nice to him. The Nationalist party oppressed him; our Communist party members in Shanghai also punished him—he was getting it from both sides; but Lu Xun still wrote. Nowadays essays on economics can also be written. [Whether] articles are good or bad will depend on their results. From time immemorial every assessment has been made on the basis of results.*

At this point, the Chairman asked the representative of the *Guangming Daily* whether he was a Communist party member.

That comrade replied: I am a Communist party member.

The Chairman remarked, "A Communist party member running a newspaper for the democratic parties isn't good, is it?" The Chairman went on, "[But] your newspaper is still readable; [it] has many supplements."

The Chairman then asked Comrade Zhu Muzhi, the representative of the head office [and deputy director] of the New China News

---

[17] Cheng Fangwu was Hunanese but not from Mao's county. Cheng was a prominent Communist editor and cultural figure from the 1920s. He was at this time President of Northeast Teachers' University in Changchun and a delegate to the NPC; see *Who's Who in Communist China*, vol. 1 (Hong Kong, URI, 1966), pp. 120–1.

Agency: *Are your dispatches welcome or not? [I] heard that some people in your place raised the question of whether or not the news [provided by] a news agency had a class character.* Following Comrade Zhu Muzhi's reply, the Chairman said: *Until the elimination of classes, no matter [whether it comes from] a news agency or a newspaper, news always has a class character.*[18] [He] said: [The term] "freedom of the press" **[82]** is deceptive; there's no reportage that's completely objective. [Even] the news agencies and newspapers in the United States now carry reports on new China's economic construction. The reason is that they want to do business; therefore [they] deliberately strike a pose for people to see, because they're pressed by the economic crisis. Chiang Kai-shek in times of necessity can also strike a pose, creating an impression of [wanting] peace talks. Because the United States had been pressing him, and wanted to get an even more pro-American person like Hu Shi to replace him, he created an impression of [wanting] peace talks, so that the US would not dare to press him too hard. Now [the US] has learned from our past policies: we in the past united with the democratic parties to isolate Chiang Kai-shek; now the US unites Hu Shi and others to isolate Chiang Kai-shek.[19] It would be better if Chiang Kai-shek did not fall from power. [If he] fell from power, [then] the more pro-American elements like Hu Shi and the like would come to power. [Then] it'd be even worse. Chiang Kai-shek created the impression of [wanting] peace talks to resist pressure from the United States; We need not expose him or criticize him. [If] he creates [that impression], we can do likewise. Of course, Chiang Kai-shek is still anti-Communist, [he] still calls us names; [if] he didn't call [us] names, [he'd] be left without any capital.

Shu Xincheng of the Zhonghua Publishing House (recently reemerged from three years of retirement) reported on the current situation in publishing circles and on what he saw during his [tour of] inspection in Changsha, Hunan, and adjacent places.[20] People said that books currently being published were in "short [supply]" and

---

[18]The translation here has been adjusted to accord with the slightly different version in *Mao Zedong xinwen gongzuo wenxuan* (1983), p. 191.

[19]The standard works on Taiwan give no hint that the US government ever thought of Hu Shi as someone to replace Chiang Kai-shek.

[20]Shu Xincheng (1893–1960), editor and publisher. Famous for supervising the publication of the encyclopedic dictionary *Cihai* in 1936; see *BDRC* 3, pp. 135–7. He was from Hunan.

"poor [in quality]"; [but] he considered that actually the main problem was the shortage of supplies. Therefore he requested the Center to try to resolve the problem of paper supplies. He also said that currently various departments of the Center all had [their own] specialized publishing houses, [each] covering the whole gamut of professional tasks [including] editing, publishing, and so on. Was this [all] necessary? Could [they] be responsible only for the editing of [their own] departments' professional books [and] journals, leaving the rest of the publishing work to be done in a unified manner so as to economize on human [and] material resources? [He] also [said] that various localities had collected large amounts of archives and old books for recycling and thereby destroyed large quantities of archives, books, and newspapers which were rich resources. The Committee for the Protection of Cultural Relics was responsible only for cultural relics [and] had nothing to do with [research] materials. Were this to continue, it would be difficult in the future to find [research] materials.

On the problem of paper supply the Chairman said: Can the Ministry of Light Industry consider some increase in investment? This is something [you] won't lose any money on.

(A comrade from the Ministry of Culture said: [We've] already asked the premier for instructions [and] after some calculations it was thought impossible to increase investment.)

The Chairman interrupted him to say: What people are talking about is wanting [more] paper, [and] you say there is no paper. People don't want to hear that, [so] say no more. [83] On the problem of recycling archives and old books, the Chairman remarked: This is a new version of the burning of the books.[21] [If] one province [acts] this way, other provinces will do likewise. [I'm] afraid [it] may be even worse around Zhejiang. (Asking XX:) This problem deserves [our] attention.

At this point XXX spoke. He said that the talks the Chairman

[21]Mao is presumably alluding here to the burning of the books by Li Si under the Qin dynasty in 213 BC; see Derk Bodde, *China's First Unifier* (Hong Kong, Hong Kong Univ. Press, 1967), pp. 162–6.

was having with the press and publishing circles today would open up a new era in the history of China's journalism. [He] hoped that the Chairman would give a directive on the question of the essential nature of journalistic work. XXX considered that the key question in current newspaper work was the problem of how to carry out criticism correctly. He said that this problem had existed for a long time in the past; but from now on, at a time of correctly handling contradictions and problems among the people, the ability to publish could have a great bearing [precisely] on the handling of contradictions among the people. Therefore could [we] think of a few guidelines [for everyone] to follow?

Comrade Kang Sheng also interjected: At present, publishing criticisms in the newspapers has met with many difficulties. Weren't there people saying: "[If you] criticize veteran cadres, [they] say you don't have a firm [class] stand; [if you] criticize democratic personages, [they] say you're destroying the United Front"?

The Chairman said: *When criticizing, [you] should prepare a ladder for people; otherwise [when] the masses encircle [them], they won't be able to come downstairs. [It's] the same with opposing bureaucratism. During the Three-Antis, many ministers came downstairs precisely because the Center provided a ladder for them.* In the initial period of the Three-Antis, [some] said so many tigers were driven out; after subsequent investigation, [they changed their minds and] said only 2 to 3 percent were [tigers]. It was similar in the campaign against counterrevolutionaries. The Three-Antis was actually for rectifying the Communist party, whereas the Five-Antis was for rectifying the capitalists. *In the past is was necessary to wage campaigns. It wouldn't have done not to have waged [them]; but when [we] waged [them], [we] hurt too many people. We should learn a lesson. It's not currently in the interests of the great majority of the people to have big democracy* [da minzhu]. *If you overthrow the people's government, Chiang Kaishek would come back. Some people always want to use democracy against other people; [they] want to rectify others. [But when it] comes to rectifying themselves, [then] the smaller the democracy the better. In resolving the problems in literature, the press, and so on, I think [we] should use ultra-small democracy* [xiao xiao minzhu], *adding another "small" on top of small democracy—that is a drizzle* [mao mao yu]

[which] falls incessantly.[22] The Rectification Campaign will begin
formally next year. This year [we'll] first issue a directive to let people
be prepared. There'll be an informal period.[23] During the informal
period, [if] you find you have subjectivism, **[84]** bureaucratism, [or]
sectarianism [and] correct [yourself], [then we] won't investigate in
the future. It was like this not long ago when Comrade Chen Boda
returned to his native heath, Fujian, to work on grass-roots elections.
Some cadres [were guilty of] corruption, [and they] were asked to
fork out the money and admit their mistakes to the masses. As a
result, after the masses had criticized them, [those] cadres were nevertheless elected. This is a very good experience. The Communist
party's Rectification Campaign will unavoidably affect the democratic personages, but make absolutely sure never to rectify people to
death. [We] should use the method of small democracy first to rectify
the Communist party. Currently, some of our comrades are very pre-
tentious. They don't have [any] "capital," yet want to be officials.
[They] have to assume great airs. [When] the Communist party has
[its] Rectification [Campaign], everyone will become modest.

*Speaking of running newspapers, the Communist party is not as
[adept] as the non-party personages. In Yan'an [we] had a short history of
running newspapers, [so we] have no experience in running newspapers
nationwide. It's the same with running schools, publishing, [and] scientific research. There are about five million intellectuals nationwide;
[among them] the Communist party's members amount to but one
small finger [of the ten].* The game we're good at is fighting battles,

[22]By "big democracy," Mao meant large-scale struggle sessions at which offenders were
denounced by the "masses"; these had typified the campaigns he cites in this passage and
others. "Small democracy" implied intimate gathering at which faults could be raised and
criticized in a comradely manner. For a perspective on how such "small group" criticism
operated, see Martin King Whyte, *Small Groups and Political Ritual in China* (Berkeley,
Univ. of California Press, 1974).

The Chairman's comments here confirm a sense of unease among party members at the
prospect of the methods of "big democracy" being sanctioned for use against them in the
projected Rectification Campaign. Some had apparently suggested that "big democracy"
could lead to a toppling of the regime. Mao ruled out "big democracy" in order to minimize
party opposition to outsiders participating in its rectification. "Small democracy" was signified in the actual rectification directive by the phrase "gentle breeze, mild rain," which
Mao foreshadowed in this passage and first used a week later in Shandong; see Text 11, n. 15.
For a more extensive discussion, see *Origins* 1, pp. 178, 212, 225–7.

[23]For a discussion of why the decision was taken to advance the timing of the Rectification
Campaign from 1958 to 1957 see below, Text 13, n. 5.

[excercising] dictatorship; [we know] a little about literature and art, [but] not many [of us]. *[They] say the Communist party cannot lead science; this is half true. At present we are laymen leading experts; the leadership [we've been] exercising is administrative [and] political. As for the hard sciences and technology, such as geology, the Communist party does not understand [them]; but the Nationalist party does not understand [them] either. After being in power for more than twenty years the Nationalists trained only something over 200 geologists, [whereas] after seven years of liberation we've trained more than 10,000. The administrative leadership* is simply "one Li Xiannian plus one Li Fuchun": one in charge of eating, the other of planning.[24] *Now is a transitional period; [it] has to be like this. This situation will change in the future. Currently [we] should try to get the more than 80 percent of intellectuals who adopt a neutral position to study Marxism, ask them to obtain a preliminary understanding of Marxism rather than demand that they achieve a thorough understanding all at once. Even Marx himself, the creator of Marxism, didn't understand everything all at once. The publication of the* **Communist Manifesto** *in 1848 was only the beginning of the Marxist system, certainly not the completion of the Marxist system. To demand that all intellectuals accept Marxism at once is unrealistic. [When one] speaks of understanding Marxism, actually, the degrees of understanding also differ. I, too, have not read many Marxist works.* **[85]** I don't know how many they wrote. Probably those that we have translated do not amount to one-half.

(Comrade Zeng Yanxiu[25] of the Peoples' Publishing House [Renmin chubanshe] said about 47 percent had been translated.)

[Chairman:] *Those who are experts should read a bit more; we don't have that much spare time, [so it's] OK to read a bit less. The important [point] is to pay attention to study methods. Many cadres at present don't have the habit of reading; [they] use [their] spare energy to play poker and go to the theater [and] dance. People should not waste time [like this].* This time you've raised many questions; upon [your] return you

---

[24]Li Xiannian was then Finance Minister; he was head of state 1983–88. The late Li Fuchun was then Chairman of the State Planning Commission.
[25]Zeng Yanxiu was director and editor-in-chief of this, the most important publishing house in China; he was among those later denounced as a rightist.

should study [these questions and] try to search for answers your-selves. [When you] hold meetings, [you] should have party and non-party people together. The Communist party should not hold meetings behind closed doors. It's advantageous to hold [meetings] jointly. This is dialectics [which] could unify opinions from both sides.

(Comrade Kang Sheng interjected: Everybody is still unused to this method of holding meetings: The non-party personages have some misgivings. Party members also hesitate to speak. [But] what the Chairman has described is a good method.)

The Chairman: You go back and try to see whether it'll work; [if] not I'll make [them] do it. As to the question of numbers, I think that non-party personages could make up a third and Communist party members two-thirds.

[In] the article by Ma Hanbing and several others, their policy [*fangzhen*] is incorrect and their methods are incorrect, too. Their pol-icy is in opposition to that of the Center; [and] they used the method of suppression, which can't convince people.

(Kang Sheng interjected: There are now three factions in relation to this policy of the Central Committee: Chen Qitong, Ma Hanbing, and the like represent the "left" faction, suspecting this policy is bad, and believing that it should not be propagated from now on.[26] The right faction, by contrast, doesn't care about anything else, thinking it advantageous to stir things up in the newspapers. It is advantageous to stir things up a bit, but it depends on how it's done. There's also a faction in the middle [that] recognizes the policy as good, but [they are] not certain in [their] minds, [and they] fear difficulties.)

The Chairman: What's [there] to fear? If in criticizing the youth [you've] helped the youth, [in] criticizing the veteran cadres [you've] helped the veteran cadres, [and in] criticizing the democratic person-ages [you've] consolidated the United Front, isn't that good?

(Kang Sheng again spoke up: Now the army cadres are confused

[26]See Text 3, pp. 168–9.

about this policy, believing that what the army is engaged in is positive education, which allows only fragrant flowers to bloom and not poisonous weeds.)

The Chairman: In fact, there are also poisonous weeds; **[86]** it's just that [they] don't emerge in the guise of poisonous weeds.

[This is] because everyone takes his own opinion as the blooming of a fragrant flower. Of course the army is different from other departments. The army does business by orders. But our armed forces have had democratic discussion from the very beginning, [that is,] soldiers can criticize officers; [if] an answer is not satisfactory, [they] can criticize again. Aren't there also corruption and waste and warlordism in the armed forces? Therefore the armed forces should also have rectification; but [it] wouldn't do for it to be run too chaotically, [it] would have to be directed. During the Three-Antis in the past, a theater could put up a sign "Beating Tigers" and stop performing for a few days, [but] newspapers can't do that. If there are mistakes, [you] can hold a meeting to discuss [them], but [you] can't fail to publish the next day.

(Comrade Kang Sheng interjected: As far as the armed forces are concerned, [they] should "Open up the channels of speech and pay attention to effects.")

The Chairman: That's very good; it should be like this everywhere.

On the question of the speed of news, journalists participated in the discussion at this propaganda conference. On this question the Chairman said: *[We] should conduct concrete analysis of concrete problems; the same is true [with regard to] the speed of news.* For instance, on the campaign to ban opium, the problem with us was not [one] of speed, but rather [one of] not publishing [it]. Because the United States insulted us in the United Nations General Assembly [with the allegation] that we sold opium; [if] we published [it], wouldn't [we] be providing them with propaganda materials? *The same holds with regard to the news of the land reform. To avoid spreading some half-baked, mistaken experiences, we did not publicize it in the newspapers. At the end of the year before last, Beijing accomplished in [just] a few days [a changeover to] state-private joint management for whole trades, and publicized this as entry into socialism.*[27] *With this kind of news, we ought to have thought things through [before publishing]. Thereafter, once the* New China News Agency *had spread the news—*

(Comrade Zhu Muzhi of the New China News Agency's head office said: It was the radio station that first broadcast [it].)

[Chairman:] —*each locality straight away followed suit without any concern for its own concrete conditions. This [put us in] a very passive [i.e., difficult position].* Or as [in the case of Imre] Nagy's coming to power during the Hungarian incident: we were not clear about the situation, but couldn't keep calm either, [so we] published [the news] three days too early. As a result when we published the news on day one, we didn't say if he was good or bad. In day two's news, we said he was good. On day three, we said he was bad. [So] the masses became confused. Since the original situation was not clear, [we] really didn't have to publish [the news]. The French Communist [party] was wiser than us in this regard. *L'Humanité* is published in Paris, surrounded by bourgeois newspapers; it just wouldn't publish [the news] before understanding the situation clearly.

[87] When discussing the need to train some people to write articles, the Chairman said: [We] must find people who can write articles, indeed, have already found some. On whether articles criticizing matters [i.e., contradictions] among the people should be sharp, the Chairman remarked: *[One's] cutting edge can be sharp even when advancing criticisms among the people. I also want to write a few articles for the newspapers, but [I would have to first] resign from the office of chairman. I could start a column in a newspaper and become a columnist. Articles should be sharp; only sharp knives can cut paper. But the sharpness should be to help people not to hurt them.*

[Questioner:] Can [articles] criticize certain problems in the localities with policy implications?

[27]Mao has misremembered the timing of this transformation. Though businessmen were softened up at meetings in autumn 1955 and some transformation by trades took place in December, the big push in Beijing occurred in January 1956. For a discussion of the process and a hint of Mao's contemporaneous scepticism at what had been accomplished, see *Origins* 1, pp. 19–25.

The Chairman said: Some can be criticized. [I] heard that a county in Xinjiang set up twenty-four companies in the commercial system alone. Aren't you at the *Dagong bao* engaged in commercial reporting? You can set up a few models for criticizing.

(XX of the *People's Daily* said:[28] [If] newspapers don't handle the problem of contradictions among the people well, the impact will not be good. But in the past we lacked experience in this regard, [so our] style of writing was stiff. Now the situation is different, but writing styles can't adjust.)

The Chairman: [They] didn't adapt in the past [either]; some articles made people [feel] uncomfortable after [they] read [them]; [they] don't discuss in a reasonable manner; [their] immediate objective is to suppress people.

(XX went on to say: This is of course related to the ideological methods and ideological style of work of us comrades working in the press. The wind often starts in the press. The newspapers themselves are also aware of this and try their best to avoid starting a wind or being one-sided. Take for example current propaganda on birth control and late marriage: the *People's Daily* has from the beginning paid attention to preventing one-sidedness. But once more and more reports and articles were published, problems emerged at the grass-roots.)

The Chairman: *As soon as there are more articles, [people] think [we're] revising the marriage law, [so they will] hurry to get married. This indeed makes it hard to run a newspaper. In the old society the masses read things in the newspapers, but it was as if they hadn't read anything [i.e., they didn't take any notice]. Nowadays if [something is] published in the newspapers, it can be [very] different.*

(XX continued: For example, on the problem of letting a hundred schools contend, some take it that contention is mainly limited to academic thought, and it is inappropriate to apply this to actual work. [But] the relationship between the two is easily confused. Another

<hr>

[28]XX may again be Deng Tuo, see nn. 7, 8.

example is the discussion of the ready-for-labor-and-defense system
and of teaching students in accordance with their aptitude: Once the
number of articles in the newspapers increased, the thinking of some
students and teachers became confused. Perhaps [we'd] better delimit
the scope [of these policies].)

The Chairman: *[Regarding] purely academic [matters], endless
debate won't have adverse effects. As for issues with policy [implications],
perhaps [we'll] have to differentiate* **[88]** *situations. But there are also
difficulties in delimiting the scope [of policies], since there are so many
policies. If [you] discover that propaganda on birth control and late marriage has had some harmful consequences, then [you] can immediately
write articles in the papers to explain [things]. Our articles are often late,
though. As to how to delimit the scope [of a policy], each paper can consider [this] on [your] return.*

Comrade Zhu Muzhi of the New China News Agency's head
office said: Currently there are so many problems—can [we] hold a
special meeting to discuss [matters] and summarize [our conclusions]?

The Chairman: [We're] only raising problems this time. Later on
[we'll] have to hold a discussion meeting. In addition, this conference
is [attended by people from] all corners of the land; what the effect
[of that] will be, [we'll] see in the future. The problems that I talked
about in [my] speech to the Supreme State Conference, [I] had
already thought about for a long time. I had already talked about
them several times last year; later on [I] observed a few more things.
[When I] read the article by Chen Qitong, Ma Hanbing, and others,
[I] thought some people might think their article represented the
opinion of the Center, [and] therefore [I] felt it necessary to talk
about it in a thoroughgoing manner. [This was] because [the article]
"More on the historical experience of the proletarian dictatorship"
resolved only international issues.[29] Within our country now, <large-

---

[29]This article, the second published by the CCP in its attempt to limit the damage caused
to the international communist movement by the repercussions of Khrushchev's "secret
speech" attacking Stalin at the CPSU's 20th Congress in February 1956, appeared in *RMRB*
on 29 Dec. 1956. For a translation, see *Communist China, 1955–1959: Policy Documents
with Analysis* (Cambridge, Harvard Univ. Press, 1962), pp. 257–72.

scale, turbulent > [30] class struggle has basically ended. Contradictions among the people have come to the fore. So then one trend is [people] saying that there are [too] many criticisms, that the people are making trouble, [and the people saying this] are in a constant state of anxiety. On the other hand some people feel they've not enjoyed themselves to the full yet. Some want to restrict, others want to bloom. Everyone wants to fathom what is the Center's policy at bottom. In reality, the Center has no other fundamental axiom; the policy is just that one [policy], but there are some new problems. Worker and student strikes are all problems among the people. Student strikes [have taken place] because too many students were enrolled last year. [When one] enrolls a lot, [then] some people fear [they cannot] enroll enough, and so [they] cheat; [if you] cheat, naturally the students are dissatisfied. [When] problems accumulate, they take on an ominous appearance. This kind of thing will happen again in the future. Among the people, the absolute majority is the petty bourgeoisie, a part is the national bourgeoisie. [There are] many democratic parties and non-party personages. [We are] now [in the midst of] a great social transformation; the ideological confusion simply reflects [this] great transformation. It'd be hard to understand [if it] weren't reflected. Bureaucratism is precisely the direct cause of troubles; since bureaucratism doesn't want to change, the masses [inevitably] create disturbances. The Chinese people are a most discipline-observing people. The supply of non-staple food in Shanghai was so short, **[89]** [but] we laid out the situation and explained the reasons clearly [and] told people to come up with ideas, [and] wasn't the result that the Spring Festival went very well this year? At present, the period of transition is not yet over, [so] problems, big and small, happen every day.

---

[30]The phrase "large-scale, turbulent" (*da guimo jifeng baoyu*), in square brackets in the original Chinese text, was clearly inserted by editors, either during the Cultural Revolution or perhaps earlier. This phrase is lifted from the officially published version of Mao's "Contradictions" speech; see *XJ5*, p. 389. The qualification was inserted when the speech was released in June 1957 to extricate Mao from the embarrassment of being on the record as proclaiming the end of *all* class struggle just as the Anti-Rightist Campaign was getting underway! Even this qualification could not really disguise Mao's blunder, since the Anti-Rightist Campaign certainly qualified as large-scale and turbulent.

(XXX said: Also we didn't link up enough with press circles in the past.)

The Chairman: Isn't it that [you] had no liaison at all? From now on, we'll have a meeting every year. We get by comparatively well these days. The Soviet Union [had] the October Revolution in 1917; by 1927 [it] was still very chaotic. Literature and the arts were even more chaotic. They were poorer [than we are]. The intellectuals complained more. Now [it's] been thirty-nine years, [but their supply of] commodities is not necessarily more than ours.

At this point, some one asked whether the problem of one-sidedness had existed in propaganda about the Soviet Union in the past.

The Chairman said: Of course, the Soviet Union has shortcomings [that] we don't want to publish. We don't want to publish India's weaknesses either. At present only the capitalist states in the West propagate [them]. With respect to these, we precisely need to be one-sided. Some say the development of production in West Germany is faster than that of East Germany. Why [then] do you always say West Germany is no match for East Germany? In [our] propaganda we still must not say West Germany is better than East Germany, but equally [we] shouldn't say everything in East Germany is better than in West Germany. We socialist states also have shortcomings, because our history is short, [and] Marxism broke through and achieved revolutionary victory first of all at the weakest link of capitalism. I once told [some] German comrades Marx was currently very busy in the East [and] temporarily could not return and so their revolution could not succeed. Today Asia is more progressive politically than Britain and the United States, because Asians' living standards are much lower than theirs. We were exploited in the past [and] were very poor; [if you're] poor [you] want revolution. Their living standards are high, their levels of education are high, [so] they're just not revolutionary. Naturally, the United States also has [its] advantages, with a short history, without the burden of history: When they study history, they don't have to make as much effort as we do. Neither do [they] need to discuss the problem of periodization of history. Sometimes bad things can turn into good things. Now it is the

East that is advanced [and] the West that is backward. After several decades, the countries in the East will completely drive away Western imperialism. At that time, they won't have any colonies to exploit, [90] [they] won't have much profit, whereas we countries in the East will become rich. [When] their living standard decreases, their people will become progressive. Today Asia is in ferment, Africa is in ferment. If Latin America, too, were in ferment, things could then be easily managed.

A Letter to Zhou Enlai and Other Comrades

17 MARCH 1957

[256]

Comrades [Zhou] Enlai, XX, XX, XX[1]

Universities [and] middle schools should all be required to strengthen ideological [and] political leadership and improve ideological [and] political education. [Academic] classes should be be reduced; middle school political classes should be restored, [and] constitutional [law] classes canceled; ideology [and] politics textbooks should be edited afresh; groups of cadres from [both] the party and govern-

---

Sources: 1:256; alternate text, 6A:48. See also Text 10, Mao's speech at Tianjin given the same day.
[1]The excised characters may be given names of Deng Xiaoping, party General Secretary; Lu

ment systems capable and suited for school work should be transferred to work in universities and middle schools; the responsibility
of leading ideological [and] political work shall be vested in the Ministry of Higher Education and the Ministry of Education. Please
[have] the Center discuss the above-mentioned points [and] issue a
decision. I have already reached Tianjin.

Mao Zedong
17 March 1957

Dingyi director of CC Propaganda Department; and Hu Qiaomu, an alternate member of
the party secretariat dealing with ideology. Or Mao may have been addressing Premier
Zhou and his ministers responsible for education, Zhang Xiruo (Education) and Yang Xiu-
feng (Higher Education).

Talk at a Conference of Party Member
Cadres in Tianjin Municipality

17 MARCH 1957

[74] (There is a long enthusiastic standing ovation as Chairman Mao, accompanied by four Comrades, XXX, XXX, XXX, and XXX, appears on the rostrum.)

XXX: Comrades, I will now ask Chairman Mao to speak to us. (Applause)

Chairman Mao: What problems do you have?

Sources: 10:74–90, alternate text, 1:239–55; see also Text 9, Mao's letter to Zhou Enlai and others the same day.

XXX: If there are any problems you want the Chairman to give answers to, you may write them out. And now the Chairman will speak to us first.

Chairman Mao: What shall I talk about? What problems do you have, comrades?

There are many comrades [here] I have never met before. Today I would like to discuss a number of issues with you comrades. I hope you comrades will raise some questions with me. Since they have not been sent up yet [i.e., to the rostrum], and there is still some time, I would like to say a few words first. So I'll talk about "Let a hundred flowers bloom, let a hundred schools contend," is that OK? (Applause)

For this is an issue about which our entire party, society at large, democratic personages, and personages of various circles are all concerned. Opinions among our comrades on this issue are not entirely unanimous. Some comrades think this policy is all right and approve it; others outwardly seem to favor it, but inwardly [they] are generally [75] a bit uncomfortable. "Let a hundred flowers bloom"? With so many flowers, how terrible it would be if some bad things happened to spring up! "Let a hundred schools contend"? We the Communist party are counted only as one "school." How terrible it would be if the ninety-nine [other] schools surrounded us! Is there such a problem, comrades? In other words, there are those who have a better understanding of the policy, those who understand it a little but not much, those who are skeptical about it, and those who don't accept it. In our party there are all sorts of different opinions.

What was our party's major task in the past? At present, don't we have construction work? In the past few decades, our prime task was class struggle. [It was] class struggle, not construction. Class struggle means the overthrow of various systems such as imperialism, bureaucratic capitalism, and feudalism. It was a revolution; socialism is the overthrow of the capitalist system. All this falls into the category of class struggle. Fighting Chiang Kai-shek, resisting America and aiding Korea, suppressing counterrevolutionaries, land reform—and in the cities there were in addition democratic reform and socialist transformation. All this falls into the category of class struggle. The momentum of [all] that was tremendous, wasn't it?

In the past few decades, from the time when our party was

founded up to the socialist transformation of the first half of last year [1956], I mean the high tide between the second half of the year before last [1955] and the first half of this year,[1] when there was a deafening noise of drums[2] and a great deal of excitement, our party concentrated its efforts primarily on this task. It was a prolonged struggle. If we begin with the year 1840, when our forefathers fought the Opium War, which marked the beginning of the resistance to imperialism, and count to 1940, that's a hundred years. [And if we count] up to last year, 1956, then it was only with the passage of 116 years that we took the superstructure, the relations of production, and changed the old relations of production into new relations of production, the old superstructure into a new superstructure. Relations of production refer principally to the system of ownership. The system of ownership we now have is socialist ownership. Superstructure refers to government, organs of state power, and the army. All these have been changed. This was a massive struggle. In the past when we were engaged in this struggle, people initially had no faith in us. Who in the world would believe that the Communist party could succeed? At the time when the Communist party first came into existence, people were sceptical. **[76]** They remained so throughout the intervening period, for this was the period during which we suffered defeats. After our defeat during the Northern Expedition and later the failure of the agrarian revolution,[3] after these two major defeats, no one had faith in us. What about now? Now people believe in us, saying the Communist party is competent. Competent at what? [They] say, you are competent in politics as well as in military affairs. You are experts in these two fields. Since people say the Communist party is strong in these two fields, can it contest with imperial-

---

[1]This must be a slip of the tongue: Mao almost certainly again meant "last" year, as in the previous phrase; for he was referring to the socialist "high tide," which by customary Communist dating, extended from mid 1955 to mid 1956, covering the collectivization of agriculture, followed by nationalization of industry and commerce, and the collectivization of handicraft trades.

[2]When commerce and industry were taken into joint ownership by the state in January 1956, businessmen in various cities marched through the streets celebrating by beating gongs and drums.

[3]Mao is referring here to the massacre of communists in Shanghai and elsewhere by Chiang Kai-shek in 1927, the failure of the CCP to maintain an alliance even with Chiang's leftist rivals within the KMT, and the subsequent failure of various communist rural uprisings, such as that led by Mao himself in Hunan; see C. Martin Wilbur, "The Nationalist Revolution: From Canton to Nanking," in *CHOC* 12, pp. 620–38, 650–81.

ism? In the contest with Chiang Kai-shek, between the Nationalist party and us, who emerged victorious? Who won, who was defeated? We won. Indeed you won, that certainly counts! Being able to win always deserves credit. Since you won, what else is there to say?

[Now,] what about construction? People have long [felt] that this is probably beyond the Communist party's competence. How do things stand now? We are carrying out revolution and construction simultaneously. When I was talking a moment ago about [our] "major" [task], about class struggle being [our] major [task], this was not to imply that we had not undertaken construction. We have carried out some construction, but we are still a novice in this respect. But though I talk [of us] as novices, we do know a bit. For when we were occupied with class struggle in the past, we did, more or less, learn a bit in the base areas. When it comes to building large factories, however, which requires [technical] know-how as to design, construction, and installation, we are ignorant. As for science, natural science, engineering, technology—if [we] want to teach [these subjects to] college students, [the number of] college professors [in our party] is very small.

How many of you are professors? (Rises and asks the audience:) Are there any? Those who are professors, please raise your hands! Not even one? Are there any professors?

(One comrade in the audience raises his hand.)

[Chairman:] One. One over there. How pitifully few! Comrades!

(Huang Huoqing:[5] Some haven't raised their hands.)

Chairman Mao returns to his seat and continues:) How many didn't raise their hands? Well, there are not too many of you, so you didn't dare to raise your hands.

Today some people are saying that the Communist party is unfit to run science, that the Communist party can't teach in the universities, can't be a doctor in a hospital, can't run engineering in factories, and doesn't know how to be an engineer or a technician. In a word,

---

[4]Huang Huoqing was both Mayor of Tianjin and first secretary of the city's party committee at this time.

we are inadequate in many respects. How about that kind of talk? Have you heard such comments? Comrades, I have heard such comments, and I say they are correct and correspond with reality. That is to say, we don't have scientists, engineers, technicians, doctors, or university professors. There are also few high school teachers. In literature [99] and art, we have some [strength] but it's still a case of 30/70. That's to say, just like Stalin's mistakes—wasn't Stalin 30 percent wrong, 70 percent right? In our case it is 30 percent competence, 70 percent incompetence. As far as literature and art are concerned, superiority still lies outside the Communist party. Almost all professors and doctors are outside the Communist party, right? There are two million people in the field of education, in universities, high schools and primary schools. The "teachers" in the category of government employees and teachers, total over two million. What is the Communist party doing? In name it is the leader in the schools; but in reality it is not able to lead, because you don't know how [to lead]. Therefore we must admit that this is one of our weak points.

[While] what they say is correct, it's also not comprehensive. I should say half of what [they] say is correct, but the other half is incorrect. They are correct in saying that the Communist party is unable to lead. But the Communist party is also able to lead. This, however, they didn't say. Why is [the Communist party] also able to lead? I say it's because what we don't understand we ask you to do. The Nationalist party is ignorant, too; so, too, is "Generalissimo Chiang"[5] or Chiang Kai-shek. That party, the Nationalist party, is as ignorant about the several specializations I've just mentioned as we are. It has also engaged in class struggle. That party has specialized in undertaking class struggle and did not undertake construction. Over the past seven years we have undertaken some construction while pursuing class struggle. For twenty years under Nationalist party rule, the output of steel was merely a few tens of thousands of tons. Now we have been in power for seven years, this year is our eighth, and what is our steel output? It may reach 5 million tons. According to our plan, [the target is] 4.12 million tons, which can be surpassed. Per-

---

[5]"Generalissimo" is the translation used by the editors of Mao's *Selected Works* for *weiyuan zhang* (chief of commission), which was Chiang Kai-shek's title as Chairman of the Nationalists' Central Military Affairs Commission; cf. *SW2*, p. 271, and Mao, *XJ2*, p. 579. "Generalissimo," or "the Gimo" for short, was the appellation by which Chiang was known to his Western allies during World War II.

haps less than 5 million tons, but definitely more than 4 million tons. Whereas they in twenty years only [managed] a few tens of thousands of tons, we in eight years [turned out] 4 million tons. This is because we have planning. Furthermore, the Ministry of Finance has fed the people. The Nationalist party didn't have a plan, nor did it feed the people. Comrades, without anything to eat I wouldn't be able to talk, nor would you be able to listen. Be they scientists or professors, doctors or engineers, they all must eat. The Nationalist party had food, but being preoccupied with class struggle, would not feed that kind of person, but gave it to the army and the politicians. I talk of a Li Fuchun and a Li Xiannian: Are there others like these two in the world? One is in charge of planning, the other in charge of finance; they take the scientists, university professors, engineers, and doctors, and fit them into their plans. They produce [78] long-term plans, annual plans, and in this way they lead them [i.e., those types of intellectuals]: they use the plans to lead them.[6] Is there anything else in which [we] can lead them? [We] can lead them in politics, in other words, with Marxism-Leninism. However, no matter how, we are at present still ignorant. But anything in the world can be learned. We must now study. The task of class struggle is now basically completed; by basically completed, is meant that it is not yet totally completed, [but] large-scale class struggle with mass participation is basically over. We said this at the [CCP's] Eighth Congress.[7] Our whole party demands [that we undertake] construction, that we study science, that we learn how to be university professors, that we learn how to conduct experiments and scientific research in a scientific institution, that we learn how to be engineers, technicians, and doctors, and how to struggle with nature, how to lead the whole society to struggle with nature. We must change the face of China. Once the political face has been changed, the economic face must be

[6]This generous tribute to the abilities and plans of Li Fuchun, Chairman of the State Economic Commission, and Li Xiannian, Minister of Finance, is somewhat ironic. At the onset of the Great Leap Forward less than a year later, Mao was excoriating the planners in general and the Finance Ministry in particular for their excessive caution.
[7]The CCP's Eighth Congress was held in September 1956. Its verdict that class struggle was basically over was modified by Mao in private after the start of the Anti-Rightist Campaign in mid 1957. During the Cultural Revolution it was implausibly argued that Liu Shaoqi was guilty of slipping this idea into the political report in defiance of Mao; see *Origins* 1, Appendix 5. This passage in Mao's Tianjin speech is further proof of the insubstantiality of this allegation.

changed as well. We spent several decades to change the political face. To change more or less the economic face so that it will look different from the past will also take several decades. Just as we didn't know how to conduct class struggle in the past—who knew anything about class struggle? Nobody did. I for one didn't know anything about it. I was an elementary school teacher and had no idea of joining the Communist party. I believed whatever propaganda the capitalists directed at me. I believed in what they said, because the school I had entered was a bourgeois school. Later I was driven, so to speak, to join the rebels. How about each of you? Did you make up your mind so early that as soon as you were born you joined the Communist party? Is that how it was? Being assigned a duty, [to join], then one becomes a Communist party member; but my mother never assigned me such a duty. So I learned it [by myself], right? We didn't know how to run land reform, nor did we know many other things such as how to fight a battle. Only after suffering countless defeats and reversals, and with increasing experience, did we learn and become expert in class struggle. Right? Not until having gone through numerous defeats. At the present time to learn how to carry out construction will also take a few decades. Can it be learned at a price somewhat lower than that which we paid to learn class struggle? For the price we paid for learning class struggle was very high. Several times the revolution was defeated. In 1927 the revolution was defeated. Base areas in the South were completely wiped out on the eve of the Long March.[8] In the White Areas, too, there wasn't much [79] left. That was because of "leftism." [Our] defeat in 1927 was a result of rightism. Rightism in class struggle. Afterwards it was because of "leftism." Having had these two experiences, we learned our lessons. So no matter what one thinks of them, people like Chen Duxiu and Wang Ming (Chen Duxiu went over to the enemy and later died. Wang Ming has not yet gone over to the enemy) have been of great benefit to us. Not them as individuals, but the movement which they led and which was defeated at a certain time. This taught the entire party and the people of the whole country a very great lesson. Well, the price was very great. Do we now have to pay an

---

[8]The main Long March began in October 1934. For the Maoist version of the history of the 1920s and 1930s, see the "Resolution on certain questions in the history of our Party," in Mao *SW* 1, pp. 177–220. For White Areas, see Text 3, n. 83.

equally high price in our construction? Take Hungary; their former leaders were defeated in class struggle and in construction because of the turmoil—the turmoil of October last year. I say the turmoil was a very good thing. Some people were very displeased by [what has happened in] Hungary, but I was very happy. A bad thing is, in fact, a good thing. Would Hungary have been better off with or without the turmoil? That is not the question; for in the last analysis it had to happen, and that's all there is to it. A pustule will sooner or later burst! In my opinion, we can succeed [in avoiding turmoil], for we have already paid a very high price to learn class struggle; and if now we don't practice right opportunism—[9] Why is it that we paid so very high a price? Wasn't it because we practiced "left" opportunism, that we came to grief? [Wasn't it] because we practiced dogmatism and "left" opportunism that we came to grief? In undertaking construction now, if we don't repeat our past errors, we may [end up] paying a relatively lower price and avoiding what has occurred in Hungary.

Now we must think carefully. It is very necessary to do so. We must realize that there is this situation, [namely] that undertaking class struggle is nearly completed, this is the point. In the past, during high tides of class struggle—for instance, socialist transformation, [the campaign to] suppress counterrevolutionaries and so forth—people didn't much notice our shortcomings during the high tide. We understood our shortcomings; and on the construction front, and in science and running the schools, we have asked for the people's forgiveness [for not having done much], and they have forgiven us to a certain degree. In society [at large] today that play [i.e., class struggle] is no longer being performed—Wan Xiaotang.[10] Is he here or not? That's [the play] about suppressing counterrevolution. There are not many [performances] left of his play, but there will still be some. Here among you there are military officers and military

---

[9]Mao seems here to change direction in mid thought and speech. Perhaps he suddenly realized that he should not be dwelling too much on the perils of rightism, because conservative critics considered that Hundred Flowers policy rightist—hence his abrupt return to the perils of leftism.

[10]Wan Xiaotang was at this time a deputy mayor and a senior party official in Tianjin who had had a close connection with the public security organs there from early on in the Communist period. He can therefore be presumed to have had a particularly close connection with class struggle. Mao appears to be giving Wan a public warning to behave himself during the Hundred Flowers. (Wan's name is given as XXX in one of the available texts.)

cadres. If you don't have a part to play, what do we still want you to do? **[80]** Of course, you still have a part to play, but not at this very moment. As a saying goes, maintain the army for a thousand days.[11] We haven't heard the boom of guns yet. Hence many problems in our society are now being exposed. [Now] there is this problem. Because of the gongs and drums, the gongs and drums of class struggle and the great excitement, ever since the deafening noise of gongs and drums in the first half of last year and the Eighth [Party] Congress passing a verdict on [all] that, it [i.e., the problem] has floated to the surface, it has been put on the agenda, [indeed] on our party's agenda. The people are now even more demanding of us. What can you Communists do? We answer, "Comrades, we also have a specialty, which is called class struggle. Ha ha! You people always look down upon us, don't you? But we [*laozi*] have been doing this for decades." (Laughter) But if we keep telling people that same thing all the time, it doesn't seem proper. Because everyone acknowledges that you have this specialty. They admit you are competent in politics and military affairs, that you have been working very hard for decades. There is no question of that. Our names can be found in the record of merit. But, comrades, how to teach in a university? How to perform an operation in a hospital? I never learned those things. How to run a middle school? How to solve a scientific problem? What is atomic physics? We know nothing about such things as engineering, design, construction, installation, transshipping. We are just beginning to learn. It takes time for such a situation to be remedied; maybe three Five-Year Plans are needed. At least fifteen more years are needed to bring about a change. For a bigger change, even more time will be needed. Because all of this needs to be learned, and it needs time. Can we learn? Of course, we can. There is no short cut. If you don't study, you'll never learn natural science or how to perform an operation. If I were to perform an operation, I'm sure I could do no better than the surgeon in a comic cross-talk [*xiangsheng*].[12] As long as you set

---

[11]This four-character phrase, *yang bing qian ri,* is normally completed with another, *yong-zai yichao,* the whole meaning: "Maintain an army for a thousand days, to be used in one morning."

[12]*Xiangsheng* is a popular style comedy dialogue of vaudeville humor in Peking dialect employing the performers' facial expressions (*xiang*) and the sound of their voices (*sheng*). Usually, *xiangsheng* includes two performers, a "joke cracker" and a "joke getter." In a well rehearsed exchange, the audience is treated to jokes, songs, imitations, and pointed satire.

your mind on learning something, however, you can learn it. Are there people studying now? Yes, there are, and we are going to send more people to study. For example, today's college students, Communist party members, and Communist Youth League members, they are all studying at this time. Fifteen years from now they'll be university professors and engineers. Perhaps they won't need fifteen years. But for some, it does take fifteen years before they can graduate. In addition, among today's scientists, engineers, university professors, and high school teachers, there are some who want to join the Communist party. Those of them who are qualified **[81]** can be admitted into the party. Therefore, given another three five-year plans things can be learned. If we compare it with class struggle, which one of them is easier to learn? I think this thing is relatively easier to learn. After all, it should be easier than fighting a battle or suppressing counterrevolutionaries. During the campaign against counterrevolutionaries, they were invisible. You [might] say there weren't any, but there were; you [may] say they exist, [but] the name counterrevolutionary is not written [on their faces]. As a matter of fact, when we were fighting the Americans during [the War to] Resist America and Aid Korea, we hadn't much assurance [of winning]. The United States was such a colossus, and we struck it with only one finger. I think, after graduating from high school, it is still necessary to spend five years in college, and after that, work for five or ten years, and then a person can qualify as a university professor, an engineer, an engineering technician, or a surgeon. Some people can't foresee these changes and so [say] the Communist party can never learn. But I think we can, and our task at present is to learn. Who are our teachers, then? Our teachers are none other than today's democratic personages. They are our teachers. We want to learn something from them and, as long as we adopt a proper attitude, to put away our bureaucratic airs, and stop trotting out the same old stuff about our [revolutionary] seniority, [and asking] where were you during the revolution. Let's put away all this stuff, because it's meaningless. Let the historians write about those decades. If every day, when we meet each

---

See Perry Link, "Hou Baolin: An appreciation," *Chinese Literature*, February 1980, pp. 84–94. Hou is the greatest living *xiangsheng* actor, who for a period went to Mao Zedong's residence every Wednesday and Saturday evening to perform (Link, p. 93). Mao apparently is referring to a certain *xiangsheng* routine satirizing incompetent or fake surgeons.

other, we have nothing better to say than we have been making revolution for decades, that's equivalent to doing nothing. Because that thing's finished. The problem of class struggle is basically completed. Now let's talk about science. I want to learn from whatever strong points you have. Do I know anything? No, I know nothing. First, [we must] admit our total ignorance. What, then, did you do in the past? In those days I was involved in class struggle, which kept me very busy. Such an answer is appropriate. It means I was deprived of education during my childhood. Hence my ignorance. Now would you please teach me? Some of the teachers still may not readily comply; but as long as we are earnest in our requests, they will teach us. In the old days, believe me, when paying respect to a master artisan, you had to burn incense and kowtow three times.[13] Is this still [the custom] in Tianjin today? I think it is still the custom. Do people still kowtow?

(Huang Huoqing: No, they don't kowtow.)

[Chairman:] Oh, they don't kowtow.

(Huang Huoqing: They sign a master-apprentice contract.)

[Chairman:] They sign a master-apprentice contract. [82] Now the ordeal of kowtow has been dispensed with. But suppose you still had to go through with it, then what would we do? Suppose it is still necessary, suppose they won't teach us until we kowtow three times. There we have a problem. Must we observe the established practice? I think we should kowtow three times, because you want to learn his skill, and his practice is that you must kowtow! Although now we don't have to kowtow, we must learn from them conscientiously; we must respect our teachers! We must study hard! This is equivalent to kowtowing. That spirit is still needed. Now within our party there is an unhealthy tendency. Instead of developing new habits, [some people] still have their minds stuffed with those past decades. When they

[13]"The full kowtow was no mere prostration of the body but a prolonged series of three separate kneelings, each one leading to three successive prostrations, nose upon the floor. The 'three kneelings and nine prostrations' left no doubt in anyone's mind, least of all in the performer's, as to who was inferior and who was superior." John King Fairbank, *The United States and China*, 4th ed. (Cambridge, Harvard Univ. Press, 1979), p. 160.

are not busy they idle. What do you play here, mah-jong or poker? Or is it going to the theater or going dancing? In any case, they are idlers who have never acquired the habit of reading. They do not devote their remaining energy to study. This is the general [situation]. As for our functionaries in schools, factories, scientific research institutes, and hospitals, they can all study. If you can learn [just] that bit, that's fine; if you can comprehend the content, that's fine[, too]. If you remain totally ignorant, but still want to lead there, then no wonder people say we're incompetent. [If] you are totally ignorant, and you [have to] study, then it's inappropriate for you to put on airs. We must study. A policy like "Let a hundred flowers bloom" for the arts is also the same. For a time [things] will appear in bold relief. "Let a hundred flowers bloom, let a hundred schools contend" means competition. What shall we do if bad things come into the open? Just now there are many bad things and much strange talk. I say it doesn't matter. We can simply criticize such strange talk. People are afraid that some of the flowers when [they] bloom may look ugly or be poisonous. As for [the policy] "Let a hundred schools contend," they say the Communist party represents only one school and the other ninety-nine schools can surround us. This is clearly a misconception. As far as problems of the social sciences and world outlooks are concerned, there are only two schools contending with each other, not a hundred schools. One is the proletariat; the other is the bourgeoisie. In terms of their very nature, these hundred schools can be divided into two contending schools. In today's world, there's the proletarian school and the bourgeois school, proletarian thinking and bourgeois thinking; and these two schools [are locked in] ideological struggle. In the realm of social sciences, is the petty bourgeoisie to be considered as representing one school? [83] Of course, it can be considered a school; but [as it] aligns itself with the bourgeoisie on basic issues [of principle], the petty bourgeoisie belong to the category of the bourgeoisie. Is there contention within the school represented by the Communist party? In fact, there is. Historically, the Second International represented one such faction, which practiced revisionism under the guise of Marxism. Today there is still revisionism—Yugoslavia. Does it also exist in our country? It also exists in our country; you can find that sort of person [here]. They can be called right opportunists.[14] [But] there is no need for us to talk about revisionism in China, [for] it might seem as though there is a revisionist faction within our ranks. There is none at present, but in the past there was. Chen Duxiu was one. Chen was a revisionist [or] right opportunist. Later, during the latter years of Wang Ming, [this was] the mistake of the second Wang Ming line. Do you comrades know about it? The second [Wang Ming line] occurred at the time when we began fighting Japan, in the early years of the War of Resistance against Japan. That was revisionism. Now we can use Zhong Dianfei as another example.[15] Didn't he write an article on movies in which he negated all our previous achievements? There are also some comrades who tend to affirm everything. They not only fail to see our shortcomings and mistakes, but also don't allow other people to criticize the shortcomings and mistakes in our work. Who are these people? Chen Yi and Ma Hanbing, to name only two. In the *People's Daily* of 7 January there is an article by Chen Qitong and Ma Hanbing.[16] I'd say the intentions of these comrades are good; they are loyal and devoted, seeking to uphold justice and protect the party. When they saw outsiders opposing us with a deafening noise of gongs and drums, they voluntarily came out to fight without waiting for orders. Such people who voluntarily come out to fight showed a spirit of hating what is hateful. We must recognize that, though their spirit is good, their policy and the method they use are wrong. Whether there are such things in Tianjin, you may find out for yourselves. "Left" and right, affirming everything and negating everything, these are two kinds of one-sidedness. In appraising our own work, it is not right to affirm everything without analysis. That's how the dogmatists have always behaved. Rákosi was that way and so was Stalin. Can we call Stalin an out-and-out dogmatist? We can't say that either.

---

[14]"Right opportunism" was the sin attributed to Bukharin and his colleagues at the CPSU's 16th Congress in 1930; see Leonard Schapiro, *The Communist Party of the Soviet Union* (London, Eyre & Spottiswoode, 1960), pp. 388–9. It would be the accusation leveled at Marshal Peng Dehuai and his fellow victims at the Lushan conference in 1959; see MacFarquhar, *Origins* 2, p. 248.

[15]See Text 3, n. 53.

[16]For these two men and their article, see Text 1, n. 16; and Text 3, under "Blooming Flowers and Contending Schools," esp. pp. 168–9.

That man had many achievements, but he was afflicted by dogmatism. His dogmatism once affected China, causing our revolution for a time to suffer reverses. Had we followed his instructions, [84] the subsequent revolutions would have been doomed to fail, too. We wouldn't have been able to hold this meeting here today. Who put up this building? Didn't we build it? [Had we listened to Stalin,] we wouldn't have had the chance to do so; for the rule of the Nationalist party and imperialism would still be in place. He had two sides, and also dogmatism; [he wanted us to] copy everything from the Soviet Union. We must learn from the Soviet Union. Both the mistakes and achievements of the Soviet Union are worth studying. Our slogan is to learn the advanced experience of the Soviet Union. We've never said we will learn their backward experience. When did we ever put forward such a slogan? Though we have never said that, however, in the past seven years that sort of thing has been brought in along with others. But, generally speaking, we have never copied things in a totally uncritical manner, because we have criticized dogmatism, the very source of which can be traced back to Stalin.

As regards all sorts of different opinions among the public, because class struggle has basically finished, all sorts of things have come into the open. There are various kinds of grievances. People are dissatisfied with the Communist party, saying we are incompetent. This is what I've just been talking about. When we are incompetent, we ought to acknowledge that we are incompetent. People say we are unable to lead science. As far as specific professional work is concerned, we are indeed unqualified to lead. But when it comes to the overall development of science, we are capable of assuming leadership, that is to say with politics and state plans. So we have a duty to study. What policy should we adopt in dealing with the numerous misguided criticisms that are around? We should adopt the policy "Let a hundred flowers bloom, let a hundred schools contend," and try to settle things in the course of discussion and debate, [and find out] what is right and what is wrong. We have only this method. All other methods are not needed. But there is a tendency in our party to continue with old practices, punishing people by military law. If you don't obey orders, you'll be court-martialed and summarily executed. (This is what punishing by military law means, for we are accustomed to these simplified methods.) This was Wan Xiaotang's method. (He meant methods used in [the campaign] to suppress counterrevolutionaries—Stenographer's note.) That method won't do, because it's for dealing with the class enemy. In dealing with the class enemy, in dealing with those who owe a blood debt, you simply have them executed; that's military law. As we have been used to that method, **[85]** we used it out of habit for decades in class struggle. In fact, even [class struggle] is not that simple. There are many other more finely tuned methods. But since what we were dealing with in those days was the enemy, we were full of energy. Today, however, we are not dealing with the enemy, but with problems among the people, [including] the democratic parties, non-party democratic personages, the national bourgeoisie, university professors, and doctors. The [old] simplified way of doing things, then, won't work. We must go through a learning process. They are right. With science, technology, and so on, we have only one option, and that's to learn from them—and there is nothing that cannot be learned. If we have ten to fifteen years, we can learn. Then we'll be able to lead them not only in politics, but also in technology. As for the various different opinions, they can be divided into two types. One has to do with science. No matter whether we understand it or not—today we don't, in the future we will—the policy is the same: there must be no resort to "punishment by military law." Wan Xiaotang's methods won't work. We can only adopt the policy "Let a hundred schools contend" and let people express their views. In any scientific discipline there may be several schools which [should be allowed to] argue [with one another], eventually to arrive at the truth. Social sciences are the same. Problems having to do with science must be solved through discussion, not by punishing people whom we don't like. To convert these people requires a process of persuasion. There is absolutely nothing to be afraid of in such discussions. What is there to fear? How is Hu Feng?[17] He was arrested, wasn't he? That was because he ran a small secret organization. Hu Feng is still alive, and will certainly be released one day. Indeed he will have expiated his mistakes and crimes by being in prison for a while. But Hu Feng's ideas have not perished yet; they still exist in many people's minds. This is bourgeois ideology. Scientific problems, ideological problems, spiritual problems such as religion, Marxism-Leninism, the bourgeois world outlook or the proletarian outlook, as well as artistic problems, none of them can be solved by using crude methods. There are two

[17]For Hu Feng, see Text 1, no. 7.

methods: One is coercion; the other is persuasion. If we are to adopt one of these two methods, should we adopt the method of coercion or the method of persuasion? **[86]** At present [we can see that] some of our comrades have lost patience and cannot wait to exert pressure. Coercion cannot convince people. People will not give in to such pressure. By suppressing problems, [we] will end up putting ourselves in a disadvantageous position, and they will add another entry in the record they have been keeping of the mistakes made by the Communist party. When the Americans crossed the 38th Parallel, it was right for you to resort to coercion. It was also right to take coercive measures to deal with the counterrevolution. But why, in dealing with science, do you employ coercive methods that are used for dealing with Chiang Kai-shek, the Nationalist party, and the landlord class? Why should you employ coercive methods to deal with literature and art, religion, and different opinions? If we employ coercive methods, then we are in the wrong [*mei li*] and cannot hold our ground, and we lose. That' why we must employ the method of persuasion. What if we don't know how to persuade people? If that's the case, then we should learn. In the South we have a saying about the beggar beating the dog. What we [in the South] call *jiaohuazi*, [i.e., beggar] you call *yaofande*, [i.e., beggar]. Beating dogs was his special skill: "To beat a dog, a beggar only has to exercise one skill." We have this saying in the countryside. Indeed we are ignorant at present, not knowing how to deal with things, or how to persuade. We must learn how to persuade, how to write persuasive articles, and how to give persuasive reports. It's always been a single blow. Once a comrade said to me: "Why bother about persuading them? I've never got used to it. [I've] always [set things straight] with a single blow." He said [he'd set things straight] with a single blow, but I told him you can't [settle] problems with a blow, or even with two or three. We must analyze and study things, and the articles we write must be convincing. As for publishing the various misguided criticisms in our newspapers and magazines, holding forums, and [letting people] criticize [us], will all this cause an upheaval and lead to the downfall of the People's Government? I'd say such an outcome is totally impossible, because they are not counterrevolutionaries, nor are they spies. The great majority are willing to cooperate with us. Even the tiny minority who hate us are not spies either; but they do hate us. Many still have no faith in the Marxist world outlook; they've studied a little, but, in fact, still don't believe it. Others, including party members, have some, but not total faith in Marxism. Comrades in our party understand Marxism a little, their understanding is still not yet total, they still don't understand it. So you see, both biases are represented by our party. The dogmatists and those who affirm everything **[87]** will tolerate no unpleasant remarks; they don't allow people to criticize us, even though we do have shortcomings. There are also people who say everything is bad, everything, and negate everything. Apparently these two kinds of bias or metaphysics still exist.

We now publish a newspaper called *Reference News* [*Cankao xiaoxi*].[18] Probably everyone in the audience has seen it. Could it be that many? Really? People may say the Communist party and the People's Government have done imperialism a service by publishing a newspaper for them to condemn us without even asking for a penny. Is it true that the Communist Party publishes a newspaper without charge for the imperialists to condemn itself? From the looks of it, it does. I read it through every day. Many of the articles do condemn us. Now we are going to expand the run to three hundred thousand copies, so that about a million people will be able to see it. It is issued down to the county level. To what level is it issued in the cities? We should temper ourselves. Both party members and non-party members should undergo this test, thereby broaden their horizons and get to know something about the world. For example, how does our enemy curse us? What's happening in our enemy's home? Some say this may lead to chaos [*luan*]. No, there will be no chaos. On the contrary, what would be very dangerous would be to stay behind closed doors, shut our eyes, and stop up our ears. One person maintains that as soon as the issuing of *Reference News* is expanded, the reactionaries will become more rampant. Consequently, this comrade (I was told of this by your municipality committee [secretary], Comrade Huang Huoqing) hopes that an editor's comment can be added to every single dispatch from foreign news [agencies]. What a hassle, comrade! Everything has to have an editor's

---

[18]*Cankao xiaoxi* began publication in late 1956 with the aim of exposing trusted officials to foreign news agencies' coverage of the world. Already by this time circulation was planned to reach 300,000; by the early 1970s it was six million and, though access to it was still "restricted," it was hardly a secret publication. See Henry G. Schwartz, "The *Ts'an-k'ao Hsiao-hsi*: How well informed are Chinese officials about the outside world?" *The China Quarterly*, No. 27, pp. 54–83; and *Origins* 1, p. 343, n. 17.

comment. Our very purpose is to let people think for themselves, hold forums by themselves, and talk things over among themselves. Possibly many strange things will be said, but I think the more the better. That is to say, we should under no circumstances seal ourselves off. Marxism was created and developed in the struggle against forces hostile to it. Now it still needs to be developed. For instance, we want to get things done in China, but we won't do things well if we don't develop. The principles of Marxism, when applied to China, must take on a Chinese color, and must solve problems in the light of concrete conditions. [Some comrades] have no confidence in the policy of letting a hundred schools contend. They are afraid that poison will seep out if we let a hundred flowers bloom. But we see things in a completely different light. If we employ coercive methods **[88]** and do not allow a hundred schools to contend or a hundred flowers to bloom, our nation will be sapped of its vitality and become simplistic and impervious to reason, and our party will not study, learn how to persuade people. As for whether Marxism can be criticized, whether the People's Government can be criticized, whether the Communist party can be criticized, or whether veteran cadres can be criticized, I'd say none of them cannot be criticized, as long as the criticism is well intentioned. Who is afraid of criticism?[19] A Chiang Kai-shek–type party and Chiang Kai-shek Fascism [are afraid of criticism.] We are Marxist-Leninists. They are the Nationalist party, we are the Communist party. "Veteran cadres" like Chiang Kai-shek—[for] they are also "veteran cadres"—cannot tolerate criticism because they cannot stand firm. Our capital is great[er]. We are not here to put on a temporary show—our show has lasted for decades. But when we are at work, we should not wear an expression designed to tell people we have been making [revolution] for decades. As a matter of fact, people already know about this. Are veteran cadres so easy to criticize that the moment they are criticized, the moment you blow on them, they immediately fall over? Are you all veteran cadres? Are there any new cadres? There must be some. But now I'm talking particularly about veteran cadres. I think they can't be blown over by an ordinary gust of wind, only if it's a force-12 typhoon. A force-12 typhoon can uproot trees and knock down

---

[19]One of the texts used omits the word "fear" (*pa*) here, but the resulting sentence is almost impossible to translate in the context.

houses, but it cannot blow down veteran cadres, nor can it blow down the Communist party, the People's Government, or Marxism. Nor will veteran cadres or new cadres be brought down, provided they are correct.[20] But if you have mistakes, then exposing yourself to a little wind is just what you need. This room doesn't have any electric fans, does it? That's because it's winter. But when it gets to be summer, we will certainly need to put on fans. Perhaps people are apt to have minor illnesses in the summer. We use the washing of one's face as an analogy. Do you wash your face once every three days or once a day? No one ever bothers to inquire into the question of why people wash their faces once every day, or even twice a day. This is because [our faces] get dirty. This is [because] the skin not only forms a boundary with the outside world—[a boundary similar to] the 38th Parallel; it has contact with the air, or the "Yellow River boundary,"[21] the skin makes up the face—but also serves as an excretory organ. The skin is a huge excretory organ that discharges a tremendous amount of wastes. In my opinion, the face is the dirtiest part of the entire human body, because it has [89] seven holes which discharge things, and in addition very many small excretory organs as well. That's why we have to wash it every day. Now, doesn't the party's face also need washing? The party also needs to wash its face. Poisonous weeds and anti-Marxist ideas that emerge are not to be feared. As a matter of fact, having them around is useful. We need to be exposed to these things so that we can develop by struggling against them. It's like getting a smallpox vaccination. Just now I said the publication of *Reference News* is going to be expanded. Isn't vaccination being recommended now? What is vaccine? It is a kind of virus or microbe. When a tiny bit of it is injected into your body,

[20]Mao seems to change his mind in mid paragraph here. At first, he appears ready to concede that some criticism might be excessive even for veteran cadres. Then—perhaps sensing that it would be politically unwise to give his conservative opponents within the CCP the loophole of being able to claim that certain criticisms were "force-12" and should be banned—he changes tack and asserts that to succumb even to such a typhoon would only be an acknowledgment of sins.

[21]"Yellow River as the boundary" (*Huanghe weijie*), refers to the division of China between the Chu and the Han around 203 BC shortly following the collapse of the Qin. The negotiated boundary, after much fighting between two contending forces, was actually along the Honggou canal in Central China. The canal gets its water from the Yellow River, hence the expression, "Yellow River as the boundary." The phrase *Chu Han xiang zheng, Huanghe weijie* (Yellow River was the boundary in the rivalry between the Chu and the Han) is often seen printed on Chinese chess boards.

you'll develop an immunity from smallpox by fighting with it, and so you won't get pockmarks. A person with a pockmarked face will get no more pockmarks because he has developed this immunity. It is very dangerous if a person never suffers from an illness. Someone wrote an article saying that I had discussed something, that I had said something about a minor illness.[22] [But] what I was talking about was those who go through life without suffering any illness whatsoever, and if one day they do fall ill, it could be very dangerous. Because the germs or viruses that have [previously] penetrated their bodies are far too few. What about those who catch some disease or other every now and then? These people are relatively more secure as they never stop struggling. The proletariat can only develop by means of struggle against bourgeois ideology; Marxism can only develop in the struggle against non-Marxism. This is why the policy of "Let a hundred flowers bloom, let hundred schools contend" is needed. The development of art in its various forms cannot be achieved without letting a hundred flowers bloom, nor can the various forms of art be compared with each other if there is no competition. Only by letting a hundred schools contend and compete with one another, only through criticism and discussion, can we develop what is correct. So we mustn't fear these things. Don't be afraid. Instead of staying in houses with heating facilities, we must go out into the open air.

I hear that some people even doubt the APCs. All sorts of skepticism has emerged just now. There's nothing to be afraid of, however, if a few people make cynical remarks. We can gradually persuade the skeptical. It will take five years for collectivization to be accomplished, and last year is only the first year. We need five years, at least five years, to consolidate the socialist system throughout the nation. Generally speaking, at least five years or so are needed before the socialist system of ownership can be consolidated, and before [people can get] used to it. Only collective production can enable the poor peasant's per *mou* [90] yield to reach what the well-to-do middle peasant formerly [achieved], but it takes a bit of time. Having watched for a year, during which some APCs went under because of mismanagement, while the income of well-to-do middle peasants was

[22]This is an obscure passage, but Mao seems to be flinging out a reference to an article in which he has been misinterpreted.

reduced, it's not unreasonable that people have become disappointed and pessimistic. What you're saying is not totally without grounds. Indeed there are some APCs that have been mismanaged; there are some well-to-do middle peasants whose incomes have decreased. We should persuade these people and show them the facts. If they still cling to the view that socialism doesn't have any superiority, you may reserve your own opinions.[23] Just [wait and] see. If we can have the support of the majority, that would be good enough [for us].

And then there's a rectification [campaign]. We in the Center intend there should be a rectification [campaign] this year, [or] next year, [or] the year after,[24] to rectify subjectivism, sectarianism, and bureaucratism. The way to change these bad phenomena is rectification. There is nothing to be feared about rectification. We went through it in Yan'an. As long as it is not linked with a campaign to suppress counterrevolutionaries, there is nothing to be feared. What it involves is some study, some research, some self-criticism, and a little discussion in small groups, the purpose of which is to spur us on to study Marxism and to get rid of subjectivism, sectarianism, and bureaucratism. Those comrades who have made serious mistakes of that nature will of course get nervous. We must help them. We must not use the methods of calling mass meetings [to] struggle [against them]; we will not select the struggle method but [rather] that of helping them to correct their mistakes. We can first conduct some experiments in a few [party and government] organs or various different places, and see how it works out. The Center has not yet issued a directive. Such a directive [will get people] to prepare for a period of experiment. This year, for instance, will be the year of experiment. The movement won't start formally until next year. It will only involve party members, [but] those outside the party may participate on a voluntary basis. The Center's directive has not been issued yet. It will take a little time, and there are still things to be talked over. Because I got to talking about this subject, I took the opportunity to report on it.

---

[23]Mao appears in the same sentence to be talking both *about* the doubters and *to* them, in the latter case as if to show his audience how to treat them.
[24]On the question of timing, see Text 13, n. 5. Here Mao may be raising the possibility of holding the campaign in 1957 for the first time; but in the light of his remarks a little further on, he is probably thinking of 1957 as a year of preparation.

OK now, how long have I talked, comrades? After all, it's already evening. What! An hour?

You haven't given me a single question. Just let me keep talking. Are there any questions to be collected? See if there are any.

(Huang Huoqing: Don't you have any questions? Anyone who has a question should raise it. It's OK if you put them down on a slip of paper.)

[Chairman:] Every one of you people is unwilling? Aiya, you people won't even give me a break! OK, let's wait until next time; you can prepare some themes. Since I'm passing through your place—I've passed through this place many times, but never called you comrades together for a talk. Because a conference was convened in Beijing—have you heard of it? It was [a session of] the Supreme State Conference, at which I gave a long speech. What I gave to you comrades here today was a short one.

That's all.

(The entire audience rises. Prolonged applause.)

[Chairman:] OK, goodbye, comrades!

(Prolonged applause.)

Talk at the Conference of Party Member Cadres of Shandong Provincial Organs

18 MARCH 1957

[257] A moment ago Comrade Shu Tong[1] suggested some topics and asked me to say something about them. Once you are assigned a topic, you must deal with it. But he raised too many topics—what am I going to do? Of the many topics [he suggested], I'll talk about only one: ideological problems.

Ever since the latter half of last year there has been ideological confusion both within the party and among the public. For example, many people now criticize the Communist party; non-party person-

---

Source: 1:257–77; alternate text, 10:91–111. A very brief portion of this talk, given in the provincial capital of Jinan, is excerpted in Mao, SW5, p. 436, and is italicized here.
[1]Shu Tong was at this time the party first secretary of Shandong province.

ages are bolder than before in speaking out and criticizing our short-comings. (Comrades, it would be best if you didn't take notes. Taking notes will interfere with your listening. Not that I want to keep things in secrecy; I'm here to exchange views with you. But if you take notes, you'll be all rushed. You'll be more relaxed not taking notes.) [They] are saying that the Communist party is unqualified to lead [the development of] science. They are also skeptical about the superiority of socialism. Some say that socialism doesn't have any advantage, that the APCs are mismanaged. And indeed some APCs are not well managed, and the Communist party doesn't understand much about science. Then again, the Soviet Union used to be [considered] quite good, but since last year it has been [considered] rather bad, for what reason, I don't know. In short, it was quite good the year before last, last year it was quite bad, this year it's been getting a little better again. [Yet] the Soviet Union is still the same Soviet Union. Some intellectuals say that the United States is better than China and that the United States is better than the Soviet Union, that the United States is turning out much more steel than the Soviet Union. Apart from that, [our] people have been creating disturbances frequently. Last year, particularly the latter half of the year (I don't know what it was like in Shandong, [but] I gather there were a few [disturbances] here, too), there were strikes by workers and by students [as well as] demonstrations; discipline was somewhat lax. This doesn't mean that discipline in factories and schools, [and] work attendance in the APCs were not generally maintained. On the whole, these were maintained quite well, but there were exceptions. [Then take] newspapers: I don't know how it is with your newspapers in Shandong, [but] in Beijing, Shanghai, and Tianjin, more and more essays, [258] sarcastic and satirical articles have appeared in magazines and newspapers, criticizing our shortcomings and scoffing at us. Under such circumstances, as I see Comrade Shu Tong has said, some people have begun to take a negative view of the APCs which, they said, [not only] showed no superiority, but were full of darkness. Others, on the contrary, have adopted a highly positive attitude toward the APCs, so much so that they completely ignore their short-comings. This being the situation, some Communists have been led astray by other people. Some party members and Youth League members have followed in the footsteps of the bourgeoisie, negated everything without analysis, and perceived the situation as being pretty bad. Other Communists are uncomfortable [with the situation], say-ing that all this trouble has resulted from "Let a hundred flowers bloom, let a hundred schools contend." Did things such as this also happen in your province? Have you implemented the "Let a hundred flowers bloom" [policy]? It has been tried elsewhere. "Let a hundred flowers bloom," but so far barely a dozen or so flowers have bloomed. (Laughter) They haven't all bloomed yet. "Let a hundred schools contend"; yet perhaps only ten or twenty schools have come out to compete. In the course of blooming and contending, [people] have said that certain things are not quite right, so some comrades were quite offended. They wanted to call it off, saying that there has been too much blooming and it must be brought to a halt. In other words, blooming should be either abolished or restricted. "Let a hun-dred schools contend" should also be restricted. [These comrades] favor the idea of restriction. So there are two types of people in our party: One type echoes whatever is said outside the party and follows in other people's footsteps; the other type wants to bring everything to a halt and considers resorting to coercion when they are dis-obeyed. This is how things stand at present. [That] is the internal cause. Of course, what happens abroad also affects us. The Twentieth Congress [of the CPSU] which criticized Stalin, the incidents in Poland and Hungary, the worldwide anti-Soviet and anti-communist agitation, the speeches of Tito and Kardelj[2] (have the Shandong news-papers carried this article?), all this has caused confusion in people's thinking. Moreover, there have been many mistakes in our work; whether it was in the campaign to suppress counterrevolutionaries, in land reform, in the collectivization movement, or in socialist trans-formation, we have made the mistakes of subjectivism, bureaucra-tism, and sectarianism, thus causing some confusion in people's thinking. But there has been no major turbulence. I'd say that here in China things are not so turbulent as abroad, certainly not so turbu-lent as in Hungary and Poland. Compared with other socialist coun-tries, too, there isn't so much turbulence in China. For example,

---

[2]It is not clear to which utterance of Edvard Kardelj, the Yugoslav Vice-President, Mao was referring. Conceivably it was his article explaining the Yugoslav road to communism pub-lished in *Pravda* on 2 June 1956 to coincide with the arrival of the Yugoslav President, Mar-shal Tito (1891–1980), in Moscow at a period of Soviet-Yugoslav rapprochement; see Wolfgang Leonhard, *The Kremlin Since Stalin* (London, Oxford Univ. Press, 1962), p. 204. In Tito's case, Mao is clearly referring to his Pula speech; see Text 3, n. 2.

Vietnam has been in upheaval for quite a while. Let us [259] now analyze the causes. There are external causes, to be sure, but it is primarily because we are in the kind of period, the kind of conditions
under which large-scale class struggle has basically been concluded
and socialist transformation has basically been accomplished. The
Eighth Congress reached a conclusion on this, [and] that conclusion
was in conformity with the actual situation. In the past our whole
nation fought against Chiang Kai-shek, the War of Liberation, these
were large-scale class struggles; land reform, the campaign to suppress
counterrevolutionaries, and the campaign to Resist America and
Aid Korea, these were [also] large-scale class struggles. Socialism is
also class struggle. Against what class is this struggle waged? It is a
struggle against the bourgeoisie and the individual economy linked
with capitalism. We had to wipe out the bourgeoisie together with
the individual economy, the base that produced capitalism, and that
massive struggle was basically concluded in the first half of last year.
With the end of this big struggle, problems among the people have
become prominent. Herein lies the fundamental cause. This is why
problems among the people have increased and been exposed, and
why many ideological problems have been exposed and people's
thinking has become somewhat confused. Did we have ideological
problems in the past? I'd say we did, especially during the period,
which you comrades all went through, when we first entered the
cities, when the big cities were liberated. Weren't the years 1949, '50,
'51, '52, and '53 chaotic? Were those years more chaotic, or is it more
chaotic now? In fact, those years were more chaotic. For instance, the
bourgeoisie at that time were so uneasy that it was like having fifteen
buckets at the well, seven up, eight down—they didn't know what to
do. But differences of opinion in the past were covered up by large-
scale class struggle. Many people were so scared by the War of Liberation, [the campaign to] suppress bandits, [the War to] Resist America and Aid Korea, the campaign to suppress counterrevolutionaries,
and land reform, that they didn't dare open their mouths. It certainly
wasn't [the case] that there were no problems; problems were legion
at the time. [But] we did solve many problems. For example, the fact
that in the past six or seven years the democratic personages have
made tremendous progress is precisely because we cooperated with
them in those struggles, and we should acknowledge that they have
made progress. Class struggle was basically concluded in the first half

of last year. By saying "basically concluded," I mean there is still class struggle, particularly in the ideological sphere; it has only been basically concluded, not completely concluded. This must be made clear so that no room is left for misunderstanding. **[260]** This is quite a long tail to drag. Particularly when it comes to class struggle in the ideological sphere, I'd say there are not "a hundred schools contending," just two. Of these two among the hundred schools, one is the proletariat, the other is the bourgeoisie. This contention will indeed go on for decades.

So the problem of how correctly to handle contradictions among the people has now been placed on the agenda. The correct handling of contradictions among the people is not large-scale class struggle. As I just said, there is still class struggle, particularly in the ideological sphere, but we treat it as a contradiction among the people. We treat the national bourgeoisie as a contradiction among the people, not as Nationalist spies. [Take] the bourgeoisie, [take] your Miao Hainan.[3] We drew a distinction between Miao Hainan and Chiang Kai-shek or a spy. We declare that he is not a spy, nor is he a Chiang Kai-shek, he is simply Miao Hainan. We cooperate with him. Seeing, this, he says OK; he says he is willing to cooperate with us. So our two schools can easily do things [together] for both us and you are willing. As I mentioned just now, there are quite a few comrades in our party who don't understand very well "Let a hundred flowers bloom, let a hundred schools contend," nor, what's more, [the policy of] "Long-term coexistence and mutual supervision." Some even don't really endorse such policies. Whether you comrades here endorse them or not, I'm not sure, because I've just got here, and besides, we don't ordinarily work together. In other places where I've been, for instance Beijing, I'd say among high-ranking comrades, [those at the level of] minister, perhaps only one out of ten did come around to the idea and endorse it. Of the rest, some sort of endorsed it, but not totally and in varying degrees. As for comrades of the

---

[3]Miao Hainan (b. 1902, in Shandong) joined the CCP while studying at a textile college. In 1949, he was the manager of Chengtong Textile Mill in Jinan. He became a leading member of the All-China Federation of Industry and Commerce and the China Democratic National Construction Association. He was made a Vice-Governor of Shandong in 1950. From January tô September 1956, he served as a Deputy Secretary of the Secretariat of the Shandong provincial party committee. See *Who's Who in Communist China*, vol. 2 (Hong Kong, URI, 1969), pp. 519–20. Mao clearly still thought of Miao as non-party.

ranks of department, bureau, and section chiefs, most of them initially expressed considerable doubts. What is this "Let a hundred flowers bloom" which allows that many flowers to bloom! (Laughter) "Let a hundred schools contend"–isn't that very dangerous? We the Communist party represent only one school; how terrible it would be if we were to be surrounded by the other ninety-nine schools! (Laughter) Then we'd have to get help from the PLA and fight our way out. Only by fighting a bloody battle would we be able to get away. "Long-term coexistence" they also [261] didn't endorse. To have those democratic parties around for seven or eight years would be about enough! Let them dig a hole and bury us? Who is going to supervise whom? Why ask them to supervise the Communist party? Would you say these comrades had some justification [to say] this? I think [what they said] was quite logical. What right do the democratic parties have to supervise the Communist party? Who actually did the fighting and won state power? Was it the working class and the peasantry under the leadership of the Communist party, or you democratic parties? That's why what they said sounds quite plausible. But still it is better to adopt this policy. What are the reasons? "Let a hundred flowers bloom, let a hundred schools contend": This is both a method and a policy. It is a method that can promote the flourishing of literature, art, and science. No matter how many flowers you are, you must always bloom! Among them there are beautiful flowers, and some that are not beautiful, [but] are ugly, and even poisonous weeds. All may bloom. What are we going to do if poisonous weeds spring up? There are [certainly] poisonous weeds in the world. But what about people? Will they die if they are in contact with poisonous weeds? This way there's a comparison. It's easier to deal with things by making comparisons. It's not all that easy, but very complex. Every kind of flower should be allowed to bloom (art in its various forms). People then say, in this event won't ghosts emerge, won't monsters and demons all swarm onto the stage? What sort of plays do you put on here? Are there any monsters and demons in the plays? Elsewhere there are, particularly in Shanghai, where many previously unstaged backward pieces are being brought back on the stage again. For instance, the Judge Bao shows never go without the beating of somebody's buttocks on the stage. Now we are talking about abolishing corporal punishment, aren't we? Yet on stage our Judge Bao still demands buttock-beating. Such practices will sooner or later be abolished. At present should we let it be continued in plays for a while? I think it doesn't matter if we let it be continued for a while. When such plays become too numerous, people will start complaining. The more people complain, then audiences will diminish. Then these plays won't be acted. In the past we imposed a harsh ban through administrative decree to prohibit such plays from being staged, but it is not so good a method as free competition of letting a hundred flowers bloom. As for "Long-term coexistence and mutual supervision," what this means is: because our party has made great contributions, **[262]** because it is a political party of workers and peasants, workers and poor peasants are the chief elements of our party, which by virtue of its very character is the vanguard of the proletariat; and because it has high prestige among the people, when this prestige grows too high, it produces the dangerous [consequence] that [the party finds it] easy to run things by itself by simply resorting to administrative decree, [thinking that the party] has got both numerical strength and tremendous prestige among the people. In view of this, we specially invite some people to supervise us, and [to partake in] long-term coexistence. As long as we exist, they will also exist. We don't need to say that if the Communist party lasts for a hundred years, they will be allowed only fifty years; if the Communist party lasts fifty years, they are to be allowed only twenty-four years. In a word, they must die first, they must die decades before us. Is this necessary? Will it be easier to get things done if they die first? Will there be more grain? (Laughter) Will there be more steel, more lumber, and more cement? Will auditoriums be built even better? Not necessarily. It can't be proved that if the democratic parties become extinct, we would be able to build better auditoriums. It can be argued that it would be better if some democratic parties put on a rival show and made sarcastic comments, revealing our shortcomings with sarcastic comments several times a year. Therefore, instead of tightening up [control] now, we must loosen up more. There is insufficient loosening up just now. We shouldn't try to suppress it; on the contrary, we should not suppress it. Ideological problems, problems in the spiritual sphere cannot be solved by using crude or coercive methods. We should all of us develop discussion on the basis of democracy and equality, and debating among ourselves. This is the method of persuasion, not the method of coercion. Of these two methods, which one should be adopted? One is coercion;

the other is persuasion. The method of coercion is for dealing with the enemy. Those of us who have fought battles all know that since the time we began the struggle on Jinggangshan, whether it was in the Dabie Mountains or elsewhere, we have learned that in dealing with the enemy we can use only this method. In dealing with the Americans in North Korea, that is during [the War to] Resist America and Aid Korea, we used the method of coercion. What method should we use in dealing with counterrevolutionaries and spies? We simply suppress them! First ferret them out, then persuade them. The method of coercion is to be used to deal with the enemy and to solve contradictions between the enemy and ourselves. It involves the use of force. Contradictions among the people doesn't call for the use of force. The superior man only uses his mouth, but never uses his fists. [263] (Laughter) Among the people persuasion rather than coercion should be adopted. It just won't do to settle things by force. When one uses administrative orders to enforce a prohibition, though nominally no force of arms is being used, in reality the PLA is there. The fact is, administrative orders can be carried out only because of the presence of the PLA, without which such orders cannot be enforced. Who would obey your orders? In other words, one has to rely on its strength to enforce administrative orders. Later [sic] we had the PLA, which was several million strong. We also have the common people. We have a basic mass [following], namely the workers and peasants. First, we've got the basic mass [following]; second, we've got armed force. This explains why those democratic personages cannot get their own way. They've not got these two things. First, they don't have a basic mass following; second, they've got no armed force. If, instead of imposing restrictions, we employ the method of encouraging the free airing of views along with the method of persuasion, then our country will become prosperous and flourishing. Since there are now contradictions among the people, we mustn't use methods for dealing with the enemy among the people; we mustn't use methods for dealing with the enemy in dealing with the people. These two things must be distinguished from each other. What is dictatorship? Don't we talk about the dictatorship of the proletariat? Dictatorship is over the enemy, whereas democracy is among the people. Mutual relationships among the people are democratic relationships. Of course, democracy must be under centralized leadership. [I'm] not saying one doesn't want leadership. At present in some places discipline is rather lax. There is a lack of discipline. This is going a bit too far. We must use the method of persuasion to overcome this problem. We must talk to them patiently and hold meetings with them. If things cannot be cleared up by holding one meeting, then hold a second and a third. Can we persuade students, workers, and peasants? I think we can, as long as we are in the right, that is to say we use the method of talking sense with reasoning. If we get it wrong and extend the scope of dictatorship to [include] the people, if whenever there is a contradiction or problem the method of coercion is employed, then our country will suffer losses, tremendous losses. And sooner or later we would have to turn back, when we cannot convince the people by coercing them. The superior man uses only his mouth, never his fists. You [may] want to use your fists, but sooner or later you'll have to desist, because this is not the way to solve problems among the people, but the way to handle the struggle between us and the enemy.

[264] Is there something to be afraid of? Contradictions among the people have been growing, yet neither coercion nor administrative orders are to be used—isn't this very dangerous? In my own view, there's no danger at all, because differences of opinion can only be correctly resolved through debate and democratic discussion from which the truth emerges. In the arts, that's the only way there'll be more liveliness and creativity; that's the only way literature, art, and science can develop. The results won't be visible in one or two years. It might take a few years, a dozen years, or decades before we can see the effects. Here and now we must get prepared in case of truly bad people and opinions. That is to say, in the realm of art there are poisonous weeds, weeds with poison, and very ill-looking flowers will spring up. What shall we do if they crop up? We believe those things can also be useful, because they allow everyone to take a good look [and see that] there are these kinds of poisonous weeds and these kinds of flowers. If a person is compelled every day to see only good things but no bad ones—[4] Truth develops through its struggle against falsehood. Both Marxism and our party have developed like that, through the struggle against false opinions. Unless we let false opinions be expressed, we won't know what they are. The beautiful devel-

---

[4]Mao appears to have left his thought unfinished; presumably he was implying that someone exposed only to good things would not recognize a bad one when confronted with it, as he indicates later.

ops through the struggle against the ugly; the good man develops through his struggle against the bad man. Ten thousand years from now there will still be truth and falsehood, the beautiful and the ugly, good men and bad men. Some bad men are indeed bad and not good, [but] they are also the teachers of good men. [As long as] there are bad men, people have [negative] models and won't emulate their wickedness. [As long as] there are good men, people can learn from them. But without the contrast between good men and bad men, people won't be able to distinguish the good from the bad. When a kid of a certain age watches a play, the first question he will ask is, Who's the goodie and who's the baddie? (Laughter) So don't be afraid of things like bad men and false arguments. There's no point in being afraid. Given this, it'll be relatively easy to overcome the mistakes of our party and government. If it were the other way round, namely adopting the method of coercion, that would be bad, [and] really fearful.

Our party is used to struggling against the enemy. Having practiced class struggle for decades, we know how to do it; and since we won, we proved ourselves to be qualified. Decades, indeed! That's why people admire us for this, [but] what do [people] feel the Communist party is competent at? You are quite adept at politics and military affairs. There are these two things for which people [265] admire us. Now, did they admire us from the outset? Not necessarily so. At the time when we first founded the party, no one admired us. The slogans we raised then— "Down with imperialism!" "Down with feudalism!" "Down with the warlords!"—people only listened, [but] effectively never paid attention. Later we also made blunders, [which is why we had to] make the Long March. Few adults survived it. At that time we advocated the overthrow of imperialism, but people still wouldn't pay much attention to us. After that, however, we had some achievements to show. By 1948, many people changed their attitude. It looks as though the Communist party all of a sudden had become popular and admirable. Particularly when the outcome of the Civil War had become a foregone conclusion in 1949, even more people expressed their admiration. Despite all this, comrades, when it came to construction, they didn't admire us: "The Communist party is capable of undertaking construction?" They wanted to look for a while. Now it appears that we are quite up to the job: "These people really know how to get things done; there's such animal energy!" (Laughter) Who would have credited us with being capable of carrying out construction? As far as construction is concerned, by now they have gradually built up a little confidence in us. After watching you do it for six or seven years, it looks as though you do have some qualifications. But when one talks of science, that's something entirely different. "Things like physics, chemistry, mathematics," they say, "you can't handle, and we still have to come [and help]." What should we do? What do you think we should do? All of you here are scientists, aren't you? (Laughter) There aren't many scientists in our party. The reason is simply that there aren't many scientists, professors, and engineers. Of the various types of artists, there are some but not many. There are few men of letters. In other words, in these various fields we are not adequate. University presidents are mostly non-party personages. Who is the president of Shandong University?

(Answer: Chao Zhefu)

[Chairman:] Is Chao Zhefu a party member or non-party?

(Answer: A party member)

[Chairman:] A party member university president still has to listen to non-party personages. You don't have any professors. (Laughter) Some hold the position of vice-president, but the non-party personages don't think highly of them. A large proportion of our party members are students and teaching assistants. There are also some lecturers but very few. Professors are even fewer. Now, should the students lead the teachers or the teachers lead the students? Should the teaching assistants lead the professors or the professors lead the teaching assistants? That this question should arise is very natural. I believe there is justification [for it]. What they have said is right. The Communist party is indeed unqualified; for very few of us are professors, scientists, or engineers, **[266]** almost none. The same can be said about the many fields of literature and art. What's the reason? This is because [we] were too busy in the past. For decades we were engaged in class struggle and were too preoccupied with class struggle to be able to do [all] these [other] things. In those days you had to have territory under your control to do what you did. In those days they simply wouldn't allow us to come to Jinan or other places. They simply wouldn't allow us to enter universities such as Shandong or Qilu. They wouldn't even allow us to come! I once lived in Beijing, but for thirty-one years I couldn't go there. I couldn't enter the city. If I had come, they would have invited me to stay in the jail. (Laughter) So we admit all this. But can we still learn? We studied class struggle for twenty-four years, right up to the [CCP's] Seventh Congress, 1921 through 1945; after twenty-four years we finally summed up [our experience]; only then had we basically learned these things, [after] making numerous mistakes. To these must be added [the mistakes we have made in] the many years since the Seventh Congress. So can we learn how to carry out construction, how to run science, how to be professors, how to be a doctor in a hospital, performing surgery? Is it as difficult as class struggle? I think that that class struggle business is more difficult; for as soon as you strike, it runs away. (Laughter) It's easier to conduct an operation, because the patient doesn't run away. (Laughter) In the natural sciences it takes five years to graduate from college. With five years of work that's ten years. Another five years of work, that'll be fifteen years. Couldn't he become an engineer [by then]! Can't this kind of person become a professor? Yes, he can. Given ten to fifteen years, he can learn. Now we've already learned a great deal about design, construction, and installation. We also have learned quite a bit about how to manage factories. With class struggle basically finished, what task should we switch to next? We should switch to learning those things and carrying out construction. So the whole society, [all] 600 million people, must wage a struggle against nature. We must bring prosperity to China and transform it into an industrialized nation. This can be learned. Don't be afraid of "Let a hundred flowers bloom, let a hundred schools contend," nor of "Long-term coexistence and mutual supervision." It's good if there's criticism; it's bad not to have criticism or to suppress criticism. Stalin made exactly this mistake. Stalin did a lot of good things, but he [also] did some bad things. He confused two things. He used method [appropriate] for the enemy towards the people and contradictions among the people. The government couldn't be criticized; [267] the party couldn't be criticized. As soon as one made any unpleasant remarks, at the first sign of trouble, a person would be labeled a spy and put under arrest. So currently we don't encourage strikes, student strikes, demonstrations, or petitions, but we must oppose and overcome bureaucratism. [If this can be done,] things such as strikes and student strikes will decrease. But there may still be some, [and] then what do we do? When such things occur, we should deal with them by using the methods appropriate for contradictions among the people. Is the People's Liberation Army still needed, then? Or should we disband it? Would that work? "Maintain an army for a thousand days to be used in one morning,"[5] to be ready to cope with imperialism. The People's Liberation Army is for dealing with imperialism, not for dealing with the people. The People's Liberation Army is the son of the people. How could the son [of the people] ever oppose the father of the people?[6] (Laughter) It doesn't bear discussing! The son of the people opposing the people! The people fighting the people? That won't do. The People's Liberation Army is an instrument of class struggle and a weapon of dictatorship. We must be different from the Nationalist party. Who is more afraid of criticism, the Communist party or the Nationalist party? I think the Nationalist party is. That party is terribly afraid of criticism. They are terrified of such things as "Let a hundred flowers bloom." We alone dare to advocate "Let a hundred flowers bloom, let a hundred schools contend." As for "long-term coexistence," we say we want to coexist with them for a few years, but they absolutely won't do it. Once they set up a so-called National People's Participation Council [*guomin canzheng hui*]. The Communist party was represented by several members; I was one of them. What was our status? We were not representatives of the CCP, but were called worthy and prominent personages. (Laughter) It sounded good but that was all, "worthy" as well as "prominent." (Laughter) They didn't recognize us as representing the CCP. They wouldn't accept short-term coexistence, let alone long-term coexistence. (Laughter) So we're the only ones who will talk about "Let a hundred flowers bloom, let a hundred schools contend" [and] "Long-term coexistence and mutual supervision." The proletariat is relatively selfless, because its goal is the liberation of all mankind. Only by liberating all mankind will it itself be liberated. The CCP should have the least fear of criticism. No criticism can topple us, and no wind can blow us down. We are not even afraid of a force-

[5]See Text 10, n. 11.
[6]Mao seems to have got carried away by his metaphor. He presumably means "How could the son of the people oppose his father (i.e., the people)?"

12 typhoon. A force-12 typhoon can sweep away a large auditorium or a tree as thick as this (with a gesture [which indicated one] about 2 feet [in diameter]). But as for the CCP, the People's Government, Marxism [268], and the veteran cadres, I believe it cannot blow them away, nor can it blow them down. (Laughter) Even a force-12 typhoon cannot blow them down, let alone a force–5-6 or a force–6-7 one. (Laughter) Have you been to Qingdao? I have never been there, but I would like to.[7] I have been to Beidaihe. [Even] when there is a force-7 wind [there], one can swim perfectly comfortably in the ocean. Normally there's not a breath of wind and no waves, and to propel oneself forward takes a lot of effort. But when there's a typhoon, the waves can reach the height of a man or [even] two. I've never seen a force-12 typhoon. Criticism can't topple us; nor can it topple the CCP, the working class, or the peasantry; for truth is in our hands. And since we have truth on our side, [since] we have grasped the truth, the path upon which we are set is truer than that [taken by] any other class. We have the basic mass [following] of the workers and peasants. How can a party and government such as ours, which is rooted in a basic mass [following] of the workers and peasants, be toppled by criticism? How can Marxism be toppled by a breath of criticism? Anything which can be brought down by a puff of wind must be bureaucratism. Perhaps bureaucratism doesn't need a typhoon, just give it a push like this and bureaucratism will fall to the ground. (Laughter) I think it would be better if such things as bureaucratism, subjectivism, and sectarianism got blown down a bit. That sort of thing should be blown down. We Communists sometimes still need the help of non-party forces. This is called attack from both within and without. Let bureaucratism, subjectivism, and the like get blown away a bit.

Just a moment ago Comrade Shu Tong brought up the issue of the superiority of socialism, because there are some people who doubt the superiority of socialism. Once one talks about superiority, then it's all superior and there's not a single shortcoming; once one talks about the lack of superiority, then there's not a single good point. There are two kinds of one-sidedness to be found both within and without the party. In the struggle between the two systems, which one is to win and which one is to lose? In other words, which of the

[7]Mao soon got his wish; a major party conference was held in Qingdao in July 1957. See *Origins* 1, pp. 285–9.

two social systems is to overcome the other, socialism or capitalism? Has this issue been resolved or not? Do you think the final outcome can be determined? According to the resolution of the Eighth Congress of our party, one should say that the final outcome has been determined. Who has won and who has lost? Of course capitalism has lost and socialism has won. Basically socialism has won. Is it the final victory? Not really. In the competition between these two system, socialism as a social system basically has come out as the winner. But this is not yet the final victory. It still hasn't been consolidated. We still have to [wait and] see. People still want to [wait and] see. Capitalists, peasants, **[269]** the capitalist class, the petty-bourgeois peasantry, and urban petty-bourgeois handicraftsmen still want to [wait and] see. Some people in the Communist party also still want to [wait and] see. In the struggle between the two systems, who's won, who's lost, which has won, which has lost, one can say has basically been decided; but the final victory will still require a period of time, perhaps two or three five-year plans. It will take at least five years for the APCs to be consolidated. Most APCs as of now only have a history of little more than a year. If we look at the struggle between the two ideologies—capitalist ideology and proletarian ideology, Marxism and non-Marxism—and [try to find out] which is going to win and which is going to lose in the ideological sphere, then the situation becomes even more problematic. That's why there's such chaos now. [Speaking of] the ideological aspect, it's intentional that the general topic of my talk today is the ideological issue. Despite all the changes in social systems, ideas will continue to exist quite stubbornly, particularly [people's] world outlook. In other words, whether it's the bourgeois world outlook or the proletarian world outlook, materialism or Idealism, dialectical materialism or metaphysical idealism, or metaphysical materialism, the struggle between these two types of ideology will last even longer.

How many intellectuals are there in our country today? Approximately five million. Of these, two million are associated with schools: universities, middle schools, and elementary schools. Besides them, there are intellectuals in the party system [*xitong*], the government system, and the army system; intellectuals in the economic, commercial, and industrial systems; and intellectuals in literature and the arts. Altogether these people, it's said, amount to as many as five million; but only a minority believes in Marxism. Ours is a culturally backward country, yet five million is by no account a small figure. Therefore we must make good use of this contingent of intellectuals. This body of intellectuals can all be considered bourgeois intellectuals; [and] having studied in bourgeois schools—I was one of them, namely a bourgeois intellectual who went through bourgeois schools and was subject to the influence of bourgeois society; and I only became a proletarian intellectual afterwards. I think [270] this is also true for many of you comrades sitting here who are intellectuals. When your mother gave birth to you, she didn't pass on the duty of having to join the Communist party, or having to believe in Marxism. I had the same experience. When my mother gave birth to me, she never told me these things. (Laughter) She didn't know that there were in the world [such things as] Marxism and the Communist party. It was social struggle that eventually drove me to go up the Liangshan.[8] My Liangshan was called Jinggangshan. Each of you has his own Liangshan, which is here in your Shandong. Those who truly believe in Marxism are the minority, about 10 percent perhaps; out of five million there are probably 500,000, maybe a little more. There are the ones who truly understand Marxism. In addition, there are always a few percent who basically oppose Marxism and adopt an antagonistic attitude toward us. But they are not spies, these democratic personages, though they do nurse a grievance and are basically opposed to us. Are there such people? I think there are. They are also the minority. In the middle, more than 80 percent are the middle faction. Of true Marxism, [they] understand very little. They show no interest when told to go to the countryside. When they visit a factory, they just make a cursory tour and then come back. Instead of becoming as one with [*dacheng yipian*] the workers and peasants, they are divorced from them. We call on them to become as one; but they say it would be better if they could remain separate, because there is no harmony of feelings, [and so] it's impossible for them to unite with the people. The intellectuals don't feel close to the working people, and there remains a gap between them. The world view of these people has not changed; the basic cause is still their bourgeois world view. Their ideological confusion arises in this way. Why

---

[8]For Liangshan, see above, Text 8, n. 4. Jinggangshan, the Jinggang mountains in Jiangxi, was the first base of Mao and Zhu De when they began to build up a guerrilla force in the late 1920s.

are they confused in their thinking? Because they keep wavering like grass on the top of a wall, which sways with every wind, which stands still only when there is no wind. Whenever a wind blows, they sway. The Hungarian incident came as a gust of wind; the Twentieth Congress of the CPSU came as a gust of wind; from somewhere else came still another gust of wind. As wind will never stop blowing in the world, so they keep swaying back and forth all the time. They are also very proud, with their tails held high. They consider themselves important because they are intellectuals. In a country such as ours, intellectuals indeed are valuable, but as far as world outlook is concerned, genuine proletarian intellectuals they are not. These are still bourgeois or petty bourgeois intellectuals. The overall category is bourgeois intellectuals. Some people call them petty bourgeois intellectuals, [271] and that's all right. When you call them bourgeois intellectuals, they will be offended. Nevertheless, the overall category is still that of bourgeoisie. It will probably take as long as three five-year plans (a few years have already passed); maybe a dozen years or so are still needed before Marxism can win a decisive victory. We must win them over to our side. Do you want to know who are the people now teaching? It's them. All of them are teachers. They run newspapers; they teach in schools; they plan and manage everything in our offices; and they are engineers. Not even for a single day can [we] do without them. There are intellectuals here in your midst as well, comrades; but they are rather few. If you say we can leave the intellectuals [alone], that won't wash. We can't leave them; we wouldn't have anyone else to teach. Two million of them are teaching and working in universities, middle schools, and elementary schools. In addition to literature and art, there are all kinds of newspapers. The acrobatic actors and [those who sing] the drum songs in Shandong cannot be considered as intellectuals, can they! But Mei Lanfang[9] must be counted as one; Mei Lanfang is an intellectual. What is the name of that Mei Lanfang of yours in Shandong? Don't you Shandong folks know who the Mei Lanfang in Shandong is?

Now I would like to talk again about the issue of working-class intellectuals. In the course of leading the revolution, the proletariat from the very first won over a group of intellectuals to serve it. This

---

[9]For Mei Lanfang, see Text 3, n. 66.

is how Marx was won over. Marx, Engels, and Lenin were all bourgeois intellectuals who served the working class. Our Chinese intellectuals are the same. Now there is a group of intellectuals who understand Marxism. They make up, as I said a moment ago, about 10 percent of the 5 million. That's 500,000. They are the nucleus of the intellectuals.

Of the various classes, which one has a future? Only the working class has a future. How many do we have in the working class? Prior to the revolution, before Liberation, there were only a few million. [The number] has increased to 12 million in recent years. Now there are 12 million industrial workers working in the factories. In a population of 600 million, only 12 million are workers. That's a little more than 1/50th, only one worker in every 50 people. [272] Though so few in number, they alone have a future. All others are transitional classes. It means [they have to] keep going. Go where? Go where [the working class is]. [Take] the peasants, for instance, the peasant in the future will become an agricultural worker and collectivized through mechanization. As for collectivization, it will in the future become socialism, and [then] will be transformed into national ownership, ownership by the whole people. A few decades from now, the current APC ownership by the peasants will be transformed into something like a factory, an agricultural factory. In this factory, corn, millet, rice, sweet potatoes, peanuts, and soybeans will be planted. The capitalist class now is, as you know, in the middle of the transition. They, too, will become workers. The several hundred million peasants and handicraftsmen, who now have already become collective farmers, in the future will become state farmers, agricultural workers, operating machines. Apart from a minority, the rest of the 5 million intellectuals all endorse and support the socialist system, even though in their world outlook and their thinking they are still wavering. Generally speaking, with the exception of a small number of people, they all support socialism and are willing to serve it. OK, then, the working class has already won them over. Through the Communist party it has won the intellectuals over to our side and to cooperate with us. But to cooperate and serve socialism is one thing; their world outlook and their souls are quite another thing. It will take time for them to change their world outlook into that of Marxist dialectical materialism and historical materialism, or, to put it in a simple way, into that of Marxism.

Most intellectuals have not changed their bourgeois thinking and bourgeois world outlook so far. Some have changed, but only slightly, or have not greatly changed it. As I just said, they still remain estranged from, and still haven't integrated themselves with, the working people. Writers and artists are unwilling to go down to the factories and the countryside; and when they do, they come back almost immediately. With their attention turned elsewhere, they don't have much interest in the workers and peasants. They want to go home and be with other intellectuals. I'd say these people are half-hearted. Half of their heart wants to serve socialism; this half of their heart is good. And since half of their [273] heart is good, we can take our time to change the other half. The other half still belongs to the kingdom of the bourgeoisie, to bourgeois ideology. If I were to say this to intellectuals, they would jump up and say, "How can you say we are half-hearted?" I would say, "Of course I can; even if you jump on the roof, I will still say so. (Laughter) Because you are still wavering in this manner. You are willing to serve the working class, but only half-heartedly, not wholeheartedly. Is there any proof? [The proof] is [that] instead of becoming one with the workers and peasants, you remain estranged from them. You have no friends among the workers and peasants. All your friends are intellectuals. It would be better to make friends with the workers and peasants than with intellectuals." But they won't listen. Even if you try to drive them down [to the grassroots], they still won't go. Those who have been driven down will come back right away. The working class requires the intellectuals to serve it wholeheartedly. It not only makes this demand, but also asks them to change their world outlook and give up their bourgeois world outlook. In the newspapers I once said that we must destroy capitalism and build socialism. Destruction and construction always go hand in hand; without the destruction of the one, the other cannot be established. Hence the task of carrying out destruction. Destruction entails some pain. In that case, you capitalists should let us know now. Among the capitalists are a large number of intellectuals. We must use them. The working class needs a great number of intellectuals to serve it wholeheartedly. If not a 100 percent, then the majority of them should believe in Marxism and have interests in common with us. Now we do have interests in common. As far as socialism is concerned, they have some interests in common with us—except for a few of them who have no interests in common with us, who are happy upon hearing that the APCs are not running well, who are pleased when the APCs are having bad luck, and who rejoice when the Communist party gets into trouble. There are a few such people, but the majority are willing to cooperate with us. But they are still hanging in mid air. Consequently, our task is to win them over.

Our party is now recommending that we prepare for rectification. In order to win over the intellectuals as well as non-party personages, we must first rectify our own style of work. The Central Committee plans to hold a conference this year, but it hasn't been decided yet. Today I might as well talk about it briefly. [274] We haven't had rectification for years. The Three-Antis and the Five-Antis[10] were sharp struggles, but they didn't solve the ideological problem. We are preparing for rectification; and it is our expectation that, if through such rectification the work style of the Communist party can be improved, then we can win over the vast numbers of non-party personages. Speaking of the non-party personages, there remains a problem: Should we or shouldn't we cooperate with them? This is not their problem; it is not a problem of whether they want to cooperate with us, but rather whether we want to cooperate with them. There is still another problem. It's easy to talk about cooperation. You democratic personages, you Miao Hainan, we want to cooperate with you. But the question is whether we should use them. Some say they are not of much use and even call them waste matter. Well, waste matter can also be made use of. Why can't waste matter be made use of? Today I can't talk concretely. Miao Hainan has been called waste matter, but he is perhaps a very useful person. Even those who are not very useful can still be made use of. Some have coined the epithet "waste matter," but waste matter can also be made use of. When holding a conference, we mustn't adopt a perfunctory attitude. Every year, as a mere formality, a Political Consultative Conference and a session of the People's Congress are convened, but afterwards nothing happens. Probably only one or two weeks are spent on the matter in a year. Such an attitude is a negative attitude. I think we must adopt a positive attitude. These democratic personages are largely non-party intellectuals. They are veteran intellectuals, a legacy left over by the old society.

---

[10]For details of these two campaigns in the early 1950s, see Text 3, n. 35.

How many students currently in college are from workers' and peasants' families? Twenty percent according to the nationwide statistics. Out of a hundred college students, only twenty are from workers' and peasants' families. Eighty percent are sons and daughters of landlords, rich peasants, and capitalists. [The situation with regard to] middle school students is not very clear; the ratio is probably 4:6, that is, 60 percent are from the families of landlords, rich peasants, and capitalists, while 40 percent are from workers' and peasants' families. It could be half and half. Do you have statistics on this? I don't have them. Of those who enter senior middle schools, I'm afraid they still constitute the majority, it's still those of exploiting class origin who are in the majority. When will a hundred percent of the college and senior middle school students come from workers' and peasants' families? It will take at least three five-year plans, or at least **[275]** eleven to twelve years for these conditions to be fundamentally changed. Perhaps it will take an even longer time, and another two five-year plans won't be long enough; perhaps three more five-year plans are needed.[11] As a species, sooner or later they will become extinct. There is no doubt about that. What is awaiting them is their extinction. Will the bourgeoisie remain as a species? Will the landlord class remain as a species? They won't remain as a species, and our very goal is to bring about their extinction! In the future there will be no capitalist system, nor will there be a feudal landlord system. Thereafter for 10,000 years there'll be a system of workers and peasants and all [children] will be workers' children.

The proletariat is the class with the brightest future. But currently [it is beset by] a temporary shortage [of proletarian intellectuals]. As you know, we can't move a single step without them [i.e., bourgeois intellectuals]. Suppose we abandon them, there will be no teachers, no engineers, and no scientists. Most professors as well as middle and elementary school teachers come from these people, so do most writers and artists. We can't move without them. If we leave them, we won't be able to move a single step. This is why we must take pains to unite with them. After a number of five-year plans then there'll be a change. By then they, too, will have changed; the capitalists will

[11]Mao's customary reckoning of a lengthy period required for major social change was three five-year plans, starting with China's first FYP (1953–7), with success in sight by 1967. Here he is taking the precaution of adding in the fourth FYP, i.e., three five-year plans from 1957, or 1972.

have become workers, and the landlords peasants. Their children will have changed, too. They are undergoing changes now.

Rectification is a method to solve intra-party contradictions through self-criticism. It is also a method to solve contradictions between the party and the people. Dogmatism, sectarianism, and bureaucratism, these three styles of work must be rectified. These aside, other problems are also to be addressed: for instance, the problem of corruption, which exists in political institutions, particularly in such basic level units as APCs, factories, and mines; *the problem of the decline of the spirit of serving the people with heart and soul, and that of waning revolutionary will; such phenomena as striving for position and fame and fighting for personal gain have become more widespread. The death-defying spirit some of our comrades used to display in class struggle, that is, in the struggle against the enemy, now has disappeared. [Now they] are fastidious about food and clothing, and try to match each other in terms of salary; and if the wage grades [they get] are below their expectations, [they] would cry their hearts out. Everybody has two eyes, right? The water in our eyes is called tears; that in a teacup is called tea. When their wage grades fall short of what they think they deserve,* [276] *these people become all tears. (Makes a gesture and the audience burst into laughter.) During the time when they were fighting Chiang Kai-shek, during the War to Resist America and Aid Korea, and during land reform and the campaign to suppress the counterrevolutionaries, they never shed a tear, nor in the construction of socialism. But when their personal interests are affected, they become all tears. (Laughter) Someone is said to have refused to eat for several days. This person, who I've heard is from here, didn't eat anything for three days. We think not eating for three days is no big deal, but eating nothing for a whole week is a bit dangerous. (Laughter) In short, striving for fame and position, trying to match each other in terms of salary, clothing, and luxury, all these things have emerged; and they are also to be seen as contradictions among the people. Two streams of tears trickle down; starve and weep for personal interests. There is a play called* **Lin Cong Flees at Night [Lin Cong ye ben]**[12] *in which a line reads, "A man [nan'er] does not easily shed his tears ([Chinese] Editor's note: According to the play's text, this line should read "A real man [zhangfu]*

---

[12]This is a scene from a Ming dynasty opera, in the Kiangsu Kunqu style, called *The Story of a Sword;* see *SW5,* p. 439.

does not easily shed tears until his heart is broken").[13] *We at present have some comrades who are also [real] men or perhaps [real] women. Look, a man should not easily shed his tears until the time when his wage grade is to be reviewed. Comrades, don't you need to rectify this style of work of yours! Let's go back and talk them round. That a man doesn't easily shed his tears is right. What is it that really breaks our hearts? It's when the survival of the working class and the peasant class is in the balance. It is quite all right if you shed a few tears at such a time. As for your wage grade, even if it were not fairly determined, you still must accept it. Don't let your tears flow outwardly, let them flow inwardly (Laughter) so that you can swallow them. Indeed, there are numerous cases in which things have been unfairly settled, and it is very likely that some people's wages are not fixed correctly; but as long as everybody gets enough to eat, they don't matter very much. Ours is a revolutionary party and our principle is that no one should die of hunger. Those who have not died of hunger are all revolutionary comrades. We must struggle. Ten thousand years from now we still must struggle. We must struggle when there is a Communist party. Even when the Communist party no longer exists, by that time when it will have disappeared, leaders and a group of managers will always be there. They will also be serving the people. In short, we must serve the people wholeheartedly, not half-heartedly, nor one-third–heartedly or two-thirds–heartedly. Those whose revolutionary will has waned must bestir themselves.*[14]
This year we propose, this year is the preparatory phase. We'll serve notice to people, telling them we are going to have a rectification. Each locality may also conduct its own pilot rectification. There are a few corrupt elements, and they must wash their hands quickly this year. If you took **[277]** some things, you had better put them here; then we won't treat you as a criminal. Next year rectification will formally be launched, so this year you should stop embezzling and disgorge what you have stolen. What about things that have already been gulped down, digested, and turned into shit? If they have already turned into shit, then, depending on each different case, they

---

[13]This correction of Mao's misquotation was perhaps the work of a party editor with a tendency to bourgeois pedanticism! More interesting is that this note underlines the unwillingness of compilers of Mao's speeches to correct or elucidate any of the Chairman's *own* words.
[14]The italicized paragraph corresponds fairly closely to *SW5*, pp. 436–7. Compare New Mao Texts 1, pp. 275–6, to *XJ5*, pp. 419–20. The unitalicized part of the fourth sentence has no parallel in the previously published excerpt.

must be compensated in installments. No one can get away with it in the APCs. In the eyes of the peasant, 30 yuan is a very big issue. In that case, you may pay them back in three installments. Ten yuan this year, ten yuan next year, and ten yuan the year after next. Those who have disgorged everything and have become thoroughly remolded will not be viewed as criminals next year. That's why we make the announcement this year. Once bureaucratism has been overcome, both our relations with the people and our relations with subordinates will be improved. Indeed it's not easy to be the chief of a provincial department! Most of the subordinates ordinarily don't say anything; but when the rectification campaign comes, they begin to speak up. Some of you here must be department, bureau, or section chiefs. Is it that, after throwing a bomb, the rectification will get started? I'd say no. I think we shouldn't blow things up; we only need to correct them. In dealing with our own shortcomings, in dealing with the shortcomings of the people, we mustn't resort to big democracy or a large-scale movement. They are to be applied to the enemy only. What we need is small democracy. If one small still won't do, another one may be added to it; then it becomes ultra-small democracy. In short, what we need are a gentle breeze and mild rain [*hefeng xiyu*].[15] Though a typhoon may not be necessary, the fine drizzle [*maomao xiyu*] will keep coming down and the gentle breeze will keep blowing. (Laughter) Let it blow for three years. This year we get prepared, but next year and the year after next, there will be a little drizzle [*maomao yu*] and a little breeze [*weiwei feng*]. It will blow away our bureaucratism and subjectivism. Our point of departure is to protect our comrades. Start from the desire for unity and arrive at a new unity through proper criticism. That's it, comrades.

[15]"Gentle breeze and mild rain" was the phrase used in the actual Rectification Campaign, see Text 8, n. 22. In that earlier talk on 10 March, Mao used a similar phrase, "drizzle" [*maomao yu*], also used here. The Chairman appears to have been groping towards a characteristically memorable phrase with which to delineate the methods of the forthcoming Rectification Campaign and this may have been when he devised the final formulation.

On Ideological Work (Talk at a Conference Attended by Party Cadres from People's Liberation Army Units under the Nanjing Command and from Jiangsu and Anhui Provinces)

19 MARCH 1957

[278] Giving a talk at every stop on my journey, I have turned myself into a wandering lobbyist. In the present period, a number of questions need to be answered. That's why I have talked all the way here to your place. This place is called Nanjing, and I've been here

---

Sources: 1:278–301; alternate text, 10:112–35. In the full title of this text, the date is given as 20 March 1957; but a short extract from the speech, published in *SW5* (p. 436) is dated 19 March. If Mao was traveling south by train, he would have reached Nanjing before Shanghai, where it is known that he gave a speech on 20 March (see Text 13). It seems more likely that he made the speeches on successive days than that he spoke in Nanjing, made the four-hour trip east, and spoke again in Shanghai on the same day. We have, therefore, accepted the *SW5* date.

before. I think this place Nanjing, a coiling dragon and a crouching tiger,[1] a good place. But a gentleman named Zhang Taiyan[2] asserted that [the expression] "a coiling dragon and crouching tiger" is a "false statement made by the ancients," a lie told by the ancients. It appears that when applied to the Nationalist party, the expression is indeed a false statement. For having ruled from here for twenty years, the Nationalist party was driven away by the people. Now in the hands of the people, Nanjing is again a good place, I think.

The problems that exist in various places are more or less the same. We now find ourselves in a period of transition, a period in which the old struggle—class struggle, has basically ended, has basically been completed. The struggle against imperialism was class struggle; the struggle against bureaucratic capitalism, feudalism, and the Nationalist party, the War to Resist America and Aid Korea, and the campaign to suppress counterrevolutionaries were also class struggles. Later we went on to launch the socialist movement, socialist transformation, the character of which is also that of class struggle.

Now, is the collectivization movement class struggle? The collectivization movement is, of course, not a struggle of one class against another class, but the transition from one system to another system, or from a system of individual ownership to one of collective ownership. Individual production is a category associated with, and in the domain of, capitalism. It is the source that gives birth to capitalism, often gives birth to capitalism. This domain or base area from which capitalism stems has been eliminated by collectivization.

[279] Therefore, generally speaking, what we were engaged in over the past few decades was class struggle: We transformed the superstructure, overthrew the Japanese puppet regime and the government of Chiang Kai-shek. We have established the People's Government, and changed the relations of production and the socio-economic system. As far as social and political systems are concerned, the face of our society has been changed. Look, all of us here in this auditorium are Communist party [members], not Nationalist party [members].

---

[1]"Coiling dragon and crouching tiger" (*longpan huju*) a traditional phrase for Nanjing, is attributed to Zhuge Liang, military commander and prime minister of the Shu during the Three Kingdoms period. See *Tai-ping yu-lan, juan* 156.

[2]Zhang Taiyan (Zhang Binglin) (1868–1936) was a scholar, editor, and anti-Manchu revolutionary; see *BDRC* 1, pp. 92–8.

In the past, however, people like us could not come to this place, nor were we allowed to go to any other big cities. Seen in this light, things have changed; and they have been changed for quite a few years in the realm of the superstructure and political system. The transformation of the economic system into a socialist one came about in the last few years, and now can be said to have been basically accomplished. All this is the result of our struggle over the past few decades. If one takes the history of the Communist party, it's something over thirty years; [or] if one counts from the anti-imperialist [struggle] that began with the Opium War, over a hundred years, we have done just one thing—we have engaged in class struggle.

Comrades, the change of the superstructure and the socialist economic system through class struggle merely opened the road for the transformation of other things. Now we are confronted with new problems. Domestically, the struggle we had in the past has been basically concluded; but internationally, it is still not over yet. Why do we still need the PLA? We need it, most importantly, against foreign imperialism, which may come and invade our country, given their malicious intentions. Within our country, there are also still a few surviving counterrevolutionary elements who have not yet been ferreted out, as well as some of those suppressed in the past, such as the remnants of the landlord class and the Nationalist party, who may rise up if we don't have the PLA around. The landlords, rich peasants, and capitalists now all behave themselves. The capitalists are somewhat different [from the rest of them]. For this reason, we treat them as part of the problems among the people. Unlike the peasants, who embrace collectivization, one may say the national bourgeoisie is only half-willing to accept socialism. In other words, they are somewhat reluctant. Moreover, they agree to subject themselves to transformation on terms which are quite favorable to them. Therefore, we now find ourselves in a period of change: from class struggle to the struggle against nature. To improve living conditions, we must promote construction, that is to say we must struggle against nature. From revolution to construction, [280] from our previous anti-imperialist and anti-feudal revolution and the subsequent socialist revolution to technical and cultural revolution.[3]

In order to build our country, we must have technology and

[3]Mao here seems to mean only the modernization of culture in the narrow sense, not the

machines; we must also understand science. In this regard, in the past we did hand work; we used hand tools to make tables, chairs, and stools, using our hands to grow food and plant cotton, everything by hand. But now [we have to] change to using machines; [to acquire] the skill to operate machines is indeed a tremendous revolution. Without such a revolution, if we have only changed our politics and our social system, ours will remain a poor country, an agricultural country, and a country with only handicraft industry and handicraft skills. For this reason, we must carry out a cultural revolution. I think you all understand and are all aware of the changed circumstances. It seems, however, as though some people are still not quite clear or still haven't recognized this kind of change.

Now a number of new problems have arisen: the problem of science and technology; the problem of culture; people are making demands upon us; and some people are making trouble. What are these problems? Temporary workers, hard-pressed households in the countryside, students, and collectivization have all given birth to new problems. A small number of workers go on strike; a small number of students boycott classes or take part in demonstrations or petitions; among demobilized soldiers, some are also inclined to stir up troubles; also some APC members, well-to-do middle peasants, not many but they are dissatisfied and want to drop out of the APCs. There are still other things with which they are dissatisfied, and so they make trouble with us.

What is to be done? How to handle trouble started by the people? We must discuss these questions in clear and unequivocal terms.

Contradictions should be divided into two types: the first type is called contradictions between ourselves and the enemy; the second type is called contradictions among the people. What we solved in the past few decades was the first contradiction, and now we must solve the second contradiction. It manifests itself in various areas. For instance, [the current transformation] from an agricultural country to an industrialized country is also a contradiction.

[281] We don't possess enough technology; we don't have

---

total and wholesale transformation of the human soul undertaken later in the "Great Proletarian Cultural Revolution."

machines and culture; and we are not well off. Some people say, "Now that we have entered socialism, perhaps we are going to live a better life." Don't they also say: "Socialism has already succeeded. Last year the Communist party convened a congress at which it was proclaimed that socialism had been basically accomplished. It seems as though we are about to live a happy life." This indicates that they are ignorant of what socialism means. Socialism, when seen as a social system, is nothing but the relations of production. We have established a relationship that differs from the old one. To carry out production, there existed in the past the capitalist-worker relationship and the landlord-peasant relationship. Now we have established a socialist relationship, and use that kind of interrelationship to promote production. Speaking of production, we have just started. As for the new relationship, it has just been established and has not yet been perfected. The APCs have still not been consolidated. When people use these methods to engage in production, the relations between them are socialist relations. For the old methods are unsuitable and relatively inadequate for [promoting] production and development, but also have, over a long period of time, caused the Chinese people to remain poverty-stricken and illiterate, and to be looked down upon by other peoples of the world. Now these [old] relations have just been changed, but production has not yet started. Without production there can be no life; without a great deal of production there can be no good life. How many years are needed? I think probably a hundred years are needed. A hundred years from now I won't exist in this world to enjoy the good life. It certainly won't take that long if we proceed step by step; perhaps a decade or so from now life will become slightly better; two or three decades from now it'll be a little bit better still; fifty years from now it'll become more or less enjoyable; and a hundred years from now things will be truly extraordinary and very different from what they are today. A hundred years is a very short period. Even if ten thousand years are needed, people still must live on.

How can life be made better when revolution and socialism have just begun? How can grain production be increased? Has grain production been increased? Yes. In 1949, the year in which the People's Government was established, we got only 220 billion catties of grain. Last year we had already got 360 billion catties, an increase of 140 billion catties.[4] But how many people are to be fed? One of the advantages of our country is its large population, but its disadvantage [282] is also that large population. The more people, the more mouths to feed; and the more mouths to feed, the more grain is needed. The additional 140 billion catties of grain have all disappeared. At times we even feel a shortage of grain. There was a shortage of grain in 1949; today, there is still a shortage, there is still not enough grain. In order to live well, we have now already drawn up a twelve-year plan for the development of production, a science plan, an agricultural plan, and an industrial plan, which are to be carried out step by step in our work and production.[5] Such a matter is easy for us older folks to understand, but not for the youth. It seems as though everything must be made perfect as soon as they come into the world. Therefore, we must educate them, we must educate the broad masses of the people, and in particular the youth, why they have to work hard and start from scratch.

Today, we must start from scratch, for our ancestors left us very little. Who were our ancestors? Imperialism, feudalism, and Chiang Kai-shek. They are the previous generation, and the previous government. What they left to us was a people fleeced to the last bit. Nevertheless, they are all gone; things will get better. Since they are gone, a piece of land is made available. This piece of land of ours stretches 9,600,000 square kilometers from the seacoast in the east to the Kunlun Mountain Range and the Pamir Plateau in the west; and from the Amur River in the north to Hainan Island in the south. Together with the entire people of our country, together with everybody, together with the youth, let's devote decades to working on this land. Without looking to the distant future, let's work for fifty years. If the first half of this century is for revolution, then the second half is for construction. Forty years are still left of this century; this means the central task at present is construction.

[We] must clearly distinguish the two types of contradiction. The first type, contradictions between ourselves and the enemy, should not be mixed up with the second type, contradictions among the

---

[4]Mao is using approximations of contemporary statistics; his figures translate into 110 million tons for 1949 and 180 million tons for 1956. For official figures, see State Statistical Bureau, *Ten Great Years* (Beijing, Foreign Languages Press, 1960), p. 119.

[5]The only twelve-year programs to be drawn up formally were for agriculture and science; see *Origins* 1, pp. 18, 35.

people. That there are contradictions in socialist society, that contradictions persist in socialist society, this is something Lenin once pointed out. He recognized that there were contradictions in socialist society. During the first years of Stalin's leadership, the period following the death of Lenin, domestic life in the Soviet Union was still quite lively and not very different from ours today. There, too, were different parties, different factions, and well-known personages such as Trotsky. Trotsky had many followers, but he was perhaps only a democratic personage within the Communist party. **[283]** Moreover, he played a mischievous role in making trouble with us. Besides these, there were still other people; and in society at large, one could speak out and criticize the government. At that time, there was such a period, but afterwards it didn't last. Afterwards, under an increasingly dictatorial government, criticism was no longer to be tolerated. If someone made a criticism, or a hundred flowers were to bloom, that was something very much to be feared. Only one flower was allowed to bloom. A hundred schools contending was also feared. Whoever caused the slightest trouble would be branded a counterrevolutionary and thrown into jail or executed. In this case, the two types of contradiction were being confused with each other, with contradictions among the people mistaken for contradictions between ourselves and the enemy. Your Nanjing comrade Xu Jiatun[6] says that when a host of students came to him to present petitions, their ranks remained in good order. Governor Peng Chong[7] also says they maintained good discipline and behaved well on the street. But once inside his yamen, they began to shout: "Down with bureaucratism!" in an effort to get their problems solved. If anybody had given such a case to Stalin, I think he would have arrested some of them, and it is very likely that several people would have lost their heads.

[6]Xu Jiatun had become a secretary of the Nanjing party committee in Nov. 1954. In April 1957, he would explain the Hundred Flowers policy to non-party personages at a session of the provincial CPPCC. See *Chinese Communist Who's Who*, vol. 1, (Taipei, Institute of International Relations, 1970), pp. 279–80. In 1983, Xu became head of the Xinhua News Agency in Hong Kong, and thus Beijing's "ambassador" to the colony.
[7]Either Mao or the editor of this speech got Peng Chong's position wrong: he was not provincial governor (*sheng zhang*) of Jiangsu, but mayor (*shi zhang*) of Nanjing. Peng, who like Xu Jiatun had moved from Fujian to Nanjing in the mid 1950s, was also secretary of the municipal party. See *Who's Who in Communist China*, vol. 2, p. 544. After the Cultural Revolution, Peng Chong was appointed to the Politburo of the CCP's 11th Congress in 1977, but dropped from it at the 12th Congress in 1982.

Down with bureaucratism, isn't this counterrevolutionary? As a matter of fact, not a single one of them was a counterrevolutionary. They were all good young students. Not only that, the problem should have been solved. There had indeed been some bureaucratism, for the case involving overseas Chinese students who caused trouble was not properly solved. By presenting petitions, the students helped us. They themselves also learned a lesson, as did many cadres, and the overseas Chinese students as well. Those who had started the trouble and beaten up people also stopped. Why did they have to fight every day? Because in the past we didn't educate them well, and because we didn't mobilize the masses to criticize them. Similar to this problem, there are also some [cases of] demobilized soldiers making trouble. Comrade Zeng Xisheng is from your neighbor, Anhui province.[8] The demobilized soldiers there caused trouble and went to see him. He spoke to them for forty minutes and their problems were solved. At the outset they were filled with anger, but later their anger somehow disappeared. In short, [their] problems became only a few, and they were all resolved. One of these people has been found to be a crook who tried to pass himself off as a revolutionary soldier. He was a bad hat, and he was one of the leaders.

When the people cause trouble, we should never use the methods we employ with the landlord class, the Nationalist party, and imperialism. We must adopt an entirely new approach. Except for those who violate the law—for example, those who kill people with knives, those who injure people, or those who break into offices [284] and smash furniture, must be dealt with according to legal procedures—all the rest, even if they have made mistakes, even if they are leaders, even if they have taken the lead in making trouble, should be subject to persuasion and education, and mustn't be expelled from factories, schools, or offices. Suppose you expel a person, where will he go? When expelled from this school, he'll enter that school. Does it make any difference? When expelled from this factory, he'll go to that store. After all, he must find himself a place. He cannot go to the Sun Yatsen mausoleum and make a living there.[9] Without food and shelter, he cannot survive there. He cannot live in the wilderness, but must

---

[8]Zeng Xisheng was the Anhui provincial party's first secretary at this time.
[9]Nanjing was the capital of the Nationalist Republic of China from 1928 to 1937, and the Nationalist party's founder's mausoleum was completed there in 1929.

find a place to stay. By expelling him, you may find peace and quiet; but it is only by shifting your problem onto someone else. I think too much peace and quiet won't do you any good. It's not a bad thing at all if there are a few troublemakers in an office, a school, or a factory.

Now let me talk again about the first type of contradiction—contradictions between the enemy and ourselves, between the enemy and the people, or between the people and the enemy and counterrevolutionaries. Currently there exist two erroneous viewpoints. One is the right-deviationist viewpoint which holds that peace and tranquility now prevail in the world. Consequently, the few reactionary elements as well as evil doers are not brought to justice as they deserve. This is not right. This is the right-opportunist viewpoint. Since it now exists in various provinces, each of these provinces must pay attention [to this problem]. Some of our friends among the democratic personages or democratic parties also share the right-deviationist viewpoint. Sometimes their right-deviationist viewpoint is more to the right than ours, as some of the counterrevolutionaries now kept in jail or having been executed are their old friends. They feel somewhat disheartened because [we] have executed their relatives or friends. There are such viewpoints [and] we must make explicit our attitude. It is unhealthy to have such viewpoints within party ranks. Second, there is also the exaggerating or "left" viewpoint,[10] which claims that there are still many counterrevolutionaries. Such a claim is wrong. At present, hidden counterrevolutionaries still exist, and this must be affirmed. The campaign to suppress counterrevolutionaries in the past was basically correct. Had we not suppressed the counterrevolutionaries, what might have happened can hardly be imagined. One of the reasons why things like the Hungarian events have never occurred in China is that we have eliminated counterrevolutionaries, whereas in Hungary they were not eliminated. Therefore, to say that there are still many counterrevolutionaries doesn't correspond [285] to reality. It is an exaggeration.

As class struggle has been basically completed, the second type of contradiction, contradictions among the people, now becomes more revealed and further exposed. Regarding problems of this kind, consensus has not yet been reached among our comrades. There are still

---

[10]For Mao's use of "left" in quotations, see Text 3, p. 138.

different opinions. Only through explanation, discussion, and study can our comrades reach unanimity of opinions on these problems. Mentally we are ill prepared for dealing with trouble caused for us by the people, because in the past we fought the enemy alongside the people. Now since the enemy is no longer there or can no longer be found, only the people and we remain. If they don't argue with you when they have grievances, who else can they argue with? In the past, to make things difficult for the enemy was to make revolution. But what they are doing now cannot be called revolution. After getting rid of me, then what? Ask Chiang Kai-shek to come back? Nevertheless, because you fail to handle things properly, they still won't stop making trouble. If things are properly handled, if in nine out of ten places things are properly handled, if nine out of ten problems are properly handled, but in one place there is one problem which is not properly handled, then trouble will occur in that place. Their causing trouble is normal—for if you fail to handle [their problems] properly, why shouldn't they argue with you? Now tell me, if they don't argue with you, who else can they argue with? With "Generalissimo Chiang Kai-shek"? But he's gone to Taiwan. That's why they want to argue with the factory director, the APC leader, the *xiang* [township] government, the city government, the People's Government, or the school principal: because you fail to handle [their problems] properly. In our work there exist bureaucratism, subjectivism, and sectarianism. Bureaucratism exists because there are too many people and too many opinions. Here again we come across both the "left" and the right viewpoints. When the people make trouble, some maintain that we should use the old methods to deal with them. Having tried them out for decades, we know how to handle them. You know how long we've been fighting for the revolution, don't you? After all, we have a set of methods, namely our methods for dealing with the enemy. Sometimes we can use them, call in the police to suppress them. In several places the police have indeed been sent for to make arrests. Calling in the police to make arrests when the students go on strike, this is the Nationalist party's way of doing things. The Nationalist party used these methods. There are also people who feel completely helpless and don't know what to do. In the old days when they were dealing with the imperialists, [these same people] displayed tremendous daring and courage. Armed with nothing [286] but millet plus rifles, they nevertheless showed no signs of fear. You [were] not afraid of the imperialists and Chiang Kai-shek, or [their] warplanes and artillery. Not afraid of imperialism, but when the people make trouble, [you] are somehow a bit afraid. Now listen, if you are not afraid of imperialism, why should you be afraid of the common people? And yet, strange as it is, [they] are just afraid of the common people. They may not be afraid of imperialism; but as soon as people start arguing with them, they become helpless. This is because they have never learned how to deal with [such situations]. They still haven't learned well. What they learned in the past was how to deal with imperialism and Chiang Kai-shek; if one talks about struggling against local despots and allocating land [to the people], that they were good at. But when it comes to dealing with discontented people, they have not studied well. They have never taken this class. Therefore, [this problem] really deserves our attention, and we must openly raise this problem with people both within and outside the party and start discussing it. Then a solution will be found.

Comrades, confronted with imperialism and the common people, which after all is easier to deal with? Which one is more difficult to deal with, the enemy or the common people? No matter how long you try to drive them away, the enemy simply refuses to go. How shameless they are! The spies who have wormed their way into our government, schools, factories, and the countryside simply refuse to go. But in no way are the common people spies, nor are they imperialists, landlords, or capitalists. As common people and working people, they can be easily brought to reason. That's why when a large group of students, indignant at the overseas Chinese students' use of violence, went to present petitions, Comrade Xu Jiatun and Comrade Peng Chong successfully settled the case by the method of persuasion.

My position is that, nationally, our policy is "Overall consideration and proper arrangements"[11] and strengthening ideological education. You may call this a strategic policy, for what is involved here are "Overall consideration and proper arrangements" for 600 million people including the landlords, rich peasants, national bourgeoisie, counterrevolutionaries who have not been executed, and all sorts of unemployed people. All must be properly taken care of, so that they

---

[11]This is a major theme of Text 3; q.v., under "Overall Consideration and Proper Arrangements," pp. 159–62.

can live and have something to do. Among [all] these [600 million], approximately five million are intellectuals. In China, the number of intellectuals is rather too small. Nevertheless, there's still a group of them, about five million of them. Of these, less than a million have joined the Communist party. There are still four million outside the party. What are they doing? They are working in our government [287] systems [*xitong*]: A small fraction of them is affiliated with the army; two million of them are in the educational system, including colleges, middle schools, and elementary schools; one million are in the financial and economic system. In addition, there are scientific workers, literary and art workers, writers, poets, artists, painters, actors, as well as journalists, newspaper editors, and so on. Many of them are in Shanghai.

Of this big group of intellectuals, some have integrated themselves with the workers and peasants, accepted Marxism, and joined the Communist party; some haven't joined the party, but are very close to us. Those who actively support and endorse Marxism constitute only a small proportion, perhaps 10 percent or slightly more than that. Jiangsu reportedly has 17 percent. At the other end are those who are hostile to us, but who are not spies. They are hostile to us and do not accept Marxism. Reluctantly they accept the socialist system, for they are incapable of reversing the historical trend. Such people do exist. They perhaps make up a few percent in the entire population. Those in the middle constitute 80 percent. Maybe not that much, but somewhere between 70 percent and 80 percent. These are the centrist faction, the vacillating elements. To a certain degree they subscribe to Marxism, and they have also read a few books, but never really dug into it. They only learned it here (pointing at his own forehead), but never really got into it deeply.

There is one way in which we can put the intellectuals to the test. Some say we must distinguish between a petty-bourgeois intellectual and a bourgeois intellectual. The idea is that it is better to be labeled as a petty-bourgeois intellectual than as a bourgeois intellectual. But I think this is not true. I myself used to be a bourgeois intellectual and went to a bourgeois school where the social atmosphere was infused with the air of capitalism, and what I learned there was all Idealist stuff. [For a time] I believed in the Idealism of Kant. Can you call it petty-bourgeois? Sometimes you may and should draw a distinction; but when it comes to world outlook, such a distinction can hardly be made. How would you define the petty-bourgeois world outlook? Semi-materialist? As for myself, not until afterwards did I dig into Marxism and learn it. Moreover, it took a very long time for me [288] to be transformed gradually in the struggle against the enemy. There is one thing by which we can test the intellectuals, that's to see which of them can identify with the workers and peasants, which of them can become one with the working people. Some of the intellectuals are able to do so; but most of them keep a considerable distance from the workers and peasants, so that, even if they want to, they can hardly merge with the latter. They don't feel affection for the workers and peasants; they aren't friends with them. If they have something to say, the workers and peasants won't tell it to them; they, in turn, also look down upon the workers and peasants. The intellectuals have all got a tail, so we must throw cold water on them. When you throw cold water on a dog, it will tuck its tail between its legs. But if you don't, it will stick up its tail and look quite cocky. Since they have read some books, they are indeed quite proud of themselves. But when the working people see their grand airs, they feel uncomfortable.

Our task is to win over this 70 to 80 percent wavering centrist faction. They generally endorse the socialist system, but they haven't completely accepted Marxism as a world outlook. I would say they are not serving the people wholeheartedly, but only half-heartedly. Half of their hearts wants to serve the people, that's fine. Yet there is still another half, which they don't know where to put. Do you think they support Taiwan? Apparently they don't support Taiwan. But when it comes to foreign countries, I'm afraid they would still say the United States is admirable. "Look, the United States has so much steel. Science in the United States is so advanced." Are the foreign countries, capitalist countries, or Western countries really admirable? I think they are indeed admirable. They have so many machines and so much steel, whereas we have nothing. But the fact that they are admirable doesn't mean you are admirable, too. For no matter how much steel your United States has, it is the steel of the American people, not the steel of us Chinese people. What's the use of us talking about their being admirable all day long? Every year the United States turns out 100 million tons of steel, but not us. If every year we could increase our steel output by tens of thousands of tons, we would be delighted. Now we've only got 4 million tons of steel.

According to the first FYP, we may achieve 4.12 million tons, which
is likely to be surpassed, [the real output] probably will be slightly
more than that, that is, 4 million and several hundred thousand
tons.[12] The figure for 1949 was a mere 100,000 tons plus a few tens of
thousands. The annual output record was set in 1934, in which the
Japanese played a major part,[13] [289] but still there were no more
than 900,000 tons. Chiang Kai-shek ruled for twenty years. When I
said Chiang Kai-shek should fall from power, it was with justification. We didn't throw him out for no reason. For twenty years under
his rule, steel output remained at the level of several tens of thousands of tons. Even this might not have been maintained had he not
benefited from what Zhang Zhidong[14] and others did in the late
Qing period. We have been in power for seven years or, if we count
this year, eight years; yet already we are able to turn out more than 4
million tons of steel. Therefore we'll be happy even if our steel output increases by one ton only, because it is our own doing. But when
your United States raises its steel output by a few million tons, we
won't be happy. The more steel you have, the unhappier we are.
What are you going to do with the additional steel? It is very dangerous when you greatly increase your steel output; they will attack us.
Yet some of our intellectuals still keep trumpeting how much steel
the United States has. Steel! Steel! So much! We must persuade them
out of this. We must persuade the intellectuals.

Some intellectuals work as teachers. Scientists are all teachers; so
are college professors, middle school teachers, and elementary school
teachers. They all teach the people. Journalists and those who run
newspapers are doing the same thing. Broadcasters, writers, and

[12]The first FYP steel output figure for 1957 was finally given as 5.35 million tons; see
Zhongguo guojia tongji ju, comp., *Zhongguo tongji nianjian, 1983* (China Statistical Yearbook, 1983) (Beijing, Zhongguo tongji chubanshe, 1983), p. 245. Mao's deprecating references here to the gradual increases in China's steel output contrast strongly with his ever
escalating calls for sharp increases during the GLF a year later. But what does emerge from
this passage is how large steel loomed in Mao's mind.
[13]Mao is referring to the development of the steel industry in Japanese-occupied Man-
chùria after 1931.
[14]Zhang Zhidong (1837–1909) was one of the great Qing officials who pioneered the modernization of China. Mao is presumably referring to Zhang's establishment of an iron and
steel works at Hanguang; see William Ayers, *Chang Chih-tung and Educational Reform in
China* (Cambridge, Harvard Univ. Press, 1971), pp. 100–1.

artists are all teachers of the people. Technicians and engineers are indispensable in our factories. Those who think we can look down upon these several million intellectuals, those who think we can do without them, are all wrong. We can't do without them; we can't get anywhere without these several million intellectuals. We can't even make one step, so to speak: Our schools will have to be closed, and the publication of our newspapers will have to stop. Speaking of literature and art, the Communist party has never produced either a Mei Lanfang[15] or a Zhou Xinfang.[16] Now an actress named Yuan Xuefen[17] has joined the party, but we still haven't got a Mei Lanfang, a Zhou Xinfang, or a Cheng Yanqiu;[18] and we still haven't got any professors. Now we are beginning to have some engineers, but still they are very few. Some technical personnel are beginning to join the Communist party, but the bulk of them are still outside the party.

So our several million intellectuals have their use, no matter how wavering they are. They are the property and the teacher of our people. For the time being, there is only them to work as teachers. No other teachers are available, because they are what the older generation and society left to us. If we look at their class origins, they invariably came from landlord, rich peasant, and bourgeois [290] [families]. But they can be changed through education. We mustn't use the theory of the unique importance of class origin. Otherwise, Lu Xun would have been a landlord, a rich peasant, or a bourgeois; Marx would have been a landlord, a rich peasant, or a bourgeois; and so would Lenin. Isn't this absurd? This is why we mustn't talk of the theory of the unique importance of class origin. This is because today they—the landlords, rich peasants, and the bourgeoisie—have been cut off from the source of their social power. Their social basis

---

[15]Mei Lanfang, see Text 3, n. 66.

[16]Zhou Xinfang (1895–1975), a well-known Peking Opera singer, did join the CCP in 1959; *Who's Who in Communist China*, 1, pp. 166–7. He later got into trouble for writing and staging a Peking Opera about the Ming official Hai Rui, because it allegedly sniped at Mao. See Tom Fisher, "'The Play's The Thing': Wu Han and Hai Rui Revisited," *The Australian Journal of Chinese Affairs*, No. 7 (1982), p. 23.

[17]Yuan Xuefen (1922–) was a Shanghai actress close to the CCP even before 1949; see Guo Hualun, ed., *Zhonggong renming lu* (Biographical dictionary of Chinese Communist personnel) (Taipei, Institute for International Relations, 1967), pp. 331–2.

[18]See above, Text 5, n. 33. All three of them, Mei, Zhou, and Cheng, joined the party in 1959. Zhou Enlai personally introduced Cheng Yanqiu into the party.

or their roots in society have been eradicated. Now suspended in the air, they are like parachutes hanging in the sky, and can be easily remolded; and we should not be afraid of them.

Some comrades of worker-peasant origin or worker-peasant cadres are somewhat annoyed when they see the intellectuals; perhaps they can't stand them or make headway with them. It is true that the intellectuals are hard to deal with. This is precisely because they are intellectuals. The trouble lies in [the fact] that whereas they have read a few books, we haven't. And because we haven't, they get so stuck up that it's really hard for us to deal with them. If you think it's hard, then it's hard; but if you think it's easy, then it can be easy. After all, over the past seven years, these several million intellectuals have made some progress, and we must recognize this. You people in Jiangsu can testify to it, for there are more intellectuals here than anywhere else, am I right? After all, they are reckoned to have made some progress.

What are the democratic parties? The democratic parties are all intellectuals. There are very few worker-peasant cadres in the democratic parties. Where are there any worker-peasant cadres? Such democratic parties as the Revolutionary [Committee of the Nationalist party], the [China] Democratic League, the [China] Democratic [National] Construction [Association], the Jiu-san Society, and the Peasants and Workers Democratic Party are all groups of intellectuals.[19] That's why our party put forward the policy of "Let a hundred flowers bloom, let a hundred schools contend" and the policy of "Long-term coexistence and mutual supervision."[20] It is comrade Jiang Weiqing's suggestion that I speak on this issue.[21]

There are reasons why we put forward such policies. As regards "Let a hundred flowers bloom, let a hundred schools contend," should we still "bloom" or should we "rein in"? Now the non-party personages are saying that the "blooming" is not enough. They are deeply worried lest we should "rein in." On the other hand, from what has taken place, our comrades think that things don't seem to be right

[19]For a discussion of the origins of these parties, see Lyman P. van Slyke, *Enemies and Friends: The United Front in Chinese Communist History* (Stanford, Stanford Univ. Press, 1967); the current fate of these parties is covered in James Seymour, *China's Satellite Parties* (Armonk, N.Y., M. E. Sharp, 1987).

[20]See Text 3, n. 42.

[21]Jiang Weiqing was the Jiangsu provincial party first secretary at this time. He survived the Cultural Revolution, and in 1977 he was elected to the 11th Central Committee.

and are somewhat reluctant [to continue] "blooming," and would prefer to sound the retreat. What about us? The Center's opinion has already been discussed with comrades in various provinces, at the second plenum of the Central Committee last November and at the conference of provincial party secretaries this January. We have a unanimous opinion. [291] We consider that the policy of "Let a hundred flowers bloom, let a hundred schools contend" must be adhered to. We must "bloom" and not "rein in." What is incorrect should be criticized. Wrong ideas and wrong works—or, if only part of an article or a work is wrong, then that part—should be criticized. But we must use the method of persuasion. In short, we must choose between the method of persuasion and the method of coercion. We must select one method. Should we "bloom" or "rein in"? We must pick one. It is our opinion that "blooming" should continue, that there should be no "reining in." However, in the course of "blooming" many things will come forth, many things that will not be right will come forth: then what to do? Should we "suppress" them, or should we adopt a different method and persuade them? Some comrades have itchy hands and want to suppress people in much the same way as they would the class enemy: they would either resort to military law, using simple methods; or when the army is not called in, then use administrative orders to suppress people intolerable in their eyes. The Center believes this way is bad. You can never win people's support by suppressing them. Ever since ancient times, no one has been able to change people's minds by means of coercion. In dealing with the enemy, of course, we must take repressive measures; but after that, we still have to persuade them. For example, as soon as a captured enemy soldier is disarmed, we begin to persuade him. So long as a counterrevolutionary is not executed, we must win him over, educate him, and remold him. High-handed policy cannot solve any problems. In dealing with problems among the people, high-handed policy must be discarded.

If [we] "bloom," if [we] use only persuasion, and don't use administrative orders to suppress, could there be chaos in the world? We can assure you this is never going to happen. But won't people criticize all aspects of our work? Won't they criticize our shortcomings in the newspapers, periodicals, and at forum discussions, so much so that we are unable to back down with good grace, and the People's Government, like its counterpart in Hungary, would be toppled?

Could this happen? I say it's not possible. China is not Hungary; here the Communist party and the People's Government enjoy considerable reputation among the people. Marxism represents the truth; it won't fall apart when being criticized. Neither will the veteran cadres; therefore, the veteran cadres should not be afraid of criticism. As a matter of fact, criticism can do much good to the veteran cadres. If we are tainted with bureaucratism and shortcomings, first let people within the party criticize us, then let people outside the party criticize us. Let them criticize our **[292]** shortcomings; let them help us reform our bureaucratism and overcome our shortcomings. Wouldn't that be a good thing? Could [we] be toppled? Of course, not. How can the People's Government be blown down? Last year Shanghai was hit by a tornado, and some very huge things were blown away. Houses and petroleum containers were all swept up into the air. But the Shanghai People's Government didn't get swept away. No matter how hard it blows, I believe a typhoon could never bring down the People's Government, the Communist party, Marxism, the veteran cadres, and the new cadres, provided they genuinely and sincerely serve the people. Those who serve the people half-heartedly will get half-blown away, while those who never want to serve but to oppose the people deserve to be blown down.

What's to be done if there is poison? With the hundred flowers springing up, many carry poison in their bodies, as if they have grown out of the mouth of a snake. Speaking of poisonous things, there is an article entitled "More on the historical experience of the proletarian dictatorship." You comrades have probably already read it. In this article there is such a passage which says that under democratic centralism, if there are shortcomings, they should be criticized: "There is no doubt that the centralism in the system of democratic centralism must rest on a broad basis of democracy, and that the party leadership must maintain close ties with the masses. Any shortcomings in this respect must be firmly criticized and overcome. But such criticism should be made only for the purpose of consolidating democratic centralism and of strengthening the leadership of the party. It should in no circumstances bring about disorganization and confusion in the ranks of the proletariat, as our enemies desire."[22] Is this correct? This is correct and very well said. You

---

[22]The translation of this passage is taken from the English version of this article issued by the Foreign Languages Press and reproduced in *Communist China, 1955–1959: Policy Doc-*

should discuss this article with the democratic personages. You should ask university students to discuss it. As is made clear in this article, criticism surely is allowed, but the result and purpose of it must be the consolidation of democratic centralism and the leadership of the party. It must on no account lead to the disorganization and confusion in the ranks of the proletariat that our enemies hope for.

These principles must be adhered to, but care must also be taken to show flexibility. When people are allowed to speak out, they may say things that are very unpleasant to hear; when a hundred flowers bloom, some may appear that look very ugly. Labor strikes, student strikes, petitions, and demonstrations may lead to a bit of chaos. Their purpose is not necessarily **[293]** consistent with the above principle. Since 80 percent of the intellectuals have not learned Marxism and still retain the bourgeois world outlook, how can they possibly understand that principle when they see the masses start disturbances? When people criticize us at forums, we may find ourselves in a bad situation. On such occasions, if you try to silence them by saying, "Look, I've got a book here, have you ever read it?", it won't work. At any rate, you must learn to solve problems in the same way as Comrade Peng Chong and Comrade Xu Jiatun handled them. Had they at the time kept reciting what I quoted a moment ago but said nothing else, I'm sure they would not have remained in the positions as mayors. Since what [the masses] want to see solved are concrete problems, it is inevitable that sometimes they may go to extremes.

Some of the literary works are not so correct. In Shanghai they have put on a play called *Substitute a Wild Cat for the Prince.*[23] It is said that in this play, which I have not seen, demons and ghosts of every description all make their appearance on the stage. I think it's quite all right if only a few monsters appear on the stage. Many people have never seen monsters in their life. I for one have seen very few. Therefore, I'd like very much to watch *Substitute a Wild Cat for*

---

uments with Analysis (Cambridge, Harvard Univ. Press, 1962), p. 268. For the circumstances of the article's original publication, see Text 3, n. 2.

[23]*Limao huan taizi*, based on a corrupted version of a story about the Empress Liu, consort of Emperor Zhenzong (998–1023) of the Song dynasty, is a traditional Chinese opera in which the childless empress, out of jealousy, substitutes a wild cat for a baby prince born to an imperial concubine.

the Prince. How can one afford to miss that play if one wants to live in this world? Nevertheless, we mustn't watch that kind of stuff too often, nor should we put on monster shows every day—today, tomorrow, and so on. A few such shows may help us broaden our horizons and widen our knowledge of the ideology left over by the feudal society in its artistic form, which is different from fairy tales. For example, *The Monkey King Turns the Heavenly Palace Upside Down*[24] is everybody's favorite piece, to which no one seems to have any objection. Other pieces, such as *Cleave the Mountain and Rescue the Mother* [*Pishan jiu mu*], *The Golden Mountain Submerged* [*Shuiman Jin shan*], and *The Broken Bridge* [*Duan qiao*], and so forth,[25] are also fairy tales and are not opposed by anyone either. Even if there were other [undesirable] things, we would not get perturbed. Let them be performed for a while; sooner or later people will criticize them. When there are only a few novels, and poems are written and published, and plays, those like *Substitute a Wild Cat for the Prince* are staged, why should one be so worried? We should be patient and let people form their own judgement. Gradually literary and theoretical works will change for the better. Under no circumstances should we try to ban them by administrative orders. Comrades, don't be under any misapprehension that I am trying to promote demons and ghosts. I don't advocate those things, but rather want to eliminate them. But the way to eliminate them is to let them appear and be judged by public opinion. Sooner or later they will either slowly die our or gradually be changed. In the past we tried to use orders **[294]** to ban them. We banned them for seven years, and now they have slowly reappeared. From this you can see that the ban we imposed wasn't effective.[26]

Finally, I will talk a bit about letting people both within and outside the party discuss the issues raised by our party. We must say the same thing: those outside the party must be told the same as those

---

[24]*Sun Wukong danao tian gong* is an opera drawn from the immensely popular novel, *Journey to the West* (also known by Arthur Waley's translation, *Monkey*). For details on this favorite literary image for Mao, see Text 3, n. 6, n. 47.

[25]*Pishan jiu mu*, also known as *Baolian deng* (Precious lotus lamp), is a traditional Chinese opera based on a Yuan dynasty play, in which the son of a fairy mother and a human father performs a legendary feat in rescuing his mother. *Shuiman Jin shan* and *Duan qiao* are operas drawn from the popular novel *Baishe zhuan* (The white snake).

[26]Mao also mentioned the ban on 8 March, see pp. 242–4.

within the party. For instance, we shouldn't avoid using such words as "half-heartedness" when speaking to them. "I insist on saying that you are half-hearted. What can you do about it?" "No way! You call me half-hearted, no way!" No way, I want to beat you! I'm not afraid of having a fight with you. But if you are half-hearted and I say so, why should you feel uncomfortable? After all, at least half of your heart is good! You are still half-hearted, and this is talking about your world outlook, not your attitude toward the socialist system. Certainly you support the socialist system, but not necessarily all of it. For instance, some are skeptical about the APC system. But if you ask them whether they endorse socialism in general and the five-year plan, the answer will be yes. Their answer will also be yes if you ask them whether they endorse the Constitution. They generally endorse the Communist party. When it comes to world outlook and dialectical materialism, however, then they don't endorse, or only partially endorse. It's for this reason that we say they are half-hearted. Therefore, you have another task—to further remold [yourselves]. Yours is a dual character: On the one hand, you support socialism; on the other hand, your support is not without reservation, that's why you are half-hearted. You have the desire to get close to the people, but you can't get close enough and become one with them. After spending a few days in the countryside, you remain basically unchanged.

I hear an incident took place [here] in Nanjing. During the Three-Antis, a writer, who was secretary-general, or something like that, of the Writers' Union, went down to the countryside to experience real life, and yet he took with him city food to eat. When he was ready to return, he informed Nanjing. As soon as they got the message, members of the Nanjing branch of the Writers' Union lined up on both sides of the street to welcome him. This writer, who had just tasted real life, passed through in the middle, feeling, in a word, very proud of himself. There was another person who happened to get married in the middle of the Three-Antis who insisted on spending his wedding night sleeping in the bed that Chiang Kai-shek once used in the presidential palace. In short, various kinds of weird things can happen in this world. All these things were exposed during the Three-Antis and Five-Antis.[27] The reports sent by Nanjing [295] to Beijing

---

[27]For the Three-Antis and Five-Antis, see Text 3, n. 35.

we saw. Being curious is the common feature of these people: Here is the bed on which the President once slept. The President's surname is Chiang, [and he is no other than] Chiang Kai-shek! Today I'm getting married. I must spend the night on that bed.

We must make use of the democratic parties and democratic personages. A moment ago I spoke of the intellectuals. Those in the democratic parties are all intellectuals. We must make use of them. People all agree that making use of them is right, but they also say these people are useless, these old good-for-nothings. Even waste materials must be utilized. Waste materials also have their good points. [We] should make use of them; [we] should hold meetings [for them]. At the [Chinese People's] Political Consultative Conference held recently in Beijing, I also told them that they should not adopt a perfunctory attitude toward such annual meetings. On the contrary, each province should hold such a conference once or twice a year, and take advantage of the opportunity thus offered to work on them, persuade them, and make them work for us.[28] Since they are in contact with other people, we can persuade those other people through them. Such an approach is an active one, which differs from the passive approach of merely using them. Ours is the policy of "utilization," "restriction," and "transformation." Our comrades like the last two aspects, namely, "restriction" and "transformation," but not the first one, that is, "utilization." We only want to transform and restrict you people. Clearly that policy is meant for the capitalists; it is inappropriate to talk in this way to the democratic personages just now. It is inadvisable to talk about the policy of "utilization," "restriction," and "transformation" to the democratic personages. But our comrades, in fact, only [want to] restrict [them]. They don't "transform" them, nor "utilize" them. They know how to do certain things we are unable to do. We must be honest with them. In most cases, we mustn't play a double game with them, saying one thing to those within the party, but another to those outside the party. Whatever I've told you I can tell them, too.[29] Of course, any party will keep cer-

[28]The CPPCC, the principal organ of the United Front in the PRC, is specifically intended to symbolize the unity of the CCP and the democratic parties. Mao presumably was exhorting the CCP delegates to it to take more interest, since they would be more likely to query its usefulness.
[29]Evidently, as the title of this talk indicates and this remark confirms, Mao in Nanjing was talking only to party members, so it is hard to understand his frequent use of "you" as if talking to non-party people.

tain things secret from outsiders. The democratic parties have certain things which they don't want to tell us, and vice versa. But things having to do with policy can all be discussed, both within and outside the party. Materials should all be made accessible to those outside the party. Certain materials such as those on labor strikes, student strikes, and demonstrations as well as those exposing our bureaucratism may be printed and distributed for them to read. **[296]** Since they normally have no access to such materials, this would be better. Sometimes the two parties [sic] may hold joint meetings in which people both within and outside the party can participate. Recently a propaganda conference was held in Beijing. It was quite a success. About 150 to 160 non-party personages attended the conference. They made up 20 percent of the attendance. When you hold meetings with them, you may give them even more seats and let them take 40 percent. We don't play two-faced games on issues that have a bearing on policy. Let them see the materials.

Hard struggle [*jianku fendou*].[30] Both Comrade Jiang Weiqing and I have discussed this. How long will it take before our people's life can be improved? Now we must encourage hard struggle. This, however, doesn't mean that female comrades should not wear bright-colored clothes. They can still wear bright-colored clothes. According to one study, bright-colored clothes are less expensive. Currently, women have to make two suits of clothes, and wear the bright-colored one underneath a blue jacket. That's too expensive. We must practice thrift, and wearing bright-colored clothes is one way to achieve economy. From the standpoint of thrift and hard struggle, much work still needs to be done.

Now some comrades evidently have become rather sluggish and don't do much work. When there is nothing to do, they while away their time playing poker and mah-jong. I hear that playing poker has become a fashion, and sometimes people play it all night. We must cultivate the habit of reading. I have no objection to people's playing poker, dancing, or going to the theater; but they must know when to stop. Our strong points are no longer any use. Our strong points are class struggle, politics, and military affairs. Our weak points are our lack of culture, lack of science, and lack of technology. We must learn these things. I've already said this in my 1949 article "On the

---

[30]By struggle here, Mao probably means living austerely.

people's democratic dictatorship."[31] I said our strong points, our specialties, and the things we comprehended soon would become useless, and what we found before us were things unfamiliar to us. Therefore, our task was to learn. Now after seven years, I feel even more strongly that we must encourage people to study, to acquire the habit of reading, and to spend their spare time reading. Once they concentrate their spare energy on reading, they won't be as interested in playing poker as they were before. They will find their new interest in books **[297]** and study.

*It appears that some comrades not only have lost their revolutionary will, but also lack the death-defying spirit. What does a "death-defying" spirit mean? In **All Men Are Brothers**,[32] there is a fellow named the "Death-defying Third Brother" Shi Xiu. His was the embodiment of the death-defying spirit. In the old days while we were making revolution, we also displayed that kind of death-defying spirit and strong will. In recent years, however, some comrades have begun to lose their vigor.[33]* They created such a storm over their wage grades that some even went on a hunger strike for three days. It's really a disgrace! I think one can go without food for four days and still be all right. But on the third or fourth day of their hunger strike, people began taking food to them. I think it's too early. Let them starve for four to five days. It may get serious if they don't eat for a whole week, but eating nothing for three days is no big deal. Why should you bring them milk and eggs in such a hurry? Some even cried their hearts out when their ranks, their wages, or the style of their clothes could not match those of others.

People's wages probably will be adjusted, but the Center hasn't made the decision yet. Didn't we propose a wage reform and increase wages last year? Wages should be increased; but in some cases they have been increased more than they should have been, such as in the administrative system and perhaps the educational system. Here I'm not talking about the workers, nor the factories, but the administrative system. There are 1.7 million administrative personnel in our country (including township [level] cadres, but not those in the

---

[31]Translated in *SW4*, pp. 411–24.

[32]For the novel *Shuihu zhuan*, see Text 8, n. 4.

[33]This italicized passage and the five subsequent ones correspond roughly to the three paragraphs in *SW5*, pp. 437–9. New Mao Texts, Vol. 1, pp. 297, 298–9, 299–300, likewise corresponds roughly to *XJ5*, pp. 420–2.

APCs). In the education system there are 2 million people; in addition, there are the commercial system and the enterprise system not affiliated with factories. Finally, there are 3.8 million PLA personnel. Altogether, there are 10 million plus. This is the number of people who together form the state we have organized. Formerly there were a few million industrial workers, now they have increased to 12 million. Since ours is a big country, we do need more functionaries. There should be no question about that. But over 10 million is a bit too large a figure. Therefore, as soon as we are ready, I mean, as soon as outlets can be found, we plan to send a number of people back to the factories and APCs. Production is mainly carried out in two sectors: one is industry; the other is agriculture. These are the two sectors on which we rely in terms of production. Now it appears that there are inequalities in our current wage system which have caused discontent among the people. I think the more people complain, the easier this problem can be solved. Because the more people complain, **[298]** the more justification for us to make an adjustment. We must maintain the spirit, the vitality, and the enthusiasm we used to display in the years of revolution and class struggle. Revolutionary enthusiasm means carrying one's work through to the end. *Everybody has a life, but how long that life can last varies from person to person—sixty [years], seventy, eighty, ninety.* There's a painter named Qi Baishi who is 98.[34] We'll see how long you people can live. When you are not truly able to work, you should more or less do something; and *when you work, you should show enthusiasm. Lacking enthusiasm and not moving forward is not a good phenomenon, and we must criticize it.* Sometimes it is because there are more hands than needed in an office, where too many people sit around without anything to do. If they don't play poker, what else can they do? When you have a bunch of people and there are no more than a few minor things for them to do, don't you think they will end up playing poker?

We must strengthen our ideological and political work. How are things going in the army? There are quite a few military cadres here today. Isn't peacetime political work different from wartime political work? During the war, we had to stay close to the masses; we had to maintain unity between officers and men, and between the army and the people. At that time, because it was wartime, people tended to for-

---

[34]Qi Baishi (1863–1957) was at this time actually only 93. He died six months later in September. *BDRC* 1, pp. 302–4.

give us our shortcomings. Now we are in time of peace. We have no enemy before us, nor is there a war going on. All we do is training. Now if we have shortcomings, very naturally people will find it hard to forgive us. The same can be said if you work in the government or in local party organizations. At a time when class struggle is over, it is more difficult for people to forgive us. Now we have instituted the system of military ranks as well as various other systems. While these systems are being implemented, we must continue to maintain the unity between officers and men by integrating ourselves with the soldiers. We also must allow them to criticize us. For example, when a party congress is convened, they should be given the opportunity to criticize us. Comrade Chen Yi[35] *once made an apt remark in the East China Military Region during the movement against the Three-Antis, saying that we had been exercising dictatorship for several years, could we now let other people exercise dictatorship over us for a week? If we can order people around for years, why can't we let our subordinates say something in criticism of us for a week, just a week? What he* **[299]** *meant to say is that we should let them [criticize us]. I agree with what [he] said. We should brace ourselves and let our subordinates criticize us for a week. But before they make the criticism, we should first get ready and give a talk about our shortcomings, such as one, two, three, four— Just three or four examples would be enough. Then let comrades have their say to supplement or criticize what you have just said. Those who have rendered great service can rest assured that people won't forget the history of our achievements. As for the soldiers, they should also be given the opportunity to criticize their platoon leaders and company commanders. It would be best if such criticism meetings could be held once a year for a few days. We have tried before, and the outcome was beneficial. This is what we call democracy in military affairs, democracy in the army. If this [could be maintained], then the close relations between superiors and subordinates, between officers and men, between the army and the people, and between the army and local authorities would not be damaged because of the system of military ranks and various other systems. There is no question that the relationship between superiors and subordinates should be a close one, a comradely one; that officers and men, military cadres and soldiers should form an indivisible whole; and that the army and*

---

[35]Marshal Chen Yi, one of the victorious commanders in the civil war, was at this time a Politburo member and a vice-premier. He was to succeed Zhou Enlai as Foreign Minister in February 1958.

the people, [the army] and local party and administrative authorities should remain close to each other.

The entire party should put emphasis on ideological work. The general theme of my talk today is ideological work and ideological problems. This is because these problems have become relatively prominent of late, particularly those caused by the policy of "Let a hundred flowers bloom, let a hundred schools contend" and that of "Long-term coexistence and mutual supervision." People are asking whether "blooming" should be allowed to continue, lest it should involve too much risk. Long-term coexistence—why should people be afraid of long-term coexistence? "You democratic parties, where were you when we were making revolution?" Whenever you bring this up, they have to endure humiliation without knowing what to say. But we say [that] at this time we should not bring up old scores, *nor should we rely on our titles, our positions, and our seniority. Speaking of your seniority, that is, the number of years you have been a revolutionary, there is indeed no question about that. You should not, however, rely on it. You may have great seniority, [stretching back] decades; but if one day you blunder, or say something impudent, then people won't forgive you. If you fail to get things done right, even though you have done many good things, even though your position is high, if today you have done something wrong and hurt the people, they won't forgive you. Therefore, we must not rely on our seniority to earn our keep, but on our ability to settle things correctly. We can rely only on our being correct; never should we rely on our seniority. Will you rely on being correct,* **[300]** *or will you rely on seniority? Relying on seniority won't earn your keep if you do the wrong thing or handle problems in the wrong way. People won't forgive you for that despite your seniority. In view of this, we might as well forget about our seniority and try to deal with things as if we didn't have any official titles at all. In other words, don't put on bureaucratic airs. No bureaucratic airs. Drop them. Meet the people, meet subordinates. Don't assume bureaucratic airs. Don't rely on seniority to earn your keep. We must take all this seriously, particularly the veteran cadres. Junior cadres don't have such a burden. They are relatively unencumbered.* They say: "Being old does not necessarily mean you're good! You have indeed been making revolution for decades. And at the time when you were making revolution, we were still crawling on the floor." They can never beat us on that score. That's why they are free of encumbrances.

We must treat the new cadres as our equals. In many aspects, we are inferior to them. Take knowledge for example, we must learn from them. The current generation alone is able to pass on knowledge to the working class and the peasantry. For do we have any other intellectuals at present! No, we don't! About 80 percent of today's college [students] are the sons and daughters of landlords, rich peasants, and capitalists. At secondary school, according to Jiangsu statistics, over 60 percent of higher middle school [students] and over 40 percent of lower middle school [students] are also the sons and daughters of landlords, rich peasants, and capitalists. Only in elementary schools [is the balance reversed]: sons and daughters of landlords, rich peasants, and capitalists make up 20 to 30 percent, whereas children of workers and peasants possibly make up 70 to 80 percent. It will take a very long time, probably ten to twenty years, before such a situation can be changed. Therefore, today's intellectuals are bourgeois intellectuals, and we must patiently win them over. On the other hand, we must persuade them, help them to make progress and accept Marxism; in other words, we must educate them. In order to become teachers, first they must learn [to be students]. On the other hand, we must learn from them. We must learn from the bourgeois intellectuals, for no other intellectuals apart from them are available.

The proletariat must have its own intellectuals. Our country is under the leadership of the proletariat, which alone has a bright future. All other classes are moving toward becoming one with it. For example, **[301]** take the peasants. In the future, they'll become agricultural workers. The APC will become a state farm within a few decades and APC members will become agricultural workers. The capitalists today are changing; and within a few years, they, too, will become workers. Everybody in our society will become a worker. That's why the working class alone has a future. All others are classes in transition. The proletariat must have its own intellectuals, intellectuals who will serve it heart and soul, not half-heartedly. It is roughly estimated that by the time the third FYP is fulfilled [i.e., 1967], instead of the current percentage of a dozen or so, or 15 percent, or 17 percent of the five million intellectuals—(This includes some of those who have joined the party but should not be counted as party members. For joining the party doesn't necessarily mean they have accepted the Marxist world outlook completely. Some who do accept the Marxist world outlook never join the party. Lu Xun was that kind of person. Who was better, Lu Xun or Chen Duxiu, Zhang Guotao, or Gao Gang? I think Lu Xun was better. On the one hand a party member, on the other a non-party personage. When we examine individuals, those who have joined the party are not necessarily better than party members.)—[by then] we will have expanded [our proportion] to one-third of the intellectuals. They will either join the party or, while remaining outside the party, accept the Marxist world outlook and get closer to the workers and peasants. The other two-thirds will also change for the better during those ten-odd years, from being half-hearted to being 70-percent–hearted. Their tails partly cut, they will make certain progress. We must strive for such a future. Because I have been speaking of ideological problems, I have linked them with the problem of the intellectuals.

As for the many problems in connection with the collectivization movement, I can't talk about them [today]. Collectivization is a good thing, which has definitely displayed its superiority. Since this has been borne out by many of the APCs, there should be no question about it. But some comrades still remain skeptical, while some non-party personages still disagree. Therefore, we must explain [things] to them.

Talk at the Meeting of Party Cadres in Shanghai

20 MARCH 1957

[302] Comrade Ke Qingshi[1] has mentioned just now that the present is a period of transition. In the past, we engaged in the revolutionary struggle. But this struggle has now basically come to an end at home. The former regime of the class enemy has been overthrown and the reformed social system has basically replaced the old one. The new task we are facing now is construction. Construction is also a sort of revolution. It is a technical and a cultural revolution: to unite all the members of society and people all over the country to struggle with

---

Source: 1:302–12; alternate text, 10:136–46.
[1]Ke Qingshi, the Shanghai first secretary and member of the Politburo, was a close supporter of Mao's during this period and subsequently during the Great Leap Forward; see
Origins 1, pp. 205, 281–2, 290–2; *Origins* 2, pp. 21, 36, 62, 83, 89, 164, 250.

the natural world. Of course, the struggle persists between man and man in the process of construction. At the present stage of transition, the struggle between man and man still includes class struggle. When we say that class struggle has basically come to an end, we mean that it has not yet completely ended. The struggle between the proletariat and the bourgeoisie will continue for quite a long time, particularly in the field of ideology. Our party has taken notice of this situation. At the Eighth National Congress of the party, Comrade XXX's report[2] and the resolution of the Congress both stated that large-scale mass class struggle had basically ended. As the contradictions between ourselves and the enemy at home have been essentially solved, the contradictions among the people now become more obvious than in the past. So far, however, many comrades have not yet quite realized this situation, and they are still using some of the old methods to solve the new problems. It ought to be made clear that for a time in the past the Center itself did not specifically address this problem because this change did not mature until recently. For example, among the ten relationships discussed at the conference of the provincial and municipal party secretaries last April,[3] one was the problem of the relationship between ourselves and the enemy, and another was the problem of right and wrong. [The idea that] class struggle had basically finished was not discussed at that time. It was not until the latter half of last year, **[303]** when the party congress was held, that we could declare this definitely. Now the situation has become even clearer. Therefore, we need to explain to the whole party in even more detail that we should not use the old methods to deal with the new problems, and that we should distinguish contradictions between ourselves and the enemy from those among the people.

Are there any contradictions in socialist society? Lenin once talked about this question and thought there were contradictions. But Stalin in reality did not admit this for a long time. During Stalin's later life, people were neither allowed to speak ill of the society nor to criticize the party of the government. In fact, Stalin mistook

---

[2]This is clearly a reference to Liu Shaoqi's political report at the 8th Congress, with Liu's name excised because of his fall. Again, Mao is here endorsing a position which he himself had earlier laid down, but for which Liu was denounced during the Cultural Revolution.
[3]Mao is referring to the "Ten great relationships"; see *SW5*:284–307.

contradictions among the people for those between ourselves and the enemy, and consequently regarded those who bad-mouthed [the party or the government] or who spread gossip as enemies, thus wronging many people. In his book, *Economic Problems of Socialism in the U.S.S.R.*, written in 1952, Stalin mentioned that there remained contradictions between production relations and productive forces in socialist society, and [said that] if the contradictions could not be handled correctly, they would be transformed into antagonistic ones. Nevertheless, Stalin talked little about contradictions within socialist society and those among the people. In my opinion, we must currently discuss this problem in public—not only within the party, but also clearly in the newspapers, so as to arrive at an appropriate conclusion to this problem. It is better this way.

Let's take for example the problem of people making trouble. This is obviously not a universal phenomenon; rather, there are isolated cases. Nevertheless, they may occur frequently because the phenomenon of bureaucratism always exists. We must rectify [our errors], and solve the problem of bureaucratism. But no matter [how hard we try], it will always remain difficult to avoid bureaucratism, since our party is so big, our work is so complicated, and the country is so large. Wherever bureaucratism arises, people there may make trouble. How should we respond when disturbances occur? We ought to think of it as a common phenomenon, and we should not make a fuss over it. We ought to realize that it is a way to adjust the social order under unusual circumstances. If a problem can't be solved with correct methods after a long period of time and so the people begin to make trouble, and then the problem is solved, why then should they not make trouble? Of course, we by no means encourage [people] to cause trouble. Solving problems without [people] making trouble, solving them through the democratic-centralist [304] system in accordance with the formula "unity-criticism-unity" is what we advocate. In order to carry out this policy, we must oppose bureaucratism. If a leader of a certain unit is thoroughly bureaucratic and very stubborn, and it is impossible for the people there to express their opinions, while the higher authorities have failed to detect and correct [the situation] in time, nor have they removed the leader from his office—well, then, the people there would doubtless make trouble. Under such unusual circumstances, what does it matter if some trouble arises?

There are always different viewpoints—both rightist and "left"[4] within our party, whether about contradictions between ourselves and the enemy or about contradictions among the people. The rightist attitude is to see no enemy in respect of the problem of contradictions between ourselves and the enemy. Don't we say that the domestic class contradictions have been basically solved? Some people understand basically solved as meaning completely solved. Hence, they would not deal with the bad people whom the people hate very much, the true spies, and the real evil-doers. This kind of thinking is obviously wrong. It is also incorrect to exaggerate the contradictions. Exaggeration is the "left" viewpoint. Class contradictions have already been basically solved; but some people say they haven't yet, and maintain that contradictions are still very great. As for contradictions among the people, some people ignore the facts and consider that all's right with the world. [In their minds], our Communist party was the representative of the people in the struggle against imperialism and the Nationalist party, and later on against the bourgeoisie. How could the people turn against us? Hitherto, they have never imagined that the people could feel dissatisfied and that they would demonstrate against us, present petitions, go on strike, or boycott classes. They cannot quite believe this even now. This is one type of emotion. The other type of emotion is to be scared. They think things could not be worse when a little trouble occurs—there will be a massive upheaval throughout the land and the People's Government will collapse. If a tornado strikes, will our Communist party, the People's Government, and Marxism be blown away? We can say impossible with confidence. So there's nothing to be scared of. Moreover, if in reality a situation arises when people feel they must make trouble, it is better to allow them to do so rather than prevent them. You, comrades, may ponder whether such a view is appropriate. This is one problem.

[305] Next, I'd like to say something about the question of the intellectuals. There are about five million intellectuals in the whole country. They may all be considered bourgeois-type intellectuals as far as their education, their family background, and their past service are concerned. Among them, about a little over 10 percent have joined the Communist party. Some others have been proletarianized

---

[4]See Text 3, p. 138.

and have accepted Marxism for quite a long time, although they have not yet joined the party. They account for several percent of the intellectuals. Some comrades estimate that if we put these two groups together, they account for about 15 to 17 percent. On the other hand, there are a few intellectuals who are antagonistic towards us. Yet they are not counterrevolutionaries, and they may cooperate with us on some problems, for example, on the problem of opposing imperialism. Nevertheless, they doubt Marxist ideology and the socialist system. Such people also account for several percent. The remaining 70 to 80 percent of the intellectuals have a middle-of-the-road attitude. They understand a little Marxism, but not much. They may approve of the socialist system, but they are easily shaken. It is also difficult for them to accept the Marxist world view. They often use the terms "yours" and "ours." Unlike most workers and poor and lower-middle peasants, they do not take our party as their party. Looking at their relationships with workers and peasants, we can also see that their world view is not a Marxist one. When they visit factories and the countryside, they can't identify themselves with the workers and peasants. Although they have been there, they keep a distance from the workers and peasants, and can neither make friends nor have heart-to-heart talks with the latter. Their relationship with the workers and peasants is still that between "yours" and "ours." They, too, serve the people, but they cannot do it wholeheartedly. They cannot be of one mind with the people, nor are they totally apart from them; they are half-heartedly with the people. Our work is to win them over. We should try, for example, within a period of three FYPs (eleven years remain) to enable the entire intelligentsia to go one step forward in learning Marxism and in combining themselves with the workers and peasants. And from them, one-third should either join the party or become non-party activities. After that, we will try further to win over the rest of the intellectuals. In this way we must step by step change [306] the state of the intelligentsia and transform their world view.

It is still a problem for some intellectuals to accept the view that literature and the arts are for the workers, peasants, and soldiers. This is one kind of manifestation of the fact that intellectuals have not yet formed a new outlook on life. We should tell them that in our country there are no people other than workers and peasants, because capitalists are to become workers while landlords are just changing into peasants. In addition to these two kinds of people (workers and peasants), the third kind is the intellectual. Intellectuals serve the workers and peasants. They themselves are also changing their very essence, and will transform step by step into working-class intellectuals. Therefore, literature and the arts will certainly be for the workers, peasants, and soldiers; there can be no other orientation. Can you still serve the landlords, the bourgeoisie, or imperialism? These forces have already disappeared from the political stage, and they have lost their base in society. As regards the several hundreds of millions of petty-bourgeois elements, they have collectivized and can no longer be called bourgeoisie because they have become collectivized peasants and collectivized handicraft workers. Of course, there remains in their minds a petty-bourgeois tail, particularly in the case of the well-to-do middle peasants and upper-middle peasants. They still have quite a strong sense of bourgeois and petty-bourgeois ideology. Those intellectuals who now doubt the orientation towards the workers, peasants, and soldiers actually reflect the ideology of the bourgeoisie and the rich section of the petty-bourgeoisie. Though both bourgeoisie and petty-bourgeoisie still have a tail left, however, no matter how long the tail is, it will eventually vanish. So we have every possibility to unite and win over the bourgeois and petty-bourgeois intellectuals. But it takes time. The period will be at least as long as ten or twenty years. We should not be imprudent or hasty. Marxism can only be accepted gradually through persuasion, not through cramming [it down people's throats]. Cramming it down cannot solve problems.

Currently, there is a theory popular among a section of the intellectuals, which says that the Communist party is not capable of leading science. Is there any truth in their claim? We think it is a half truth. At present, there are indeed few party members among the engineers, professors, doctors, and other high-level specialists. Generally speaking, at the moment we actually don't understand science. [307] In the past, our people had neither the time nor money to attend universities and study abroad. Moreover, the imperialists and the Nationalist party did not allow us to stay in the cities to study science. Many intellectuals say that we are not capable of leading science though we are good at politics as well as military affairs. Actually, even this they were not willing to admit until recently. In the past, before we had won our victory and when we were still engaging in guerilla warfare, they did not speak in this way. At that time, they thought we were good for nothing. In short, [they thought that] we wouldn't get anywhere. People want to see results. Therefore, so long as we still have not established our leadership of science, it is impossible for us to convince them that we are capable of such leadership. However, what they say is only partially true. They have not realized the other half [of the truth]. Although we now don't understand science, we are using the state plan and politics to lead scientific enterprises. Under the leadership of the Communist party and the People's Government, China's industry has developed, and science has developed, too. Is this not a fact? In this respect, if scientists are not working under the leadership of the Communist party and the People's Government, then under whose leadership are they working? Besides, like politics and economics, science can be understood through study. Now that we have grasped politics and military affairs, we can also learn science. If in the process of political and military struggle, from 1921 to 1949, it took us as long as twenty-eight years to win our victory, then it will not take us such a long time to reach the level of the average [scientific] specialist. Fifteen years will be enough—five years of university [training] plus ten year's working [experience].

Another problem closely linked with the problems of the intellectuals and of science and the arts concerns the policies of "Let a hundred flowers bloom, let a hundred schools contend" and "Long-term coexistence and mutual supervision." We still need to do a lot of work to explain this policy within the party. Some comrades think the policy is too dangerous. If we let a hundred flowers bloom, may we not let some devils out? As for the policy of "Long-term coexistence and mutual supervision," they say, "What right do the democratic parties have to [be allowed] long-term coexistence with us? A short time is quite enough!" [Others say,] "I can supervise you, but you are not in the position to do that to me. Where were you democratic parties when we were fighting for power?" All these [308] viewpoints oppose "blooming" and favor "reining in." Are these viewpoints correct?

The Center considers that those favoring "reining in" are wrong. "Let a hundred flowers bloom, let a hundred schools contend" is the basic policy for the development of science and the arts. It is not a temporary policy. During the present transition period, the policy has particular significance for uniting and educating intellectuals. That is to say, as long as they are not counterrevolutionaries, people should have the freedom to speak not only on purely scientific and artistic problems, but also on matters of a political nature in terms of right and wrong. What shall we do if they have said incorrect things? Shall we use the method of coercion or that of persuasion? The Center considers that the method of coercion is not good. Coercion does not involve convincing someone. It is impossible to convince someone with coercion. The contradictions among the people, the ideological problems, and problems involving the mind can only be dealt with through persuasion, not through coercion. The dictatorship exercised by the proletariat should be used only to deal with antagonistic classes and enemies, that is, imperialism abroad and the surviving domestic enemies. We must not use the measures of dictatorship but those of democracy to deal with average people who have said the wrong thing or who have made trouble. Here is an important line of demarcation. In handling contradictions among the people, some of our comrades nowadays are apt to resort to a "military solution." This is very dangerous and must be firmly corrected. What should be done if [some of us] don't know how to persuade? We must learn. We ought to learn how to argue, and we can do it. What shall we do then, if, after using the method of persuasion, people still continue making trouble? Could it cause massive upheaval throughout the land? I don't think so. As long as we persist with our explanations and explain fully, disorder will not come about. In addition, we shouldn't fear trouble. A little trouble can do us some good; for in this way, we will be able to gain experience. We should criticize and struggle against poisonous writings and other harmful things, but we needn't be scared. In the struggle against those harmful things, we will be able to strengthen ourselves and develop Marxism. Marxism has grown up from the very beginning in the struggle against antagonistic ideas.

In order to wage a struggle against antagonistic ideas, we must first rectify our own shortcomings. We have achieved great successes. Our party is a great party, a glorious [309] party, and a correct party. This must be affirmed. But we also have a lot of errors. This fact must also be affirmed. We should not affirm all that we have done, but only the most important and correct things. At the same time, we must not negate all we have done, but only some [of our] mistakes and shortcomings. Those who negate everything are opportunists while those who affirm everything are dogmatists. Dogmatism is also a form of metaphysics, because it affirms everything without analysis. If we analyze our work, we can see that our achievements are the most important aspect of our work, but that there are shortcomings. Therefore, we need to promote rectification.

The Center has not yet made a formal decision on rectification. We plan to do it in this way: making preparations this year, and getting the movement under way in the two following years.[5] We will adopt the measures of the Yan'an period, studying Marxism calmly and unhurriedly and with the spirit of self-criticism. We will use proper methods to criticize subjectivism, sectarianism, and bureaucratism in our style of work. Criticism will be carried out in small groups, not in large meetings. Errors will be neither minimized nor exaggerated, and [everyone will have an opportunity for] self-examination with the help of one' comrades. In sum, the method is "unity-criticism-unity." That is to say, we will begin with the desire for unity and reach the result of unity by way of criticism; we will learn from past mistakes to avoid future ones, and we will cure the sickness in order to save the patient. We will adopt this attitude in conducting rectification in order to raise the level of our Marxist ideology. Since the Yan'an Rectification [Movement], we in fact have not had any systematic party-wide rectification in over ten years. I believe the result of rectification this time will be to enable our party to make substantial progress. Shall we lose our prestige if we ourselves criticize our own bureaucratism, subjectivism, and sectarianism? I don't think so. On the contrary, I think our prestige will increase.

[5]As these translations reveal, on 8 March, 10 March, 17 March, and, as we see here, as late as 20 March, Mao apparently still envisaged holding the Rectification Campaign in 1958, with a preparatory (*zhunbei*) or informal (*fei-zhengshi*) period in 1957. In fact, the campaign was formally launched on 30 April 1957. For a discussion of the importance of the rescheduling of the campaign, see *Origins* 1, pp. 177–83, 207–10, where it is incorrectly suggested that the decision to advance the timetable was probably taken in February, before Mao made his "Contradictions" speech, but that the actual launch date was not settled until after 22–23 April. This new evidence suggests that even the decision to advance the timetable was not taken until late April, or that if Mao had taken the decision already, he was not yet prepared to tip his hand. Either way, the decision-making process would serve to underline the foot-dragging antagonism Mao faced on rectification, and would indicate that he nevertheless considered the issue so important—presumably out of a concern to avoid East European-type unrest in China—that he was prepared to use his authority to hustle his colleagues down a road they were reluctant to travel.

The Yan'an Rectification proved this.[6] It increased the party's prestige, our comrades' prestige, and the veteran cadres' prestige; the new comrades were also educated. Which of the two fears criticism, the Communist party or the Nationalist party? It is the Nationalist party which fears criticism and forbids it, but they still could not save themselves. The Communist party does not fear criticism, [310] for we are Marxists and truth is on our side, and the workers and peasants and the masses at large are on our side. If we can rectify our errors, we will be able to exercise more initiative in our work and we will increase our capabilities. In addition, we will be more modest. Those of us who in the past did not know how to persuade people will learn how to do it bit by bit. Non-party personages may also be allowed to participate in the movement on a voluntary basis. We will initiate rectification, and they will join in later. If about 60 to 70 percent of the intellectuals took part in the movement, that would be very good.

One of the duties of rectification is to carry on the tradition of hard struggle. Owing to the victory of the revolution, some comrades' revolutionary will has been somewhat sapped and their revolutionary enthusiasm has been waning. An increasing number of people now pay more attention to remuneration and seeking ease and comfort. We should make them regain ardor through rectification. After the long span of the revolutionary struggle, feeling somewhat tired and desiring some relaxation is understandable. We are not opposed to going to the theater or to dancing or to dressing up in colorful clothes. What we oppose is the pursuit of position and privilege, extravagance and waste, and distancing [oneself] from the masses. In our work and our life, we must cut down on all things which can and should be cut down. Class struggle and several decades of revolution have combined to pave the way to construction. In order to construct, we must use manpower and material resources sparingly. Construction takes a long time and it is another kind of war. We hope that before too long China will become better, richer, and stronger than it is now. The revolution was for this purpose: That battle was in order to fight this battle, and that war was in order

[6]Indeed, the 1942–44 Party Rectification in Yan'an is generally considered one of the key contributors to the CCP's success in 1949. For a positive description of the Yan'an Rectification Movement, see Mark Selden, *The Yenan Way* (Cambridge, Harvard Univ. Press, 1969).

to fight this war. This war is more arduous and will be much longer; for example, it may be at least ten thousand years long. To construct faster and better, we must continuously adhere to the work style of hard struggle, maintain close ties with the masses, and oppose such bad practices as extravagance and waste, the pursuit of privilege, the putting on of airs, and so forth.

We should make further progress in our relationship with non-party personages. This is also one of the tasks of rectification. It is necessary to have a line of demarcation between party and non-party personages. It is inappropriate to make no distinction. So, there must be some difference. That's the first point. Secondly, there should not be a deep trench between them. The present situation is that the trench between the party and non-party personages is too deep in many places. The trench must be [311] filled. We should tell non-party personages the whole truth, not half the truth, keeping the other half within the confines of the party. They will thus be enabled to make faster progress.

Will the party's leadership be weakened if we adopt the aforementioned policy? In the article "More on the historical experience of the proletarian dictatorship," there are the following words: "But such criticism should be made only for the purpose of consolidating democratic centralism and of strengthening the leadership of the party. It should in no circumstances bring about disorganization and confusion in the ranks of the proletariat, as our enemies desire."[7] I have just now said that it does not matter if there are a few disturbances or a few incorrect articles published. We can gradually criticize and educate and argue. Does this view point contradict that of the article? What the article discusses is the principle, and what I am now talking about is flexibility. The principle should be applied with flexibility. Otherwise, whenever there is a strike, we would rush there and shout, "Hey! You are destroying the party's leadership!"; [or] if intellectuals criticize us, we would reproach them, "Do you want to weaken the proletarian ranks? Do you want to destroy the party's leadership, and thus harm the system of democratic centralism? Do you want only democracy but no centralism?" Is it right to use this article as a shield everywhere? No, it is not. We in principle do not encourage strikes, class boycotts, harmful essays, plays with poison-

---

[7]Mao cited the same passage in his Nanjing speech the previous day; see p. 338.

ous elements, and so forth. But if in fact a few strikes or class boycotts have occurred, if a few incorrect articles have appeared in the
newspapers, and if a few bad plays have been staged, then we'd better
adopt the policy of "blooming" and use methods of persuasion and
education regarding such matters. [This policy] will not cause any
great trouble; on the contrary it will be helpful, whereas the policy
of suppression would actually be harmful. With this policy it is
easier to adjust the social order and the relations between the leaders
and the led, between the government and the people, as well as
between the party and the people. The result of such an adjustment
will consolidate the party and the system of democratic centralism.

We hope to make ours a lively country, where people dare to criticize, dare to speak, dare to express their opinions. [We] should not
make people fearful to speak. People like us must correct our errors
and shortcomings whenever we find them. It will not do otherwise
because it would be unreasonable. Whether inside or outside the
party, we should not practice bureaucratism nor force people to do
[312] unreasonable things. If we adopt such a policy, I am sure that
the people's political conditions and relations between the people
and the government, between the leaders and the led, and among the
people themselves, will become reasonable and lively. Thus, our culture, science, economy, politics, and our whole country will surely
develop and prosper more quickly.

TEXT FOURTEEN

Transcript of a Talk to a Gathering of Responsible Persons from Various Democratic Parties and Non-party Democratic Personages

30 APRIL 1957

[146] For several years [we've] all been thinking of rectification, but haven't found the opportunity. Now [we] have. Anything that involves a large number of people cannot be done without a campaign. [We] need to create an atmosphere; it won't work without an atmosphere. Now an atmosphere of criticism has been created. This atmosphere should continue; [and] with handling contradictions among the people as its subject, [it should] analyze various aspects of [these] contradictions.

Sources: 10:146–52; alternate text 1:316–22, with extra sentence, p. 321. This is the long-suspected, but officially unacknowledged, talk Mao gave at a hastily called session of the Supreme State Conference in Beijing following his provincial tour. Because there was much

In the past there were contradictions which were blindly identified in industry, agriculture, culture, and education. Now, let's line up the contradictions [and] figure out what's what. In the past, it seemed as if as soon as contradictions were mentioned the heavens would fall. Actually what was so disastrous? Chiang Kai-shek had four million troops; the American troops reached the Yalu River. Nothing disastrous about that. Every day [we] all live among contradictions; contradictions exist everywhere; everyone puts on a rival show, yet [we] are unwilling to recognize or [we] confuse the two different types of contradictions.[1] [We] should recognize them, then analyze them [in order to] find ways to solve them. Just now, the newspapers discuss the problem of contradictions daily. Some people worry that the People's Government might be toppled. But it's been two or three months already, [and] the government has not been toppled at all. What's more, the further the discussion evolves, the more consolidated the People's Government becomes. Both the Ministry of Higher Education and the Ministry of Education are under fierce attack—the more [they're] attacked, the better. [We should] divide contradictions into different categories. [If you] want to attack, [then] take advantage of this opportunity. As long as proof can be found, [you] can hold your ground. Problems that have been insoluble for years and even decades, once they are debated, may be resolved in a matter of a few **[147]** months. People have not suggested breaking

---

controversy about this meeting and Mao's subsequent rush into rectification, the text appears in both sources only as a "Transcript of a talk to a gathering of responsible persons from various democratic parties and non-party democratic personages." A one-page extract appears in *Ziliao xuanbian* (n.p., n.pub., 1971), p. 184.

Another text from around this time is an April 1957 speech to the Hangzhou meeting of the Shanghai bureau, which appears in the New Mao Texts three times: 1:323-31; 7:59-74; and 9:113-29. We have not translated it because it appears in *Wansui* (1969), pp. 100-9, and is translated in *JPRS* 61269-1.

A set of relevant texts, from July 1957, also appears three times in the New Mao Texts: 1:349-67; 544-53; and 10:153-62. They are largely covered in *SW5* in "The Situation in the Summer of 1957" (pp. 473-82). Another related text, "Talks at the Shanghai conference of various figures" (New Mao Texts 1:368-81 and 10:162-75), appears in *Wansui* (1969), pp. 109-22, and is translated in *Chinese Law & Government* 10.2:35-56 (Summer 1977).

The last important set of talks for 1957 are the ones Mao gave in Moscow, 14-18 November (New Mao Texts 8:5-22, with extracts in Vols. 2 and 12B). They are translated in *The Journal of Communist Studies* 2.2:109-26 (1986). Extracts also appear in *XJ5*, pp. 496-500.
[1]Alternate text 1:316-7 gives minor variants in wording here and at eight other points in this and the next two paragraphs.

your rice bowls, nor [do they] intend to club you to death with a single blow. On the contrary, [they] desire improved relations [with you]. [We should] classify contradictions by categories: higher education, general education, literature and arts, science, and so on. Health [matters], too, deserve to be attacked. Attack more, attack earnestly. Publish [the attacks] in the newspapers, [where they] can arouse the people's attention. Otherwise, bureaucratism can never be resolved. In order to find a way, [those] inside and outside the party should get together. [We] used to hold small meetings, but they weren't effective. So we have to hold large meetings like the enlarged eleventh session of the Supreme State Conference and the Propaganda Conference, at which people inside and outside the party will meet together and the two elements will combine in a chemical reaction and become something else. [That] will be effective. All provinces and cities must hold [such conferences]. As soon as they're publicized in the newspapers, the oppressive atmosphere will be dispelled. It's more natural to mention rectification now. The general theme of rectification is handling contradictions among the people and opposing the three "isms."

There's a special stipulation in the directive of the Central Committee of the Chinese Communist Party, namely, the requirement to participate in manual labor. This is not a recommendation that everyone present should go plough the fields; sweeping the streets would be good enough. What's important is expressing a certain attitude: eliminating bureaucratism, subjectivism, and adding on the method of participating in manual labor. In essence [you] should mingle with the workers and peasants, participating more or less in a bit of manual labor. The peasants say, "In the past you and we waged land reform together. Now you've become officials [and] no longer pay attention to us." In the past the directors of APCs didn't participate in manual labor, and they didn't win the hearts of the masses. The masses were very unhappy. Without participating in manual labor, [you] can't become one with the peasants [and] the common people won't trust you, won't tell you the truth. Now cadres in the townships and prefectures are participating in production together with the masses, [and] the masses immediately tell them the truth. What the masses tell the representatives of the [National] People's Congress and the [People's] Political Consultative Congress has not been the complete truth. Especially since we are all intellectuals [and] are like square pegs in round holes among the laboring masses, there's one way to be together with them: that is to participate in some amount of manual labor. For instance, it's not difficult at all in the south to weed rice seedlings. Of course, the old and the infirm do not have to go. Our country has one special feature: a population of over 600 million with an area under cultivation of less than 1,600 million *mou*. Without adopting some special methods, [I'm] afraid the country can't be managed well.

[148] Rectification will influence [life] outside the party. It is stipulated that non-party members may voluntarily participate [or] freely withdraw. It's been this way for the past two months; this is the way of rectification: I attack you, you attack me; [if you] have an opinion, then express it. [Those] inside and outside the party are becoming one. This is rectification; it's already been going on for two months.

The contradictions in united front work have been insoluble for several years. Problems, such as [non-party figures] having position but no power and so forth, were very difficult to resolve in the past; now [they] can be resolved. The most important source of this difficulty in solving [contradictions] in the past was that [our] thinking wasn't straight. In the past Communist party members had position, power, and responsibility, [while] democratic figures had only position and neither power nor responsibility. Now everyone should have position, power, and responsibility. Democratic figures are hard put to work alongside communists; [they're] rather annoyed, [and] it's hard to get things done. Now the relations between those inside and outside the party should change to one of equality, with [non-Communists having both] position and power in fact, not just in form. From now on, no matter where, whoever is the chief is in charge.

(Ma Yinchu:[2] Luckily in the past there was [a party] organization. All that I [know about] is old hat; if [I] had really been in charge, what exists today could not have come about.)

---

[2]Ma Yinchu (1881–1982): a noted non-party economist and President of Peking University at this time, though in practice the university was administered by the Vice-President, who was a party member. Ma was dismissed for his advice on population control in 1959 and since 1980 has become the patron saint of China's one-child family policy.

[Chairman:] What you have said is not the whole story. Contradictions exist, [and] muddling along can't solve [them]. I suspect it makes sense for professors to run education. Should we divide into two organizations: a committee on college affairs in charge of administration [and] a council of professors in charge of education? One article in the party constitution³ stipulates that factories, villages, army units, and schools should adopt the system of party committees. Now it seems that the system of party committees in schools is perhaps inappropriate. It should be somewhat modified [*gai yixia*]. [Power] should be concentrated in the committees on college affairs and the councils of professors. If the Communist party and democratic parties have any ideas or suggestions [they] can go there and have them discussed. What people approve should be implemented; what they do not, should not be. This problem should be studied. Let Comrade XXX⁴ be responsible for finding non-party democratic figures and [members of] the Democratic League, the Jiu San [Society], and so on, to hold some forums in which to solicit suggestions on the problems of having [both] position and power and the school party committee system.

Don't work on dialectical materialism just now, work a bit on political relations [and] the three "isms." Don't bury [yourselves] in the methodology of world-view ideologies so that [you] slight political relations. Go back to working on dialectical materialism later on.

³See Chapter VI of the 1956 party constitution.
⁴XXX: almost certainly Deng Xiaoping; see Li Weihan, *Huiyi yu yanjiu* (Recollections and research), *xia* (Beijing, Zhonggong dangshi ziliao chubanshe, 1986), p. 831. Li Weihan, director of the CC United Front Work Department, convened a series of forums of senior non-party personages from 8 May, at which the issue of running universities was raised; see Roderick MacFarquhar, *The Hundred Flowers Campaign and the Chinese Intellectuals* (New York, Praeger, 1960), p. 47.

In fact, the role of the party in institutions of higher education became a key issue in the Anti-Rightist Campaign, for leading "rightists" like Luo Longji and Zhang Bojun were attacked for advocating the abolition of the party committee system. This passage clearly indicates that their advocacy was prudently based on Mao's willingness to see that system abolished in its then current form. Knowing this, critics of the rightists had to cling to Mao's concluding directive that the problem should be "studied," claiming that he had gone no further than that; *Origins*, 1, pp. 277–8.

The editor of the alternate text of this speech evidently realized what a hornet's nest this passage was and omitted the whole paragraph after the words "thinking wasn't straight." In addition, at the start of the next paragraph, this editor omits the words "Don't work on" and "just now" in the passage "Don't work on dialectical materialism just now"! (New Mao Texts 1:318.)

This problem will have its influence on the democratic parties [and] democratic figures. [As for] dialectical materialism, we can't expect a large number of people to accept the Marxist world view at a stroke. [I] hope that within three FYPs, of the five million intellectuals **[149]**, one-third, or some 1.5 million intellectuals, will be able to accept dialectical materialism. That'll be very good. From now on, all [political] study should be voluntary, worked on by oneself; small groups can be voluntarily formed. A [new] textbook on dialectics should be compiled every year. Some are out of date, [and] the old language needs to be freshly phrased. World view is a long-term problem. The five million intellectuals who served the old society in the past ought now to turn to serving the new society. Theirs is the old world view; only a small minority have the new world view. It is both unnatural and impossible for a large number of people to believe in a new world view so soon. [I] estimate that in ten years something more than one-third but less than two-thirds of the intellectuals will still have the old world view. But these people are first of all patriotic [and] second of all believe in socialism. That is enough. Some professors talk about Marxism-Leninism when they lecture. This is so that they can eat. But when talking among themselves, they say they don't believe in dialectics. There is one left-wing professor in Shanghai who said that since Liberation [his] "body and soul have been restless," [and that it's like] "having fifteen buckets at the well, seven up, eight down."[5] Those who teach the social sciences find themselves in a passive position every day. History must be rewritten and taught anew. In the old society, teaching was [simply] putting out what was available; one textbook could be used for years; [and] there weren't so many meetings. Natural scientists are a bit better. [It's] a period of great social upheaval, [and] intellectuals, primarily [those in] the social sciences, have suffered. This involves a problem of the economic base. The economic base on which the five million intellectuals relied in the past has now collapsed. Imperialism, feudalism, [and] bureaucratic capitalism have long been overthrown; even national capitalism has basically disappeared, [and] the system of individual ownership, too, has been smashed. Some people say, "If the system of private ownership no longer exists, what dual

---

[5]I.e., he is so agitated he does not know what to do, as in the English expression, "I'm at sixes and sevens." See also pp. 300, 499.

nature can there be?" This is incorrect. "When the skin is gone, to what can the hair adhere?" With the old skin gone, the hair will adhere to the new skin; [it] can't hang in the air. [It] will adhere to the skin of the working class. At present the 5 million intellectuals are eating off the workers and peasants, eating off state and collective ownership. Now there are 12 million industrial workers [and] 14 million party, administrative, military, educational, and economic functionaries (excluding factory and cooperative directors); all told, 26 million people. Of these, 14 million people do not directly produce; those who truly produce are the [150] 12 million workers. All the rest have to make the transition toward becoming workers. At the time of Liberation there were only 5 million industrial workers; the Soviet Union, too, at the beginning had only 3.5 million workers. Social progress is not determined by the number of people; there are several hundred million peasants, but they cannot determine whether society will progress or not. In the end, peasants must become agricultural workers, [and] APCs [must] become state farms, probably several decades from now. The hair of 5 million intellectuals will adhere to the skin of the 12 million–strong working class. Hair detached from the skin can't survive; [you] should always have to eat together in the same family. At present, the intellectuals are somewhat lacking in self-awareness; their footing (the economic foundation) has long since been undermined. The old economic system having experienced an earthquake, they are suspended in the air. The old economic system is gone, but their minds have not yet changed. It takes years for ideology to seep in. Now the hair has already adhered to the new skin, but in [their] minds they still consider Marxism no good. People can't be forced to believe in the Marxist world view. If people are to believe, there must be a process. [Among] old world views the bourgeois and petty-bourgeois world views are one and the same. [Some] say the petty-bourgeoisie produces dualism [while] the bourgeoisie produces monism; some people, [if you] say [they] are petty-bourgeois intellectuals, feel quite comfortable, [whereas if you] say [they] are bourgeois intellectuals, they feel uncomfortable. Actually this is a superstition, a social convention. For example, I was originally a bourgeois intellectual and was influenced by bourgeois social practices and bourgeois education. I believed in Buddhism, Kant, [and] anarchism. All of these amount to anarchistic Idealism, and so [I] was a bourgeois intellectual. Petty-bourgeois intellectuals are themselves bourgeois intellectuals; there was only one old world view. There is no such petty-bourgeois world view to be subdivided out of it.

Industrialists and businessmen can get elementary knowledge of politics from textbooks. But textbooks are textbooks, [and] ideology remains ideology. There are always some people who will never change. [It's a] conditioned reflex. Childbirth originally is actually not painful; but once public opinion says it's painful, [it] becomes painful.[6] To turn pain into painlessness, doctors have to do lots of work. There should be a conditioned reflex of another sort. Don't believe that all intellectuals, democratic parties and Communist party members all believe in communism. Within the Communist party [151] there are still many who don't believe in communism, [and] what's more don't believe in socialism. What they believe in is democracy; they've not prepared for the socialist revolution. The former Vice-Governor of Hebei Province, Xue Xun, opposed [the states'] unified purchasing and marketing;[7] [he] advocated free trade. Not to have unified purchasing and marketing won't do; neither will it do to have too much [of it]. [We] plan to have the majority of the APCs, except in the cash crop regions, handle their own grain, edible oil, and meat by themselves next year. Quite a large number of party members do not believe in socialism. They are engaged in socialism because they were swept into the mainstream. I just don't believe that all the democratic parties believe in socialism. A large group of people don't believe in socialism but are unwilling to talk about it in public. A portion of the Communist party, the democratic parties, the national bourgeoisie, and the peasantry, as well as a portion of the workers (the composition of the workers is also complex; having increased from 5 million to 12 million, they're not of one mind), still want to wait and see whether or not socialism will succeed and whether or not the Communist party will make a go of it. Quite a group of people in society has boarded the pirate ship (the ship of communism); [they] had no choice. Whether or not the ship will capsize is up to heaven. This is quite natural.

What [we] did in the past was class struggle. It was like this during both the democratic revolution and the socialist revolution. People making war on people, people fighting people, rebellion among the

[6]Half the world's population is unlikely to view this statement as anything but "subjective idealism"!

[7]Mao was to refer to the system of state grain procurement and resistance to it at greater length at the first Zhengzhou conference; see Text 18, pp. 473–4.

people. We have expended decades of our energy. Counting from the Opium War it's already been over a hundred years. The Opium War was class struggle as far as the masses were concerned. For Lin Zexu[8] it was a struggle between Chinese exploiters and foreign exploiters. Just take for example the past few decades; in the thirty-six years since the establishment of the Communist party, all our energy has been spent on this. Some people say the Communist party can't lead in science; it can only wage class struggle. The Communist party has tactics but no learning. This is half right. To say that we have tactics but no learning depends on [how one defines] learning. For instance, class struggle is a great field of learning, [and you] can't say we haven't any. It's been garnered through so many years of making mistakes and conducting self-criticism. There'll still be class struggle in the future; for example, wars against imperialism [and] diplomacy with capitalist states are in the nature of class struggle. Now [we] are entering upon another type of war, namely the war on nature, [and we] must understand the natural sciences. If not, what can we do? As I said in an article in 1949, we shall soon put aside the things we know well;[9] **[152]** we must master those things we don't know anything about. Not knowing is not knowing; don't pretend to understand. [We] must study with all sincerity; perhaps it will take decades, as with learning class struggle in the past. From the establishment of the party to the Seventh Congress (1921–1945) we expended twenty-four years, shed much blood, and suffered many setbacks before learning how to wage class struggle. Now [we] are learning the new war of construction [and] need to learn from scratch. Can [we] master it or not? Certainly [we] can. Some parties have many experts; for instance, the Democratic League, the Jiu San [Society] and the Democratic [National] Construction [Association] have quite a few. In general, [this] is a new era with new tasks; class struggle has ended, [and] war has been declared on nature.[10] It is still a transitional period. The old relations of production have been destroyed, [but]

---

[8]Lin Zexu (1785–1850) was the imperial commissioner sent to Canton in 1839 to try to stop the opium trade; his forthright challenge to the British led to the Opium War.

[9]From "On the People's Democratic Dictatorship." Mao does not quote himself precisely; see *XJ*4, p. 485; *SW*4, p. 422.

[10]These clauses on the end of class struggle and the war on nature are deleted from the primary text but appear in alternate text 1:321. The editor of New Mao Texts, vol. 10, may have excised this brief passage because Mao stated here baldly and without qualification that

the new economic base has not yet been consolidated. Fighting this battle will take decades, probably two or three decades. Because we have no experience, nor cadres. With the experience of the Soviet Union before [us], we may do a bit better or a bit worse or the same as them. How [we'll] do, everyone wants to see; I'd like to see, too. [We] can't boast that [we are] 100 percent correct. Some people say that the Communist party, especially the Ministry of Higher Education, issues orders in the morning and rescinds them in the evening; that the Nationalist party had too many taxes, [and] the Communist party too many meetings. With so many meetings [things] must change. This year [the figure for] basic construction has been altered by over 2 billion. The budget should be finalized the previous November, then sent to the Standing Committee of the National People's Congress. By December it should be distributed for discussion. In January of the following year [it] should be put into operation. Sending [it] to the National People's Congress is in reality approval after the fact.[11] Lacking experience, [we] need to learn, to study the natural sciences, to study the experience of planning; [we] need to accumulate experience, decades of experience. There are [cases of] issuing orders in the morning and rescinding them in the evening, [and] they're due to a lack of experience. In the beginning in my mind, I, too, craved for greatness and success. Only as recently as March and April of last year did [I] begin to change. [First I] talked with comrades from some thirty ministries, later at the Supreme State Conference [I] spoke on the ten great relationships, five of which concern economics.

Beijing is a place that is both good and not good. Responsible cadres in the Communist party should spend four months a year outside and eight months in Beijing. You may do so as well. The characteristics of central institutions are first, emptiness, and second, comprehensiveness. The weak point is the emptiness. Once away from Beijing, [you'll] feel comfortable.

"class struggle has ended" (*jieji douzheng jieshu*). An alert editor would have known that on other occasions, Mao qualified "class struggle" with the phrase "large-scale, turbulent" and qualified "ended" with the phrase "in the main," as in the officially published version of his February 1957 "Contradictions" speech; see *SW5*, p. 408.

[11]Mao is alluding to the pointlessness of discussing the budget at the annual session of the NPC, which was then normally held in mid year, after the budget had been in effect for several months.

The Great Leap Forward

TABLE 4 Date Summary, September 1957–1958

	1957
September 20–October 9	Third Plenum of the CCP's Central Committee: Revised draft of Twelve-Year Program for Agriculture accepted.
November 2–21	Mao in Moscow for fortieth anniversary of Bolshevik revolution; pledges China will overtake United Kingdom in output of major products in 15 years.
December 12	Major water conservancy drive in China.

	1958
*January 3–4	CCP's Hangzhou conference; Mao backs campaign against "four pests" (rats, sparrows, flies, mosquitoes).
January 11–22	CCP's Nanning conference; Mao starts drafting "Sixty articles on work methods," which will include idea of "uninterrupted revolution." Mao denounces the anti-"blind advance" policy, which halted the 1956 little leap forward, and the senior economic officials who espoused it.
January 31	Mao signs "Sixty articles on work methods"; one article reveals he will retire as head of state (but not as chairman of party).
February 1–11	NPC session: 1958 steel target fixed at 6.2 million tons.
March 8–26	CCP's Chengdu conference: Mao encourages party to smash superstition and not blindly follow Soviet model.
*April 1–6	CCP's Hankou conference.
May 5–23	Second session of CCP's Eighth Congress; Liu Shaoqi gives political report launching Great Leap Forward.
June 1	*Red Flag* publishes recent article by Mao in which he says that the Chinese people are "poor and blank" but that this is advantageous because it makes them eager for revolution.
June 22	Mao endorses report advocating a target of 30 million tons of steel for 1959, and 80–90 million tons for 1962.

TABLE 4 *(Continued)*

July31–August 3	Khrushchev visits Beijing to discuss Mideast crisis.
August 4–10	Mao tours Hebei, Henan, Shandong.
August 9	Mao endorses People's Communes in Shandong.
*August 17–30	CCP's Beidaihe conference; 1958 steel target raised to 10.7 million tons (double the 1957 figure); nationwide formation of communes ordered.
August 23	PLA starts shelling KMT-held offshore islands.
September–October	High tide of commune formation and steel drive.
*November 2–10	CCP's first Zhengzhou conference; first signs of Mao's moderating GLF egalitarianism.
*November 21–27	CCP's Wuchang conference; retreat continues.
November 28–December 10	Sixth Plenum of CCP's Central Committee held in Wuchang; communes endorsed, but ideological claims modified.

Note: *Texts from these dates are translated in this section of Part Two.

Talks at the Hangzhou Conference (Draft Transcript)

3–4 JANUARY 1958

[30] 3 JANUARY 1958

Rightists are oppositionists; those on the right of center also oppose us; the middle-of-the-roaders are doubters. [But] the masses at large and the leftists among the bourgeoisie [and] bourgeois intellectuals support us.

With regard to the treatment of the bourgeoisie, many countries wonder whether China has turned right, in a way unlike the October Revolution. Because instead of doing away with [*gediao*] the capi-

Sources: 2:30–9, alternate text, 6A:86–95. The nature of the prose leads the translators to conclude that this text is a transcript of a tape recording.

talists, we are transforming them away [*huadiao*]. In reality, in the end [we] (will transform away) the bourgeoisie: How can that be branded rightist? [It's] still the October Revolution. If [we] do everything like the Soviet Union after the October Revolution, there will be no cloth, no grain (without cloth you can't exchange for grain), no coal mines, no electricity, no nothing. They lacked experience, while [we gained] a lot when running our base areas. [We] have left bureaucratic capital (the system of production) intact, even more so in the case of the national bourgeoisie. But there's change within non-change. Nationwide, there are 700,000 households of capitalists and several millions of bourgeois intellectuals; without them [we] can't run newspapers, engage in science, or operate factories. Some people say [you've] turned "right." Such a "right" is necessary, [we] must transform [them] slowly. The correct handling of contradictions among the people is precisely the implementation of this policy. Some are half enemy, half friend; others are one-third or more enemy.

We've spent seven years and 1.2 billion renminbi to harness the Huai River. [This] amount for harnessing the Huai is worthwhile even if [we] give it a 30 percent discount (there are some quality problems). Our estimate in the original plan was low; later [we] incurred cost overruns. Criticizing rightist conservatism is very comforting; the more [one] criticizes, the happier [one] is. The enthusiasm of more than 10 million people in Gansu is very high; [it's] worth studying.

The Twelve Articles must be grasped; from now on, [we'll] compare and appraise. First, water [conservancy]. Second, fertilizer. Third, soil. Fourth, planting (of fine varieties of food products). Fifth, system changes, like double cropping, changing from late to early planting, changing from dry to paddy rice. Sixth, eliminating plant diseases and pests (100 million catties of grain were lost in Zhejiang to insect pests; then in one summer all the insects were wiped out. Japan has no [31] Marxism but is already free of insect pests. We have Marxism). Seventh, mechanization (new farm tools: two-wheeled, double-shared plows,[1] water pumps, and so on). Eighth, live-

---

[1]These plows had already proved to be white elephants in southern China; see *Origins* 1, pp. 90, 123, 127.

stock. Ninth, side-line occupations. Tenth, making things green, afforestation. Eleventh, eliminating the four pests.[2] Twelfth, curing disease and practicing hygiene.

Another Twelve Articles must also be grasped, [and] must be compared and appraised, too. First, industry. Second, handicraft industry. Third, agriculture. Fourth, side-line occupations. Fifth, forestry; Sixth, fisheries. Seventh, animal husbandry. Eighth, transportation. Ninth, commerce. Tenth, science. Eleventh, culture and education. Twelfth, health.

The Forty Articles[3] will be revised in the third, fourth, or fifth year of the second FYP; [then we'll] criticize [our] right deviation with pleasure. In 1956 the value of industrial production increased by 31 percent; without the leaps and bounds of 1956, [we] wouldn't have been able to fulfill the [1953–1957 first FYP]. [We'll] make comparisons in March this year, again in the summer, then again when [we] hold the Party Congress in October.[4] Provinces [should be] compared with provinces, counties with counties [and] APCs with APCs. If everyone agrees, [we'll] discuss how to do it again. Everyone should go visit other provinces; if you go visit but don't get out and about, then if [you] lose by comparison, it serves you right. It's well worthwhile to make a trip to Gansu.

[We] must plan thoroughly, check up a few times [a year], compare and appraise at the end of the year; hold a few meetings, hold small meetings, making sure we've got the prefecture and county secretaries on board. Meetings of prefectural party secretaries should be held once every two months, each time for no more than five days; the county committees should go to the prefectural committees to hold meetings (it's more interesting to have several prefectural party committees holding a conference jointly). Large-scale "extraordinary

[2]Four pests: rats, sparrows, flies, mosquitoes. In 1960, bed bugs were substituted for sparrows when it was realized that the extermination of these birds had permitted insect pests to flourish; see *Origins* 2, pp. 21–4, 305.
[3]Forty Articles: The extravagant 12-Year Agricultural Program, which had 40 articles, had been launched in January 1956, quietly dropped later in the year, and revived in autumn, 1957; see *Origins* 1, pp. 27–9, 90–1, 314–5.
[4]The 2nd session of the 8th Party Congress was, in fact, held in May 1958, presumably brought forward to provide a launching pad for the GLF.

sessions" should be held only once or twice a year. [We] must pay some attention [to this] once every two months; otherwise, a year will fly by just like that. The comparison and appraisal of the provinces [can be done] at Central Committee meetings.

I myself talk with people four times a year. I travel a bit everywhere, each time for two or three days, visiting five or six units.

There should be forty articles for industry, as well. Science and culture and education should have them, too. First [let] a few people draw up some suggestions, then others will have their input [and] we'll get somewhere.

Nationwide, [we should] establish several economic coordinating regions;[5] some provinces can have overlapping [jurisdictions]. [We] should identify temples rather than deities. There should be this tradition: As long as there is a temple, no matter who's in charge, we'll let him take the lead; as long as he can make a go of it, that'll be fine. Sha Wenhan and Yang Siyi are something else.[6]

There is a report from the Hubei provincial party committee on leading cadres personally running experimental fields; the Center has approved it and passed it on. Have [you] read it? It's very important. [We] must make widespread experiments.

[32] On the problems of accumulation and consumption. Exactly how large should accumulation be? Some suggest 45 percent, some 50 percent, some 55 percent. The best is half and half. Depending on the year's harvest, and on the area, [we should] make several types of regulations. Distributing 60 percent [of the harvest] is not the normal rule; [it's used] when there is a drop in production. [We] must be industrious and thrifty in managing [our nation]; individual consumption should be kept down; [we] must oppose extravagance at weddings and funerals. Every province should put up a proclamation banning gambling. Weddings and funerals should all be kept simple. Make your own wine at home; it's not good to ban [that] completely. Don't forbid firecrackers, for they have the effect of inspiring enthusiasm.

Politics and professional work should be combined; this again is the problem of red and expert. Politics is called red (for us it's red, for

[5]These regions were established in 1 June 1958. See Text 17, n. 18.
[6]Sha Wenhan and Yang Siyi were senior members of the Zhejiang provincial party who had been purged as "rightists" the previous month; see *Current Background* 487 (Hong Kong, U.S. Consulate General).

the United States it's white). Red and expert are the unity of opposites. The two are not the same; they differ. One has to do with the
spirit, the other with material things. Some responsible comrades in
professional departments seldom mention politics when they talk; it
shows [they] normally don't talk much about politics. [They're] too
busy; once [they] start talking, it's always about professional work. It
could be worse in the case of those in charge of professional work in
the provinces. [We] must definitely criticize any tendency to lack
interest in politics; at the same time, [we] must oppose empty-headed
[*kongtou*] politicians. It's good to understand something about professional work; otherwise [you'll] be red in name but not in reality. [If
you] don't understand agriculture, [you'll] be no good at directing
agriculture. Get involved in running experimental fields, and the
problem of red and expert will be solved. One type is the empty-
headed politician who doesn't understand any professional work; the
other type is the economist or other technocrat who has lost his bear-
ings; neither is good. Analyze it a bit. But when [you] criticize
others, examine yourself first. You yourself are a little empty-headed,
[and you] don't know much about it [either]. Last year, the Premier
looked into the problems of wages and welfare. I've visited an industrial exhibition in Beijing; seeing once is not enough. [I] still need to
see more.

Rectification should be carried out thoroughly; it should not be
left half finished. What Shanghai calls the third type of person knows
only how to be an official; [we] must wipe out bureaucratic airs.
Shanghai suggests [we] must have enthusiasm: very good. *Zhejiang
Daily's* editorial "Promoters or Regressers" should be reprinted in the
People's Daily.

Rectification should combat waste; it shouldn't take too long; a
few days will do. Rectification and reform [*zhenggai*] should be combined. Make it a special topic for blooming; after blooming, everyone will be alert. Every member of a family should promote [this]
through education [and] should be industrious and thrifty in managing households.

When should the plan be handed in? Provinces, prefectures, counties, and APCs should all be engaged in it. Start with a rough outline
on how to economize; the assignment should be finished in six
months.

[33] 4 JANUARY 1958

Everyone should take a look at Li Da's article in the fifth issue of *Philosophical Research* and Feng Youlan's in the sixth issue.[7] Formal logic is the science of the stage of quantitative change; [it's] a component of dialectics. Quantitative change and qualitative change form the unity of opposites. Everything has its relative regularity. Making a plan or a resolution, each has its relative balance. After [everything] is set, there is still change. Balance, consolidation, unity . . . all are temporary, while imbalance and contradiction are absolute. Everyone who attends conferences thinks of the break-up time; the longer the conference lasts, the more [you] want the meeting to be over.

Formal logic is very like elementary mathematics; dialectical logic is like advanced mathematics. This idea is worth studying. Cut the circumference into tens of thousands of pieces and it'll become square.[8] Circles and squares are the unity of opposites.

The modes of thinking comprise concepts, judgment, [and] inference. Formal logic is the study of the mode of thinking. Formal logic contains quite a few incorrect major premises. Therefore, it cannot arrive at a correct judgment; but from the perspective of formal logic [that judgment] is not at all incorrect. [Formal logic] is concerned only with quantity and not with content. Content is the business of various departments of science.

[I] talked about the two Twelve Articles yesterday; no [I'll] make some additional remarks:

First, [we] need to grasp firmly [all] the Twelve Articles on water, fertilizer, soil and so on, to achieve the proper balance. To have water and not fertilizer or to have manure and no water will not work; [they're] interrelated. After ten years (or perhaps even longer), electrification will be adopted in agriculture, in plowing. Livestock farm-

---

[7] Alternate text 6A:89 gives the full names of the two authors, while the primary text gives only Xs. Li Da's "Criticize Fei Xiaotong's comprador sociology" appeared in *Zhexue yanjiu* 1957:5:1–14. No article by Feng Youlan appeared in the sixth issue, but his "Once again on the problem of inheriting China's philosophical legacy" did appear in *Zhexue yanjiu* 1957.5:73–81; 73–81, and to this Mao presumably refers. Both articles reflect the returned constraints on intellectual life that had come about in the Anti-Rightist Movement.

[8] In the text, the word is "straight" (*zhi*); but "square" (*fang*), which is in the alternative text, 6A:89, fits better with the next sentence.

ing is related to manure [collection]; [it's] also [a source] of energy, meat, and industrial raw materials. Eliminating the four pests concerns labor power; [it] improves physical strength and unleashes the spirit.

Second, [we] must firmly grasp the Twelve Articles on industry, handicraft industry, and agriculture.

Third, combat waste. [According to] reports from Shanghai, the Meilin Canned Food factory wasted 450,000 [yuan] in four years, amounting to half its capital. Eight years [of this] and you could build an identical factory [from its wastage]. This is a widespread problem. If every factory, school, [governmental] organ, and APC would practice [thrift], much material could be saved. Everything must have its proof; without proof people will not **[34]** believe. One report is enough. It's enough to dissect one sparrow; it's not necessary to dissect all that many.

In rectification, ten days should be used exclusively to combat waste (from starting blooming to reform, ten or fifteen days should be enough). [We] can save billions [of yuan].

Fourth, the ratio between consumption and accumulation should be seriously studied. The ratios include 45 percent, 50 percent, 55 percent, and 60 percent, and so on. All the various ways of division should be studied. It should be grasped by the spring or there will be no time for it. This is a major problem. If [we] don't handle it well, the workers and peasants will be dissatisfied. In 1954 [we] collected 96 billion catties [of grain], thus offending hundreds of millions of peasants. This year [we will collect] 85 billion catties,[9] a target temporarily set for three years. I am inclined toward [the ratio of] 50 percent, depending on whether the harvest is poor or a bumper one. Combining this with industrious and thrifty domestic management, [we] can make a go of it. Weddings and funerals and other celebrations should all be kept simple.

Fifth, [we] should run experimental fields. (The report) of the Hubei provincial party committee on experimental fields is a good report.

---

[9]Eighty-five billion catties [*jin*] is approximately 42.5 million tons. In fact, collection in 1958 was 55.7 million tons; see table in Nicholas R. Lardy, *Agriculture in China's Modern Economic Development* (Cambridge, Cambridge Univ. Press, 1983), p. 34.

(XX interjects: Because of the editorial note appended by the *People's Daily*, the report of the Zhejiang provincial committee is getting public attention.)

[Chairman:] From now on no book of translations can be published without a preface. The first edition should have a preface; the revised second edition should also have a preface. The *Communist Manifesto* has any number of prefaces. How should we view today the many things from the seventeenth and eighteenth centuries? This, too, is the combination of theory and Chinese reality; it is a very important matter.

Sixth, red and expert, politics and professional work, are the unity of opposites. Both aspects should be criticized. Being concerned only with politics without familiarity with professional work is not good. Politics together with professional work are precisely red and expert. To require all those who engage in politics also to be experts presents difficulties, but [they] should specialize a little in the principal part [of their work]. The experimental fields under the Hubei provincial party committee seem very effective. Yet they haven't been running [them] very long.

Seventh, wipe out bureaucratic style. That's what Shanghai has proposed. Don't act like an official; wipe out the bureaucratic style altogether, and be on the same plane as the common people.

Eighth, hand in plans on time.

Ninth, eliminate the four pests.[10] Begin a patriotic health campaign with the elimination of the four pests as its center. Have a thorough checkup once every week. "Five years depends on three years; three years depends on the first."[11] This is well said.

Tenth, making things green, afforestation. We must master it this year, make a plan and do it in a big way. I have heard that a tree of over three *zhang* [35] in height absorbs and diffuses in one day more than one ton of water. Will this effect underground water?

---

[10]The campaign against the four pests figures very little in Mao's remarks at the Hangzhou conference, but it was his visit to a model health unit in the city that sparked the massive drive that started later in the month; see *Origins* 2, p. 22. The admonition in this paragraph must have ranked as a preliminary directive.

[11]This slogan means that success in a FYP depends on going all out in the first three years and that success in a three-year enterprise depends on going all out for a breakthrough in the first.

Eleventh, [during] the second FYP, the value of the output of local industries in the provinces should surpass the (value) of agricultural production (including the industries which have been decentralized to local management). There should be equilibrium in the whole nation; there cannot be anarchism.

Twelfth, methods of holding meetings. There should be large, medium, and small scale [meetings]. "Extraordinary meetings" (for each province) (such as party congresses) once or twice a year. Medium-sized [meetings should be] a few dozen to two or three hundred people (such as county committee secretaries' conferences); small-sized ones [are] like prefectural secretariat conferences. Go down and attend their conferences to understand them. "Extraordinary meetings" should discuss politics. Professional meetings should also discuss politics.

Thirteenth, provincial party secretaries and members of the provincial party committees should take turns getting out of their offices. [Tour around] for four months a year. Go everywhere. Use two methods: [you] can view flowers from horseback or get off your horse and look at the flowers. Staying at a place to talk [only] for three or four hours, or staying a week or two, either is fine. There is no need to stay at one place for three or four months.

Fourteenth, within our ranks, don't do any entertaining. Don't ask others to treat you at a restaurant; don't give welcome and send-off parties; don't specialize in giving dance parties; and don't take people to the theatre. Whoever goes to greet a guest at the airport, this person who is being greeted will be punished. This is one way of wiping out bureaucratic practices.

Fifteenth, on the two types of contradictions. One is contradictions between the enemy and ourselves. The other is contradictions among the people. There are two types of contradictions among the people. One has the character of class struggle. The other has the character of [contradictions] among the working class, the laboring people, between the advanced and the backward. Contradictions among the people divide into two types. One is the contradiction between the proletariat [on the one hand] and the bourgeoisie and petty bourgeoisie [on the other]—this is a class contradiction. There are also contradictions among the laboring people—this is the contradiction among the laboring people. Some [of these contradictions] have the character of class struggle, such as wife-beating, even going so far as wife-killing because of the influence of feudal ideas. Or, for instance, liberalism, individualism (which is bourgeois and petty-bourgeois ideology), absolute egalitarianism (a petty-bourgeois ideology) all reflect problems of the private ownership system. Others [of these contradictions] belong [to the realm of problems between] the advanced and the backward. [This] is a problem of cognition, the inability to see through problems. For example, the agricultural collectivization high tide—[I] couldn't see quite clearly when [we] held [our] conference in Beijing.[12] After the conference [I] went down south to Shandong and other places only to find great changes in the situation there. Only then did [I] feel certain about writing the preface.[13] This was a contradiction between the advanced and the backward—[36] the inability clearly to size up the situation. Some people obstinately refuse to try to increase output, asserting that the conditions [for increase] don't exist. [When] we launched rectification, the rightists suddenly jumped up. After a few editorials, by June and July things had settled down. There are many things that cannot be completely predicted.

The main and the quantitatively greatest contradictions: Class struggle is the main [contradiction]; it aims at overthrowing something. The Constitution stipulates three transformations. In reality there are two transformations—transforming the bourgeoisie and transforming the petty bourgeoisie. Class contradiction is (the main contradiction) of the transitional period. [If] it is carried out well, all will be over in another XX years. XX years plus eight years makes XX years. It won't take XX years. [If] we have a rectification like this every year, we'll get rid of bourgeois ideology. The quantitatively greatest [contradiction] is between the advanced and the backward. The contradiction with the vast number of middle-of-the-roaders is a class contradiction. Among well-to-do middle peasants 40 percent

[12]The primary text says "at the beginning" (*kaishi shi*); the alternate text's reading translated here seems more likely.

[13]Mao appears to be explaining away his sudden shift to a more ambitious collectivization policy in May 1955, which led to the criticism of the director of the CC's Rural Work Department, Deng Zihui, who was loyally pursuing the more moderate policy agreed by Mao only weeks earlier; see Jiang Boying, *Deng Zihui zhuan* (A biography of Deng Zihui) (Shanghai, Renmin chubanshe, 1986), pp. 314–28. The preface to which Mao refers was to the compilation of reports on cooperativization published under the title *Socialist Upsurge in China's Countryside* in January 1956; see *Origins* 1, pp. 15, 26–7. It is not clear which of a number of possible conferences Mao means.

endorse the APCs, 40 percent are not so enthusiastic, [and] 20 percent want to withdraw from the APCs. [But] they don't really want to withdraw from the APCs, because those who are determined to do so are in the minority. About 5 percent are probably rightists, [but] they are still laboring people. Don't categorize them as rightists; capture and release them seven times [to win them over].[14]

The causes that produce contradictions among the people:

1. The influence of bourgeois and petty bourgeois ideology on the laboring people. Individualism, liberalism, absolute egalitarianism [and] bureaucratism (now attributable to the bourgeoisie) are all the influence of bourgeois and petty bourgeois ideology.
2. Subjectivism as a cause. [When we] can't aim accurately, can't estimate adequately, that is rightist. [We] must regularly alert [ourselves] to advance in accordance with the situation.
3. Leadership as a cause. [If] leadership is bit better, the advanced will be in the majority and the backward in the minority. [You] can lead in this manner or in that manner (for instance, Pingyang and Huangyan, two counties in Zhejiang, are different).

[You] need to dissect only one sparrow to understand the overall climate. How to exercise leadership merits study. A certain Liu Chuanyou of Shouzhang county in Shandong, goes deeply [among the masses] to lead [them]. In western Shandong there was no tradition of raising pigs, now every household raises two pigs, which also helps improve the soil. In Zhejiang the oil plant and the winery in Tonglu competed on their output under identical conditions. [Such] reports on laggards pressing forward to catch up with the advanced are good. The short commentary by Wang Pu in the *People's Daily* is well written, containing dialectics (for both, see the 3 January *People's Daily*). [We] should propagandize theory; talk about dialectics; talk about materialism, such as the superstructure and the economic base, production relations and production forces, which are the basic content of historical [37] materialism.

Turn problems over in [your] mind often, talk them over with a few comrades together, talk them over with your secretaries on a

---

[14] A set, four-character phrase, *qi qin qi zong*, taken from one of Mao's favorite novels, *The Romance of the Three Kingdoms*, in which the third-century AD statesman Zhuge Liang captures and releases an adversary seven times until he gains the voluntary submission of his rival.

basis of equality, see what their viewpoints are, seek out a few party secretaries to discuss [things] with, not as decisions [already taken], but as brainstorming. To think over a few problems within a certain period of time, to talk them over, is a very important method. Don't call conferences before using your brain, before thinking things over. Some things mature gradually.

Sixteenth, let's talk about the theory of uninterrupted revolution [*buduan geming*]. The uninterrupted revolution I am talking about is not the same as Trotsky spoke of. They are two [different] theories of uninterrupted revolution. The steps of our revolution are:

1. Overthrowing the enemy and seizing power. This was accomplished in 1949.
2. The land revolution, which was basically completed in the three years between 1950 and 1952.
3. Another land revolution, a socialist one, now [I'm] talking about collectivizing the principal means of production. By 1955, this was also basically completed. Some leftover work remained in 1956. These three things followed closely upon one another—two were resolved in three years, striking while the iron was hot. This was strategic: the intervals cannot be too long; there cannot be any loss of momentum. [We] can't go and establish a "New Democratic Order"; for if [we] do, [we'll] just have to spend more energy tearing it down again. Poland and Hungary "interrupted" the "momentum" of the time [and] bourgeois ideology took root. The next push [for uninterrupted revolution] did not go well, for middle peasants and those even better off didn't want to go in for collectivization. Bulgaria is a bit better—30 percent is cooperativized.
4. The socialist revolution on the ideological and political fronts—the rectification campaign. This time it can be finished in the first half of this year. [But we'll] have to do it again in the first half of next year.
5. There is still the technological revolution.

Steps 1 to 4 are all in the sphere of the economic base and the superstructure. Land reform is the destruction of the feudal system of ownership. It has to do with production relations. The technological revolution has to do with the production forces, management methods, and operation. [This] must be done in the second FYP. [Steps] 1, 2 and 3 are over. The revolution on the ideological and political fronts persists. A person can go moldy again after a year or two. The emphasis, however, will be on the technological revolution. Great numbers of technicians must be produced; we must encourage [people] to learn from those good at technology. In factories and villages there are elementary technicians. [38] The leading cadres of Hongan county were originally empty-headed politicians. Later [they became] both red and expert. In industry, follow the direction of Tonglu county, linking experiments with technological revolution and combining politicians with technicians.

Beginning in 1958, [we] should emphasize the technological revolution while continuing to finish the ideological and political revolution. Emphasize doing the technological revolution well. When Stalin raised the slogan that cadres are decisive in everything, he also put forward the [slogan of] technological revolution.

To emphasize doing a good job in the technological revolution doesn't mean there is no need to engage in politics. Politics and technology cannot be separated. Ideology and politics take command, and politics is the guarantee of professional work.

The withering away of classes will be complete in another XX years. After that, there will still be ideological and political struggle (or call it revolution) between people, but of a different nature. It won't be class relations, it will be a contradiction between the advanced and the backward [among] the laboring people. The [nature of the] struggle at that time will also be twofold: one will be the influence of bourgeois ideology on the laboring people; the other will be subjectivism—caused by consciousness or caused by leadership. Those who understand the art of Marxist leadership will be better than those who don't. The "theory of the nonexistence of conflict" is metaphysics. Why did the Moscow Declaration include a paragraph on dialectics? Because it applies to the past, the present, and the future. In the future, when the whole world is unified, there will still be two factions scrambling for power, because they do not hold the same opinions. Putting out various newspapers, putting on various shows, each side will try to win over the masses. There will be ideological contests. Superstructure and ideology will still exist then. So long as there are contradictions between production relations and production forces, and between the superstructure and the economic bases, there will be three kinds of people; the left, middle, and right. If the superstructure is in the hands of those who are stubborn and backward, there won't be any big contending and blooming. If mistakes are not corrected, there will be conflict. Even without armies, it is still possible to fight with fists and clubs. At that time, there will be no classes. If things are managed well, there will be no antagonism; if they are not handled well, there will be antagonism. [Two lines,] one progressive and one backward, are mutually exclusive and antagonistic. After XX years, the function of state power in domestic affairs will gradually cease to exist; all will have become laboring people. Even now, as far as the laboring people are concerned, that power is already basically nonexistent. Only persuasion can be used against the laboring people, not suppression. State power cannot be used on the laboring people; using that power is suppression. It may appear to be very "left," [but] in fact it's very right, the style of the Nationalist party. It's absolutely necessary to dispel bureaucratic airs. [39] To put on an awe-inspiring air in front of the enemy is correct, [but] it simply won't work with the people.

Seventeenth, politicians must understand some professional work. In agriculture, run experimental fields; in industry, run trial products. Make comparisons; comparisons are the unity of opposites. There is an imbalance between enterprise and enterprise, between workshop and workshop within an enterprise, between small group and small group, between individual and individual. Imbalance exists not only in social laws but also in the laws of the universe. Just as soon as equilibrium is reached, it is immediately disrupted. No sooner is there equilibrium than there's disequilibrium. If you want to criticize and appraise under broadly similar conditions, comparisons can be made between the backward and the advanced; it's not impossible.

Politicians should always understand some professional work. There should be comparison in technology, and in politics, too. Combine technology and politics, and see which one does better.

Everyone look at a few articles (the *Liberation Daily* story of the launching by Shanghai's Meilin factory of contending and blooming on opposition to waste, the report in the 3 January *People's Daily* on the factories in Tonglu comparing output rates and Wang Pu's commentary). One affair reflects on the affairs of the whole nation, and so everyone must consider other people's good jobs as their own. In practising socialism, no matter where the problem occurs, we should make it our own.

As for the rightists among the students, 80 percent may remain in school to continue studying. [We] should strengthen [our ideological] work with them, [we] should keep interacting with students, gradually transforming them. If they do some good deeds, they should be praised. Of course, there are also some bogus activists.

Don't think that, following this rectification, everyone will take the Yellow River as a boundary, as if the boundary could be marked that clearly.[15]

---

[15]Mao is warning that even after rectification (and, of course, the Anti-Rightist Campaign) the boundaries between right and wrong, progressive and backward will still be difficult to discern.

Criticism of People's Daily, Which Should Not "Oppose Adventurism" (Draft Transcript)

JANUARY 1958

[159] Everyone's reaction to the press is relatively good. Newspapers have made progress. News, commentaries, have improved. [They] can be improved still more; don't be self-satisfied.

Recently news [reporting] has been more lively.

Let everyone write commentaries. The responsibility system, for each section is a good method. The editor-in-chief is the commander-

Source: 9:159–61. These remarks appear to have been made to a group of journalists at either the Hangzhou or the Nanning conference. A related text is Mao's "Talk at the Nanning conference" of 11 and 12 January 1958, in which he brings up *RMRB* and its "pedant editor," Deng Tuo (New Mao Texts 2:40–7 and 6A:95–102), which appears in *Wansui* (1969), pp. 145–53, and is translated in *JPRS* 61269–1.

in-chief; he should organize everyone to write. Leaving the writing to just a few people is not good.

Organizational form. Whether or not this kind of production relationship impedes the development of production forces should be studied.

Each department, each page section may compete [with one another].

In writing commentaries, [you] should integrate [current] conditions with the political climate. Changes must be quick.

The writing shouldn't be stereotyped; there should be a variety of forms.

Political commentary should resemble political commentary, but certainly shouldn't exclude all emotion.

People in newspaper offices ought to go frequently down [into society], breathe fresh air, [and] develop good relations with the provincial committees.

The people who are sent down should do their [share of productive] work and be journalists at the same time. Don't live always in Beijing. Move around a bit. [You] should regularly roam around outside.

The *People's Daily* is a department of the Central Committee, like the Organization Department and the Propaganda Department. All [of you] should learn from the localities. One very important task of the paper is to carry reprints of new things from local papers. Make this a political responsibility. This will encourage the local papers, and make them have to read the *People's Daily*.

[160] Ideological commentaries can be made.

Red and expert is still an important question, but it should be integrated into discussions of current conditions.

Headlines should catch people's attention. This is very important.

There should be a special section on getting rid of the four pests.

X X X[1]

The circumstances surrounding the propaganda against adventurism [*fan maojin*] after June 1956 should be investigated. Investigate the commentaries and news [reports] of that time.

[1]Three Xs, the meaning of which is unclear, appear across the page in the original.

The editorial of 20 June [1956] had errors in principle.[2] [It] said that it opposed both conservatism and impetuosity. When anti-rightist [work] wasn't even half a year old, this editorial held that great accomplishments had been achieved. This was an overestimate and incorrect. [I] can't say there was not a single bit of Marxism in the editorial. However, after the "but," it was anti-Marxist.[3] The way the editorial was put resembled the methods of Wei Zhongxian: [We know that] there were both superior men and small men in the Dong Lin party, as well as at the imperial court. His idea, in fact, was to say that everyone in the Dong Lin was a small man.[4] When quoting from my remarks [they did so] out of context, quoting only a couple of sentences on opposing "leftism" and not quoting the whole passage. This is incorrect. As [is the line] in *Qin Qiong Selling His Horse,* omitting the beginning and the end, [preserving] only the middle section.[5] It's a one-sided method. The first part [of the editorial] discussed the [conservative] minority, but the second part discussed how the majority [was inclined towards adventurism]. In appearance, it opposed both. In fact, it opposed "leftism"; it opposed "adventurism".

[It] criticized the [use of the] two-wheeled, double-shared plow as "adventurist," saying the south couldn't use it. Wrong. In fact it has been used [there]. [It's] very good. There should be a reversal of verdicts restoring [its] good name.[6]

[2]The bulk of this paragraph is nearly identical to a text of remarks by Mao, allegedly made in June 1956 (New Mao Texts 1:415, 6A:35–6, and 12:227). For a discussion of the politics behind this editorial, see *Origins* 1, pp. 86–8; see also *Dang shi yanjiu* (Research on party history) 1980.6:34–41 (Beijing).

[3]A common style of *RMRB*'s editorials was to praise achievements in the first half of the text and then, after a "but" [*danshi*], to be critical and indicate the changes that were required to remedy the situation. The 20 June 1956 editorial was couched in this form. It effectively halted the "little leap" of the first half of 1956.

[4]Wei Zhongxian (1568–1626) was a notoriously evil eunuch in the late Ming court who in 1624 ordered the bloody suppression of a group of reformist Confucian scholars, the Dong Lin academy. Wei was executed by the following emperor. Mao's meaning is that this villain and *RMRB* both condemned the good with the bad. "Superior man" and "small man" are traditional Confucian terms for ethical and debased personalities.

[5]Qin Qiong: a great warrior of the Tang period who fell on hard times and had to sell his horse and his mace, but later joined the founding Tang emperor to set up the new state. This line comes toward the end of the Peking Opera, *Qin Qiong Selling His Horse,* when Qin offers to give a brief demonstration of the use of his mace to two prospective buyers. "Omitting the beginning and the end" refers to his not going through the entire exercise in his sales demonstration. Mao appears here to be using the quotation literally, that is, the shortening of the original, without further metaphorical intent.

[6]On the two-wheeled, double-shared plow, see Text 15, n. 1.

As for the question of "disrupting normal practice," the editorial said that "normal practice was disrupted inappropriately." This was incorrect. Revolution must disrupt normal practice. "Opposing adventurism" cannot be spoken of as a policy; only "adjustment" [*tiaozheng*] can be. If we took ["adventurism"] as a tendency to be opposed, then we would be opposing [the policy of] "More, faster, better and more economically."[7]

The editorial said that especially after the Center put forward "More, faster, better and more economically" and the Forty Articles, adventurism was engendered.[8] That was a one-sided way of putting it, which made it look as if the errors emanated from the Center.

[161] Have you opposed rightism or not? Putting it this way seems dialectical in form, [but] in fact is a vulgarization of dialectics. [We should] oppose "leftism" and rightism simultaneously, [and] in a balanced fashion. The policy, "More, faster, better and more economically" is a complete one, a single whole. [You] can't say this fits and that doesn't.

According to experience, errors in work are normal, not abnormal. Revolution should make leaps. Individual errors are unavoidable. [You] should distinguish whether nine fingers or just one finger is the problem. [Going] a little to the left or the right in the course of work is a normal phenomenon. The question is, what is the policy and the direction? In the future do not raise [the issue of] "opposing adventurism"; don't do it under any circumstances.

[7] Mao's meaning here, presumably, is that to "oppose adventurism" is to oppose "More, faster, better, and more economically."
[8] For a discussion of the 40 Articles (the 12-Year Agricultural Program) in the blind advance of the first half of 1956, see Text 15, n. 3. For a discussion of the slogan, see *Origins* 1, pp. 27–32.

Talks at the Beidaihe Conference (Draft Transcript)

17–30 AUGUST 1958

[295] 17 AUGUST

This is an enlarged Politburo conference; responsible comrades from all provinces and autonomous regions are participating. The topics are [listed in the documents] distributed here, [and] comrades may refer to them.

The key point is the first problem: the problem of the Five Year Economic Plan next year—mainly it has to do with industry, [but] it's also somewhat relevant to agriculture. It's unfair just to issue

---

Sources: 2:295–321; alternate text, 10:389–407. This long text, a "draft transcript" (*jilu gao*) of Mao's talks at the Beidaihe conference, appears to be an accurate transcript of a tape recording. We have found no other edition of this text except a one-page extract on agricultural

reference figures; [we] should be fairer [and] more correct [with our figures]. Let's take three days [to work on it]; Comrade [Li] Fuchun[1] will be responsible.

The second problem: the problem of iron, steel, copper, and molybdenum [production] this year. Steel [production] has to double from the 5.3 million tons of 1957; [but] there's a danger that we may not be able to reach [the target] of 11 million tons, [and] the key problem is iron. Now we[2] have all made telephone calls [and] mobilized [people], but [those in the localities] must still be sure to return [those] phone calls to confirm.

The third problem: Comrade XXX[3] will be in charge of agriculture next year.

The fourth problem: Chen[4] and Li[5] will be in charge of water conservancy next year.

The fifth problem: the problem of agricultural collectivization; [we have] printed a copy of Henan's regulations for the experimental operation of people's communes.

The sixth problem: [Li] Xiannian[6] will be in charge of commercial purchases and distribution this year (including the handling of this year's grain). Grain production will probably reach XX hundred

---

universities as noted in John Bryan Starr and Nancy Anne Dyer, *Post-Liberation Works of Mao Zedong: A Bibliography and Index* (Berkeley, Center for Chinese Studies, Univ. of California, 1976), item 244, and translated in *Current Background* 888 (Hong Kong, U.S. Consulate General), p. 8. Mao's wild romanticizing of the Yan'an experience and his equating dining halls and a non-monetary economy with "communism" are startling aspects of this speech and reflect his terminological laxity, exemplified also by the loose terms and inaccuracies noted in Text 3.

[1]Li Fuchun, Chairman, State Planning Commission.

[2]Presumably the Center.

[3]XXX: presumably Politburo member Tan Zhenlin who took charge of agriculture during the GLF; see *Origins* 2, pp. 82–5.

[4]Chen: Almost certainly Chen Zhengren, Deputy Director of the State Council's 7th Office, which was in charge of agriculture and forestry, and chairman of the National Water and Soil Conservation Commission. Chen, a former private secretary to Mao, had emerged as one of the Chairman's agricultural trouble-shooters in 1955, when he became a deputy director of the CC's Rural Work Department and apparently played a major role in the collectivization drive; see *Origins* 1, p. 18.

[5]Li: almost certainly Li Baohua, a vice-minister at the Ministry of Water Conservancy (later the Ministry of Water Conservancy and Electric Power) from the founding of the PRC. Li was the son of Li Dazhao, one of the intellectual leaders of the early communist movement and an important influence on Mao.

[6]Li Xiannian: Minister of Finance.

million catties this year, per capita XX catties. Strive to reach XX catties per capita next year [and] XX catties the year after. Whether or not this will reach 2,500 to 3,000 catties [per capita], [we'll] discuss later. Can we indefinitely develop grain [output]? I think it's not going to be easy to exceed 3,000 catties [per capita].

The seventh problem: the problem of education. Comrade XXX[7] is writing an article. Once a resolution is [made], it'll be printed and distributed.

[296] The eighth problem: the problem of cadres participating in manual labor. Officials, no matter who, whether big or small, including us here, all should participate in manual labor as long as they're [physically] able, excepting [only] those too old or too weak. We have millions of officials; adding [those] in the army there are more than ten million. [We] don't even have a clear idea as to exactly how many officials. Cadre children number in the tens of millions, and [they are] in a favored position [from which] to become officials. When one has been an official for a long time, it's easy to get separated from reality [and] the masses. The construction of the Ming Tombs Reservoir has been completed; many people went to the reservoir to perform manual labor for a few days.[8] Can [we] do manual labor for one month a year, making assignments according to the four seasons of the year? Workers, peasants, and commercial personnel are all able to combine manual labor and [their ordinary] work; everybody should be like that. If other people can do manual labor, is it acceptable that our officials should not? And then there are all those many cadre children. In the Soviet Union, graduates of agricultural colleges don't want to go to the countryside. Isn't it absurd to run agricultural colleges in the cities! Agricultural colleges should all move to the countryside. All schools should run factories. Even the Tianjin Conservatory is running a few factories; [that's] very good. Participating in manual labor is easy [for cadres] at the county and township levels, [but] it's hard to manage [for those] at the level of the Center, provinces, and prefectures;[9] [they] probably can't operate a machine! How is

[7]XXX: almost certainly Lu Dingyi, alternate member of the Politburo and director of the CC's Propaganda Department. His article "Education must be combined with productive labor" was published on 1 September in *Hongqi* (Red flag), No. 7 (1958).

[8]Mao himself had led his senior colleagues to work there in May to symbolize the importance he placed on manual labor.

[9]Mao uses the abbreviation *zhuan* for *zhuanqu* or prefecture (literally: special district), an

it that people who can eat with chopsticks and write with brushes can't operate a machine? Is it easier to operate a machine or to climb a mountain?

The ninth problem: the problem of the labor system. It should be worked out by the Ministry of Labor.

The tenth problem: the problem of sending tens of thousands of people to the border regions.[10]

The eleventh problem: the problem of maintaining technological security.

The twelfth problem: the problem of the international situation. It was I who raised this problem, because everywhere people are asking whether there'll be [another] world war. What to do if [the war] starts? What exactly is the nature of the Western military bloc? To whose advantage is a tense [international] situation? Is it better for the United States and British forces in the Middle East to withdraw soon or to stay a bit longer?[11] Embargo or not embargo—to whose advantage would it be?[12] Is it advantageous for the United Nations to recognize us or not to?[13] In the last analysis who fears whom? Who fears whom more? These questions have not been completely resolved even within the party. Some say, "The east wind prevails over

---

administrative division between the provincial and county levels not laid down in the 1954 state constitution but in widespread use; in 1971, the term *zhuanqu* was replaced by the term *diqu*. See Theodore Shabad, *China's Changing Map*, rev. ed. (New York, Praeger, 1972), p. 29.

[10]Presumably Mao is referring here to the nascent program to transfer unemployable urban youth to the countryside, including border areas. In fact, this program was set aside in 1958; see Thomas P. Bernstein, *Up to the Mountains and Down to the Villages* (New Haven, Yale Univ. Press, 1977), pp. 34–6.

[11]A Middle East crisis had erupted after a coup in Iraq on 14 July, which had resulted in the replacement of the pro-Western monarchy by a radical leftist regime and the collapse of the anti-communist Baghdad Pact (later reshaped as the Central Treaty Organization). In the aftermath of the coup, the Western members of the Pact, the USA and Britain, had landed forces respectively in Lebanon and Jordan to safeguard the pro-Western regimes there (neither of which was actually a member of the Pact). The crisis unleashed a flurry of diplomatic activity, with the Soviet leader Khrushchev calling for an emergency summit meeting and the Chinese press advocating the dispatch of "volunteer" armies (something like the "Chinese People's Volunteers" in the Korean War, only presumably this time coming from the USSR). So great was Sino-Soviet disagreement on this issue that Khrushchev flew secretly to Beijing for talks with Mao at the end of July. (See *Origins* 2, pp. 92–96.)

[12]Mao is referring to the Western embargo on trade with the PRC, total in the case of the US.

[13]Mao is referring to the fact that at the UN, Taiwan held the Chinese seat.

the west wind"; but it's clear that [the east wind] has not prevailed, otherwise how dare the Americans and British land in the Middle East? [Our] views are not unanimous on this problem: both within and outside the party there's fear of the West, there's United States–phobia. Who fears whom more? [I think] perhaps it's the West that fears us a bit more. There are three "isms" in the world: communism, imperialism, and nationalism. The latter two are both capitalist. One is national capitalism, the other is [297] the capitalism which oppresses other people—imperialism. Nationalism was originally the rear base of imperialism; but once it opposes imperialism, it becomes our rear base. India and Egypt both practice [nationalism], but [their position] is more to our advantage. If our two "isms" stand together, [our] strength will be greater. Both sides have atom bombs; [but] the might of the people is greater on our side, so there won't be a war. But a war is still possible, [so] we had better be prepared to fight. It's hard to predict monopoly capitalism. If they want to fight, is it better to fear fighting or not to fear it? Steel yourselves; be implacable towards the enemy; fight with all your might; destroy first and reconstruct later. Let's say clearly it's better not to fear a fight.

As for the three groupings of imperialism,[14] in our propaganda we say that [imperialism] is an aggressor because it launches aggression against nationalism and socialism, but [we] should not see this as anything that alarming. It will only attack us under one circumstance: that is, if we're in great disorder, and are overthrown by counterrevolutionaries. The Hungarian counterrevolution has already been suppressed; they dare not return. The socialist camp is consolidating; with 70 to 80 million tons of steel our China will be consolidated. As for those imperialist treaties, they're not so much for offense as for defense. They are organizations suffering from calcification like lungs afflicted by tuberculosis and shouldn't be taken too seriously. The Baghdad Pact sprang a leak; its center collapsed, and in a [single] morning Iraq was turned around. Communist ideology can infiltrate; I quite appreciate XXX's[15] saying that they fear our penetration. The imperialist military blocs are [protected by] walls of thin boards,

---

[14]Mao presumably means NATO, the South East Asian Treaty Organization (formed in 1954) and the now defunct Baghdad Pact.

[15]XXX: possibly Liu Shaoqi, or someone almost as senior with a right to voice opinions on foreign policy, to whom Mao might think it obligatory to be mildly flattering.

standing on shaky foundations. NATO is relatively more consolidated; it's keeping the intermediate zones in order. They have no
chance of keeping us in order, so [they] do it to the intermediate zones.
[They] also give each other a hard time: the British and the Americans
keep France in order, [and] restrict West Germany.[16] In our propaganda, we say that we oppose tension and strive for detente, as if
detente is to our advantage [and] tension is to their advantage. [But] can
we or can't we look at [the situation] the other way round: is tension to
our comparative advantage [and] to the West's disadvantage? Tension is
the West's advantage only in that they can increase military production, and it's to our advantage in that it will mobilize all [our] positive
forces. On the morning of 14 July the lid was taken off Iraq. Tensions
can [help] gain membership for Communist parties in different countries. [It] can [help] us increase steel as well as grain [production]. It's
better if the United States and Britain withdraw from Lebanon and Jordan later [rather than sooner]. Don't make the Americans seem kind-
hearted people. Every extra day they stay is an additional advantage to
us. [We can] capitalize on the United States' mistakes, and make an
issue of it. American imperialism will become a target of public criticism, but in [our] propaganda [we] can't talk like this. We still have to
say [they] should withdraw immediately.

[298] As for the embargo, the tighter the better; the longer the
UN refuses to recognize us the better. We have experience [in this].
During the anti-Japanese war, Chiang Kai-shek and He Yingqin[17]
refused to give us supplies or money. We raised [the slogan of] unity
and self-reliance, developing production on a large scale. The value
[of our production] was more than 400,000 yuan. We even had cotton-
padded clothes to wear, many more than what He Yingqin gave us.

[16]Mao's remarks here reflect an analysis that emerged in 1964 as his theory of the two intermediate zones (between the two superpowers), one consisting of third world countries, the
second of Western countries other than the USA. At that time, encouraged by de Gaulle's
recognition of the PRC in defiance of the USA, Mao focused particularly on France; but
this passage indicates he had long derived satisfaction from tensions between that country
and the "Anglo-Saxon" powers. See King C. Chen, ed., *China and the Three Worlds* (London, Macmillan, 1979), p. 3. For a suggestion of an earlier origin of the intermediate zone
theory, see Warren Kuo, ed., *A Comprehensive Glossary of Chinese Communist Terminology*
(Taipei, Institute of International Relations, 1978), pp. 99–100.
[17]Gen. He Yingqin (1890–1987) served as Chiang Kai-shek's Minister of War (1930–44). He
was also chief-of-staff (1938–44) and subsequently army commander-in-chief (1944–6). In
September 1945 he accepted the formal Japanese surrender in Nanjing on behalf of the
Nationalist Government. See *BDRC* 2, pp. 79–84.

It was like that then, so it's to our advantage now to have various countries put an embargo on us. It would be best if [they] recognized us seven years from now. Divide seven years into three periods: struggle hard for three years, [then another] two years, [then still another] two years. By that time, we produce from XX to XX million tons of steel. To have an enemy in front of us, to have tension, is to our advantage.

The thirteenth problem: the problem of communist education in the villages this winter and next spring.

The fourteenth problem: the problem of cooperation [*xiezuo*].

The fifteenth problem: the problem of deep ploughing. Currently the main orientation in agriculture is the problem of deep ploughing. Ploughing deeply is like [creating] a big reservoir for water and a big cistern for manure, otherwise no amount of water and manure will work. In the north [we should] deep plough [to a depth of] over a foot [*chi*], in the south to 7 or 8 inches [*cun*], then apply manure in different layers so as to enhance the granular structure of the soil. Every granule is both a small reservoir, [and] and small manure cistern. Deep ploughing brings water above ground into contact with underground water. Close planting is based on deep ploughing: otherwise it is useless. Deep ploughing helps weeding. Digging up roots in turn helps eliminate insects so that one *mou* of land [can produce as much] as three *mou*. Now each person nationwide has three *mou* of land. Once we go down [to the grass roots], [we] can increase production. What's the use of planting that much land? In the future we can use one-third of the land for afforestation, and after a few years again decrease the acreage [for grain] by another *mou* [per capita]. In the past [we] weren't able to afforest the plains, but by that time [we] will be able to. Without deep ploughing there's no such possibility.

[Our] views on population should change. In the past I said that [we] could manage with 800 million. Now I think that one billion plus would be no cause for alarm. This shouldn't be recommended for people with many children. When [people's] level of education increases, [they] will really practice birth control.

The sixteenth problem: the problem of fertilizer.

The seventeenth problem: the problem of the people's militia. The coordinating regions [*xiezuo qu*][18] or the larger provinces can pro-

---

[18]Mao is almost certainly referring, as in problem 14, to the seven economic coordinating

duce small arms, such as rifles, machine guns, light artillery, and so forth; [they] arm the militia, establish large cooperatives, [and then] everything is under one roof: industry, agriculture, commerce, education, and military affairs.[19] Producing that many guns is probably a waste, since we are not at war **[299]**. [But] a little waste is still necessary. "Everyone a soldier"[20] helps boost morale and courage. Sing more of Mu Guiying, of Hua Mulan, and of Sizhou fortress, sing less of Zhu Yingtai.[21] In another six years there will be a gun for a quarter of the population, nationwide [we'll] need 100 million guns; everyone will be given a score or more of bullets, which should all be used.

19 AUGUST

The [provincial party] first secretaries must personally grasp industry.

"Unified [i.e., centralized] planning, management by levels; priority construction projects; branches and leaves supporting each other."[22] The Tianjin prefecture has set up a steel mill of 40,000 tons [capacity]. This is their priority [project]. [Lower] levels [of management] are under centralized planning, a small portion, or two out of ten, of the total projects will be under the management of the Center (both investment and profits can be the Center's business); the majority,

---

regions (*jingji xiezuo qu*) to which mysterious reference began to be made in the press in 1958, but which thereafter received scant attention; see Audrey Donnithorne, *China's Economic System* (London, Allen and Unwin, 1967), p. 20. From post–Cultural Revolution publications, we learn that these regions were set up on 1 June 1958; see Fang Weizhong, ed., *Zhonghua renmin gongheguo jingji dashi ji (1949–1980 nian)* (Economic chronology of the People's Republic of China (1949–1980) (Beijing, China Social Sciences Publishing House, 1984), pp. 213–4.

[19]Interestingly, Mao still refers here to large cooperatives rather than people's communes as he does in his next speech two days later. Even more oddly, there is no suggestion in this speech of the momentous change in the countryside that was about to be ordered. Yet Mao's image of the large cooperative corresponds to the blueprint for the communes.

[20]"Everyone a soldier" was the name of a current campaign to enlarge the militia.

[21]Mu Guiying, a fictional heroine of the Northern Song dynasty, commanded troops in defeating invading Liao forces. Hua Mulan, a folk heroine, in male disguise took up arms in her father's place and fought brilliant battles. Sizhou fortress in Sizhou county, now in Anhui province, was the site of the defeat of a female water demon. Zhu Yingtai is the main female character in a popular romance, which ends with her suicide.

[22]These slogans exemplify Mao's attempt during the GLF to encourage the maximum possible initiative at the lower levels without sacrificing an overarching central guidance.

or eight out of ten, will be assigned to local regions for management. By 1962 [we'll] produce XX tons of steel. How to manage at that time, [we'll] have to wait and see. Where we should put our priority [projects] will depend on where [we find appropriate] conditions. Decentralization without dictatorship will not do. If we are to pursue speed, Wuhan Steel [Mill] can go a bit faster; [but] if all counties and communes champion "steel activism," it will be disastrous. [We] must have control; [we] cannot talk only about democracy. [The ways of] Marx and Qin Shihuang have to be combined.[23]

The entire party running industry, each level running industry, [but] all must be under unified planning; [and] there definitely must be priority [projects]. There [must be] branches and leaves. Whatever does not impinge upon priority [projects], people at large can run; [but] those which do must all be centralized. Each level should run only those things it is able to; it's not necessary for every APC to produce steel. APCs should mainly process grain, produce indigenous fertilizer, repair and produce farm tools, and dig small coal mines. Only when you don't do everything, can you then do something.[24] Every coordinating region must have a [complete] set [of economic activities],[25] but the provinces should divide up the work properly [among them], and not [try to] run every kind of [project themselves]. How much grain, [and] how much steel should each province produce? Eventually every province should produce and consume its own [products]. No province should think of selling [its products] elsewhere while planning to receive some allocations from the Center. Fujian [province] produced XX thousand tons of steel. Where should it be used? Big steel mills belong to the Center; small- and medium-sized [mills] can be run by more or less every province.

Decentralization of power to the localities: Every level (province, prefecture, county, township, APC[26]) should have power. The sub-

---

[23]For Qin Shihuang, see Text 18, n. 5.

[24]Mao is clearly referring here to the Daoist concept of "no action" (*wu wei*) although he says *bu wei*. A literal translation of the sentence would be: "Only when there is no action, then there is action." But Mao clearly means selective action rather than no action at all.

[25]Mao was here, as often, concerned with local self-reliance and self-sufficiency, particularly in the event of war and invasion. Conscious that total self-sufficiency in an industrializing economy is impossible to achieve at a very local level, he seems here to see the economic coordinating regions as the smallest independently viable units. His long-term vision, however, seems to be self-sufficiency at very local levels.

[26]The final term in his list is simply *she,* which could refer to either an APC or a com-

stance and scope [of that power] may vary. Management by different levels, but do not divide up all the raw materials.[27]

All levels should gradually strengthen their planning [system]. Production and distribution in APCs should also gradually be brought under unified management. It won't do not to have tight planning and organization. Grain production **[300]** should also be [well] planned. Should so many types of potato be planted next year or not? Do [we] want to plant so much cotton or not? [If we] strive hard again next year, and get the per capita gain [figures] up to XX catties, then [we'll] see [what next.]

A socialist state is a tightly organized network. In ten thousand years [there'll be] many people, many automobiles; [we'll] have to line up even to go shopping (*shang jie*). [There'll be] many airplanes, [and] it won't do not to have control of air traffic. When monkeys were evolving into human beings, there was much freedom; later there was less and less freedom. On the other hand, humanity [experienced] a major liberation, consciously taking control of the cosmos, uncovering limitless forces.

[We] must eradicate the ideology of bourgeois right. For instance, competing for position, competing for rank, demanding overtime pay, high salaries for mental workers and low salaries for physical laborers—these are all vestiges of bourgeois ideology. "To each according to his worth"[28] is stipulated by law; it's also bourgeois stuff. In the future should [we] ride automobiles according to rank? [We] do not necessarily need specially [assigned] automobiles. It's OK to make some allowances for the old and infirm; for the rest there should be no ranking [for automobiles].

Do [we] need to strive hard for grain production next year or not? [We] do, indeed. Struggle arduously for three years, storing up one year's worth of grain (500 catties per capita). [But we] can reduce [the output of] sweet potatoes a bit.

All plans should be made public; there should be no concealment of production. It won't do not to have control over prefectures,

---

mune. At this stage in the Beidaihe conference, APC seems more likely, especially since communes and townships tended to coincide.

[27]Presumably Mao is concerned here to prevent central enterprises' being starved for raw materials and so is prepared to have them under centralized allocation.

[28]Mao does say "worth" (*zhi*).

counties, and townships. [If] you can't transfer things, then [transfers] must be enforced by administrative orders. From now on, [performance] appraisal [among localities], must be by comparing assignment fulfillment, technological creativity, work methods, organizational discipline, [social] order, and responsible dictatorship. [But] only after great contending and blooming can [you] practice dictatorship. At present, iron can't be transferred [out of localities], neither can steel; [there exist] hundreds of thousands of governments—how outrageous!

[We] still need to talk about current affairs. On the domestic front, [we] need to talk about [taking] the whole nation as a big commune [*da gongshe*]; on the international front, [we] need to talk about the possibility of the imperialists launching a war. With the whole nation as a big commune, it's impossible not to have priority [projects]; it's impossible not to have unified planning. From the Center [down] to the APCs, there must be unanimity. There must be flexibility; but flexibility has to do with the branches and leaves, it can't impinge upon the main trunk. Next year's target of XX million tons of steel must be fulfilled; this year's XX million tons of steel must be guaranteed.

When the provincial [party] secretaries return home, [they] should immediately establish proletarian dictatorship [with] effective regulations: one chief for each region, one head to a province. "Every injustice has its perpetrator, every debt has its debtor."[29] [Someone] from an APC in Handan [Hebei] drove a cart to the Anshan steel [mill] and wouldn't leave until given some iron. In every place [there are] so many people roaming around uncontrolled; this must be banned completely. [We] must work out an equilibrium between levels, with each level [301] reporting to the next higher level—APCs[30] to the counties, counties to the prefectures, prefectures to the provinces—this is called socialist order. A Center, too, has only one head. The Center's head for steel is Wang Heshou[31] and the head for machinery is Zhao Erlu.[32]

The Center's plans [should] be formulated with [the participation

[29]I.e., someone has to be responsible: "the buck stops here."
[30]See n. 26.
[31]Wang Heshou: Minister of the Metallurgical Industry.
[32]Zhao Erlu: Minister of the 1st Ministry of Machine Building.

of] all provinces and cities; provincial level plans should be formulated with [the participation of] prefectures and counties. Perhaps [things] can't be resolved in one sitting, [so we] must talk a few more times.

Now on the problem of the people's communes: What should they be called? They may be called people's communes, or they may not. My inclination is to call them people's communes. This [name] is still socialist in nature, not at all overemphasizing communism. They're called people's communes, first, [because] they're big and, second, [because] they're public. Lots of people, a vast area of land, large scale of production, [and] all [their] undertakings are [done] in a big way. [They] integrate government [administration] with commune [management] to establish public mess halls, and private plots are eliminated. But chickens, ducks, and the young trees in front and behind a house are still private. These, of course, won't exist in the future. [If we] have more grain, [we] can practice the supply system; [for the present] it's still reward according to one's work. Wages will be given to individuals according to their ability and won't be given to the head of the family, which makes the youth and women happy. This will be very beneficial for the liberation of the individual. In establishing the people's communes, as I see it, once again it's been the countryside that's taken the lead; the cities haven't started yet, [because] the workers' wage scales are a complicated matter. Whether in urban or rural areas, [the aim] should be the socialist system plus communist ideology. The Soviet Union practices the use of high rewards and heavy punishments, emphasizing [only] material incentives. We now practice socialism, and have the sprouts of communism. Schools, factories, and neighborhoods can all establish people's communes. In a few years big communes will be organized to include everyone.

In Tianjin municipality one million people could have participated in manual labor yet did not. In the second FYP period, mechanization can finally be basically realized. Only with mechanization can the labor force be completely liberated.[33]

[There must be] centralized power on major issues; decentralized

---

[33]Mao appears to be voicing contradictory attitudes here: On the one hand he is reproaching Tianjin citizens for not participating in morally therapeutic manual labor; on the other, he is anticipating with pleasure the eventual liberation of the work force from manual labor.

power [applies to] minor issues [only]. Once the Center makes a decision (the Center and the localities decide jointly), each locality should implement that decision; implementation also means making decisions, but not in violation of principles. Party committees should take the responsibility of investigating work [as it is carried out]. These [points] still need emphasis. Centralized power is the main trunk; decentralized power is the branch and leaves. On the one hand there's policy-making; on the other, there's investigation [of results]. The special small group for steel must carry out a check-up every ten days. After you've returned [home from this conference], do nothing else but concentrate on industry for a few months. Without giving up something, [you] can't specialize. Without a specialization, [you] have no priorities. The grain problem has been basically solved; high output satellites should not be given too much attention.³⁴ Imperialism oppresses us; [and so] within three, five, or seven years **[302]** we must build our country into a great industrial power. For this goal we must concentrate our strength on building up [our] large-scale industrial base; [we must] grasp the main things; [and] as for things of secondary importance, [if we] don't have enough capability, then get rid of some. It's just like pruning cotton plants for the growth of cotton bolls. Will this hurt the initiative of the lower levels? [If] APCs³⁵ don't produce steel, [they can] produce something else. Who produces and who does not produce iron and steel must be on the basis of a decision. [We] must issue an emergency order requisitioning iron and not allowing it to be dispersed. The plans of medium- to large-sized steel mills must be fulfilled, [and we must] strive for overfulfillment.³⁶ In a specified period, only a few things can be done. [If] you want to sing *Xiaoyaojin*,³⁷ then you cannot sing

---

³⁴After the launch of the Soviet Sputniks in 1957, high achievements were often called launching satellites in China. In this passage, Mao is referring to APCs or communes claiming massive outputs. Such claims were commonly the grounds for emulation campaigns that resulted in enormous exaggerations, a typical feature of the GLF which Mao seems here to be anticipating.

³⁵The text does say APCs, not communes, here and in a few subsequent instances. The translation is literal each time.

³⁶At this point, Mao clearly hoped to fulfill his extravagant steel target from the output of regular steel mills. It was only in October, when this aim could be seen to be unrealistic, that the mass steel campaign started. See *Origins* 2, p. 44.

³⁷*Xiaoyaojin* is the name of a Peking Opera. Although its story has nothing to do with the discussion here, Cao Cao, one of Mao's favorite characters from *Romance of the Three King-*

other operas at the same time. [We] must drive home the principle "only when you don't do everything, can you then do something."

We must go all out for the next two years on [the production of] iron, steel, copper, aluminum, molybdenum, and other nonferrous metals. It won't do not to go all out. Steel [targets] must be fully met; iron can be a little less, [but we] must also strive to fulfill [that target].

When [we] sent people to Vietnam, I said [to them, "You should cherish and protect every tree and every blade of grass in Vietnam. That's not [just] the business of Ho Chi Minh, but global business, the business of [all] laboring people. Attacking the enemy is also Ho Chi Minh's business [but equally] global business, [and] the business of [all] laboring people. [If you should] die in battle there, then be buried there." In the future we'll establish a global committee, [and] make plans on global unification. Then wherever grain is short, we will supply it as a gift. But [this will be] possible only when the opposing classes are eliminated. Now each of the two classes has its own plans. in the future [we'll] achieve [the goal of] from each according to his ability, to each according to his needs; there'll be no distinction between what's one's own and what's another's; [and when we] help a place that's in dire straits, [we] won't ask for even a single penny. [We've] fought wars for so many years, so many people have died, yet no one asked for compensation for losses. Now construction is also a fierce battle; struggle desperately for a few years, [and] after these few years [we] will still have to struggle. But at least all this kills fewer people than fighting wars. [We] can't count time by the clock [or,] how could [we be] considered to have superior morality?[38] Hebei province has estimated that teenagers of fifteen could graduate from university after [a further] fifteen years; with part-work, part-study, people's consciousness will be raised. Too great a reliance on material rewards, with high rewards and heavy punishments, won't do. We won't hand out any medals from now on. Officers should go down [to the ranks] to be [ordinary] soldiers: those who've had no

---

doms, is the lead character; and two paragraphs later, Mao does quote his denunciation of the emperor Xian from the opera. In colloquial Chinese, the name has been appropriated to mean "leisurely and carefree," "unconcerned," "relaxed," etc. It appears to be used in that sense here.

[38]Mao appears to mean it is ignoble to keep a minute profit-and-loss account in human transactions.

experience of being soldiers should have the experience; it's also good for those who have had the experience to do it again. Division and army commanders should go down to be under the command of squad leaders for three months, then come back to be division and army commanders again. There's a division commander in Yunnan [province] who spent a few months as an ordinary soldier, getting to understand the soldier's life and mentality. That's very good. Some say that cadres [should] participate in manual labor for two months [a year]; even one month would be fine. It's beneficial for us to be as one with the workers **[393]**; our feelings will change, [and this] will influence some tens of millions of cadre children. Cao Cao's condemnation of Emperor Xian of the Han as "born in the secluded courts, raised at the hands of ladies" was justified.[39] As long as everyone struggles hard with all their might, with all their effort, in three [or] five years, we'll have achieved something.

It won't do for the [economic] coordinating regions not to engage in politics; they must engage in some politics. In the past some people said that coordinating regions only do economic [work], not politics. I think [we] still need politics in command; only when [our] thinking is unified can [we] run the economy well. Grasp planning with politics in command. To establish big communes, to have unified planning, to have priority construction [projects], [and] to get rid of some branches and leaves, that's [all] politics.

21 AUGUST, MORNING

[If] priority [projects] can be guaranteed, next year XX to XX million tons of steel [and] XX tens of thousands of machine tools can be [produced]; completion of these will be a victory. Therefore, we must struggle with all our might. [We] must stress [this point] once a week; [since we] still have over a dozen weeks [left this year], it should be stressed over a dozen times. At the conference of [party] secretaries for industry and on factory party committees on the 24th [of this month], [we'll] see whether there can be any certainty [of fulfilling our targets]. [We've] given repeated injunctions that whoever

---

[39]Cao Cao was a leading Han general who controlled North China as that dynasty disintegrated into three parts in the third century AD. This quotation comes from the Peking Opera, *Xiaoyaojin;* see n. 37.

refuses to hand over their iron will be disciplined. [For those] practicing dispersionism: first, warning; second, record a demerit; third, relief from duty while remaining in office; fourth, dismissal; fifth, probation within the party; sixth, expulsion from the party.[40] Otherwise it will be disadvantageous [to the fulfillment of the plan]. I'm afraid there's a danger of not fulfilling the plan of producing XX million tons of steel. I asked Wang Heshou in June whether or not steel [production] could be doubled. It was I who brought up the subject; [if the plan] can't be realized, I will have to make a self-criticism. Some people don't understand that failure to produce XX million tons of steel is a serious matter affecting the interests of the people of the entire nation.

[We] must work hard, with all our might. In Shanghai over 100,000 tons of scrap steel were resmelted. [We] should retrieve scrap steel in a big way. Those railways that are temporarily of no economic value, such as the Ningbo and the Jiaodong lines, can be dismantled or moved to [economically] important places. First of all, [we must] guarantee [production of] metallurgical equipment, blast furnaces, open-hearth rolling mills, electrical machinery, major railways, priority engineering [projects], lathes, and cranes. [We] must make it clear to the cadres and the people that only by first guaranteeing a number of important tasks can [we] obtain] ten thousand years of happiness. Every injustice has its perpetrator, every debt has its debtor; a province can have only one head: [I'd] like to see whether [you] agree or not. If [you] agree, then permit no one to roam around uncontrolled. [You] can still make a few adjustments outside the state plan between various coordinating regions and between provinces. There are still 133 days, 19 weeks [left in the year]; pay special attention to it once every week, take good charge of it.

Our people are very disciplined; this has impressed me profoundly. During my visit to Tianjin **[304]** tens'of thousands of people gathered around me, [but] at a single wave of my hand everybody dispersed. There are 29,000 households with a population of 130,000 in Xiuwu county, Henan, and [they] have established a big commune

---

[40]These six sanctions, which are part of the CCP rectification process, are detailed in Frederick C. Teiwes, *Politics and Purges in China: Rectification and Decline of Party Norms, 1950–1965* (Armonk, N.Y., M. E. Sharpe, 1979), pp. 33–8.

with four levels: commune, wings, squadrons,[41] and action groups [*zhandou xiaozu*]. Being big, [communes] are easy to manage and easy to incorporate into the [general] plan. With the concentration of labor force and land management, [you acquire] a different [level of] capability. When the crops double at the autumn harvest, the masses will realize the advantages. [We've] drawn water up hills from the Tiao River in Gansu [province]; the completion of such a large project is the result of the party's leadership and the people's communist spirit. Why is the enthusiasm among the people so great? The reason is that we take little from the people; [and] unlike the Soviet Union, we don't use a system of obligatory sales. We are one party with one "ism" [and] the masses support us. We have become one with the masses,[42] and since the great rectification [of 1942], of one heart. The Hongan experience is a [good] model.[43]

[Our] comrades must be made to understand that [the theories of] Marx, Engels, Lenin, and Stalin on the relations of production consist of the interrelationships among three elements: the system of ownership, the interrelationships [among the people], and distribution. They have heard about these ideas but have not begun to understand them. I don't think economic theory has clarified this properly. The Soviet Union, too, has failed to resolve this matter since the October Revolution. The interrelationship among the people when laboring is the important element in the relations of production. To stress relations of production and not stress [human] interrelationships is impossible. Equality among people will not automatically emerge following the transformation of ownership. If China fails to solve the relationship between people, the Great Leap Forward will be impossible.

---

[41]"Wings" (an air force formation) and "squadron" underline the militarization ethos of the early commune movement.

[42]*Women yu renmin dacheng yipian:* Mao's key populist phrase became ubiquitous in the Cultural Revolution and contrasts nicely with the equivalent phrase used by the managerial elite—*miqie de lianxi qunzhong,* or "intimately link with the masses." For an example of this second term, see Liao Mosha, et al., eds., *Yi Deng Tuo* (Commemorating Deng Tuo) (Fuzhou, Fujian Peoples Publishing House, 1980), p. 109.

[43]Hongan county in Hubei province pioneered the experimental plot movement. Cadres transferred to the grass roots experimented with new methods of cultivation on small plots. This system was lauded for two reasons: it united cadres and masses, and aided output, thus combining redness and expertise. The CC had publicized and promoted the experimental plot system since February 1958. See *Origins* 2, pp. 346–7.

After the transformation of the system of ownership, bourgeois right still exists, such as the system of ranks [and] the relationship between leaders and the masses. Since rectification, the system of bourgeois right has been almost completely destroyed; leading cadres no longer lead by virtue of their power and prestige [or] bureaucratic airs, but [instead] rely on serving the people, seeking benefits for the people, and on persuasion. [We] should consider the question of eliminating the wage system [and] restoring the supply system.[44] The army of the past had no salaries, no Sundays [off], no eight-hour work system; superiors and subordinates were as one; officers and soldiers were as one; the army had become one with the people,[45] [and thus] we were able to mobilize tens of thousands of people. This communist spirit is very good. If human beings only live to eat, isn't that like dogs eating shit? What meaning is there [to life] if [you] don't help others a bit, [or] don't practice a bit of communism? [If] the wage system is eliminated, there will be, one, food to eat—nobody will die—two, physical health. When I was in Yan'an I wasn't very healthy, but once Hu Zongnan[46] launched his attack, six of us—I, the premier [Zhou Enlai], Hu XX, Jiang Qing,[47] and so on—moved into a two-room cave dwelling [and my] health got better. In Xibaipo,[48] too, I had [only] a small **[305]** house. Since coming to Beijing my housing has become better and better, [but] my health has deteriorated; [I come down] with the flu more often. Since the Great Leap Forward, [my] health has improved again. One night in three or four, I stay up all night. We should put into practice some of the ideals of utopian socialism. The life of Protestant Puritans was very hard. Sakyamuni who created Buddhism was also a product of an oppressed people.[49] The Buddhist "Sutra of the Six Patriarchs" of

[44]For a discussion of the public promotion of Mao's views on bourgeois right by the Shanghai propagandist Zhang Chunqiao, see *Origins* 2, pp. 106–8.
[45]Literally: *dacheng yipian*, the same idealistic phrase used above, see n. 42.
[46]Hu Zongnan (Hu Tsung-nan) was a leading KMT general. His forces captured Yan'an on 19 March 1947 after CCP forces had slipped out. See Jacques Guillermaz, *A History of the Chinese Communist Party, 1921–1949* (New York, Random House, 1972), pp. 398–400.
[47]Hu XX: almost certainly Hu Qiaomu, then Mao's political secretary, who was in the group that left Yan'an with the Chairman. Jiang Qing: Mme. Mao.
[48]Xibaipo: a village in Pingshan county in the Jin Cha Ji border region in southern Hebei, where the 7th CC held its 2nd plenum in March 1949.
[49]The Buddha was, contrary to Mao's assertion, the scion of a princely house.

the Tang dynasty records that the monk, Huineng,[50] from Hebei, was illiterate but very knowledgeable; while doing his missionary work in Guangdong, he affirmed the emptiness of everything. It was Idealism through and through, [but] he highlighted [the role] of subjective activity, a great leap forward in the history of Chinese philosophy. Huineng dared to negate everything. Someone asked him, "Will we reach the Western Paradise after death or not?" He replied "Not necessarily so. [If we] all reached the Western Paradise, what about the Westerners?" He lived in the period of Tang Taizong; his theories prevailed during the time of [Empress] Wu Zetian. In the turbulent years at the end of the Tang dynasty people had no spiritual sustenance, [and his theories] became very popular.

Marx's thinking on equality, democracy, persuasion, and on the interrelationships among people, [and] becoming one [with the masses] have not been brought into full play.[51] The people's relationship in labor is a relationship of equality and a relationship of becoming one [with each other]. The Soviet Union didn't do well [on this point] after the October Revolution. The old system of [hierarchical] rights was not completely destroyed; [as a result] mental labor is divorced from physical labor, [and] education is divorced from production. Lenin once said [the Soviet Union] should abolish the standing army [and] instead should arm the people. [As long as] imperialism exists, there remains a need for a standing army. But the hierarchical system [and] the relationship between officers and soldiers in the Soviet armed forces have been influenced somewhat by the Tsarist period. The majority of Soviet Communist party members are cadres' children; ordinary workers and peasants are not admitted [to party membership]. That's why we need to find our own road. We must thrust cadres' children in among the masses; [they] should not enjoy the advantage of being in a favored position. Our army officers [should be] like the division commander in Yunnan [who served as] a soldier for one month in the year; I think this

---

[50]For a discussion of the life and teachings of Huineng (638–713), the Tang dynasty's sixth Chan patriarch, see Kenneth Ch'en, *Buddhism in China* (Princeton, Princeton Univ. Press, 1964), pp. 353–7. Either Mao or the editor of New Mao Texts, vol. 2, got his origins wrong, for Huineng was from Hubei, not Hebei.

[51]An alternative reading would be: "Marx's thinking on combining equality, democracy, persuasion, and the interrelationships among people has not been brought into full play."

is a good method. Perhaps [we] should extend this [practice] every-where; then our army will be forever invincible.

Red Flag will publish the regulations of Chayashan Commune.[52] Other places need not necessarily copy them; [they] may create various patterns. [We] should give [this] some good publicity; let ten or more people in each province do the publicity. [In their organization], big communes [*da she*][53] should integrate the natural environment, population, and [local] educational levels. Comrade XXX[54] in Hebei got together ten or so people to promote the communist ideological work style, and they were all quite enthusiastic about it. You, too, should do this kind of promotion when you return to your posts. Since entering the cities, some have commented that we have a "rural work style" or a "guerrilla work style." This [criticism] is bourgeois ideology corroding us. We have cast aside some of our **[306]** good things; the rural work style has become unpopular; cities demand regularization [of procedures]; government offices [*yamen*][55] proliferate; [and we] have become distant from people. [We] should become one [with the people], use persuasion and not coercion. This has been [our tradition] for years: How is it that now they have become problems? It is because [we] have become divorced from the masses [and] have become privileged. We have always advocated unity between superiors and subordinates, unity between officers and soldiers, unity between the army and the people, support the government [and] cherish the people, support the army [and] give preferential treatment to the families of revolutionary martyrs. The supply system was more equitable, clothing was more or less the same; but since entering the cities, this has changed.[56] After going

[52]*Hongqi* No. 7 (1958), pp. 16–22. This commune in Henan province was more often known by the second half of its full name: Chayashan Sputnik Commune.

[53]Mao's occasional use of the term *da she* suggests that the final decision on the appropriate name for the new organization had not yet been finalized, despite his own stated preference for "people's communes."

[54]XXX: possibly Hebei's recently appointed governor, Liu Zihou.

[55]*Yamen* is a pejorative term used here instead of equivalent communist terms; it projects a powerful image of corrupt and useless local government in China before 1949.

[56]Mao is idealizing the degree of Yan'an egalitarianism, as we know from the famous case of Wang Shiwei, whose 1942 polemical essay, "Wild Lilies," pilloried the party for "instituting three classes for clothing and five levels for food." While Wang was purged as an "absolute egalitarian," most Yan'an observers agree that material distance between superiors and subordinates did not begin with the CCP's entry into major cities around 1949. See Simon Leys, *Chinese Shadows* (New York, The Viking Press, 1977), pp. 124–6.

through [the 1957] Rectification, the masses said the Eighth Route Army[57] has again returned. Clearly [it] had earlier disappeared. It is precisely the cities that should carry out the "rural work style and guerrilla practices." Chiang Kai-shek's ghost remains in the cities; the bourgeois stink is influencing us; [and] when we meet them face to face, [we] want to cut our hair, shave, assume a gentleman's air, and put on a bourgeois style—really distasteful. Why shave? Isn't it good enough to shave and cut your hair four times a year?[58] A secretary of the Hunan Provincial Party Committee, Zhou Hui, says when he worked in a county, he could be one with the masses; when he worked in a prefecture [party] committee, he could still be close to the masses; [but] in the three years since he's been on the provincial committee, it's been hard [for him] to find the cadres and the masses. Last year's rectification produced changes. In the past, millions of us steeled [ourselves] through class struggle into communist fighters supported by the masses. [We] practiced the supply system, led a communist life—this was a Marxist style of work as opposed to a bourgeois style of work. In my view, the rural work style and guerrilla practices are, after all, better. In twenty-two years of war we were victorious: Why is it that building communism doesn't work? Why do [we] have to use a wage system? This is a concession to the bourgeoisie; [we are] allowing the rural work style and guerrilla practices to be used to belittle us, [and] the result is the development of individualism. The emphasis on persuasion and not coercion has also been forgotten. Should the cadres take the lead in restoring the supply system or not? In the old base areas of North China [we] conducted tunnel warfare, [so] all [the cadres] in the north have been steeled through war. Hebei adopts militarization [because] it's used to this pattern. Many places in the south were not steeled through war, [so] the life style of cadres who grew up there is somewhat different. The cadres of the 25,000 *li* Long March have even produced some bad eggs, for example, XX [and] XX. XX is very backward in [his] consciousness, very secretive; it's hard to see what he's thinking. It seems that the [party's] Control Commission hasn't been effective;

[57]The 8th Route Army was the wartime appellation of the communist forces. It is used by Mao to signify the untarnished original virtue of the communists prior to their capture of power and entry into the corrupting cities.
[58]The average Chinese man does not shave every day and generally gets himself shaved when he has a hair cut.

even Gao Gang [and] Rao Shushi[59] were not "controlled." [The commission] merely checked on the "Qingsen No. 5" (rice) in Hunan and Hubei. [What] really worked was the 1,400-man conference of the Military Affairs Commission this time.[60]

We have already destroyed the system of bourgeois right to a great extent, but not thoroughly enough yet. [307] [We] must continue working a bit. Don't immediately advocate the abolition of the wage system, but in the future it will be eliminated. [We] must stress the rural work style and guerrilla practices, participating in manual labor one month a year, [and] going down to the countryside in groups [to do so]. Lenin wrote an article on his visit to a worker's family on the eve of the October Revolution. The worker could find no bread; later he did and was very happy, [saying] "This time I finally found some bread." Lenin only learned of the importance of bread from this. [If] our cadres participate in manual labor one month a year and become as one with the people, it will greatly influence their state of mind. This time [we] must restore our military tradition—the tradition of the Red Army, the Eighth Route Army, [and] the PLA—the tradition of Marxism; [and we] must get rid of bourgeois ideological work styles. We may be a bit "uncouth," but [our ways] are genuine [and] most civilized. The bourgeoisie appear a bit more civilized, [but] in reality they're hypocritical and uncivilized. Restoring the supply system seems like "retrogression," [but] "retrogression" means progress, because we've retrogressed since we came into the cities. Now [we] must resume our forward march [and] take the lead [in getting] the 600 million people to adopt the communist work style.

The people's communes contain the sprouts of communism. When products are bountiful, we will implement communist [distribution] of grain, cotton, and edible oils. By that time morality will have greatly improved. Labor will no longer require supervision; even if [you] want someone to rest, he won't. The Jianhua Machinery Plant practices the "*ba wu*."[61] In the people's communes, [people]

---

[59]For Gao Gang and Rao Shushi, see Text 1, n. 10.

[60]This meeting took place 27 May–22 July 1958 and was designed in part to restore some of the Yan'an ethos to the PLA; see *Origins* 2, pp. 66–8.

[61]*Ba wu*: lit., eight have-nots. This term is obscure, but one Chinese respondent who was a high school student during the GLF partially recalls learning a chant, "The Eight Proletarian Points" (*bage wuchanjieji zhuzhang*), the first point of which was "poor" (i.e., *yi, qiong, er . . .*). *Ba wu* would not be an unusual contraction, just as *si hua* is the contraction for *sige xiandai hua* (the four modernizations slogan).

practice cooperation in a big way, bringing [their] own tools and food. The workers beat drums and gongs [and] don't ask for piece-rate wages. All of these are the sprouts of communism, [and they] destroy the system of bourgeois right. I hope everyone will publicize [this] way of looking at the problem, read the two relevant documents, and publicize the actual situations in which there is increasing growth of the elements of communist morality.

In the past during the revolution numerous people died without asking anything in return. Why can't it be like that now? If we can eat without paying for it, this will be a tremendous change. Probably in about ten years our production will be very bountiful [and the people's] morality will be very noble; [then] we can practice communism in eating, clothing, and housing. Eating without paying in public mess halls is communism. In the future everything will be called a commune. [We] won't say factories; for instance, Anshan Steel Mill will be called Anshan Commune. Cities and villages will be called communes, [and] universities and neighborhoods will establish communes.[62] Townships will be integrated with communes, [local] government will be integrated with commune management; temporarily [we] put up two signs. Set up a "department of the interior" (administrative section) in the people's communes to administer registry of birth and death, marriage, census, [and] civil administration.

[308] X X X[63]

Some people ask, "should there still be flexibility after centralization?" Flexibility is still needed. Apart from the guarantee of XX million tons of steel, flexibility is permitted. [This is] like fruit trees or cotton plants that need pruning, [while] others do not. Centralization is needed mainly in [the production of] steel and in machinery. Allocate XX million yuan to stimulate [production] so that the vitality of the APCs will have something to aim at. XX million tons of steel should be guaranteed for the state, leaving the remaining XX million tons of steel to be used by the provinces, prefectures [*di*], and counties at their discretion; if [we] can surpass [the target] a bit, all

---

[62]Yet, when Zhang Chunqiao and Yao Wenyuan wanted to establish the Shanghai Commune in 1967, Mao ridiculed the idea; see *Wansui* (1969), pp. 666–72.

[63]Three Xs, the meaning of which is unclear, appear at the top of 2:308.

the better. Plans can't be completely accurate; [it's] impossible for everything to be planned ahead of time: Some things are difficult to anticipate; blindness is unavoidable; there may be a little chaos, but the achievements would be great, unprecedented. We didn't pay attention to this in the past; now the whole party should manage it. The first secretaries should grasp industry in their right hands and agriculture in [their] left hands. Party committees at all levels should have several secretaries.

21 AUGUST, AFTERNOON

The problem of grain policy for 1959: Should our effort be greater than this year's or be about the same? [I believe] the greater the effort we make, the better. [Our effort] next year should be still greater than this year. Don't worry about a bumper harvest containing [the seeds of] famine, don't diminish your efforts for fear of overproduction.[64] But there should be a rhythm to production. At present, the intensity of labor is very high; the peasants must be allowed to have proper rest, two days a month, one day a fortnight. During the busy season, rest a little less; at other times, rest a little more. [Those] living relatively far away from the work site can eat and sleep [there], so as to save on commuting time and have more rest. This point should be written in the documents but not be talked about too much.[65]

There's plenty of grain, but edible oils are still insufficient. The production of grain, cotton, and edible oils should all be increased, [and] the key is deep ploughing. This year most [places] didn't plough deeply, and close planting has also been insufficient. [Of course], planting so closely that no air gets through is no good, either. Only by ploughing deeply [can you] plant closely, conserve water, store manure, and kill insects.

(XX interjected: Close planting above ten million plants may fail, though five million should pose no problem; large scale close planting will create experience.)

---

[64]This is an obscure passage.
[65]It was not only 9 Nov. that *RMRB* warned openly that peasants had to get more rest.

[Chairman:] Some of the problems in the theory of political economy and historical materialism should be written afresh. We've solved a theoretical problem in Marxism. First take care of agriculture, while at the same time taking care of heavy industry. The arguments Khrushchev had with Molotov were precisely over too much heavy industry. We take a road opposite to that of the Soviet Union: [we] first take care of agriculture in order to facilitate industrial development; [we] first take care of the green leaves, then the red flowers. What's wrong with this approach? It seems some questions need reinterpretation. Economic **[309]** theory and historical materialism require new development and amplification. The three aspects of the relations of production, [namely] the system of ownership, the interrelationship among workers, and distribution all have yet to be brought into full play. The collective farms and handicraft cooperatives in the Soviet Union are still under collective ownership. Why haven't they introduced the system of ownership by the whole people? Ownership by the whole people [means that things] belong not just to the Center but to all the people. In the past, [our] system of ownership was expressed in the ownership of Wang Heshou and Zhao Erlu; this is the way of the Soviet Union. At present, we can't even manage twenty-eight provinces, municipalities, and autonomous regions[66] except to hold four conferences a year. We did even less in the past, merely issuing some directives and reporting on developments. Now 20 percent is controlled by the Center and 80 percent by the localities. Provinces should also decentralize power, even down to the individual enterprises which should also have prescribed jurisdiction and independence. The Shijingshan Steel Mill has responsibility [*baogan*] for investment. It can raise production from 600,000 tons to 1.3 million tons [per year]; in the second state it can produce 3 million tons. What's the reason? Is there some trick to this? Think about it. [It's simply that] the initiative of the masses has come into play. When Wang Heshou was in charge it was actually the dictatorship of the planners. Here's a problem for you all to ponder. In my opinion this is a problem to do with the people [and the motivations] which are the same as in national independence [movements]. Activism in independent India is higher than it was under American

---

[66]At this time 26 provinces plus Beijing and Shanghai were directly under the Center. (Tianjin was demoted to sub-provincial level, 1958–67).

[sic] rule; once there is independence, there is more activism. Of course, this has manifested itself in class struggle. In the neighborhoods, factories, and popularly run [*minban*] schools, progress has been made in a transformation from collective ownership to ownership by the whole people.

The problem of the struggle between flexibility [*huo*] and "inflexibility" ["*si*"]. The struggle between "flexibility and inflexibility" will exist ten thousand years from now; [should we] control "inflexibility" or not? No inflexibility won't do; overly inflexible control won't do, either; [and] absolutely no inflexibility also won't do. If the [target for] steel for 1959 is XX tons, XX tons [of it] must be inflexible and XX tons is flexible; if [the target is] XX tons, then [something like] XX tons is flexible;[67] if XX tons is surpassed it can be allocated [like] edible oils; [if you have] more, eat more; less, then eat less. This is flexibility. Guaranteeing priority projects is what's inflexible; what's outside the priority projects and won't impede the priority projects is what's flexible. Implementing a responsibility [system] in a big way contains both inflexibility and flexibility; everybody should keep an eye on this. Inflexibility and flexibility are expressed in terms of centralization and decentralization; both are needed. The responsibility system is expressed in this unity of the contradiction between inflexibility and flexibility. This is the principle of centralizing power on major issues and decentralizing power on minor issues. After all, who's in charge of the Center? To what extent should we centralize power on major issues? Is it enough to have only a [State] Economic Construction Commission?[68] Is it possible to establish [both] an Industrial Production Commission [*Gongye shengchan weiyuanhui*] and a Basic Industrial Construction Commission [*Gongye jijian weiyuanhui*]?[69] In the final analysis, "every injustice has its perpetra-

[67]In 1958, Mao promoted a dual system of dependable steel targets and higher targets to be striven for; see *Origins* 2, pp. 165–70. In this passage, the inflexible amount is the dependable target and the flexible amount is the difference between the dependable target and the target to be striven for. We have scrupulously retained the Chinese editor's use of quotation marks with regard to *huo* and *si*.

[68]It is unclear whether Mao is being loose in his terminology or simply forgetful. There was no body called the Economic Construction Commission. The passage could also possibly be rendered "[State] Economic and Construction Commissions," but in February 1958 the State Construction Commission had been abolished and its functions taken over by other bodies, including the State Economic Commission.

[69]Here Mao may have been airing alternative ideas of central government restructuring cur-

tor."[70] Contracts and responsibility for tasks [*baogong baogan*] [will] give people something to strive for. We talk about the six points on discipline as a war of nerves, [310] primarily [meant] to scare people, not to send them to jail; just as long as people don't break the law, that's fine.[71]

The problem of the superstructure in historical materialism is the problem of political power; it's already been solved. The people's communes integrate government [administration] and commune [management]. Gradually political power will disappear there. Estimate one scoundrel for every few people in the people's communes and so dictatorship is exercised. Sentencing 1.3 million criminals to remolding through labor from a population of 600 million is not really very many. The army in the past said it was backward; but since [they] met in [that] conference, the interrelationships [among their people] have improved and a new atmosphere emerged. At the moment, the army is holding conferences everywhere; the Great Leap Forward in the army is starting; [it] can do all kinds of things. By taking one-third of [its] time to engage in politics, culture, and manual labor, will the army's military training be affected? Not only will it not be affected, but it will be improved. Public Security and the courts are in the midst of rectification, too. This business of law, it won't do to be without it, but we have our own way—investigation and research settle problems on the spot and mainly through mediation—or is the way of Upright Judge Ma[rx] better?[72] Since the Great Leap Forward, everyone's been engaged in production, blooming and contending in a big way, and freely writing big character posters, so they haven't had time to break the law. In dealing with thieves it won't do not to rely on the masses.

(Liu XX[73] interjects: In the end [do we] rule by law or rule by people?

rently under top-level debate. No body with either of these titles existed, but in November 1958 a State Capital Construction Commission (*Guojia jiben jianshe weiyuanhui*) was created, presumably because the abolition of the State Construction Commission was now felt to have been a mistake.
[70]See n. 29.
[71]See n. 40.
[72]This is an obscure passage. Mao seems suddenly to realize that perhaps Marx, whom he respects, might not approve of his preference for an unstructured system of justice.
[73]Liu XX: unidentified, possibly Liu Shaoqi.

Judgments are dependent on people; laws can function only as references in the conduct of business. If everyone acts according to the decisions of the Nanning conference, the Chengdu conference, the second session of the Eighth Party Congress,[74] and the Beidaihe conference, then . . . The Meilin company in Shanghai practices two sets of laws [*shuang fa*];[75] as soon as it's published in the newspapers, [it will be] adopted nationwide.)

[Chairman:] [We] can't rule the majority of the people by relying on law. The majority of people [can be ruled only] by relying on the cultivation of [good] habits. The army's reliance on rule by law didn't work; what's actually worked has been the 1,400-man conference. Who could remember so many clauses of a civil code or a criminal law? I participated in the formulation of the Constitution, even I can't remember [it]. Han Feizi[76] advocated rule by law; later the Confucianists advocated rule by men. Each of our draft resolutions is law; holding conferences is law, too. Observing public security regulations is possible only when people have cultivated good habits. [If this] becomes public opinion [and] everyone becomes conscious [of it], then communism is achievable. The great majority, some 90 percent, of our rules and regulations are created at the departmental and bureau [level]. Essentially we do not rely on these; mainly we rely on resolutions, holding conferences—four held annually—and not on a civil code or a criminal law to maintain social order. The National People's Congress and the State Council in conference have their ways, and we rely on our ways. This has to do with the superstructure.

The impact of ideology, world view, methodology, newspapers, culture, and education is enormous. The more bourgeois freedom is destroyed, the more proletarian freedom there is. The Soviet [311] Union didn't completely destroy bourgeois freedom, [and] consequently hasn't fully established proletarian freedom. Our revolution in politics and ideology has been relatively thorough: the cadres

[74]These three major meetings had all been held earlier in 1958 and were crucial in the development of the GLF; see Table 4.
[75]The exact nature of the Meilin company's legal procedures is obscure; possibly the company used persuasion and mediation initially in cases of rule-breaking and punishment by the rulebook only when all else failed.
[76]Han Feizi (fl. 3rd century BC): a leading philosopher of the Legalist school of statecraft.

participate in production and become one with the masses, [and] rules and regulations have been thoroughly reformed. This is precisely the complete destruction of bourgeois freedom, [and] the enthusiasm of the workers has been soaring. These questions are touched upon ever so slightly in a few sentences in [the text on] political economy.

[On] the problem of distribution: Wage grades among Soviet cadres are too numerous and the gap [between the cadres and] the workers and peasants is too wide. The peasants are obliged to sell their [grain], shouldering 48 percent of the burden [of the states's economic investment], which has restricted agriculture from developing for forty years. We only take 5 to 8 percent (aside from indirect obligations), thus storing wealth among the people. "With ample grain, how can army provisions be insufficient?" When Khrushchev came [to power] he talked only of how much grain the state must have, but not of how much to produce. We are the ones who talk about production. People know that we are in the end [doing so] for them, so [their] enthusiasm is very high. Some say, "With a big country and a large population it's hard to get anything done." It depends on what methods [you] use. As long as the methods are right, even with an additional billion or more people, we can easily get things done. Our method is big contending and blooming, and the exercise of self-management. We obey the truth; if truth is on the side of the subordinates, [then] the superiors obey; if the soldiers are wiser than the officers, [then] the officers obey the soldiers; if students can compile textbook materials better than the teachers, [then] the teachers obey the students. The compilation of teaching materials needs the "three-in-one combination" of activist elements in the party, and among students and teachers. [We must] sort out the bourgeois monopoly in science, field by field, and achieve our own breakthrough. The director of the Research Institute on Traditional Medicine in the Academy of Sciences, Zhao Chenggu, was able to extract herbs (from snake root grass [*shegen cao*]) for treating high blood pressure, but all along he refused to tell others [how]. Young scientists refused to admit defeat, and after a few days of struggling, they got it as well. Therefore we should pay special attention to young scientists so as to isolate these professors. This is a fierce kind of struggle, so it may take a few years.

Now, on to the importance of ideology: Ideology is the reflection of objective reality. It concerns itself with the [economic] base and serves that base. Reform the system of rules and regulations. Holding conferences is making ideology; [this] Beidaihe conference is making ideology. At last year's [CC's] Third Plenum, this year's Nanning conference, the Chengdu conference, and the Party Congress, [we] put forward the slogan of doing away with superstition; it's had quite an impact. The Great leap Forward was possible only because of this. Incorrect reflection of objective reality is very harmful. Eight-legged essays[77] and the thoughts of Confucius have been passed down for thousands of years; there are people who'd eat the shit and dirt the Dalai Lama offers[78]—idiotic in the extreme. Zhang Daoling had every worshipper donate 5 *dou* of rice; [anyone] donating 5 *dou* of rice **[312]** could then eat [for free]. [But] the Celestial Master Zhang, introduced to [the people of] Jiangsu, changed for the worse.[79] There's a pattern in the consumption of grain: Both big and small eaters should eat 3 *dan*, 6 *dou* a year. Let them eat to their heart's content. Xue Rengui ate 1 *dou* of rice every day, but this is rare.[80] In running the public mess halls, we can [let the people] take [food] to eat at home. The provision of free meals can be gradually adopted. [We won't] decide on it for the time being. Whether or not [we] adopt it in 1959, [we'll] see next year, and also whether clothing can be free, too. Eating without payment may not have to wait until the third FYP.[81] The dormitories for workers and staff should be arranged in proper proportions. Large dormitories are better than small houses. The vestiges of bourgeois right cannot be completely

[77]A tradition of classical scholarship, this type of essay had long been excoriated by Mao as the reflection of bureaucratism; see *SW3*, pp. 50, 53–68.

[78]Even in a closed party gathering, this slighting reference to the Dalai Lama at a time when he was still formally in good standing with the PRC government is unusual.

[79]Zhang Daoling, also known as Zhang Ling, was a Daoist priest in the 2nd century AD who founded the so-called "Southern School." He personified the transformation of ancient Daoist principles and doctrine into a religion with a magic-making priesthood. Regarded as a miracle worker, he came to be called "Celestial Master" *(Tian Shi)*; but his custom of asking dues in rice also brought him the sobriquet "rice-thief" and his teachings "The Way of the Five Pecks of Rice." See Holmes Welch, *Taoism: The Parting of the Way* (Boston, Beacon Press, 1957), pp. 113–4.

[80]The Tang general, Xue Rengui, was said to have been a great trencherman; see also Text 3, n. 48. Mao's point appears to be that with grain production increasing mightily, even if rationing were ended, individual grain consumption would not increase very much except in rare cases.

[81]The 3rd FYP was due to start in 1963.

eradicated; [therefore] university professors can eat better than students. Henan cultivates 8 billion square meters of land and doubles its grain output. If Henan can do it, the whole country should do it.

Next year will be the tenth anniversary of the founding of [our] state. [Should we] propagandize this in a big way or in small way? Since we'll be propagandizing for the Chinese people, and to motivate them, we need not consider impressing foreign countries. Actually foreign countries will be affected. If [we propagandize] in a big way, should we invite foreigners or not? [If yes, then] how many should [we] invite?

When [you] return from this conference, tell your comrades in the army, officers must serve as soldiers one month a year, beginning with a few officers. Once someone starts, others will want to do it. Once there's one October Revolution, the whole world wants to make revolution; once one APC produces 1,000 catties [of grain] per *mou* [of land], the entire nation will want to do the same. [After all,] does the minority obey the majority or the majority obey the minority? It's always been the majority obeying the minority, because the minority [has always] reflected the opinion of the majority. When you came to this conference, wasn't it because of a notice from Deng XX?[82] Isn't this the majority obeying the minority? Darwin's theory of evolution and Copernicus' theory of the solar system were each created by a single individual; others all followed. Marx [and] Engels both reflected objective laws or the opinions of the majority. The formula for protein has not yet been discovered, [but] the 167 types of reactive dyes have. The world's first, marsh gas, is H_4C; farts are H_2S; gypsum is calcium sulphate. From this perspective, the opinion of the minority reflects the opinion of the majority.

Xushui county in Hebei province is working on militarization, combatization, and disciplinization.[83] These three slogans may or may not be raised. Organization need not necessarily conform to regiments, battalions, companies, platoons and squads; brigades, detach-

---

[82]Deng XX: Deng Xiaoping as party General Secretary would have been formally responsible for issuing the notices ordering the attendance of officials.

[83]This slogan in expanded form was altered to "Organize along military lines, work as if fighting a battle, live in the collective way"; see Kuo, *Communist Terminology,* p. 432; *Hongqi,* No. 7 (1958), p. 15; T. A. Hsia, *The Commune in Retreat as Evidenced in Terminology and Semantics* (Berkeley, Center for Chinese Studies, 1964), pp. 29–35. Despite the key nature of this slogan, Beijing translators did not agree on an English version at first: cf., official trans-

ments, and teams will also do.[84] Actually it's a problem of labor organization and democratization. Imperialism has spread rumors about this development, but we're not afraid of it. Coercion and orders, of course, are not good, but a bit of coercion is also necessary. This is discipline. Your coming to Beidaihe for this conference [313] is a case in point. War communism in the Soviet Union was a system of collecting surplus grain.[85] We've had twenty-two years of military tradition, [and] the supply system is our war communism. [If] we practice communism among our cadres, not including the common people, then they will be affected. Engels said that many things start in the army, and indeed they do. [When] we went from the cities to the countryside, we united with the semi-proletariat to form the party and the army. We ate from the same pot, no deference, no salaries. This was the communist supply system. Since coming into the cities, [we've] acquired an inferiority complex. The old ways no longer worked. [We] want woolen garments, [we want] to shave, and we want the cadres to become intellectualized. The salary system has negated the supply system. Garments are divided into three colors and grain into five grades, and we have followed the mass line insufficiently in the cities. From liberation until 1952 it was still all right. The years 1953–1956 mainly reflected China's bourgeois ideology. The second [problem] has been our indiscriminate imitating of the Soviet Union. In the past we were compelled to have bourgeois advisors. We were unaware of the concept of bourgeois right. [We have] hundreds of millions of peasants, 7 million industrial workers, over 20 million cadres and teaching personnel. As the sea of the bourgeoisie has risen up to our chests, it has drowned some. Liu Shaotang has become a rightist, [but] Yao Wenyuan's not bad, better than Liushahe.[86]

---

lations of *Hongqi* and *RMRB* editorials in *Communist China, 1955–1959: Policy Documents with Analysis* (Cambridge, Harvard Univ. Press), pp. 458, 462. Mao would again mention these "three transformations" in his 6 November speech to the Zhengzhou conference, see Text 18, n. 6.

[84]"Brigades" and "teams" (here *da dui* and *xiao dui*) were the terms eventually universalized.
[85]"War communism" lasted from 1918 to 1921.
[86]Liu Shaotang was a prominent young communist writer who fell from grace because of criticisms he made during the Hundred Flowers; see Merle Goldman, *Literary Dissent in Communist China* (Cambridge, Harvard Univ. Press, 1967), esp. pp. 194, 231–6. Yao Wenyuan, the future bugler of the Cultural Revolution, appears to have caught Mao's eye during

Once the draft Resolution on the People's Communes is issued, every county [must] conduct tests at one or two selected points. It is not necessary to get [them] fully under way immediately. Neither do you have to start with regiments, battalions, companies, platoons, and squads. [But] there must be leadership and [we must] proceed with the planning in a systematic manner. It won't do not to start now; that would be to commit an error. The increase in the size of private plots, livestock being raised mainly by private individuals, big cooperatives having to establish small cooperatives, and so on, were concessions to the rich peasants. It was all right to go through this stage; it was not an error of principle. In the conditions of that time [such measures] even had a certain positive significance.[87] [But] now it has again been negated. One or two pigs may be raised by private individuals. The bigger the commune, the better. The characteristics of the people's communes are one, big, and two, public; most important is that many cooperatives combine into one big commune. The several comments in *Socialist Upsurge in the Countryside*[88] said big cooperatives were good; mountain areas could establish big cooperatives, too, [in order to] develop a diversified economy and to ensure all-round development. [However,] establishing slightly small cooperatives to begin with also had its advantages. The youth and women are happy about the [new] wage system. The rationale of increasing private plots and so on were all proposed by the [party's] Rural Work Department.[89] As early as 1955 I recommended establishing big cooperatives. Establish 15,000 to 25,000 communes nationwide, [averaging] 5,000 to 6,000 households or 20,000 to 30,000 people per commune—rather large and convenient for running industry, agricul-

---

the Anti-Rightist Campaign; see *Origins* 1, p. 396; see also Lars Ragvald, *Yao Wen-yuan as a Literary Critic and Theorist: The Emergence of Chinese Zhdanovism* (Univ. of Stockholm published doctoral dissertation, 1978). Liushahe was a Sichuanese poet purged in the Anti-Rightist Campaign. Mao had mentioned him in his Hundred Flowers talks; see Text 1, n. 5.
[87] Mao has been describing the measures adopted to achieve peaceful collectivization in the early and mid 1950s.
[88] The full title of this collection of essays on collectivization edited by Mao and published in January 1956 was *Socialist Upsurge in China's Countryside (Zhongguo nongcun de shehuizhuyi gaochao)*. Mao seems to be concerned here to demonstrate the consistency between his views of late 1955, when he completed his editorial notes to this book, and August 1958.
[89] This is a dig at the then head of the department, Deng Zihui, who was criticized in 1955 for being too cautious on collectivization.

ture, commerce, education, **[314]** [and] military affairs [side by side], as well as farming, forestry, animal husbandry, sideline production and fisheries. With this way [of doing things], I think in the future a few large cities will be dispersed; residential areas of 20,000 to 30,000 people will have everything; villages will become small cities where the majority of philosophers and scientists will be assigned. Every large commune will have highways constructed, wider roads of cement or asphalt, with no trees planted [alongside] so that airplanes can land—they will be airports. In the future, every province should have a couple of hundred airplanes, averaging two planes per township. Large provinces will set up their own factories for aircraft construction.[90]

Each area need not implement communization according to Xushui [county's] methods. Each area [should] have the three slogans (militarization, combatization, disciplinization). The general regulations of five Star Commune[91] will be published in *Red Flag*, [and] in the main they can be followed; each area should use them as a reference [in their own] implementation.

30 AUGUST, MORNING

The people's communes have been set up as a result of the masses' initiative; it wasn't us who advocated it. We advocated uninterrupted revolution, eradicating superstition, liberating thought, and daring to think, daring to speak, daring to act; [and] the masses have risen [to the occasion]. [We] did not anticipate this at the Nanning conference, the Chengdu conference, or the second session of the Eighth Party Congress. The spontaneity of the masses has always been an element inherent in communism. First there was utopian socialism, classical materialism, and dialectics; then came the summation [of these theories] by Marx and others. Our people's communes have been developed on the basis of the APCs; they've not come into being from nowhere. We need to understand this clearly in order to system-

---

[90]This utopian vision seems redolent of Sun Yat-sen's earlier visions of the industrialization of China; see C. Martin Wilbur, *Sun Yat-sen, Frustrated Patriot* (New York, Columbia Univ. Press, 1976), pp. 23–6. In addition, it was clearly the source of Mao's colleagues' extravagant claims; see, for instance, Tan Zhenlin's description of communism in *Origins* 2, p. 84.
[91]*Wu xing gongshe* must be a misprint for *Weixing Gongshe* (Sputnik Commune) whose regulations were indeed published in *Hongqi*, No. 7 (1958), see n. 52.

atize this question. The characteristics of the people's communes are one, big, and two, public. [They have] vast areas of land and abundant resources [as well as] a large population; [they can] combine industry, agriculture, commerce, education, and military affairs, as well as in farming, forestry, animal husbandry, sideline production and fisheries—being "big" is terrific. [With] many people, there's lots of power. [We say] public because they contain more socialism than do the APCs, [and they will] gradually eradicate the vestiges of capitalism. For example, the eradication of private plots and private livestock rearing, the running of public mess halls, nurseries, and tailoring groups so that all working women can be liberated. They will implement a wage system and agricultural factories [in which] every single man, woman, old person, and youth receives his own wage, in contrast to the former [system of] distribution to the head of the household. Direct payment of wages is much welcomed by the youth and by women. This eradicates the patriarchal system and the system of bourgeois rights.[92] Another advantage of [communes'] being public is that labor efficiency can be raised higher than in APCs.

Currently there are 700,000 APCs nationwide. It would be best to establish big APCs of 10,000 people or 10,000 households. **[315]** Henan advocates 2,500 households or so in each; that's all right, too. This is a new problem, but once you disseminate the news, explain the reasons, [then] perhaps in only a few months—through the autumn, winter, and spring—it could be accomplished, more or less. Of course, it will still require a transition period to achieve a wage system and free meals, perhaps a year; for some places perhaps three years. In [our] draft resolution there's a passage [about its taking] one to two or four to five years or even a bit longer to make the transition from the system of collective ownership to the system of communist ownership—almost the same as in the factories—that is, public ownership of all eating, clothing, and housing. The Soviet Union still encourages the construction of houses by private individuals. We will eliminate private housing in the future.

The problem of making things green, of afforestation: beautifica-

---

[92]Mao's pro-feminist ideals for ending patriarchal domination via the commune system did not come to pass. His comments here fall squarely in the utopian tradition of Chinese thought.

tion of the landscape, the cities, and countryside—all [should look like Zhongshan Park or the Summer Palace. It's not good that Zhongshan Park does not produce grain. China has just started its construction. [We] must think how the construction can be done more rationally and better. Some say, "In the cities, unlike in the countryside, factories take up too much land." In China there are 3 *mou* of land per person, but 2 *mou* would be sufficient for us. [If] the production per *mou* is raised in a few years, [then] one-third [of the land] can be used for planting trees, one-third for grain, and one-third allowed to lie fallow. If the production per *mou* is 1,000 catties, as much as today's "satellites,"[93] [then] one *mou* will equal 40 *mou* or 80 to 90 *mou* [in output], so why then plant so much? Planting trees must be done in a planned way. Sowing the land must be planned. The French have made their streets, houses, and boulevards very beautiful. If capitalism can do it, why can't we? [We] should do it in a more orderly manner. In an antithetical couplet praising the West Lake, Kang Youwei[94] said, "I have not found gardens like this, touring the four continents." Actually, why tour the four continents? Once we start the greening process, [you] will be able to tour the whole country—why must you visit the West Lake? In the West Lake the water is shallow; the trees aren't good either. Housing must be arranged well. It can't be done in a big way this year. [We] can make a start on a few this year, some next year. If [we can] produce XX catties of grain [per capita] (perhaps XX catties this year, double that next year), then we can go ahead with our plans for transforming [places] into parks, making things green, animal husbandry, and housing, and so forth. I took a look in Hebei and Henan to see what they meant by making things green. How can it be called afforestation without trees? True afforestation, I think, can only be carried out in a big way when [we produce] several thousand catties of grain per capita so that one-third of the land can be taken out for planting trees. Agriculture, forestry, and animal husbandry are interrelated and interactive.

There are still many problems about the people's communes, as yet unknown, so that continued study is still needed. There is already [a set of] regulations; the twenty-four articles of Henan's

---

[93]Mao is referring here to trailblazing production areas rather than to the Weixing or Sputnik Commune.

[94]For Kang Youwei, see Text 1, n. 22.

Sputnik Commune, its "constitution." Once it is **[316]** published, many will respond to the call throughout the nation. Can the people's communes make the transition from collective ownership to ownership by the whole people in the next two or three years (next year and the year after)? As for implementing state ownership of land, the wage system, and establishing agricultural factories, there's a document that says the transition to communism will start from the third FYP; I added [or the] fourth or fifth FYP. One document says next year will be the decisive year. This is well said. To double grain [production] again, to produce XX to XX tons of steel and to strive for XX tons, that's a big battle. [We] still can't rest; the machines can't rest. There are still four months [left in] this year. I made a mistake: it would have been better to have paid attention to [this matter] a month earlier. [I] raised the subject on 19 June, but failed to [suggest] any concrete measures. Everyone went off to work on the plans. Their enthusiasm is worthy, but [attention] to production this year has slackened. I didn't do well; the responsibility is mine, not yours. From 21 August there were still nineteen weeks or 133 days [left in the year], not a day more, not a day less. Now another ten days have passed. [It's] quite dangerous. [We] must have emergency mobilization. I have doubts about whether we can fulfill [our targets.] I'm a "tide-watcher."[95] Can we [fulfill our targets] by 1 January next year or not— I'm up in the air about it. If we fail to fulfill [our targets], then, one, the wrong subject was raised in the wrong way and, two, the work was not paid close enough attention to, and those were my mistakes. When the Ministry of the Metallurgical Industry estimated in its briefing report a production figure of 9 million tons, I said, "Be quick about it! Double it—why procrastinate?" I asked many people about producing 11 million tons [of steel]; they all said it was possible, there was hope. [The target for] 1956 was even more solid [but] the actual increase in production was not much, only XX catties [of grain].[96] Whether it's

---

[95]Mao is being ironic. This was the term he had used as the 2nd session of the 8th Party Congress to criticize those who were reluctant to commit themselves one way or the other on the GLF; see *Origins* 2, p. 57.

[96]This sudden comparison of the reliability of the 1958 steel target with the setback to the 1956 grain target seems strange, and possibly the editor has mistaken *dun* (tons) for *jin* (catties). On the other hand, Mao had hoped for a breakthrough in grain production in 1956 to consolidate and justify collectivization, and the failure to achieve it may have rankled and made him worry that the GLF would not achieve a breakthrough either. Mao is also, of course, safeguarding himself from appearing wildly optimistic.

realistic or not [to aim for] 11 million tons of steel this year, I have doubts. It only counts when we see it. "[The work in] iron and steel is not yet completed. Comrades should continue to exert themselves."[97] Next year [we'll produce] XX tons, increasing another XX tons the year after; struggle hard for three years [i.e., 1958–1960] to obtain XX tons—then the foundation will be laid. In a further two years, that is by 1962, [if we] produce XX to XX tons of steel, [then we'd] be close to XX tons. How many tons of steel [should we have] for a population of 700 million? One ton per capita, I think; make it 700 million tons. Grain production could be half the figure for steel; make it 3,500 billion catties.[98] Grain produce should be diversified, it shouldn't always be the good old sweet potato.

The first precondition for communism is plenty; the second is to have a communist spirit. Once an order is issued, everyone automatically goes to their work, idlers are few or none. Communism does not differentiate between superiors and subordinates. We have a twenty-two year history of war communism, with no salaries, [which is] different from the Soviet Union. In the Soviet Union [it's] called the system of surplus grain collection. We didn't [317] practice that. Ours was called the supply system, [in which] army and civilians, officers and men are equal, [and there are also] the three great democracies.[99] Originally we divided up the leftovers from the mess and had small subsidies. After we came into the cities, it was said that the supply system was backward, guerrillaism, a rural work style, [and] that it couldn't boost initiative, nor stimulate progress. [They] wanted to establish a salary system. [They] endured for three years, [and] in 1952 the salary system was established. [They] said bourgeois ranks and rights and such were very fine and called our old supply system a backward method, a guerrilla practice that affected activism. In effect [they] turned the supply system into a system of bourgeois right, [thereby] promoting bourgeois ideology. Did initiating the 25,000 *li* Long March, the Land Revolution and the War of Liberation rely on salaries? Two to three million people during the anti-

[97]This appears to be an adaptation of a passage from Sun Yat-sen's will: "The work of the revolution is not yet completed. Comrades should continue to exert themselves."
[98]This figure translates into 1,759 million tons by 1962, which compares with a 1957 production of 185 million tons and a Beidaihe projection of 350 million tons for 1958. It is not clear whether the editor mistook the figures or Mao mistook the possibilities.
[99]Democracy in military affairs, politics, and economics.

Japanese war, from four to five million during the War of Liberation lived a life of war communism, no Sundays [off]—didn't [they all] risk their lives? The party, the administration, the army, the civilians—numbering several million—all were together with the masses, supporting the administration and loving the people. The party, the administration, and the army under a unified leadership had nothing "to spend," but [with] unity between officers and men, and between the army and civilians, and the support for the administration and love for the people, [we] drove off the Japanese devils and defeated Chiang Kai-shek. Nor did [we] have anything "to spend" when we fought the United States. Can it be said [we did all this] because we handed out salaries? Now [we] have something "to spend," issuing salaries according to rank, dividing [them into] generals, field rank officers, and junior officers; but some of them have not even been in battle. Whether or not they're any good has yet to be tested. The result is divorce from the masses; the men don't love their officers, and the masses don't love their cadres. Because of this we're not much different from the Nationalist party: our garments are in three colors, our food is divided into five grades, even the desks and chairs of our offices are ranked; [and so] the workers and peasants don't like us, saying, "You're officials—party officials, government officials, military officials, commercial officials"—so many officials, how can there be no "isms"?[100] Too many bureaucratic airs, too little politics, so bureaucratism emerges. Since the Rectification [Campaign] we have been rectifying bureaucratic airs and putting politics in command. [Since then] the cases of competing for rank and scrambling for special treatment have not been many. I think [we should] get rid of this thing. The salary system does not have to be abolished immediately, because there are professors. But [we should] prepare for it in one or two years. Once the people's communes are established, [this] will force us gradually to abolish the salary system. Since we came into the cities, [we have been] under the influence of the bourgeoisie. [When] we launched a campaign, it was a really Marxist practice and a democratic work style, [but] they branded us [as using] "rural work style" and "guerrilla practices." "Guerrilla practices" are capitalists' words. [It was] probably during the period from

---

[100]Mao is presumably referring to the three sins combatted in the previous year's Rectification Campaign: bureaucratism, sectarianism, and subjectivism.

1953 to mid 1957[101] when they did things together with the bourgeoisie, local tyrants, and evil gentry [that they began to] straighten
their clothes, sit properly, and study the bourgeois style—having hair-
cuts and shaves, shaving three times a day—all learned from the same
source. Just after Liberation, **[318]** in 1950 and 1951 when we were
performing Yangge,[102] we prevailed over the bourgeoisie. They dared
not say anything. Later the Yangge became unpopular, [it was] said
there was nothing to it. Mei Lanfang[103] appeared; [the opera] *Yu
Zhou Feng*[104] prevailed over the Yangge, and shaving had to be done
once every three days. What was truly Marxist stuff became unpopular. Now it's back again: "rural work style" and "guerrilla practice"
are Marxist work styles. Thus, speak of equality, the equality
between officers and men, and between the army and civilians, and
no Sundays [off]; the common people say, "The old Eighth Route
[Army] has come back." They are seeing the Eighth Route Army of
the past again.

I asked Comrade Chen Boda to compile a book, *Marx, Engels,
Lenin and Stalin on Military Affairs.* I have read one or two chapters.
One of the quotations says that from ancient times many things
started in the army. Our communism, as well, started in the army.
China's party is a very special party. Through several decades of battle, it always practiced communism. During the eight years of the
anti-Japanese war and four years of the war of self-defense, the masses
witnessed our hardships [and] supported us at the front. There were
no wages; [they] brought their own food. In battle people died; even
so they supported us the way they did. Some say [that] egalitarianism
produces idlers. In the past twenty-two years, how many idlers have
been produced? I haven's seen many idlers. Only grade-ism[105] produces idlers. What are the reasons? Primarily, putting politics in command, class struggle, beating Japan, beating the reactionaries, sharing

[101]In mid 1957 the bourgeoisie was counterattacked in the Anti-Rightist Campaign.
[102]Yangge were dramatized combinations of folk songs and peasant dances used by the
CCP in Yan'an in the 1940s. For the significance of this dramatic form in propaganda and
its importance for Mao, see David Holm, "Folk Art as Propaganda: The *Yangge* Movement
in Yan'an," in Bonnie S. McDougall, ed., *Popular Chinese Literature and Performing Arts in
the People's Republic of China 1948–1979* (Berkeley, Univ. of California Press, 1984), pp. 3–35.
[103]For Mei Lanfang see Text 3, n. 66.
[104]One of the most popular plays in Mei Lanfang's Peking Opera repertoire. In the act usually performed, there is much dancing, for which he was widely acclaimed.
[105]I.e., worrying about one's rank in the cadre scale.

a common goal, and suffering on behalf of the majority of the people. Now [we] struggle with imperialism abroad, and at home our main struggle is with nature. Our goals are also clear. We're now engaged in production and construction. Whom do our more than 10 million cadres throughout the land serve? [They serve] the happiness of [all] the people, not just a few. Today, if one invents something, one is given 100 yuan, which in the end will produce laziness and strife, but not activism.[106] Were the many creations and inventions of the past bought with money? Piece-rate wages are not a good system. I don't believe the adoption of the supply system will make people lazy, inventions fewer, or activism lower. Because decades of experience prove otherwise. The sources [of our problems] are twofold: one is socialism, which has been borrowed from Elder Brother [the Soviet Union], and the second is capitalism, which is home born and bred.

In some places the people's commune have adopted a military organization with divisions, regiments, battalions, and companies, and in other places they have not; but "Organize along military lines, work as if fighting a battle, live in a disciplined way,"[107] this three-transformations slogan is very good. This is a great industrial army, capable of increasing production, improving life, providing rest; capable of learning; and capable of engaging in military democracy. It seems as soon as [we] talk of the military, we just exclude democracy, but democracy—namely the three great democracies in military affairs, in politics, and in economics—originated precisely in the military. In battle everyone helps each other. [When] officers oppress soldiers in our army, it's a violation of our discipline, it's a disgrace. The "three transformations" in the communes are very good. In the past few years we have learned this stuff, first from the bourgeoisie which is indigenous, second from the proletariat—our Soviet Elder Brother. Luckily, it hasn't been long, so the roots are not deep; revolution is

[106]Mao's contempt is given added bite by the relative paltriness of the sum he quotes. In fact, when the Academy of Sciences set up a system of science prizes in 1955, the sums involved—10,000 yuan for first prize, 5,000 yuan for a second, and 2,000 yuan for a third—were extremely attractive by comparison with a 350 yuan salary range for the highest paid scientists. See Richard P. Suttmeier, *Research and Revolution* (Lexington, Lexington Books, 1979), pp. 61–2.

[107]This is the full version of the slogan mentioned by Mao in his speech on the afternoon of 21 August; see n. 83. However, Mao (or his editor?) is still referring to discipline rather than collectivism to describe the desirable life style.

still easy to make. Since [the 1957] Rectification, various kinds of rules and regulations have almost all been discarded, [and] much of the bourgeois stuff has been jettisoned. This time the army is going to hold a conference to eliminate "spending."[108] We've written a resolution on cadres participating in manual labor: the members of the Center must [do] a month a year; other cadres will [need to do] more, excluding the old and infirm. How can it be as little as a month when you plant an experimental field? A division commander in Yunnan went down to be an [ordinary] soldier in a company. I think many "commanders"—army commanders, division commanders, and so on—all ought to serve as soldiers for at least a month [a year]. In the first year, it'd be best [to do it] for two months. They must obey the commands of squad leaders and platoon leaders. Every year you command the others for eleven months—why can't you let others command you for one month? Some were [ordinary] soldiers once, but have not been for many years. Now they should become soldiers again for a while. Civilian cadres should participate in manual labor for at least one month a year. During the construction of the Ming Tombs Reservoir, even many ministers participated in manual labor. Learn agriculture one year and industry another. Learning them in turn, one is bound to master these two skills. Militarizing the people's communes is not militarization in a bourgeois manner. There is discipline and democracy; the interrelationship is one between colleagues, persuasion rather than coercion. Manual labor needs strict discipline.

As the whole people [begins] to run industry, a certain amount of chaos has temporarily appeared, [because] the boundaries [of authority] are not yet clearly drawn. At this conference, industry, agriculture, commerce, education, and the army have all been topics; but the priority is industry, the whole party and the whole people running industry. From now on the [provincial] first secretaries will be enlisted in the field of industry. In the past we enlisted them in the field of agriculture; [we] used agriculture to repress industry, checked [industry's] king. Agriculture has taken off; it's on track, [but] not industry as yet. Industry must be the focus. Some say, "Sleep on the

---

[108]Presumably Mao means the abolition of wages and salaries and the readoption of the supply system in the PLA.

work sites and sleep beside the machines: Only that way will it get
off the ground; it won't work if we do not sleep beside the
machines." The three provinces in the Northeast focused on industry
in the past, but they have not done well in agriculture. The Northeast should pay attention to industry, on the one hand, and pay attention to agriculture, on the other. Other provinces and autonomous
regions must focus on industry. Next year is the year of the decisive
[320] battle and the most important thing is to direct industry, particularly steel and machinery. With steel and machinery, digging coal,
producing electricity, everything will be easy. They are called "Marshals" for a reason.[109] We must grasp this and actively, not inatten-
tively. When we are tested in the future, it will be on this. The six
[rules of] discipline [are]: first, warning; second, demerit; third, relief
from duty while remaining in office; fourth, dismissal; fifth, probation within the party; sixth, expulsion from the party, but without
imprisonment as imprisonment wastes labor power.[110] These rules
are all a war of nerves, [we] can't do without them. They are penal in
nature. Nine of our fingers stand for explaining, relying on politics,
and conscience; [only] one finger is for discipline. Marxism doesn't
depend on punishments. [Once you] depend on punishments to get
the job done, [you] commit errors. Our party has consistently relied
on persuasion, education, as well as class struggle. For instance, XX,
XXX, Gu Dacun,[111] Sun Zuobin[112] and whatcha-ma-call-it Labalay-
efu[113] in Xinjiang, in all only a few dozen people, such a small minority, just one finger of ten. If you can't persuade them, they deserve

[109]The military title, *yuanshuai* or "marshal," was given to priority products during the
GLF.
[110]See n. 40, above.
[111]Gu Dacun had been exposed as a rightist at the 2nd session of the 8th Party Congress,
but was allowed to retain his CC membership, partly as a result of Mao's intervention; see
Klein and Clark 1, pp. 449–50; *Origins* 2, pp. 358–9.
[112]Sun Zuobin, a senior official in Northwest China in the early 1950s had been dismissed
from the party earlier in 1958 for promoting "local nationalism;" see Klein and Clark 2, pp.
780–2.
[113]Labalayefu: jibberish which sounds like a Uygur name. Possibly, Sepollayev (Saifula-
yefu), party secretary of the Xinjiang Uygur Autonomous Region 1956–8 and today one of
the Vice-Chairmen of the Region's NPC Standing Committee. Sepolloyev at that time
favored USSR-style Soviet "Republics"–perhaps too decentralized a plan after Gao Gang's
"mutiny" attempt in 1953–4. Mao often confused Uygur names, as in his July 1957 speech
at Qingdao where, according to a Uygur from China, Zhou Enlai had to correct him on one.

punishment. Exhort and warn [them first]; in emergency cases there could be summary dismissal. XX[114] is a rightist in the army (but not counted among the rightists) XXX is a local rightist; Wang Ming[115] is also a rightist. Why elect Wang Ming to the Central Committee? Because he's a senior party member, [he's] worked for many years, [we] can't let him off the hook so easily. He must serve [on the Central Committee]. You don't want to serve; I want you to serve. [Don't think] everything will be all right if you don't serve as a member of the Central Committee. His modus operandi is to take sick whenever there is a conference. Letting him be [a member] has its benefits. It's also good for XXX to be a member. Either he changes or not, [in which case] sooner or later he'll be expelled [from the party]. This is the relationship between persuasion and discipline.

The problem of life and death, not the "death" of corpses, but inflexible and flexible control. It won't do not to have [this kind of] "death" in this world. It is unacceptable for our steel target of 11 million tons to be short a single ton. This is "inflexibility." Next year's [target of] XXX to XX tons: [we should] strive for XX tons, of which XX tons are "inflexible" or "inflexible steel." Beyond that, XX to XX tons are flexible, placed under the disposal of the localities. Some comrades fear there will be no flexibility. Complete flexibility won't work; there must be inflexibility as well as flexibility, unified planning and decentralized management. All levels [should] run industry, and all people [should] run industry. There are priorities; there are branches as well as leaves. Only when a tree has a main trunk can there be branches and leaves. Human beings rely on their backbone, they are vertebrates and superior animals. Dogs are superior animals quite capable of understanding human nature, but the only thing is that they don't understand Marxism, they don't understand steel production—more or less like capitalists.

[321] [Our] next conference will be held two-and-a-half months from now. We'll hold a small conference in mid November in the South. It won't be as long as this one, because we still won't be able to

---

[114]Just possibly this XX refers to a young writer in the General Political Department of the PLA, Bai Hua, whose purge as a rightist in 1957 was mitigated by the intervention of Marshal He Long and General Xiao Hua; see Richard Kraus, "Bai Hua: The Political Authority of a Writer," in Carol Lee Hamrin and Timothy Cheek, eds., *China's Establishment Intellectuals* (Armonk, N.Y., M. E. Sharpe, 1986), p. 187.
[115]See Text 1, no. 10.

summarize [our work] then. After October there will still be about a month's time [before the next conference]; there's still time to grasp matters.

I would like to ask that the book, *Marx, Engels, Lenin and Stalin on Communism* (Stalin didn't do very well), be printed in every province and widely distributed for everyone to read. It's very enlightening, although there are still some inadequacies, because of the limitations imposed by conditions in [the authors'] times. They had little experience, so naturally their views are vague and inexplicit. Don't think the ancestors all fart fragrantly and fart no foul farts. [When you] talk about the future, there must inevitably be some vague spots. The Soviet Union has had forty-one years of experience; we've had thirty-one years. We should break free of superstition.

On eliminating the four pests:[116] We can focus on this during the National Day holidays, the New Year, and the Lunar New Year. The less we have of these four pests, the better for us; because these four pests harm the people and directly affect the health of the people. [We] must wipe out various kinds of diseases on a large scale. At one place in Hangzhou, only one person took sick last year. The rate of attendance [at work] exceeded 90 percent. [When] the physicians have nothing to do, they can go till the fields and do research. The day China eliminates the four pests [we] should hold a celebration. [It] should be recorded in history books. The capitalist states have not done it; those so-called civilized [states] still have many flies and mosquitoes.

[116]See Text 15, n. 2.

Talks at the First Zhengzhou Conference

6–10 NOVEMBER 1958

[173] 6 NOVEMBER 1958

We've been going at it for only two months and have already achieved something. If next year we go at it another year, we'll have the knack. For next year the most important things are to take steel as the main link, the three big marshals, and the two advance guards.[1]

What is meant by "completing the construction of socialism"? What is the "transition to communism"? Definitions are needed.

Source: 13:173–95. An alternate version (2:195–214) has expurgated certain names and numbers found in the primary source. Shorter versions are found in 9:181–4, and *Wansui* (1969), pp. 247–51, from which extracts were translated in *JPRS* 61269-1 (1974), pp. 129–32.
[1]Marshals: grain, steel, machinery. Advance guards: railways, electric power.

Three years of hard struggle, and then twelve more years, fifteen years is the transition to communism. Don't publish that, but it won't be good if we don't do it.

[174] How long will the transition from collective ownership to ownership by the whole people take? Three, four, five, six years or a bit more—isn't that a bit short? Or is it too long? Sometimes [I] feel it's too long, at other times worry that it's [too] short. [I'm] more often worried that it's too short. When will the people's communes be able to reach a [level] akin to the Anshan Steel Works?[2] Is it possible to transform agriculture into a factory? [When] products and accumulation can be allocated—we are not going to allocate accumulation completely, but products that have to be transferred should be transferred unconditionally—then it can be considered ownership by the whole people. Henan province talks about four years [for the transition to communism]. That's perhaps a bit short; double it, eight years. Fan county [in Shandong province] talks about making the transition to communism after two years of hard struggle.

One has to look at the things Stalin wrote. His strong point is that he alone talks about a socialist economy, but his greatest shortcoming is that he sets up a rigid framework, saying that the *kolkhozy*[3] are willing to exchange commodities but won't go for allocations [of goods and capital by planning authorities]. This was because [he] did not want uninterrupted revolution, but wanted to consolidate the socialist order. The Russian peasants cannot be that selfish; it cannot be that they don't want uninterrupted revolution. Russia has built up a socialist order, but this type of order cannot be consolidated. With us it's the other way round. We disrupt a part of the socialist order; the supply system [i.e., payment in kind] is what disrupts that order.

Public grain, accumulation and labor power are allocable; they are owned by the whole people. A million soldiers went south of the [Yangtze] river—why can't we similarly allocate people to [manual] labor? For the moment allocations can only be partial; this cannot be done for whole provinces or the entire country. For instance, Anguo plans to give 500 pounds of wheat to each person in Fuping next

---

[2]Anshan Steel Works: the major steel complex owned by the state (or "the whole people"), located in the Northeast.
[3]*Kolkhozy:* collective farms—Mao calls them collective villages—in the Soviet Union.

year;[4] that kind of thing has never before happened [anywhere] in the world. For allocation there must be feasibility as well as necessity; one shouldn't allocate disruptively. Qin Shihuang [conscripted and] allocated 700,000 people to build a tomb for him; as a result [his dynasty] was toppled. Sui Yangdi also fell because of the disruptive allocation of the labor force.[5]

When King Wu attacked Zhou, didn't he [carry out the] three transformations [*san hua*]? From the oldest times on there were three transformations, and they started with military affairs.[6]

How many years are needed for the transition from collective ownership to ownership by the whole people? Will four years do? Henan says four years; Fan county says two. The standard is the Anshan Steel Works. In Anshan, apart from the capital depreciation of 7,200 yuan, the remaining [value produced per worker] is 10,800 yuan [of which] the worker gets 800 yuan, and accumulates 10,000 yuan for the state. That's the way we should allocate.

(XX: We have to mechanize and diversify the economy.)

[175] [Chairman:] This transition seemed immensely difficult to Stalin and he didn't set a deadline [specifying] how many years would be needed. This is the first transition [i.e., that from collective ownership to ownership by the whole people]. The second transition is that from "To each according to his work" to "To each according to his need." Now we have already begun to prepare for the second tran-

---

[4]Anguo and Fuping are two counties, fairly close to each other, in Hebei province. Fuping is more mountainous and poorer.

[5]Qin Shihuang unified the warring Chinese states into a single empire in 221 BC, but the Qin dynasty collapsed under his son only fifteen years later. Yangdi was the second of the two major emperors of the Sui dynasty, which reunified the Chinese empire in AD 589 but then collapsed after only twenty-nine years. Both the Qin and the Sui dynasties have traditionally epitomized oppressive dynasties. The construction of the Great Wall in the case of the Qin and the Grand Canal in the case of the Sui are seen as the principal examples of their brutal use of mass labor.

[6]King Wu overthrew Zhou Xin, the last, wicked ruler of the Shang dynasty in 1122 BC. The "three transformations" (*san hua*) refers to the GLF slogan "Organize along military lines, work as if fighting a battle, live in the collective way" or "Organization militarized, action martialized, and life collectivized" (*zuzhi junshihua, xingdong zhandouhua shenghuo jitihua*). See Text 17, n. 83. It is not clear how Mao links these transformations to King Wu, except that the latter did overthrow Zhou Xin by military means.

sition, one doesn't have to pay for one's food. The Soviet Union also brags [about entering communism] but you only hear a noise on the staircase, you don't see anyone coming down. Our [system of] food without pay is the sprout of "To each according to his need." At present we eat too little oil, normally not even four *liang;* some have one, some two, some three, some four, and some five *liang;* but normally it is between three and five. Nourishment is got from grain, therefore people eat a lot of rice but that could be changed [to include more oil]. Don't go about it rashly; all that can be done should be done gradually. This certainly can be said to be an element of communism.

Self-sufficiency, the supply system, and internal allocation within the people's communes on the one side and commodity exchange on the other have to be developed simultaneously. Without a development of the commodity economy, no wages can be paid. A professor visiting the Xushui University found that the monthly wage paid [there] was 15 yuan, and that wasn't even enough to pay for two packs of Qianmen brand cigarettes a day—can you call that superiority [of the socialist system]?[7] There are three counties in Hebei in need of emergency aid; [in] some ten counties [people] have only rice to eat; the third type pays wages, between a couple of dimes and a few bucks.[8] Beijing and Shanghai have a lot of money. In the villages water and fuel is not counted in monetary terms. One has to discuss a standard.[9]

In the womb of the mother is the baby, and socialism contains the sprouts of communism. Stalin failed to see this dialectical law.

We cannot do [everything we want to do for] agriculture within two or three years; at present we have to manage industry and continue to develop agriculture, although we are also concerned about lagging behind with agriculture.

[7]Xushui county in Hebei was the site of one of the earliest communes, formally inaugurated after Mao's inspection tour on 4 August 1958; see *Origins* 2, p. 80. Commune "universities" were effectively technical schools of rather variable quality. Qianmen was at that time one of the best native brand of cigarettes, and very popular among intellectuals.
[8]Literally, two *mao* (about 20¢) and a couple of *kuai* (the measure word used with *yuan* in formal speech and substituted for it colloquially).
[9]Mao presumably means a standard for comparing rural and urban living standards; it was a habitual complaint that rural standards lagged far behind. Mao seems here to be implying that rural living standards include many unquantified elements, which brought them closer to the urban level.

(Tan:[10] Use 50 percent of the labor force in agriculture, 25 percent in commodity crops, 20 percent in steel making, coal mining, and so on, and 5 percent in the service trades.)

[Chairman:] One has to encourage each people's commune to produce commodities, and one shouldn't always [just] talk about the word commodity.

China has extremely irrational production methods: 500 million people are engaged in producing foodstuffs, [but] producing only this much – 370 billion catties of grain. We have obtained from this two experiences: to promote mechanization and to decrease the sown [area] while increasing output, [in order] to save labor power, [and thus to be able to] run industry in a big way.[11] If we could achieve this during the next two years it would be good. Hebei province intends to plant 10 million *mou* next year [and get] 10,000 catties per mou, which would give 100 billion catties. Last year they [planted] 88 million *mou* but [harvested] only 25 billion catties, and this year they also **[176]** will have only 45 billion catties. Using power machinery, planting a smaller area will yield more grain.

Don't brag about it so loudly. The result might be as Huang Yanpei[12] says, that in Zhengzhou you can only eat vegetables. Having blown one's trumpet, but when there's only 1.5 *liang* of oil per month, what kind of superiority is that?

(XX: Communism mustn't mean lower standards.)

[Chairman:] Of such lowered standards there still are several gradations. According to the standard of Fan county, 95 percent industry connotes communism. The present cannot be called communism, the level is too low; one can only talk about elements and sprouts of communism, and one shouldn't lower the high standards of communism.

[10]Evidently Tan Zhenlin, who was in charge of agriculture during the GLF; see *Origins* 2, pp. 82–5.

[11]For a discussion of the attempt to obtain greater output from a smaller sown acreage, see *Origins* 2, pp. 119–28.

[12]Huang Yanpei, a prominent educator prior to 1949, was a leading "democratic personage" at this time, a former Vice-Premier and Minister of Light Industry (1949–54), and currently active in two non-Communist "democratic parties," the China Democratic League and the China Democratic National Construction Association; see *BDRC* 2, pp. 210–13.

The supply system is a form adapted for the transition; it does not create an obstacle. Completing the building of socialism is designed to lay the basis for the transition to communism.

The Soviet collective villages don't engage in industry; they only do agriculture, an agriculture, furthermore, that goes with planting large areas and [garnering] small harvests. That's why they don't manage to make the transition. Soviet socialism has collective ownership and ownership of the whole people. Stalin's transition to communism was hardly possible; there was no transition to the ownership by the whole people; he did not promote the elements of communism at all, split heavy and light industry, and openly advocated putting but small emphasis on the production of consumer goods. Various differences became greater.

[We] have to reread Stalin's *Economic Problems of Socialism* and look at the *Collection of Articles on the Problem of Bourgeois Right*.[13]

There ought to be a discussion on the nature of the people's communes, on how the transition will go, how much time will be needed, and on the Forty-Point Program [for Agriculture].[14] How are we to run urban people's communes?[15] Should we not lower standards for different kinds of people as a matter of principle? Cadres within the party [may] make slight adjustments [with regard to standards], but this [should] not be publicly communicated. When

---

[13]For discussions of Mao's study of Soviet economic ideas, and of the issues of "bourgeois right" during the GLF, see *Origins* 2, pp. 106–8, 295–7. Mao's notes on the Soviet *Political Economy: A Textbook* are translated in Mao Tse-tung, *A Critique of Soviet Economics* (New York, Monthly Review Press, 1977). Stalin's book appears in English as *Economic Problems of Socialism in the U.S.S.R.* (Moscow, Foreign Languages Press, 1952).

[14]The 40-point Program, also known as the 12-Year Agricultural Program, was launched in January 1956, shelved in mid 1956, and revived for the GLF. It was characterized by over-ambitious targets; see *Origins* 1, pp. 27–9, 90–1, 314–5. It had thus been a barometer of Mao's attempts to achieve leaping progress from January 1956 on. When moderation prevailed, the program was shelved; see Parris H. Chang, *Power and Policy in China* (University Park, Pennsylvania State Univ. Press, 1975), pp. 9–40, 122–5. Mao's comments later in this speech suggest that there was at least one other version of this plan, perhaps under consideration at this meeting; we do not have that version. The text of the 12-Year Agricultural Program we do have is "The Draft Program for Agricultural Development in the People's Republic of China, 1956–1967," passed by the CCP Central Committee in January 1956 in the form of 40 articles or points, see *Communist China 1955–1959: Policy documents with Analysis* (Cambridge, Harvard Univ. Press, 1962), pp. 119–26.

[15]At this time there were no urban communes, apart from a few experiments. The idea was shelved after the CC's 6th plenum in December 1958 and revived after the 8th (Lushan) plenum in August 1959; see *Origins* 2, pp. 305–6.

professors [already] have their salary reduced and can smoke only a few Qianmen brand cigarettes, [if] standards are still to be lowered, what superiority is there? Shouldn't we go about [making such adjustments] step by step? Only if [the level] is raised can this be counted as "superiority." The workers, I'm afraid, will have to have their wages increased, the [living standards] of the peasants have already risen. We should also institute the supply system in the cities.

On the first of January next year the change will take effect, a full eight hours of sleep, four hours for eating and recreation, two hours for study. The system for the peasants is 8-4-2-10 [hours of work]; for the workers the best is 8-4-2: make a timetable for work and rest; otherwise it cannot be sustained. Sunday [**177**] is for rest.[16]

Not to rest, that is the communist spirit. Work is not done for money [*renminbi*]. It has already stopped being only a means of life, and has become a necessity of life As for me, I don't [work] for the 530 yuan [I get] but because it's a necessity.[17] One should make an investigation.

(XX: It's mainly manifested in a disregard of pay and time, and going to the opposite [extreme, of resting only] six hours. With the abolition of piece-rate wages, [earnings] dropped by 20 percent, yet it wasn't considered a fabulous thing. [One has to] manage it so that no money is needed for food; pay somewhat lower wages. When those with few members in the family have somewhat lower wages, they "will not worry about their sons and daughters.")[18]

[Chairman:] Worrying about sons and daughters, [or] about oneself, will [then] change into worrying about the cause of society.

During this year there have been so many good things: trails have been blazed, many things have been realized about which we did not

---

[16]Unless there is a misprint here, it is not clear what contrast Mao is making between rural and urban work schedules.

[17]This figure of 530 yuan was presumably Mao's official monthly salary as party and state Chairman. The average *annual* wage for workers and staff in 1958 was about 650 yuan; see Christopher Howe, *Wage Patterns and Wage Policy in Modern China, 1919-1972* (Cambridge, Cambridge Univ. Press, 1973), p. 31.

[18]The full meaning of this intervention is unclear; the gist seems to be that the communist spirit has been manifested in long work hours in disregard of remuneration, and that, as long as people get free food, they will not worry too much about money wages. For a discussion of "shock" work during the GLF, see *Origins* 2, pp. 119-20.

even dare to dream earlier. Therefore we dare dream about people's leisure time, a leisure time of one-third.[19]

Forestry is quite amazing; one shouldn't look down on it. Vil'iams[20] says, "Agriculture, forestry, and livestock-raising must be combined. One shouldn't think of afforestation just in terms of making a place green." In the South fifteen to twenty-five years will be needed, in the North forty to fifty years. In planting trees, too, close planting is needed. With company they grow easily; when they all grow together, they will be comfortable; a lone tree doesn't grow. There is a way to planting trees. Raising fish is like raising pigs; planting trees is like sowing grain: you have to dig one *zhang* deep[21] and apply fertilizer to each layer.

This year we are emphasizing doing [things in] the small, native, and mass manner. Some people say that there is considerable waste of wood and coal, but there's also a great saving. Several tens of millions of people have gone into the mountains and identified resources [i.e., fuel], and [in the process] have got themselves some experience: that's a net gain.[22]

You cannot talk entirely in terms of living standards, otherwise those rotten emperors and nobles would have been in communism a long time ago. You have to talk about needs, and quantities of heat [i.e., energy available to the body]: 2500 calories should be adequate; even an emperor or a duke couldn't take more, and less wouldn't do, either. Foodstuffs contain seventeen kinds of elements, like nitrogen,

---

[19]Mao is presumably envisioning leisure time doubling from the currently mandated four hours discussed above, with the extra hours coming from working hours when modernization makes that possible.

[20]Vailii Robertovich Vil'iams (1863–1939): Soviet soil specialist and founder of agronomical soil sciences in the USSR, who set the standard for range land agricultural planning there and now has a scientific medal for achievement in agriculture named after him. His *Principles of Agronomy and Soil Science* emphasized an agronomical system of combining agriculture, forestry, and animal husbandry. Translated into Chinese, it had a great influence in China in the 1950s. See *Great Soviet Encyclopedia*, vol. 5, (New York, Macmillan, 1974), pp. 464–5.

[21]A *zhang* is about 3.3 meters, as advocated for deep ploughing at the time.

[22]The phrase "small, native, and mass" (*xiao, tu, qun*), as contrasted with large-scale, foreign or modern, and capital-intensive, reflected a key element of the GLF, the desire to increase output without massive new investment in large factories by using what China had plenty of: surplus labor and native ingenuity. Mao was apparently referring here to the 1958 "backyard" steel campaign, in which millions of Chinese smelted iron in small, homemade furnaces to help reach the national target of doubling output. In 1959, it was admitted that this locally produced metal could not really be called steel.

hydrogen, carbon, oxygen, potassium, magnesium, sodium, germanium, phosphorus, and sulphur; and communism, too, will just have a certain number of elements to make up its nourishment; [but] it shouldn't have too many.

The Forty Points will be achieved in fifteen or ten years, this year included.[23]

[178] 7 NOVEMBER 1958, AFTERNOON

Ownership by the whole people [as instituted] in Xushui[24] cannot be counted as the completion of the building of socialism. There is little [ownership by] the whole people; a lot [belongs to the] collective labor power, financial and material resources; none of them can be allocated. This point has to be made quite clear: to mix up the two is not advantageous. At present quite a few cadres are confused about this, [and] if one says this is not [the completion of socialism] that's a "rightist tendency."

There are two systems of ownership, that by the whole people and that by the collective; but what is of decisive importance here is whether things can be allocated. Things that cannot be allocated by the state cannot count as being owned by the whole people. [Things] allocated under ownership by the whole people are not "commodities" any more as defined in political economy. If the "two transformations" are not completed, there can be no abundance of products, there cannot be direct exchange, and there cannot be any abolition of the exchange of commodities.

To the three differences (between industry and agriculture, city and countryside, physical and mental labor) still needs to be added that between skilled and unskilled.

At present the relations of production are still [developing] from the small collective to the big collective; the mutual aid team[25] bore

---

[23]For the 40-Point or 12-Year Agricultural Program, see n. 14. What is extraordinary in this remark is that by this point in 1958, most provinces were vowing to fulfill the program long before the 12 years were up in 1967. Mao had earlier shown signs of wanting to moderate excessively ambitious projections (see *Origins* 2, pp. 42–3), but this is the first indication of his envisioning the program taking much longer than the original time scale.

[24]See above, n. 7.

[25]Mutual aid teams were the rural organizations set up by the CCP in the early 1950s to accustom peasants to working together in order to make them more amenable to collecti-

the sprouts of socialism within itself. From the lower-stage APC to the higher-stage APC, from the higher-stage APC to the people's commune, private plots have been reduced; the sphere of management [by the collective] has widened; [the responsibility for] education, communal mess halls [*gonggong shitang*], and child care has been taken on by the communes; the patriarchal [family] system has been abolished; and one can eat without paying—these are great changes, but all of them are within the confines of a single commune or a single county and do not go beyond the commune. From the viewpoint of the state as a whole, they don't represent a fundamental change. This does not compare with the Anshan Steel Works. [Only] on the question of eating without paying is this more advanced than Anshan. At present there are some places that have abolished [production] norms, [and instead] fix norms on the basis of labor intensity, technical level, and on whether one's attitude is good or bad, so that in both norms and salaries there have been changes.

The essence of the commune is to be the basic unit of socialist social structure, combining industry, agriculture, commerce, education, and military [affairs]. Its main function is to be the organizer of production and life while at the same time embodying some functions of political [i.e., state] power, which it must retain. At present there are people who don't understand that the functions of political power are the supervision and remolding of landlords, rich peasants, counterrevolutionaries, and bad elements as well as the protection of socialist **[179]** construction vis-á-vis the outside [world], but that it cannot be used to deal with and solve problems among the people. Currently some people mistakenly use political power to handle [matters] among the people, in the way a battalion commander hits a company commander, but that is resorting to coercion and commandism. The commune is a product of the Great Leap Forward. It is not fortuitous. It is the best form for the two transitions [*guodu*].[26] It is both big and public, and advantageous for the realization of the

---

vization in due course. See Franz Schurmann, *Ideology and Organization in Communist China*, rev. ed. (Berkeley, Univ. of California Press, 1968), pp. 439, 447–51.

[26]The two transitions were from collective ownership to ownership by the whole people (i.e., the state), and from a socialist distribution system ("to each according to his work") to a communist one ("to each according to his need").

two transitions. It is also the basic unit of the future communist society. The law of value [*jiazhi faze*] is an instrument; it only has calculating functions, but not the function of regulating production. Stalin's writings contain a lot of good things.

Ownership by the whole people means there must be product allocation.

Go back and hold meetings; solicit comments; don't say there has been a meeting in Zhengzhou. Can what [they have] be considered ownership by whole people? Have they already reached communism or not? Have the elements that make up communism been taken into consideration? Don't take upon yourself right away to extend [the meaning of] the resolution [of this meeting]. [To talk about] abolishing the family is not really telling the truth. It would sound very leftist [as if we intended to] chop off the head and cut away the tail, [forcing] the separation of children from their parents.[27]

As to county federations of communes and one commune [comprising] one [whole] county, each county's different; one commune [comprising] one whole county [can] easily produce a Qin Shihuang while county federations of communes do not easily produce Qin Shihuang; it's not easy to play the role of Qin Shihuang.[28] Xushui county is an independent kingdom, a lot of things are not being discussed with the provincial and prefectural committees; these two can't handle [Xushui county].

Xushui is no match for Anguo: from now on [we] must propagandize Anguo, not Xushui.[29] Xushui concentrated the good pigs [in one place] for people to see; that is not seeking truth from facts.[30] The "Sputnik" figures for steel [production] releases in some places are also not accurate. Such methods are no good; one has to stop them, to oppose exaggeration. One has to seek truth from facts, not make

[27]The final portion of this paragraph is somewhat obscure.

[28]During the leftist "high tide" of September 1958 it was thought that the larger a commune, the nearer it would be to communism. Thus some counties converted themselves into communes. But the preferred form was to have a number of smaller communes in each county linked up "federally."

[29]Anguo, like Xushui, is a county in Baoding prefecture, Hebei; see n. 4. Mao referred approvingly to the "Anguo documents" (presumably for propaganda purposes) at the 2nd Zhengzhou Conference in February–March 1959; see *Chinese Law & Government* 9.4:66.

[30]Xushui's device was presumably designed to convince visiting officials that pigs produced by many units had been produced by just one.

empty reports. On matters of major orientations and policies there should be some discussion; the leadership organs should be sober.[31]

In [agricultural] field management, it is not good if no one is responsible. Institute a responsibility system; don't let chaos reign; arrange things under a unified plan.

In the future, [we] will select the "three-thirds system" for the distribution of products.[32] Urban communes have to be organized, some earlier, some later, [and] organized very well. In Beijing and Shanghai they should be organized slowly—if they went about it fast, what would Huang Yanpei[33] do? One city, one commune—I'm afraid that here, too, [we'll have to have] federations of communes. Each will certainly need its own economic base. XXX praises our communes, saying that the communes which the Soviet Union had earlier **[180]** handled only consumption. Our people's communes are an organizational form with production at its center. The cities divide into two types: in a city with big industry, where citizens are after things, welfare should be open to all. The big factories and the universities belong to the state. But while their employees can join the [urban] communes, their cadres and products cannot be transferred [to the communes]. They can be assigned some welfare benefits, help to set up "Sputnik" factories, and enjoy rights as commune members, while also fulfilling obligations. These are the relationships between state-owned factories and [urban] communes. [These relationships] are the same [between] the army [and the urban communes].[34]

[31]Mao is being a bit disingenuous (see also n. 47). Carol Lee Hamrin argues that the "hot-headedness" which produced such "Sputnik" figures came out of the August 1958 Beidaihe conference, (see Text 17); and that even three months after what Mao says here, it was impossible for the director of the CCP's Central Party School, Yang Xianzhen, to speak honestly on inflated reports from Henan discovered by his field group; see "Yang Xianzhen: Upholding Orthodox Leninist Theory," in Carol Lee Hamrin and Timothy Cheek, eds., *China's Establishment Intellectuals* (Armonk, N.Y., M. E. Sharpe, 1986), p. 67.
[32]The term "three-thirds system" was normally used to describe the base-area political system around Yan'an in the 1940s, dividing nominal power among the CCP, non-party leftists, and middle-of-the-roaders. Perhaps Mao means that goods will be distributed partly freely, partly on a ration system, partly in return for payment; or perhaps that the peasant will retain one third, the commune another third, with the final third going to the state, as is implied on p. 459.
[33]See n. 12. Mao is evidently using Huang Yanpei as a symbol of the bourgeoisie whose cooperation in running urban commerce and industry he does not want to lose by hasty "leftism."
[34]Mao evidently forgot or did not bother to mention the second type, presumably smaller cities.

Stalin's last letter is nearly entirely wrong; he thought that giving machinery to the *kolkhoz* was a step backward.[35]

The communes are not to assign all sorts of tasks to the factories; industries and schools that serve the state or the province as a whole generally should not be handed down to ownership by the communes. If things are not handled this way, troubles could come about as in the pharmaceutical factory in Shijiazhuang where work came almost to a halt when personnel were dragged off to do deep ploughing and make steel.[36]

The value created by workers is very large, [so] they should [have an income] slightly higher than that of the peasants. Next year [we] should think about making small [wage] increases to make up for the losses due to the abolition of piece-rate wages.

[There should be some] small freedoms [within] the great collectives. Each family does some cooking;[37] while the historical role of the family has been destroyed, consumption [in the framework of the family] continues in part, as does bearing and raising children. The patriarchal system and monetary relations [within the family] are destroyed, [because there is] widespread social security. The old Chinese family is family communism—in each family one ate without paying—but there was no equality.

As for times of work and rest, commune members should have at least two days [rest] per month (women need five days; during their menstruation they should be compelled to rest). In the future there will be a six-hour work system with four hours for study; there should be some variation for capitalists, professors, democratic personages, actors, and athletes.

Fixed interest [payments] to capitalists will not be abolished (if they don't want them, that's fine; but this should not be made public),[38] and [their] entering communes should be according to the

[35]This refers to Stalin's reply to A. V. Sanina and V. A. Venzher, which is appended to his *Economic Problems of Socialism in the U.S.S.R.* The Peking Foreign Languages Press reprinted Moscow's English-language edition in 1972. Stalin's discussion of the disadvantages of giving machinery to the collectives (*kolkhozy*) is on pp. 90–9 of this edition.

[36]The example seems to imply that Shijiazhuang, a city in Hebei approaching a million inhabitants, had already formed an urban commune.

[37]Literally, "handles some pots and pans." By small freedoms, Mao means things like cooking occasionally at home rather than eating always in a public mess hall as collectivist-minded cadres were encouraging at this time.

[38]When the socialist high tide engulfed private industry and commerce in early 1956, the

‌‍‌‌‍‌‌‌

‌‍‌

principle of voluntariness. The problem of cadres' wages has to be handled with great care: first some experiments, don't publish [decisions] too early. (Wage reductions for party members should also not be made publicly.)

[181] 9 NOVEMBER 1958

Abolish the patriarchal [family] system [that derives] from history. Ensure that homes are built which are conducive to men and women, old and young living together; when [work] is intense, they may be separated. Building homes without proper arrangements is a coercive method.[39] Abolish only the patriarchal [family] system [deriving] from history. At present a family still needs a head, namely the most capable, not necessarily the most senior.

[We] generally avoid this aspect [when discussing] the problem of commodities and commerce: it seems as though if it is not handled this way, it will not resemble communism. The people's communes have to produce socialist commodities suitable for exchange in order to promote the gradual increase of individual wages. As far as the means of subsistence are concerned, socialist commerce has to be developed. Furthermore, making use of the form of the law of value is an instrument of economic accounting during the transitional period, and beneficial for the gradual transition to communism. Present-day economists don't appreciate economics. Shortly before his death, Stalin said, "Whoever talks about the law of value is not appreciated"—he said that in a letter to Yaroshenko.[40] Some people in

---

government announced that it would recompense businessmen by paying 5% of their invested capital annually for 7 years; see Barry M. Richman, *Industrial Society in Communist China* (New York, Random House, 1969), pp. 897–8. Though the valuations of the businesses were typically on the low side, these "fixed interest" payments were sometimes very large, and during the GLF they seemed to some firebrands like capitalist "tails" which should be eliminated. Hence Mao's warning.

[39]In the early commune period, cadres in some areas wished to promote collective living by building single-sex dormitories.

[40]Mao's reference does not seem to be correct; see Stalin's comments on Yaroshenko's errors, in *Economic Problems of Socialism in the U.S.S.R.* (Moscow, 1952), pp. 59–86. In this pamphlet, Stalin does talk of planners who are poorly acquainted with and tend to ignore the laws of value (p. 20). L. D. Yaroshenko was a Soviet economist who survived Stalin's strictures only to be criticized later by Khrushchev! See Robert Conquest, *Power and Policy in the U.S.S.R.* (London, Macmillan, 1961), p. 110.

the Soviet Union don't come out in favor of commodity production, thinking communism has already come, while in fact they are quite far away from it; we've been at it for just a few years, so that we are even further away.

Lenin in his time vigorously promoted the development of commerce, because city and countryside were cut off from each other. In the year 195X that happened to us, too. At present transportation is not in good shape, so that there is a situation of a semi-cutoff and I think things have to be developed in two directions: one is to expand allocation and transfer; the other is to expand commodity production. If not, we will not be able to pay wages, nor to raise living [standards.]

Bourgeois right has to be demolished in part. For instance, strict hierarchy, lording it over those below, separation from the masses, not treating others as one's equal, not earning a living on the basis of capacity but on the basis of seniority or power—all these things have to be abolished day by day. Once smashed, they regenerate; once they regenerate they have to be smashed again. After Liberation, we didn't make use of the advantages of the supply system, but switched to a wage system. It seemed that we had no choice but to switch in 1953, because the people from the liberated areas were in the minority [and] the working class was also on a wage system. The personnel newly added to government organs and industries were very numerous; they had all been under the influence of the bourgeoisie, and it would not have been easy to require them to switch to the supply system, and so it was necessary at the time to make a concession. [182] But there were shortcomings. We accepted a rank system with a strict hierarchy, and too many ranks: There were over thirty ranks to be evaluated, and [they caused] struggles over ranks and remuneration. These concessions were not right. Through the Rectification [Campaign] this tendency was reduced. This type of unequal relationships between cadres and the masses—[similar to] relationships between cats and mice or fathers and sons—has to be abolished: such relationships are completely unnecessary. From last year to this year we fought a major battle against bourgeois right. Last year we introduced experimental fields; the cadres were transferred down [to the grass roots], and we correctly solved contradictions among the people by using persuasion and not coercion. As a consequence the climate improved greatly; without this change, the GLF would not have been possible. Why else don't the masses sleep and rest, but work over ten hours? Because party members are together with them; in Hong'an county [Hubei province] the cadres had quite lordly airs in the past, and they were cursed by the masses. A change came about in the second half of 1956; they made much progress, and the masses welcomed them.

Another part [of bourgeois right] must be preserved. One has to preserve an appropriate wage system, some necessary [income] differentials, and something of the principle [that] he who works more earns more. Then there is one part which has the character of a deal, such as the maintenance of a system of high salaries for the bourgeoisie, bourgeois intellectuals, and democratic personages. One can allow a bourgeois to be a member of a commune, but he will still wear his bourgeois hat (no concession is to be made [on the question] of the hat). Commune members are divided into two kinds: first the worker and peasant members, second the bourgeois members.

For purposes of unity the three levels of the Center, the provinces, and the prefectures should have a program. How would things work out if [those responsible for] the provincial committees and above are not clear about the production targets and interrelationships? At present there are some problems which are rather chaotic. Once something is transmitted [to lower levels], it is transmitted all the way. Down to what level [things] are to be published has to be a matter for political judgment. People are not nervous about grain [quotas]. It is the four items—steel, machinery, coal, and electricity—that make them nervous. As for the time [needed for the achievement of this program] one might suggest "fifteen years or a little bit more";[41] as to the target, fix XX, and just explain orally: Forestry will become one of the basic problems. After forestry it's the turn of animal husbandry and fisheries; sericulture and soybean [production] also have to be added. Forestry is the basis of the chemical and construction industries. [When talking about] eliminating floods and droughts, [we] have to add "to the maximum degree"; for the most part these things fall into man's domain, but they are partially caused by nature,

[41]Mao is presumably referring here to the commitment he made a year earlier to overtaking Britain in the output of major industrial products within 15 years; see *Origins* 2, pp. 16–7. But later in this passage, he seems to be referring to the 12-Year Agricultural Program, probably to the version never published, circulated at the CC's 3rd plenum in September–October 1957; see *Origins* 1, pp. 27–9, 314–5; 2, p. 305. This may have had references to urban communes. See also n. 14.

and this is still going to be so after ten thousand years. As to fertilizer, organic fertilizer is the main thing. [Concerning] the elimination of the four pests[42] and other major [agricultural] pests, one should add also "to the maximum degree." As for labor, sleeping and rest is not to be reduced below twelve hours per day, plus two hours for study; the maximum labor time is not to exceed ten **[183]** hours. This is a big problem throughout the country. Service work in the mess halls has to be regarded as a noble task in the service of the people, as has service work in nurseries and kindergartens. Every laborer is a state worker.

I fully agree with Article 36 [on] commodity production and allo-cation and transfer.[43] [If] the communes can practice a system of con-tracts with each other, why can't contracts be made between the state and the communes? Perhaps this would offend the "left" faction. Our present commodity production is not regulated by the law of value, but by the plan—or can you say steel, grain, and cotton in our coun-try are regulated by the law of value? Copper and aluminum were not [so] regulated in the past; from now on we have to devote some energy to managing [these items under the plan].

In the past we said, "First on behalf of the state, second on behalf of the commune, third on behalf of oneself." But the producers turn this around: [For them] the self comes first, the commune comes second, and the state third, even when we use slogans like "Protect the family, guard the state"; "To prosper, plant cotton"; "Plant more cotton for love of the state and family."

In Article 38, [we] should add, "In order to be prepared utterly to defeat an invader in the event of an invasion, [we] must implement an everyone-a-soldier system."

On Article 39: Because, on the one hand, they are pleased [if capi-talists] (become commune members), and on the other they are concerned[44] [in view of the capitalists having] (housekeepers and high salaries), it has to be made clear to the workers that preferential

---

[42]See Text 15, n. 2.

[43]Again, Mao seems to be referring to a revised version of the 40 Points, since Article 36 in the available published text concerns rural credit cooperatives, not commodity production, etc. See *Communist China 1955–1959*, p. 126. Or he may be referring to an unpublished 40 Points on urban communes. His subsequent reference to Article 39 suggests this.

[44]Mao is taking the literal meaning of a classical quotation from the *Analects* of Confucius out of its original context: *"yize yixi, yize yiju,"* from Chapter 21 of *Liren*. Legge translates

treatment for the capitalists serves the purpose of isolating them, allows them to be something special, where they stand out individually. The small [capitalists] should enter [communes] early; as for the middle ones, it's not certain.

As to Article 40, [it's just] a heap of viewpoints.[45] [I am] dissatisfied. No one will bother to read the seven viewpoints.[46] The crux [of the matter] is [how] to solve [the problem of] work methods by implementing the mass line. One shouldn't tie people up, beat them, curse them, argue with them, or punish them with hard labor; even battalion commanders are treating company commanders in this manner, "[I'll] argue the hell out of you, you villain." Xushui is not alone in tying up, beating, shouting at, and disputing with company commanders. Therefore each and every one is afraid of debates, which they have turned into struggle meetings, into some kind of punishment. [For the] two kinds of contradictions [there are] two different kinds of debates: the first is directed against the rightists, serving to isolate them; the other kind is among the people, designed to persuade.

[We should] encourage seeking truth from facts: [people] should not give false reports, shouldn't give out someone else's report on pig [raising] as their own; **[184]** and 300 catties of wheat should not be reported as 400.[47] This year's [reported] 900 billion catties of grain are at most 740 billion catties; that should be taken as the [real] figure. It would be more appropriate to consider the remaining 160 billion catties as being falsely reported. The enemy can't be fooled; in the old days, false reporting in battle news could only fool the people, not the enemy. The enemy just had a good laugh when they saw them. On the Fujian front the loss in aircraft is six of ours as against fourteen of the enemy, a ratio of 1 to 2.33. But the Nationalist party blew

the full sentence as "The years of the parents may by no means not be kept in the memory, as an occasion at once for joy and for fear." See James Legge, *The Chinese Classics*, vol. 1 (Taipei, Southern Materials Center, 1983), p. 171. For another example of this rhetorical habit of Mao's, see Text 16, n. 5.

[45]The original point 40 refers to the exchange of experiences between workers and peasants to reduce the subjective side of their differences. The text in the present form here is not comprehensible.

[46]There is no indication of what the seven viewpoints are.

[47]This is Mao's second admonition to moderation in reporting gains in the GLF in this speech, and, again, seems a bit disingenuous; see n. 31.

its own trumpet; there is some truth, but there is also falsehood, so that they mixed up the true and the false.[48] Yanshi county [Henan province] originally intended to hide its production and underreport. But we also have cases of overreporting. The *People's Daily* would do best to take things a bit more coolly. Some problems they have become accustomed to talking about should be handled in a manner more appropriate to the present. The main emphasis has to be on solving problems of work style, [that is] party leadership, the mass line, seeking truth from facts.

∗ ∗ ∗ ∗ ∗ ∗ ∗ ∗ ∗ ∗ ∗ ∗ ∗ ∗ ∗ ∗[49]

Stalin's book on the economic problems of socialism[50] has to be reread. The cadres from the standing committees of the prefectural and provincial [level] and above should study it; they all have to study the economic problems of socialism. Reading the first three chapters in the past may not have been very interesting, [but] now it's different. In Chapters One, Two, and Three, there are many things deserving attention. There are some inappropriate things, and then there are some about which he himself was not quite clear. The first chapter on objective laws postulates the antithesis between a planned economy and an anarchic situation. He says there is a difference between the laws of planning and [specific] policies; that's very good. He brings up the issue of subjective planning striving to match the objective laws, but he does not pursue this; perhaps he was not quite clear about that himself. In his mind he felt that Soviet planning basically corresponded to the objective laws; but to what extent deserves study. For instance, the relationship between heavy and light industry, the problem of agriculture—they [the objective laws] were not entirely reflected, and he had to pay for that. People cannot see from this [Soviet experience how to] combine long- and short-term benefits. Down to the very present, they [the Russians] have fewer commodities than we have; [the Soviet economy] walks like Iron Crutch Li, one leg long, one leg short, the hands holding the

[48]Mao is referring here to the air duels over the Taiwan Strait during the confrontation there in August–September 1958.
[49]A row of stars appears at this point in the original text.
[50]For Stalin's book, see n. 13.

crutches, quite out of balance.[51] At present, what we advocate is [this]: on the premise of assigned priority to the development of heavy industry, [we say] the development of industry and agriculture [should be] simultaneous, [in other words] walking on two legs. Which [of the two methods] is in the final analysis better adapted to the objective laws? Not having any [interest in the] masses or in politics, [Stalin] talks only about technology and specialists; that also is [walking on] one leg. **[185]** In the internal relations between heavy and light industry, [Stalin] did not bring out the main aspect of the contradiction; this dialectical law we, too, have mastered only very recently—to take steel as the key link—this brings out the main contradiction. He didn't bring that out.

(XX: He only attached importance to machinery, and suggested that machines were the centerpiece.)[52]

[Chairman:] Without steel, you can't have machines; but with steel you have machines, coal, electricity, oil, transport, and [equipment for] the Navy, Army, and Air Force. In a lot of areas, Stalin just raised the questions, but didn't provide the answers.

In the second and third chapters he talks about commodities and the law of value. Have you any comments? I pretty well go along with many of the views in these [two chapters]. It is really necessary to get a clear understanding of these problems. "Means of production are not commodities," [Stalin says], and we say, "They are and they are not." With us, means of production are still in part commodities. We sell agricultural machinery to the APCs [sic]. The last letter [of Stalin's][53] is fundamentally wrong, setting the state and the masses against each other, distrustful of the peasants, and rigidly holding onto the machines without letting go. The reasons [he gives] are

[51]Iron Crutch Li is one of the legendary "Eight Immortals" (*ba xian*). Once, while his spirit was roaming outside his body, his disciples, mistaking him for dead, cremated his body. His spirit therefore attached to the corpse of a beggar who had just died of hunger; thus he had a different (and ugly) incarnation. By his magic, he changed the beggar's bamboo stick into an iron crutch. The subject of many literary works, from Yuan drama to Ming novels, he is a figure in a Peking Opera, *The Eight Immortals Crossing the Sea* (*Ba xian guo hai*), which is most likely the origin of Mao's reference.

[52]The printed text includes the phrase *mei you gang* inside the parentheses. Linguistic sense moves that phrase outside and into the following sentence, as it is rendered here.

[53]Reply to Sanina and Venzher in Stalin, (Moscow, 1952), pp. 63ff.

unconvincing; he deceived himself. [He says he] is not afraid [of the consequences], but he also did not want to let go. He did not want to sell the tractors to the peasants. He finally said that the peasants who bought them might not be able to cover their losses, but that the state could absorb those losses.[54] In sum, he has not found a method of the two transitions, has not found a way out from the system of collective ownership to that of the entire people.

(XX: He didn't understand that before receiving, there must be giving.)[55]

[Chairman:] Exactly! If you go for rigid control over the peasants, the peasants also will want to control you. It may be as he says [that] as the differences between workers and peasants, and city and countryside are eliminated, these essential distinctions are also eliminated. However, [despite] thirty years of experience he did not find a way out, and from his letter one can see that he was very frustrated. Nevertheless, he said he would not preserve the [form of] commodity handed down from the old society. The main regulator is planning, not the law of value—there he is quite right. This has become very clear [to us] during the last few years. The Great Leap Forward has the [party] secretary taking command, has politics taking command.

(XX: He [Stalin] only saw the contradiction between workers and peasants.)

[Chairman:] His criticism of Yaroshenko is correct. He does not, however, talk about the relationship between superstructure and base, nor about how the superstructure adapts to the economic base, [yet] that is a very big problem. We run rectification [campaigns]; we send cadres down [to the lower levels, and promote] the two participations and the one reform; the cadres participate in physical labor; and we eliminate inappropriate rules and systems and so on.[56]

[54]Ibid., p. 94.
[55]This is a version of a saying in Chapter 36 of the *Dao de jing:* "He who is to be taken away from, Must first be given;" see Lin Yutang, *The Wisdom of Laotse* (London, Michael Joseph, 1958), p. 183.
[56]Mao refers to the "one reform" (of inappropriate rules) and to one of the "participations" (in physical labor). The other "participation" was of workers in management.

[The Soviet] *Political Economy[: A Textbook]* only talks about economic relations, not about politics. The newspapers talk about "selfless labor," but in fact [people] do not forget themselves for a single hour. In his economics, everything is cold **[186]** and cheerless, wretched and miserable, and totally gloomy. The strong point is that he brings up problems. Lenin did the same, but his slogan "Attack on the entire front" when the New Economic Policy had just been implemented for one year was a bit rash. In the Soviet Union, people like [the businessman] Rong Yiren[57] were all driven into the sea. [Stalin] does not discuss bourgeois right, the ideology of rights, and the system of rights, and so forth. The educational organization, too, is bourgeois in form. How does one get to communism without a communist movement? Stalin saw material things, not people; he saw only the cadres, and not the masses.

(XX: One group thinks of going for communism, another of stopping at socialism, and a third of returning to capitalism.)

[Chairman:] One group (the landlords, rich peasants, counterrevolutionaries, bad elements and rightists, some cadres, and those who want to preserve bourgeois right) think of turning back [to capitalism]; the majority want to build communism.

The entry into communism must be step by step. [We must] expand in two directions, on the one hand in developing production [for] self-sufficiency, and on the other in developing commodity production. At present [we] have to make use of commodity production, commodity exchange, and the law of value as useful tools. Stalin gave many reasons. Are there no negative aspects? Refute him!

Ours is a state with a very undeveloped commodity production. Last year we had 370 billion catties: 30 billion catties were tax grain; 50 billion catties were sold to the state as a commodity, which means not even a third was commodity grain. Apart from grain, cash crops are also very undeveloped, like tea and silk, neither of which has regained its historically highest production level. There has to be a stage during which commodity production is developed, otherwise we cannot pay wages. As an example, Hebei province is divided into three kinds of county: in one group [people] have just rice to eat; in

[57]See Text 1, n. 6.

another they need relief [grain]; in a third they can pay wages. The last category divides again into different groups, one of which pays just a few *jiao*.[58] Therefore each commune has to develop some things besides grain, which it can sell for money. On steel they lose money. First, [money will pay for] school fees; second, it will support the state's industrialization.

[We have to] develop socialist commodity production and commodity exchange. Unequal wages will have to remain for a whole. We must affirm that socialist commodity production and commodity exchange still have positive uses. Only a portion [of commodities] is to be allocated and transferred, the great part [is exchanged through] buying and selling. We have to expand socialist commodity circulation. At present there is a deviation, as if the more communism, the better. Communism has to come step by step. We have to investigate Fan county's [plan to] achieve communism within two years.

[187] In short, commodities are not developed in our country, and to enter communism one has first to eliminate the attitude of being the overlord and the three kinds of [work] styles and the five airs;[59] and second to maintain wage differentials. At present a few people persist in wanting to achieve communism in a matter of three to five years.

The economists are "left"; they get by under false pretences, and thereby expose their vulnerable side. The Forty Point draft program is the proof.

AFTERNOON, 10 NOVEMBER 1958

Change the minutes [of this meeting] into a resolution of the Politburo. When you go back to the lower levels, carry it out. The Politburo will reaffirm it retroactively according to legal procedure.[60]

---

[58]A *jiao* was worth roughly a dime in the 1950s.

[59]Here Mao is citing the Shanghai First Secretary, Ke Qingshi, a leading advocate of the GLF, who had been raised to the Politburo in May 1958. Early in the year Ke Qingshi had attacked military cadres for exhibiting the "three [work] styles and five airs" (*san feng wu qi*). The three bad work styles were those criticized in the 1957 Rectification Campaign: bureaucratism, subjectivism, and sectarianism. The five airs were arrogance, bureaucratism, extravagance, laziness, and apathy. To counteract these sins, an order was issued in September for officers to spend spells in the ranks as ordinary soldiers. See Warren Kuo, ed., *A Comprehensive Glossary of Chinese Communist Terminology* (Taipei: Institute of International Relations, 1978), p. 428; *Origins* 2, p. 67.

[60]It is not clear which session's minutes are to become a resolution.

What the newspapers report is pure poetry. The Great Leap Forward has something about it which makes people dazed and befuddled. [I] can't sleep, and want to talk a bit, try to copy Stalin,[61] and go on and try a little persuasion on some comrades. I believe I'm right. But if my opponent is right, I would obey [him].

First there's the question of whether or not one has to draw boundaries. Then there's the question of blending these various forms of ownership. As for collective ownership, some forms left behind by the bourgeoisie have to be used. At present this is still the peasant question. Some comrades suddenly rate the peasants very highly: they think the peasants are number one, the workers number two; the peasantry is thus superior even to the working class, they're the elder brothers! On some questions the villages are ahead, but this is just appearance, not substance. In the last analysis, is Anshan Steel the elder brother or is it Xushui? Some people think that the Chinese proletariat is in the villages, while Anshan Steel with its eight-tiered wage system and not even having established a people's commune, has fallen behind. Some comrades have run about Xushui for two days, and then conclude that Xushui is the elder brother. It's as if the peasants were the proletarians and the workers were the petty-bourgeoisie—is such a view Marxism? Some comrades are Marxists when they are reading Marxist textbooks; but once they run into real problems, [their belief in Marxism] is discounted. This is quite a fashion. Among the cadres there are some hundreds of thousands or even some millions whose thinking is muddled; the masses, too, are quite confused. So you are careful and cautious, shunning the use of capitalist concepts that still have a positive meaning—commodity production, commodity circulation, law of value, and the like—to serve socialism. **[188]** Based on Article 36,[62] you make utmost use of this unclear wording to get by under false pretenses in order to make it seem as if the peasants had entered communism. That is an attitude lacking in thoroughness and seriousness towards Marxism. It is an

---

[61]Mao may mean he is copying Stalin in liking to work late; see Milovan Djilas, *Conversations with Stalin* (London, Hart-Davis, 1962), pp. 72–3.

[62]Although this Article 36 does not correspond to any such article in published versions of the 40-point Twelve-Year Agricultural Program, it, like the Article 36 mentioned on the previous day (see n. 43), seems to be concerned with commodity production and may appear in a revised, unpublished version of the Program.

affair concerning several hundred million peasants. The reasons Stalin gave why one could not expropriate the peasants are as follows:[63] (1.) The peasant's labor power belongs to the commune in the same manner as seeds; that is different from Anshan where they produce for the entire people. The collective village or commune not only owns the seeds, but also fertilizer and products, the ownership of which is with the peasant; and if you don't give him things, don't trade on the basis of equal value, he will not deliver to you. Should this problem be treated rashly or cautiously? On the surface, it looks as if whatever is needed is given, but in reality there is much pain [in the giving]. The first secretary of the county [party] committee of Xiuwu[64] did not dare to proclaim ownership by the whole people, first because he was afraid he might not be able to pay wages if there were a natural disaster and a decrease in production, as the state would neither guarantee nor subsidize; second he was afraid that after a rich harvest the state might take [the surplus] away. This comrade thought about things and did not get into frenzy; he did not rush madly forward in the manner of Xushui. We have not proclaimed state ownership of the land but commune ownership of the land, the seeds, the animals, and the large and small agricultural implements. In this period it is only through commodity production and circulation that we can get the peasants to develop production and to enter ownership by the whole people.

In the second paragraph on page four of the first chapter of *Economic Problems of Socialism in the U.S.S.R.,*[65] it says "Freedom is the appreciation of necessity."[66] Objective laws exist independently of human consciousness; objective laws are the opposite of human subjective understanding. Only by understanding objective laws can one control them.[67] As to the laws of the political economy of socialism, one has to study their necessity. The suggestions made at the

---

[63]The text gives no second numbered point.
[64]Xiuwu county is in Henan province.
[65]Stalin (Moscow, 1952), p. 4.
[66]It was clearly Mao's citation of Stalin's use of this quotation from Engels' *Anti-Dühring* that emboldened Chen Yun to refer to it when he was called on by Mao to restore order to the Chinese economy in 1959. See *Origins* 2, p. 164, where (not having seen the text of the present speech) I mistakenly suggested that Mao picked up this quotation from Chen Yun.
[67]Mao uses the term, *jiashi,* as in piloting an airplane, which we translate here as "control."

Chengdu conference seem to have had positive results when enacted. At the second session of the [party's] Eighth Congress there was a report made which still seems efficacious,[68] but do they [i.e., the suggestions and this report] accord with [objective] laws or do they not? And are these all that was [needed]? Will they tumble head over heels? [We] still need to continue to test them in practice. Some years, even a decade, will be needed for this. I once said to Gomulka, look again after ten years.[69] In our own past the revolution was doubted by people: did China need a revolution or not? did political power have to be seized or not? Internationally some people resolutely opposed it; but the revolution itself has proved that our course was correct, practice has provided its rightness. But that was still only proof for one phase. Collectivization, joint state-private enterprises, production increases are [further] proof of it. Increase there was indeed; but after eight years of [economic] construction, **[189]** we only did 370 billion catties of grain. This year [we'll] do a bit more—[who] knows how next year will be? Comrade Tan Zhenlin has suggested that during the four months from December this year through January, February, March next year, the first secretaries should again take agriculture into their hands, which would influence the wheat harvests.[70] Please, would everybody think about this. Grasp agriculture at the same time as grasping steel. The first secretaries should call meetings to distribute labor power, make some announcements, give some orders, and hand the responsibility over to the agricultural [department] secretaries. The provinces, prefectures, and counties all have to take responsibility; and bad performances won't do. Otherwise nobody is going to take responsibility; each one will say he himself is right, [with the result] that everyone is going to turn to steel-making [and agriculture will be neglected]. Shanxi province talks

---

[68]Mao's March 1958 speeches at the Chengdu conference are in *Wansui* (1969), pp. 159–80; and translated in *Issues and Studies*, November, December 1973. The report referred to is presumably Liu Shaoqi's political report to the 2nd session of the 8th Party Congress (May 1958); see *Communist China, 1955–1959*, pp. 164–20ɔ.

[69]The only time Mao is known to have met the Polish Communist leader Gomulka, who was rehabilitated in August 1956 and made first secretary that October in the face of Soviet objections, was at the 40th anniversary celebrations of the Bolshevik revolution in Moscow in November 1957.

[70]For Tan Zhenlin, see Text 17, n. 3. The 1958 autumn harvest had been neglected in favor of steel-making with calamitous consequences for grain output; see *Origins* 2, pp. 113–21. Tan was presumably trying to ensure that there was no repetition of this in 1959.

about three victories: in industry, agriculture, and ideology. That is a good slogan. Going at it by leaving out one would be like Iron-Crutch Li. Neglect agriculture and you become a Stalin. Those doing agriculture must be hell-bent on doing agriculture. Write it down again in the resolution that agriculture is not to be thrown out.[71] The first secretaries must put their minds to two, three, or four tasks and acquire many-sided abilities. One day a month, four days in four months, is too little [for taking care of any one task]. "Industry, agriculture, and ideology" was [a slogan] suggested at the Chengdu conference; this time it's a creation of the people from Shanxi, just like people from Henan suggesting "Three years of hard struggle," which has now become a national slogan; "Making experimental fields" was a slogan from Hubei. Nothing comes out of the brains of the few of us. All we do is to put together the experiences of the different regions and then popularize them to bring forth a few products [i.e., ideas] like those from the Chengdu and Beidaihe meetings. This time we came up with two products; one will be implemented immediately, and the other will [be held] in draft form.

Do our measures entirely correspond to objective laws? If they by and large correspond, that is already all right. Stalin said: "The Soviet power at that time had to create new, socialist forms of economy, 'starting from scratch,' so to speak. That was undoubtedly a difficult, complex and unprecedented task."[72] We have a precedent; we have the experience of the Soviet Union's successes and failures. This book of Stalin's is exceedingly useful; he has put together a text book [for us]. I have not looked at it in detail, and at present I am forced to read it; the more I read, the more interesting it becomes. Chen Yun and [Li] Fuchun are more knowledgeable [from practical experience], but have not yet learned from the Soviet experience.[73] It's useful, and we have to do a bit better than they. If we make a mess of it, China's Marxists aren't of much use.

This book says in the second paragraphs of pages six and seven

---

[71]Mao is presumably referring to the resolution on the communes which would be passed at the CC's 6th plenum in December 1958 and which might have by this time been in the drafting stage. For the resolution, see *Communist China, 1955–59*, pp. 488–502.

[72]Stalin (Moscow, 1952), p. 5. Mao's version does not correspond precisely to the official version.

[73]*Qujing* is a popular PRC idiom, drawn from the idea of "making a pilgrimage for Buddhist scriptures," but now meaning "learning from others' experiences."

that [talk about] eliminating and creating [economic] laws is wrong, objective laws and policy directives should not be talked about in the same breath, the law of planned development **[190]** has arisen as the antithesis to capitalist competition and anarchy. There there's anarchy, here there's governance. We, too, do planning, and we, too, have experience: a spate of mobilization, and there's too much coal; another mobilization, and there's too much sugar; yet another mobilization, and there's too much steel so that we are forced to sell it to the Soviet Union, but the next day we scrap the contract because again we don't have enough. Last month it was said there's too much; the following month the word is it's not enough. We are frustrated. We don't know how to handle it properly. Like a fly in a glass house, blindly banging against the glass. Having experienced the twists and turns of the small leap forward in 1956 and the leap backward in 1957, we compared [them] and came up with a way, calling it the general line. The Forty Points for agriculture also experienced twists and turns; at one time we called them operative, at another time inoperative; but in the last analysis they are operative and have already been basically accomplished, and in general cannot be said to be wrong. Are the new Forty Points operative or not?[74] I still have my doubts. [We should] prepare to talk about it again. Will we be able to catch up with England in per capita [production] within fifteen years?[75] To avoid frightening people to death, don't broadcast [the concept of] three years of hard struggle. Once that time comes, we will shock imperialism, and also our friends. Ten million, 30 million [tons of steel]—after a couple of years they'll get used to the shock and won't be afraid anymore.

Does the general line package reflect objective law pretty well overall, or has it been wrongly devised? Steel gets made and there's no coal. In Shanghai and Wuhan there is nothing to eat. An understanding of the objective world has to come gradually. Until things have

---

[74]This is the clearest indication that at the Zhengzhou conference a radically new, supercharged version of the Twelve-Year Program for Agriculture was discussed. Mao's subsequent expression of caution is a typical example of his preference for seeming sober while implicitly spurring on his colleagues to more extravagant objectives, because he always shrank from damping enthusiasm. See text above and n. 31; his remarks at the Chengdu conference earlier in 1958 (for which, see n. 68); and *Origins* 2, pp. 42–3.

[75]Mao apparently misremembers that the goal of the leap was to overtake the UK in gross output not per capita output, a totally fanciful idea. This may be a slip of the tongue, but it illustrates that for Mao targets were more for mobilization than for implementation.

reached a certain point, contradictions will not manifest themselves: they will not be reflected in people's brains, and [therefore] cannot be understood. For eight years [we] didn't understand [we had] to take steel as the main link, and in September this year we finally got that point, and grasped the main aspect of the contradiction. This is monism, not pluralism. Once we have grasped the main contradiction, everything else will follow. Coal, iron, and machinery don't stand as equals next to each other. Large, middle-sized and small [factories?] have the large ones as the main link [*yi da wei gang*]; and in the case of the Center and the regions, the Center is the main link. It's the same as in dancing. When a man and a woman dance together, how could it work if the woman fights for independence? She has to achieve independence in the process of following; if she doesn't follow the man, there's no independence. [If] you don't dance, you are culturally impoverished, and I have no language in common with you.[76]

Stalin's statement, "One has to study this economic law [of balanced development of the national economy], has to master it, to learn to apply it with full understanding, and to compile such plans as fully reflect the requirements of this law," is excellent.[77] We still have not fully mastered this economic law nor have we learned to apply it with full understanding. [191] It can't be said that during the past eight years we have carried out the planning of production in a fully correct manner, in a way which completely reflects the requirements of economic laws. Of course, there are achievements; and they are the main thing, while the defects and mistakes are secondary. What are the planning organs? The Central Committee, the large regions, each province and each level are all planning organs, not just the Planning Commission. There is a potential for good planning, but one should not confuse potential with realization. In order to transform [potential] into reality, you have to study [this economic law], have to learn to apply it with full understanding, and compile plans that fully reflect objective law. You have to pay attention. The small, native, mass [-run blast furnaces need] 10 tons of coal for 1 ton

[76]There are a number of reports of Mao's fondness for Western-style ballroom dancing in Yan'an; see, for instance Harrison Forman, *Report from Red China* (New York, Henry Holt, 1945), p. 97; Dick Wilson, *Mao: The People's Emperor* (London, Hutchinson, 1979), pp. 185, 462 (notes). Mao apparently had occasional dance parties in Lushan during summer visits in the 1950s and 1960s.
[77]See Stalin (Moscow, 1952), pp. 7–8.

of iron—is that a law? Foreign [i.e., modern, ones] need only between 1.7 and 2 tons of coal for a ton of iron. Here there's a problem of laws.[78] One ton of steel needs 2 percent of copper and aluminum. It can't be said that the plans of the past eight years have completely reflected the law, and you can't say that this year's fully reflects the requirements of this economic law.

Stalin stops here and does not develop this question further. I have my doubts as to what level he reached in his studies. Why didn't he walk on two legs? Why does heavy industry need so many rules and regulations? The problem is, have we studied [this law], mastered it, and applied it with full understanding? At least this has not been done fully. Our plans, like theirs, don't fully reflect objective law, and therefore we have to study it.

Chapter Two [of Stalin's book deals with] commodity production. At present, some people are big on abolishing commodity production. Not a few people get all worried on their march towards communism whenever commodity production is brought up, because they think this to be something capitalist. They disregard the essential difference between capitalist and socialist commodities and have not understood the importance of making use of their [respective] functions. This is a symptom of not recognizing objective law, and not understanding the problem of 500 million peasants. During the initial phase of socialism [we] must make use of commodity production in order to unite the several hundred million peasants. I think that during the period of socialist construction, once there are people's communes, commodity production and commodity exchange must be ever more developed; socialist commodity production must be developed massively in a planned way, like livestock, soy beans, jute, casings [for sausages], sausages, fruit trees, skins and furs. At the moment, Yunnan ham no longer tastes good. While destroying superstition, [we] also restore superstition. Some people lean to [the idea] that [we] don't need commodities, [and] there are at least several hundred thousand people who think we no longer need commerce. That is an incorrect standpoint, which disregards objective law. Take Zhang Desheng's[79] **[192]** walnuts and eat them without paying a

---

[78]Here Mao is clearly beginning to rethink his grandiose steel targets, a process he completed at Wuchang later in the month, see *Origins* 2, p. 128.
[79]Zhang Desheng was first secretary of Shaanxi province, where the valley of the Wei River

penny—are you willing to do that? [If we] don't understand the five hundred million peasants or what kind of attitude the proletariat should adopt towards the peasantry, would it be possible to allocate without recompense the cotton of Qiliying?[80] You'd instantly get your head cracked open. In the old society, products had a controlling function over men. We [the state] own only a small fraction of the means of production and the social product. Stalin's analysis of Engels' statement is correct.[81] Our [sphere] of ownership by the whole people is very small; [and] only when all means of production are [thus] owned and the social product has become abundant will we be able to abolish commerce. It seems our economists have failed to understand this point. I use dead Stalin to bear down on the living. Stalin still retained his reservations on the question of the abolition of commodity production after [eventual] success of the English revolution,[82] and I think it would be best if England and Canada got together to form one state (page 10, para2). I'm afraid at least a part [of commodity production] can't be abolished; Stalin, however, does not arbitrarily decide the question; he does not give a conclusion.

Page eleven, paragraph three says there are some "half-baked Marxists" who want to expropriate the middle and small producers in the villages—in China, too, there are such people. Some comrades are impatient to proclaim ownership by the whole people. It isn't necessary to talk of expropriating the small producers, you just have to talk about abolishing commerce and implementing allocation and transfer, which amounts to expropriation, to get Taiwan all elated. In 1954 we made some mistakes, compulsory purchase [*zheng gou*] was too high—93 billion catties of grain—and the entire peasantry was against us; everybody was talking about grain, each household was talking about compulsory purchase.[83] This, too, was [the work of]

---

is noted for its walnuts; see T. R. Tregear, *A Geography of China* (London, Univ. of London Press, 1965), p. 215.

[80]Qiliying: a pioneer commune in pioneering Henan province; see *Origins* 2, pp. 80–1.

[81]Stalin (Moscow, 1952), pp. 9–11.

[82]Ibid.

[83]Compulsory grain procurement was introduced in 1953, partly to enable the government to control a key commodity as the 1st FYP got under way, partly to eliminate the disequilibrium between its current acquisitions and its essential disbursements; see Kenneth R. Walker, *Food Grain Procurement and Consumption in China* (Cambridge, Cambridge Univ. Press, 1984), pp. 42–3. Mao's figure of 93 million catties equals 46.5 million tons.

"half-baked Marxists," because they did not know how much grain the peasants had in their hands. Having gone through this experience once and made that mistake, we later decreased [our procurement] and fixed it at 83 billion catties. The first to oppose [this change] was Zhang Naiqi, which shows that the capitalists only desire to see our world plunged into chaos.[84] In sum, we had not hitherto figured out this law. The Chinese peasants are the owners of their labor, land, [and] means of production (seeds, tools, irrigation works, forests, fertilizer, etc.) and therefore of their products. For whatever reason, our philosophers and economists have suddenly forgotten these things and we are again in danger of becoming separated from the peasants. Therefore to achieve the "Three-Thirds System" with one-third delivered to higher levels (including adjustments within the counties) might require ten years. You (Tan)[85] want to leave [only] 25 percent [for the peasantry]; if the peasants come to blows [with us], **[193]** you [certainly] won't win. The Chinese workers are used to poverty; once they get to work, they work very hard. Furthermore, when cadres go down and become one with them, they work for twelve hours, and when called upon to go home, no one goes. After smelting iron and steel, the peasants said, "Our elder brothers, the workers, are quite extraordinary." The peasants are too poor, wages are too low; to take more from them now would not be good. [Taking the whole population], those who make an average of 5 yuan are in the minority.[86]

Lenin's answer, "The political power expropriates industry," has been accomplished by us.[87] The communes are a step ahead of the

---

Walker gives two figures, both over 52 million tons, for gross procurement (i.e., compulsory purchases and taxes) for 1954; Lardy's figure is 45.1 million tons; see Nicholas R. Lardy, *Agriculture in China's Modern Economic Development* (Cambridge, Cambridge Univ. Press, 1983), p. 34. Whatever the correct figure, Mao is clearly referring to gross procurement, not just to compulsory purchase, though he may not have been clear about that. The reaction of the peasants was sharp and this made a strong impression on the Chairman, for this was not the first time he had referred to this crisis; see Walker, pp. 56–67.
[84]Zhang Naiqi was a prominent non-Communist former businessman who was Minister of Food from 1952 to 1958, when he was dismissed for "rightist" remarks made in 1957; see *Origins* 1, pp. 282, 284. Presumably he opposed reducing grain procurements because of its negative impact on the food supplies for which his ministry was responsible.
[85]Presumably Tan Zhenlin; see n. 10.
[86]Mao is presumably referring to cash income distributed by the collective; see Lardy, p. 160, where the average figure for 1958 works out at 3.45 yuan.
[87]Stalin (Moscow, 1952), p. 12.

Soviet Union. Develop industry, strengthen the villages[88]—we are doing that, too. We should not expropriate the villages. [Having] the communes run industries is bolder than Stalin. Will that lead to capitalism? No. Because there is the political power that depends on the poor and lower middle peasants, there is the party, there are the county [party] committees, and hundreds of thousands of party members. In the past [we] though that profit-making industries should be run by the township government, and shouldn't be given over to the APCs. In this there was some lingering influence of Stalinism. To merge the political administration and the communes into one, and to permit them to run industries under the administration of the district committee, so that there is development everywhere and there are flowers opening all around—this does not diminish money, but increases it. Li Xiannian[89] has also become convinced of this. At present the communes are too poor; beyond providing food, wages are very small. Some pay only a few *jiao;* food, too, is very poor, substandard. It's still a case of poor and blank.[90] I say that's a good thing. [But] people are not enthusiastic about [going back to] the old base areas [days]. "Don't think about the future; don't think of the past: think only about pre–higher-level APC and the post–land-reform period." [This is their saying, and they] consider that the Golden Age.[91] "Revolution has come to a head, but what gets revolutionized is not the leadership's but our own head," they say in Shanxi. We didn't go for uninterrupted revolution [*buduan geming*], [and the revolution] has come to a standstill. I say [we] have to reach out to the middle peasants, and get them moving. "If the monk paws you, why can't I?"[92] Lenin said commodity production (exchange through purchase and sale) should be preserved for a certain period, it alone

---

[88]Ibid., p. 13.

[89]Li Xiannian, see Text 8, n. 24. His Finance Ministry had been attacked for conservativism by Mao in January 1958; see *Origins* 2, pp. 25–7.

[90]Mao first formulated this phrase in his speech on the ten great relationships in April 1956; see *SW5*, p. 306. His conception was that China's backward economic ("poor") and cultural ("blank") state was an advantage because it made the people eager for revolutionary change.

[91]The period in question is roughly 1953–5. Mao's remark is very revealing of peasant happiness with land reform and dissatisfaction with collectivization.

[92]Mao is quoting a rather vulgar line from the anti-hero of Lu Xun's famous short story, "The True Story of Ah Q." We use the translation by Yang Xianyi and Gladys Yang in *Selected Stories of Lu Hsun,* 3rd ed. (Peking, Foreign Languages Press, 1972), p. 78.

being acceptable to the peasants, and trade should be developed to the full.[93] Once we made a big fanfare out of this phrase [saying] that this was trade with a socialist essence. When Stalin says this is the only appropriate way, I think he is right. You can only trade, not expropriate. In 1954 we nevertheless still resorted to [compulsory] purchase and overdid it, which the peasants opposed.

We have followed all of Lenin's five points,[94] and moreover established the people's communes, and exerted all our energy to develop industry, agriculture, and commerce. The question is still the peasant question, [and] we have to be prudent and cautious. The root of the mistake in 1956 basically was that we did not look at the peasant question. Now **[194]** again it's a case of not understanding the peasant question. Once the heaven-storming enthusiasm of the peasants emerges, it's easy to think of them as workers, [and] to consider the peasants to be superior to the workers. This is a transformation of a rightist [deviation] into a leftist [deviation].

Commodity production should not be confused with capitalism. Why fear commodities if not from fear of capitalism? At present it's the state that is doing business with the people's communes, capitalism has long been discarded—why are [we] afraid of commodities? Don't be afraid: I think [commodity production] has to be greatly expanded. China is a state with an extremely undeveloped commodity production, even further behind than India and Brazil. India's railways and textiles are more developed than China's. Is there the exploitation of workers by capitalists in our state? No. Why be afraid? One cannot look at commodity production in an isolated manner: Stalin is entirely right (p. 13).[95] Commodity production depends on the kind of economy to which it is linked. Commodities linked to capitalism give rise to capitalism, whereas linked to socialism they give rise not to capitalism, but to socialism. Commodity production has existed since olden times; the Shang dynasty conveys the idea of doing business.[96] To regard King Zhou, Qin Shihuang, and Cao Cao as bad people is completely wrong.[97] King Zhou

[93]See Stalin (Moscow, 1952), p. 13 for the precise quotations.
[94]Lenin's five points are cited in Stalin (Moscow, 1952), pp. 12–3.
[95]Ibid., p. 14 (p. 13 in the Chinese edition).
[96]The character for the "Shang" dynasty is the same as that for "commerce" (*shang*).
[97]For King Zhou, see n. 6. For the tyrannical Qin Shihuang di, see n. 5. For Cao Cao, see Text 17, n. 39.

attacked the barbarians of Xuzhou and scored a victory, losing cadres [*ganbu*] and having all too many prisoners of war, "the stream of blood making the poles float (flag poles)." Mencius says: "To have complete faith in the *Book [of History]* is worse than having no *Book [of History]* at all." Which is to say he didn't believe in this incident of "the stream of blood making the poles float."[98] The slave society[99] did not lead to capitalism, [but] in the last stage of feudalism[100] the embryo of capitalism had already formed; on that point Stalin was not correct.[101] In the womb of capitalism, the proletariat and Marxism were already being bred, socialist ideology was already being produced.

At the second plenum [of the Seventh Central Committee] in 1949 we spoke about restricting [capitalism], and capitalism did not go beyond these restrictions. In 1950 we started to let them [the capitalists] expand for a period of six years, but already we were giving them state orders for processing; and when in 1956 it came to joint state-private ownership, actually we had already gained control.[102]

[98]Mao's ramblings here about ancient Chinese history were obviously triggered by his remark on commerce and the Shang dynasty, the last of whose emperors was King Zhou. Digression is typical of a Mao speech. The incident he cites is irrelevant to his point about the need for commodity production, but one of his concerns is evidently to rehabilitate these three negative characters in traditional historiography, King Zhou, Qin Shihuangdi, and Cao Cao, with the latter two of whom he from time to time gave evidence of identifying. Here he clearly derives much support from the revisionist historiography of Guo Moruo, the intellectual with whom he seems to have had the closest relationship after 1949; see *Guo Moruo quanji* (Collected works of Guo Moruo), "Lishi pian" (Historical section), vol. 1, 454; vol. 3, pp. 457–76, 486–8.

In the case of King Zhou, Mao evidently agrees with Mencius that no large-scale slaughtering of enemy troops was committed by King Zhou's troops, though his explanation is different; see Legge, vol. 2, *The Works of Mencius*, p. 479. Mao seems to be arguing that King Zhou's magnanimity is evidenced by his failure to slaughter all his prisoners despite the loss of his officers (i.e, *ganbu*) in a battle. In fact, this whole episode can be interpreted quite differently; see Legge, vol. 3, *The Shoo King* [The Book of History], p. 315.

[99]According to a standard Communist Chinese text, "Shang society was a slave society divided into slave, peasants, and nobles"; see *An Outline History of China* (Beijing, Foreign Languages Press, 1958), p. 15. The text goes on to state that the nobles made slaves of their prisoners of war, which suggests a more ignoble motive for King Zhou sparing his prisoners than that implied by Mao.

[100]According to official Communist Chinese analysis, the "feudal" period lasted from the unification of the country under the Qin until the collapse of the last dynasty, the Qing, in 1912; ibid., pp. 39, 293.

[101]Stalin (Moscow, 1952), p. 14.

[102]This translation is based on the assumption that *kongzi* (opening) is a misprint for *kongzhi* (control).

"The decisive economic conditions"[103]—we have all of them. May I ask how [commodity production] can lead to capitalism? This question is very important. Having swallowed up the ghost already, should one still be afraid of it? Don't be afraid; [commodity production] cannot lead to capitalism, because the material base of capitalism has already ceased to exist. Commodity production can obediently serve socialism and lead the five hundred million peasants toward the system of ownership by the whole people. Is commodity production a useful instrument? On behalf of the five hundred million peasants, the all-out use of this instrument [195] for the development of socialist production must be reaffirmed and this problem has to be on the agenda for discussion among cadres.

Labor, land, and the other means of production belong altogether to the peasants, and belong to the people's communes; therefore the commodities belong to the communes, too. Simply exchange commodity for commodity, no other linkage will be accepted by the peasants. We must not consider the Chinese peasants to be particularly progressive. The secretary of Xiuwu county committee was quite right in his assumptions.[104] The necessity of commodity exchange is something communists have to think about. Only after the abundant development of products would the liquidation of commodity circulation be made possible. Comrades, it's been just nine years, and already [we're] pressing [to say] we don't need commodities. Only when the central authority has the power to allocate all products might we get to the point where the commodity economy is not needed anymore and dissolves. Comrade Wu XX also does not have to manage [to get to communism] at the same time as comrade Chen XX.[105] [They are imbued with] too much Marxism. One does not have to rush to achieve it within four years. Don't think that after four years the peasants will be like the workers of Zhengzhou. Guerrilla war took twenty-two years—how can socialism be managed

[103]Stalin (Moscow, 1952), p. 14. These "decisive economic conditions"—social ownership of the means of production, the abolition of the system of wage labor, and the elimination of the system of exploitation—are said to be sufficient to prevent commodity production from being strictly confined and to make it incapable of producing capitalism.
[104]See n. 64.
[105]Comrade Wu XX could well be Wu Zhipu, the leftist first secretary of Henan province at this time; but if so, it is not clear who Comrade Chen XX was, since there was no provincial first secretary in 1958 with that surname.

without patience? Without patience it won't work. We have already [once] patiently awaited victory. With Taiwan it's the same thing. Is it better to have [John Foster] Dulles and Chiang [Kai-shek] supporting each other, or to win over one part to our side? We are cautious and careful; Chiang, too, is cautious and careful. We constantly warn the United States, making it clear that we are suffering wrongs.[106] A lot of people don't understand our warnings. I think we have to warn thirty-six hundred times. At present the Americans are doing nothing, which shows the effectiveness [of our warnings].

As long as two systems of ownership persist, commodity production is extremely necessary and extremely useful. Are you going to refute Stalin? The question of how to make the transition from one form of ownership to the other was not solved by Stalin himself. He was very clear, saying it required separate discussion.[107] In many places [in his booklet] you just have to change "our land" into "China" and things get interesting. [Stalin's statement that "our," i.e., Soviet, commodity production] "is confined to items of personal consumption" does not work.[108] Agricultural implements and handicraft tools, are also commodities, and can this lead to capitalism? It cannot. Hasn't Khrushchev sold machinery to the *kolkhozy*?[109] Historically there was commodity production, and now a kind of socialist commodity production is being added.

[106]The PRC had started issuing "serious warnings" to the US during the Taiwan Straits crisis in August–September 1958.

[107]Stalin (Moscow, 1952).

[108]Ibid.

[109]Under Stalin, agricultural machinery was under the control of the Machine Tractor Stations (MTS), which additionally exercised surveillance over the collectives (*kolkhozy*). In January 1958, Khrushchev abolished the MTS and forced the *kolkhozy* to buy the machinery; see Martin McCauley, *Khrushchev and the Development of Soviet Agriculture* (London, Macmillan, 1978), pp. 109–13.

Talks at the Wuchang Conference

21–23 NOVEMBER 1958

[196] 21 NOVEMBER 1958, MORNING

I couldn't get to sleep, [with] things on my mind; [I] turned [them] over as with an account book. [Now I have] suggested a few topics for everyone to think over. You [all] write articles; I have some ideas of my own.

. . . .[1]

(2) Planned and proportionate[2] [development:] if steel goes up,

---

Source: 13:196–217. The alternate text, 10:275–87, provides only the 23 Nov. talk, but identifies several names and has the 7th section of that talk, which the primary text lacks.
[1]Ellipsis dots in the primary text appear to indicate excision of Mao's first point.
[2]*You jihua an bili.*

everything else goes up, too, and the sixty-four kinds of rare metals must all be in proportion. What is proportion? At present no one among us has any idea what proportion is. I don't know what it is; perhaps you're a bit brighter. What planned and proportionate is has to be gradually figured out. Engels said one has to recognize objective law, master it, and apply it with full understanding.[3] I think Stalin's recognition [of this law] was not complete either; in [his] application [of it] there was no flexibility, and as to application with full understanding, in that [he] was even more deficient. His [handling of the relationship] between light and heavy industry was not so correct; too much emphasis on heavy industry, is like Iron Crutch Li,[4] . . . At present we have achieved some proportionality, namely by walking on two legs, with heavy industry, light industry and agriculture. He Changgong[5] did not come [to this conference], his legs are not in proportion. We do the three simultaneous promotions [of agriculture, light industry, and heavy industry]: That is walking on two legs, that is proportion. The relationship between big, medium, and small [factories promoted by us] also exhibits proportionality. With everything in the world there are large, medium, and small [sizes]. The twelve current reports[6] [before me] I have read; most of them are well written, some are particularly good; the combination of spoken language with scientific terminology is also a combination of native [*tu*] and foreign [*yang*].[7] In the past I have often said that if economic and scientific articles are not well written, you yourself might understand them, but others won't. I hope everybody will have a look [at these reports]. We have quite a few days [at our disposal];[8] if we read one a

[3]Quoted in Stalin, *Economic Problems of Socialism in the U.S.S.R.* (Moscow, Foreign Languages Press, 1952), pp. 4–5. See also Text 18, n. 66.

[4]For Iron Crutch Li, see Text 18, n. 51.

[5]He Changgong, Vice-Minister of Geology, received a serious leg wound around the time of the Long March, see Klein and Clark 2, pp. 292–5.

[6]Mao discusses and praises these reports from 12 central ministries in his noon talk of 23 November, below.

[7]Mao discussed how best to combine the best of Chinese and foreign ideas in his "Talk to music workers" on 24 August 1956; see the translation in Stuart Schram, *Mao Tse-tung Unrehearsed* (Harmondsworth, Penguin, 1974), pp. 84–90.

[8]In fact the Wuchang conference only lasted 21–7 November, but the CC's 6th plenum which followed it 28 November–10 December would have given delegates the requisite reading time. It is interesting that Mao knew from the start that the two meetings would last about two weeks, for central meetings and plenums varied in length and often give the impression that no fixed timetable has been agreed upon in advance.

day, we can easily read them all. It seems as if we have [achieved] some proportionality [with the] three simultaneous promotions; and we have a priority, taking heavy industry as the key link; but there still are problems in [our] truly recognizing objective law, and applying it with full understanding.

(About entering communism, [and what happens] if we enter it first) . . . [We] had better hang out **[197]** the shop sign of socialism while implementing communism in practice.[9] For this [kind of] having the reality but not the name, can one not use the analogy of a man of great learning like Confucius, Jesus, or Sakyamuni [the Buddha]? No one every gave them the title of PhD, but that did not prevent them from effectively doing what PhDs do. Confucius was later extolled and made famous, during the Han dynasty, by Dong Zhongshu;[10] afterwards he was not all that well regarded until the Tang dynasty when things got a bit better again; especially after Zhu Xi of the Song dynasty,[11] his sagehood was firmly established; and by the Ming and Qing dynasties he was eventually invested with the position of the "All-Perfect Ultimately Sage Prince Wenxuan." The May Fourth Movement dumped him again,[12] but whether [he] is a sage or not, it would not work any more. We communists are historical materialists, we recognize his position in history, but we don't recognize such [categories] as sage or non-sage. His mathematics was no match for ours, equivalent to lower middle school level, and perhaps only to higher primary school level. If we talk about mathematics, our university students would be sages and Confucius was merely a worthy. [All of] which is to say that when we make the transition to communism, we will not ennoble [ourselves] as sages, just carry on as worthies or common folk. What is the hurry in ennobling one-

[9]Presumably Mao's audience did not need to be told until much later in the speech that this was an extremely sensitive issue in Sino-Soviet relations (see *Origins* 2, pp. 132–5); but possibly this was all explained in the excised passage.
[10]Dong Zhongshu (ca. 179–104 BC): the Confucian scholar principally responsible for the adoption of Confucianism as the state ideology by the Emperor Han Wudi (r. 140–134 BC).
[11]Zhu Xi (Chu Hsi) (1130–1200): the principal synthesizer of Neo-Confucianism who reinvigorated the orthodoxy in the light of the challenge posed by Buddhism, which had more or less supplanted Confucianism as the dominant philosophy of the elite in the Tang dynasty.
[12]The May Fourth Movement, deriving its name from the patriotic, anti-Japanese student demonstrations of 4 May 1919, is the term applied to the iconoclastic search for a new, modern Chinese culture around that time.

self as a sage? Being ennobled as a worthy does not inhibit one's essence [from being that of a sage]. There are three kinds of people—common people, worthies, and sages—and becoming a worthy is quite enough. We communists are sages in essence, but not ennobled; carrying on as worthies in no way inhibits our essence. Is that not better?[13]

We, too, have our shortcomings. When the Beidaihe conference spoke of three, four, five, or six years or a little bit more until we would make it to communism, luckily it [mentioned] five conditions, too:[14] (1) extreme abundance of products; (2) an elevation of communist ideology, consciousness, and morality; (3) popularization and elevation of culture and education; (4) disappearance of the three differences[15] and of the remainders of bourgeois right;[16] (5) gradual disappearance of the functions of the state other than in relation to the external world. The disappearance of the three differences and bourgeois right cannot be achieved in less than one or two decades; I'm not in a hurry, but the young people are; [but] if the three[17] conditions are not completely fulfilled, then [we've attained] only socialism and no more. Would everybody please give some thought to this question. I am not saying that we should advance at a leisurely pace; [the slogan] "More, faster, better, more economically" is something [in accordance with] objective [law]. Where acceleration is possible, accelerate; but things should not be forced. The TU 104 airplane reaches an altitude of over 10,000 meters, our planes only a few thousand meters. Old Ke[18] riding the train is even slower, and walking is slower still. Speed is an objective rule. I don't believe this year's grain [harvest is] 450 million tons; 370 million tons would mean a doubling

[13]Mao's long-winded, historical justification for not proclaiming China's transition to communism is illustrative of the disappointment he anticipated the more fervent cadres would feel after the euphoria earlier in the year.

[14]See Text 17, p. 434ff.

[15]The three differences were between town and country, industry and agriculture, and mental and physical labor.

[16]Bourgeois right was, in the context of the GLF, material incentives, payment according to work.

[17]"Three" must be a misprint for "five."

[18]It is not clear whether Mao is using the name "Ke" simply to mean anyone traveling by train or is referring to someone specific he sees in the audience, like, say, his close collaborator during the GLF, Shanghai first secretary, Ke Qingshi. The former seems less likely, since it would have been more normal for him to have chosen a commoner surname (like Zhang, Wang, or Li) in that case.

[of the previous harvest and] that is possible, and I would be satisfied with it. I don't believe in 400 million, **[198]** 450 million, or 500 million tons. There are two possibilities with regard to speed: either it is relatively high, or it is not that high. We envisage producing 400 million tons of steel [annually] within fifteen years; perhaps we'll manage it, perhaps we won't. One question is whether we can or not, the other whether we need [so much] or not. Will we, in the last analysis, need that much; who will be the buyers? Only Lü Zhengcao[19] to construct railroads with it; or [it will be used] for building ships, that would be a matter for the Transport Ministry. Will we need it for mechanical and electrical facilities and still other things or not; will we achieve [such a quantity] or not? Generally speaking we have a pretty good grasp on the agricultural side, [but] industry is more difficult than agriculture. You who are in charge of industry, what do you say: Can we do it or not? If the whole party and the entire population really concentrate on industry, with only two months [to go] who can be sure of it? That touches upon the Forty Points. Whether that will do it, [we are] not sure. We might discuss the Forty Points once on this occasion, but we shouldn't make a focal point out of it.[20] We held the Zhengzhou meeting; [that was] very good, it had very great historical significance. But continuing on from there, a discussion will not be productive as far as whether we can produce those 400 million tons of steel, and whether we will need them. Comrade XXX has given me an explanation that does not solve the problem; he only explains how it is possible, but does not answer the question whether we need it or not. The United States produce 100 million tons; their exports are a bit over 10 million tons (which includes machinery), that is about 10 percent. With at least three years of arduous struggle we can edge a bit closer next year and the year after. On an impulse, [I] thought of a figure and came out with it. Can we make 30 million tons of steel next year? The need seems to

---

[19]Lü Zhengcao was Vice-Minister of Railways; but at the end of the 1950s (as Mao's reference confirms), he gradually took on the role of minister though not formally named to that post till 1965; see the biographies of Lü and of his superior, Teng Daiyuan, in Klein and Clark, pp. 655–8, 828–31.

[20]The "40 Points" is presumably the 12-Year Agricultural Program (see Text 18, n. 14), perhaps revised (see Text 18, n. 74). If so, then Mao appears to suggest setting aside the tasks of the program, at least for the last two months of the year, in order to fulfill the industrial targets.

be there, but can we do it? Let's all discuss that. This year we have 11 million tons, but we started late; next year [we will] have twelve months.

(XX interrupts: [If] 30 million tons [of steel] is a marshal, how are [we] going to handle the rest?)[21]

[Chairman:] The problem of the Forty Points: if it is publicized, it would be very bad. You are producing so much, how much does the Soviet Union produce?[22] That is known as vanity inviting disaster. Not only will there be no boasting, no one will believe you, and [people will] just say "The Chinese are boasting; and if [you] suffer a real disaster, the Americans might use the atomic bomb [against you]; it will throw you into confusion." Of course, that's not certain. If in the future we first can't do it, and secondly we don't need [it]—wouldn't we have toppled ourselves? I think we should continue to be a bit cautious. There are people having illicit relations with foreign countries, giving reports to embassies; and the Soviet Union above all may be startled. How should we handle this? A little surplus grain doesn't matter; but [if] everybody has 5,000 kilograms [a year], that is not good either and will lead to disaster, unless [people] don't sow their fields for three years, and start again only when everything is eaten up.[23] I have heard that some girls say that if they don't get 40,000 kilograms per *mou* [199] they won't marry. I think they intend to practice celibacy and use this as a pretext. According to [Chen] Boda's [24] investigations they are still thinking of getting married, [but] 40,000 kilograms just won't happen. That is the second question: In the last analysis what would be best? Let's talk about it again in two or three years; anyway it does not matter. I have said in the past we should not make long-term plans as we had no grasp of things but just one-year plans. However, it is also necessary that there

[21]The three "marshals" in the GLF were steel, grain, and cotton; but the term *marshal* was also applied more widely; see, for example, Text 18, n. 1.
[22]Mao's point appears to be that the publication of a revised and even more extravagant 40 Points would annoy the Russians by making them appear laggard.
[23]The disaster Mao foresees could be either that the proclamation of an excessive claim would cause everyone to relax their efforts with unfortunate results, or that, if the claim were actually achieved, there would be no storage space and the harvest would have to be eaten before production could be resumed.
[24]Chen Boda: alternate member of the Politburo and editor of *Hongqi* (Red flag).

should be ideas in the heads of a few people. We can adopt two types of approach to the Forty Point Program: first conscientiously to discuss things and make it a draft to be discussed and passed by the entire meeting; the second method is not to discuss nor to pass [it] at all but just to make things clear by explaining that the numbers at the Zhengzhou conference are not definite but have positive meaning for mobilizing purposes.

(3) The tasks of this conference are, first, the people's communes; second, the arrangements for next year's plan (especially the arrangements for the first quarter). Of course, some other things may be dealt with too, like the "two transfers, three unifications, and one guarantee" in finance and trade, and so forth.[25]

(4) The question of drawing the line: should one or should one not draw a line? And how? At the Zhengzhou conference there were five criteria [put forward], [but] Shanxi had objections; the essential manifestation for the completion of the building of socialism is ownership by the whole people. That is different from what Stalin proclaimed in 1938. What does complete achievement of ownership by the whole people mean? What does completion of the building of socialism mean? Stalin's two reports of 1936 and 1938 (the former being the report on the constitution, the latter the report to the Eighteenth Party Congress) put forward two indicators: one was the extinction of classes, and the other was that industry should occupy a 70 percent proportion [of the economy]. But [since then], the Soviet Union has gone through [another] twenty years and XXXX[26] will have another twelve years; that is, after thirty-two years they will eventually make the transition, and at that time collective ownership and ownership by the whole people will finally merge. On this ques-

---

[25] *Liangfang, santong, yibao:* This formula was apparently devised by Finance Minister Li Xiannian. The two transfers were of personnel and assets to the lower levels; the three unifications were of policy, planning, and control of working funds at the commune level; the one guarantee was the commune's undertaking to pay an appropriate portion of its revenue to the state; see Warren Kuo, ed., *A Comprehensive Glossary of Chinese Communist Terminology* (Taipei, Institute of International Relations, 1978), pp. 319–20, where a somewhat different translation and explanation is given for *yibao.*

[26] It is not clear what the four missing characters are, but Mao may be referring to Khrushchev's prediction, published in the "theses" for the Soviet Seven-Year Plan (1959–65) just before the Wuchang conference, that by 1970 the USSR would overtake the USA in per capita as well as total output of major industrial and agricultural products; see *Origins 2*, p. 16.

tion, we don't do things according to their pattern. We talk about the five criteria; and we don't say that when industry accounts for 70 percent, that means the building [of socialism] is completed. Up to this year, we have had nine years; with another ten that would make nineteen. Counting from 1921 to 1938, the Soviet Union had had eighteen years, but [by then] only had 18 million tons of steel. By 1968 we, too, will have had eighteen years; in terms of time that will be about the same, but for sure we will have more things. Next year we will have exceeded 18 million tons of steel. For us, the criterion for the completion of the building of socialism will be the unification of the systems of ownership. Everything will be owned by the whole people. We take the achievement of ownership by the whole people as the primary criterion. By this criterion, the Soviet Union has not [200] completed the building of socialism. They still have two systems of ownership. This has given rise to a question: people all over the world ask, has the Soviet Union even now still not completed the building of socialism?

(Zeng Xisheng[27] interrupted: This point should not be made public.)

[Chairman:] Even if we don't publicize it, it still will be passed on. Another method is not to put it that way, [but do] as we did at the Beidaihe conference, where we only mentioned some conditions [for the completion of the building of socialism] but did not say at what time the building would be completed; perhaps [in this way] we would gain more initiative. The Beidaihe conference documents had a shortcoming, namely that the time [set there] was a bit too ambitious, as a result of the influence of Henan. I thought the north would need a minimum of three to four years, and the south a maximum of five to six years; but that cannot be managed, and one will have to revise [that timing]. Living standards in the Soviet Union are generally higher than ours, but they have not yet made the transition. There is a professor at Peking University who went to Xushui to have a look and said, "One-yuan [*yikuai qian*] communism is not for me." The salary in Xushui is in fact not more than two or three yuan. Ten years of the three-thirds system [*san san zhi*], with one-

---

[27]Zeng Xisheng: Anhui province first secretary.

third [of output] being allocated and transferred annually, which means one-third ownership by the whole people; of course, there also is one-third for accumulation, and there still has to be the part for the peasants' own consumption. So we are close to ownership by the whole people. At present we still eat meagerly. And as to these public mess halls, they were [set up] too quickly, at least three to four and as a maximum five to six years [will be needed]. I am a bit panicked; I fear I may have committed the mistake of adventurism.[28] Wu Zhipu[29] is also less adamant, and thinks it would be quite all right if things took a bit longer. And then there is the completion of the "three transformations" [*san hua*]: mechanization, electrification, and transformation [of the land] into parks [*yuanlin*], for which five to ten years will be needed. Once [mechanization, electrification and afforestation] have become preponderant, one can speak of transformation.

(XXX: Once a consumption level of 150 to 200 yuan is reached, one batch can be transferred; in the future one batch after another will be transferred. There are advantages doing things this way, but if one waits until [the consumption level] is still higher, transfer will pose a lot of problems, and that in turn will not be of much use.)[30]

(XXX: The transformation of agriculture into factory[-style work] should actually be called mechanization and electrification.)

(XXX: The problem is that the three transformations cannot be easily brought about, in particular the transformation [of the land] into parks.)

(XX: After we did land reform, we went in for collectivization in a big way and [then] set up the people's communes; we can make the transition only when per capita income is between 150 and 200 yuan. [If the income level] is too high, as in Rumania, when peasant

---

[28]Mao is presumably being ironical, having blasted some of his senior colleagues earlier in the year for opposing what they called adventurism.

[29]Wu Zhipu: Henan province's first secretary who had made his province into a GLF path breaker.

[30]The unknown interrupter appears to mean that people will be readier to accept transfer of ownership to the state (i.e., the whole people) if they are not too poor and not too rich.

income is higher than worker income, transfer does not go smoothly. Keep the three transformations in low key, strike while the iron is hot, early transformation is better than late transformation; after three or four years one will be ready to make the transformation.)

[Chairman:] According to your way of talking, there is great hope that the building of socialism will be completed within eighteen years.

(XXX: Mechanization and electrification are not easy.)

(Ke Qingshi: Does collective ownership [201] promote production or not? Is it advantageous [for the collective] to guarantee everything?)[31]

(XXX: If we work on the basis of transferring and allocating one-third according to the three-thirds system, I'm afraid we'll need ten years; three years or so won't be enough.)

[Chairman:] According to the opinion of XX and XX, it is necessary to take advantage of a situation of poverty to make the transition; transition in poverty perhaps has advantages, otherwise it might be difficult to make the transition at all.[32] In sum, a line has to be drawn; but would you please discuss how, and set up some criteria, which must absolutely be higher than those of the Soviets.

(5) The question of the abolition of classes: the question of the abolition of classes deserves some thought. According to the Soviet theory which they promulgated in 1936, after sixteen years [classes] were abolished. The same might be true for us after sixteen years; this year it's nine years and we have seven more to go, but one should not state it so definitely. There are two kinds of abolition of classes: One concerns classes that engage in economic exploitation; they are easily abolished, and we now can say they are already abolished. The second concerns classes in terms of political thinking (landlords, rich peasants, the bourgeoisie, including their intellectuals); these are not

[31]Ke Qingshi, the Shanghai first secretary, presumably is asking whether communes should guarantee all consumer expenditure, e.g., food, clothing, housing. As one of the "leftists" of this period (see *Origins* 2, p. 221), Ke presumably was in favor of a total guarantee.
[32]This is a rare insight into a high-level argument being conducted in public. After Mao's death, the concept of "transition in poverty" was ridiculed and blamed on Chen Boda; see *Origins* 2, p. 131.

easily abolished, and they have not yet been abolished—that is what we discovered during last year's Rectification Campaign. In a comment I wrote on a report [*piyu*] in 1956, there was a passage: "The socialist revolution has been basically accomplished, the question of the system of ownership has been basically solved."[33] I now think that was not appropriate, [for] after this we were confronted with the Zhang [Bojun] and Luo [Longji] alliance.[34] The landlords in the villages liked reading the *Wenhu bao*[35] once the *Wenhui bao* arrived, rumors spread, and the landlords, rich peasants, counterrevolutionaries, and bad elements seized the opportunity to rise. That is why [after] the Qingdao conference [of July 1957] we started making arrests and executions. In Hunan a hundred thousand people were struggled against, ten thousand were arrested, one thousand executed; in other provinces it was the same, and thus the problem was solved. These landlords, rich peasants, counterrevolutionaries, and bad elements did not practice economic exploitation; but, as a class in the political and ideological [sphere], like the landlords and bourgeoisie who were with Zhang Bojun, they still exist; and when the people's communes were set up, above all [it was] the intellectuals and professors [who] were most concerned and were in a constant state of anxiety. There was a woman professor in Beijing who had a dream in the middle of the night: the people's communes had been set up and her child had gone into a [collective] nursery; she burst into tears, and only when she awoke did she know it had been a dream. Things are not that simple.

In 1936, Stalin proclaimed the abolition of classes—so why in 1937 did he kill so many people, and [why were] spies so thick on the ground? I think one has to leave this question of the abolition of classes in suspense, and that it's best not to proclaim it hastily. In the last analysis, at what time would the proclamation of the abolition of classes be most advantageous? If one does proclaim **[202]** the abolition, the landlords will all be peasants, and the capitalists workers: Is that advantageous or not? The bourgeoisie are permitted to enter the people's communes, but they must still wear their bourgeois hats;

[33]See chapter by Roderick MacFarquhar in this volume, p. 4.
[34]On Zhang and Luo, see MacFarquhar chapter above, n. 20.
[35]The *Wenhui bao* was accused by Mao in 1957 of inciting rightist disaffection in 1957; see *Origins* 1, pp. 224–5.

fixed interest is not abolished. In view of Stalin's too early proclamation, one should not be hasty in proclaiming the abolition of classes, and I'm afraid one can only proclaim it when there is fundamentally no more harm in doing so. Is the abolition of classes within the Soviet intelligentsia in any way complete? In my opinion, not so. Just recently a Soviet author has written a novel that created a worldwide, small, anti-Soviet movement; the Hong Kong papers made noisy propaganda for it, and Eisenhower said: "If this author came, I would receive him."[36] Among their authors there are still [members of the] bourgeoisie, and among their university graduates there are still so many who believe in religion and become priests.

(XXX: If Ehrenburg[37] were in China, he would be a rightist.)

[Chairman:] I'm afraid they had no previous experience, while we have had it; we should be a bit careful.

(6) As to the question of economic theory, do we in the last analysis need commodities or not, and what falls into this category? At the Zhengzhou [conference], we restricted [commodities] to the means of livelihood, and added a part of the means of production of the communes. This is Stalin's theory; he maintained that the means of production should not be sold to the collective farms. Our country has proclaimed that the land is nationally owned; we make the machinery for mechanization ourselves, the peasants cannot make it, and we deliver it to them. Recently there was news that the third edition of the Soviet *Political Economy: A Textbook* had enlarged the scope of [what should be considered] a commodity, which now is not restricted any more to the means of livelihood, but also includes the means of production. This question should be studied. One point made by Stalin did not make sense. Agricultural products were commodities, while industrial products were not: one a commodity, the other a non-commodity (the products of state industries). How

---

[36]Presumably Mao is referring to Pasternak's *Dr. Zhivago*, the English translation of which was published in Britain in September and in the USA in October 1958. In the latter month, Pasternak was awarded the Nobel Prize for Literature; see the introduction by Patricia Blake in Max Hayward, *Writers in Russia, 1917–1978* (London, Harvill, 1983), p. liii.

[37]Ehrenburg always managed to stay on the right side of the Soviet authorities, albeit sometimes promoting unorthodox attitudes, as in his novel *The Thaw* (1954–6); see Hayward, pp. 138–9.

can anyone explain the exchange between the two ([e.g.] the exchange between cloth and the grain from the villages)? I think the way [we are] defining it at present is rather good: The means of production, Wang Heshou's[38] steel, can't be eaten or worn; with Zhao Erlu's[39] machinery it's the same. Many of the [products] of the chemical industry can be worn; [but] your stuff, Zhang Linzhi,[40] can't be eaten. Li Baohua's[41] water can be drunk, but [his] electricity can't be eaten. In the last analysis, the means of production serve to manufacture the means of livelihood. (Including clothing, food, shelter, and transportation, cultural entertainment, the *Erhu*[42] and flutes for singing performances, and the four treasures of the scholar's studio,[43] etc.) There was a period when [we] seemed to think that the fewer commodities the better, and the shorter time [they were around] the better, and to the extent that after two or three years they would not be needed anymore. This raises problems. I think that extending the commodity period a bit **[203]** is better. If one does not need a hundred years, one might still need thirty, or at the minimum there may be fifteen years—what's so harmful about that? The question is, what disadvantages does this have? Does it obstruct economic development or not? Of course, there are periods when [commodity production] obstructs the development of production. So the statements in the Forty Points[44] dealing with commodities are inappropriate; they are still written according to Stalin's [opinions]. But Stalin did not make clear the relationship between the means of livelihood produced by state-owned [industries] and those produced by collective farms. Would you all please discuss this; it is in the third edition of *Political Economy*. As to the rest there is little to change. Thus one can repudiate only a part of Stalin's things and should not throw them out altogether. The reason being that he is scientific, [and] to repudiate him altogether would not be good. Who was the first to write a study of the political economy of socialism? It was none other than

---

[38]Wang Heshou: Minister of the Metallurgical Industry; Mao had mentioned him at Beidaihe.

[39]Zhao Erlu: Minister of the 1st Ministry of Machine Building, whom Mao had also mentioned at Beidaihe.

[40]Zhang Linzhi: Minister of the Coal Industry.

[41]Li Baohua: Vice-Minister of Water Conservancy and Electric Power.

[42]*Erhu:* two-stringed bowed instrument, a sort of Chinese fiddle.

[43]Four treasures: brush, ink stick, ink slab, paper.

[44]I.e., the 12-Year Agricultural Program.

Stalin. Of course, there are partial shortcomings and mistakes in this book. Such as in [his comments on] the third letter[45] [where he says] agricultural machinery should not be sold to the collective farms, in order to keep a hold of the peasants' pigtails. He laid down the rule that they should have only the right of use, but not the right of ownership; this simply [demonstrates] a lack of trust in the peasants, whereas we gave [the machinery] to the cooperatives, . . . I once asked Comrade Yudin[46] why, since their villages had trucks, small factories, and work tools, they couldn't be given tractors. We here, me included, have in the past not paid attention to the political economy of socialism, and have not studied the texts, and at present a few hundred thousand people throughout the country are discussing it vigorously; ten different people have ten different theories, a hundred different people have a hundred different theories. It's time to study the texts again; those one had not read should be read, and those one had read should be reread; and furthermore *Political Economy: A Textbook* should be read. Have you done so or not? Everybody should be issued a copy of this textbook. First read the section on socialism— aren't we discussing ideological guidelines?

(7) Should one pour cold water [on enthusiasm]? People must eat their fill, and sleep sufficiently, especially those who go all out and battle hard for days and nights. Once they come off work, they must—except under special circumstances—sleep for a while. At this point [we] should alleviate [people's] tasks. In the construction of irrigation works, between last winter and this spring we moved, nationwide, over 50 billion cubic meters of earth and stone, but from this winter to next spring we want to move 190 billion cubic meters nationwide, an increase of well over three times. Then we have to deal with all sorts of tasks: steel, copper, aluminum, coal, transport, the processing industries, the chemical industry—[they all] need hordes of people. In this kind of situation, I think if we do [all these things simultaneously] half of China's population unquestionably will die; and if it's not a half, it'll be a third or ten percent, a death toll of 50 million people. When people died in Guangxi, wasn't Chen Manyuan dismissed?[47] If with a death toll of 50 million you didn't

---

[45]See Stalin, pp. 87–99.

[46]P. F. Yudin: Soviet ideologist, then serving as ambassador to China; see Text 3, n. 45.

[47]Chen Manyuan, then Guangxi first secretary, was dismissed in June 1957, along with

lose your jobs, I at least should lose mine; [whether I would lose my] head would also be open to question. **[204]** Anhui wants to do so many things, it's quite all right to do a lot, but make it a principle to have no deaths. One hundred ninety billion cubic meters of earth and stone is an awful lot; discuss it—if you insist on moving [that many], I can't do anything about it; but if people die [as a result], you cannot cut off my head. Last year must be surpassed by a bit, moving [say] 60 to 70 billion [cubic meters], but one doesn't want an excessive amount. In the document by Tan Zhenlin[48] and Liao Luyan[49] there is a passage on this that I hope you will talk over. Apart from this, if there are other tasks that press on you to the point of suffocation, how to alleviate them a bit can also be considered. Tasks will have to be increased, but they cannot be increased too much. One has to look at it from the opposite side; doubling [of output] is possible, but multiplying by several tens has to be thought about. As to 30 million tons of steel, do we really need that much? Are we able to produce [that much]? How many people do we have to mobilize? Could it lead to deaths? Even though you say that it is necessary to work on the basic points (steel, coal), how many months do you need to get that done? Hebei says half a year, which will have to include iron-smelting, coal, transport, steel rolling, and so forth; this has to be talked over.

(XXX: The tasks for next year will be discussed severally by each province. Will they agree to 30 million tons or not? If not, [this target] will have to be changed and we'll have to consider whether it should be 30 million tons.)

(Interruption: Sixty million people turn out 10 million tons of iron. In fact, it is only 7 million tons, of which good iron amounts to only 40 percent; it is not as [claimed in] the high estimate. Once a base is established, bring back the [farm] laborers, or else there won't be anyone left even to harvest the seeds, and there won't be any

---

other officials, for failing to prevent deaths by famine in spring 1956; see *Survey of the China Mainland Press* 1562 (Hong Kong, U.S. Consulate General), pp. 13–20.
[48]Tan Zhenlin: Politburo member in charge of agriculture during the GLF.
[49]Liao Luyan: Minister of Agriculture.

exports [of agricultural products] either. Of 11 million tons of steel, good steel represents no more than 9 million tons or perhaps 8.5 tons. If we are aiming at 30 million tons, that is a two-and-a-half-fold increase.)

[Chairman:] This year there are two aspects [to be considered]. How many 60 millions can China's population be divided into? If of the several million tons of local iron and local steel, only 40 percent are good, should we make an earnest effort to double that to get from 10.7 million tons this year to 21.4 million tons next year? If we produce yet another ten thousand tons, we should be able to manage 21.4 million tons next year. In my view, we should be a bit prudent. If water conservancy [construction] sticks at 50 billion cubic meters and doesn't multiply in any way, won't that still be 500 billion cubic meters after ten years? I say we should leave some things for our sons to do. Why should we finish everything?

Furthermore, as to the arrangements for different types of work—coal, electricity, oil, chemicals, afforestation, building materials, cloth and paper making—at this conference we should adopt a low-keyed approach and pipe down a bit. If, after having worked through the first half of next year, things go [well], there are reserve forces and circumstances are favorable, then we might be a little more [205] ambitious and ratchet up on on the first of July. But one should not do it like the people who play the *huqin*[50] at the opera, who risk breaking the strings when they tighten them too much. Perhaps this sounds a bit like pouring cold water, and the cadres at the lower levels who run the communes may have some objections and will not fail to curse us for rightist tendencies. [But] don't be afraid, toughen your scalps and let those below curse you. Doubling [output] has never happened in the world since Pan Gu separated heaven and earth[51]—how is this a rightist tendency?

What are the targets for agriculture?

(Tan Zhenlin: Publicly we say we aim at about 10 billion catties, which would give about two thousand catties per head.)

[50]*Huqin:* bowed instruments used in Chinese opera.
[51]A common term for "since the beginning of the world"; Pan Gu was the mythological creator of the universe.

[Chairman:] These things from the Beidaihe conference have to be discussed again. You talk of right opportunism, [so] I proceed to double [targets]! [This year the target is] 80,000 machine tools, next year a fourfold increase, producing 320,000—can that really be true? At the time of the Beidaihe conference we still had no experience in running industry; but when, after a bit more than two months, the transportation of iron and steel has clogged things up everywhere, we have become relatively experienced. Generally speaking it's best if there's a practical possibility. There are two kinds of practical[52] possibility: one is a real possibility, the other is an unreal possibility. For instance, it is unrealistic at present [for us] to make a satellite, but in the future this might be realized. Isn't it true that there are two kinds of possibility? Comrade [Chen] Boda![53] A possibility that can be transformed into reality is a real possibility; the second kind is the possibility which cannot be transformed into reality: As an example, dogmatists in the past maintained that all they said was a hundred percent correct, [and] didn't we lose all the regions as a consequence? I think not to marry if the production per *mou* does not reach 40 tons is also [an example of aiming at an] unrealistic possibility.[54]

(8) The people's communes have to be overhauled for four months; in December, January, February, and March. An inspection force consisting of ten thousand people should be set up, mainly to see if people get eight hours of sleep a night. When they sleep only seven, that means they are not [able] to finish their tasks—I never finish my tasks; you can also investigate [me] and stick up a big-character poster. [Also] how the mess halls are doing; they should have regulations, and the people's communes should discuss them. [We'll] issue a directive. Can the overhaul be completed in four months? Isn't that a bit short—does one need half a year? According to current reports from Hubei, at present 7 or 8 percent of the communes are running relatively well. I belong to the skeptical faction; I count it a success if I see one out of ten people's communes is being run really well. The provincial ([or] city) and prefectural com-

---

[52]A portion of this text in a significantly different form appears in Helmut Martin, ed., *Mao Zedong Texte*, vol. 3 (München, Carl Hanser Verlag, 1980), pp. 504–5.

[53]Chen Boda (see n. 24) had helped Mao in the study of dialectics in the 1930s; see Raymond F. Wylie, *The Emergence of Maoism* (Stanford, Stanford Univ. Press, 1980), pp. 59–66.

[54]See Mao's references to young girls wanting to marry only if certain levels of productivity were reached, in this text, above, p. 486.

mittees must concentrate forces to help see to it that one commune is run well. They have four months; then the ten-thousand-member inspection force has to be set up, otherwise there is danger that the country will go under. [John Foster] Dulles **[206]** and Chiang Kai-shek both slander us for setting up people's communes. They put it this way: "If you don't set up people's communes, you won't go under; but if you set them up, you will go under." I think one can't say they don't have a point. Generally speaking there are two kinds of possibility: one, we go under; the other, we don't. Of course, having gone under, there may still be a chance of staging a comeback; it [may be only] a temporary catastrophe. The mess halls may go under, and so may the nurseries; in Gucheng county in Hubei province, there's a mess hall where things went like this. A number of the nurseries will most certainly be abolished. It only needs a few babies to die, and parents will certainly take [their children] back home. In Henan there is a happiness home[55] where after 30 percent [of the residents] had died; all the rest ran away. I, too, would have run away: how could it not collapse? Given the fact that nurseries and happiness homes can collapse, why can't the people's communes? I think as with everything there are two possibilities: collapse and non-collapse. There were APCs in the past which collapsed; there were instances of collapse in Henan and Zhejiang,[56] and I don't believe that in such a big province as your Sichuan not even a single APC collapsed. It's just that it was not reported. From the time a child is three, a part of the cells in the human body start dying; peeling skin and loss of hair are all manifestations of partial decay. Dead cells contribute to the process of growth, a process of metabolism contributing to growth. Within the party a section of the membership became rightists; from the branches to the Center, everywhere were people who fell from power: Didn't Chen Duxiu, Zhang Guotao, Gao Gang, and Rao Shushi fall from power in the Center? Wang Ming[57] has still not fallen; at present his attitude has improved (his letter to the Center should be printed for him), perhaps . . . this line of ours actually does seem to be a hundred percent correct.[58]

[55]I.e., an old people's home.

[56]The "collapse" in Zhejiang in 1955 was held against the then party agricultural chief, Deng Zihui.

[57]Mao mentioned most of these examples from time to time; see Text 1, n. 10.

[58]Judging from analogous cases where alternate texts can fill in excisions, the ellipsis dots here

It's a good procedure for me to bring up problems and topics for discussion. Every comrade can bring up problems. At times like these, such problems lodge in my head and [it's like having] fifteen buckets at the well, seven up and eight down:[59] In the end, which method is best—for instance, with regard to steel, in the end is a 30 million ton or a 21.4 million ton [target] better?

This is a conference to sum up this year; it's already [virtually] December. In making arrangements for next year, the key is the first quarter.

[207] 23 NOVEMBER 1958, NOON

(1) I'll start with remarks about writing articles. Comrades from twelve central ministries have written twelve reports: Would those Central Committee members and alternate members who have come to this conference please have a look at them, discuss them, and make amendments. I have read the articles with much pleasure. The line is still that line; the spirit is still that spirit; but the bases for the plan targets are not fully substantiated. [They] only talk about what is possible, and not about the basis [for it]. [One] says 400 million tons [of grain] is possible: [but] why is it possible? The targets have to be realistically studied; they have to be made a bit more solid. The report on electric power is very well written. Who wrote it? Li Baohua? Liu Lanbo?[60] Liu Lanbo is not here. Without electric power, you people who are present cannot achieve anything. Everyone in the Central Committee has to read it, and one can make it available to the party committee secretaries and the managers of the eighteen key enterprises to let them all read it so that they get an overall perspective. Some of the articles might even be published in the papers after having been revised to let people know. There is nothing secret [about them]. When I said one should compress the atmosphere,[61] I did not mean reducing it; matter does not disappear, and there is always so much air

indicate that lines have been twisted or a point uncongenial to the Cultural Revolution editors deleted.
[59]See Text 14, n. 5.
[60]Li Baohua and Liu Lanbo were Vice-Ministers of Water Conservancy and Electric Power.
[61]*Yasuo kongqi:* translated earlier in this text, toward the end of Mao's speech of 21 November, as "pipe down." See p. 496.

around that you can only compress it and bring it to a liquid or a solid state. As for the question of not having got through the pass,[62] we should clarify them a bit more and explain at what time we will get through. When can we get through? There is some reason and basis for saying next year in March, April, or May (as an example both ends of the metallurgy facilities—mining equipment and steel-rolling equipment have not got through the pass.) Why don't complete sets of machinery fit together? When after all will they finally fit? On what basis? Talk it over with [your] Number Two's. Another example: When and how will the technical [problems] of [running] modern furnaces with local iron be solved? Another example: What is one to do when electrical power is insufficient? At present we have found a way out, and that is that [units which need electrical power] manufacture for themselves, build for themselves, and equip for themselves [their own] electric power plants. That factories, mines, [governmental] organs, schools and military units take care of their own electricity, and that water, fire, wind, gas (methane) are all made use of [to produce it], is one of the successes achieved by the Northeast. Can the other regions use similar methods? How much [of the electricity shortage] will be solved [in this manner]?

Shouldn't we discuss the twelve reports for another two or three days and then get the revision done? The amendments [should be] based on real needs [that are] reliable, [then] revise the [plan] targets again.

[208] The regulation we are promoting at present is each year to take a grip [on matters] four times, with the Center and the localities doing joint inspections and consulting together. Next year's things should be arranged this year, and a framework for the year should be put up first. Next year, as spring, summer, fall, and winter come, each time one must get a grip. This year with the Nanning conference, the Chengdu conference, the second Session of the Eighth Party Congress, the Beidaihe conference, the Zhengzhou conference and this Wuchang conference, we have got a grip on things altogether six times. The Nanning conference indulged in verbiage [but] solved mutual relations. The Chengdu conference was a bit more concrete, and solved some

[62]*Guoguan:* There was much talk in 1958 of achieving a fundamental breakthrough, for instance in grain, whereby food would no longer be a problem. By late autumn, such ideas had begun to seem unrealistic.

specific problems. The Wuchang conference is the continuation of the Chengdu conference.

(2) As to the problem of the comrades from the party committees of various provinces, cities, and autonomous regions writing reports: The comrades from the Center's different ministries have written twelve reports. Comrades from the different provincial and city committees, it just won't do for not a single one of you to write a report; [we'll have to] put some pressure on. Is it possible that each [of you] could write a report? None of you is saying a word. When we put on the screws this time, perhaps people will be pressured to death. Can't everybody write a piece for next time? Five or six thousand characters, maybe seven or eight thousand, either on particular aspects or on the overall situation, both are fine; but the first secretaries have to get down to it personally, and even if they don't write it with their hands, they should work on it with their brains and mouth, revise and supplement [it]. Have the reports by the different ministries of the Center been written by the ministers personally? The next meeting starts on 1 February next year,[63] these articles should be sent in before 25 January to facilitate examination; they will be printed for distribution at the meeting itself, and can be discussed and revised at the site of the meeting. Each province is to hold a party congress to sum [things] up. It does not work if there are too many problems [dealt with in an article]; if you deal with a hundred problems, no one is going to read it. Cut out ninety-nine, write about a few or one single problem; at a maximum don't exceed ten problems. Something must be emphasized. Man has eight systems (respiratory system, reproductive system . . .); local work, too, has many systems; therefore some points may be left out, others have to be kept in suspense for some years, and others have to be emphasized.

Our line is still the line of constructing socialism by going all out, aiming high, and achieving greater, faster, better, and more economical results. The methods still are "Politics takes command," the mass line, the simultaneous development of a variety of things, plus a combination of native and Western [i.e., modern] methods, and so forth.

(3) Let me talk about the question of tomorrow evening:[64] taking steel as the key link to spur on everything else. As to the steel target, in

---

[63]This would seem to foreshadow the 2nd Zhengzhou conference, held 27 Feb.–5 March 1959.
[64]We have found no text dealing with the evening of 24 November 1958.

the last analysis how much do we settle on as best? The Beidaihe conference fixed on 27 to [209] 30 million tons; that was in the nature of a proposal, [but] this time we have to finalize it. I am in favor of 27 million tons for steel; I'm also in favor of the 30 million tons, the more the better. The problem is whether or not we can manage it—is there a basis [for it]? The Beidaihe conference did not settle this question because [conditions] were not ripe then. Last year's 5.35 million tons were all good steel; this year [that figure] is being doubled; [but] 10.7 million tons was a risky plan. The result was that 60 million people went to that front, that everything else had to give way, that everything became very tense. There is a county in Hubei which had a batch of pigs to send to the Xiangyang special district; when they could not get any transport, they left them and went away.[65] Xiangyang has a lot of local products and iron that could not be transported out, and industrial products needed by the peasants [there] could not be transported in. Even Marshal Steel itself could not get by. The roughly three months of experience since the Beidaihe conference have been of great benefit for us. To fix 27 to 30 million tons for next year just will not work. Can't we lower the plan target? I suggest we don't triple [output] next year, but just double it. Is there some assurance that we can manage 22 million tons? The day before yesterday I got together with a few comrades—Li Fuchun, XXX and XXX, and so on[66]—in the evening to talk about this, to see whether we could be sure of success for 18 million tons. The bases which have now been mentioned still cannot convince me. I've already taken the opportunist standpoint and I am fighting for this. If my butt is thrashed, this will have nothing to do with you; it will simply [mean] that we will in the future again have U-shaped [development].[67] In the past you all opposed my reckless advance [*maojin*], [but] I'm not opposing anybody's reckless advance here today. From yesterday evening's discussion, it seemed as if 18 million tons of steel could be

---

[65]Presumably they took the pigs to the railway station or truck depot from which they would normally be shipped and found all the transport tied up with the steel drive.

[66]There can be no certainty as to the identity of Li Fuchun's colleagues, but one must almost certainly have been Bo Yibo, Chairman of the State Economic Commission, who was definitely involved later in setting the 1959 target; see *Origins* 2, p. 166.

[67]Literally "saddle-shaped" (*ma'an xing*). This conceptualization of China's development cycle derived from the observation that a surge in output one year was often followed by a trough the following year.

achieved, that with effort it was attainable, that it would not be a reckless advance. Next year we have to make 18 million tons of good steel; of the 11 million tons of steel this year, only 8.5 million tons were good. If we double that, it would be 17 million tons, and 18 million tons is even more than doubling it—can you call that opportunism? You say I am opportunistic; Marx may come out in my defense. He will say I am not opportunistic. Only if he says [I am] will it count. [You] also say I am [for] a great leap forward. It's not a great leap forward, I disagree. I think 18 million tons still has an insufficient basis; quite a few passes have not yet been crossed. When you revise the document,[68] you will have to explain which pass is going to be crossed when, the passes for ore dressing, mining, crushing, smelting, transport, and quality. Some of them can be passed in January-February or in March-April-May-June. At present some localities already have no reserve supplies (coal, iron, ore); **[210]** some factories, because of transport difficulties, have now come to the point where they cannot even deliver meals [to their work sites]. These are examples from steel, but in other spheres things are the same. If there is no assurance at what time some of the passes can be crossed, [the target plan] will have to be lowered still further—15 million tons would still be all right. If there is an assurance [of success], make it 18 million tons; and if there is still more assurance, make it 22 million tons; and if still more, then 25 or 30 million tons are all fine with me. The question is only whether there is an assurance. Yesterday, comrades were in favor of 18 million tons, saying there was an assurance. Last year the Northeast had 3.5 million tons. This year it was originally fixed at 6 million tons, and [they] actually produced 5 million tons. For next year they are prepared only to produce 7.15 million tons. They say, too, that with special efforts they may make 8 million tons. I think if we talk about opportunism, it's they who are opportunistic. In the Soviet Union, however, they would be in good standing; for with only 5 million tons this year and 8 million tons next year, they would have a 60 percent increase, an increase of more than half, which amounts to half-opportunism. North China produced only 600,000 tons last year, and this year 1.5 million tons; next year's plan

---

[68]Presumably the Communiqué of the CC's 6th Plenum (which met in Wuchang immediately after the Wuchang conference), in which the 1959 steel target was set at 18 million tons.

is 4 million tons; this year's increase was 1.7-fold—that is Marxism-Leninism. Next year's increase to 4 million tons is several Marxism-Leninisms: Can you manage that? Can you spell out the bases for your planning to produce that much next year? East China produced 220,000 tons last year, and this year 1.2 million tons (adding to this the bad steel, it would be 1.6 tons); next year it's 4 million tons, an increase of more than 200 percent. Shanghai is truly proletarian: first, it does not have coal; second, no iron; it has only fifty thousand people.[69] Last year Central China produced 170,000 tons and this year 500,000 tons; next year it'll be 2 million tons, a threefold increase. This person originally was very bold and planned to go after 3 million tons; if only everyone made a great effort to cross the passes, they might succeed, nobody would object, and we would furthermore hold a celebration meeting. The Southwest had 200,000 tons last year and this year 700,000 tons, next year 2 million tons, a twofold increase. The Northwest last year had only 14,000 tons, somewhat less than Chiang Kai-shek; this year they have 50,000 tons, surpassing Chiang Kai-shek;[70] for next year it'll be 700,000 tons, an increase of thirteen times. Is there opportunism in this? South China made 2,000 tons last year, and this year 60,000 tons, an increase of 30 times. The further you get to the south, the higher the Marxism; next year [it'll be] 600,000 tons, ten times [this year].

These numbers still have to be checked; there has to be a basis for each one; would Comrade [Li] Fuchun please [211] check how much there is this year and how much next year, and whether they don't just make reckless announcements. Speaking about these numbers simply proves that there is no opportunism and no danger [of my] losing my party membership. Adding up the different regions, next year is 21.3 million tons; and the question is, can that really be managed? One should arrange a lot of safety coefficients; let's take 18 million tons for the first account book,[71] pass it at the People's Congress, and let's really strive for it; there will furthermore be need for

[69]Presumably Mao means the number of people in steel production, since the total population of Shanghai was at this time about 7 million.
[70]Planners on Taiwan did not see the development of a steel industry as an economic priority during this period, but concentrated instead on tropical foodstuffs and light industry.
[71]Mao's reference to account books (*diyi ben zhang* and *dier ben zhang*), here and in the next paragraph, seem to hark back to the two types of targets the regime used during the GLF: a public one that had to be achieved and a private one to be striven for.

ideological preparation. If we can only come up with 15 million tons of good steel, and besides that there are 3 million tons of local steel, I'll be satisfied, too. If we cannot fulfill our target, I have local steel. The Soviet *Metallurgy News* praises our "small, local and mass" method. It says that although there may be some loss of quality, it will be very useful, that it can be used for making agricultural tools. If you look at it this way, then you can relax.

The first account book is 18 million tons, the second account book is 22 million tons. With that as an example, the targets for the different departments should all be lowered appropriately. Take electricity generation for example: use small, native, and mass to generate and use [electricity] for themselves. [This] has to be coerced and commanded. For those places where this is already being practiced, one has to adopt the measure of not issuing pay.

(XX, XX: [We] still need equipment.)

([Li] Fuchun: [This] can't be completely resolved [now].)[72]

[Chairman:] A further example is the railways: Originally it was fixed that they should only lay 20,000 kilometers in five years; now in a few years they are to lay 20,000 kilometers. What is needed is needed, but can they manage that much?

(XXX: During the first quarter of next year there will only be 2.9 million tons of rolled steel; if imports are added, it [still] does not exceed 3 million tons, not enough to distribute. When they ask for 30,000 tons, we can give them only 10,000.)

[Chairman:] Lü Zhengcao,[73] we don't have the steel. What shall we do?

(Lü Zhengcao: One can go for modular cast iron.)

---

[72]This exchange between Li Fuchun and two unnamed colleagues appears only in alternate text 10:279.
[73]Lü Zhengcao's name is given in alternate text 10:280, here and in the next sentence by Mao, whereas the primary text gives only XXX.

[Chairman:] The Chengdu conference [fixed] 20,000 kilometers in five years, and now in 1958 we have already laid 20,000 kilometers. The report by Lü Zhengcao is very daring, I greatly enjoyed it; the question is only whether we can achieve it, whether there is a basis. Do you have a method for finding a basis?

(Ke Qingshi: His method is that each region should manufacture its own.)

(XXX: For some months we have only looked at material factors and not human factors; looking at the reports by the ministries, one gets a start and can't write a thing.)

[Chairman:] There is a contradiction. Lü Zhengcao, have you really ideologically solved this? The Center can talk big, but the burden eventually is on the shoulders of the regions.

(XX: The tasks are the third account book; the raw materials are the first account book.)[74]

[Chairman:] For example, during the first quarter, Hubei has a local need of 80,000 tons of steel products, the Wuhan steel [plant] needs 75,000 tons, altogether 155,000 tons; but the Center gives only 70,000 tons; therefore these projects cannot be built. If you don't give rice, the cleverest housewife will be hard put to make a meal. The peasants have all sorts of measures to resist us. For instance, in some area they will specially appoint a falsifying reporter whose duty is exclusively to fill out those forms. [This is] because the higher levels absolutely want reports, and if too little is reported it looks bad; [the fake reports] will be reported up from level to level, and the higher-ups believe **[212]** them to be true, although in fact they lack any basis. In my opinion there are quite a few problems of this kind at present. In the last analysis, are there really 8.5 million tons of good steel this year? Do they really exist or have they [just] been reported? Is there no faking? [Wherever steel] cannot be transferred to higher levels, there is falsification. I think, in fact, there is not that much [good steel].

---

[74]We do not know what the "third account book" (*disan ben zhang*) means nor how it relates to the first two.

(XXX, Wang Renzhong:[75] People don't dare to misreport good steel, but [figures for steel produced] by small, local, and mass [methods] are unreliable.)

[Chairman:] (4) As to the question of falsification, the resolution on the communes has to be changed into a directive and has to have a special paragraph on the question of falsification. Originally there were two sentences, but that's not enough—a special paragraph has to be written. If you lump it in with work methods, people won't pay attention. Now, no matter what, they want to launch "Sputniks," strive for fame, and don't care whether they fake it or not. When they don't really have all that many things, they fabricate them. There is a people's commune which itself had only a hundred pigs. To cope with a visit, they borrowed another two hundred fat pigs, and returned them after the inspection was over. If you have a hundred, you have a hundred; you don't have what you don't have—what is the purpose of making it up? In the past, during the war, when we published news of victories and said how many prisoners of war [we had], the same thing went on. We made unfounded reports of successes in order to bolster our cause. The common people saw them and were pleased, but the enemy just had a good laugh when he saw them. Later we opposed this [practice] and after many orders and much educational effort on the need for honesty, eventually [people] didn't dare to give false reports. In fact, are [we] that truthful? People are not of one mind. I think there still is some falsification around. There are some people in this world who are not all that honest. I suggest you talk this over seriously with the secretaries of the county committees and the secretaries of the commune party committees and require that they should be honest and not falsify. If [you] truly lag behind, let others write it up; and if there is no glow [of success] on your face, it's not important. One should not strive for empty fame. For example, with regard to wiping out illiteracy, there is talk about doing it completely in half a year, a year or two; I don't have much faith in that; if it's wiped out during the second FYP that

---

[75]Wang Renzhong, a Long March and Yan'an veteran associated with Li Xiannian, had been a leading party official in the Central-South China Administrative Region and in Wuhan Municipality. Wang had been promoted to alternate member status in the CC in May 1958. Alternate text 10:280 gives the second name in full, while both texts give only XXX for the first name here.

won't be bad. Or take afforestation: each year afforestation is done; each year nothing comes of it; and the more afforestation is [reportedly] done the fewer trees one sees. [We] say the four pests have been eliminated [and ours] is a "four-without village," but in fact it's a "four-with village." When tasks have been handed down, they always say they have been fulfilled. There is nothing in the world without a bit of falsification; where there are true things, there will by necessity be fakes. Without having fakes for comparison, where would there be truth? This is just human nature. The serious question at present is not only that the lower levels fabricate, but that we believe them; from the Center, the provinces, and the prefectures down to the counties, everybody believes them, primarily the first three levels—that's the danger. [But] if [you] don't believe anything, it becomes opportunism. The masses, in fact, do achieve successes. Why write off the successes of the masses? But by trusting fabrications, one will also commit mistakes. Take the 11 million tons of steel: to say that **[213]** not even ten thousand tons exist is of course wrong. However, how much is there really? Or grain, how much is there in the last analysis? Tan Zhenlin,[76] you are a Marshal, having been commissioned as such.[77] Some people say 900 billion catties: do they really exist?

(Tan Zhenlin: About 750 to 800 billion catties.)

(XXX: The amount of 900 billion catties is already a reduction to 70 percent.)

(Li Xiannian: 750 billion catties really do exist.)

[Chairman:] Last year there were 370 billion catties; this year's 750 billion catties would be twice that much; that is terrific. Don't get nervous over the amounts discarded; matter does not disappear, [the lost grain] changes into fertilizer. The peasants are very careful with things; I have heard they took in a second harvest.

If you demand comparison, the result will be fabrications. If you

---

[76]Only alternate text 10:281 gives Tan's name here in Mao's questions and the response in parentheses.

[77]The original text reads *ni shi yuan shuai, suan liao zhang de,* which obviously contains a typographical error: *suan* should read *sheng. Sheng zhang* ("rising up in his tent") is a Peking Opera term meaning that a military general appears onstage.

don't compare, there is no competition. You have to come up with methods for competing. You have to check and examine as you do with export goods, using a microscope. What is the water content of a pound of grain? How many bugs? If it does not conform to standard, it will not pass. Economic endeavors must be ever more detailed, penetrating, realistic, and scientific. It is completely different from writing poetry; you have to understand the difference between writing poems and managing the economy. "He lifted Chao Lake as his water ladle":[78] that is poetry. I have not lifted anything, [but] it seems you Anhui people have. How are you able to lift it up? The examination must also pay attention to work style, taking into consideration the possibility of fabrications, [because] some fabrications can't be discovered under examination. A meeting is called [and] things will all be neatly arranged.[79] I hope that the Center, the provinces, and the prefectures will all understand this principle; they must have clear heads. At present it is generally said that reported successes should be discounted, split 30/70—can three out of ten be taken as fake, and the seven as true? Would that be an underestimation of the successes, distrust of the cadres and masses? Partial distrust is needed; the minimum is that there is not less than 10 percent fake, and there are cases where it's 100 percent. Sometimes nothing has been done, and they say it has been successfully completed.

(Jiang Weiqing:[80] The masses know.)

[Chairman:] Talk about a district or a province; the masses only know their own village. These are the bad fabrications. But there are also excellent fabrications, fabrications about which one has to be elated. For example, the hiding of output; this contradiction has its advantages. The cadres want to report much, [but] the common people want to hide output.[81] This is precisely the point where it is

[78]A familiar Anhui saying implying Herculean strength. The Chao Lake is in Anhui province.
[79]Under the guise of holding meetings, the origins of fabrications could be concealed and then the falsifications presented as true facts. By Nov. 1958, Mao was becoming aware of the extent of false reporting of production increases in the GLF.
[80]Jiang Weiqing: first secretary, Jiangsu provincial party committee. Interestingly, the alternate text, which has so far been more revealing of names, gives only XXX (10:282).
[81]I.e., in order to keep it for themselves and not have it procured by the state.

good: some places have suffered losses and reported increases. The higher levels demand a lot, [but] they say they don't have any more. Then there is a kind of fabrication that also has its benefits, which is against subjectivism, coercion, and commandism. Zhongnanhai has a cadre who went down to the countryside; he wrote a letter back saying that an APC had determined to pull up three **[214]** hundred *mou* of maize and plant sweet potatoes; on each *mou* 1.5 million clusters of sweet potatoes would be planted. But the maize had already grown above a man's head, and the masses felt this was deplorable, and thus the maize was not pulled out. They pulled it out on only 30 *mou*, but reported 300 *mou*. This kind of fake reporting is good. XXX says that in his native village, wheat is irrigated on New Year's Day and rest is not allowed. What else could the common people do but fake it? During the night lanterns were blazing in the fields, but in fact the people were at home resting. The cadres saw the glare of the lamps all over the fields and assumed they were not resting. In Hubei there's a county where day and night battles were demanded, no sleep at night; but the masses wanted to sleep, and so they got little kids to stand guard; and when they saw the cadres coming, everyone got up and made a big hullabaloo; [but] once the cadres had gone, they went back to sleep. That too is a good fake. Altogether I think this kind of thing is not rare at all. Number one, you have to have a clear head; number two, you have to instruct [cadres] that they should not let themselves be fooled, nor resort to coercion and commandism. At present there is an atmosphere in which there is only talk about successes and not about shortcomings; when there are shortcomings, there is loss of face; and when you speak the truth, no one listens. If you say that a cow's tail grows on its rump, no one listens; if you say it grows on its head, that's news. Fabrications, much talk, that's glory. Education is needed. Speaking clearly and being honest and truthful—if we achieve this within a few years, it would be good. I think if within a few years we get on the right track, we can be on firm ground.[82] { The USSR is on relatively firm ground, honest and frank, producing every year 50 million tons of steel.

(XX: Not necessarily, the USSR also falsifies.)

---

[82]In the primary text, this paragraph ends here. The remainder of the passage within braces comes from alternate text 10:283.

[Chairman:] I, too, know they have numerous fabrications, but steel [production] cannot in the end by fabricated. They still have a margin left over; [they] haven't fully utilized [their] equipment.

(XX: [Once a] certain level[83] of development is reached, there will be all sorts of surpluses.)}

[Chairman:] Make a list of the steel plants that are under construction or have been built, how many there are in a given province and their capacity. I think we might have a second look at what we thought earlier—perhaps this is opportunism. In the past we thought next year 30 million tons, and in the year thereafter 60 million tons to reach 80 to a 100 million tons in 1961/1962. Now let's rethink this: if next year we only make 18 million tons, in the year thereafter 30 million tons, and after three years of arduous struggle surpass West Germany and become the world's number three, that would be quite splendid. How much annual [output] in 1961/1962? If our yearly increase is 10 million tons, the second FYP will reach 50 million or 53.5 million tons; that is a tenfold increase over 1957: Can you still call that opportunism? Even if Marx cursed us as opportunists, we would no longer accept him. As to need and possibility, need is a problem, and so is possibility. Several programs must be devised for the FYP, and the 30 million tons cannot be the primary program; [we] will have to see next year's results. If everyone exerts himself, the leadership is correct, superstition is shattered, and native and Western [techniques] are combined; large, middle and small-sized [factories] are run in harness; [215] if we go all out and can reach 30 million tons in five years, that would be very fine; and if we surpass that by a bit, it would be even better. { At that time, even the USSR will not surpass 70 million tons; when they see our 50 million tons, they will be surprised and pleased.

([Li] Fuchun: The USSR may well [produce] a bit more.)}[84]

---

[83]Literally, "period" (*shiqi*), which in Marxist thinking means a level of productive development.

[84]These lines within braces are taken from the identical paragraph in alternate text 10:283. The primary text gives only ". . . . . ."

[Chairman:] Generally speaking, I think we will not be able to cross the technical and various other passes next year; we will need at least a further year; but if we cross all of them, of course, that's all the better. The first FYP [envisaged] 200,000 machine tools; this year [we made] 80,000; next year it will be 180,000 to 200,000, and in the year thereafter 250,000 to 300,000; thus the plan target originally fixed for next year has been deferred by one year. If after three years of arduous struggle the overall number reaches 800,000 machine tools, that will surpass Japan. If in 1961/1962 we make another 600,000, we will reach 1.4 million; that would be an increase from 260,000 to 1.5 million, which would be excellent. If we are making only 50 million tons of steel], we won't need 1.5 million machine tools—1.1 million will be enough.

For the distribution of steel products, there has to be a queue: Machine building comes first (within that realm, machine tools come first, and mechanical equipment second), rail communications and transportation second, and agriculture third.

This kind of tentative plan to lower our sights a bit is very necessary. After two five-year [plans] plus three years, we reach over 50 million tons. Our thirteen years correspond to the Soviet Union's forty years. In 1939, [after] twenty years, they produced only 18 million tons of steel. Our 50 million tons together with our 1.5 million machine tools are greatly superior. The reasons: (1) We are a big country with a large population; (2) the three [sectors][85] are simultaneously promoted, [plus] the party's line; (3) the Soviet experience. Without that third point, things would not have worked. [After] twenty years they made 18 million tons, and we made 50 million tons after thirteen years. Looked at in this way, it's still [our way that] pays. There is a bit of opportunism, but not much; perhaps it's a bit more realistic.

Agriculture is [developing] very fast; next year we'll make it another [such] year. As to grain, once we have reached 1,500 billion catties the peasants can rest, they can take a year off. When there is too much grain it will not all be eaten; of course, that cannot be applied to cotton.

(XX: There is a policy problem with agriculture; if grain [output]

[85]Presumably heavy industry, light industry, and agriculture.

per capita has gone up to [about] 750 to 1,000 kilograms [a year], is that still insufficient? In order to consolidate the communes, they have to make some things that they can exchange, and the emphasis might be shifted to cash crops; they might produce rather [216] more commodities.)

(Zheng Xisheng:[86] We are concerned about the problems of outlets for crops.)

(XX: There are outlets for oil-bearing crops.)

[Chairman:] True, when Hebei has gone from 550 kilograms to 750, Guangdong, Jiangxi and Anhui from 750 to 1,000, that is enough. For cash crops you have to enter into contracts; we will settle that at this conference. Let's do some business at this conference; the Center, the provinces, the counties, and the townships should conclude contracts [at their] four [respective] levels; the various provinces throughout the country must have a division of labor; if more bamboo, wood, silk, tea, oil, and hemp is produced, that will be no problem.

(5) Eradicate superstition, but don't make science a superstition to be eradicated; for example, people have to eat, that's scientific, and shouldn't be abolished. No one has yet proved that people can go without eating. "Zhang Liang abstained from grain,"[87] but he ate meat. At present there are a lot of reports that the masses are not left free to eat. If you produce 350 to 400 million tons and are still unwilling to let people eat more, perhaps there has been over-reporting. If people don't eat their fill, there is no leap forward. People have to sleep; that, too, is scientific. All animals need rest, even bacteria. The human heart beats 72 times a minute; that makes more than 100,000 heartbeats a day; if he neither eats nor sleeps and these two things are eliminated, he will die. Outside these areas, there are quite a few other superstitions that are being eradicated, the result of which has

---

[86]See n. 27. This is only the second case where the primary text identifies a name that the alternate text fails to identify.
[87]Zhang Liang (d. 186 BC) was enfeoffed as a noble by Liu Bang, founder of the Han dynasty, but later forsook officialdom and sought immortality by abstaining from eating grain.

been that people are squeezed to death by machines. Man subdues nature and uses tools on the objects of production; and, of course, these objects resist and react, that's a piece of science. When people walk on the earth, the earth has some resistance, without which you could not walk. Walking on grass, you don't meet much resistance, and it's not easy to walk there. In a swamp you sink in and can't pull yourself out; that kind of land has to be filled in with sand. Nature resists, that is a piece of science. If you don't acknowledge this, it will punish, maim, pound, and kill you. Since we eradicated superstition, the effects have been extremely great: [we] have dared to think, dared to speak, and dared to act. But a small part of that eradication goes too far, and eradicates scientific truths as well. These should not be eradicated, for instance by saying that one hour of sleep is sufficient. The policy is to eradicate superstition, but science cannot be eradicated.

An estimate of successes and empty claims should be made. In the end, how much [of each] is there? You should discuss whether their proportion is 70/30 or 80/20; perhaps you can take that back and research it with prefecture and county committee comrades. If the estimate of falsification is too high, [that means] distrust in the masses and one will make a mistake and be disheartened. Not to take account of the falsification is also [217] to commit a mistake. I am talking in general terms; but there are particular cases where everything is true, and others where everything is fake. Take the elimination of illiteracy, or the elimination of the four pests: Even if illiterates come in droves, they still say illiteracy has been wiped out; if basically [an area] has not been made green, it is [nevertheless] reported that it has become green. Four-withs are reported as four-withouts,[88] and so on. This has to be analyzed. Superstition absolutely has to be eradicated, but truth absolutely has to be safeguarded. Bourgeois right can only be partly abolished; for example, the three work styles and five airs, excessive [income] disparities, patriarchal attitudes, old-style relationships, definitely have to be eradicated, and the more thoroughly the better. Another part, like salary levels, the relationships between higher and lower levels, and a certain amount of state coercion cannot yet be eradicated. Sixty million people are

[88]I.e., areas with the four pests are reported as areas free of them.

sent to the [steel] front; Fuyang[89] [has] a population of 50,000 people, who have neither coal nor iron: Isn't it because [they think] "It can't be wrong to listen to the Communist party?"[90] To order 60 million people to make steel has something coercive about it; it was rammed through at the Beidaihe conference and the four telephone conferences.[91] We cannot at this time do without this coerciveness to enforce a division of labor. If there were freedom of reporting; free choice of one's profession—whoever wants to go fishing, goes fishing; whoever wants to paint, paints; to sing, sings; and to dance, dances— and if 100 million people were [thus] singing and another 100 million painting, would we still have grain to eat? We would go under. A part of bourgeois right has to be abolished; another part still has a use in socialism and has to be preserved and made to serve socialism. To beat it black and blue (as in the civil war when, during the movement to clean out counterrevolutionaries, good people were arrested and beaten to a pulp),[92] would be a mistake, and would put us into a passive position, and we would have to admit mistakes. As to the useful part [of bourgeois right], you have made a mistake if you have beaten it to a pulp, and you still have to apologize and straighten things out again. One has to analyze which [parts] have their use, and which have to be eradicated. The Soviet Union did not eradicate [parts] that should have been eradicated, and these are still relatively persistent. As to us, we should eradicate what has to be eradicated, and preserve the useful part.

(6) As to the Forty Points,[93] it is best not to enact them on this occasion; at present we have no basis; there's no point in having a discussion.[94]

[89] A prefecture in Anhui.

[90] Alternate text 10:286 places this phrase in quotation marks.

[91] It is not clear when these "telephone conferences" took place, whom they involved, nor even how many there were: alternate text 10:286 gives *jici* instead of *si ci*, which would make the phrase read, "and in several telephone conferences."

[92] This refers to the Campaign to Eradicate Counterrevolutionaries in Yan'an, which formed the last stage of the famous Rectification Campaign of 1942–4. These purges were run by Kang Sheng, head of security in Yan'an; in the post-Mao period he has been given primary blame for the excesses Mao here describes as more general to the movement. See Zhong Kan, *Kang Sheng pingzhuan* (A critical biography of Kang Sheng) (Beijing, Hongqi chubanshe, neibu faxing, August 1982), pp. 77, 82–95.

[93] This would appear to be a new 40 Points, and not the existing 12-Year Agricultural Program. Perhaps they were to deal with industry or urban communes or both.

[94] This is the end of the primary text. The alternate text provides a further 24 lines under item (7).

{[10:286] (7) Who will first enter communism! Will the Soviet Union enter communism first or will our country? This has become a question in our country. Khrushchev raised the conditions for entering communism in twelve years; they [the CPSU] were very prudent; we, too, should be a bit prudent on this question. Some people say, [we'll] enter communism in two to three, three to four, five to seven years: Is that possible or not? To enter [communism], first Anshan Steel Works goes, then Liaoning [province] (8 million of their population of 24 million is urban); it won't be another province. Then [will come] Old Ke [Qingshi][95] [and his] Shanghai, if they want to wait for others; [they] can't enter alone. XXX, Shouzhang [and] Fan [counties] want to enter [communism], but isn't that a bit hasty? [We] sent Comrade Chen Boda to investigate, [and he] said it would be tough [for them] to enter. At present, no one in prefectures or provinces say [they'll] be the first to enter; they would rather be prudent, [10:287] only some counties want to be the vanguards. How much time it will take for all of China to enter communism, no one knows that now; it's hard to estimate—ten years? fifteen years? twenty years? Twenty years? For the Soviet Union forty-one years, plus twelve more is altogether fifty-three years, and that's just to prepare conditions [for entering communism]. Is China so formidable? With just these few years we get ambitious—is this possible or not? Considering it in terms of benefit to the proletariat of the whole world, perhaps it would be better if the Soviet Union entered [communism] first. Perhaps on the hundredth anniversary of the Paris Commune (1971) the Soviet Union [will] enter communism. What of our [plan for] twelve years? Perhaps it's possible, but I don't think so. Even if in ten years, by 1968, we have completed our preparations, [we] still [should] not enter; at least wait two or three years after Soviet Union enters, then enter, lest [we] cause Lenin's party, the country of the October Revolution, to lose face. [If] in fact you are able to enter but don't, it doesn't matter. You have this ability, but neither announce it nor put it in the newspapers to say [you] have entered communism. Isn't that falsification? It doesn't matter. Many people think China might just enter first, because we have found the way of the people's

---

[95]Lao Ke (old Ke) refers to Ke Qingshi, first secretary of Shanghai and a strong supporter of the GLF.

communes. [But] there is an impossibility here; there's also [the question of whether we] ought to.

(XX: How can you enter communism if the only thing you have to eat is sweet potatoes.)

[Chairman:] How can [one] enter communism on a salary of one dollar? It's not a good idea to discuss these questions publicly, but this ideological questions should be clarified inside the party.}

Appendix
Select Bibliography
Glossary-Index

Comparison of Texts from 1957 in New Mao Texts, Volume I, with Versions in Other Sources

The impression that the newly available volumes not only are reliable sources but represent an informal archive of the Mao texts from which both "collective wisdom" and "historicist" versions have been drawn is suggested by a close comparison of them with the officially published sources. That previously available Red Guard sources also contain some of the same material points to the obvious fact that there is a real archive, in the hands of the Central Committee of the CCP, from which all these sources come but which is unlikely to be released in our lifetime. Results of comparing the first volume in the new series with other types of Mao publications are reported below. To date this has been thoroughly done only for the first two volumes. Complete analysis awaits further study.

In the newly available *Xuexi wenxuan,* (New Mao Texts, Volume

1; see Table 1 in Timothy Cheek's chapter), texts appear chronologically from the April 1956 "Speech at the expanded meeting of the Politburo of the CCP" to the 8 July 1957 "Speech at the Shanghai conference of figures from various circles." While many of the texts for April 1956–February 1957 and then for April–July 1957 have appeared in the official *Mao Zedong xuanji* (and their translations, the *Selected Works of Mao Zedong*), there is a huge gap in the official texts for February–March 1957. That gap can be partially filled from the newly available texts and in part justifies the present translations. The overlap of the new with the previously published texts, furthermore, helps to establish the authenticity of the new as well as point out where they may modify or expand our knowledge, especially for 1957.

In the group leading up to February 1957, the first piece (1:134–139), the April 1956 speech, first appeared in the 1969 *Wansui* (pp. 35–40). The second, "Talk with music workers" from August 1956 (1140–145), first appeared in another "Red Guard" publication and has been translated in Stuart Schram's *Mao Tse-tung Unrehearsed* (pp. 84–90). After two short selections (new but not translated here) and a variant version of Mao's opening address to the Eighth Party Congress (1:145–150), of which the official version is widely available, comes the 12 November 1956 "In commemoration of Dr. Sun Yat-sen" (1:152–153), which appeared in the 1969 *Wansui* (pp. 59–61) and later in the 1977 *Selected Works*, Volume 5 (pp. 330–331). The "Summation speech at the second plenum of the Eighth Central Committee (main points circulated from notes)" (1:154–168), dated 15 November 1956, is a variant of the official version in the *People's Daily* of 16 November 1956, which is translated in *Selected Works* (*SW5*, pp. 332–349; *XJ5*, pp. 313–329). The January 1957 "Summary of conference of provincial and municipal party committee secretaries" (1:169–178) is identical to the 1969 *Wansui* version (pp. 81–90) and appears in highly edited and longer form in the *Selected Works* as "Talks at a Conference of Secretaries of Provincial, Municipal and Autonomous Region Party Committees" (*SW5*, pp. 350–383; *XJ5*, pp. 330–362). Mao's occasional remarks at the same conference (1:179–187) appear in the 1969 *Wansui* (pp. 73–81). The "Letter discussing poetry" (1:188) first appeared in Ding Wang, *Mao Zedong xuanji buyi* (1971, p. 94); it is followed by a one-page text that we have not translated. Next in our Volume 1 comes the original transcript of the famous 27 February 1957 speech on handling contradictions among the people (1:190–323), which we have translated. We have translated eight texts from Mao's provincial tours of March 1957 for which Volume 1 is a source (1:233–312). From this period only two texts have been available in previously published collections. First, four pages of extracts from the 18 and 19 March talks in Jinan and Nanjing are found in the *Selected Works* (*SW5*, pp. 436–439; *XJ5*, pp. 449–452); and the 1986 *Mao Zedong zhuzuo xuandu*, pp. 799–802; the talk at Nanjing being more fully represented by our "On ideological work" (1:278–301). Second, some portions of the 10 March talk with journalists (but none of the dialogue) appeared in the 1983 *Mao Zedong xinwen gongzuo wenxuan*, pp. 186–194.

For April 1957, Volume 1 provides "Speech at a banquet in honor of Chairman Voroshilov" of 17 April (1:313–315), which is available in part in *Peking Review*, 24 April 1970, p. 5; "A talk to responsible democratic personages" (1:316–322) which is Mao's address to the officially unacknowledged 30 April meeting of the Supreme State Conference, where he initiated the ill-fated May 1957 Rectification Campaign; and a text from the April 1957 Hangzhou Conference of the Shanghai Bureau (1:323–331), which is also found in the 1969 *Wansui* (pp. 100–109). Next is a new one-page letter to Li Shuyi (1:332). Then comes a speech, "Things are beginning to change," from 15 May 1957 (1:333–339), which is *identical* to the published version (*XJ5*, pp. 423–429; *SW5*, 440–446). Next a brief new text of a 22 May talk to representatives of the Youth League's Third Congress (*tuan san da*) (1:340). Then the 14 June 1957 *People's Daily* editorial criticizing the *Wenhui bao* (1:341–342). A separate text, "The bourgeois orientation of the *Wenhui bao* should be criticized" of 1 July 1957 (1:343–348) is identical to the officially published version (*XJ5*, pp. 465–470; *SW5*, pp. 451–456). The next text, "The situation in the summer of 1957" (1:349–357), delivered in Qingdao in July 1957, was officially published (*XJ5*, pp. 456–465; *SW5*, pp. 473–482). There follow two new texts on similar topics (1:358–367). Finally, the untranslated 8 July "Speech at the Shanghai Conference of figures from various circles" (1:368–381) appears in the 1969 *Wansui* (pp. 109–122) and bears some resemblance to the published speech of the next day in Shanghai (*XJ5*, pp. 440–455; *SW5*, pp. 457–472).

I. CHINESE WORKS

Note: The use of traditional and simplified characters in this bibliography reflects actual usage on the title pages of the publications listed.

Selected Mao Texts by Date of Publication:

Mao Zedong, "Xin minzhu de zhengzhi yu xin minzhu de wenhua" " 新 民 主 的 政 治 與 新 民 主 的 文 化 " (New democratic politics and new democratic culture), *Zhongguo wenhua* 中 國 文 化 (Chinese culture) 1.1:1–24. (Yan'an. February 1940).

Mao Zedong xuanji 毛 澤 東 選 集 (Selected works of Mao Zedong). Deng Tuo, ed. N.p., Jin Cha Ji Xinhua shuju, May, 1944. Five *juan,* sometimes bound in one volume.

Mao Zedong xuanji Dalian, Dazhong shuju, August 1946; 3rd printing November 1947. May 1944 preface (abbreviated); same selections as 1944 edition, with three additional texts.

Mao Zedong xuanji. N.p., Jin Cha Ji Zhongyang fenju, March 1947. Expanded version of 1944 text in six *juan.* Reprinted by ARL-CCRM, 1970 (Microfilm 19).

Mao Zedong xuanji. 5 vols. Beijing. Renmin chubanshe, serially: 1951, 1952, 1953, 1960, 1977. The first 4 volumes have been reprinted several times.

Mao Zedong zhuzuo xuandu (jia/yi zhong ben) 毛 泽 东 著 作 选 读 甲／乙 种 本 (A reader of works by Mao Zedong: supplementary volumes A and B). Beijing, Renmin chubanshe, 1965.

Dahai hangxing kao duoshou 大海航行靠舵手 (Sailing the seas depends on the helmsman). N.p., n.pub., preface by Lin Biao dated 16 December 1966.

Mao Zedong sixiang wansui 毛泽东思想万岁 (Long live Mao Zedong Thought). 9 vol.; new series, circa 1967. See New Mao Texts, Vols. 5–11B, in Table 1 in Timothy Cheek's chapter above.

Mao Zedong sixiang wansui. 3 vols. N.p., n.pub., 1967–1969. Three separate volumes of apparently original material, released by the Institute of International Relations, Taipei.

Xuexi wenxuan 学习文选 (Study selections). 4 vols. N.p., n.pub., circa 1967. See New Mao Texts, Vols. 1–4, in Table 1 in Timothy Cheek's chapter above.

Xuexi ziliao 学习资料 (Study materials). 3 vols. N.p., n.pub., n.date. See New Mao Texts, Vols. 12A–12C, in Table 1 in Timothy Cheek's chapter above.

Xuexi ziliao: xu yi 学习资料：续一 (Study materials; supplement one). N.p., n.pub., n.date. See New Mao Texts, Vol. 13, in Table 1 in Timothy Cheek's chapter above.

Mao Zhuxi jiaoyu yulu 毛主席教育语录 (Chairman Mao's sayings on education). Beijing, Hong Dai Hui, Beijing tianji xuexiao, Dongfang hong gongshe, July 1967. Preface by Lin Biao.

Mao zhuxide geming luxian wansui: Dangnei liangtiao luxian douzheng da shiji (1921–1969) 毛主席的革命路线万岁：党内两条路线斗事大事记 *(1921–1969)* (Long live the revolutionary line of Chairman Mao: Major events in the two line struggle inside the party, 1921–1969). N.p., n.pub., n.date. See New Mao Texts, Vol. 14, in Table 1 in Timothy Cheek's chapter above.

Mao Zhuxi wenxuan 毛主席文选 (Selected writings of Chairman Mao). N.p., n.pub., n.date. Fully translated in *JPRS* 49826, 12 February 1970, and *JPRS* 50792, 23 June 1970.

Mao Zedong de geming wenyi luxian shengli wansui 毛泽东的革命文艺路线胜利万岁 (Long live the victory of Chairman Mao's revolutionary line in literature). N.p., n.pub., n.date.

Ziliao xuanbian 资料选编 (Selected Materials). N.p., n.pub., 1971. Note on title page: "Classified materials, Have not been corrected, Only for reference, Be careful to protect." Over a hundred brief extracts from Mao's writings 1919–1967. Published by ARL-CCRM (1980); translations in Schram, "New Texts by Mao Tse-tung, 1921–1966" (see below, Section II).

Ding Wang 丁望, ed., *Mao Zedong xuanji buyi: disan juan (1949–1959)* 毛澤東選集補遺：第三卷 *(1949–1959)* (Addenda to *Selected Works of Mao Zedong, Vol. 3, 1949–1959*). Hong Kong, Ming bao yuekan, February 1971.

Takeuchi Minoru 竹 内 實 , ed. *Mao Zedong ji* 毛 澤 東 集 (Collected writings of Mao Zedong). 10 vols. Tokyo, Hokobosha, 1971–1972; rev. ed., 1983.

——. *Mao Zedong ji bujuan* 毛 澤 東 集 補 卷 (Supplements to *Collected writings of Mao Zedong*). 10 vols. Tokyo, 1983–1986. The tenth volume, which is unnumbered, contains a chronology of Mao's writings.

Mao Zedong Texte, Chinese texts accompanying German translations; see below under Helmut Martin, in Section II.

Mao Zedong junshi wenxuan: neibu ben 毛 泽 东 军 事 文 选 (内 部 本) (Selected military writings of Mao Zedong: Internal edition). Beijing, Zhongguo renmin jiefang jun chubanshe, 1981. Reprinted, Tokyo, 1985.

Mao Zedong zhexue sixiang jiaoxue (yanjiu) cankao ziliao 毛 泽 东 哲 学 思 想 教 学 (研 究) 参 考 资 料 (Reference materials for teaching [and research] on Mao Zedong's philosophical thought). 5 vols. Printed by the Mao Zedong's Philosophical Thought Research Room of Department of Philosophy, Peking University. Vol. 1 (lacking *yanjiu* in title), July 1983; Vols. 2–5, October 1983. See New Mao Texts, Vols. 15A–15E, in Table 1 in Timothy Cheek's chapter above.

Mao Zedong shuxin xuanji 毛 泽 东 书 信 选 集 (Selected letters of Mao Zedong). Beijing, Renmin chubanshe, December 1983.

Mao Zedong shuxin shouji xuan 毛 泽 东 书 信 手 迹 选 (Selected letters of Mao Zedong in his own hand). Beijing, Wenwu chubanshe, 1983.

Mao Zedong xinwen gongzuo wenxuan 毛 泽 东 新 闻 工 作 文 选 Selections on journalism by Mao Zedong). Beijing, Xinhua chubanshe, December 1983.

Mao Zedong zhuzuo xuandu 毛 泽 东 著 作 选 读 (Selected readings from Mao Zedong). *Shang* and *xia* volumes. Beijing, Renmin chubanshe, 1986.

Reference Works and Studies

"Deng Tuo yu diyibu *Mao Zedong xuanji*" "邓 拓 与 第 一 部 毛 泽 东 选 集 "(Deng Tuo and the first *Selected Works of Mao*), *Dang shi xinxi* (Information on party history), No. 17, p. 1 (1 September 1986).

Gong Yuzhi 龚 育 之 . "Tong Shi Lamu jiaoshou de tanhua" " 同 施 拉 姆 教 授 的 谈 话 (A conversation with Professor Schram), in *Wenxian he yanjiu: 1984 nian huibianben* 文 献 和 研 究 :1984 年 汇 编 本 (Documents and research: 1984 compilation). Beijing, Renmin chubanshe, 1986, pp. 243–260.

——, Pang Xianzhi 逄 先 知 , and Shi Zhongquan 石 仲 泉 , eds. *Mao Zedong de dushu shenghuo* 毛 泽 东 的 读 书 生 活 (Mao Zedong's reading life). Beijing, Sanlian shudian, 1986.

Li Weihan 李维汉 . *Huiyi yu yanjiu* 回忆与研究 (Recollections and research). 2 vols. Beijing, Zhonggong dang shi ziliao chubanshe, 1986.

Liao Gailong, see *Zhonggong dang shi wenzhai*, below.

Lin Xiling. "Letter to Comrade Deng Xiaoping," *Chinese Law & Government* 17.4:5–91 (Winter 1984–1985). Translated from *Guang jiaojing* (Wide angle), Nos. 9–10 (Hong Kong, 1983).

Liu Guokai, "A Brief Analysis of the Cultural Revolution," *Chinese Sociology and Anthropology* 19.2 (Winter 1986–1987). Translated from *Renmin zhi sheng* (Voice of the people), No. 2 (Guangzhou, December 1980).

Liu Lantao 刘澜涛 , et al., eds. "Sishi nianqian de yibu *Mao Zedong xuanji* "四十年前的一部毛泽东选集" ' (An edition of the *Selected Works of Mao Zedong* from forty years ago), *Liaowang zhoukan* (Outlook weekly) 1984.17:11 (23 April 1984).

Shi Zhongquan. "A Comment on Some Theoretical Issues in the 'Annotated Edition of the "Historical Resolution" (Revised),'" *Jiaoxue yu yanjiu* (Teaching and research) 1985.3:2–11 (28 May 1985), translated in *JPRS-CPS*-85-113 (7 November 1985), pp. 24–34. A briefer version of this appears in *Guangming ribao*, 18 December 1985, p. 3, translated in *FBIS-CHI* 2 January 1986, pp. K13–K16.

Wenxian he yanjiu 文献和研究 (Documents and research). Periodical publication of the Central Party Documentary Research Office; see Gong Yuzhi, 1986, above, for annual compilation.

Zhonggong dang shi dashi nianbiao 中共党史大事年表 (Chronological table of major events in CCP history). Beijing, Renmin chubanshe, 1987.

Zhonggong dang shi wenzhai niankan: 1982 中共党史文摘年刊：1982 (Annual selection of articles on CCP history: 1982). Edited by Zhonggong zhongyang dang shi yanjiu shi. Chief editor (listed on cover), Liao Gailong 廖盖隆 . Hangzhou, Zhejiang Renmin chubanshe, 1985.

Zhonggong zhongyang shujichu, ed. *Liuda yilai—dangnei mimi wenjian* 六大以来党内秘密文件 (Since the Sixth Congress—secret inner party documents). *Shang* and *xia* volumes. Beijing, Renmin chubanshe, 1941. Revised ed. preface dated February 1980.

———. *Liuda yiqian* 六大以前 (Before the Sixth Congress). Beijing, Renmin chubanshe, 1980.

Zhonggong zhongyang wenxian yanjiu shi, ed. *Guanyu jianguo yilai dangde ruogan lishi wenti de jueyi zhushiben (xiuding)* 关于建国以来党的若干历史间题的决议注释本（修订）(Annotations, revised edition, on the resolution on certain historical questions of the party since the founding of the nation). Beijing, Renmin chubanshe, 1985.

Zhongguo gongchandang liushi nian dashi jianjie 中 国 共 产 党 六 十 年 大 事 简 介 (A synopsis of the major events in sixty years of the CCP). Beijing, Guofang daxue chubanshe, 1985.

Zhongguo shehui kexue yuan Ma-Lie suo Mao Zedong sixiang yanjiu shi, eds. Du Weihua 杜 魏 华, chief editor. *Mao Zedong shengping, zhuzuo yanjiu suoyin* 毛 泽 东 生 平 , 著 作 研 究 索 引 (Index to research on Mao Zedong's life and works). 2 vols. Beijing, guofang daxue chubanshe, 1987.

Zhongguo shehuizhuyi geming he jianshe shi jiangyi 中 国 社 会 主 义 革 命 和 建 设 史 讲 义 (Teaching materials on the history of China's socialist revolution and construction). Hu Hua 胡 华 , ed. Beijing, Zhongguo renmin daxue chubanshe, 1985.

*Zhonghua renmin gongheguo jingji dashi ji (1949–1980 nian)*中 华 人 民 共 和 国 经 济 大 事 记 (1949–1980 年) (Record of major economic events of the People's Republic of China, 1949–1980). Fang Weizhong 房 维 中 , ed. Beijing, Zhongguo shehui kexue chubanshe, 1984.

Zhongyang dang'anguan, ed. *Zhonggong zhongyang wenjian xuanji* 中 共 中 央 文 件 选 集 (Selected documents from the CCP Central Committee). Beijing, Zhongyang dangxiao chubanshe, 1982–.

Zhou Enlai tongyi zhanxian wenxuan 周 恩 来 统 一 战 线 文 选 (Selections by Zhou Enlai on the United Front). Beijing, Renmin chubanshe, 1984.

Zhushiben, see Zhonggong zhongyang wenxian yanjiu shi, ed., *Guanyu jianguo yilai dangde ruogan lishi wenti de jueyi zhushiben (xiuding)*.

II. WESTERN TRANSLATIONS

Jerome Chen. *Mao*. New York, Prentice Hall, 1968, pp. 62–123.

———. *Mao Papers: Anthology and Bibliography*. London, Oxford Univ. Press, 1970.

Chinese Law & Government (New York), a journal of translations:

    1.4 (Winter 1968–1969): "In Camera Statements of Mao Zedong."

    9.3 (Fall 1976): "Mao Zedong: Previously Untranslated Documents, 1 (1957–1967)."

    9.4 (Winter 1976–1977), "Mao Zedong: Speeches at the Zhengzhou Conference (February and March 1959)."

    10.2 (Summer 1977): "On Party Unity and Revolutionary Successors: A Selection of Mao Zedong's Speeches and Conversations, 1953–1968."

    10.4 (Winter 1977–1978): "Mao Zedong's Oral Report to the Seventh Party Congress (24 April 1945)."

    11.4 (Winter 1978–1979): "Mao Zedong on Intellectuals: A Selection of

Speeches and Writings from the 1950s" (includes April 1957 critique of *People's Daily*).

Current Background, translations by the U.S. Consulate, Hong Kong:

CB 891 (8 October 1969), full translation of *Wansui* (April 1967).

CB 892 (21 October 1969), translation of "Collection of Statements by Mao Zedong (1956–1967).

CB 897 (10 December 1969), translation of *Zuigao zhibiao* (Supreme directives), preface by Lin Biao dated 16 December 1966.

Joint Publications Research Service (U.S. Government Printing Office):

JPRS 49826 (12 February 1970) and *JPRS* 50792 (23 June 1970), translation of entire *Mao Zhuxi wenxuan.*

JPRS 61269-1 and 61269-2 (20 February 1974), translations from *Wansui* (1967) and *Wansui* (1969).

Kau, Michael Y. M., and John K. Leung, eds. *The Writings of Mao Zedong, 1949–1976.* Vol. 1: *September 1949–December 1955.*Armonk, N.Y., M. E. Sharpe, 1986.

"Mao Tse-tung's Concluding Speech at the Supreme State Conference (2 March 1957)," *Issues & Studies* 10.12:110–115 (September 1974). Published by Institute of International Relations, Taipei.

[Mao Zedong]. *Selected Works of Mao Tsetung.* 5 vols. Peking, Foreign Languages Press, Vols. 1–4, 1975; Vol. 5, 1977.

Martin, Helmut, ed. *Mao Zedong Texte.* 6 vols. in 7. München, Carl Hanser Verlag, 1979–1982.

McDougall, Bonnie S. *Mao Zedong's "Talks at the Yan'an Conference on Literature and Art": A Translation of the 1943 Text with Commentary.* Michigan Papers in Chinese Studies, No. 39. Ann Arbor, 1980.

Roberts, Moss, and Richard Levy. *Mao Tse-tung: A Critique of Soviet Economics.* New York, Monthly Review Press, 1977. Translations from Mao's "Political Economy" notes in *Wansui* (1967 and 1969). See also, Levy, "New Light on Mao," *The China Quarterly,* No. 61 (1975).

Schoenhals, Michael. "Mao Zedong: Speeches at the 1957 'Moscow Conference,'" *The Journal of Communist Studies* 2.2:109–126 (June 1986). These texts are drawn from New Mao Texts, Vol. 8, pp. 5–22; see Table 1 in Timothy Cheek's chapter.

Schram, Stuart. *Mao Tse-tung Unrehearsed.* Harmondsworth, Penguin Books, 1974.

——."New Texts by Mao Tse-tung, 1921–1966," *Communist Affairs* 2.2:143–165 (April 1983). Translations from *Ziliao xuanbian.*

III. SOURCES FOR FURTHER BIBLIOGRAPHY

For pre-1949 Mao *Xuanji*, see as cited above, Gong Yuzhi, "Tong Shi Lamu jiao-shou de tanhua," in *Wenxian he yanjiu: 1984 nian huibianben*, pp. 244–245.
For *Mao Zedong sixiang wansui*, see below, MacFarquhar, *Origins*, vol. 1, p. 410.

Fogel, Joshua A. *Ai Ssu-ch'i's Contribution to the Development of Chinese Marxism.* Cambridge, Harvard Council on East Asian Studies, 1987.
Hamrin, Carol Lee, and Timothy Cheek, eds. *China's Establishment Intellectuals.* Armonk, N.Y., M E. Sharpe, 1986.
MacFarquhar, Roderick. *The Hundred Flowers Campaign and the Chinese Intellectuals.* New York, Praeger, 1960.
———. *The Origins of the Cultural Revolution.* Vol. 1: *Contradictions Among the People 1956–1957.* New York, Columbia University Press, 1974.
———. *The Origins of the Cultural Revolution.* Vol. 2: *The Great Leap Forward 1958–1960.* New York, Columbia University Press, 1983.
Martin, Helmut. *Cult & Canon: The Origins and Development of State Maosim.* Armonk, N.Y., M. E. Sharpe, 1982.
Schram, Stuart. *The Political Thought of Mao Tse-tung.* 2nd ed. Harmondsworth, Penguin Books, 1969.
———. "Mao Studies: Retrospect and Prospect," *The China Quarterly*, No. 97 (1984), pp. 95–125.
Starr, John Bryan. *Continuing the Revolution: The Political Thought of Mao.* Princeton, Princeton University Press, 1979.
———, and Nancy Anne Dyer. *Post-Liberation Works of Mao Zedong: A Bibliography and Index.* Berkeley, Center for Chinese Studies, University of California, 1976.
Weigelin-Schwiedrzik, Susanne. "Party Historiography in the People's Republic of China," *The Australian Journal of Chinese Affairs*, No. 17 (January 1987).
Wylie, Raymond F. *The Emergence of Maoism: Mao Tse-tung, Ch'en Po-ta, and the Search for Chinese Theory 1935–1945.* Stanford, Stanford University Press, 1980.

Note: Terms that appear in the New Mao Texts are glossed exactly as they appear in the original documents. Other Chinese terms, names, and titles are given in simplified characters, except in the case of a few words that are more recognizable in traditional form. Book titles that appear in the bibliography are not glossed in the Glossary-Index.